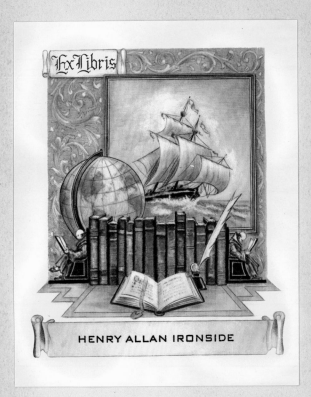

MRS. EDDY

THE BIOGRAPHY OF A VIRGINAL MIND

MRS. EDDY

The Biography of a Virginal Mind

By

EDWIN FRANDEN DAKIN

"It must be borne in mind that my design is not to write histories, but lives."
—PLUTARCH.

BLUE RIBBON BOOKS

NEW YORK

IN GRATEFUL ACKNOWLEDGMENT

TO

MY MOTHER

ELMORE JAMES DAKIN

who by devoting many weeks to research and transcription, poring laboriously over yellowed files, and exploring with painstaking care the obscure haunts of data, made possible through her enthusiastic collaboration the writing of this book. —E. F. D.

PUBLISHERS' NOTE

THE publication of this popular edition of *Mrs. Eddy* marks the failure of an organized Minority to accomplish the suppression of opinions not to its liking.

We published the book on its merits—one of which was its presentation of a highly interesting and significant character, about whom people were entitled to know, in a conscientious and impartial manner. And since a publisher, whatever his personal views of the subject, is required by his profession to publish material of such interest and value, we could not properly have done otherwise.

The book appeared on August 16, 1929. In the ensuing weeks it was reviewed by a score of men of character and of knowledge of the subject, outside the organized Minority, in complete confirmation of our opinion of its importance and fairness.

This enthusiastic reception accorded by non-partisans was accompanied by so virulent a campaign for suppression that if the issue had been only a commercial one, it might well have seemed the part of practical wisdom to withdraw the book.

But the issue now was that of freedom of speech: if this interested Minority could force the suppression of this book, so could any strongly organized minority force the suppression of any book of which its members did not approve. The situation required us to fight it out and take the consequences.

For many weeks it seemed as if the sale of *Mrs. Eddy* might actually be so reduced that the book could not be kept on the market. Many stores were forced by threats to renounce its sale, and many to conceal it. Others openly defied those who came to threaten boycott, and in all but a few cities the book could always be bought somewhere. The American book trade recognized the principle at issue, and the moment it gained public support—as it did when the public became aware of the attempt at suppression—it so valiantly rallied against this tyranny that the sale of *Mrs. Eddy* rapidly increased.

Except for the indignant resistance of booksellers and public to the arrogant assumption of a Minority that it had the right to dictate the sources of information on a given subject, a precedent extremely dangerous to freedom of the mind would surely have been established.

Grateful acknowledgment is due *The New Republic, The Saturday Review of Literature*, the New York *Nation*, the Hartford *Courant*, the New York *World*, the Portland (Me.) *Evening News, The Carnegie Magazine, Harpers Magazine, Plain Talk*, The Authors' League, and scores of publications and organizations and hundreds of individuals for their aid in informing the public of the situation.

—*Charles Scribner's Sons*

FOREWORD

Popular conceptions of Mrs. Eddy have shown an extraordinary variance. To some of her followers she has appeared as nothing less than a Christ incarnate. Other observers have portrayed her as a bigger humbug than Barnum and the worst virago since Xantippe. Such a wide range of concepts cannot solely be accounted for by mere variation in human points of view. Rather is the conclusion justified that few individuals have ever had an opportunity to weigh the facts regarding this extraordinary woman at something approaching their true relative values. And it is indeed true that many of the facts have been purposely concealed; others are obscure; and still others appear on the surface so contradictory that they seem to bear no relation to any accepted picture of the woman, and hence have been more or less ignored.

It is the task of the biographer to reconcile, as well as to recount; to omit, in selecting his data, only material representative of that already included. Otherwise he must cast the values of the picture out of balance. In particular it is necessary to avoid that state of mind which accompanies a desire to prove a preconceived thesis—the attitude which has resulted in attempts to show variously that Mrs. Eddy was an earthly archangel and a maniacal fiend. Certainly neither interpretation can suffice to explain her glamorous rise from the lot of a simple country girl to a position of unique eminence and wealth, such as few men or women through their own efforts ever attain.

There undoubtedly prevails a certain notion that all those who dare to talk intimately of God should conform in character to a conventional pattern, much as the designs for sacred faces on church windows must all have an orthodox stare. This is a notion that has been shared alike, strangely enough, both by the devout and the ribald ungodly. Whenever the disciples of a proclaimed Messiah have met with evidence that their saint was indeed quite different from their ready-made concept of what the design should be, they have often denied the legitimacy of the facts. On the basis of the same evidence, the ribald have denied the legitimacy of the Messiah.

There is obviously a fallacy here somewhere. Perhaps it lurks in the idea that anyone can ever know how a Messiah should really appear.

*   *   *

Some effort must be made to avoid all such deplorable pre-conceptions in seeking to form a just understanding of a figure so unpatterned as Mrs. Eddy. Those who would carve her down until nothing remained but a marble saint, on whom there settled somehow a mystic glow from heaven, have actually done her an even greater injustice than those others who wagged their heads gleefully on discovering she was too vital a being ever to be hewn into such a shape. The miracle-hungry canon-izers rob her of far more stature than the belittling scoffers, who have at least left her her human foibles; for while strip-ping her of humanity they cannot possibly give her divinity in its place.

Now it is because Mary Baker Eddy was a woman with an impassioned urge for life and self-expression throbbing in her veins, and not a passive figurine, that she has any possible hu-man significance. It is because of this that hers was a gorgeous adventure—gorgeous no matter what the beginning and what the end. What if she was indeed a soul obsessed? Few who have become instruments for great ideas were ever less. What if she was indeed ignorant, distraught, fearful—lustful of power and glory—tortured by self and the universe—eager for wealth and grandeur? What if she made mad mystery out of ignorance, inspiration out of dread?

The streets of the whole world are thronged by those who are her kin.

In these pages, then, will be found no fumbling apologia for Mary Baker Eddy, and no effort to fit her into the image of a saint on calloused knees. Any attempt to understand reality must at least be a braver human tribute than any feeble effort to extenuate. When she said that her course was "impelled by a power not one's own," it would not matter if she erred. For at least she was impelled. This is enough. The force in her of that great inner Will which in every being creates its own fulfilment—compensate how it must—needs no justification. It is beyond the little human labels of "good" and "evil." Such a force in all things, in all men, is that which is.

✐ ✐ ✐

It is a characteristic of logic that facts correctly arranged usually explain themselves; thus it is that biography is so largely a science of ordering and organization. Unfortunately great effort has been exerted toward keeping many of the facts regarding Mrs. Eddy from the world; and it appears probable that some of this material may never be released. There are now, however, sufficient facts at hand to portray all the highlights of her remarkable story; and these may be arranged in such natural and logically compelling order as to suggest that any additional information which becomes available in the future should serve merely as explanatory detail.

No matter what further biographical material is yet to be discovered, it is certain that to Georgine Milmine every subsequent biographer must owe an important debt. For Miss Milmine, not waiting until death had destroyed opportunity to record recollections that were invaluable, set out during Mrs. Eddy's lifetime to tramp up and down New England in the quest for those who still remembered the Mary Baker Glover of earlier years. The strange doors upon which Miss Milmine knocked, the unknown streets and country roads that she explored, yielded a mine of golden material not merely for the biographer but also for the psychologist and the neuro-pathologist—material which otherwise would have been utterly lost within a few years' time. That her book was withdrawn, and even the plates destroyed, does not lessen the obligation to her which the future must acknowledge—an indebtedness to a pioneer which footnotes can but partially express, and which this author is proud to record.

✦ ✦ ✦

Since first publication of this work a few months ago, the agents of Mrs. Eddy's church have left nothing undone in efforts to effect its suppression in turn, and—failing that—to discredit it utterly. As the book now goes into its fourth edition, and opportunity is presented to add important material further validating its viewpoint, it must be recorded that the officials of the Christian Science Church, despite their general denunciations, have not produced specific evidence to refute a single important statement the volume contains.

In consequence, what few small corrections appear in this edition have not been inspired by the church officials, except in a single instance where they pointed out a minor misstatement in connection with the description of the number present at Mrs. Eddy's funeral. The other changes—those that might well be necessitated in any compilation of this scope—are listed for the convenience of scholars on page 550.

In the Appendices the author is fortunate in now being able to present some of the extraordinary source material in the sensational Frye diaries. A short history of these important documents is included. To make the volume as complete a reference book as possible, a brief interpretation of Mrs. Eddy's literary sources has also been added.

It is of interest to note that the description of the duties of the Christian Science publicity forces which begins on page 392 appeared in all earlier editions of this work, and was an accurate forecast of these agents' recent manœuvres. That their campaign against this biography has not met with the success their efforts have previously enjoyed is a phenomenon for which the author desires to express deep appreciation not alone to the many booksellers who have resisted intimidation, but also to his publishers, who have stanchly ignored powerful pressure.

E. F. D.

January 15, 1930.

CONTENTS

PART I

✦   ✦   ✦

PART I

A QUEST FOR MINERVA'S PARENTAGE

"The most glorious exploits do not furnish us with the clearest discoveries of virtue or vice in men; sometimes a matter of less moment, an expression or a jest, informs us better of their characters and inclinations than the most famous sieges, the greatest armaments, or the bloodiest battles whatsoever."

—PLUTARCH.

I

Born in 1821, Mary Ann Morse Baker lived forty years of her existence before she found a real objective in life, and spent another twenty before she began to attain the recognition which eventually made the name of Mrs. Eddy famous. She had already reached the age of sixty before she even sighted her goal. And she was over eighty when she had fully revealed the illimitable resources of one of the most gallant and infinitely pathetic figures in modern times. Nor was it in her achievements that the real measure of her magnificence emerged. Rather was it in her very human weaknesses, and finally in her crushing defeats, when she stood alone yet indomitable in a universe where she never once found adequate understanding, that she proved her right to be called unique in her degree: above censure and beyond praise.

If hers had been only the ordinary span of life, she would have had hardly a mention in the pages of history. Thus it happened that few were ever interested in the story of her childhood until she reached a ripe old age; and when in her latter years she sat down to gratify this public interest and make an account of her memories, the record was not wholly to be relied upon. As with so many old people, the years had dimmed some events, idealized others, wholly obscured several passages, and in at least a few instances inserted recollections of occurrences for which no confirmatory evidence can be found.

It is known, however, that she was born in 1821, that the Baker family for some six generations had tilled the New England soil, and that the family stock was the hardy pioneer stuff in which indomitability of will seems a recognized and general characteristic.

Her birthplace of Bow, in New Hampshire, was a small village five miles from Concord, consisting in reality only of a group of farms loosely tied together under a town government. There was the usual district school as well as the homely meeting house, where the lean farmers and their overworked wives gathered weekly according to their established sense of Sabbath pleasure and duty.

The Baker family, of which Mary was the youngest, was not an unduly ample one in view of the contemporary fecundity of most New England fathers. Mary had three brothers, Samuel, Albert, and George; and two sisters, Abigail and Martha. Mark Baker, the father, was an imposing individual who in tintypes of the period shows the high forehead and piercing eyes which might belong either to idealist or zealot; the great heavy pout of the underlip and the harsh, set lines of the mouth reveal the zealot's mind. His daughter in later years was probably erring only by understatement in saying, "My father possessed a strong intellect and an iron will."

Abigail Baker, the mother, seems to have been endowed with the best qualities of those outstanding pioneer women who could work eighteen hours a day in providing necessities for their families and still find time and spirit left to be a mother. Cooking, spinning, weaving, sewing, mending, scouring, doctoring, teaching, were all a part of her usual routine duties, yet she managed somehow to be more than a laboring automaton. Like so many others, Abigail Baker died early, worn out with the struggle; and her husband, like so many contemporary husbands, promptly married again. Of the mother Mary later wrote, "I cannot speak as I would, for memory recalls qualities to which the pen never can do justice."

The family was not without good connections, which long years after its most eminent daughter delighted to recall. A relative on the Baker side was General Henry Knox, who acquired his title in the Revolution. Through a great-grandmother Moor Mrs. Eddy claimed relationship with Hannah More, "the pious and popular English authoress," and she also described other important forebears. In *Retrospection and Introspection* she said:

My ancestors, according to the flesh, were from both Scotland and England, my great-grandfather on my father's side being John McNeil of Edinburgh. . . . In the line of my Grandmother Baker's family was the late Sir John Macneill, a Scotch knight, who was prominent in British politics, and at one time held the position of ambassador to Persia.[1]

In later years this claim of connection with the Scottish peerage was challenged, after Mrs. Eddy had not only published it widely but had put the crest of the McNeil family upon her stationery. When both crest and claim were reproduced in a biographical sketch of Mrs. Eddy in the *Ladies' Home Journal*, Mrs. Florence Macalister of Aberdeen, Scotland, wrote a protest to Mrs. Eddy and also sent a corrected statement to be published in the London *Truth*. She said:

I am the only married grandchild of the late Right Honorable Sir John MacNeill, G. C. B., of Edinburgh, "who was prominent in British Politics and Ambassador to Persia," and Mrs. Eddy is certainly not my daughter. . . . I wrote to the Editor of the *Ladies' Home Journal* who published Mrs. Eddy's statement, asking him to publish a correction, and I sent a copy of the letter to Mrs. Eddy herself. She did not reply at all, and he excused himself from publishing it on the ground that the correction could not appear for five months.

After Mrs. Macalister's protest had been copied by numerous American papers Mrs. Eddy herself issued a statement saying that the whole thing was a misapprehension, and that genealogical writers should no longer take the statement about the Sir John MacNeill connection literally. Regarding the coat-of-arms, she explained that "Fannie McNeil, President Pierce's niece, afterwards Mrs. Judge Potter, presented me my coat-of-arms, saying that it was taken in connection with her own family coat-of-arms. I never doubted the veracity of her gift."[2]

It is a matter of record, however, that Mrs. Eddy used the coat of arms on her stationery almost until the end of her days, some years after expressing the wish that genealogical writers ignore the aristocratic claim.

---

[1] Page 1. Here, as in all subsequent annotations, the page reference applies to the most recent edition, unless otherwise noted.

The assorted spellings here accorded the MacNeill patronymic are apparently Mrs. Eddy's own.

[2] *Miscellany*, page 311. The use of *veracity* for *authenticity* is a typical Eddyism.

Mrs. Eddy displayed a tendency to idealize her youth as well as her ancestry. She made only the most cursory mention, for instance, of the sickness that is one of the most important threads running through Mary Baker's childhood. It was a strange sickness, inducing a lack of physical vitality, with a pronounced tendency to attacks of childish temper, hysteria, and sudden pains in the spine.

The tendency to temper she came by naturally. Mark Baker, her father, had a reputation for quick, hot angers and fierce prejudices. Known as "Squire" in the vicinity, and thoroughly respected as a God-fearing man who was honest to the smallest penny—even while he paid his workers the slimmest wages in the neighborhood—he managed nevertheless to make even his religion an occasion of embroilment. The Congregational Church at Tilton, where the family moved in 1836, entered on its records the story of numerous such quarrels. Mark did not hesitate to bring charges of backsliding and delinquency against "brethren and sistren" who failed to attend church regularly or to live up to his idea of their proper religious obligations.

The move to Tilton, named after its most prominent family and later christened Sanbornton Bridge, occurred in 1836. The Bakers undoubtedly improved their circumstances by the sale of the weather-beaten and unpainted old homestead at Bow; for Sanbornton Bridge was a larger centre, where manufacturing was developing. Here an opportunity for more real social life was presented to the Baker children, some of whom were now approaching the marriageable age.

Mary continued in that state of precarious health which from her infancy had so troubled the other stalwart members of the family. Her "fits," as they were known, were sufficient even to make the redoubtable Mark Baker pliant to the whims of his youngest daughter. During these seizures she exhibited symptoms that the modern psychologist would classify as hysteria in an unmistakable form, sometimes screaming, sometimes lying on the floor and pounding her heels up and down, and not infrequently passing into a state of apparent unconsciousness. These seizures were usually brought about by flashes of anger following some thwarting of desire. As a result, it soon became easier for the Bakers to allow Mary her own way than to try to oppose her. During long periods Mary was allowed to stay away from the district school and amuse herself around the house instead.

She was a brooding child, quick in her likes and dislikes, highly imaginative, and with a strong religious instinct. The Bible formed the regular and sometimes the only intellectual fare in the Baker household, and much of it doubtless was deeply etched on the child's consciousness. The story of Samuel was familiar to her through long repetition; and it is not difficult, knowing the love of self-dramatization which was with Mary Baker all her life, to understand how one of the incidents she relates of her childhood may have seemed wholly real. In her latter years she described it thus:

Many peculiar circumstances and events connected with my childhood throng the chambers of memory. For some twelve months, when I was about eight years old, I repeatedly heard a voice, calling me distinctly by name, three times, in an ascending scale. I thought this was my mother's voice, and sometimes went to her, beseeching her to tell me what she wanted. Her answer was always, "Nothing, child! What do you mean?" Then I would say, "Mother, who *did* call me? I heard somebody call *Mary,* three times!" This continued until I grew discouraged, and my mother was perplexed and anxious.[1]

Poor Mrs. Baker, with all her worries, must indeed have been perplexed. She knew how to make a home, but plumbing the intricacies of human psychology was undoubtedly out of her line. She was even more worried when Mary told her that Mehitable Huntoon, Mary's small cousin who occasionally came for visits, had also heard the mysterious call for "Mary." Perhaps, indeed, child minds being what they are, Mary had actually convinced Mehitable of the reality of the call. Finally Mrs. Baker caught the idea—that this must be a modern experience akin to that of Samuel's. She told Mary to answer the next time by saying "Speak, Lord; for Thy servant heareth."

[1] *Retrospection and Introspection*, page 8.

plumbed. And it would not be until several generations later that Emile Boirac would write:

The majority of hysterical symptoms belong to cryptopsychism, as may be realized by the list of such symptoms: fixed ideas, anesthesia, amnesia, paralysis, contractions, etc. It might be stated in confirmation of what Durand (de Gros) and Pierre Janet said, that it could be considered as the "key of all hypnotic phenomena." And better still, it might contain in itself the explanatory key to suggestion itself.[1]

Undoubtedly Mary Baker herself never realized the real nature of these recurrent attacks—attacks which followed her through all her life, as will be seen, recurring particularly during periods of great mental stress. And she always denied vigorously that they were associated with "temper." Thus she wrote, "My mother always presented my disposition as exemplary for her other children to imitate, saying, 'When do you ever see Mary angry?' When the first edition of *Science and Health* was published, Dr. Ladd said to Alexander Tilton, 'Read it, for it will do you good. It does not surprise me, it so resembles the author.' "[2]

Certainly between these periods of fierce emotional paroxysm, Mary was a child in many ways lovable, appealing, and of real charm. This is shown by a group of letters that were written just before and just after the family moved from Bow, and addressed to her brother, George Sullivan Baker, whom she called by his middle name. She loved her brothers dearly. Albert was her favorite, a talented lad who went to Dartmouth and afterward read law in the office of Franklin Pierce, at Hillsborough—the same Pierce who was later to be President of the United States. Albert was finally admitted to the bar, was elected to the legislature of his native state, and died at the age of thirty-one, just after he had been nominated to Congress.

George, whom she called Sullivan, has received less mention in her memoirs, but these letters to George show a close attachment between this other brother and his youngest sister.

[1] Émile Boirac, *La Psychologie Inconnue*, page 67.
[2] *Miscellany*, page 310.

The letters well illustrate the character of the girl as it was developing—affectionate, replete with little affectations, inclined to moments of brooding and loneliness. The first letter of record—and she calls it the second she ever wrote—is penned in her fifteenth year, on a day when her parents went to a funeral and drove over later to look at a farm at Sanbornton—perhaps the very farm Mark Baker eventually purchased. It includes a strange mixture of formality in style, which she had absorbed from the talk of her elders, and utter informality in spelling, the result of her long absences from school. Its reference to the gift of a toothpick that never arrived suggests the aroma of an age now almost beyond recall.[1]

Stating that the family had gone to attend the Sabbath funeral of a neighbor, so that she was "left alone to review past events," she went on to mourn her brother's absence:

There is one thing if I have not improved it aright I have learned from expperience to prize more perhaps than ever I did *before* that is *Dear brother* the *friendly advice* and *council* you was ever giving me and the lively interest you ever manifested in my welfare but now when I sit down to my *lonely* meal I have no brother Sullivan to encourage me as formerly—but there is no philosophy in repining I must extend the thought of benevolence farther than selfishness would permit and only add my health at presant is improveing slowly and I hope by dieting and being careful to sometime regain it. . . .

I have written much more than I intended as sister M. and I have both written and will now close giving you much thanks for the present you sent me by Mr. C. although I did not receive the tooth pick I shall take the will for the deed and think much of them for coming from you. Write every opportunity excuse all mistakes as this is the second letter I ever wrote and accept the well wishes of your *affectionate sister.*[2]

In the following year we see Mary writing in a less brooding and more spritely mood. The "Brother S." she refers to is

[1]This and the letters following, including the one written in Mary's twenty-sixth year, are among the very few Eddy documents which have not been subjected to extensive editing. Their immunity is due to their manner of discovery. A Mr. A. A. Beauchamp, antiquarian of New York, found them in an old trunk in the former home of Mrs. George Sullivan Baker at Tilton, when he went there searching for Americana after her decease. They were published for the first time in *Munsey's Magazine*, April, 1911, in connection with a critique prepared by Isaac F. Marcosson.

[2]Dated Sept. 7, 1835.

Samuel, who had gone to Boston with the son of a neighbor, one George Washington Glover, with the intention of learning the trade of a stone mason. She could not guess that in just a few years she would be George Washington Glover's widow as she wrote in 1836:

We have just finished our morning vacations, and I am engaged in the sweet emplyment of writing (or rather talking) to brother S. at Conn, and to comply with good *ton*, I shall first enquire for your health, spirits, and the like of that, hopeing time sill continues to glide smoothly as in former years, it continues to do so with us only when we are obligeed to ride in a *wagon* and then it is rough. . . . You cannot imagin the disappointment I felt on receiveing your letter that you should not return, but I hope it will not be long before I shal again see you, do not disappoint me but come and see us if you cannot stay.

Another letter in the same year is interesting because it tells in Mary Baker's own contemporary words of her home life. It is evident that neither Mary's occasional periods of illness, her father's outbursts of temper, nor the iron routine of the struggle of a farmer's family with the barren New England soil prevented honest gaiety and happiness.

Saying that "Esqr. Pierce" had been elected Senator to Congress, and that Albert was considering attractive "proposals" which Mr. Pierce had made to him, Mary continued in her primitive spelling:

We saw Uncle Baker not long since he is strangely altered and to appearence is wasting verry fast, enough enough of this. . . . We attended a party of young Ladies at Miss Hayes last evening she was truly sorry our Brother from Conn. was not there, but she is soon to be married and then the dilemma will close as it is your fortune to have some opposeing obstacle to extricate you. Oh brother I wish I could see you, and I hdly think Abby and I would be as sleepy as we wer the last night you spent with us; but could amuse ourselvs (if not you) by telling you things that would excite laughter if nothing more, but when are we to realize this this happiness? I am impatient to learn soon verry soon I hope; but if we are not to see you soon, to hear of your health and prosperity is a pleasure that none but those to whom we are most nearly can experience.[1]

And now comes what is perhaps the most important letter of

[1]Dated Dec. 20, 1836.

the entire group, containing as it does a reference to the neighboring Shakers and the curiosity in which they were held. Later commentators have noted that Mary Baker seemed to have owed something to Shaker theology in the final assembling of her ideas, but much has been conjecture. It has been pointed out that the main contribution of the Shakers to modern religious theory was the idea that God is both masculine and feminine, that they raised their prayers to "Our Father and Mother which are in Heaven." It is also worth noting that Ann Lee, the Shaker Leader, was claimed by some of her followers to be greater than Christ, and that she was also identified by some of these enthusiasts with the woman of the Apocalypse, described in Revelation. "Mother Ann" proclaimed that she had the gift of healing; felt that she assumed the sins and sufferings of her followers as they became freed of these burdens; governed her followers to some extent through fear; and allowed them to believe that she had some strange mental power which could inflict torture on them if she would. Her traditional sayings were treasured by her New England followers long after she died, and were a subject of profane discussion in communities where Shakers lived and gathered.

The Shakers called their church "The Church of Christ," and their main organization the "Mother Church."

Declaring that her spirits were "rather depresed tody," Mary wrote in her sixteenth year:

I will give you an abridged sketch of a gentleman recently from Boston, now reading medicine with a doctor of this town, a *perfect complet gentleman I met him a number of times at parties last winter* he invited me to go to the Shakers with him but my superiors thought it would be a profanation of the Sabbathe; and I accordingly did not go. But I have since then attended a wedding with a Mr. Bartlett he was groomsman and I bridsmaid; we had a fine time I assure you. I have been studying evry leisure moment this winter I shal attend school this summer if I possibly can as my health is extremely poor occasioned by a cold I hope as almost everry one is complaining of some disseas occasioned undoubtedly by our severe seasons. . . .

The following excerpts from the letter are of interest because they suggest moments of brooding and loneliness, together with

regret that she is too poor even to take writing lessons from
the itinerant master:

> Abigail is prepareing for the celebration of her nuptials, probbably,
> as soon as June; then there will be another tie severed, she will be lost
> to us irrevocably, *that is certain,* although it may be her gain. How
> changed in one short year! Dear brother can you realize it with me? if
> so just take a retrospect view of home see the remaining family placed
> round the blazing *ingle* scarcely able to form a semi circle from the loss
> of its number. . . .
> I believe I have written nearly all I intended to and perhaps all
> that will interest you, althoug I will tell you we had a call yesterday
> from the writeing master that is teaching at the village; he gave us a
> verry urgent invitation to attend, but Martha is not able and I have not
> wherewith. Although there is need enough of it it is evident. . . .

After the move from Bow to Sanbornton, Mary's health
showed some improvement. It is evident in her letters of this
period that she found herself more in harmony with her environment; that as she grew, she found more opportunity for
self-expression with consequently less frustration of emotional outlet. In her better moments she was quick, vivacious,
could even be charming, being endowed with a more or less
natural desire to please which apparently all her life was in
conflict with that other inborn desire to rule.

For many years Sanbornton residents remembered her as a
rather slight girl with fair and clear complexion, large gray
eyes that in moments of excitement could become almost
black, and rather dainty hands and feet that she used with
evidence of grace. At school she was not particularly bright,
for when she began attending school at Sanbornton she was
obviously handicapped by previous lack of educational training; at Bow she had been frequently absent. In later years
one of her old schoolmates said that "in spite of her back-
wardness she assumed a very superior air, and by her sentimental posturing she managed to attract the attention of the
entire school. She loved to impress us with fine stories about
herself and her family."

Mary's desire to "show off," her little affectations, her tendency to haughtiness, are all characteristics of the same complex which the psychiatrist would recognize in her emotional

seizures. It is not to be wondered at that she did not absorb much of a formal education; for the business of mastering spelling, punctuation and composition was a slow and boring task for a girl who had ambitions to be a poetess before she hardly passed her teens. Some of this childhood verse, which she sent to local newspapers and saw published, she saved to republish in later years after she became world-famous. These early literary creations show nothing unusual; rather they are the obvious products of an immature and introspective mind struggling for some form of self-expression—even if that form must be imitative. And so we have, preserved to us from those years, such stanzas as this:

> Here fame-honored Hickory rears his bold form,
> And bears[1] a brave breast to the lightning and storm,
> While Palm, Bay, and Laurel in classical glee,
> Chase Tulip, Magnolia, and fragrant Fringe-tree.

In her old age Mrs. Eddy was destined to be pricked by many sharp-pointed shafts for preserving these poetic creations of her childhood. Mark Twain, who crossed some of his best lances with her, wrote of the stanza quoted above:

"Vivid? You can fairly see those trees galloping around. That she could still treasure up, and print, and manifestly admire those Poems, indicates that the most daring and masculine and masterful woman that has appeared in the earth in centuries has the same soft, girly-girly places in her that the rest of us have."

Probably Mark Twain never even guessed about some of the strange places that were hidden in Mary Baker Eddy's heart.

---

[1]This spelling was corrected to "bares" after Mark Twain's comments, and so appears in present editions of *Retrospection and Introspection*, page 17 ff.

II

Mary Baker carried out of childhood a frail physique; a rudimentary education that was far richer with what she had absorbed from the book-talk of her brothers than with what she had learned at school; a tendency to long periods of depression and attacks of hysterical spasm, best described as neurasthenia; and a desire to get married.

Long years later she spoke glowingly of what she had received in tutelage from her brothers, and rebuffed the critics of her grammar and her various literary and historical allusions by declaring, "After my discovery of Christian Science, most of the knowledge I had gleaned from school books vanished like a dream. Learning was so illumined, that grammar was eclipsed."[1]

Unfortunately we have scant record of that side of her nature which is of far greater interest to the historian—the emotional, rather than the intellectual, development. It was at the age of twenty-two that she married George Washington Glover, who was the friend of Samuel Baker and the son of the Bakers' old neighbors, John and Nancy Glover, at Bow. The ceremony was performed two weeks before Christmas in 1843, at the Baker farmhouse near Sanbornton. It was a family gathering, and the sisters and brothers were there in full panoply with their respective husbands and wives.

Abigail six years before had married the most sought for beau of the village, Alexander Tilton, who was proprietor of a woollen mill bearing the Tilton name. She and her ample purse were eventually to prove a haven for Mary in time of trouble.

[1] *Retrospection and Introspection*, p. 10. For further statements of Mrs. Eddy regarding the extent of her learning, vd. *Miscellany*, p. 304: "I was early a pupil of Miss Sarah J. Bodwell, the principal of Sanbornton Academy, New Hampshire, and finished my course of studies under Professor Dyer H. Sanborn, author of Sanborn's *Grammar*. Among my early studies were Comstock's *Natural Philosophy*, *Chemistry*, Blair's *Rhetoric*, Whateley's *Logic*, Watts' *On the Mind* and *Moral Science*. At sixteen years of age, I began writing for the leading newspapers, and for many years I wrote for the best magazines in the South and North."

Samuel Baker was there from Boston with a wife who had previously been a missionary to the Indians. Martha with her husband, Luther Pillsbury of Concord, and George Baker, still unmarried, filled out the family circle. Albert had died before this event occurred.

"Wash" Glover, as he was nicknamed, was a hale and hearty fellow who had gone south following his apprenticeship at masonry in Boston; in Charleston, South Carolina, he had succeeded in forming a small contracting business. Some doubt has been thrown over his exact financial standing, although Mrs. Eddy later claimed that he owned several slaves and was an exceedingly prosperous young citizen. Whatever his own slave-owning status, his wife immediately caused a small local furore by advocating abolition among all her new Charleston acquaintances and friends.

Mr. Glover found it necessary to make a trip to Wilmington, North Carolina, to transact some business. He did not dare leave his wife behind to pursue the discussion of abolition, for arguments over slave owning were scarcely tactful in a community whose economic structure was founded on slavery, and were particularly to be avoided by the wife of a man who hoped to make a financial career there.

In consequence Mr. Glover took Mrs. Glover along to Wilmington. News travelled slowly in those ante-bellum days, and on arriving they found Wilmington in the midst of an epidemic of yellow fever, a now almost forgotten scourge which science was not to conquer until the dawn of the twentieth century.

Mr. Glover contracted the fever and died within nine days. It is related that he was a Mason and was cared for by fellow Lodge members, who considerately excluded his wife from the dangerous sick-room. It has further been recorded, with his widow's approval, that he was buried with elaborate Masonic rites in the local Episcopal cemetery in Wilmington.

Young Mrs. Glover was now left in a wholly dependent financial condition, and she was carrying the child who as George Washington Glover the second would cause one of the most poignant chapters in her history. She later authorized

the statement that she allowed the slaves of her husband to go
free, no record existing of this transaction because of South
Carolina's statutes on emancipation. Whatever young Glover's
business amounted to, there were no real assets following his
death. His widow therefore came North, was met in New
York by her brother, George Sullivan, and returned home to
the farmhouse of her parents, where in September she gave
birth to her son.

All in all, for a girl of Mary Baker's temperament it was an
unfortunate experience, one that might well have undermined
the strength of an emotionally far more stable temperament.
Sex always played a rather large part in her life; how large a
part indeed is revealed to the psychologist not so much by her
several marriages as by her subsequently constant efforts to
deny sex an orderly place in her scheme of existence. So persistently in later years did she deny the legitimacy of the demands of sex that many of her followers came to believe that
even cohabitation between husband and wife was unspiritual,
if not ungodly.

Had "Wash" Glover lived, and had Mary Baker Glover
retained this marital outlet for the tempestuous emotional
storms that swept over her regularly, the whole course of her
history might have been changed. As it was, for a long period
after her return to her father's home her life was despaired
of. She was unable even to nurse her child; and the boy was
put in charge of the wife of one Amos Morrison, local me-
chanic and locomotive builder. Mrs. Morrison had only recently given birth to twins.

So terrible were the attacks of hysteria to which Mrs.
Glover was now subject that her father had the local roads
covered with tan-bark and straw to shield her from the con-
vulsive shudders that were aroused even by the cheerful patter of horses' hoofs. When the tan-bark failed, old Mark
Baker would take his daughter up and rock her in his arms
like a baby.

Such rockings undoubtedly seemed to help. When the strain
at home grew almost unbearable, the Bakers sent Mary over
to visit her sister Abby Tilton, whose large house was well

able to accommodate an invalid; and Mrs. Tilton took turns with the rocking. Years later old neighbors told Georgine Milmine how Mrs. Tilton, hoping to end this onerous practice, devised the bright scheme of importing a large and commodious cradle, built from an old sofa with a balustrade so that the occupant could not fall out, and attached to a rocker in which the hired man could sit and rock both himself and the invalid by the hour.[1]

So effective was the cradle that Mrs. Tilton also had a swing installed in her sister's room, hung on hooks in the ceiling rafters. When Mrs. Glover grew weary of being cradled she could sit up in the swing and be pushed by her boyish nephew, Albert Tilton. If these sessions waxed long and Albert grew weary, sometimes the neighborhood boys would be called in to lend their services; and one of them later related how when Mrs. Glover was too nervous even to have some one in the room with her, it was the custom to tie a rope to her swing and pull it back and forth from outside her chamber door.

In after years it was related by neighbors that during some of these seizures Mrs. Glover would take morphine, which seemed to ease her pain temporarily, but made matters worse for the rest of the family. For morphine only aggravated her hysteria, and John Varney, the hired man, had to be sent for to hold her in the bed, to prevent her harming herself. In words attributed by the New York *World* to Mrs. H. L. Philbrook, of Tilton, wife of a Methodist clergyman and a former schoolmate of Mary's:

I knew Mary Baker from the time she was fourteen. I knew of John Varney's being sent for to keep her from harming herself during her hysteria after taking morphine. It made her crazy. . . . I myself have gone to get the Lang boy to rock Mary Baker.[2]

When every known device would fail to calm her, a local mesmerist was sometimes called on—one "Boston John"

---

[1]Mrs. Eddy, on page 313 of her *Miscellany*, denies the tan-bark story and also the cradle incident. But the tan-bark episode is included in her approved biography by Sibyl Wilbur, on page 43, and the cradle incident seems well authenticated.

[2]New York *World*, October 30, 1906.

Clark, whose trade was bridge building and whose hobby was the new Ism which was titillating the curiosity of all New England. Practitioners to-day regard suggestion, whether or not associated with the use of hypnotism, as a most effective method of dealing with cases of hysteria showing symptoms such as those displayed by Mrs. Glover. Clark knew little of the scope of his hobby, but he was delighted to have a chance to test its possibilities on anybody; and he found Mrs. Glover peculiarly suggestible.

It must not be thought that a deplorable situation of this character lasted for twenty-four hours a day and seven days a week. Had such been the case Mrs. Glover's relatives would only have had the choice of two alternatives: either to go to the insane asylum themselves or to send Mrs. Glover there. These seizures, as they may well be termed, were spasmodic and recurrent, and would pass as swiftly as they came. Mary would then be up on her feet again and appear little the worse for the recent nightmare.

She even tried to make an effort at self-support. Twice she attempted to teach school. And twice she failed. The attempts are worth mention, not because of their failure but rather because they reveal how little real judgment or self-knowledge Mary Baker Glover must have possessed at this time. A temperament less fitted for schooling children is difficult to imagine. One story of these attempts has survived, to the effect that Mrs. Glover made her scholars march around the room singing a popular roundelay:

> We will tell Mrs. Glover,
> How much we love her;
> By the light of the moon
> We will come to her.

Mrs. Eddy in the dignity of her later years resented the fact that this inconsequential rhyme should be brought to light, took her pen in hand, denied authorship, and asserted it was only a paraphrase of a current song, as indeed it was.

On her better days Mrs. Glover was able to attend the town sewing circle, write verse for the local newspapers, and find occasion to impress the neighbor women with details of her aristocratic life in the South. Sometimes she would refer to Glover as "Colonel," sometimes as "Major."[1] Always she took pains to create the picture of a young Southern gentleman, wholly different from the plain Wash Glover that Tilton had known. It would seem that her health was never sufficiently robust to permit her to care for her young son, who was with his mother only on rare occasions. Her state of mind at this time, pensive, with a tendency to affect light social graces, is well shown in a letter addressed to Martha Rand, then visiting at Bath, in Maine. Martha was destined to marry George Sullivan Baker in 1849. The letter was undated, but was evidently written when Mrs. Glover was about 26 years old. It hints very definitely that the young widow had found a temporary beau in one John M. Burt.

After a long introduction written in what she describes as a "mood lachrymal," in which she declares herself "so weary of solitude, I have half determined this very moment to throw aside my pen and wait to weep," Mrs. Glover once again mentions her straitened financial circumstances:

—Little of real marvel has occurred since you were an inhabitant of S. B. The Sem. ladies are getting up a fare to defray the expense of *building* opperations, such as fitting up an assembly room. Miss Lane is figurante and directress. Wonderful! that a girl of *twenty two summers* can be so sage in counsel!!! I have had an invite to join but *dis child* won't spend a whole *shilling* of *borrowed* money again on charitable occasions, I think. Prof Sanborn is going to leave the venerable shades with his most worthy spouse, children and chattels! Goodale is for taking exit soon; after so many ladies are intoxicate with the *"critter."* John M. Burt has *paid* an annual visit to the homestead (not I) recently, and spoke of Miss Rand very kindly—wished me to send a little love to her. He now intends to go to Withsconsin after he graduates in August. I hope then people will mind their business about either of us, as I am getting a little *mad* at their *lies,* for such they are . . .

I feel anxious to hear from you and how you found your dear Aunt. Be careful of your own health to preserve it, tis the greatest of earthly blessings and without which little else can be enjoyed. My own health

---

[1]This confusion in titles was carried by Mrs. Eddy into her later records. Vd. *Miscellany*, page 312, for comparison with *Retrospection and Introspection*, page 19, and *Message to the Mother Church for 1902*, page 15.

is *poor* this Spring, the consequence of the Season only, I hope. . . . And I trust the future has stores of joy for you; and with life in its endless vicissitudes let us ever remember, there is one "who careth for us"—too wise to err, too *good* to be unkind. On Him may you rely, and find a Father and a friend. Yes, dear Mathy, this is my only consolation, *unworthy* as I am—and tis the greatest I can recommend to those I love. Please excuse this hasty hasty scrawl. George has been constantly at my elbow, which must account for the execution.

Mrs. Glover's writing was by no means confined to letters. She had apparently developed a nebulous desire some years previously to become an "authoress" and a "poetess," and she sent the occasional creations of her more reflective hours to any nearby editors who gave promise of literary hospitality. One of these early poems is preserved in the pages of *The Covenant* of May, 1846. Called "The Emigrant's Farewell," it obviously was written shortly after Mary left her New England home to accompany young Glover southward. Nine long stanzas repeat the farewell theme; the fourth indicates that the verses were autobiographical—the product of some homesick hours during which the writer found solace in tying up her grief in a formal package:

> Home of the heart,—New England Shores
> Long since I bade adieu,
> And shall I view those scenes no more
> Where childhood revelled free,—
> The foliage o'er each wild nook flung,
> Where birds in wanton glee
> 'Mid azure skies the echo rung
> Of pastime's liberty?

In *The Covenant* of November, 1846, we find an example of her contemporary prose. This publication was an organ of the Odd-Fellows fraternity, to which Mr. Glover appears to have belonged and in which his wife seems therefore to have taken a passing interest. Her article was evidently written with the purpose of defending the Odd-Fellows against the resentment of small town wives who disliked the mysterious disappearances of their husbands on Lodge nights. With an amusing mixture of pomposity and play on words—all the airs of a Bishop tickling a kitten—young Mrs. Glover wrote:

Can a feeling pervade the benevolent bosom in any one of Eve's fair daughters, opposed to the best interests of her sex,—the extension of benevolent institutions,—simply because they are of secret origin? . . .

Let woman, sympathizing woman, be the *last* to lift up a voice against unobtrusive charity, simply because its modest claims are not wholly understood, but sufficient unto the end are the manifestations thereof. . . .

To bid bold defiance to what the world might tolerate, would constitute her *Odd*, by proof unequivocal, in past or present ages. Again, she must have had some coevals in virtue to nerve the hand and encourage the heart of *associated* cooperation; else, little good could have resulted from unbefriended and unsustained effort. Hence, let it be the pride of purity, to be Odd, as is defined, secret if wise, and ever associated in pious endeavors.

Her literary ambitions did not die with the passing of young Glover, and she continued her contributions to local journals after she returned north as a widow with a posthumous child. These effusions were, of course, extremely spasmodic in their production—their chances for preservation in the thin periodicals of the day were at the same time precarious. But they at least afforded their author a pastime.

Thus several years were passed. Mrs. Glover's young son was farmed out to the care of one Mahala Sanborn, daughter of a neighboring blacksmith. Mahala at times had played nurse to Mrs. Glover herself. In 1849 Mrs. Glover's mother died, and Mark Baker promptly set about the business of looking for another wife. His financial circumstances had for a long while been improving. George Baker had gone into the mill of Alexander Tilton, husband of Abigail, and had worked his way up to become a mill agent and eventually a partner. George and his partner both took a kind interest in Mark Baker's finances, advising the old man on investments. As with so many others in that New England country where per capita savings accounts still average highest in the nation, Mark Baker had always spent less than he earned in income from his crops; and this surplus was now managed in a fashion that brought him a comparative independence. He built what was for that time an imposing residence in town, adjoining the white-columned house of the Tiltons, turned his love for disputation into politics, and in the autumn of 1850 took unto his bosom a widow from Londonderry, New Hampshire, by the name of Mrs. Elizabeth Patterson Duncan.

Mrs. Glover in 1850 had been a widow for five years. She had lived now with her sister Abigail, and now with her father, a rather aimless, inconsequential existence, punctuated with her racking illnesses, and, during more buoyant periods, with social and literary flutterings. Besides her flights into verse there were occasional articles of a political flavor, usually mentioning the evils of slavery as discovered from her sojourn in the South. She was now thirty years old, and her son was five. And the future loomed without incident before her.

It was at this time that she developed more than incidental interest in the strange influence called sometimes mesmerism, often magnetism, sometimes hypnotism, that was engaging the attention of all New England. Mesmer had electrified Paris with his theories as far back as 1778, and magnetism arrived in Britain only ten years later. Interest in the strange phenomena associated with this mysterious force seems first to have blossomed in New England in 1836 under the ministrations of Charles Poyen, a young Frenchman who had emigrated the preceding year. Again, in 1848, another New Englander by the name of Grimes dabbled in hypnotic phenomena, and published some observations under the title of "Electro-Biology."

In a day when newspapers were scant both in size and content—when a town twenty miles away was a day's journey distant—and when life was a business of hard routine and recreations were few—any subject of fresh interest in a community was talked and re-talked and discussed still again until its last drop of life was wrung away.

Thus Sanbornton had its mesmerism craze, as it later had its spiritualism sensations; and just as Mary Baker had heard "calls" when she first learned about the experiences of Samuel, so she now proved to be highly susceptible to the influence of mesmerism, and made a subject to warm the heart of any parlor investigator who sought to exercise his amateur powers. The new Ism provided entirely too good an opportunity to be missed by one who had always gloried in being the centre of interest in any circle she occupied.

And so it happened that Mrs. Glover developed a habit of falling into trances.[1] Sometimes, *mirabile dictu*, this would happen right in the midst of an ordinary social call, and on such occasions she could delight her breathless audience by describing "scenes and events." Old neighbors long remembered that "Boston John" developed an idea of putting these interesting clairvoyant powers to practical use; thus he hypnotized Mrs. Glover and questioned her regarding the location of lost and stolen articles, and once even of the body of a boy who had been drowned. She never managed to give any useful information, but it is related that she described the hiding place of some fabled Captain Kidd's treasure, which was dug for near Lynn several days after she had directed her auditors to that spot.[2]

There is no evidence that Mrs. Glover ever developed any clairvoyant ability that might interest the modern psychological investigator; there is also no evidence that she was insincere in her various manifestations. With a temperament such as hers, with a nature so extravagantly susceptible, a mind that was suggestible to an obviously high degree, the threshold between her subjective and objective world was shadowy and constantly shifting. It is probable that Mrs. Glover herself believed—for the moment—in the reality of these trance-like states.

A little later, when the Fox sisters electrified the country with their Rochester table rappings, spirit seances arrived in Sanbornton, to provide its inhabitants with new mental fodder, and these little social events were staged in the best front parlors of the town, including Mark Baker's. Again it was too tempting an opportunity for the lover of an audience to miss; and Mrs. Glover now began to receive messages from

---

[1]Despite the statement on page 71 of *Science and Health* that "I never could believe in spiritualism," Mrs. Glover's dabblings in this hobby have been too specifically described by old neighbors, and too painstakingly recorded by Miss Milmine, to leave any possible room for belief that Mrs. Eddy's later denials should be taken seriously.

[2]Vd. Milmine, *Life of Mary Baker G. Eddy*, page 30.

the dead. Like the Fox sisters, she was also highly successful in producing table rappings. The Foxes later confessed to using their knees; Mrs. Glover perhaps thought that she was really a channel for occult forces.

On the whole she was and long remained a neighborhood curiosity. She never formed any close friendships, and her oddities did not escape comment. She was still an "authoress" as well as an occasional "seeress"; she used large and unfamiliar words in her speech; and she combined them in a fashion, as indicated by her letters, that was evidently intended to be impressively sweeping. Despite a complexion that remained fair and beautiful to the end of her days, she affected rouge and powder—toilet accessories that were almost unknown to most simple New England girls of 1850, that were indeed, until several generations later, regarded generally as the mark of a "gay woman." There is, let it be emphasized, no suggestion that this toilet make-up was with Mrs. Glover the mark of anything but a rather pitiful vanity; she was merely an unstable little creature, eager in her frail conceits.

There was one cosmetic, however, which she never employed—and for the same reason that she always liked flowers only because of their color, and not their scent. Mrs. Glover never used perfume. She was entirely without a sense of smell.

She was at all times romantic and sentimental, read a great deal of poetry while she was trying her own hand at verse-making, and spent long hours with such romantic novels of the day as she could lay her hands on. She never felt too poorly to exhibit a new vivacity in the presence of an eligible young man, and she liked to think herself such a heroine as some of her favorite novels described. She developed a sentimental fancy for John H. Bartlett, of Hill, New Hampshire, the young gentleman who had once played groomsman to her bridesmaid, as described in an earlier letter to her brother Sullivan. Even after young Bartlett went to California, she continued to have amorous day dreams that centred about his manly form.

When word came back at the end of three years that Bartlett had died and was buried on an inaccessible part of the coast, Mary was for a while inconsolable. She at once put on mourning, dramatically made a public announcement of her grief, and insisted that Bartlett's father hold a funeral service for the son, even though the corpse was missing. This was done, and neighbors long told how Mrs. Glover appeared at the ceremony wearing full widow's weeds—borrowed from several considerate friends who really thought that she and the handsome John had been secretly married—and how she wept copious tears as chief mourner.

There now came another brief climax in her career—the necessity for making a decision regarding her son's future. Shortly before Mark Baker became betrothed to the London-derry widow, Mahala Sanborn had herself decided to get married; she had grown into the graces of one Russell Cheney, of Groton, a town distant by thirty or forty miles in the mountains. Mahala wanted to take George with her, for her constant mother-care of the child had made a warm place for him in her spinster heart.

Mahala's desire seemed a fortunate solution for a problem that must have burdened both the Tiltons and the Bakers. Mark Baker's new wife could hardly be expected to undertake the care of a foster-grandchild; and poor Abigail Tilton felt that she had her Christian hands more than full in caring for Mary alone. A new wife in the Baker home meant obviously that Mary was a permanent inheritance for the Tilton estab-lishment.

Thus it was decided that Mahala should have George. There is no record, other than Mrs. Glover's own version of the incident, written many years later, to show that she was more deeply affected by the parting than would be expected in a rather volatile and irresponsible soul. The final separation came just before Mark Baker's second marriage. Mrs. Glover celebrated her sorrow by writing a poem. She tells about it in this wise:

A few months before my father's second marriage, to Mrs. Elizabeth Patterson Duncan, sister of Lieutenant-Governor George W. Patterson of New York, my little son, about four years of age, was sent away from me and put under the care of our family nurse, who had married, and resided in the northern part of New Hampshire. I had no training for self-support, and my home I regarded as very precious. The night before my child was taken from me, I knelt by his side throughout the dark hours, hoping for a vision of relief from this trial. The following lines are taken from my poem, "Mother's Darling," written after this separation :—

> Thy smile through tears, as sunshine o'er the sea,
> Awoke new beauty in the surge's roll!
> Oh, life is dead, bereft of all, with thee,—
> Star of my earthly hope, babe of my soul.

. . . The family to whose care he was committed very soon removed to what was then regarded as the Far West. After his removal a letter was read to my little son, informing him that his mother was dead and buried. Without my knowledge a guardian was appointed him, and I was then informed that my son was lost. Every means within my power was employed to find him, but without success. We never met again until he had reached the age of thirty-four, had a wife and two children, and by a strange providence had learned that his mother still lived, and came to see me in Massachusetts.[1]

Mrs. Glover in later years made the statement that she entered into a second marriage with the hope of making a home where she could have George with her, but that his step-father was unwilling so to yield to a mother's love.

She further declared that this second marriage was "very unfortunate." Daniel Patterson, the other partner to the ceremony, came to the same conclusion. But he could hardly have known, when he fell in love with Mary's volatile charms, the nature of the volcanic explosives which lay beneath the little mannerisms which struck his fancy.

[1] *Retrospection and Introspection*, page 20.

III

Daniel Patterson was a great hearty, bluff fellow who was handsome, genial, and over six feet tall—the very sort of male who feels all his protective instincts aroused in the company of a slight, yielding, clinging little piece of feminine humanity.

He was drawn to Mary Glover on his first sight of her, and determined to marry her. Mary Glover for her part could be charming when she chose; her airy vivaciousness, her volubility, her desire to please could all be readily converted into courting assets. Patterson was a dentist with a trade scattered over the countryside and headquarters in Franklin, New Hampshire. He dressed in the grand manner becoming his handsome frame, affected a frock coat and silk hat, wore a full beard, and was altogether a Beau Brummel.

When Mark Baker heard of the Doctor's intentions, he told the dentist frankly of Mary's nervous physical condition, but this warning served only to heighten the lover's ardor. The wedding took place June 21, 1853; it was a period in which Mary was again afflicted with a "spell," and her lover carried her downstairs for the ceremony and then hoisted her up again after the bonds were tied. When she was sufficiently recovered the bride and groom repaired to Franklin where he had made a payment on a house. He was not particularly well-to-do, but his patients liked him, and his income seemed sufficient for the two.

Mrs. Tilton was amazed and relieved to find her burden so miraculously lifted from her hands; it had never occurred to her in her wildest dreams that any person could have the temerity wilfully to assume the burden of ministering to her neurotic sister. Mary had made neither a pleasant invalid nor an agreeable guest; she had never hesitated, for instance, to argue heatedly with any of Mrs. Tilton's other guests who disagreed with her own ideas on slavery; and her political views had involved her in tactless disputes on more than one occasion. Whether or not she had any warm convictions on

the subject, she at least enjoyed the opportunity of holding
the centre of the stage in any argument; and she could always
win an important point by referring grandly to her Carolina
observations and experiences.

As Mrs. Patterson, Mary Baker now had far less opportunity to display her forensic inclinations. Franklin was a
drab factory town where she found no friends, few acquaintances, and no recreation. For the three years she lived there
Mrs. Patterson was bedridden much of the time. Although
she later denied memory of "any such stuff"[1] it is recorded[2]
that she sent for her cradle, and that Patterson went and
fetched it in a large wagon.

Dr. Patterson was often away from home, seeking for
teeth in need of a pull and aches that demanded a dentist's
care; and his wife was consequently left often to herself for
many days at a time. It was not an experience which could
benefit her egocentric and rather brooding disposition. After
three years in Franklin, the Doctor having discovered no
great number of patients who yearned for his care in the
surrounding villages, a move was made to North Groton.

Groton occupied a valley in the White Mountains, inaccessible to travellers except by stage coach, and a lonely and
isolated place. For Mrs. Patterson the move could not have
been wholly a happy one. When in the centre of the stage and
with people around her to be impressed, she had incentive to
wake her sleeping vitality and overcome some of her handicaps; but alone and without even a near-neighbor in that
rugged mountain country, she fell prey to all her old moods
of depression and moroseness, with punctuating periods of
emotional paroxysm. Part of this time the Doctor managed
to supply her with a housekeeper, and there were frequent
attacks when the old woman would find her mistress lying
absolutely rigid, with foam upon her lips.[3] For these attacks
Mrs. Patterson kept a supply of "medicine,"[4] which the old
woman would duly administer.

[1]*Miscellany*, page 313.   [2]Milmine.
[3]Vd. Sibyl Wilbur, *Life of Mary Baker Eddy*, page 62.
[4]*Ibid*.

It will be recalled that it was at Groton that the Cheneys and young George Glover had settled down. Despite their proximity Mrs. Patterson saw little of her son, and in 1857 the Cheneys packed up their household goods and moved west. George, who was now thirteen, was taken along with them, but before his departure on this exciting adventure he said his farewells not only to his mother but also to his relatives in Tilton, where he was taken for a final visit with his grandfather and his Aunt Abigail. The Cheneys settled at Enterprise, Minnesota, and wrote at length and often to their many friends and relatives in the old neighborhood. When, in 1861, George wrote his mother that he was going to join the army, she was as pleased and proud, according to an old neighbor, as any other mother with a boy in the army.

Mrs. Patterson was not wholly without a certain evanescent love for her son; she was only lacking in that yearning and tender self-abnegation which makes for motherhood. She had never held friends, for she had nothing to share of friendship; and similarly she never held her son, for she had nothing of motherhood to give.

Her existence in Groton became more and more self-centred, brooding, miserable. Dr. Patterson kept up his wandering travels in search of paying patients. When patients or pay were scarce he remained at intervals in Groton, running a small mill that adjoined the Patterson house and drew power from the nearby mountain stream. His sojourns at home were far from satisfying, made dreary as they were by the ills of a neurotic wife whose strange spells and fierce tempers became a byword over the whole neighborhood. Long afterward a North Groton correspondent addressed a letter concerning this period to the *Plymouth Record*, at the time of the dedication of a Christian Science Church at Concord, July 16, 1904: And he said:

With the announcement of the dedication of the Christian Science Church at Concord, the gift of Mary Baker Glover Patterson Eddy, the thoughts of many of the older residents have turned back to the time when Mrs. Eddy, as the wife of Daniel Patterson, lived in this place. These people remember the woman at that time as one who carried herself above her fellows. With no stretch of the imagination they remember her ungovernable temper and hysterical ways, and particularly well do they remember the night ride of one of the citizens who went for her husband to calm her in one of her unreasonable moods. The Mrs. Eddy of today is not the Mrs. Patterson of then, for this is a sort of Mr. Hyde and Dr. Jekyll case, and the woman is now credited with many charitable and kindly acts.

The night ride referred to was long a chapter in neighborhood history. Dr. Patterson had finally learned that one of the most efficacious treatments which could be administered to his wife during her periods of consuming hysteria was to leave her severely alone, as Mark Baker had himself discovered, after long experience. It is related that after Mary had grown to womanhood, her father once so far yielded to the opinion of the neighbors that her spells were merely temper tantrums as to try an experiment. When his grown daughter threw herself violently to the floor after he had challenged her in an argument, he walked away and left her lying there alone. An hour later, when he returned, Mary had retired to her room; and when supper was called she came down in the calmest of moods. Thereafter Mark Baker had ceased to take her seizures so seriously.

Like old Squire Baker, Dr. Patterson had also become acclimated. One night in Groton, when he was absent on one of his usual trips, Mrs. Patterson was overcome by one of her dark and nervously brooding moods that ended in the usual hysteria. When a neighbor was hastily called she cried that she was dying and that her husband should be sent for immediately. It was a bitter winter's night; the roads were almost impassable with snowdrifts. Nevertheless the neighbor hitched up his team, bundled himself into muffler, gloves and greatcoat, and set out in the middle of the night to make the thirty-mile drive to Franklin, where the Doctor was stopping.

He paused only once in the terrific journey, for a change of horses. When he reached Franklin he found Dr. Patterson leisurely working away at a patient. He told his news breathlessly. The dentist grinned good-naturedly. "She'll probably hold over until I finish this job, anyway," Patterson remarked. And he went on with his work.

When the two of them got back to Groton late that night they found Mrs. Patterson rocking away quietly in her chair, her illness completely vanished and everything serene.

Mrs. Patterson was seldom wholly alone during her illnesses. She had the old woman housekeeper for a while, and afterward a blind girl who one day "knocked at the door"— according to the later story of Mrs. Patterson—and stayed after the housekeeper left.[1]

Mrs. Patterson, as previously, had her good days as well as bad, and occasionally found time to indulge her old hobbies. The neighboring Kidders showed an inclination to be friendly because of an interest enjoyed mutually by Mrs. Patterson and Mrs. Kidder in the mysteries of Spiritualism. Mrs. Patterson became rather attached to a child that was born at this time to the Kidder household, and named him Mark after her father. To an older son of fifteen, Daniel, she gave spasmodic school lessons.

Dr. Patterson did not remain at home longer or oftener than necessary. Rumors were not lacking that his journeys around the country-side held more pleasant rewards for him than swollen jaws. An amiable, easy-going, handsome chap, he could undoubtedly appreciate the smile of a buxom country lass after some of his sessions at home, and if he was sometimes given more than a smile there are few who could have begrudged him his moments. There is a story that one of his gallantries once resulted in his being pursued to his very door by the husband of one of his conquests. Such events doubtless did not help Mrs. Patterson's state of nerves.

Financially the Doctor went from bad to worse. According to the fixed habits of mortgages, the one on his house at Groton came due. It was a week when both the cupboard and the Doctor's pockets were bare. The farmer holding the mortgage decided to evict the debtor and regain his property. Dr. Patterson resorted to a fist-fight, and the farmer resorted to law.

[1] *Miscellany*, page 311.

The farmer won. Word was sent to Mrs. Tilton to come and do her duty. She came in a carriage, and as she and Mrs. Patterson drove back down the mountain side the ironic farmer went into the church and slowly tolled the bell. It was a dramatic moment, and Mrs. Patterson broke into sobs. Back of the carriage followed the blind girl, stumbling along in the dust and also shedding tears.

The blind girl, at least, had found some happiness in that unpainted, dreary little house on the mountain side. She ran along after the carriage for six miles. Mrs. Tilton doubtless felt that she already had enough on her hands without worrying about a blind orphan. And Mrs. Patterson was busy weeping for her own woes.[1]

Shortly thereafter the Doctor took his wife to room and board with a Mr. and Mrs. John Herbert at Rumney Station. Mrs. Patterson seemed now to have settled down into a chronic state of invalidism. It was not long before her exacting ways, her petulant humors, her sudden hysterias, became too much for the tranquil Herberts. Dr. Patterson got her a small cottage to herself in Rumney Village where only a servant need bear the brunt of her moods.

It was not long thereafter that the Doctor went to Washington for the purpose of discharging a commission for Governor Berry of New Hampshire, who had collected a fund to be distributed among Union sympathizers in the South. The great war had now become almost the sole topic of village and town discussion everywhere; Mary Patterson's minor adventures into magnetism and spiritualism were no longer of interest to any one but herself. Dr. Patterson, when he got to Washington, seems to have sought a commission on the army's medical staff, and to have got involved in the Battle of Bull Run. He was taken prisoner by the Confederates, escorted to the famous old Libby prison, and held for duration.

Mrs. Patterson, as usual when life took a dramatic turn, wrote a poem on the occasion and published it in the local paper. The date is June 20, 1862. It is addressed "To a Bird

[1] Vd. *Wilbur*, page 65.

Flying Southward." After an apostrophe to the "sweet thing" the poetess writes:

> I, too, would join thy sky-bound flight
> To orange groves and mellow light,
> And soar from earth to loftier doom,
> And light on flowers with sweet perfume,
> And wake a genial happy lay—
> Where hearts are kind and earth so gay.
> Oh! to the *captive's* cell I'd sing
> A song of hope—and *freedom* bring—
> An olive leaf I'd quick let fall,
> And lift our country's blackened pall;
> Then homeward seek my frigid zone,
> More chilling to the heart *alone*. . . .

There were four other stanzas of equal length, all expressive of a formal grief.

There is no doubt that from Mary Baker Patterson's point of view she was now, and had been for years, a very sick woman. She had great spinal weakness and periods of complete catalepsy; her nervousness even during comparatively well periods was responsible for a sort of palsy. These symptoms, as well as the others which so long had been familiar to every one with whom she came in contact, may well have been only phases of the hysteria from which she had suffered since a child. But an illness whose cause is only a neurosis is to its victim none the less oppressive and real.

Of this long and poignant period in her career, Mrs. Eddy had in later years little to say. It is not even mentioned in her autobiography. From 1844 to 1866 the years had flowed by in a sluggish stream, utterly wasted. She had let them carry her whither they would, had made only one or two fleeting attempts to help herself, and had never raised her hand to do anything for any one else. At forty she found herself alone, unloved even by her relatives and her own son, poverty-stricken, pain-racked, purposeless. Regarding her son old Mark Baker once declared, "Mary acts like an old ewe that won't own its lamb."

It was now, when she had almost reached middle age and had spent half of her allotted span, that she first met Quimby.

Before Dr. Patterson had left for Washington his wife had heard strange reports and seen interesting circulars describing the work of Phineas P. Quimby, of Portland, Maine. Quimby was reported to be performing miraculous cures throughout the New England states, solely by the use of mesmerism or hypnotism, two terms which were used interchangeably. He used no medicines, and his methods never failed to heal even chronic diseases of long history.

Mrs. Patterson, who had always had a penchant for the esoteric, was immediately interested; and her husband, who had tried to yield to her every whim, wrote to Quimby on October 14, 1861.[1] He had heard that Quimby was coming to Concord. Dr. Patterson wrote that his wife had been an invalid from a spinal disease for many years, that she had heard of Quimby's "wonderful cures" and that she would like to see him either in Concord or Portland. Quimby did not come to Concord as he had planned, and Dr. Patterson soon left for Washington on the journey that ended in his subsequent imprisonment. His wife, without resources of her own, once more had to fall back on her relatives. Again it became the duty of Mrs. Tilton to play the good Samaritan, and again she gave her sister a room in the Tilton home at Sanbornton.

But Mrs. Patterson had suddenly developed a new interest, an unwonted air of determination. She was obsessed with the thought of managing a way to see Quimby. She had written to the healer before she left Rumney, expressing her "full confidence" in the Quimby methods, "as explained in your circular." She expressed a conviction that "only you can save me," begged Quimby to come to Rumney, and declared that if this were impossible then she felt sufficiently "excitable" to try to make the trip to Portland despite her state of health.

After returning to her sister's house Mrs. Patterson still could think and talk of nothing but Quimby, and she begged

[1]For this letter and all subsequent correspondence between the future Mrs. Eddy and Dr. Quimby, see *The Quimby Manuscripts*, edited by Horatio W. Dresser, Thomas Y. Crowell Co., page 146 ff. (1921), first edition. The letters do not appear in the second edition, the editor declaring that "we are not at liberty to print the text." Miss Milmine was given access to these letters in 1906–7, and summaries of some of them are presented in her own work.

Mrs. Tilton to send her to Portland. That lady, with a firmness born of long suffering from Mary's whims, refused point blank, with the statement that she thought Quimby a quack and his cures highly exaggerated. She sent Mrs. Patterson to a water cure at Hill, New Hampshire, as a sort of compromise.

Mrs. Patterson on arriving at Hill found that even the patients at the water cure were busy speculating as to the possible superiority of the Quimby healing methods. So she wrote Quimby once again from Hill, saying that she could sit up only a few minutes at a time, but declaring that she was going to make the attempt to reach him.

She knew that she could never get enough money to make the trip by taking Mrs. Tilton further into her confidence. So she kept her counsel, and quietly hoarded the extra money that Mrs. Tilton sent her from time to time for incidental expenses. In October of 1862 she counted her coins and decided that she had enough to set out.

She registered in Portland at the International Hotel and then went immediately to Quimby's office. She had to be assisted up the stairs.

George Quimby, son of the healer, who was acting as his father's secretary, received her in the midst of the bevy of patients that thronged the ante-room. Her weakness and emaciation were evident to all. As she sank into a chair the man she had talked of and dreamed of for so long came from the inner office. She recognized him immediately.

He was a slight man, weighing only about 125 pounds. His hair and his closely cropped beard were white. His mouth was cut generously, the lips held together in a firm, clear line. The eyebrows were level, the dark eyes set wide apart above an aquiline nose. There was in his gaze the shrewd, kindly look of the philosopher who has beheld many human ills and still retained hope.

Even as he bent down to her chair and took her hand she felt his dynamic, vital power. She took a deep breath, and a thrill ran through her.

Mary Baker Patterson had reached Quimby at last.

IV

No one had ever looked square into the face of Phineas Parkurst Quimby (Dr. by courtesy only) and doubted his rugged honesty and sincerity. There were those who called him faker and charlatan, but they were the ones who had never met him. Nor did his virtues end with honesty—for even fools are honest. "Of his rare humanity and sympathy," wrote Mrs. Eddy afterward, "one could write a sonnet."

When Mrs. Patterson first came to him in 1862 he was sixty years old. He had been delving into the strange powers of the mind since 1838, when he had first heard Charles Poyen, French hypnotist, give a course of lectures and experiments in Belfast, Maine, where Quimby then was living.

He had been born at New Lebanon, New Hampshire, one of seven children. His father was a blacksmith. "Park," as the son was called, was early apprenticed to a clockmaker. There are still many old Quimby clocks to-day, hidden away in New England garrets. As a lad he acquired no formal education beyond the three Rs. But he had the inquiring, curious, observing type of mind which is the gift of the born philosopher. In no way religious, in the then accepted, orthodox sense, he was vitally interested in the world around him and in the many people who made up that world. He became engrossed in philosophy and science, read as deeply as the meagre facilities in his town would permit, and was one of the most interested persons in the audience when Poyen came to Belfast in 1838 to lecture.

Quimby stayed after the lecture, made Poyen's acquaintance, and the Frenchman assured him that he had unusual hypnotic power. Thereafter Quimby followed Poyen around from town to town, and inevitably began seeking to try out his powers on any friend who would volunteer to be "subject." Returning to Belfast, Quimby made quite a stir with his strange ability to fix his eyes on a person, and send him into a sound sleep—so sound that there was no response even to pin-pricks and pinches.

There were of course many scoffers; on the other hand there was a stirring interest in hypnotic phenomena abroad over all New England in 1840, and not a few, even in Quimby's home town where a prophet could not expect honor, believed in his strange power. Many believed that he was able, after fixing his eyes upon a man, to make that man perform his will.

Among his various volunteer subjects, Quimby found a youth still in his teens, named Lucius Burkmar, who was extraordinarily suggestible, and thus made a most responsive and unusual subject. Quimby and this lad travelled all over New England together, giving demonstrations before large audiences. Eventually, when Quimby returned to Belfast for another session of clock-making, young Burkmar was employed by another exponent of the hypnotic art by the name of John B. Dods, who is now remembered as author of a book called *The Philosophy of Electrical Psychology*. Dods seems to have been a business man as well as a philosopher; for he soon found that it was a very profitable undertaking to read the minds of ailing patients by clairvoyance, and then to prescribe medicines of his own manufacture.

Dods himself did not do the reading; it was young Burkmar who performed this service for him, and also prescribed the proper remedies under Dod's influence. Out of what was probably a rather unholy alliance, at least so far as Dods was concerned, came a very interesting development. When Quimby again employed Burkmar he himself began to experiment in the diagnosing of disease with Burkmar's aid.

Quimby, however, had no interest whatever in selling remedies; and when he found Burkmar prescribing costly or unavailable medicines he would tell him to consider the case again, and Burkmar would suggest a simpler or more inexpensive prescription. To Quimby's delight, the simple prescription secured results just as effective as the costly ones. He soon reached the conclusion that the virtues of the medicine did not lie in the drug itself, but rather in the patient's own faith in the remedy's efficacy.

It was a most significant discovery in therapeutic psychology. That others had also made it detracts no whit from Quimby's own honor, working in his small field alone.

Having gone so far, Quimby soon took another step. He dispensed with Burkmar's diagnosing services, and also with drugs. For he was now convinced that the curative process was wholly a mental one. It was induced by establishing in the patient a certain attitude of mind and emotion which would result in a buoyant faith as to his cure.

He therefore changed his methods radically. A correspondent in the Bangor *Jeffersonian* in 1857 has thus described this new method of approach:

> His theory is that the mind gives immediate form to the animal spirit, and that the animal spirit gives form to the body as soon as the less plastic elements of the body are able to assume that form. Therefore, his first course in the treatment of a patient is to sit down beside him and put himself *en rapport* with him, which he does without producing the mesmeric sleep.

The last clause in that quotation is important. Quimby had made another important advance in his psychology—the discovery that suggestion is effective without inducing the hypnotic state. As one authority has recently said, "Far from suggestion being a function of hypnotism, it is hypnotism which is a function of suggestion."[1] In other words, Quimby had now discovered that he might use suggestion to heal his patients just as previously he had used it to hypnotize them.

Quimby oftentimes used the laying on of hands as a part of his treatment, first dipping his hands in water. He stated, however, that his "manipulation" was not a necessary part of the treatment; that it was primarily directed to establishing confidence in the patient. The attitude of the patient he deemed most important.

He felt, undoubtedly, that he had a mission in the world— that of spreading what he regarded as a great discovery. He

[1] Émile Boirac, *L'Avenir des Sciences Psychiques*, page 111.

made no definite charges to his patients, kept no accounts, and practised largely upon only the poor and extremely ill. He said that people sent for him and the undertaker at the same time; and the first one who arrived got the case.

Because he felt that the secret of his healing must not die with him, he made a number of his patients promise to teach it to at least two others before they died. It will be noted, in this connection, that he had taken one other step in the development of his theory: he had reached the conclusion that therapeutic psychology could be practised not alone by one with unique hypnotic powers, but rather by any one who learned the principles of its application.

In seeking to make the record of his discoveries permanent, he wrote in six years some ten bound volumes of manuscripts in long-hand. In these he not only set forth the principles of his new discovery, but endeavored to give these a philosophical and historical basis. These manuscripts were made available to any of his patients who desired also to become a student; for the old philosopher was delighted and flattered at any opportunity to spread his message.

He believed, in particular, that he had come across the method so effectively employed by Jesus and his disciples in their work of healing the sick, and was convinced that not only was this work the principal mission of Jesus, but that it was achieved by the employment of natural forces and not by supernatural means. When Dr. Warren F. Evans, a Swedenborgian clergyman, visited Quimby for treatment in 1863 and became a convert, he declared that Quimby "seemed to reproduce the wonders of Gospel history." Quimby made a particular point, however, of disclaiming any divine revelation, and wrote a lengthy essay entitled "A Defence Against Making Myself Equal With Christ." His writings extended over a number of topics then being much discussed by New England, and generally associated in the popular mind with mental healing—subjects such as Spiritualism, Disease, Religion, Clairvoyance, Curing the Sick, Truth, and Error. One treatise was called "Scientific Interpretations of Various Parts of the Scriptures."

The usual name which he gave to his discovery was the "Science of Health."[1] Other times he called it the "Science of Christ."[2] And once or twice he used also the name "Christian Science."[3]

He was convinced that it was really a science to which he had gained the key. He declared: "This is my theory; to put man in possession of a science that will destroy the ideas of the sick, and teach man one living profession of his own identity with life free from error and disease." He maintained that health was man's natural state; that only man's false ideas, suggesting impotence and misfortune to his whole self from earliest childhood, were responsible for holding the race in the thrall of disease. Justifying this belief on philosophical grounds, he maintained that a beneficent God could and would not have created disease and suffering—only man himself was to blame because of the falsity and error in his concepts.

Patients flocked to Quimby in great numbers, and in the same throngs were apparently cured.[4] Among the patients who became convinced of the efficacy of his methods were Julius A. Dresser, who was born in 1838 at Portland, Maine, and Miss Annetta G. Seabury, who later became Mr. Dresser's wife.

Like all of Dr. Quimby's students, the Dressers were given free access to his manuscripts and writings, and made numerous copies for their own use, and for the later use of their friends. After they began practising mental healing in Boston in 1882, teaching from these manuscripts and using the Quimby method, they made the material in their possession available to the general public, and in 1921 their son, Horatio, obtained and published the complete documents.

---

[1] Vd. *The Quimby Manuscripts*, edited by H. W. Dresser, page 249. Here, as elsewhere when reference is made to *The Quimby Manuscripts*, the reference is to the second edition unless otherwise specified. This procedure has been followed for the convenience of those readers who may desire to follow the references through, but who may be unable to obtain ready access to the first edition, with its reproduction of Mrs. Glover's correspondence with her teacher. Copies of this first edition are already rare.

[2] *Ibid.*, page 131.   [3] *Ibid.*, page 388.

[4] In 1865 he wrote: "Within the last seven years I have sat with more than twelve thousand different persons." (*The Quimby Manuscripts*, pages 276-7.)

Two others who were partly responsible for disseminating the old doctor's ideas were the Misses Ware, daughters of Judge Ashur Ware of the United States Admiralty Court. Highly intelligent young women, they were deeply interested in the new theories which they heard from Quimby's lips, and it was they who first suggested that he put his thoughts in writing. Thus were formed many of the originals of the manuscripts that subsequently were copied by other patients. As George Quimby, the son, has told the story:

From that time he began to write out his ideas, which practice he continued until his death, the articles being now in the possession of the writer of this sketch. The original copy he would give to the Misses Ware, and it would be read to him by them, and, if he suggested any alteration, it would be made, after which it would be copied either by the Misses Ware or the writer of this, and then re-read to him, that he might see that all was just as he intended it. Not even the most trivial word or the construction of a sentence would be changed without consulting him. He was given to repetition; and it was with difficulty that he could be induced to have a repeated sentence or phrase stricken out, as he would say, "If that idea is a good one, and true, it will do no harm to have it in two or three times." He believed in the hammering process, and in throwing an idea or truth at the reader till it would be firmly fixed in his mind.[1]

When Mrs. Patterson reached Dr. Quimby in 1862, much of this material had already been put in written form. According to Mr. Dresser[2] there were over 800 closely written pages covering more than 120 subjects. She was fascinated by Quimby from the first moment she saw him. She had always been given to sudden and violent in-sweeps of emotion, and now she felt a great enthusiasm. For three weeks she hardly left him during the entire day. When he was treating other patients she would remain constantly near, a privilege Quimby was flattered to grant.

They talked together a great deal. It is not difficult to imagine her,—a little faded creature with her hair in ringlets around her face, in the fashion she then affected; her woollen

[1] *New England Magazine*, March, 1888
[2] *The True History of Mental Science*, Pamphlet by Julius A. Dresser.

dress shabby and poor, with its shabbiness emphasized by her affectation of tawdry and excess beribbonment; her deeply sunk, shadowy eyes turned up to the white-haired Quimby in soulful gaze.

Her first stay in Portland lasted about three weeks, and she made an impression upon all with whom she came in contact. She had explained to Quimby that she was poor, and he had helped her to find a modest boarding place. Her poverty, however, did not prevent her from affecting those usual little oddities of air by which she always sought to make an impression, regardless of the circle she entered. She had been introduced to Quimby as "the authoress," a title which she carefully nurtured as she carried it around with her for a number of years; and her somewhat languishing demeanor, no less than her unique costuming and rather birdlike flutterings, were all regarded as a part of the "authoress" atmosphere.

Quimby saw in her self-confessed literary gifts another opportunity for putting his ideas before the world, and was immensely pleased and taken with her. During her first stay she hardly left his side, and he answered all her questions patiently, and put all his manuscripts before her. From the very first day her health improved. At the end of her brief stay she felt an entirely different woman. Her old spinal weakness seemed to have disappeared. She had a vitality such as she had hardly ever known.

Immediately following her recovery, she sat down and wrote a pæan of praise to the Portland *Courier,* which published it in the issue of November 7, 1862. Because there has been so much uninformed controversy regarding the debt which Mary Baker Eddy owed Quimby, this letter is presented in full. In after years, when she had denied any obligation to Quimby whatever, even stating that Quimby's influence had been detrimental in its effects upon her, she explained this document, when it was brought to her attention, by the mere comment that she was "mesmerized" when she wrote it: "My head was so turned by animal magnetism and will power, under his treatment, that I might have written something as hopelessly incorrect as the articles now pub-

lished in the Dresser pamphlet."[1] This same explanation she
also applied to other contemporaneous documents in which
she expressed her fealty to the man who had given her so
much.

In the Portland *Courier* she said:

When our Shakespeare decided that "there were more things in the
world than were dreamed of in our philosophy," I cannot say of a verity
that he had a foreknowledge of P. P. Quimby. And when the school
Platonic anatomised the soul and divided it into halves to be reunited by
elementary attractions, and heathen philosophers averred that old Chaos
in sullen silence brooded o'er the earth until her inimitable form was
hatched from the egg of night, I would not at present decide whether
the fallacy was found in their premises or conclusions, never having
dated my existence before the flood. When the startled alchemist discovered, as he supposed, an universal solvent, or the philosopher's stone,
and the more daring Archimedes invented a lever wherewithal to pry
up the universe, I cannot say that in either the principle obtained in nature or in art, or that it worked well. But when by a falling apple, an
immutable law was discovered, we gave it the crown of science, which
is incontrovertible and capable of demonstration; hence that was wisdom
and truth. When from the evidence of the senses, my reason takes cog-
nizance of truth, although it may appear in quite a miraculous view, I
must acknowledge that as science which is truth uninvestigated. Hence
the following demonstration :—

Before proceeding it would be useful to pause for breath
and go back to ask what all this means. The reader's first impression is that most of the sentences are lacking either in subject or verb, or both. Close study will show that these exist. But
it will also reveal evidence of a rather badly ordered mind.

Let us resume:

Three weeks since I quitted my nurse and sick room *en route* for
Portland. The belief of my recovery had died out of the hearts of those
who were most anxious for it. With this mental and physical depression
I first visited P. P. Quimby; and in less than one week from that time
I ascended by a stairway of one hundred and eighty two steps to the
dome of the City Hall, and am improving *ad infinitum*. To the most
subtle reasoning such a proof, coupled too, as it is with numberless
similar ones, demonstrates his power to heal. Now for a brief analysis
of his power.

[1]Boston *Post*, March 7, 1883.

Is it spiritualism? Listen to the words of wisdom, "Believe in God, believe also in me; or believe me for the very work's sake." Now, then, his works are but the result of superior wisdom, which can demonstrate a science not understood; hence it were a doubtful proceeding not to believe him for the work's sake. Well, then, he denies that his power to heal the sick is borrowed from the spirits of this or another world; and let us take the Scriptures for proof. "A kingdom divided against itself cannot stand." Now, then, can he receive the friendly aid of the disenthralled spirit, while he rejects the faith of the solemn mystic who crosses the threshold of the dark unknown to conjure up from the vasty deep the awestruck spirit of some invisible squaw?[1]

Mrs. Patterson there goes on record, once and forever, in denying that Quimby's work had any relation to the spiritualistic doctrines that to her had previously been so familiar. Now she proceeds to deny that it is at all related to the practice of hypnotism or "animal magnetism":

Again, is it by animal magnetism that he heals the sick? Let us examine. I have employed electro-magnetism and animal magnetism, and for a brief interval have felt relief, from the equilibrium which I fancied was restored to an exhausted system or by a diffusion of concentrated action. But in no instance did I get rid of a return of all my ailments, because I had not been helped out of the error in which opinions involved us. My operator believed in disease, independent of the mind; hence I could not be wiser than my master. But now I can see dimly at first, and only as trees walking, the great principle which underlies Dr. Quimby's faith and works; and just in proportion to my right perception of truth is my recovery. The truth which he opposes to the error of giving intelligence to matter and placing pain where it never placed itself, if received understandingly, changes the currents of the system to their normal action; and the mechanism of the body goes on undisturbed. That this is a science capable of demonstration, becomes clear to the minds of those patients who reason upon the process of their cure. The truth which he establishes in the patient cures him (although he may be wholly unconscious thereof); and the body, which is full of light, is no longer in disease. At present I am too much in error to elucidate the truth, and can touch only the keynote for the master hand to wake the harmony. May it be in essays, instead of notes! say I. After all, this is a very spiritual doctrine; but the eternal years of God are with it, and it must stand firm as the rock of ages. And to many a poor sufferer may it be found, as by me, "the shadow of a great rock in a weary land."

MRS. M. M. PATTERSON.

[1]Referring to the "little Indian guide" who even yet seems useful in spiritualistic seances.

Not only is this final paragraph interesting because of the adulation which it heaps at Quimby's feet; it is of importance because it contains phrases which Mrs. Patterson found herself repeating very often in the later days of her career. Here is "truth" as opposed to "error." Here is a "science capable of demonstration." And here, finally, is set forth the "error of giving intelligence to matter."

The Portland *Advertiser*, rival to *The Courier*, had a merry laugh over this letter. "What!" exclaimed the editor. "P. P. Quimby compared to Jesus Christ?" Mrs. Patterson delighted in this new opportunity to practise authorship. She wrote immediately. "Christ healed the sick," she informed *The Advertiser*, "but not by jugglery or with drugs. As the former [Quimby] speaks as never man before spake, and heals as never man healed since Christ, is he not identified with truth? And is not this the Christ which is in him?"

This great experience in her life would hardly have been complete unless Mrs. Patterson had sat down to compose the usual poem. This time her brainchild was in sonnet form. It was sent to *The Courier*, which had already been so liberal to the "authoress" with its space:

SONNET

SUGGESTED BY READING THE REMARKABLE CURE
OF CAPTAIN J. W. DEERING

To Dr. P. P. Quimby

'Mid light of science sits the sage profound
Awing with classics and his starry lore
Climbing to Venus, chasing Saturn round,
Turning his mystic pages o'er and o'er,
Till, from empyrean space, his wearied sight
Turns to the oasis on which to gaze,
More bright than glitters on the brow of night
The self-taught man walking in wisdom's ways.
Then paused the captive gaze with peace entwined,
And sight was satisfied with thee to dwell;
But not in classics would the book-worm find

> That law of excellence whence came the spell
> Potent o'er all,—the captive to unbind,
> To heal the sick and faint, the halt and blind.
>
> MARY M. PATTERSON.

For the *Courier*

It was a rather labored piece of verse, but it was at least obviously sincere.[1] Mrs. Patterson at the moment worshipped Quimby as the sun and entire firmament of her life. She went back to Sanbornton Bridge, astonished the long-suffering Mrs. Tilton by her new found buoyance, talked of nothing but Quimby to all of her friends. As intimated in her letter to *The Courier*, she had enjoyed such moments of apparent recovery before,—"but in no instance did I get rid of a return of all my ailments." We shall see later whether this cure was more permanent than the others. Meanwhile, however, she had come across something which she had never previously gained—an approach to a philosophy of life. It absorbed her. She had not understood all of Quimby, but she had digested enough to let her see a whole new universe of interest which she had never glimpsed before. Her mind labored on it.

Worshipfully she kept up a current correspondence with Quimby. Mrs. Tilton and her son Albert had by this time become almost convinced of miracles themselves, and Mrs. Tilton was planning to take Albert up to be cured of his smoking and drinking habits, which he had evidently acquired as a member of the local *jeunesse dorée*.

Whenever Mrs. Patterson felt one of her old spells coming on she wrote to Quimby and received apparent relief. Thus, on January 31, 1863, she requested "absent treatment." In the same year she wrote that his "Angel Visits" were improving her. Once she requested that he make a visit in his "omnipresence." Most interesting is a letter in which she stated that she had attempted to treat the errant Albert, and that during these treatments she had herself felt a "constant desire to smoke."

---

[1]For a facsimile reproduction of this sonnet in Mrs. Patterson's own handwriting, vd. *The Quimby Manuscripts*, appendix, which presents the copy of the poem which Mrs. Patterson sent to Mr. Dresser.

In this connection it should be noted that Quimby in treating his patients had sometimes felt that he temporarily acquired their symptoms, and had so informed those whom he treated. He said that his remedy on such occasions was to go out into the garden and try to work the idea off. It will later be seen that this suggestion took firm hold on Mrs. Patterson's impressionable mind.

At this time her constant thought of Quimby amounted to a fixation. She wrote in terms of hyperbole. "I am up and around today, i. e., by the help of the Lord (Quimby)". . . . "Dear Doctor, what could I do without you?" . . . "Who is wise but you?"

She made another visit to Quimby in 1864, and received fresh benefit. That time she spent a couple of months in Portland, and Quimby managed to give his new disciple a great amount of his time and attention. Her fellow patients in later years recalled that she would spend every afternoon in the doctor's office, and then sit up late at night writing down notes of what she had learned during the day.

It is doubtful that she had then any definite idea whatever of the use she might wish to make of this knowledge. Ideas, even when they seem most spontaneous, are born of long periods of gestation and slow subconscious growth. At the time Mrs. Patterson seems merely to have been endowed with all the ardor of the enthusiast into whose drab life has suddenly come the vision of horizons never before dreamed of.

During her extended stay in Portland she formed close acquaintanceships with two women who were also receiving treatment and instruction at Dr. Quimby's hands,—Mrs. Sarah Crosby and Miss Mary Ann Jarvis. In Mrs. Eddy's authorized biography appears the amusing assurance that the chief interest which the three women had in common was the period necessarily spent together each evening when they tried to disentangle each other's hair following Quimby's manipulations during the day. Mrs. Patterson in after years sought strenuously to prove that her early benefactor was nothing but a mesmerist, relying solely on physical manipulation for his cures.

There is no doubt at all that Quimby at times did place his hands on the patient's head; and for many subsequent years Mrs. Patterson herself taught this method of establishing a working relationship with ailing patients.

When she left Quimby after his extended tutelage in the early part of 1864 she carried with her a copy of his writings called *Questions and Answers*,[1] from which she later taught extensively and which was to be largely incorporated in the pamphlet she copyrighted in 1870 as "The Science of Man, by which the sick are healed, Embracing Questions and Answers in Moral Science, arranged for the learner by Mrs. Mary Baker Glover." This pamphlet, with numerous changes, was finally to be included in *Science and Health* under the title "Recapitulation."

Some Quimby excerpts, read from the vantage point of today, will appear to contain some very familiar passages:

God is Wisdom. . . . The sick are strangers to this Wisdom. . . . This Wisdom is superior to opinions. . . . Opinions are nothing but error that man has embraced. . . . There is no wisdom in matter. . . . God is Truth and there is no other truth. . . . Understanding is God. . . . All science is a part of God. . . . Disease being made by a belief . . . is the work of the devil or error. . . . Now if you can face the error and argue it down then you can cure the sick.[2]

This material was incorporated in a Quimby manuscript dated February, 1862,[3] and consequently had been written

[1] See the New York *Times*, July 10, 1904, for a facsimile of Mrs. Eddy's copy of this manuscript, with emendations in her own hand, along with parallel quotations from Quimby's document and *Science and Health*. For the full document of "Questions and Answers," see *The Quimby Manuscripts*, pages 165 ff.

[2] In 1907 Horace T. Wentworth, of Stoughton, Mass. took oath that the manuscript called "The Science of Man" was in his hands, and that it was the same manuscript which his mother, Mrs. Sally Wentworth, had copied from another manuscript in the possession of Mrs. Mary Baker Glover. Facsimile reproduction was permitted for establishing a public record. This Wentworth copy of Mrs. Glover's manuscript was then compared with Quimby's manuscript, "Questions and Answers," which was in the possession of George A. Quimby of Belfast, Maine. The two were found to be identical, word for word, for an extent of 20 closely lined pages. In consequence the quotation here presented has an authenticity which may not be challenged, under any rule of evidence, as a concrete illustration of what Mrs. Patterson obtained from Quimby.

[3] For the full document vd. *The Quimby Manuscripts*, page 165 ff.

prior to the first meeting between Quimby and Mrs. Patterson. Thus, when Mrs. Patterson claimed, in after years, that any similarity between her own ideas and Quimby's was accounted for by the fact that she gave Quimby the benefit of her own theories, which she wrote down for him while he was treating her, and not by the fact that it was she who borrowed from Quimby—when she made such claims, Mrs. Patterson's memory was obviously not in line with established facts.

There is better evidence, however, than even the facts which are on record—the evidence inherent in the widely accepted law of human action that all effects first have a cause; that all human achievements result from logical growth and development; and that only in myth does Minerva spring full-fledged from the head of Jove.

Had Mary Baker been given that boon of fearlessness, with the ability to analyze self-motivation, which is demanded for honesty, much of the conflict which enveloped her in succeeding years would never have occurred, and her work would have been strengthened infinitely. For never in later years did she admit her debt to Quimby. Thus she wrote:

About the year 1862, while the author of this work was at Dr. Vail's Hydropathic Institute in New Hampshire, this occurred: A patient considered incurable left that institution, and in a few weeks returned apparently well, having been healed, as he informed the patients, by one Mr. P. P. Quimby, of Portland, Maine.

After much consultation among ourselves, and a struggle with pride, the author, in company with several other patients, left the water-cure, *en route* for the aforesaid doctor in Portland. He proved to be a magnetic practitioner. His treatment seemed at first to relieve her, but signally failed in healing her case.

Having practised homœopathy, it never occurred to the author to learn his practice, but she did ask him how manipulation could benefit the sick. He answered kindly and squarely, in substance, "Because it conveys *electricity* to them." That was the sum of what he taught her of his medical profession. . . .

After treating his patients Mr. Quimby would retire to an anteroom and write at his desk. I had a curiosity to know if he had indited anything pathological relative to his patients, and asked if I could see his pennings on my case. He immediately presented them. I read the copy in

his presence and returned it to him. The composition was commonplace
. . . it was not at all metaphysical or scientific. . . . He was neither a
scholar nor a metaphysician. I never heard him say that matter was not
as real as Mind, or that electricity was not as potential or remedial, or al-
lude to God as the divine Principle of all healing. He certainly had advanced views of his own, but they commingled error with truth, and
were not Science. . . .

It was after Mr. Quimby's death that I discovered, in 1866, the momentous facts relating to Mind and its superiority over matter, and
named my discovery Christian Science.[1]

There were many other and constant denials in a similar
vein, for in after years the so-called "Quimby controversy"
raged hotly, and divergent opinions had a prolonged life
primarily because few of the interested bystanders at that
time had an opportunity to learn all of the facts.

Even under the circumstances, the historian must be slow
to convict of intentioned dissimulation. The child whose disordered imagination allowed her to believe that God was calling her as he did little Samuel grew into a woman whose
strange mind never ceased to confuse a dream world with
reality. It was not difficult for her to believe about Quimby
as she wanted to believe, either in moments of her earlier
enthusiasm or her later disdain.

When Mrs. Patterson left Quimby in the early months of
1864 she went first to visit Miss Jarvis at Warren, Maine.
Miss Jarvis had a consumptive sister, and Mrs. Patterson was
delighted to try out her new-found lore by attempting to treat
the invalid. One of the most interesting ideas she had gained
from Quimby was his conclusion that any person might learn to
heal both himself and his fellows. It was this which suggested
to Mrs. Patterson the sort of opportunity in which she had
delighted from girlhood—an opportunity, once again, to become a unique and interesting figure in the small circle in
which she moved. She now determined to be a mental healer.

While staying in Warren she even lectured publicly on the
Quimby art. The notice of her appearance was posted on the
town billboards. "Mrs. M. M. Patterson will lecture at the

[1] *Miscellaneous Writings*, page 378–9.

Town Hall on P. P. Quimby's Spiritual Science Healing Disease, as opposed to Deism or Rochester Rapping Spiritualism." It is not recorded that the lecture brought her any patients. And she was having no apparent success with the consumptive Miss Jarvis. So in May Mrs. Patterson left the Jarvis household and descended on her other acquaintance from the Quimby sojourn, Mrs. Sarah G. Crosby, who lived at Albion, Maine. The visit lasted several months. Mary Baker Patterson was now entering on a long period of shifting from pillar to post, from house to house and acquaintance to acquaintance, with nothing to offer in return for such hospitality except the opportunity of hearing her talk about Quimby's work, and of seeing her try to put it into practice.

V

When Mary Baker Patterson went to visit Mrs. Crosby in May of 1864, she was forty-two years old, without a close friend in the world, and in a state of almost complete destitution. In terms of years she had lived almost exactly one half of her life; in terms of psychological development she had rounded out almost a complete cycle. Her mind had matured very slowly; emotionally she was under-matured to a marked degree. We now see her standing on the threshold of a new orientation in life as an emotionally unstable woman, rather thin and scrawny in the fashion of nervous women in middle life; her rapidly graying hair "touched up" and worn in ringlets; her cheeks still rouged; her manner replete with the little affectations that had been with her since childhood.

In the Crosby house she did not doff the grand and languid airs which were an essential part of her make-up; such mannerisms were an attempted compensation for her sense of inferiority, impressed on her for years by a temperament and a physique which could not compete on equal terms with the more nearly normal individuals around her. Thus at Mrs. Crosby's she posed as the guest of honor, and although it was a farmhouse where every member of the family had his daily duties and chores to undertake as a matter of course, Mrs. Patterson remained the grand lady who allowed even her room to be cared for by others.

Undeniably, however, there was in Mrs. Patterson an ability to charm and please which could always—for a while— delight those who came in contact with her. Inevitably such periods would pass, and then she would seem wholly another woman, and those who had been enchanted with her invigorating and stimulating influence would marvel at the sight of this totally different personality which suddenly swept all the charm away.

Mrs. Crosby found the summer in the company of Mrs. Patterson a pleasant interlude to the customary tedium of life on a somewhat isolated farm. The two women talked about Quimby until the subject was worn threadbare. Mrs. Patterson then trotted out her old interest in spiritualism, and they compared extensive notes on this other topic of perennial interest. Following every war come spiritualistic revivals, and the Civil War was no exception.

Mrs. Patterson and Mrs. Crosby whiled away many warm summer afternoons with their hands arched on a small table with the fingers spread stiffly apart, waiting to see if the spirits had a message for them. And the spirits did, just as they so often had had a message in the old Sanbornton days at any neighborhood investigation into spirit-calling at which Mrs. Patterson was present.

That these messages were not always conscious emanations from Mrs. Patterson, that they were not intended deceptions, seems quite probable from the accounts of some of the occurrences. Psychiatrists are familiar with a fairly common phenomenon in patients suffering from hysteria—a thing called disassociated personality. It is the result of suppressed emotional states which at times struggle to break through the ruling consciousness.

One day when Mrs. Patterson and Mrs. Crosby had seated themselves around a table in a darkened room they waited long and silently for the table to begin its customary rappings. The atmosphere was still and tense, and sultry with the summer heat. A heavy drowsiness was in the air. Suddenly Mrs. Patterson leaned stiffly backward with closed eyes and commenced talking in a hoarse deep voice. The voice said that it was Albert Baker, Mary's brother who had died years before. Albert had been trying to "get control" of Mrs. Patterson for many days, because Mrs. Crosby must be warned against putting too much confidence in her guest. "He informed me," related Mrs. Crosby in a sworn affidavit taken in later years, "through her own lips, that while his sister loved me as much as she was capable of loving anyone, life had been a severe experiment with her, and she might use

my sacred confidence to further any ambitious purposes of
her own."[1]

In later years Mrs. Patterson denied—and no one would
wish to contradict her—that she had ever been a "medium."
Thus she wrote:

We are aware that the Spiritualists claim whomsoever they would
catch and regard even Christ as an elder brother. But we never were a
Spiritualist; and never were, and never could be, and never admitted we
were a medium. We have explained to the class calling themselves Spiritualists how their signs and wonders were wrought, and have illustrated
by doing them; but at the same time have said, This is not the work of
spirits and I am not a medium; and they have passed from our presence
and said, behold the proof that she is a medium![2]

Other messages which Mrs. Crosby received via Mrs. Patterson were less striking, although they, too, were supposed
to emanate from Albert. In one of her trances Mrs. Patterson
announced that if Mrs. Crosby would occasionally look under
the cushion of a particular chair, a spirit writing would be
found there. Strangely enough, spirit writings there appeared.

One of these is partially quoted in the biography of Mrs.
Eddy which in later years received official sanction; but its
most interesting paragraph was omitted—one indorsing the
teachings of one P. Quimby. This is the message:

Sarah dear Be ye calm in reliance on self, amid all the changes of
natural yearnings, of too keen a sense of earthly joys, of too great a
struggle between the material and spiritual. Be calm or you will rend
your mortal (being) and your experience which is needed for your spiritual progress lost, till taken up without the proper sphere and your trials
more severe.

That is why all things are working for good to those who suffer and
they must look not upon the things which are seen but those which do
not appear. P. Quimby of Portland has the spiritual truth of diseases.
You must imbibe it to be healed. Go to him again and lean on no material or spiritual medium. In that path of truth I first found you. Dear
one, I am at present no aid to you although you think I am, but your
spirit will not at present bear this quickening or twill leave the body;

[1]Affidavit secured by Georgine Milmine. See Milmine, *Life of Mary Baker
G. Eddy and History of Christian Science*, page 66.

[2]*Science and Health*, 1878 (second edition), page 166.

hence I leave you till you ripen into a condition to meet me. You will miss me at first, but afterwards grow more tranquil because of it which is important that you may live for yourself and children. Love and care for poor sister a great suffering lies before her.[1]

This message appears to the critical mind to seem much more like a suppressed self of Mrs. Patterson speaking than like the voice of a deceased Albert Baker: "P. Quimby of Portland . . . in that path of truth I first found you . . . you will miss me at first, but afterward grow more tranquil because of it. . . ."

When Mrs. Patterson left Mrs. Crosby's pleasant farmhouse in the autumn she repaired to Lynn, a rather drab shoe-manufacturing town where the released Dr. Patterson had for a while worked in the offices of some other practitioners, and now had determined to establish a dental office of his own. The good doctor, according to an advertisement in the local paper, "offered his services fearlessly, knowing that competition is the real stimulus to success, and trusting to his ability to please all who need teeth filled, extracted, or new sets. He was the first to introduce LAUGHING GAS in Lynn for Dental purposes, and has had excellent success with it."[2]

Mrs. Patterson rejoined her husband, who had been in Lynn since the preceding year, because there was obviously no other place to go. Dr. Patterson was presumably not overwhelmed with joy to see her, for he was shortly due to leave her permanently, advising friends that he just couldn't endure it any longer. From the tone of all her subsequent mentions of her husband, Mrs. Patterson would appear also to have been anything but enamoured of her bluff, jovial and easy-going spouse.

But she could hardly return to her sister, for Mrs. Tilton had long felt that the Tilton family had endured quite enough. Mrs. Tilton was very shortly to close her door on Mary firmly and finally. As told by neighbors, the last straw that broke the

[1] A facsimile reproduction of part of this document, in Mrs. Patterson's own handwriting, may be found in Milmine, *Life of Mary Baker G. Eddy and History of Christian Science*, page 67, which is the source for this quotation.

[2] *Lynn Weekly Reporter*, June 11, 1864.

camel's back was a violent scene in which Mrs. Patterson accused her nephews and nieces of stealing some of her jewelry which had been lost. Mrs. Tilton thereupon decided that she was finished. And she meant it. She left instructions with her family that Mary was not even to be allowed to attend her funeral when she died.

Thus Mrs. Patterson's only recourse was to journey to Lynn where the doctor was eking out a fair living and enjoying his freedom from Confederate prisons and matrimonial bonds. He received his wife dutifully and kindly, took her to live at a boarding house at 42 Silsbee Street, and afterward moved her over to Buffum Street to rooms in the house of O. A. Durall.

Mrs. Patterson was just bursting to tell everyone she met about her new theories, and she buttonholed every chance acquaintance to inform him of the miracles upon which she had looked in Portland. An opportunity to make some acquaintances had come when she joined the Linwood Lodge of Good Templars with her husband. Her mannerisms went into the lodge with her, and even a kind critic has recorded that "some people would comment unfavorably through a sense of inferiority, I firmly believe, and would call her affected, for she was unusually scrupulous in the observation of social form."[1]

Mrs. Patterson, however, for a while enjoyed herself. She could always be prevailed upon to make a speech with no great effort from the persuader, and when it came time to elect the grand and exalted mistress of the Legion of Honor, woman's branch of the Good Templars, it was Mrs. Patterson who achieved the post.

While guiding the destinies of the lady Good Templars she did not allow her authoress activities to lapse, and she wrote neighborhood news letters to the Lynn *Reporter*, meanwhile not forgetting her poesy. Her authorized biography records that in this era "her poems were printed side by side with those of John Greenleaf Whittier, Oliver Wendell Holmes, and Phœbe Cary and are preserved in the files of the Lynn

[1]Sibyl Wilbur, *The Life of Mary Baker Eddy*, page 122.

papers." They were the same sort of stanzas that Mark Twain in later years pilloried with his pitiless criticism, the more unforgiving because she "profanely confers upon them the holy name 'poetry.'"

One of the gems written in this period was called "I am Sitting Alone"; two lines memorialized

> ". . . the unseen fountains of grief and joy
> That gushed at birth of that beautiful boy."

For Mrs. Patterson, Lynn presented an apparently calm and wholly pointless existence. But as her first year in this town of shoe-factory employees and their wives drew to a close, important events were gathering.

On January 16, 1866, Mr. Quimby died. For years he had been suffering from an abdominal tumor, which he had never treated medically, asserting that he had it under a mental control which prevented it from getting obstreperous. But during his last few years he had worked tremendously long hours, sacrificing himself to his patients without stint; and when he suddenly found himself growing feebler he felt that his time had come, and that his "error" had secured an unbreakable hold on him.

Toward the end Mr. Quimby allowed his wife to summon a homœopathic physician, not because he believed his days might be prolonged—for with his usual mental strength departed he felt a lack of power to combat the disease—but rather because of his family's insistence; they loved the old man dearly. As he died he said to his son George, "I am more than ever convinced of the truth of my theory. I am perfectly willing for the change myself, but I know you will all feel badly; but I know that I shall be right here with you, just the same as I have always been."[1]

When the news of her teacher's death reached Mrs. Patterson at Lynn she immediately wrote the usual poem, entitled "Lines on the Death of Dr. P. P. Quimby, Who Healed with the Truth that Christ Taught in Contradistinction to All

[1] *New England Magazine*, March, 1888.

Isms." These were duly published in the local paper, and she then sent a copy to Mr. Julius Dresser, one of Quimby's early patients whom she had met and admired in her Portland stay.

Referring to her great affection for Dr. Quimby, she said:

I am constantly wishing that *you* would step forward into the place he has vacated. I believe you would do a vast amount of good, and are more capable of occupying his place than any other I know of.

Mrs. Patterson then went on to tell Mr. Dresser that she had fallen on the sidewalk a fortnight before the date of her letter —February 14, 1866—and was now finding herself "the helpless cripple I was before I saw Dr. Quimby." She continued:

The physician attending said I had taken the last step I ever should, but in two days I got out of bed *alone* and *will* walk; but yet I confess I am frightened, and out of that nervous heat my friends are forming, in spite of me, the terrible spinal affliction from which I have suffered so long and hopelessly. . . . Now can't *you* help me?[1]

This letter was written two full weeks after the fall it described, for the mishap was chronicled in the Lynn *Reporter* as occurring on the evening of Thursday, February 1. Whether the physician told her she would never walk again is doubtful; he denied any such prophecy in later years, and family physicians do not believe in telling their patients the worst even if the worst is warranted. On the other hand, Mrs. Patterson had no dislike of making a circumstance—even a small circumstance—appear dramatic when the occasion permitted. This was another pleasant opportunity to show herself in a heroic light.

Discussion regarding the period required for her healing would be wholly pointless, but for one reason: in after years this fall came to be regarded by Mary Baker Eddy as the occasion for the birth of Christian Science.

Mrs. Eddy in her brief memoirs wrote of the event as follows:

It was in Massachusetts, in February 1866, and after the death of the magnetic doctor, Mr. P. P. Quimby, whom spiritualists would associate

---

[1]Horatio Dresser, *The Quimby Manuscripts*, first edition, page 163. The letter is also presented in full in Georgine Milmine's *Life of Mary Baker G. Eddy*, page 60.

therewith, but who was in no wise connected with this event, that I discovered the Science of divine metaphysical healing, which I afterwards named Christian Science. The discovery came to pass in this way. During twenty years prior to my discovery I had been trying to trace all physical effects to a mental cause; and in the latter part of 1866 I gained the scientific certainty that all causation was Mind, and every effect a mental phenomenon.

My immediate recovery from the effects of an injury caused by an accident, an injury that neither medicine nor surgery could reach, was the falling apple that led me to the discovery how to be well myself, and how to make others so.[1]

The founder of Christian Science was already an old woman when she wrote those words, and her memory was never wholly reliable regarding moments of historic importance in her career. The records of the doctor who attended her on that occasion confirm the earlier information in the letter to Mr. Dresser—that while she may have been out of bed in a couple of days her healing was not a matter of miraculous suddenness; nor, on the other hand, was it a healing which released an invalid who otherwise would have been bedridden for life.

In an affidavit of over a thousand words made forty years later,[2] published in the Springfield, Mass., *Union,* Dr. Alvin M. Cushing of Springfield transcribed from the record which he kept of all his cases, according to the habit of all conscientious physicians, the actual circumstances regarding this famous fall. He had found her in the home of one Samuel Bubier, who owned the shoe factory in front of which the fall occurred. She was "very nervous, partially unconscious, semi-hysterical, complaining by word and action of severe pain in the back of her head and neck." The doctor gave her sedatives, and in the morning administered one eighth of a grain of morphine, so that she could be moved without pain to her home. Much to the doctor's surprise she immediately went to sleep, was carried home limp and "doubled up like a jack-knife," and slept so long thereafter that the doctor began to fear having made a mistake in the size of the dose.

[1] *Retrospection and Introspection,* page 24.
[2] Jan. 2, 1907.

"Mrs. Patterson," said the doctor, "proved to be a very interesting patient, and one of the most sensitive to the effects of medicine that I ever saw, which accounts for the effects of the small dose of morphine. Probably one-sixteenth of a grain would have put her sound asleep. Each day that I visited her, I dissolved a small portion of a highly attenuated remedy in one-half a glass of water and ordered a teaspoonful given every two hours, usually giving one dose while there. She told me she could feel each dose to the tips of her fingers and toes, and gave me much credit for my ability to select a remedy. . . . I visited her twice on February 1st, twice on the 2nd, once on the 3rd, and once on the 5th, and on the 13th day of the same month my bill was paid. . . . When I left her on the 13th day of February, she seemed to have recovered from the disturbance caused by the accident and to be, practically, in her normal condition. I did not at any time declare, or believe, that there was no hope for Mrs. Patterson's recovery."

On the 10th of the following August, Dr. Cushing was called to attend Mrs. Patterson again. This time she had a bad summer cold and cough; he visited her three times on this occasion and prescribed for her the usual remedies.

Many eloquent lines have been written concerning this occasion which has become famous in many languages as "The Fall in Lynn"; and here, as elsewhere when testimonies conflict, the reader may take his choice of the probabilities. It must at least remain upon the record that almost two weeks after the fall, and just one day after the doctor had discharged her as physically sound, Mrs. Patterson was writing Mr. Dresser for mental aid because she was "frightened" at the thought of a possible return of "the terrible spinal affliction from which I have suffered so long and hopelessly."

As time went on other conflicts arose when it came to the fixing of dates for the discovery of Christian Science. When the Boston *Post* in 1883 published a letter from Julius Dresser telling about Quimby's pioneer work in mental science before 1866, another occasion beside the fall in 1866 was suggested for the origin of the Eddy idea. The then Mrs. Eddy wrote a letter declaring that "We made our first experiments

in mental healing about 1853."[1] Again, when Mr. Dresser in
1887 delivered a lecture on Quimby's discoveries in the
Church of Divine Unity at Boston, Mrs. Eddy replied to the
extensive public discussion resulting by a new claim inserted
in the *Christian Science Journal* of June, 1887: "As long ago
as 1844 I was convinced that mortal mind produced all disease."

The ensuing controversy between Mr. Dresser and Mrs.
Eddy is historic. Quimby's followers had generally looked
upon Julius Dresser as the logical successor to carry on the
pioneer's work; and the then Mrs. Patterson herself had this
feeling when she wrote, "I am constantly wishing that *you*
would step forward into the place he has vacated." Julius
Dresser and his wife, however, were both rather retiring people who lacked the pioneering urge; they journeyed to California and lived there for a number of years. It was not until
they returned to Boston and discovered Christian Science functioning as an institution that they made public the records
which were in their possession.

Between the death of Quimby in 1866 and the actual founding of Christian Science a number of years were to elapse.
The middle months of 1866 found Mrs. Patterson recovered
from the shock attending her fall, but exceedingly unhappy,
nervous, and hysterical, in the fashion that was recurrent at
so many times during her life. Close association with the
healthy animal spirits of her husband had always been a
source of irritation for her, and now she again found herself
in a state of mind closely bordering on the condition in which
she left the mountain village of Groton. And she had no way
to turn. Her father, Mark Baker, had died in 1865. The
refuge of her sister's house at Sanbornton was closed to her
forever. She heard from her child, George Glover, only upon
rare occasions, and had no possible claim upon him, now a
young man in his twenties.

As she brooded over this impasse, Dr. Patterson went to
her family, told them he was unable to endure life with her
any longer, and matched his word by pulling up stakes from

[1]*Boston Post*, March 7, 1883.

Lynn and going to Littleton, N. H. For several years he paid his wife an allowance of $200 a year, in small instalments. When after years of struggle he ceased his practice and returned to his boyhood town of Saco, Me., he was poverty stricken, and died a forsaken death in the poorhouse in 1896. He was buried in the Potter's Field.

In his wife's authorized biography, we are told in some detail of how his nature "craved the fleshpots, the gauds and baubles of sentimentalism"; and how "he, who had so effectively disported his frock coat, silk hat, kid boots and gloves in the rural mountain districts, making artisans' and farmers' wives yearn after his departing figure" was wholly out of place in the "keener social light of Lynn." It is suggested that he lost his standing quickly by an affair one too many, and fled precipitately before his sins could find him out. Perhaps so, even though there is no record of such a drama except in his wife's own memories. She wrote the Boston *Post:*[1]

". . . I was taken to Dr. Quimby, and partially restored. I returned home, hoping once more to make that home happy, but only returned to a new agony,—to find my husband had eloped with a married woman from one of the wealthy families of that city, leaving no trace save his last letter to us, wherein he wrote 'I hope some time to be worthy of so good a wife.'"

Even in her public agony it may have been some consolation to Mrs. Patterson to be able to say that the woman was "from one of the wealthy families." When the Doctor finally left his wife, they were living at the home of P. R. Russell, whose family had long since become slightly wearied of Mrs. Patterson's vagaries, although they had admired her and welcomed her company when the acquaintanceship was first formed. The fact that she could not pay her weekly rental of $1.50 was the leverage. She had previously refused to move upon request. Eviction papers were therefore served upon her, and she was dispossessed within a month after her husband's desertion.

[1] Letter of March 7, 1883.

VI

There now ensued a period of tragic wanderings from house to house; of a constant wearing-out of welcomes; of an endless struggle to make ends meet—a story that were it not so painful and pitiful would be wholly ridiculous.

Of this hard era the author of *Science and Health* has only said: "I then withdrew from society about three years."[1]

Mrs. Patterson, after the departure of what Mark Twain delighted to term her "husband of the period," promptly resumed the name which held for her more of romance—Mrs. Glover. Strangely enough, no matter what her circumstances or environment, she could always find heart to indulge the little fancies by which she sought to suggest to herself the aroma of other places and people and things.

And through it all, unhappy as she made those around her, she was even more desperately unhappy herself. She did not know—and presumably never knew—the implications of the blight which hovered over her life. And so she stumbled through those miserable years, indulging in her little compensations, shielding herself from obvious mockeries by hugging small conceits to her breast; demanding that her hostess of the occasion prepare meals at odd hours; remaining for long periods closeted in her room till she suddenly descended to require attention from the assembled family; receiving occasional callers with great formality and a grand gesture; and behindhand, always, with her board-bill.

Following her eviction from the Russell household she went to Mrs. Clark in Summer Street, where she stayed only a brief part of August, despite the fact that the Clarks shared her interest in spiritualism and that she went into trances for them in seances at which the whole family assembled.[2] She

---

[1] *Retrospection and Introspection*, page 24.

[2] One of the subsequent Mrs. Eddy's most advertised cures relates to this period. Vd. *Science and Health*, pages 192 f.: "I was called to visit Mr. Clark in Lynn, who had been confined to his bed six months with hip-disease, caused by a fall upon a wooden spike when quite a boy. On entering the house I met his

then found a short haven with Mrs. Armenius Newhall, who quickly requested her to move. Following this unfortunate episode she sought haven with a kindly woman, Mrs. James Wheeler of Swampscott. Things went well again for a short period, Mrs. Wheeler even providing meals for Mrs. Glover at hours not convenient for the rest of the family; but suddenly Mrs. Glover again had one of her "spells."

Mrs. Wheeler and her sister Julia were in the dining-room when Mrs. Glover one morning descended for her usual late breakfast. She appeared to be in a fury. It is recorded that "she began at once, and without any apparent cause, to talk to Mrs. Wheeler in a most abusive manner, using violent and insulting language."[1]

Very shortly thereafter Mrs. Glover was once more requested to move. Mrs. Wheeler suggested, however, that the board bill should be settled before the moving. Mrs. Glover replied that she had "treated" an infected finger for Mr. Wheeler, and that this treatment must be taken in lieu of payment.

How effective was the treatment no unbiassed record recalls. Three similar treatments during this period of her life are recorded for Mrs. Eddy in the biography to which she eventually gave her official approval. These claims, however, are made with the qualifying statements that the patients later denied the cures. Thus in the story regarding Dorr Phillips, who had a felon on his finger,[2] a lengthy account is given of

physician, who said that the patient was dying. The physician had just probed the ulcer on the hip, and said the bone was carious for several inches. He even showed me the probe, which had on it the evidence of this condition of the bone. The doctor went out. Mr. Clark lay with his eyes fixed and sightless. The dew of death was on his brow. I went to his bedside. In a few moments his face changed; its death-pallor gave place to a natural hue. The eyelids closed gently and the breathing became natural. . . .

"I told him to rise, dress himself, and take supper with his family. He did so. The next day I saw him in the yard. Since then I have not seen him, but am informed that he went to work in two weeks. . . .

"Since his recovery I have been informed that his physician claims to have cured him, and that his mother has been threatened with incarceration in an insane asylum for saying: 'It was none other than God and that woman who healed him.'"

[1] Affidavit of Julia Russell Walcott obtained by Georgine Milmine.

[2] Sibyl Wilbur, *The Life of Mary Baker Eddy*, page 148.

the circumstances under which a cure was obtained by Mrs. Glover's ministrations. Dorr was the son of a family in Lynn in which she occasionally visited. It is stated that when the felon had been healed by her "treatment" Mrs. Glover disclaimed any "miracle," saying "It is natural, divinely natural. All life rightly understood is so." But two sentences later is a further statement. "With peace restored to his body, Dorr Phillips forgot all about Divine Science."

Another similar episode is related concerning a "young man from Boston" who lived with a son-in-law of the Phillips family. He had a fever. But—"so simply was the youth's release from fever accomplished that none who knew of the case would credit her with having done anything."[1]

A third story of unverified healing is related of a Mrs. Winslow, still another relation of this Phillips family. Mrs. Winslow, it is recorded, was assisted by Mrs. Glover to rise from an invalid's chair where she had sat for fifteen years. But, says this record, "the woman's pride kept her from acknowledging a cure."[2]

It is related that there was quite a close friendship maintained between Mrs. Glover and the Phillips family; however this may be, it is certain that the Phillipses were one of the few families in Lynn with whom Mrs. Glover never lived.

Only one contemporary record of Mrs. Patterson's efforts as a healer during this period appears to exist. It is incorporated in one of the fourteen letters which she addressed to Dr. Quimby.[3] She relates here how she cured a woman of lung trouble which appeared whenever the wind blew from the east. In *Science and Health* the same general story is repeated, except that the malady is definitely described as consumption. The *Science and Health* version is as follows:

A woman, whom I cured of consumption, always breathed with great difficulty when the wind was from the east. I sat silently by her side a few moments. Her breath came gently. The inspirations were deep and natural. I then requested her to look at the weathervane. She looked and

[1] Sibyl Wilbur, *The Life of Mary Baker Eddy*, page 150.

[2] *Ibid.*, page 151.

[3] Vd. *The Quimby Manuscripts*, first edition.

saw that it pointed due east. The wind had not changed, but her thought of it had and so her difficulty in breathing had gone. The wind had not produced the difficulty. My metaphysical treatment changed the action of her belief on the lungs, and she never suffered again from east winds, but was restored to health.[1]

Unfortunately, although the author of *Science and Health* has included in her book many claims of having healed the most terrible human afflictions, including "both acute and chronic disease in their severest forms," so that "shortened limbs have been elongated; ankylosed joints have been made supple, and carious bones have been restored";[2] and although she asserts that she has cured "hopeless organic disease, and raised the dying to life and health,"[3] no specific records whatever are available as evidence. In only a small number of instances, indeed, is there even a specific mention of an individual cure. Outside the healing of Mr. Clark; the treatment of the lady who suffered from the weathervane; the remedying of a "case of convulsions, produced by indigestion,"[4] and the cure of a patient "sinking in the last stage of typhoid fever,"[5] there remain remarkably few records of any "demonstrations" by the founder of Christian Science; and these are all told in her own words. The most important story of this sort has to do with a woman who had the dropsy.

It is included in *Science and Health* in connection with the author's account of how she learned the worthlessness of drugs while studying homœopathy, which seeks to cure the patient by gradually diminishing the dose until no drug is taken at all:

A case of dropsy, given up by the faculty,[6] fell into my hands. It was a terrible case. Tapping had been employed, and yet, as she lay in her bed, the patient looked like a barrel. I prescribed the fourth attenuation of *Argentum nitratum*, with occasional doses of a high at-

---

[1]*Science and Health*, page 184.   [2]*Ibid.*, page 162.   [3]*Ibid.*, page 428.
[4]*Ibid.*, page 389.   [5]*Ibid.*, page 153.

[6]There is no evidence that Mrs. Eddy ever attended a school of medicine, and hence this reference to "the faculty" is slightly obscure. There can be no doubt, however, that she picked up a great deal of the jargon used by homœopathic physicians from direct contact with this gentry during the days of her own early illness.

tenuation of *Sulphuris*. She improved perceptibly. Believing then somewhat in the ordinary theories of medical practice, and learning that her former physician had prescribed these remedies, I began to fear an aggravation of symptoms from their prolonged use, and told the patient so; but she was unwilling to give up the medicine while recovering. It then occurred to me to give her unmedicated pellets and watch the result. I did so, and she continued to gain. . . . She went on in this way, taking the unmedicated pellets,—and receiving occasional visits from me,—but employing no other means, and she was cured.[1]

However large or small may be the importance which can be attached to these claims of healing prowess, it is at least incumbent upon the biographer to point out that all must rest upon the credibility of the author herself. The episodes are included here primarily because they belong chronologically to this period of Mrs. Glover's rapidly expanding life. The evidence relating to this material is debatable and intrinsically of questionable value. We may only conclude for certain that Mrs. Glover, despite the difficulties, rebuffs, and privations which she was enduring in this period, was finally attaining the vision of a wholly new sort of career. But it was not entirely a new vision. Her ambition was still the same as it had been in the days when she sought to hold the centre of the stage by her interest in mesmerism and spiritualism. There was only one difference—she now based her bid for public attention on her interest in Quimbyism. There is little evidence, in other words, that she took up Quimby's work out of any yearning love for suffering humanity; rather did this new activity arise from that poignant yearning for adequate self-expression which had been with her since her youth.

From the Wheelers, with their unpaid board bill, Mrs. Glover went to live with Mrs. Mary Ellis, whose unmarried son was a master in a boys' school at Boston. The sojourn here appears to have been a peaceful one, and it is related that Mrs. Glover often spent the evening with these two gentle people reading aloud from her book, at which she had been writing during the day. During all of her wanderings from home to home the news about her mysterious book preceded

[1] *Science and Health*, page 156. See also *Christian Healing*, page 13, for another mention of the dropsy case; here sugar of milk is named as the remedy.

her. Mrs. Glover was not unhappy to have it so. There was a
certain distinction in being a live and producing authoress.

Her move from the Ellis household appears to have been by
volition. At the home of the Clarks Mrs. Glover had met a
young shoe factory employee called Hiram S. Crafts, who
lived in Stoughton but had come to Lynn for the winter to
follow his trade. Crafts, who was married, was rather pleased
by the interest Mrs. Glover took in him; she, in turn, showed
him the best foot she could put forward. Crafts and his
wife had both been much interested in spiritualism, but Mrs.
Glover said she had a lore to divulge compared to which spiritualism was as nothing. She then explained something of
Quimby's works and his doctrines, and young Crafts was
greatly impressed. Shoemaker as he was, he had read something of Emerson, had become interested in the idealistic
philosophy of transcendentalism, and found hints in some of
the things Mrs. Glover told him about Quimby which made
him want to learn more.

In consequence, when he left Lynn at the end of the winter
and returned to East Stoughton he invited Mrs. Glover to
pay him and his wife a visit and teach them her Quimby
doctrines, agreeing to pay her for her trouble. How much
she was paid, and how much she was supposed to take out
in board, history does not recall. The tutelage lasted all during the spring months of 1867; and in May Mr. Crafts, feeling that he had learned enough of the science to set himself
up as a healer, assumed the title of Doctor and moved over
to Taunton, taking his wife and Mrs. Glover with him.

His advertisement, appearing in the Taunton paper, said:
"*I can cure you*, and have never failed to cure Consumption,
Catarrh, Scrofula, Dyspepsia, and Rheumatism, with many
other forms of disease and weakness, in which I am espe-
cially successful. If you give me a fair trial and are not helped,
I will refund your money."

Hiram Crafts was Mrs. Glover's first student to set himself
up in the healing business, and Mrs. Glover was enthusiastic.
Despite her attempts at applying Quimby's science to the
healing of the afflicted, she apparently was already reach-

ing the conclusion that this was not to be her forte. But she knew instinctively that the whole appeal of what she had to offer was the claimed ability of the system to cure human ailment. In consequence a partner who would undertake the healing work, while she continued with the teaching, appeared to be an ideal arrangement.

As she turned this idea over in her mind, she began to think of ways and means by which she could cement a partnership. Hiram Crafts was a rather manly and cleancut young fellow, and not at all bad to look at. It seems to have occurred to Mrs. Glover that his wife was rather a hindrance to his progress.

Mrs. Crafts was a kindly, simple and self-effacing soul who had not the intellectual interests of her husband, and expressed her love for him merely by waiting on his every wish and want. She had assumed the burden of providing for Mrs. Glover's needs because this was Hiram's wish, which in turn was law.

Concluding that her husband's devotion was being alienated to a new career, she quietly began to pack up her possessions and arrange to leave Hiram to this woman who seemed more ably to fulfil his needs. When Mr. Crafts found out that he was about to lose his wife, he announced to Mrs. Glover that she had better depart, which she did. Not long thereafter the Crafts left Taunton and returned to East Stoughton, and Mr. Crafts did not continue his healing business.

While staying with the Crafts Mrs. Glover taught, as usual, from a manuscript which she always carried with her, and Crafts was at the time allowed to make a copy of this, as were all her students for a number of years. Long afterward she paid Mr. Crafts to come to her home at Pleasant View and return to her the copy which had been left in his hands.

Having been ushered forth from the home of the Crafts, it is recorded that Mrs. Glover found another haven by going to Amesbury, Massachusetts. Here there lived a delightful old lady who was the wife of a retired sea captain, Mrs. Mary Webster. She was famed abroad for her interest in spiritualism, and so great was her delight in seances that she maintained in her house a specially furnished room for the use of the spirits. The seances were always held in this chamber.

On a dark autumn night in 1867 there came a rap at the door. Grandmother Webster was alone, as she was so often, for old Captain Webster was superintendent of some cotton mills in Manchester and was frequently away from home. When she went to the door she found a strange little woman there in the shadows, plaintively asking if she might come in. The stranger said that she needed lodging, and that she had been led here by the spirits with the injunction that this was "a nice harmonious home."

The stranger was Mrs. Glover. After Mrs. Webster had invited her in and made her welcome for the night, she settled down in the house with every sign of intending to remain there permanently, despite the objections of the good captain when he returned. As for old Mrs. Webster, the words of the spirits were law to her, and she felt that her hospitality was owing to any one whom the souls of the world beyond had directed to her roof.

There was one thing, however, that she would not do for Mrs. Glover—she would not accept the Quimby doctrines. Mrs. Glover talked constantly to the old lady about Quimby's science, and said that she herself had been inspired by Quimby to write a revision of the Bible. But Mrs. Webster remained loyal to her spirits, and would have none of any newfangled ideas.

So things continued for several months, Mrs. Glover accepting hospitality freely, and using the spirit room for a part of each day while she wrote what was known as her Bible. Finally, however, Mrs. Webster's son-in-law, William Ellis, came up for a visit from New York. It appears that Mr. Ellis made these journeys fairly frequently, with the frank and avowed purpose of cleaning out the crowd of broken down spiritualists to whom his mother-in-law was perennially giving a haven. When he looked Mrs. Glover over, he decided she must depart immediately. Mrs. Glover did not merely protest; she made words.

In consequence Mr. Ellis, assisted by Captain Webster, put

Mrs. Glover and her bag precipitately outside the door. It was night, and pouring rain. Poor Mary Baker Glover stood there shivering in the storm, alone in the world, friendless, her shabby clothes sopping in the chill downfall.

At Mrs. Webster's was another spiritualist guest, a Mrs. Richardson, whose home was at Newburyport and who was perhaps visiting for the night. Her heart was touched. She put on her coat, slipped out of the house, and led Mrs. Glover down the street to the home of another spiritualist, Sarah Bagley, who supported herself as a seamstress.

Miss Bagley was pleased to have a guest to break the monotony of her humble life, and she agreed to house Mrs. Glover permanently, taking a small sum for board and receiving in addition instruction in the marvellous new faith-healing in which she already knew Mrs. Glover was an adept.

While at the Websters', Mrs. Glover had advertised her art in the paper that was familiar to all good spiritualists, the *Banner of Light*. Signed "Mary Baker Glover," this advertisement asserted that "any person desiring to learn how to heal the sick, can receive of the undersigned instruction that will enable them to commence healing on a principle of science with a success far beyond any of the present modes. . . ."[1] Miss Bagley now embraced the opportunity to secure this valuable information; and she used it so well that she shortly went into the healing business as a calling more profitable than dress-making.

It was while staying with Miss Bagley that Mrs. Glover received an invitation to go back for a while to Stoughton to visit Mrs. Sally Wentworth. Mrs. Wentworth and Mrs. Glover had met in Stoughton, while the Crafts had still been extending hospitality; and Mrs. Wentworth had been much impressed with what she had learned of Mrs. Glover's mind healing system. It was now agreed that Mrs. Glover should teach her this system for $300, said $300 to be taken out in a long term of room and board.

Thus began a relationship which lasted something more than two years, and the memory of which lasted many years

[1] *Banner of Light*, July 4, 1868.

longer to plague a woman who, as she grew older, constantly found her past streaming up over her head to make disturbing shadows on her present.

The Wentworth family consisted of Alanson C. Wentworth; Sally, his wife; Horace and Charles, their sons; Lucy, a daughter; and a niece, Catherine. For many months the Wentworths found Mrs. Glover an engaging and entertaining figure. Catherine, in later years, recounted how Mrs. Glover would lecture long and earnestly to the family on the mysteries of mind and matter; and then folding her hands, tilting her head, and nodding back and forth in rhythm to her words, would declare:

"I *learned* this from *Dr. Quimby,* and he made me *promise* to teach it to at least *two* persons before I *die.*"

All in all, being a rather jolly family group in the beginning, they had a lot of fun out of Mrs. Glover, and enjoyed her tremendously. Whether poor Mary Baker Glover had taken to heart the lesson of eviction into a stormy night; or whether she was now enjoying one of those periods when emotional calm and a sense of well-being made peace in her soul, one cannot know. But she was worshipped by little Lucy, who followed her about, took long walks with her, waited on her constantly, and was almost her shadow. As for Mrs. Wentworth, when her family became a little ribald concerning Mrs. Glover's eccentricities, she would rejoin reproachfully that "if ever there was a saint upon earth, it is that woman."

The neighbors were not as impressed as were the Wentworths themselves, and they showed an interest in the strange guest that was not at all times flattering. In a quiet New England village Mrs. Glover could not possibly escape attention for either her customs or her doctrines. All sorts of strange tales arose at Stoughton just as they had at Amesbury—where gossips related that Mrs. Glover intended to walk on the waters of the Merrimac just as soon as she finished her Bible, and small boys actually followed her on her meanderings to the riverside to ascertain whether the book had been completed.

Mrs. Glover taught Mrs. Wentworth from a manuscript entitled *The Science of Man, or the Principle which Controls all Phenomena*, which was further labelled "Extracts from Doctor P. P. Quimby's writings." Mrs. Wentworth, as usual, was allowed to make a copy for her own use; her copy was the same manuscript which was later found to be identical in content with a manuscript dated 1862 in possession of the Quimby family. In addition to the original Quimby material, Mrs. Glover's manuscript now contained an introduction or preface, written by herself and signed by her name.

After Mrs. Glover's own introduction came extracts headed "Questions by Patients, Answers by Doctor Quimby."[1]

Mrs. Glover prized her Quimby manuscript more than anything else in her possession, and she made Mrs. Wentworth promise, while copying it, never to leave it anywhere except in a locked desk. Mrs. Glover also wrote out some instructions of her own for treating certain ailments. Here, for instance, are some of her written instructions for dealing with a fever, with an incidental demonstration that she could not deal readily with punctuation:[2]

First the fever is to be argued down. What is heat and chills we answer nothing but an effect produced upon the body by images of disease before the spiritual senses wherefore you must say of heat and chill you are not hot you are not cold you are only the effect of fright there is no such thing as heat and cold if there were you would not grow hot when angry or abashed or frightened and the temperature around not changed in the least.[3]

There were also oral instructions, which included "manipulation." Mrs. Glover taught Mrs. Wentworth to rub her patient's head just as did Quimby, stating that it was not a necessary part of the process but it was an aid to concentration of thought.

[1]Vd. sworn affidavit by Horace T. Wentworth, Milmine, *Life of Mary Baker G. Eddy and History of Christian Science*, page 126.

[2]Even in her later years Mrs. Eddy never fully mastered the punctuation problem. Almost all of her published writings and letters have received careful editing, and in consequence do not appear entirely as they were first prepared.

[3]Copy obtained by Georgine Milmine from original document, in Mary Baker Patterson's handwriting, in possession of Horace T. Wentworth. Vd. Georgine Milmine, *Life of Mary Baker G. Eddy*, page 130.

The Wentworths occasionally, during the first year or so of Mrs. Glover's stay, saw outbursts of temper and quick, hot explosions of mood, but these were few and far between. Their pleasant family life provided one of the most friendly and healthy environments that Mrs. Glover had dwelt in for a long time, and it was perhaps natural that she should experience a greater emotional serenity and calm than she long had known. All through her life her great adversary was not a cold and heartless outside world; it was not the treachery of friends, nor the lack of the ordinary decencies of living, nor ignorance and poverty, nor even disease. Her one great enemy was herself, and that strange sleeping volcano within herself with its streams of suppressed bitterness and anger that were ever waiting some opportunity to break through the thin crust of the conscious to wreak havoc in her life.

At the Wentworths', Mrs. Glover was still writing away at what she called her "Bible," by this time a thick pile of closely lined note-paper, tied up with a string. Catherine, the cousin of the house, copied some of it for her. One fine day Mrs. Glover brushed up her bonnet, put on her best dress, and announced that she was going to Boston to find a publisher. She returned with the news that she couldn't find any one willing to produce the book for less than $600, payable cash in advance. Mrs. Glover seemed rather depressed. She suggested, even urged, that Mrs. Wentworth consider mortgaging the farm to raise the necessary money.

This plea failed, but Mrs. Glover's ever active mind hit upon another possible scheme of financing the publication. From the beginning she had been convinced that with a good working-partner there were possibilities of real money-making in the Quimby Science. Her quest for such a team-mate, however, had so far been in vain.

Now she suggested that Mrs. Wentworth give up her household tasks and accompany her to some town where they could make the necessary start in a small way. Mrs. Wentworth did not like the idea; and when Mr. Wentworth heard about the suggestion he was most indignant. Thereafter a pronounced coolness between him and his house-guest arose; and it is related that once, when he was sick in bed, Mrs.

Glover shut herself up in her room and pounded on the floor above in order deliberately to emphasize her disapproval of him.

This feud between Alanson Wentworth and Mrs. Glover soon involved Mrs. Wentworth, who became terrified at the unsuspected aspect of her guest which now appeared. Indeed, in later years Horace Wentworth related that his mother was so horrified at Mrs. Glover's tempestuous outbursts that for a while she lived in a state of terror, putting a lock on the door of her room to avoid any sudden ingress by Mrs. Glover at night.

There are two versions of what subsequently happened.

Several times Mrs. Glover was requested to leave, but showed no desire to adopt the suggestion. Finally, however, she made up her mind to go on a day when the family were all away from home. When the Wentworths returned in the evening, her door was locked; not knowing of her departure they went to bed, and when there was no sign of Mrs. Glover in the morning concluded that she must have gone over to some neighbor's for the night. When several days in turn had passed, they became really alarmed, and decided to force the lock on the door and learn if anything were wrong.

Horace Wentworth later embodied in an affidavit his description of the scene they discovered. Every breadth of matting on the floor was slashed up through the middle, apparently with a knife or scissors. The feather bed was cut to pieces. In the closet on the floor was a pile of charred newspapers, with a shovelful of dead coals on the top. It appeared that the fire had died instead of blazing and destroying the house, because with the closet door closed there was a complete absence of draft, and the newspapers had merely been piled flat in their original state of tight folding, so that they did not easily burn.

This story has become more or less famous in the Eddy annals, and denials have been earnestly made despite the eminent credibility of the witness whose oath is involved. In Mrs. Eddy's approved biography the story is as follows:

The apparent foundation for such slanderous gossip is that the children playing roughly in Mrs. Glover's room tore the matting with their heavy shoes, and some dead ashes were laid on a newspaper to be removed with the rubbish. . . . It was not Mary Baker's idea of good breeding to break off long-established relations rudely or with recrimination. She recognized the limitations of this family; she knew what she had to do and that she must be about it. She acquainted Mr. and Mrs. Wentworth with her intentions and her leave-taking was made with courteous attentions on both her part and theirs. She was escorted to the train by the elder Mr. Wentworth, who carried her bag and wraps.[1]

Where the credibility of witnesses is concerned, posterity has no other standard of judgment than consistent probabilities. There were only two sets of witnesses to the facts of this incident—the Wentworths and Mrs. Glover herself.

This departure from the Wentworths' ends a period that has been likened to the sojourn in the wilderness. Mrs. Eddy was not yet quite prepared, as her chosen biographer intimates, to "be about it," referring perhaps to the Biblical mention of "My Father's business." But her long period of hopeless struggle had drawn to a close. A thin pale dawn was shortly to be apparent. She was about to find the partner whom she had been looking for so long; and her instinct had been correct when she felt that the discovery of a good working-partner would be almost as great an asset as her previous discovery of Dr. Quimby.

[1] Sibyl Wilbur, *The Life of Mary Baker Eddy*, page 188.

PART II

A BOOK TO CONJURE WITH

"Often in his speaking he would be transported into a kind
of ecstasy, as a man inspired and beside himself. . . ."
                                        —PLUTARCH.

VII

Mrs. Glover left the Wentworth home in the spring of 1870, when she was in her fiftieth year. Of her life until this period only a harsh factual outline remains. Of her subjective existence—the fleeting thoughts, moods, dreams, desires that hovered over her mind—it is possible to judge only as we see it translated into action. The written record of these years is singularly unsatisfying. One feels instinctively that there must have been a kinder reality than the records reveal, a softer outline than the surviving portraits limn.

The evidence shows only that it was a baffled life, and a miserable and unhappy one. Fear is its keynote—fear of inferiority, fear of disease and pain, fear of poverty and of dependence, fear of reality, fear of self. It would be only too easy to hold up such a struggling soul to scorn and ridicule. It is far more difficult to seek to comprehend.

It was in this atmosphere that *Science and Health* was born,—written by a woman who had merely pretensions for authorship and not a gift; whose contemporary writing shows that she could punctuate and spell only with the greatest difficulty; who had absolutely no comprehension of the demands of logic, and found it difficult even to be consistent.

If the book called *Science and Health* means anything, if it stands for anything, then it is a record of deliverance. Indeed, it was the deliverance itself. For Mary Glover it was at once a flight from external reality and from the self within. It was the crystallization of a desire that became an obsession.

Viewed from this vantage point the whole strange career of the woman suddenly becomes luminous. Her book was her release. In writing it she found a new world. Alone in her room on winter nights, huddled in shawls while the wind shook the house until the smoky kerosene lamp flickered, she could bury herself in that self-assigned task of writing, and forget utterly all the cruel trivialities of the day. And as she lost herself she could deny even that the cold and shivering outside world existed, the while her fingers grew numb under the press of the pen.

Quimby had taught the simple psychology of mental pro- phylaxis—denying evil in one's life, affirming and stressing the good. Mrs. Glover's denials themselves became an obses- sion. She denied more than Quimby had ever dared to deny. She denied existence to the entire world with which she had all her life been in conflict. Huddled alone in her room, the world of the day did indeed seem blessedly phantom-like, far away, unreal. And so she wrote, page after page after page.

The writing itself was a release from the harsh reality with which she was bounded. But gradually she must have come to feel that it might eventually mean even more than the precious hours spent with it—that it could be sold; that it would bring some money; that this money might buy a permanent freedom from the humiliation of unpaid board bills, and from the thousand and one little indignities with which she had fought for so long.

Thus in the four years between 1866 and 1870 Mary Baker Glover Patterson wrote the first draft of her book. Not until several years after its completion would she find a publisher. But as she walked out of the Wentworth house and took the train to Amesbury, there was in her for the first time in her life a sense of accomplishment.

In Amesbury she went direct to the house of Miss Sarah Bagley, who had taken her in that night when she was set out, utterly friendless, into the rain. Miss Bagley, who had seen only the better side of Mrs. Glover and had indeed profited well from her teachings, welcomed her and gave her her old room.

The charming old house in Amesbury where Sarah Bagley dwelt still stands. There is the quaint mahogany melodeon, the beautiful carved mirror, the graceful slim chairs, which even to-day seem to bear a faint fragrance of old lavender, and rose leaves dried in August to lay in the linen chest. Sarah Bagley left the house jointly to her housekeeper, Miss Gunnison, and to Richard Kennedy.

Richard Kennedy, who finally inherited full title, was the boy who made it possible for Mrs. Glover to found Christian Science.

She had first met Richard during her former stay in Amesbury, and because he was a handsome lad, and gentle and mannerly in a way foreign to the others, she had taken a real liking to him. He was eighteen when she first knew him, with a high color in his cheeks, dark hair, and a lively sense of humor which made his smile a ready winner of friends.

He had been alone in the world since early childhood; at eighteen he was supporting himself by working in a box factory, and when he went to board at Grandmother Webster's he had perhaps found a kindly home for the first time in years. Being rather a lonely and sensitive chap, he stayed around the house a great deal, and imbibed from Grandmother Webster some of her interest in the spirits. When Mrs. Glover came upon the scene, he was material to make an apt pupil; and Mrs. Glover found in his eagerness for making friendship with any newcomer an ideal qualification for a listener to the doctrine about which she so delighted to talk.

Thus this youngster and the woman of fifty established a mutual interest, for Kennedy soon became absorbed in her tales of Quimby's accomplishments. He took "lessons" from Mrs. Glover during all the rest of the time she remained at the Websters', and became so attached to her that when she was ejected he loyally left also and sought another boarding place. Mrs. Glover, who found in his flattering friendliness an evidence of appreciation which had been rare in her recent sojourns, wrote to him rather often while she was in Stoughton, and occasionally he would come over to take another lesson from her.

When Mrs. Glover returned to Amesbury in 1870, Kennedy was almost twenty-one. With her book in manuscript tied up with string in her grip, her mind now reverted with added zest to the old idea which had hovered there in the background so long—the idea that if she could only find a good healer for a partner her success would be assured.

It was with this idea that she sought out Kennedy immediately upon her arrival in Amesbury. The boy was immensely flattered and pleased; he agreed readily. It was decided between them that they should go to Lynn, then a town of some 30,000 souls, where Mrs. Glover felt that the large shoe factory population might offer good prospects.

Here they boarded temporarily at the home of Mrs. Clarkson Oliver, while Richard scoured the town for a place to establish an office. From the moment of their arrival he chivalrously assumed all the labor of making the arrangements for setting up their project. Mrs. Glover had only to remain in the background and accept his deferential service.

He finally found just what he wanted as space for an office in the home of a decorous lady named Miss Susie Magoun, who had just taken a building where she could live and teach a private school on the first floor, letting out the second in order to cover part of the rent. One warm June evening, Miss Magoun answered the ring of a very boyish and bashful chap who asked her if she would rent her floor for the offices of a "doctor." When Miss Magoun asked if five rooms would be too much space for his father, the boy was obviously embarrassed, then found tongue to explain that the incumbents would be an elderly lady who was writing a book, and himself; and that the space would not be too ample, for they both would need offices and living accommodations.

Miss Magoun finally agreed, to the boy's very evident relief; for he explained that he had been turned down by many people with rooms to rent. Several days later the new occupants moved in. Miss Magoun's first sight of Mrs. Glover revealed an elderly and bony woman who stiffly bowed and started immediately to talk about the nothingness of matter and Dr. Quimby.

Patients from the shoe-manufacturing population of Lynn started to arrive during the first week that the tree in the yard held the chaste sign, "Dr. Kennedy." At the end of the month the rent was paid promptly, and by autumn the young doctor's practice was so flourishing that sometimes lines of patients overflowed the waiting-room upstairs and were given refuge in Miss Magoun's parlor. The fact that Miss Magoun was well and favorably known in the town, and liked Kennedy well enough to put in a kindly word for him whenever possible, was perhaps of real assistance to the expanding practice.

Mrs. Glover remained a shadowy and ghost-like figure during these first months, occasionally going with Miss Magoun to the Unitarian Church, but remaining otherwise closeted for long hours in her room with the book that every one understood she was writing. Whether she was making additions to her earlier manuscript, or was revising and rewriting her first draft, may now only be hazarded; perhaps both. She rather disapproved of young Kennedy's ready friendliness with the neighbors, and the facility with which he entered into the graces of all he met did not please her. She insisted that his participation in the social life of Miss Magoun's pleasant acquaintances hardly furthered his appreciation of Science.

Kennedy's success with the healing business put the partnership on a paying basis from the first, and he was building up an excellent local reputation for effecting real and important cures. His patients talked to their fellow workmen of his mysterious powers, and they explained what a fine young fellow he was; the result was not only a greater influx of patients than ever but also a group of students for Mrs. Glover, whose cards now read "Mrs. Mary M. Glover, Teacher of Moral Science."

Kennedy, whose sense of gratitude to his teacher was very great, even though they had disagreements almost from the start of their association, had entered upon an amazingly generous financial arrangement with his elderly partner. During the whole extent of their partnership he paid the living expenses for both, and in addition gave Mrs. Glover half of whatever money was left from his practice. On the other hand, any sums which she could derive from teaching were her own.

Mrs. Glover's original price for a course of twelve lessons, or lectures, was one hundred dollars. But within a very few weeks after organizing her first class at Lynn she raised this price to three hundred dollars, and this fee was never after-

ward changed, although in later years she reduced the number of lessons given from twelve to seven. And Mrs. Glover
got her price, even when three hundred dollars meant the
wages of a half a year to a Lynn shoeworker. Replying indirectly to some of the criticism levelled in later years at the
size of this fee, she wrote:

When God impelled me to set a price on my instruction in Christian
Science Mind-healing, I could think of no financial equivalent for an im-
partation of a knowledge of that divine power which heals; but I was
led to name three hundred dollars as the price for each pupil in one
course of lessons at my College,—a startling sum for tuition lasting bare-
ly three weeks. This amount greatly troubled me. I shrank from asking
it, but was finally led, by a strange providence, to accept this fee.[1]

It will be seen that Mrs. Glover not only was led to accept
her fee; on occasion she was even led to sue for it, although
in later years when unpleasant criticism became acute, she
forbade practitioners of her church to indulge in such suits.

From the moment when she began to sense release from the
world of shabby poverty in which she had dwelt for fifty
years, Mrs. Glover began to expand and grow. Month by
month and year by year she became a more commanding,
more dominating figure, still at the mercy of the tempestuous
volcano which slept within, but ever more sure of the world
which she felt in her outer grasp.

No longer forced to constant scheming how she might live
on the charities of her acquaintances, she gradually dropped
many of those little oddities in speech, clothes, and manner
which she had unconsciously adopted as a sort of psychological barricade. Her nervous and scrawny figure developed
some curves, her carriage became erect, her gaze turned steady
and piercing.

Students soon began coming to her in goodly number; they
were either patients of Kennedy or friends of his patients, so
amazed by the cures which the Science made possible that
they were willing to pay even Mrs. Glover's exorbitant price
by yielding up more than a whole year's savings. These stu-

---

[1]*Retrospection and Introspection*, page 50.

dents were a nondescript lot. One of them, George Tuttle, was a bulky young seaman who had returned from a voyage around the world just in time to find his half-sister in a state of exalted enthusiasm because Kennedy had apparently given her entirely new life when she had been in the advanced stages of tuberculosis. She insisted that her half-brother and her husband should both join Mrs. Glover's class.

Young Tuttle, when he had had a few lessons, cured a girl of dropsy and was so amazed and frightened that he immediately dropped the mysterious art and would never touch it again. Stanley, husband of Tuttle's half-sister, also had enrolled for the course. Mrs. Glover had exacted of them an agreement to pay not only her hundred-dollar tuition fee, but also an annual 10 per cent on all of their earnings from either healing or teaching work. In addition, if they failed so to practise or teach they agreed to pay her a forfeit of $1,000. The stalwart Tuttle fell by the wayside almost before he had started. Stanley was put out of her class by Mrs. Glover when they had an argument.

As a result the Tuttle and Stanley fees were never paid in full; and nine years later, in 1879, Mrs. Glover brought suit in the Essex County Court and herself appeared to prosecute. Tuttle's testimony was most amusing. He recounted how he had had a dispute with the lady when she said, in denying the reality of Matter, that she could walk on the water, and could live without eating. He offered to share a fast with her, and then see who could do without food the longest. The dispute had gained momentum when Mrs. Glover not only denied consumption, but said that there were no such things as lungs or liver—these organs being all imagination. Following the denials of Stanley and Tuttle that they had received instruction of any practical value in Mrs. Glover's classroom, she herself took the stand and told the judge some of the details of her teaching. In rendering a decision for the defendants, the Judge said:

Upon a careful examination I do not find any instructions given by her nor any explanations of her "science" or "method of healing" which appear intelligible to ordinary comprehension, or which could in any way be of value in fitting the Defendant as a competent and successful practitioner of any intelligible art or method of healing the sick, and I am of opinion that the consideration for the agreement has wholly failed, and I so find.

Mrs. Glover, in the midst of her flourishing classes of young artisans anxious to learn how to destroy all human ills, was never without dissension of some character or other among her students. She herself was highly emotional and excitable, and so remained until the end of her days; and the thing which she had to teach undoubtedly had a curious appeal for the emotionally suggestible and high-strung.

One student, a Mrs. Otis Vickary, became so dissatisfied with her instruction that she went to the Lynn Police Court in 1872 and sued for and recovered the one hundred and fifty dollars which she had paid to Mrs. Glover as advance tuition. Mrs. Glover did not appear, and judgment was rendered by default. Another student, Wallace Wright, who was the son of a Universalist clergyman and a highly regarded young citizen of the town, took the Glover course and at first made several highly successful cures, but later failed in healing patients when he went to Knoxville, Tennessee, to make a profession of the work. Thereupon he wrote to Mrs. Glover asking her to refund his tuition. He subsequently remarked that "the result of this course was to convince me that I had studied the science of mesmerism."

The whole Glover-Wright controversy was fought out publicly, in the Lynn *Transcript,* and the files of this paper in the early months of 1872 suggest that the town must have enjoyed a titillating sensation. On February 10, Mr. Wright publicly challenged Mrs. Glover:

1st: To restore the dead to life again as she claims she can.
2nd: To walk upon the water without the aid of artificial means as she claims she can.[1]

[1]The future Mrs. Eddy never did abandon the claim that her Science, properly applied, would enable its initiate to duplicate the water-walking feat recorded of Jesus. On page 329 of *Science and Health* there is still found the statement, "Because you cannot walk on the water and raise the dead, you have no right to question the great might of divine Science in these directions."

3rd: To live 24 hours without air, or 24 days without nourishment of any kind without its having any effect upon her.[1]

4th: To restore sight when the optic nerve has been destroyed.

5th: To set and heal a broken bone without artificial means.

Mr. Wright ended the controversy, so far as he was concerned, by an exultant announcement on February 17 that Mrs. Glover and her Science were practically dead and buried.

She could easily afford to lose an occasional student; she could even afford to have her disputes with such backsliders get into the papers. For the resulting publicity, unfavorable as it must have seemed, nevertheless was far better than no publicity at all, and engendered public discussion in the town which formed new recruits for her classes constantly.

There was one of her associates, however, whom she could not easily replace. That was Richard Kennedy. Undoubtedly she realized this; and undoubtedly she was not emotionally responsible for the explosion that eventually cost her Kennedy's collaboration.

Kennedy was a level-headed youngster whose patience had already been tried by some of Mrs. Glover's vagaries, and disagreements between them had not been less as his practice had steadily increased. He had particularly sought to put a brake upon her imagination; for he was discovering through his practice that however valuable his work might be as a treatment for disease, it had natural limits and could hardly claim to be a cure-all. Mrs. Glover's statements that food was not necessary for the body, that the body did not even have organs, that she could walk on water just as easily as on dry land—such wholly irrelevant and hyperbolic flights of fancy aroused him to protest; and Mrs. Glover, who was now enjoying for the first time in her life a sense of authority, did not take these protests pleasantly.

The matter came to a climax on Thanksgiving night, when Miss Magoun, who had recently married, invited Mrs. Glover and young Kennedy in to play cards. Mrs. Glover always

[1]The claim of being able to live without food was eventually thrown into the discard. Vd. page 461 of *Science and Health*: "I do not maintain that anyone can exist in the flesh without food and raiment; but I do believe that the real man is immortal and that he lives in spirit, not matter."

liked to win; she was constitutionally unable to lose with grace
and pleasantness. When Kennedy and his partner came off
victors, Mrs. Glover threw her cards on the table and accused
him of cheating.

When they returned to their rooms, he went to the desk,
took out his contract, tore it up and threw it into the fire. He
said that he was finished. Mrs. Glover for the first time in
years resorted to the deliberate swoon that had once been so
effective with old Mark Baker. She fainted dead away. But
young Kennedy had made up his mind. Neither her swoon nor
her subsequent pleadings affected him. He immediately began
to make plans to bring the partnership to a conclusion, and in
the spring of 1872 he opened an office elsewhere in Lynn, previously settling up their mutual accounts and leaving Mrs.
Glover about six thousand dollars in cash. It was her first real
capital. Her rise to affluence dates from that day.

Mrs. Glover, while teaching students for $300 apiece, had
not lost her poetic sense in the midst of practical considerations. *The Transcript* editors were the frequent recipients of
tidbits from her pen, in one of which, "Lines on Receiving
Some Grapes," the following stanza formed the climax:

> And such, methinks, e'en Nature shows
> The fate of Beauty's power—
> Admired in parlour, grotto, groves,
> But faded, O how sour![1]

Mrs. Glover, all these years, had really been Mrs. Patterson, and when defending and prosecuting law suits had necessarily been forced to use her legal name. This recalled unpleasant memories, and it also necessitated unpleasant explanations. Consequently in 1873 she took steps to obtain a divorce
in Salem.

The divorce action was brought on the ground of desertion, and was so granted. Mr. Patterson's small annual allowance had faded away long before; she had nothing to lose and
everything to gain. Strangely enough, all her subsequent references to this closed chapter in her career were so phrased as

[1]Lynn *Transcript*, November 4, 1871.

to make it appear that she had sought and won a decision on the grounds of adultery.[1] Possibly it was because of a feeling that such grounds absolved her from all blame. As the story is told in her approved biography:

. . . Mrs. Eddy waited until nearly night for her case to be called and they thought it would not be disposed of that day. But when she was called to the witness stand the judge asked why her husband had deserted her. She replied, "Because he feared arrest." "Arrest for what?" asked the judge. "For adultery," Mrs. Eddy replied quietly.[2]

After the departure of Kennedy, Mrs. Glover retained the rooms they had shared together at South Common and Shepard Streets and went on with her teaching as usual. In a few months, however, she moved to a boarding house, and for another three-year period lived in a number of such establishments, this time well able to pay her way, but by the force of old habit not always doing so. Thirty years afterward Mrs. Allen A. Locke was claiming that a balance of $22 was still owing on a board-bill contracted by Mrs. Glover with Mrs. Locke's mother, Mrs. Geo. Allen.[3]

On March 31, 1875, Mrs. Glover ended her wanderings. On that day Francis E. Besse deeded to "Mary M. B. Glover, a widow woman of Lynn" the house at 8 Broad Street, which was thereafter always to be regarded as the cradle of the Christian Science movement. Mrs. Glover paid $5,560 for the building, all cash above a $2,800 mortgage. For years this house, a rather ugly little two and a half story affair with a fresh coat of paint, was the Mecca for pilgrimages of devout members of Mrs. Eddy's later church.

[1] Vd. *Miscellany*, page 314: "Although, as *McClure's Magazine* claims, the court record may state that my divorce from Dr. Patterson was granted on the ground of desertion, the cause nevertheless was adultery. . . . After the evidence had been submitted that a husband was about to have Dr. Patterson arrested for eloping with his wife, the court instructed the clerk to record the divorce in my favor. . . . I lived with Dr. Patterson peaceably, and he was kind to me up to the time of the divorce."

[2] Sibyl Wilbur, *Life of Mary Baker Eddy*, page 210.

[3] That this was not the claim of a harpy-like landlady who was merely disgruntled seems evidenced by the personal characters of the Mesdames Locke and Allen.

Mrs. Glover's students took entire care of the establishment, mowing the lawn, doing the chores, and looking after the wants of tenants. For Mrs. Glover had learned by the press of years of penury the art of being frugal. She rented out as much of her house as she could. For herself she reserved the front parlor, which she furnished with the cheapest of tables and chairs, and a bedroom in the attic, where the only ventilation came from a skylight. This bedroom—repainted and refurnished—in after years became a shrine. It was here that she was reputed to have finished her book.

Around her she had gathered by this time a number of local students to whom her teachings had come as a great revelation, and in whose lives she was the sole central fixture. Even those who afterward deserted her testified to the marvellous power of the woman to instil into their lives a sort of burning ardor they never felt either before or after this direct contact with her strange personality. Her great obsession became also theirs, and existence had never seemed to glow so incandescently. Some of them experienced this high exaltation only to a slight degree, while with others the experience was transcendent. They were naturally a highly suggestible group, many with the natural temperament of the mystic; and all of them were living in the mystic's world of complete negation. It was an atmosphere which would have provided James with rich material for his *Varieties of Religious Experience*.

It is not to be wondered at that under the glow of this adulation Mrs. Glover slowly lost consciousness of Quimby, as her concept of her own rôle grew. More and more her circle seemed to revolve about herself, and to hang upon her own words. Less and less did her teachings seem to be those of a man dead these ten years. As Georgine Milmine said so brilliantly, "Others of his pupils lost themselves in Quimby's philosophy, but Mrs. Glover lost Quimby in herself."

Previously at Stoughton, and now at Lynn, she had been teaching direct from Quimby's treatise, "Questions and Answers," to which she had written an introduction of her own, signed with her name. As copies of this document were recopied again, Mrs. Glover's introduction finally was absorbed into the general body of the text as if the whole were written by one person, and many of these copies were unsigned. She copyrighted this treatise under her name in 1870, but it was not published until 1876, by which time she had made a number of other changes in the context.

This was her only manuscript used for teaching purposes at Stoughton; but by the time of her Lynn sojourn she had developed another work which, when it was given a title at all, bore the name "Scientific Treatise on Mortality, As Taught by Mrs. M. B. Glover." This second manuscript was only partially Quimby's text, since excerpts from Quimby were embroidered with much that was Mrs. Glover's. A third treatise, called "Soul's Inquiries of Man," also was a combination of Quimby and Mrs. Glover.

It was from the first of these manuscripts, Quimby's own, that Mrs. Glover continued to teach; but her verbal teaching seemed so far to outshadow the manuscript itself in importance that her conscious debt to Quimby was lessened every day that she walked into her parlor to talk to her assembled students. A great number of these students said in later years that the written documents were pale and meaningless beside the marvellous vigor of her personal address; and even many who afterward were estranged from her said that these impassioned lectures had an influence upon them whose value could not be measured.

Such is the consummate power of the human being literally consumed with an idea.

As Quimby's manuscript was slowly absorbed into Mrs. Glover's own, Mrs. Glover also began teaching successfully from other manuscripts which indeed were partially hers. Then came still further changes which pushed her debt to Quimby more and more into the background.

Richard Kennedy was largely responsible for these changes. When he left Mrs. Glover, he took his sign with him and hung it out in front of his new office, and patients continued to flock as regularly as before, and in even greater numbers. Mrs. Glover resented his success greatly. Her temperament being what it was, she hungered for means to discredit him.

It occurred to her that an obvious way of attaining her purpose would be to discredit his work by disowning some of the methods of healing which she previously had taught him and which he was using to such advantage.

It was a resource which was to serve her well in later disputes with various followers. But no subsequent action of this sort that she ever took was as important in its ramifications, and in its effects on herself, as the one she adopted now. She gained her idea, evidently, from the attacks made by Wallace Wright when he asserted that her healing methods were identical with those of mesmerism.

All these years Mrs. Glover had practised, and had taught her students to practise, the "laying on of hands," as Quimby had done. Quimby himself had stated that this device had nothing to do with the actual healing: that it was merely useful as establishing a formal mode of contact between patient and practitioner. Mrs. Glover now decided not only to renounce this small adjunct to her healing system, but also to denounce it as a mesmeristic practice which she henceforth abjured as being wholly pernicious. She had her students cross out of their manuscript copies of her "Scientific Treatise on Mortality" all references and instructions for wetting the hands and rubbing the patient's head. From that moment forward "manipulation" became to her a thing as horrible as a tribal taboo of the African savage. In her first edition of *Science and Health*, she said:

Sooner suffer a doctor infected with smallpox to be about you than come under the treatment of one that manipulates his patients' heads, and is a traitor to science.[1]

This was a direct slap at Kennedy, who was calmly attending to his own prosperous business, "laying on" hands with consummate success, and paying no attention to Mrs. Glover whatever. Further on in the volume she said:

There is but one possible way of doing wrong with a mental method of healing, and this is mesmerism. . . . For years we had tested the

[1]Page 193.

never once admitted such a genesis for the name she chose. Since she was wholly unaware of the retentive memory with which the subconscious is endowed, she probably did believe, quite sincerely, that the title was an original idea.

The book was cheaply bound, crudely printed, and full of typographical errors. The copyright notice was the usual "Entered According to the Act of Congress, in the year 1875, by Mary Baker Glover, in the Office of the Librarian of Congress at Washington." There were eight chapters, named in order: "Natural Science; Imposition and Demonstration; Spirit and Matter; Creation; Prayer and Atonement; Marriage; Physiology; Healing the Sick." The chapter headings, however, do not indicate the precise nature of the subject matter included thereunder, since the material is exceedingly dispersed. Mrs. Glover wrote her thoughts rather at random; and the reader must search studiously in all her chapters to discover the totality of her views on any one topic.

This first edition did not contain the extensive discourse on animal magnetism which was added to the second with the purpose of denouncing Kennedy, Wallace Wright, and others who did not enjoy the author's favor. And hereby a strange quirk in Mrs. Glover's recollection is revealed. In after years, when this chapter on mesmerism, or animal magnetism, was considered most unfortunate even by many of her devoted followers, the then Mrs. Eddy justified it by telling a story that hinted at its divine origin and inception. So unreliable, however, was her memory that she attributed this chapter to the first edition, where it never appeared. Thus she said:

My reluctance to give the public, in my first edition of Science and Health, the chapter on Animal Magnetism, and the divine purpose that this should be done, may have an interest for the reader, and will be seen in the following circumstances. I had finished that edition as far as that chapter, when the printer informed me that he could not go on with my work. I had already paid him seven hundred dollars, and yet he stopped my work. All efforts to persuade him to finish my book were in vain.[1]

It was only then, she explains, that she "yielded to a constant conviction" that this chapter should be included. And so

[1] *Retrospection and Introspection*, page 37.

she tells how she wrote it in haste, and went to take the train
to carry it to Boston, only to meet the printer at the station
coming to say that he needed exactly this amount of new
material to fill out the book. Such a dénouement must certainly
have embodied divine intervention, hints the author, for so far
as the printer was concerned "not a word had passed between
us, audibly or mentally, while this went on."

Had the author possessed a reliable memory even for her
own motives, she could never have made this error. For it
will be seen that the chapter on mesmerism had a unique and
curious origin.

This first edition was a crude and amateurish piece of writing which bore self-evident contradictions on every page, not
to speak of errors in grammar and composition even more
striking than those in logic. In later years, when subsequent
editions had enjoyed the advantages of sundry polishings at
the hands of the author's genial literary collaborator, the book
assumed a rather different flavor—a flavor indeed so at variance with the phraseology of some of Mrs. Eddy's other writings that many critics asserted the author of Mrs. Eddy's verse
could not possibly be also the author of her chef d'œuvre.
Mark Twain's critique on Christian Science took this contention as its main thesis. What he did not then understand,
and many other contemporary critics with him, was the process
by which the original verbiage of *Science and Health* was
finally rendered civilized.

VIII

Because *Science and Health* played such an important rôle in the career of the subsequent Mrs. Eddy, and because its author can not be wholly explained unless her book is also accounted for, the narrative now is temporarily interrupted to allow for some analysis. The reader who desires to take the philosophy and theology of *Science and Health* on faith may turn to the next chapter, where the narrative is resumed. Meanwhile the genesis and evolution of the ideas which were to bring Mrs. Glover to wealth and fame must be briefly traced, their validity examined, and their implications described.

In writing her book the future Mrs. Eddy was in reality dealing with three departments of human thought: psychology, theology, and philosophy. While Quimby formed the main source of her psychology, there was undoubtedly much in her philosophy and theology that was Mrs. Glover's own modification of ideas garnered in other fields.

Quimby's psychology was actually a simple thing—a system of mental prophylaxis. One denied all evil, affirmed the reality and possession of all good. It was an application of a system of mental suggestion which would meet with the approval of almost any modern psychiatrist.

Both Quimby and Mrs. Glover, however, advocated far more than a simple Couéism. Theirs was not a mere system of auto-suggestion. Quimby started with one premise born from his experience: that suggestion would cure disease. From this grew a large conclusion: that all states either of health or disease were created solely by the mind. Then came a third idea: that a person could be affected physically either by auto-suggestion—the attitude of his own mind; or by external suggestion—the attitude of other minds. This again led to a further idea: that one mind could affect the life of another even if spacially absent and at a distance. Here lay the genesis of Quimby's theory of "absent treatment."

These theories developed still another: that not only physical health, but all experience, is the product of mental states. In other words, mind creates all objective reality.[1]

Mrs. Glover took all these Quimby beliefs over bodily, and added details of her own. For example, she developed the theory of "absent treatment" into an application which Quimby had hardly considered. She did not stop with the idea that "absent treatment" could be used to create health. She concluded that it could also be employed as a device for evil, creating untold ills in the life of the victim against which it was directed. Such absent mesmerism, for instance, might make a man sick, if the mesmerist so desired. How this idea of malicious mesmerism was expanded until it played a large part in the Eddy career will later be shown; she came to regard it as the source of all the evil which she sought to deny.

The entire genesis of Mrs. Glover's ideas regarding malicious mesmerism lay in fear, which ruled her whole life and later distorted her philosophy. Such a concept of an active principle of evil was an obvious contradiction in a philosophy based on the premise that all is good. Inconsistencies, however, seldom worried Mrs. Glover. She did not ponder them; she merely denied them.[2]

Like Quimby she had found that a philosophy was necessary to substantiate and support her propositions in psychology. A background of reasoned thought was essential if her system was to be self-contained and most effective. Following Quimby's own excursions into philosophical fields, Mrs. Glover started her philosophy with the proposition that All is God, hence All is Good.

But like every other philosopher before her, she immedi-

---

[1]Vd. *The Quimby Manuscripts*, page 193: "I will try to show that Jesus . . . not only condemned the idea of a world independent of man, but proved that there was none by all His sayings and doings."

[2]Vd. *Miscellany*, page 112: " 'Science and Health with Key to the Scriptures' is not inconsistent in a single instance with its logical premise and conclusion, and ninety-nine out of every hundred of its readers—honest, intelligent, and scholarly—will tell you this." And again, in *Science and Health*, page 345: "In this volume of mine there are no contradictory statements,—at least none which are apparent to those who understand its propositions well enough to pass judgment upon them."

ately ran into the ever-present problem of evil. If all is God, Good, then how account for the evil in the world?

It was here that Mrs. Glover really stumbled. Had she looked around her, she would have discovered many other philosophers—and not amateur philosophers, at that—who might have given her a hand. Spinoza, Leibnitz, Emerson, Berkeley,—the woods were full of them. Later she did indeed read the works of some of these erudite gentlemen. From some she subsequently quoted extensively, to show that they concurred in her views.[1] Others she denounced with ardor— particularly whenever they evinced any tendency to subscribe to Pantheism and its belief that all matter is endowed with mind.

Mrs. Glover could have said that the sense of evil is a finite limitation; merely a point of view. She could have said, as did Royce, that it is a realization of incompleteness; that as the finite individual grows into consciousness and realization of the infinite God he loses this limiting sense, and all to him is resolved into Good. Or she could even have said that the individual, being a part of God, was himself endowed with the same creative powers as God, and could thus create freely, his sense of good and evil depending only upon whether he used this godlike gift to create in complete accord with all his needs.[2]

Actually Mrs. Glover lit upon none of those possible approaches to her problem, any one of which might have offered

[1] Impressive evidence has been recently presented to prove that the founder of Christian Science, in addition to using acknowledged quotations, on numerous occasions appropriated germane material when it served her purpose. Word for word and line for line parallels can be found between her own texts and those of Ruskin, Carlyle, and Blair, Scottish eighteenth-century divine, whose texts adorned Lindley Murray's *English Reader*. No adequate research work has so far been done to establish the full extent of such indebtedness of *Science and Health* to unacknowledged writers, for the very apparent reason that no trained intellect sufficiently conversant with modern literature has devoted itself to the laborious and difficult task of rendering comparative analysis to Mrs. Eddy's famous book. Since the extent of the indebtedness would vary with almost every edition of *Science and Health*, the task involved is huge. (See Appendix.)

[2] Quimby approached this idea closely. Vd. *The Quimby Manuscripts*, page 263: "Now when the people are educated to understand that *what they believe they will create*, they will cease believing what the medical men say, and try to account for their feelings in some more rational way." The italics are Quimby's.

her fewer difficulties than the one she finally chose. How, then, did she find her way out? By the strange device of hitching evil up with matter, and then denying the existence of both. She took her cue from Quimby's assertion that there is no intelligence in matter.[1]

It should be noted, in passing, that Mrs. Glover never once defined matter in a way that would be satisfying to a logician. One may assume, however, from a study of her subsequently voluminous texts, that matter to her consisted of anything that was made evident to humanity through the five senses,—in other words, the materialist's world of reality. It was this whole world whose existence Mrs. Glover now rose bravely to blot out and deny. She took her stand on the hypothesis that there is no matter; only mind is real.

Since her whole philosophy is founded on syllogisms, it is not amiss to show how she reached this conclusion from her premise. Several syllogisms are involved, not all of them valid. Her first premise is that God is All. And God is Mind. Therefore Mind is All. The second syllogism would take this conclusion as a new premise: Mind is all; Matter is not Mind; therefore Matter does not exist. A third syllogism would cast out the reality of disease and sin in the same fashion. God, Good, is the only reality. Sin and sickness are not good. Hence, they also are not real. It is worth noting, in this connection, how Mrs. Glover now reached the conclusion that all matter is evil. She built up another fallacious syllogism: matter is not real; and evil is not real,—hence matter is evil. This fallacious conclusion sounded well in a system of thought that displayed some Puritanical tendencies. But it was destined to trouble its inventor, who when she acquired wealth sought also to acquire very material comforts.

Having now proved to her own satisfaction that neither matter nor human ailments had any real existence, Mrs. Glover's remaining problem was merely to embroider her syl-

[1] It should be stressed, in this connection, that Quimby differentiated sharply between *intelligence* and *mind*, and also between *wisdom* and *mind*. He never once said, so far as the writer can discover, that there is no *mind* in matter. There can be no doubt, however, that Mrs. Patterson failed utterly to grasp Quimby's distinction.

logistic premises with the elaborate detail necessary for applying them to human experience.

It has been said that the author of *Science and Health* probably owed much of her philosophy to Berkeley, and perhaps to
Spinoza and Leibnitz; that even if she had not derived from
them directly she had absorbed ideas from more learned readers. This is easily refuted. Mrs. Glover actually had more in
common with the realistic school of thought than with the
idealists; realists at least would have agreed with her that
mind was something distinct and apart from matter.

Certainly Mrs. Glover never glimpsed even a vision of the
wonderful world which the idealistic philosophers of her time
were even then opening up to human view; and when she
heard of pantheism she denounced it savagely as another "error."[1] This may well be a matter of regret to those idealists
who would be interested to see what heights might be reached
by a religion founded on a pantheistic philosophy—a belief
that God as mind and spirit pervades His Universe; that the
physical structure of His Universe is inseparable from His
Idea; and that matter and mind are basically kindred manifestations of the same great underlying Reality.

Mrs. Glover's syllogistic philosophy never reached such
heights: having said that mind was all, she proceeded promptly
to the conclusion that matter was nothing. Like the dramatist
who finds a few useless characters left over at the end, and
simply kills them off, Mrs. Glover merely blotted out that part
of reality which was difficult to account for.

To have any comprehension of the philosophic depths in
which the unsuspecting Mrs. Glover became involved, it is
necessary to remember first of all that the statement "There
is no matter," really means nothing whatever. Or rather, it may
mean so many various things—depending on the definition of
"matter"—that it is open to almost innumerable interpretations.

As it happens, most of the real thinkers of the world to-day
are very ready to declare that there is no matter—if by matter
is meant a reality manifest only in the terms known to Eu-

[1] Vd. her *Christian Science Versus Pantheism.*

clidian geometry and Newtonian physics. The modern scientist, indeed, has almost ceased to talk about matter, or to regard the word as anything more than a label which in the last analysis means nothing. Mathematicians and physicists are alike agreed in this conclusion, to which modern mathematics pointed the inevitable way even before the physicists reached it; and indeed the post-Newtonians, such as Einstein and Eddington, are mathematicians first of all. Far in advance even of the mathematicians were the philosophers, from Plato down through Kant and Royce to Ouspensky, reaching the same conviction by still other routes of thought. All are to-day agreed that matter is merely a form of energy. And so —presumably—is mind.

But this does not mean that the elderly Mrs. Glover, wandering around New England mill towns, was acting, so to speak, as a philosophic harbinger of Einstein. For Mrs. Glover, in denying the reality of matter, meant something vastly different from the conclusions which are so often phrased in the same terms. What she actually sought to deny was the reality of an *objective universe*. In her philosophy there was only one reality: the world of *subjective ideas*.

Berkeley alone among thinkers of modern standing ever ventured to defend such a thesis; and Berkeley has long been discredited. To Einstein, as to Royce, the objective universe —whatever it consists of actually—at least has a very real existence regardless of what any human being may ever think about it.

It was at this point, then, that Mrs. Glover became hopelessly lost—in the same depths that have swamped many other more practised minds than hers. And having become lost, she never did define the word Matter in a way that might have shown her some release from her morass. Matter remained for her the entire objective world. Having denied its reality, she left herself floating in a universe which was nothing but a void.

If, instead of denying the material world, she had merely redefined it in terms of mind, she would have avoided many pitfalls. Had she declared the identity of mind and matter; had she denied, not the valid existence of the object, but rather its independent existence apart from mind,[1] modern philosophers and scientists alike would at least respect her conclusions. It is true that at times she seemed to approach such an interpretation or definition of the physical universe, for she undoubtedly was extremely confused whenever she sought to measure her philosophy against experience. In the end, however, she always reverted to unqualified denial.

Thus she denied the existence of the entire physical universe from the most gigantic sun to the infinitesimal atom. She even denied the reality of the body—of arms, feet, stomach and lungs.

In accounting for the fact that stars and atoms and human bodies and all the rest of objective reality seem very real to humanity, Mrs. Glover made one other wild leap. She denied even the reality of the human mind which senses this material universe. She called it "carnal mind," identified it with error, and asserted that it, too, was unreal and a delusion.[2] Only Divine Mind, said she, was real. As an individual managed to suppress all human consciousness, all human senses and needs, all conception of an external reality, he would then become Divine. But until then he would live in error.

This, of course, is a wholly distorted and discredited form of mysticism. Its genesis lay first, in Mrs. Glover's efforts from girlhood to flee from a harsh external reality; second, in her puritanical training and background, through which in girlhood she came to believe that Godliness sprang only from self denial and privation; third, in her misconception of the idealistic philosophy which Quimby was seeking to evolve.

Obviously, of course, it is a philosophy wholly impossible to

[1]Quimby, to his enormous credit, hit upon exactly this idea. Vd. *The Quimby Manuscripts*, page 392: "I have shown that there is no matter *independent of mind or life.*" Again, on page 222: "There is no matter *without mind.*" The italics are the author's. There is a vast difference between Mrs. Eddy's simple assertion, "There is no matter," and Quimby's thesis. With the Quimby concept an Einstein, an Eddington, a Kant might be on perfectly friendly terms. Royce wrote his two volumes of *The World and the Individual* around this very idea. But Mrs. Eddy never once grasped the real problem here, and consequently took over from Quimby a thesis for which he was only partly responsible.

[2]Vd. *Unity of Good*, page 50: "At best, matter is only a phenomenon of mortal mind, of which evil is the highest degree; but really there is no such thing as *mortal mind,*—though we are compelled to use the phrase in the endeavor to express the underlying thought."

put into practice; and its creator herself never followed it out to its logical conclusions. Any mind which managed to do so would end up in an utter void and an endless night.

Obviously, also, the Glover philosophy would not go far to satisfy a practical thinker, who would insist that even were matter and human mind proved to be illusion, this illusion must still be explained. Puncturing the aplomb of Mrs. Glover's philosophy, however, is a task which can well be left for the diversion of the philosophers' holidays. It is sufficient merely to suggest its outlines, and to point out the essential weaknesses that account for its failure to have achieved that conquest of modern thought of which Mrs. Glover-Eddy dreamed.

Many years later, when the sanity of Mrs. Eddy was brought into question and eminent medical testimony adduced to show that she was suffering from progressive paranoia, the statement was made that her dementia had completed its period "forty years ago." It was held that evidence of this lay in her own writings, in which she solemnly asserted the non-reality of the entire physical universe. Opposing counsel immediately demanded to know if such evidence of dementia also meant that all of Mrs. Eddy's followers were also insane.

That question would indeed have to be answered if Mrs. Eddy's followers had literally and entirely subscribed to all of her philosophic theories. Actually, however, the validity of her philosophy was only a small factor in the formula she had to offer. Those few who were equipped to understand its full implications eventually left her fold. The many others who accepted it without question were generally quite unharmed, for they pursued all their normal human ways of living just as if the physical world were the very important consideration which it is, and got themselves homes and clothing and automobiles and the coin of the realm in a wholly matter-of-fact fashion. If for these followers anything was lacking in reality, it was not the physical universe but Mrs. Eddy's philosophic theories about it. And after her death her various followers quarrelled over the very material booty in her estate with such unphilosophic eagerness that her trustees were kept busy testifying in court for months.

Let it be emphasized, however, that for general purposes of usefulness her system was not much damaged by its philosophic lacks. Probably the majority of people, however trained their minds for the field of work in which they are engaged, are wholly unequipped to deal with philosophic abstractions. They can subscribe verbally to an utterly invalid philosophy without any qualms whatever, and will sense no need of giving more than verbal consent and lip-service. They will never feel an urge to harmonize this theoretical philosophy with daily experience: and if perchance they ever did, their mental training would be inadequate for the task.

It is obvious, for instance, that the geocentric and anthropomorphic philosophy of the established Christian churches— both Protestant and Catholic—is to-day so full of holes that it is in tatters; but there are few church-goers indeed who worry about it, or for that matter even know that such a condition exists. As long, therefore, as Mrs. Glover's thesis appeared water-proof on the surface, it was ready to weather any rain of average intelligence to which it might be exposed.

So far, both in Mrs. Glover's psychology and in her philosophy, we have found no evidence of any great or original contribution to human thought. But when we turn to her theology we open the door to peer in upon a very interesting achievement. It seems wholly probable, judging from any study of Mrs. Glover's previous peregrinations in the field of intellect, that her theological achievement was something of an accident, that she happened upon it almost without knowing what she was about. It does not really matter. For the achievement remains.

Human experience has tended to indicate, over a long period of years, that the force called suggestion is particularly effective when a state of high religious exaltation can be induced in the subject. Healing through suggestion has been associated with religious ecstasy as far back as there is a record of human history; and modern psychologists and psychiatrists have not been slow to recognize evidence of some important relationship between these two forces. It is known, of course, that suggestion is a psychological tool which can be used to secure results without the use of such a flux as emotional exaltation provides; but there appears no doubt that the direct effectiveness of suggestion can often be increased enormously when the mood of religious ecstasy is present.

Religious instinct, then, may be made to play a very important rôle in any system of therapeutic psychology. There are many hypotheses ventured as to why this should be so; undoubtedly a most important consideration is the fact that religious faith and an in-sweeping trust in God often serve to remove from a harassed mind its clawing fears, worries, and despairs. The whole slate of the mind is wiped clean of its previous content for the writing of a new message.

That the subsequent Mrs. Eddy never realized the theory involved here is obvious. It is equally doubtful that Quimby ever reasoned through his thesis to approach this conclusion. Quimby's religious views grew rather naturally out of his endeavors to give his psychological theories and his philosophical speculations an orthodox religious basis. We have seen that he believed himself to be on the trail of an explanation of many of the miracles recorded in the life of Jesus. And undoubtedly he realized that the faith of the patient is the controlling factor in creating a cure.

Although Mrs. Glover created her own theology—despite the fact that similarities have been found between some of her doctrines and Swedenborg's—she at least learned of the part which faith can play in a mental therapeutic system from Quimby himself. In *Mental Medicine*, copyrighted six years before the appearance of *Science and Health*, Dr. Warren F. Evans, one of Quimby's students and patients, wrote as follows of Quimby's ideas:

Disease being in its root a *wrong belief*, change that belief and we cure the disease. By faith we are thus made whole. There is a law here which the world will sometime understand and use in the diseases that afflict mankind. The late Dr. Quimby, of Portland, one of the most successful healers of this or any age, embraced this view of the nature of disease, and by a long succession of the most remarkable cures, effected by psychopathic remedies, at the same time proved the truth of the theory and the efficiency of that mode of treatment. Had he lived in a remote age or country, the wonderful facts which occurred in his practice would now have been deemed either mythical or miraculous. He seemed to reproduce the wonders of Gospel history. But all this was only an exhibition of the force of suggestion, or the action of the law of faith, over a patient in the impressible condition.

Mrs. Glover denied to the end of her days that her science had anything in common with faith cures. But as Mrs. Eddy she made many other denials, too. Actually, her declaration that her science would cure patients who were complete unbelievers was itself one of the most effective stimulants to faith in the doubting mind that could be devised.

Mrs. Glover approached her theology in much the same way as Quimby. She was seeking an orthodox supernatural cause to explain some physical results. On rereading her Bible she thought she had found the theory, which, as Quimby had indicated, seemed to be explained in some of the words and practices of Jesus.[1]

From this point, therefore, Mrs. Glover started to build up for herself a new theology derived from the Bible. It is not difficult to see how, as she proceeded, she came to regard this theology as responsible for the therapeutic results which the trained observer would have credited to applied psychology. Nor is it particularly difficult to see how she came slowly to believe as she evolved her theology that she had created an entirely original system of Divine Healing.

People had healed the sick with mesmerism long before the days of Mrs. Glover-Eddy; but no one had ever before healed them with Mrs. Eddy's theories of theology. Ergo, she had discovered a new principle. Let those who would use mesmerism. Mrs. Eddy had now discovered how to use God.

Viewed in this light much of Eddyism now looms up not as consummate humbuggery, but as sincere belief that she had really harnessed a previously unknown Principle to serve man's needs.

And to the extent that she realized the importance of religious emotionalism as an aid to applied psychology, she

[1] Vd. *The Quimby Manuscripts*, page 272: "Jesus was as any other man, but Christ was the Science which Jesus tried to teach." Again, page 199: "As it has never been explained how Jesus did these things, the people have looked on them as miracles. But to suppose Jesus performed a miracle is to suppose Him ignorant of the power he exercised."

should have recognition for this contribution to modern thought. To the extent that she credited her own theology with results that belonged either to religious emotion in general or to psychology, she can only be accused of lacking almost all equipment for logical thinking.

Actually, however, her error in logic concerning the motive force in her healing system was destined to be of great assistance to her in spreading this system abroad. Had she sought merely to market a psychological discovery, she would probably have gained only a small audience. What she had in her hand, however, was not psychology but religion—something which can be marketed on a much larger scale than any brand of psychology. There is always an audience for a new religion, and always will be. It will be a large and paying audience if the creed seems to offer precious benefits not previously secured.

Here, then, we find the amazing part of Mrs. Glover's achievement. She had committed blunder after blunder, and stupidity after mistake, and in the end she came out with the right answer.

For notice the peculiarly strategic position in which the subsequent Mrs. Eddy found herself. No matter what future claims might be made for the virtues of therapeutic psychology; no matter what claims might be made for the discoveries of Quimby; no matter what art might be shown by other mental healers, Mrs. Eddy could always claim to have something separate and distinct. Others might heal, but—no others were healing by Mrs. Eddy's system of theology. And if her theology were divine in origin—a claim which no mere logic could ever attack—then its results were also divine, and consequently not to be compared with any other healing achieved by humanly devised means.[1]

[1] Vd. *Science and Health*, page 185: "Such theories and such systems ... have their birth in mortal mind. . . . Such theories have no relationship to Christian Science, which rests on the conception of God as the only Life, substance, and intelligence, and excludes the human mind. . . ."

And again, page 112: "Although these opinions may have occasional gleams of divinity, borrowed from that truly divine Science [i. e., Christian Science] which eschews man-made systems, they nevertheless remain wholly human in their origin and tendency. . . ."

Also *Unity of Good*, page 9: "Healing, as I teach it, has not been practised since the days of Christ."

For the rest, *Science and Health* included an unbelievably varied range of discourse upon a series of topics as nearly infinite as human activity can be. The tremendous task of trying to apply not merely her theology but also her remarkable philosophy to ordinary human experience—never adequately completed—carried the author into far fields. We thus find her taking up such unique theological subjects as the necessity of washing babies. If there is no matter there is obviously no dirt, —also, incidentally, no soap and water. Mrs. Glover was at least consistent for the nonce, and she concluded that babies were being washed entirely too much. Thus she said, in a paragraph which still survives in present printings of her book:

The daily ablutions of an infant are no more natural nor necessary than would be the process of taking a fish out of water every day and covering it with dirt in order to make it thrive more vigorously in its own element. . . . Water is not the natural habitat of humanity.[1]

The word rambling is hardly adequate for the book, even now in its final form when it has had the benefits of revision incident to upward of a thousand printings. It is involved, obscure, and utterly lacking both in the simplicity and clarity which have made its chosen model, the King James version of the Scriptures, a heritage of English literature. Quimby's injunction that if an idea is good "it will do no harm to have it in two or three times" is obeyed both in letter and spirit; the book is repetitious to a degree, and many pages read on and on to nowhere.[2]

It represents, however, a monument to industry; the physical labor alone of writing out the 456 pages of the first edition in long hand must have been appalling. And it is even more an amazing monument to a woman consumed with an

---

[1]*Science and Health*, page 413. This is now qualified, however, on page 383: "We need a clean body and a clean mind . . . impurity and uncleanliness, which do not trouble the gross, could not be borne by the refined. This shows that the mind must be clean to keep the body in proper condition."

[2]The reader interested in finding a briefer and rather more intelligent and consistent adaptation of the Quimby theories and teachings may be referred to *Lessons in Truth*, by H. Emile Cady (Unity School of Scientific Christianity, Kansas City, Mo.).

ambition to rear a city even while she had only material and design sufficient to build a substantial house.

Endless pages have been written about the theology of *Science and Health* with the fulfilled intention of adding to the gaiety of nations. But in the end such criticism must be pointless, for theology is immune to the shafts of intellectual criticism. It is not concerned with the intellect and is solely a matter of belief. Its virtues or lack of them depend on whether or not it can make sufficiently strong appeal to the emotions of its followers to arouse the devotional instinct. Mrs. Glover's theology undoubtedly made such an emotional appeal, hence was effective, hence carried her to the pinnacle of fame.

We shall see in the later pages of her life how this journey to eminence affected her, in what dark chasms she stumbled time and again, through what strange storms she passed, and in what tortuous paths she was constantly losing her way.

If there is anything of the miraculous in her career, it is the fact that she succeeded despite the handicaps which not only met her on her course, but which burdened her from birth. And similarly, if there is aught of the miraculous in her voluminous writings, it is that she was inspired with courage to undertake them at all—a woman who had to struggle from the first not merely with poverty and ignorance, but with the curse of an unhappy physical and mental ailment which harried and tortured her until her dying day.

IX

Mrs. Glover's book made no commotion in a waiting world, and copies originally priced at $2.50 were shortly begging for buyers at a dollar. Copies for review were sent to the larger New England newspapers with a request to the editors that nothing at all be said about the book if the notice could not be laudatory. Some of the editors who were without a sense of the fitness of things put their opinions into print anyway. Copies were also sent to Thomas B. Carlyle, the University of Heidelberg, and several other eminent addresses with which Mrs. Glover happened to have acquired a familiarity. In addition the book was advertised by handbills and in the newspapers, with testimonials of the wonderful cures which the application of the science described therein had made possible. The original sales appeal was basically that of any patent medicine. But the book offered an advantage which no medicine could possess—the opportunity of a business career. Mrs. Glover advertised her opus as presenting "opportunity to acquire a profession by which you can accumulate a fortune." The book itself contained the statement that "men of business have said this science was of great advantage from a secular point of view."

Mrs. Glover calmly denied matter. "Obesity," she said, "is an adipose belief of yourself as a substance." She denied food. "We have no evidence," she wrote, "of food sustaining Life, except false evidence." She denied most other things. "Why," she demanded, "should man bow down to flesh-brush, flannel, bath, diet, exercise, air, etc.?" She denied the existence of any laws of science and also the validity of "the so-called laws of health." But Mrs. Eddy never denied the usefulness of money. In later years, indeed, she took pride in the wealth of her congregation; and poverty in one of her followers came to be regarded as an error as serious as sickness or sin.

When money failed to materialize on *Science and Health*, Mrs. Glover encouraged one of her students, Daniel Spofford, to go around and peddle copies personally from house to house. Meanwhile, despite this apparent failure, she immediately started in to revise the book for a second edition. The life of her book had become an obsession with her.

Daniel Harrison Spofford, who so loyally put her treatise under his arm and went out to ring doorbells, was second only to the deplored Kennedy in fervent loyalty to his teacher. Like Kennedy, he was destined to become a most influential factor in Mrs. Eddy's mental life, as well as in the development of her religion.

He had worked at rough tasks almost all his life. He came to Massachusetts from Temple, New Hampshire, when only ten years old, with a brother and his widowed mother. He was not a strong boy; but he was hired out to farmers in the surrounding country and did a man's work before he reached his teens. He enlisted at twenty, went through the Civil War, and when peace was declared came north again to Lynn and found work in a shoe factory.

It was in 1871 that he first met Mrs. Glover, and was impressed with her. A student who was taking her course gave some of her manuscripts to Spofford, and when Spofford left Lynn to wander through the southwest he carried these writings with him. He had read the Bible with reverence since his early farm days. As with so many of those silent New Englanders who drifted into Unitarianism when they gave mature study to the old theological lore, Spofford now found himself increasingly puzzled by the various paradoxes in the Scriptures which had meant so much to him as a youth.

Mrs. Glover's Quimby manuscript, in which God was defined as Principle instead of the forbidding Deity of the Puritans, interested him tremendously, and started him out on the trail of a seemingly original bit of transcendental speculation of his own. On returning to Lynn in 1875 with the manuscript still in his pocket, he tried the healing system outlined there on several friends. He made some cures which caused extensive local discussion—for in 1875 a town of

30,000 was almost entirely dependent upon gossip for incidental amusement. Mrs. Glover, hearing these stories, wrote Spofford inviting him to join her classes gratis—"without money and without price."

When he came thus to Mrs. Glover he was about thirty-three years old—a dreamy, rather melancholy sort of fellow, with small hands, finely cut features, intense blue eyes, and a gentleness of manner that marked the idealist. With him Mrs. Glover's teachings fell on ground as fertile as they had with Kennedy, and Spofford, like Kennedy, was ready to hang out his Doctor's sign before he had studied for more than a month.

For many months thereafter he played a prominent part in guiding Mrs. Glover's rather incoherent affairs. Mrs. Glover was like a head without a body—she could get ideas started, but she was utterly dependent upon others to bring them to conclusion. While attending to his own healing business he also took charge of her publishing affairs, helped with the organization of her work, and took a leading rôle in making arrangements by which a hall was hired by her students for regular Sunday preaching.

It was in 1875 that this first attempt at organization was made, although several years were to elapse before a regular church would be chartered. The students assessed themselves to provide the necessary funds. Mrs. Glover herself was given five dollars a Sunday for her services as preacher, and another five went for rental and incidental costs. Some sixty students attended the preliminary meetings at which this procedure was arranged, and eight of them signed a binding agreement to make regular weekly contributions for a year. Spofford was elected treasurer of the group.

The first services were held in Templars' Hall, Mrs. Glover delivering the main discourse of the occasion and a student, S. P. Bancroft, conducting the singing while his wife pumped a melodeon. It is reported that the audiences seldom exceeded twenty-five, and not all of these were bona fide students. Some spiritualists drifted in after the first Sunday or two, and when Mrs. Glover threw open the meeting to general discussion they arose and asked rather embarrassing questions. Thus she brought the whole project to a halt after the fifth Sunday, and declined to give any more sermons. Public services were thereupon abolished.

During these new activities her old physical trouble had by no means left her, and there were occasions when she seems to have collapsed utterly and suffered the same old tortures. Mrs. Miranda Rice, who felt under special obligations to Mrs. Glover because she had been allowed to enter a class without paying tuition, was in constant attendance upon her, and remained her close friend for twelve years—much longer than was the general custom. Mrs. Rice told in later years how her teacher would be seized with violent attacks of hysteria during which she would sometimes lie completely unconscious for many hours. In some of these attacks she would apparently become almost insane, saying that all of her friends were persecuting her, that there was no one in the world in whom she might trust, that she would run away and would never return.[1]

It was this Mrs. Rice who was the heroine of an experience that for many years, and through many editions of *Science and Health*, was to be recounted as one of Mrs. Glover's outstanding demonstrations. Under the watchful gaze of Mrs. Glover, Mrs. Rice had a childbirth that she declared to be absolutely painless.[2]

A glimpse of the goings-on in the Glover household at this period is afforded by the record of a suit later brought by a student by the name of George Barry, whom Mrs. Glover later claimed to have cured of consumption. It was Barry who, with Miss Newhall, had put up the money for financing the first edition of *Science and Health*. He was another impressionable young lad of the sort that seems to have been most readily attracted to the teaching Mrs. Glover had to offer. He called her by the name of Mother, and left on record

---

[1] Vd. interview quoted in New York *World*, October 30, 1906. Also Milmine, *Life of Mary Baker G. Eddy*, page 159.

[2] The account was deleted from *Science and Health* in the later editions. For another recital of apparently the same story, see *Retrospection and Introspection*, page 40.

a poem to her which at least compares favorably with Mrs. Glover's own rhapsodies. Mrs. Glover eventually published the verses in one of the early editions of *Science and Health*, as if to prove that Barry's later defection was due to no fault of hers:

O, mother mine, God grant I ne'er forget
Whatever be my grief or what my joy,
The unmeasurable, unextinguishable debt
I owe to thee, but find my sweet employ
Ever through thy remaining days to be
To thee as faithful as thou wast to me.[1]

George made himself constantly useful around the house, spaded the garden, mowed the lawn, did voluminous copying work after Mrs. Glover revised, went back and forth to carry messages to the Boston printer, and in general was a devoted slave. Miss Milmine has recounted that Bronson Alcott—father of the famous Louisa, who made a living for the Alcott family while her father investigated metaphysical cults—came to visit the Glover establishment, and asked George his age.

"Five years old, Sir," said George, then added that it had been five years since Mrs. Glover had first come into his life.

Shortly thereafter, however, Mrs. Glover lost another loyal adherent and devotee. George sued her for payment for five years of his services. The services itemized in his bill of complaint, which sought $2,700, were exceedingly versatile in nature. Among the listings were "Aiding in buying and caring for the place at Number 8 Broad Street; aiding in selection of carpets and furniture, helping to move, putting down carpets, etc., and working in the garden"; "moving her goods from the tenement on South Common Street, Lynn, i. e., disposing of some at the auction room, storing others in my uncle's barn, and storing trunks and goods at my father's house, clearing up rooms, paying rent for the same"; "attending to her financial business, i. e., withdrawing money from Boston savings banks, going to Boston to get United States coupon bonds."

Besides these varied duties the boy had done extensive work

[1] Edition of 1881, vol. II, page 15.

as a secretary and copyist. Other services specified were "copying Mrs. Glover's replies to W. W. Wright's newspaper articles"; "copying manuscript for classes and helping to arrange the construction of some of the sentences"; "copying the manuscript of the book entitled *Science and Health,* and aiding in arrangement of capital letters and some of the grammatical constructions"; "searching for a publisher."

The Referee, after a due examination of the evidence, made findings that Barry had copied out in long-hand 2500 pages, and allowed him compensation at more than the usual copyist rate, "on account of the difficulty which a portion of the pages presented to the copyist by reason of erasures and interlineations." Many of the other services were not valued at the complainant's rates; the total allowed by the Court was $350.

It was about this time that another student had drifted into Mrs. Glover's circle. His name was Asa Gilbert Eddy. It has been variously stated that he came to her after having taken treatment from Mr. Spofford in his Lynn office; and that he went direct to Mrs. Glover on the reference of a Mrs. Godfrey. The latter has been made the subject of a miraculous cure in the Eddy traditions; it is stated that Mrs. Glover cured overnight one of the lady's fingers which had become terribly infected, as the result of breaking a needle off in the flesh. The preferred tradition among Mrs. Eddy's followers is that Mr. Eddy went to Mrs. Glover via Mrs. Godfrey.

He was a man of wholly unpretentious origin, son of a farmer of the Green Mountains. There was nothing whatever about him to suggest the future glory that was awaiting the Eddy name from sea to sea. Gilbert had been a sewing machine agent in East Boston, and during a period of ill-health had sought out Spofford in Lynn. The two men talked together of Mrs. Glover's teachings, and Spofford advised his patient to take a course.

From the beginning the self-effacing Gilbert seems to have caught Mrs. Glover's fancy. He was a short, negative, quiet little man, capable of obstinacy but for the most part docile, dull, and utterly uninspired. Perhaps it was because he appeared so much more of a stable anchor than the ebullient and flaming souls who so often formed Mrs. Glover's student clientele that she turned to him as a real relief in the sea of fluid emotion in which she tossed.

Gilbert Eddy was the spinsterish type of bachelor, who had always lived in small rooms where he managed his own housekeeping, did his own washing, and even made his own trousers. According to his sister-in-law, on visiting her home he helped her with the housework, and he "could do up a shirt as well as any woman."

He came from a peculiar sort of family, in which the children led a rather careless existence under the eye of a mother whose *bête noir* was housekeeping, and whose main delight was a daily drive behind her horse across the countryside and through the towns adjacent to South Londonderry, where the family lived. Regarded as a neighborhood character, she was long called "the woman with the looking glass," because of a quaint invention she devised to protect her from rainy weather during her drives. Around her large poke bonnet she draped a shawl, completely enveloping her head; in this shawl she cut a hole and inserted there a pane of glass, forming in effect a little window in her unique costume through which she could gaze out serenely no matter what the storms of life might be.

Her children grew up like Topsy, eating at odd hours out of the same mush-pot, and, as they grew older, washing and ironing their own clothes. The boys as well as the girls learned to run the family loom, and when Gilbert left about 1860 to make his way in the world, he obtained a job running a spinning-jack in a woollen mill. Thereafter he went into a baby carriage factory, switching to selling sewing machines when this marvellous invention came to astonish the hardworking housewives.

Gilbert carried into later life some of the peculiarity of appearance he evinced as a youth—a mincing step, an apologetic smile, and a strange mode of hair-dressing which gave him a big roach in front and a curled effect at the rear which he tucked under in a roll.

Mrs. Glover permitted him, alone among all her students, to

call her Mary, and she in turn called him Gilbert. From the start she lost no opportunity to praise his obedience and willing service as an example to the other students, and they very quickly came to feel that he was enjoying a royal prerogative in the household wholly out of proportion to his contribution to the mutual cause. What they did not understand was that Mary Glover herself had little of the mystic in her nature; the transcendent fervor of her worshipping students indeed at times annoyed her matter-of-fact self greatly. And far from being a tower of spiritual strength on which these others could lean, or a fixed point about which they could revolve, she herself was always in quest of a stout physical support which would hold her up from her neurosis.

And so the subdued, plodding Gilbert seems to have brought quiet to her soul just as the green forest rests the gaze of the desert wanderer. Soon she began to wonder how she could establish him permanently near her. The solution came when she suggested to Spofford that he devote his entire time to the promotion of *Science and Health,* and turn over to Mr. Eddy his flourishing practice in Lynn. Mr. Eddy had now himself become a Doctor, and under this suggested arrangement Mrs. Glover saw two distinct advantages to be gained —a greater sale for *Science and Health,* as well as a job and an income for Gilbert, to whom she was turning more and more with real sentiment in her elderly bosom.

Mrs. Glover was now in her fifty-sixth year. She had grown exceedingly in dynamic personal power; but emotionally she was no less subject than in her earlier days to gusts of passion, fear, and a sense of distrust which resulted in obsessions of a great and awful loneliness. At this particular time in her career she was almost surrounded by turmoil. Mr. Eddy's entrance into her circle coincided with, and indeed caused, part of this unhappy atmosphere. Daniel Spofford particularly resented being asked to take a seat in the background, although he yielded up his practice to the new favorite —Mrs. Glover always demanding utter obedience to her wishes and commands.

In these days Mrs. Glover spoke often of an idea which

Quimby himself seems to have labored under, and which she evidently derived from that source. She had a conviction that she suffered under the ills and worries of her students, sharing their misfortunes as they managed to discard them. Particularly did she feel that when they turned their thoughts in her direction they acquired some of her own strength, and she in turn took on some of their weakness. This conviction soon gained a reasoned hold upon her mind because it helped her to explain the recurrent attacks of illness which still came to her regularly, regardless of her healing system which was supposed to destroy all disease. If she could not cure herself, she told herself that it was neither her own fault nor that of her system; it was the fault of these others who were casting upon her their own ills.

Such an addition to her philosophy was bound to result in a great deal of mental distress, which indeed was destined to grow with the years. It was in one of these moods that she wrote to Spofford a letter almost hysterical in pleading that he cease thinking of her. Spofford was already growing weary of his new minor rôle, and had hinted at a wish to discard it entirely. Mrs. Glover wrote in part:

Now, Dr. Spofford, won't you exercise *reason* and let me live or will you *kill* me? Your mind is just what has brought on my relapse and I shall never *recover* if you do not govern yourself and TURN YOUR THOUGHTS wholly away from me.

Do not think of returning to me again I shall never again trust a *man*. They know not what manner of temptations assail God produces the separation and I submit to it so must you. . . .

It is mesmerism that I feel is killing me it is *mortal* mind that only can make me suffer. Now stop thinking of me or you will cut me off *soon* from the face of the earth.[1]

[1]Letter preserved by Georgine Milmine (*Life of Mary Baker G. Eddy*, page 173), who interviewed Spofford personally and obtained from him invaluable documentary material. Mrs. Glover's conviction that she could be robbed of health by students who "turned their thoughts" on her to get strength in time of their own need still survives in the Eddy literature. In *Retrospection and Introspection*, page 71, she issued a warning against such a practice in the following threatening terms:

"Secret mental efforts to obtain help from one who is unaware of this attempt, demoralizes the person who does this, the same as other forms of stealing, and will end in destroying health and morals."

The psychiatrist cannot help noting in that letter a phrase-ology which, despite Mrs. Glover's age, indicates a definite sexual repression. The letter was written on December 30, 1876. That same evening Gilbert Eddy called on his teacher. The next day Gilbert carried to Spofford the news that he and the elderly Mrs. Glover were to be married, in a note written in Mrs. Glover's own hand and breathing the very spirit of tranquillity. Spofford expressed surprise. Gilbert stated that he too was equally overcome—that he had had no inkling of this *dénouement* until the evening before.

The wedding took place on New Year's day, of 1877, in the Broad Street house. The certificate under which it was per-formed gave the age both of bride and groom as forty years. A month later, on January 31, Mrs. Eddy's students gave her a "shower." The gifts, as chronicled in the Lynn *Recorder*, included a "bouquet of crystallized geranian leaves of rare varieties incased in glass," with a *pièce de résistance* described as a silver cake basket. Cake and lemonade were served, and a good time was had by all, including the fifty-seven-year-old bride.

In later years Mrs. Eddy wrote:

> To abolish marriage at this period, and maintain morality and genera-tion, would put ingenuity to ludicrous shifts; yet this is possible in *Science*, although it is today problematic.[1]

The thing was always problematic with Mrs. Eddy. She never quite lost her hankering for having a man around the house. But there was something in her that called the instinct evil—and led her to "deny" it—to her dying day.

[1] *Miscellaneous Writings*, page 286.

X

Following the marriage Gilbert retired from his allotted practice in Spofford's office, where, as Mrs. Eddy wrote, "he was the first student publicly to announce himself a Christian Scientist, and place these symbolic words on his office sign."[1] He moved into the Broad Street house and stayed there to wait upon his wife, who later wrote that "he forsook all to follow in this line of light."[2] It was hardly a happy household. *Science and Health* was in the throes of being prepared for a second edition, and the difficulties—particularly financial— were many. Mrs. Eddy was adamant in her resolve not to spend one cent of her own money derived from teaching on the publication of her book. She considered it the duty of her students, and particularly of Spofford, to promote the treatise.

For a long while Mrs. Eddy had entertained for Spofford the tender regard that she later transferred to Gilbert. In the fall before the marriage, for instance, she wrote him that "The students make all their mistakes *leaning on me, or working against me*. You are not going to do either, and certainly the result will follow that you will be faithful over a few things and be made ruler *over* many."[3] Not only did she thus hint darkly about possibly taking him into partnership and a larger interest in her affairs; she also took him into her confidence. In the same month she wrote again that "You know not the smallest portion, comparatively, of your ability in science. . . . Inflammation of the spinal nerves are what I suffer most in belief."[4]

From the time of her new marriage Mrs. Eddy's feelings for

[1]*Retrospection and Introspection*, page 42.

[2]*Ibid*, page 42.

[3]Letter dated October 1, 1876. Vd. Milmine, *Life of Mary Baker G. Eddy*, page 247.

[4]Vd. Quimby's statement, *The Quimby Manuscripts*, page 278: "A belief is what I call a disease." For Eddy quotation see letter dated October 22, 1876, and published in Milmine biography, page 248.

Spofford began immediately to cool. She had watched his growing popularity with his patients with some little jealousy, and was only too glad to retire him from this practice temporarily while Mr. Eddy took his place. On Spofford's side there was some natural and justified exasperation. He went about the task, however, of planning for the second edition. Mrs. Eddy wrote to him in the following April proposing the business terms under which she would share with him the proceeds from the sale of her book—after he had financed the publication and assumed the risk of promotion. Mrs. Eddy, whatever her handicaps, had a reliable business instinct. She offered to enter on a three-year agreement by which Spofford should have exclusive publication rights and in return should pay her twenty-five per cent royalty on the gross sales. These gross receipts were to be deposited into the hands of a "treasurer" before distribution. "All the years I have expended on that book," she said, "the labour I am still performing, and all I have done for students and the cause gratuitously, entitle me to *some income* now that I am unable to work." Her "inability to work" referred to her illness of this period, and she asked Spofford to "Think of me when you feel *strong* and well only, and think only of me as [being] well."[1]

Spofford, whatever he thought, was disinclined to believe that he could meet all the costs of publication, distribution, and promotion, and come out even on his investment if he paid the royalty demanded. But Mrs. Eddy insisted. "The conditions I have named to you I think are just," she informed him again. "*I give three years and more*[2] to offset the capital you put into printing."

At the time those letters were written, with their distressing complaints of ill-health, Mrs. Eddy was at times almost beside herself. It was April, 1877, only three months after her marriage; and once again—as in her previous marriage with Dr. Patterson—association with a husband seems to have aggravated all her ills.

[1] For these and subsequent quotations from the Eddy-Spofford correspondence vd. Milmine, *Life of Mary Baker G. Eddy*, pages 213–217.

[2] Referring to the years she had devoted to the book.

Thus she wrote to Spofford, "I sometimes think I cannot hold on till the next edition is out. . . . Direct your thoughts and everybody's else that you can away from me, don't talk of me."

And again: "I am in Boston today feeling very very little better for the five weeks that are gone. I cannot finish the Key yet I will be getting [a grip on] myself and all of a sudden I am seized as sensibly by some others belief as the hand could lay hold of me my sufferings have made me utterly weaned from this plane and if my husband was only willing to give me up I would gladly yield up the ghost of this terrible earth plane and join those nearer my Life. . . ."

In such hysteria did she become involved, so deeply convinced was she that her students were dragging her down into a morass of horror, that in the middle of April she fled from Lynn with her husband leaving no address, taking refuge, as she said, "in the wilderness." Spofford, whom she called "Harry" after his middle name of Harrison, received a letter from Boston postmarked April 14, its every line reeking with the hysterical fear of this excerpt:

. . . *Everything* needs me in science, my doors are thronged, the book lies waiting, but those who *call on me mentally* in suffering are in belief killing me! *Stopping my work* that none but me can do in their supreme selfishness. . . . it would be no greater crime for them to come directly and thrust a dagger into my heart they are just as surely in belief killing me and committing murder. . . .

Toward the middle of the summer her health slowly improved, and with it her buoyancy of mind. But shortly after returning to Lynn there was another explosion, this time occasioned by Spofford himself. In July he closed out the stock remaining in his possession of the first edition of *Science and Health,* with approximately six hundred dollars as proceeds from the undertaking. He immediately paid over this money to the two students who had financed the publication, George Barry and Elizabeth M. Newhall. Since these two had advanced some $2200 for the undertaking, they lost over $1500, and Spofford himself had sunk about $500 of his own funds in promoting the sales. But when Mrs. Eddy found that the money had been paid to the students instead of to her, she was furious. It was her view that Miss Newhall and Barry had contributed this money to the cause, expecting no return or recompense, and that all proceeds were rightly due her as royalties, which she could apply against the expense of getting out her second edition. Spofford, on the other hand, took the view that if the students wanted to put this money into the second edition nothing would prevent such a second gift; but that this was their privilege and not their obligation.

This incident ended all relations between Mrs. Eddy and Spofford, and in January of 1878 she expelled him from her Christian Scientists' Association on an accusation of "immorality." A notice to this effect was not only sent to him personally but was inserted in the Newburyport *Herald*. The "immorality" alleged meant nothing more than that Mrs. Eddy considered Spofford disloyal to her cause. She had quite a way with words all her life, evidenced even in her formal writings, and she never hesitated to apply a new connotation to a word if this suited her purpose. Years later she accused a woman follower of adultery. The horrified lady rushed to inquire the reason for such a terrible charge. Mrs. Eddy seriously explained that the lady had "adulterated the truth."

When Richard Kennedy left her, Mrs. Eddy had been as furious as she now felt about Spofford. She had sought to discredit Kennedy in every way, alleging that he used mesmerism and not science for his cures. She based this charge, as shown, on his use of manipulation, which she thereupon repudiated. Now, with Spofford, she also alleged the practice of mesmerism. Since Spofford, however, did not use manipulation, having been taught the revised healing system, Mrs. Eddy immediately discovered that mesmerism could be practised without any laying-on of hands. It could be practised even *in absentia*. Apparently, indeed, it differed only from absent treatment as given in Mrs. Eddy's own science in the fact that the mesmerist intended to effect harm instead of healing.

Thus it was that Mrs. Eddy now denounced Spofford, also, as a mesmerist. She assaulted him verbally with no less venom than the good-humored Kennedy, who she had prophesied would kill instead of cure any patients who sought him out. In her wrath she hastily revised the second edition of *Science and Health* which Spofford himself had helped to prepare for press; and she inserted direct and terrible attacks on the student whom she had been calling "Harry" only a few months before:

Mesmerism is practised with manipulation—and without it. And we have learned, by new observation, the fool who saith "There is no God" attempts more evil without a sign than with it. Since "Science and Health" first went to press we have observed the crimes of another mesmeric outlaw, in a variety of ways, who does not as a common thing manipulate, in cases where he sullenly attempted to avenge himself of certain individuals, etc. . . .[1]

Mrs. Eddy's assault on Spofford did not lessen her venom toward Kennedy. In the 1881 edition of *Science and Health* she still poured forth, in lines indubitably referring to Kennedy, the hatred of a woman outraged. The denunciations of his mesmeristic practices which she made in her first edition[2] were mild beside the vitriol of the third. She now declared, "His career of crime surpasses anything that minds in general can accept at this period,"[3] and she continued:

The Nero of to-day, regaling himself through a mental method with the tortures of individuals, is repeating history, and will fall upon his own sword, and it shall pierce him through. Let him remember this when, in the dark recesses of thought, he is robbing, committing adultery, and killing. . . .[4]

This "mental method" of "torture" which Mrs. Eddy so eloquently denounced is perhaps the most amazing adaptation of the Quimby psychological theories—and of his benevolent theories regarding absent treatment—that this wholly remarkable woman ever conceived.

The reader may here see the subsequently famous doctrine of malicious mesmerism—of malicious animal magnetism, as it came to be called—being born under his eyes. It grew naturally, easily, out of two dark hatreds of a woman whose com-

---

[1] Edition of 1878, page 136.   [2] Pages 193 and 371.
[3] Chapter VI, page 6.   [4] Chapter VI, page 38.

plex of inferiority, whose obsession of impotence, made her
an easy victim of fear and hatred all her life.

The second edition of *Science and Health* was got together so hurriedly to carry its freight of denunciation and
fear that it was not a complete book at all. It was labelled
"Volume 2," although the first volume was never printed, and
regardless of the fact that the second edition took over a quan-
tity of material that had appeared in the first. It contained less
than two hundred pages—a little brown book carelessly set up,
with a long list of typographical errors included so that the
reader might not be too utterly lost in the sea of misprints. It
was divided into six chapters: "Introductory," "Imposition
and Demonstration," "Physiology," "Mesmerism," "Metaphysics," and "Reply to a Clergyman."

At the conclusion of the "Introductory" was a most important note. It read as follows:

Note: None need apply to the author for consultations on disease,
or to take patients. She is not at present laboring in this department.

The biographer, seeking incontestable evidence of some of
the many cures which Mrs. Eddy claimed in her writings to
have effected by her system, comes to a halt over this notice;
here at least is some evidence that is unmistakably negative.
There is no doubt that Mrs. Eddy sought from the beginning
to leave healing work in other hands than her own.[1]

As time passed she attributed her own persistent ill-health
wholly to the machinations of the evil minds around her. Fear
and hatred of these evil minds became more and more an ob-

---

[1]Vd. *Message to the Mother Church for 1901:*
"It was that I healed the deaf, the blind, the dumb, the lame, the last stages
of consumption, pneumonia, etc., that started the inquiry, What is it? And
when the public sentiment would allow it, and I had overcome a difficult stage
of the work, I would put patients into the hands of my students and retire from
the comparative ease of healing to the next more difficult stage of action for
our cause."
This interesting paragraph is matched by another communication prepared
by Mrs. Eddy in her later years as a notice written in the third person. (Vd.
Miscellany, page 231). Here she wrote of herself:
"She has qualified students for healing the sick, and has ceased practise herself in order to help God's work in other of its highest and infinite meanings, as
God, not man, directs. Hence, letters from invalids demanding her help do not
reach her. They are committed to the waste basket by her secretaries."

session, resulting in an acute conviction that she was being persecuted and hounded by her enemies. For five years after 1872 she attributed her own unhappy state of mind and health to the horrid work of Kennedy. After the break with Spofford, he too bore the brunt of her strange complex. The malicious animal magnetism generated by these two ex-students came to be blamed for anything that went awry not only in Mrs. Eddy's own experience but in the routine of her household and the lives of her students. If a student was unable to do healing work, it was because Spofford and Kennedy were trying to disrupt Mrs. Eddy's classes.

By the time the third edition of *Science and Health* appeared in 1881, Mrs. Eddy's fears of the Spofford and Kennedy magnetism had developed into a doctrine and a dogma. Mentioned only in brief paragraphs in the first edition, mesmerism had now been exalted as an explanation of all evil. "Mesmerism was her Devil," said the Reverend Mr. Wiggin, who eventually became Mrs. Eddy's literary adviser. There was now a chapter on Demonology, showing how a hostile mind could bring utter havoc in another's life, unless that life were adequately protected by the use of counter-devices offered by Mrs. Eddy's Science. Malicious mesmerism, or malicious animal magnetism—the two terms were used interchangeably —were identified as mortal mind, or error. Technically, therefore, in Mrs. Eddy's philosophy such evils could not exist, for they certainly were not Divine Mind, which was all. This philosophical difficulty, however, hardly troubled her.

It was possible, she said, for a person to bring upon another any misfortune whatsoever—illness, poverty, business failure; to estrange dear friends and loved ones; even to create suffering which ended in death. In the third issue of her book she distinguished "Demonology" from mesmerism because it could be effective without "manipulation" or any direct contact of persons, and she said:

It has no outward signs, such as ordinarily indicate mesmerism, and its effects are far more subtle because of this. Its tendency is to sour the disposition, to occasion great fear of disease, dread, and discouragement, to cause relapse of former diseases, to produce new ones, to create dislikes or indifference to friends, to produce sufferings in the head, in fine, every evil that demonology includes and that metaphysics destroys. If it be students of ours whom he attacks the malpractitioner and aforesaid mesmerist tries to produce in their minds a hatred toward us, even as the assassin puts out the light before committing his deed.[1]

From that time on Mrs. Eddy held that any student who came to distrust her was affected by malicious animal magnetism put in force by her enemies; followers of Mrs. Eddy herself accepted this thesis; and in after years there are actually records of followers who asked to be "treated" by fellow students for this error of unbelief. The doctrine became one of Mrs. Eddy's most important means for self-justification.

As Mrs. Eddy watched the great material prosperity of young Kennedy, whose practice had now grown so large that he went to Boston to open a metropolitan office, she could not contain her bitterness and wrath, which were always intermingled with her unreasoned fear.

Mrs. Eddy herself continued in making no attempt to do any healing. The third edition of *Science and Health* contained the following notice:

The author takes no patients but takes students in the treatment of disease through the mind. Her tuition for pupils is $300.00. She has never taken over that for her usual term and oftentimes less; and has given one-third of this tuition and two-thirds of her labors and devoted all her time for the last fourteen years to the introduction of Christian Healing.

She now talked of the successful Kennedy almost continually to her students, and when she entered the classroom for the instruction period would often wander away from her subject completely to discuss the obsession of Kennedy's villainy which held her mind in chains. Kennedy was accused of curing his own patients by casting their diseases upon Mrs. Eddy. She said that when treating his patients he held her own name

---

[1]*Science and Health* (1881), Chapter VI, 35. The present editions of *Science and Health* still perpetuate these amazing ideas. Vd. the chapter beginning on page 100 which is called, with sonorous accents, "Animal Magnetism Unmasked." The material now contained under this head, however, has been radically modified and its more sensational assertions rephrased.

in his thoughts, so that she took on their torment. She cried aloud that unless this cruel and inhuman torture were stopped, she would sink entirely under the weight of all the human afflictions that were thus being thrust upon her.

This all sounded plausible enough to those of Mrs. Eddy's impressionable students who had never known the light-hearted Kennedy as he worked faithfully around the house, and their burning sympathies were aroused. They asked what they could do. Mrs. Eddy explained that they could protect her if they would all assemble together and send out counter mental currents to meet and wrestle with those coming from Kennedy. This was actually done. The students would meet in Mrs. Eddy's front parlor, form a circle, and silently concentrate on Kennedy, saying, "Your sins have found you out. You are failing in your practice. You are now leaving the town."

Let it at least be said for most of the students that they soon came to question this strange practice. One of them found that the more he tried to think bad thoughts about Kennedy, the worse he felt personally.

It was not long before Mrs. Eddy came to have Spofford preying on her mind as much as Kennedy, and this new enmity of hers resulted in one of the most bizarre court-room sessions ever held in the United States.

Mrs. Eddy first tried to sue Spofford for tuition as well as a royalty on his practice. This suit was eventually dismissed because of defects in the writ and insufficient service. Meanwhile she wrote to local newspapers asking them to publish an attack on Spofford's character. The Newburyport *Herald* of May 16, 1878, stated editorially, after the whole affair came into court: "Mrs. Eddy tried, some time since, to induce us to publish an attack upon Spofford, which we declined to do, and we understand that similar requests were made to other papers in the county."

The Spofford story is one whose only precedent can be the Salem Witchcraft cases, and the peculiar circumstances surrounding it must well have been a subject of concern to Mrs. Eddy's troubled advisers in later years. Every effort was naturally made to disassociate Mrs. Eddy herself from the

strange proceedings, and her approved biography merely says
that "instead of advising this suit, she advised against it, but
was not insistent to the point of rupture. She was engaged
with her own affairs and would not permit the frightened students to encroach too heavily upon her time. The suit brought
by themselves and in their own folly bore all the marks of
haste and fear."[1]

Undoubtedly Mrs. Eddy seems almost to have paralyzed her
highly impressionable students with fear; and even as they
walked down the street or ate their suppers in the security of
their homes they must have shuddered at the thought of the
terrible malicious magnetism that some enemy might at that
very moment be broadcasting into their lives.

But certainly, also, Mrs. Eddy was an even more abject
victim of the same awful fear herself—the result of her own
disordered state of mind. Mrs. Eddy had a student, a Miss
Dorcas Rawson, who had been a "holiness Methodist" before
she joined one of the Eddy classes and took up healing. And
Miss Rawson, in turn, had a patient whom she was treating, a
gentle maiden lady known as Miss Lucretia Brown. When
Miss Rawson could not heal Miss Brown, and went to Mrs.
Eddy for advice, Mrs. Eddy knew what was wrong immediately. Daniel Spofford was up to his old tricks. He was using
malicious animal magnetism on Miss Lucretia.

Miss Brown herself was a character in the village annals.
Georgine Milmine has written that "Essex was the cleanest
county in Massachusetts, and Ipswich was the cleanest town
in Essex, and the Browns were the cleanest people in Ipswich." The three Brown sisters were walking manifestations
of daintiness and spinsterly charm—all except Miss Lucretia,
who had been a confined invalid ever since a fall during childhood had injured her spine. Even Miss Lucretia, however,
would occasionally slip out of her snowy bed to patter ethere-
ally around the house and do a bit of dusting.

Miss Lucretia hardly knew Spofford, and when she heard
Mrs. Eddy's diagnosis from Miss Rawson she was inclined to
be incredulous. Mrs. Eddy, however, was positive in her

[1] Sibyl Wilbur, *Life of Mary Baker Eddy*, page 241.

opinion. She went to a lawyer and had him draw up a bill of complaint for Miss Brown, asking for a court injunction to restrain Spofford from his devilish undertakings. In part the allegations were as follows:

> Humbly complaining, the Plaintiff, Lucretia L. S. Brown of Ipswich in said County of Essex, showeth unto your Honours, that Daniel H. Spofford, of Newburyport, in said County of Essex, the defendant in the above entitled action, is a mesmerist and practises the art of mesmerism and by his said art and the power of his mind influences and controls the minds and bodies of other persons and uses his said power and art for the purposes of injuring the persons and property and social relations of others and does by said means so injure them.
>
> And the plaintiff further showeth that the said Daniel H. Spofford has . . . caused the plaintiff by means of his said power and art great suffering of body and mind and severe spinal pains and neuralgia and a temporary suspension of mind, and still continues to cause the plaintiff the same. . . .

The symptoms, incidentally, sound like many of those of Mrs. Eddy herself. Perhaps it was this apparent kinship of ailment that made Mrs. Eddy so absolutely certain in her diagnosis. She now set about the prosecution of Spofford systematically and thoroughly.

First, however, she sought the assistance of supernatural forces to supplement the power of the government. She selected twelve apostles from her Christian Scientists' Association to "treat" Spofford in the same way that the students' circle had previously dealt with Kennedy. At this time, however, no evening circle was formed. A sort of guard mount was established. Each student was on guard two hours out of the twenty-four, with instructions to concentrate his mind on Spofford and prevent him from getting his vibrations through to Mrs. Eddy and her followers. Under this rotating guard a constant mental barricade was erected about the Eddy homestead.[1]

The suit came up before the Supreme Judicial Court in Salem on May 14, 1878. Mrs. Eddy's usual attorney had flatly refused to be involved, so that she had arranged with one of

[1] Vd. affidavit of Henry F. Dunnels, Georgine Milmine, *Life of Mary Baker G. Eddy*, page 240.

her students, Edward J. Arens, to represent her. A whole "cloud of witnesses," some twenty of them, according to the Boston *Globe,* hovered around Mrs. Eddy as she mothered them in. One student was uncertain as to what he should say on the stand. "You will be told what to say," said Mrs. Eddy with confidence. But the witnesses were not called. The following Friday was set for the trial.

Meanwhile the Boston papers, even in a day when human-interest stories were not carefully treasured for leads on the front page, marshalled their best reporters and the *Globe* sent up a man to talk to the Brown sisters. This interview was at least instructive in showing what assistance the Browns hoped to gain by going to law. Miss Lucretia and her family "believed that there was no limit to the awful power of mesmerism, but she still had some faith in the power of the law, and thought that Dr. Spofford might be awed into abstaining. . . ."

Unfortunately for the gaiety of nations, the case never came to trial. The Court sustained a demurrer filed by Mr. Spofford's attorney, saying that it was not in the power of the law to control a man's mind, and this contention was upheld when the case was appealed in the following November.

In this whole action can be found no incident whatever casting a doubt on Mrs. Eddy's perfect sincerity. The neurosis which results in the delusion of persecution is not an uncommon ailment—but so slight in the great majority of its victims that the personal adjustment to reality is not greatly impaired. With Mrs. Eddy this delusion was a terrible thing, spreading its tentacles gradually but ever more surely through all her consciousness, and then through her teachings until it affected not only her own life, but the lives of many whose orbit of being touched hers.

XI

Mrs. Eddy's lawsuits during this period of her life were so frequent and so regular in schedule that the Boston newspapers began to keep count of them and feature a new one as a matter of jocular interest. Mrs. Eddy resented their attitude, and took a fling at it in the third edition of her book. She proclaimed that, "In the interests of truth we ought to say that never a lawsuit has entered into our history voluntarily." The author evidently meant that she never entered voluntarily into a lawsuit. She continued:

We have suffered great losses and direct injustice rather than go to law, for we have always considered a lawsuit of two evils the greater. About two years ago the persuasions of a student awakened our convictions that we might be doing wrong in permitting students to break their obligations with us. . . . The student who argued this point to us so convincingly offered to take the notes and collect them, without any participation of ours. We trusted him with the whole affair, doing only what he told us, for we were utterly ignorant of legal proceedings. It was alleged indirectly in the Newburyport *Herald* that we caused a bill to be filed in the Supreme Court to restrain a student of ours from practising mesmerism. That statement was utterly false. It was a student who did that contrary to our advice and judgment and we have the affidavit of the reluctant plaintiff certifying to this fact."

Whenever Mrs. Eddy was accused of unseemly goings-on she tried to get an affidavit in her defense. If she had such an affidavit from poor Miss Lucretia, no record thereof has been bequeathed to the historian.

The year after George Barry had sued Mrs. Eddy for $2700, Mrs. Eddy herself brought suit—in February, 1878—against Richard Kennedy. She sought to recover $750 upon a promissory note dated February, 1870, just a few months before she and Kennedy had gone to Lynn to practise. The note read as follows:

February, 1870

In consideration of two years' instruction in healing the sick, I hereby agree to pay Mrs. M. B. Glover one thousand dollars in quarterly installments of fifty dollars commencing from this date.

RICHARD KENNEDY

Kennedy won the suit on appeal, testifying that he had signed the note after already having received two years' instruction from Mrs. Glover, and only on her assurance that she had more healing secrets which she had not already imparted to him. Such further secrets, said Kennedy, were never disclosed. The lower court allowed Mrs. Eddy $768.63, but the judgment was reversed on appeal and the decision given to Kennedy.

Two months later Mrs. Eddy filed another suit. This time it was the action against Tuttle and Stanley, the two early students who had agreed to pay her a 10 per cent annual royalty if they practised, and a $1000 forfeit if they did not. This action was no more successful than the one against Kennedy.

In this same month, April, 1878, Mrs. Eddy brought action against Spofford to collect royalties on his practice under an agreement similar to that which she had made with Tuttle and Stanley. This suit was dismissed.

In May of this year came the witchcraft suit against Spofford.

And then, as if that were not enough litigation for one season, when October came Asa Gilbert Eddy and Edward J. Arens were arrested for conspiracy to murder. It was alleged that their intended victim was Daniel H. Spofford.

For some unexplained reason Mr. Eddy after marriage reversed his names. Baptized Gilbert Asa, he took the arrangement of Asa G. The mystery behind that simple rearrangement is no greater than the mystery in one of the most unusual murder cases that ever received space in a Boston newspaper.

For it was a murder without a victim.

In October, 1878, the disappearance of Daniel Spofford was announced in the Boston *Herald,* with the fact that his friends were alarmed. Some days later the paper said that his body had been found and was lying at the morgue. On the 29th of the month the paper was able to announce exclusively to its readers that Messrs. Eddy and Arens were under arrest. Arens was a young carpenter who after the defection of Spofford had become Mrs. Eddy's star pupil.

There was only one flaw in the murder story. There was no *corpus delicti.* The corpse at the morgue was not the victim's corpse. Mr. Spofford was found alive and well, and quite as puzzled as—apparently—every one else concerned.

Mrs. Eddy's hostility toward Spofford had been most freely expressed; she had openly denounced him as a malpractitioner in a paid notice in the local paper, and there is evidence that her students were "treating" him in the hope that some unfortunate blight would descend upon him. Her hatred of Spofford was now so great that she even walked the floor with it at night, crying that his mind was pursuing and seeking to enfold and crush her own, and that she could not shake it off. Mr. Eddy, submerged as he was, could not help being affected by these terrible scenes. He was known to have declared that Spofford ought to be "punished" for so persecuting a helpless woman. Asa G. took his ideas from his wife, and when she was convinced that Spofford was causing all this, meek little Mr. Eddy believed her version as a matter of course.

Poor Spofford, on his side, was almost equally harassed. He bore no ill will against his teacher, and indeed until the end of his days regarded her gratefully as one who had brought into his life its most illuminating truth. Years afterward, when he was an old man of around sixty-five, he said of *Science and Health,* "I believe it is the greatest book in the world outside the Bible. . . . I don't wish it to be understood that I have said Christian Science was Quimbyism. I said that Mrs. Eddy taught some of the Quimby doctrine when I knew her in 1870."[1] Spofford, although he knew some of Mrs. Eddy's shortcomings, regarded her as a woman with an important message, and was amazed and horror-stricken at her strange fury.

He was the more amazed when a man called at his Boston

[1]Quoted by Sibyl Wilbur from personal interview. Vd. *The Life of Mary Baker Eddy,* page 224, footnote.

office, introduced himself as James L. Sargent, a saloon-keeper, and inquired if Spofford knew two men named Miller and Libby. Spofford did not. "Well, they know you," said Sargent, "and they want to put you out of the way." The saloon-keeper explained that these two men had offered him $500 to do the murder, paying him $75 in advance. Not desiring to take the risks to which a murder is subject, Sargent explained that if Spofford would depart from town for a few days the necessity of a murder could be avoided and he could still collect the $500 before his employers learned the actual status of the intended victim.

Spofford, frightened out of his wits, immediately conferred with State Detective Hollis C. Pinkham and then departed from town. Sargent thereupon informed his two patrons, whom he later identified in court as Eddy and Arens, that the murder was a *fait accompli*, and—so the later court evidence said—collected some more money.

Shortly thereafter Spofford turned up again, reassured his friends who had meanwhile become most anxious, and Messrs. Eddy and Arens were held for trial, on a charge of conspiring to procure murder.

Mrs. Eddy afterward wrote her own view of the ensuing events in the 1881 edition of *Science and Health*, for she regarded this book for years as a sort of personal house-organ. She took occasion to denounce the whole murder proceedings vigorously. It was her indignant conclusion that "the principal witnesses for the prosecution were convicts and inmates of houses of ill-fame in Boston." This was true. The main witness for the prosecution, James Sargent, had a sister Laura who kept a pretentious establishment on Bowker Street and appeared in Court attended by a bevy of her girls.

The testimony given by Sargent was that Eddy and Arens had bargained extensively with him before the $500 price was agreed on, and also argued over the amount of the first down-payment. He said Arens directed him to Spofford's Boston office by giving him one of Spofford's advertisements. One Jessie Macdonald, who had lived in the Eddy ménage as house-keeper for eight months, testified to having heard Mr. Eddy say that he would be glad to see Spofford out of the way, since he kept Mrs. Eddy in agony. Laura Sargent testified that Arens had met her brother James in her establishment several times; and that after one of these meetings James gave her $75 to keep for him. One George Collier testified to having heard Eddy and Arens discuss the murder plot.

The case had been brought for examination before Judge May of the Municipal Court on November 7th. After hearing the witnesses the judge concluded that the case was rather anomalous but that the evidence warranted holding the accused for the Superior Court, and he fixed their bail at three thousand dollars each. When the case was called in Superior Court in December, an indictment was found on two counts, the accused pleading "not guilty." The indictment was then continued until the January term of the court.

But the case was never tried. Filed with the papers was the notice that "the District Attorney, Oliver Stevens, Esq., says he will prosecute this indictment no further, on payment of costs, which are thereupon paid. And the said Arens and Eddy are thereupon discharged, January 31, 1879."

Mrs. Eddy hastened to reach for her pen and explain the whole affair as the result of animal magnetism or demonology, diabolically conceived to injure the sale of *Science and Health*: "The purpose of the plotters was to injure the reputation of metaphysical practice, and to embarrass us for money at a time when they hoped to cripple us in the circulation of our book."[1] She immediately proceeded to publish affidavits intending to show that Mr. Eddy was entirely innocent.

Two of these affidavits, made by her students, testified that Mr. Eddy was teaching a class at a time when he was supposed to have been arranging for the murder. The third was made out by Collier, who had testified to overhearing a meeting between the plotters. Collier in this affidavit retracted his previous testimony. To-day the whole incredible affair still remains a comic-opera mystery.

This series of unfortunate legal battles, regardless of their various outcomes, ended in making Mrs. Eddy's position in

[1] *Science and Health* (1881), Chapter VI, page 22.

Lynn rather unbearable. Originally tolerated by her neighbors with a fairly humorous regard because of her somewhat quixotic eccentricities, she was now made the object of some active hostility, and the many stories of her constant conflicts with students, the raging scenes which occurred in her household, and her difficult disposition, were repeated frequently.

Mrs. Eddy was to have one more important lawsuit before this sort of unfortunate publicity ceased. After the quashing of the murder charge Mrs. Eddy began to feel a deep resentment toward Arens which grew with time; its underlying basis was probably no more logical than many more of her eccentric and sudden whims of dislike. Arens in return was slowly becoming rather tired of Mrs. Eddy; he devoted himself more and more to his own practice, and ceased to be a fixture in the Eddy establishment. Opening a Boston office, he developed a less vindictive doctrine than that which Mrs. Eddy preached, and in 1881 published a pamphlet entitled "Theology, or The Understanding of God as Applied to Healing the Sick." In this work he quoted long passages from *Science and Health* and from Quimby, writing a preface in which he disclaimed all originality for the doctrine presented, saying that it had been practised not alone by Mrs. Eddy and Quimby, but also by Jesus and his disciples and in the fourteenth century by a secret association of priests known as the "Gottesfreunde." He acknowledged his debt to *Science and Health* by saying that he had included in his treatise "some thoughts contained in a work by Eddy."

When the third edition of *Science and Health* appeared a few months later, Asa Eddy himself wrote a preface in which Arens' name was added to the list of those whom Mrs. Eddy had officially proscribed. He said that "it would require ages and God's mercy to make the ignorant hypocrite who published that pamphlet originate its contents. . . . He knows less of metaphysics than any decent honest man."

Henceforth Mr. Arens was credited by Mrs. Eddy with seeking to destroy her by the same malicious animal magnetism currents which she thought emanated from Kennedy and Spofford. It was her idea that she could distinguish between the various currents sent out by these three men, and know—

when she felt one of her "spells" coming on her—which one of the three major enemies was at that moment attacking her. Mr. Arens' attacks, she said, afflicted her as if he were seeking to poison her with a dose of arsenic; and on such occasions she would announce that she was seeking to defend herself mentally against arsenic poisoning.

Things went on in this fashion, Mrs. Eddy becoming constantly more wrought up over the thought of Arens and constantly more resentful of his quoting her in his pamphlet, until in 1883 she brought an action against him for infringing her copyright on *Science and Health*. It was in this suit that she acquired the extensive information about copyrights which served her so fortuitously in later years and played no small part in making her a millionaire. She won the Arens suit. Arens' defense was that *Science and Health* was not original with Mrs. Eddy, but that it was derived to a large extent from the writings of P. P. Quimby. Such a defense was obviously of no avail in a court of law; for Quimby's writings had never been copyrighted by himself, none had ever been published by any one except Mrs. Eddy, and the copyright on this material was now owned by Mrs. Eddy personally. Thus Mrs. Eddy was victorious, and ever after chose to construe this decision as one wholly establishing her claim to the sole and unique discovery of Christian Science, referring to it as her "vindication in the United States Court."

Actually, of course, the decision meant nothing of the sort. Even had Arens possessed the Quimby manuscripts to offer in evidence it is possible that he would have lost the suit; for Mrs. Eddy had established her copyrights, while the Quimby material languished in desk drawers. Arens was enjoined not to publish or circulate his pamphlet, and all printed copies were ordered destroyed.

George Quimby at no time during his life ever permitted these manuscripts of his father's to go out of his possession, even when Mrs. Eddy's denials of any debt to Quimby assumed the form of a challenge. This challenge, sent from Boston to the *Portland Daily Press* over her own signature, was as follows, the italics being the biographer's:[1]

---

[1]Vd. also *The Quimby Manuscripts*, page 22.

TO WHOM IT MAY CONCERN:

Mr. George A. Quimby, son of the late Phineas P. Quimby, over his own signature and before witnesses, stated in 1883 that he had in his possession at that time all the manuscript that had been written by his father. And I hereby declare that to expose the falsehood of parties publicly intimating that I have appropriated matter belonging to the aforesaid Quimby, I will pay the cost of printing and publishing the first edition of those manuscripts with the author's name:

Provided, that I am allowed first to examine said manuscripts, and do find that they were his own compositions, and not mine, that were left with him many years ago, or that they have not since his death, in 1865, been stolen from my published works. Also that I am given the right to bring out this one edition under the copyright of the owner of said, manuscripts, and all the money accruing from the sales of said book shall be paid to said owner. . . .

George Quimby utterly ignored this challenge; and Quimby's followers pointed out that Mrs. Eddy's pronouncement was obviously put out with the hope of getting these documents in her possession so that—under the terms of the challenge—she could herself sit as judge and jury and declare that all of the Quimby manuscripts were her own, "that were left with him many years ago." Mrs. Eddy no longer hesitated to claim that if there existed any similarity between her own and Quimby's manuscripts, it was because of what Quimby had borrowed from writings she left with him in 1862. She asserted this boldly in her pamphlet, "Historical Sketch of Metaphysical Healing," which she published in 1885.

George Quimby, although he allowed various interested persons to consult these documents, always refused to take any step whatever that would permit Mrs. Eddy to lay her hands on them. The manuscripts were not made available to the general public until 1921, eleven years after Mrs. Eddy's death. George Quimby died without making any provision for their publication, but they came into the hands of Horatio W. Dresser, who thereupon published them in his volume *The Quimby Manuscripts*. George Quimby was unwilling to have them published during Mrs. Eddy's life because of a very frankly expressed distrust of her. He eventually became a distinguished and rather wealthy citizen, and was undoubtedly a difficult antagonist for Mrs. Eddy and her organization to handle. In 1888 he explained his attitude toward Mrs. Eddy as follows, in a letter written to A. J. Swartz, a mental healer in Chicago, who had offered to "come to the rescue" of Mr. Quimby's father:

If I were in prison, in solitary confinement for life, I should be too busy to get into any kind of a discussion with Mrs. Eddy.

I have my father's manuscripts in my possession, but will not allow them to be copied nor to go out of my hands. Answering your further inquiries, I have no written article of Mrs. Eddy's in my possession, nor did my father ever have, nor did she ever leave any with either of us. In fact, we both have been able to make a living without stealing. . . .[1]

In a rather lengthy statement prepared for the New York *World* in May of 1907, shortly after Sibyl Wilbur had interviewed him for her inspired biographical articles in *Human Life*,[2] Mr. Quimby said of his father's manuscripts:

. . . If the fair or rather the unfair Sibyl can make herself or anybody else believe that I do not possess them, after having seen them herself, why I shall have to bear the cross as best I can and go down to the grave with the knowledge that Father did not write the manuscripts which I know he did write because I saw him do it. Sibyl says he didn't, and of course she ought to know because she knows nothing about it anyhow. The above statement is what is called logic, and it is useless to butt your head against it.

The writings I possess now belong to me. They have either been in the possession of Father or myself since some years before Mrs. Eddy ever saw Father; therefore I find it awfully hard to make myself really believe that they are the manuscripts Mrs. Eddy left with him—when as a matter of fact she never left any—or that she gave him the ideas contained in the manuscripts several years before they ever saw each other, or that she ever had such ideas.

I have never paraded these writings before the public. I have elected, so far, not to publish them. I have allowed parties to examine them under certain restrictions, as I have a perfect right to do. I allowed Sibyl the same privilege and she is the first person in forty years to doubt their authenticity. And she only doubted with her pen—for she knew they

[1] From *The True History of Mental Science*, by Julius A. Dresser, page 47.

[2] These articles were subsequently issued in book form, after due editing, as the Wilbur biography previously referred to.

were just what I told her they were and that they were authentic when she made her pen say they were not; and I'll bet her pen turned red in the face when it expressed that doubt.

George Quimby took particular exception to the statement that he hesitated to produce the manuscripts because, while he himself was a polished and educated and refined man, old P. P. Quimby had been quite illiterate, in sharp contrast to the son. So George Quimby wrote:

Now I like to have all that's coming to me, but really Father was not so illiterate and I am not as educated and refined as this article would intimate. In fact, if I could today swap personalities with my late Father, —looks, character, brain, intellect; in fact, every quality that goes to make up a man, I would pay liberal boot and think I had made a good trade.

Could we both have an audience with the President today, you would see me a sort of wall-flower wandering about the room, looking out of the window or examining the souvenir postals and attracting no attention; while the old gentleman would be the center of attraction, monopolizing most of the conversation and attention. And when we left the President would think that he had been conversing with a cultured gentleman, remarkably well-posted on most any subject and who knew how to appear in the presence of any company that he might be thrown in with; and he probably would not remember that I had been in the room, unless I had accidentally sneezed.

Mr. Quimby's animadversions on the "fair or rather the unfair Sibyl" form a sample only of the more genial altercation that has raged around the Quimby manuscripts. The greater part of the controversy, particularly on Mrs. Eddy's side, was steeped in bitterness and bile, and Mrs. Eddy came to regard all revelations touching the source of her doctrine as another phase of the persecution which haunted her. Had she had the generosity of soul which is not uncommon even among those who walk in the humbler paths of life, she would have admitted her debts and might have built on this foundation an unshakable structure, high and serene. In every way her career would then have been a far more satisfying human achievement, and all men—regardless of their creed or philosophy—might have accorded her the free, sincere, and admiring affection which is ever the historical reward of the successful torchbearer.

But intellectual honesty was not a part of the strange Eddy character. In Lynn even those students who had been most loyal were gradually disillusioned and dismayed. Mrs. Eddy found herself facing not merely the openly expressed hostility of her neighbors in the town, but the distrustful watchfulness even of her closest students. A number of the students had fallen away, utterly discouraged by the perennial conflicts, the constant assaults of malicious animal magnetism, and the unexpected gyrations of Mrs. Eddy herself, who could generate at one moment the tranquil sunshine of a warm June day and the next the fierce vagaries of an electric storm. As students declined in number finances shrank in volume, and Mrs. Eddy was now obliged to do the greater part of her own house work, even to the washing and scrubbing. Poor Mr. Eddy, who never had possessed any great energy of mind or power of will, was now reduced by his fear of animal magnetism to an almost somnolent condition. His wife was a woman who often rose to her best moments under stress of attack; Mr. Eddy merely became hopelessly dulled. He was constant in his efforts to please her and to anticipate her whims; but she showed an increasing annoyance at his slowness, his round awkwardness, and his rather rustic manners and appearance. It is related that he became deeply discouraged under the stress of these strange goings-on, and once in a burst of confidence to another student, Mrs. Rice, said that Mrs. Eddy could not be pleased by God Almighty himself. It is worth noting that Mr. Eddy, regardless of his wife's theology, always thought of God in the masculine gender.

Mrs. Eddy's own maladjustment to the world around her was increased by another delusion which psychiatrists often find associated with the delusion of persecution, and which is a not uncommon phenomenon. This was the delusion of her personal grandeur. As she grew in teaching experience and years, she came to demand explicit obedience of all her students, and sought even to regulate their personal lives. The genesis of this general supervision over her students' affairs undoubtedly lay in the theory that in order to practise Christian Science efficiently they must obey the teacher's ultimatums regarding the smallest details of life; for it was Mrs. Eddy's teaching, of course, that her healing system was not psychology but theology, and the convert must live a life under standards established first by Christ and thereafter promulgated in 1866 by Mrs. Eddy herself. Mrs. Eddy was judge and jury in decisions as to whether such standards had been maintained by a student, and she did not hesitate to interfere in a student's family affairs. She justified such an interference, as time went by, on the grounds of her own divine inspiration.

One of the members of the early circle in Lynn, Mrs. Ellen A. Locke, said in after years that "Mrs. Eddy was the unhappiest woman I ever knew. She was always imagining that some one was conspiring against her. . . . She said that she and the Pope in Rome were infallible and could do no wrong." Even as Mrs. Eddy was washing down the stairs in the absence of a housekeeper and of the previously faithful students who attended to such chores for the house and its tenants, she could find release from the reality around her by letting her mind dwell on her eminence as the bearer of a divine message.

The conviction that she was playing a miraculous rôle had by now assumed a large place in her release psychology; and she told her classes many times how, when driving through Boston in an open carriage, she had healed a cripple who came up to her carriage as it crossed a street, merely by putting out her hand. She also announced to her students the discovery that when she was in the house her house-plants could live without either sunlight or water; she could put them up in the attic, treat them mentally, and behold them flourishing just as before.[1]

Unfortunately Mrs. Eddy was never able to "demonstrate" over herself, and the Broad Street house was kept in more or

---

[1]Georgine Milmine quotes a letter, addressee unstated, written in 1896 by Mrs. Eddy in the third person, and declaring, "While Mrs. Eddy was in a suburban town of Boston she brought out one apple blossom on an apple tree in January when the ground was covered with snow. And in Lynn demonstrated in the floral line some such small things." Vd. *Life of Mary Baker G. Eddy*, page 265.

less constant turmoil by the uncertainty as to when she would have her next seizure. On such occasions she would send for those of her students in whom she had the most confidence, and have them try to "treat" her. Mrs. Rice, who excepting Miss Rawson was the only student who had borne with her from the beginning, was apparently more successful than any other in handling her during these attacks, and was sent for at all hours of the night. We are told that Mrs. Eddy turned to morphine to try to relieve her terrible seizures. Mrs. Rice, who had long lent Mrs. Eddy far more than mere moral support, since she and her husband had put up poor Mr. Eddy's bail during the murder trial, has been quoted by the New York *World* in the following words:

"I was one of Mrs. Eddy's first converts and associates. I have treated her hundreds of times. I know that Mrs. Eddy was addicted to morphine in the 70s. She begged me to get some for her. She sent her husband, Mr. Eddy, for some; and when he failed to get it she got it herself and locked herself into her room for two days and excluded everyone. She was a slave to morphine. . . . She talked so much about the evil eye and devils that she caused one of the younger children of James Howard, who lived in the lower part of her house, to have fits. For this reason Howard moved out."[1]

Mrs. Locke similarly has testified to Mrs. Eddy's use of morphine, which, as in old John Varney's time, still seems to have "made her crazy."[2]

So discouraged did a number of her remaining students become; so appalled by the prevailing atmosphere in a group of workers who were professing to cure all human ailment through a realization of Divine love; so convinced that they were being led not by an emissary of God but rather by a very foolish, grasping, unbalanced woman, that they decided to resign in a body.

Mrs. Eddy had by now assembled a regular church organization. It seems extremely probable that in the beginning she had never visualized her Science as the basis for an organized

[1] Vd. interview in New York *World*, October 30, 1906.
[2] *Ibid.*

religion. She had developed a theology largely because it followed naturally from the philosophy which she had borrowed from Quimby. Quimby certainly never thought of making a religion out of his discovery; but he did produce the genesis of a theological system. Mrs. Eddy took this over almost without alteration. It was from this point that her idea of establishing a church to bulwark her theology began to unfold. Her creation of a church through which to proselyte her message was indeed a magnificent inspiration—a tremendous step forward toward the goal she had been approaching so painfully, and indeed the most important single step of her career.

The idea must have been born in her gradually and over a long period—inspirations are only sudden realizations of meanings that have long hovered in the background of the mind. Nor is it difficult to see how this ambition that was to dominate her life took form and grew. It was a natural derivative of the thesis—developed from Quimby—that she was evangelizing the original doctrine taught by Christ when he sought to redeem men. Each time she told her disciples about the miracles she could now, through the Christ-spirit within her, perform, it must have seemed more natural to speak as if from the altar of God.

The first attempted meetings of "The Christian Scientists" in 1875 had failed to become a regular procedure owing to the "malicious animal magnetism" generated by the spiritualists who dropped in at the services. In the following year, however, Mrs. Eddy had organized her students into "The Christian Scientists' Association." By 1879 she had reached the definite conclusion that she would found an established church, and "The Church of Christ (Scientist)" was formed with Mrs. Eddy as President, Margaret J. Dunshee as Treasurer, and seven directors. They applied to the State for a charter on August 6.

All proceedings for the organization of the church were conducted in the greatest secrecy, owing to Mrs. Eddy's absolute conviction that the mesmerists, in the shape of Kennedy, Spofford, *et al.*, would undoubtedly cause the enterprise to fail if they learned anything about it. Thus Mrs. Eddy and her students acted like a group of small boys hiding from ghosts on Hallowe'en, and when it was necessary to meet before a notary and sign the agreement of incorporation, they sought long and diligently to find a man who could be guaranteed absolutely free from the taints of malicious magnetism. They pored over lists of notaries to no avail, until Miss Dunshee finally suggested a man in Charlestown for whom she could vouch. Miss Dunshee herself lived in Charlestown, and the incorporators all met at her home, then separated, and stealthily pursued their walk to the notary's by devious and winding routes.[1] This happened on August 15; the papers were filed and a charter issued on August 23, 1879. There were in all twenty-six charter members, not all of whom were active in the work, but were at least willing to permit their names to be used. Boston was named as the city in which the church should be established, and the purpose of the incorporation was to "transact the business necessary to the worship of God."

For some time Mrs. Eddy had—on those weekends when her health allowed it—gone to Boston to hold services in the house there of some student who would extend such hospitality. In her absence the Lynn services would be conducted by Mrs. Rice or some other leading student. Four, five, or six members in attendance made a good congregation in those early days. The meetings were rather simple in form; there would be prayer, a reading from *Science and Health,* a reading from the Bible, and then a talk delivered by Mrs. Eddy herself whenever she was present.

This was the status of her Lynn organization when revolution suddenly broke forth. Talking among themselves, at first a little diffidently, a number of students found that they all agreed on the subject of Mrs. Eddy's very definite limitations. Had Mrs. Eddy been present at these confidences, she undoubtedly would have assured the students that they were the unwitting victims of malicious animal magnetism which was being sent forth to destroy them and her; but at the time she was entirely unaware. The students were tired of Mrs. Eddy's outbursts, tired of being witnesses in lawsuits which had un-

[1] Recorded by Georgine Milmine. Vd. *Life of Mary Baker G. Eddy,* page 268.

fortunate repercussions all over the town; tired of having to explain the goings on in Broad Street to friends who thought that a new religion ought to have something to offer besides constant bickerings, fears, and chambers of psychological horrors.

Therefore eight students together drew up a letter of resignation from Mrs. Eddy's organization, keeping the whole matter secret until one of them arose in the regular meeting of the Christian Scientists' Association to read the document aloud. Mrs. Eddy was present as usual. As she listened she could hardly believe her ears. Every name signed to the resignation represented one of the oldest and most prominent students in her group. The resolution which she heard was as follows:

We, the undersigned, while we acknowledge and appreciate the understanding of Truth imparted to us by our Teacher, Mrs. Mary B. G. Eddy, led by Divine Intelligence to perceive with sorrow that departure from the straight and narrow road (which alone leads to growth of Christ-like virtues) made manifest by frequent ebullitions of temper, love of money, and the appearance of hypocrisy, cannot longer submit to such leadership; therefore, without aught of hatred, revenge, or petty spite in our hearts, from a sense of duty alone, to her, the Cause, and ourselves, do most respectfully withdraw our names from the Christian Science Association and Church of Christ (Scientist).

S. Louise Durant
Margaret J. Dunshee
Dorcas B. Rawson
Elizabeth G. Stuart
Jane L. Straw
Anna B. Newman
James C. Howard
Miranda R. Rice

21st October, 1881

Mrs. Eddy was amazed. She arose and said so. She also expressed her indignation. She dwelt long on the vile accomplishments of malicious animal magnetism, which even then was emanating from her enemies in its attempt to destroy not herself alone but also the eight students who at that very moment were becoming unwitting victims.

The eight had heard all they cared to, however, about malicious animal magnetism. They went to their homes without another word. The next day Mrs. Eddy got up early, donned her best clothes, and went forth to call upon the rebels. It is a rather pitiful picture—that of a woman wholly a prey to wretched impulses and delusions which she could not control, now faced with the collapse of her entire student organization in Lynn.

All of the eight students refused to admit her to their homes. Mrs. Rice has said that "she came to my house and pounded upon all three doors with a stone. She was wild. She sent me word that she intended to have me arrested for deserting her."[1]

Mrs. Eddy did not fulfil her threat of arrest; on reflection she adopted another course. She informed the students that their resignations were not acceptable, but that their desire to resign made them liable to expulsion for disloyalty. As always, Mary Baker Eddy intended to have the last word. She summoned the eight to attend the next meeting. They did not appear; instead, two more students resigned, stating that they "could no longer entertain the subject of mesmerism which had lately been uppermost in the meetings and in Mrs. Eddy's talks."

This episode marked the death-knell of Mrs. Eddy's efforts in Lynn. She tried to marshal her few remaining students around her; and four months later these students prepared some Resolutions announcing their loyalty to their teacher. The text of this document, which bore some ear-marks of Mrs. Eddy's own phraseology, was published in the Lynn *Union* on February 3, 1882. But these students were more recent arrivals in her circle, and their support was far less valuable than that which had now been withdrawn. Mrs. Eddy was definitely through in Lynn, and she knew it; she had, indeed, sensed the coming catastrophe for two or three years, and had tried to prepare for it.

Already she was an old woman, as ordinary lives go. For sixty-one years she had sought for a foothold in the world, and now once again it was necessary to move on.

[1]Vd. interview in New York *World*, October 30, 1906.

PART III

A WOMAN BECOMES A DEITY

"But the desire for glory has great power in washing the tincture of philosophy out of the souls of men."

—PLUTARCH.

XII

Mrs. Eddy's decision to move to Boston played a large part in her subsequent success, as success is measured in terms of millions of dollars and of the public acclaim accruing to the originator of any formula or brand of merchandise which can be made to sell on such a scale. She required sixty years of failure to stumble on the recipe for successful enterprise, and even then many of her hardships were not entirely behind her. But from the time she packed up her belongings in the Broad Street home at Lynn and moved them to the city, she made alliance with an invaluable force which is prerequisite to the success of any undertaking, which is indispensable to the soundly established enterprise, and which can often take even an unsound project and carry it to public acceptance and favor. That force is Publicity.

It is true that Mrs. Eddy had enjoyed publicity of a kind before. But it was often extremely unfavorable in nature. She moved in a small community where her every word and gesture were open to public gaze and comment by the neighbors. She was the traditional goldfish in the bowl, her life bared for all to see. Surrounded by the large population of Boston her personal life became immediately of less neighborly interest, less under the pitiless limelight of public curiosity. This marks the difference between existence in a small town and that in the city: that in the city personalities are minimized, back fence gossip eliminated, individuals accepted at their own appraisal until they prove themselves of different value.

Thus Mrs. Eddy, through forced transplanting to Boston, gained an advantage of untold importance to one of her temperament, persuasions, and weaknesses. The facts concerning her personal self immediately became of relatively small moment to the great, thriving city around her. On the other hand, any sensational aspect of her ideas immediately became of interest to a metropolitan press whose main business it is to provide sensations to a city population—a population which, because of its very mode of life, cannot obtain emotional outlet through the back-fence gossip route which the village environment offers, and hence depends on the daily newspaper to provide this relief from the cares which infest the day. There was little in the rather drab and colorless personal life of a sixty-year-old woman promoting a new religious cult to attract the attention of city editors. On the other hand, any sensational aspect of the doctrine which she taught was immediately worth space in their papers. The Lynn editors, writing to please a small-town clientele, were far more interested in Mrs. Eddy's doings as a quarrelsome neighbor than in her teachings. The Boston editors, on the other hand, found only in her teachings material that made any sort of news for their purposes. It was not until after Mrs. Eddy had become famous and wealthy that her personal life could have any real interest for the newspapers of the nation. And when this time came, Mrs. Eddy had gone into retirement, and was less accessible to a curious world than a Pope in the cloisters of Rome.

And yet, strangely enough, the move to Boston was not the result of any brilliantly conceived plan, but came almost wholly as a conclusion to a train of accidents which in later years Mrs. Eddy herself may well have regarded as divine, but which the historian can call nothing else than fortuitous.

Sometime before the final break-up in Lynn she had sent Mrs. Clara Choate down to Boston to do some proselyting, and Mrs. Choate, like Kennedy and Spofford, found there a paying clientele for her healing system. Mrs. Choate not only met with a certain financial success, but also established a sort of *réclame* among her patients, so that she made them want to know more about the mysterious Mrs. Eddy and her work.

As a result, Mrs. Eddy occasionally went down to Boston to address interested people in Mrs. Choate's front parlor, and as early as 1878 was giving occasional lectures in a Baptist church on Shawmut Avenue. The following year she gave Sunday afternoon talks in the Parker Fraternity building on Appleton Street. The audiences, consisting primarily of friends of Mrs. Choate, and any others in whom news of the new teaching had established curiosity, were never large; fifty or sixty people made a pretty fair gathering, and sometimes the number fell to half as many.

The trip from Lynn to Boston was of course a short one, and Mrs. Eddy was inevitably accompanied by Asa and several of her students. The students were delegated to sit in a certain pew and defend Mrs. Eddy, while she spoke, against Malicious Animal Magnetism—a force that now had assumed such proportions in her life that it came to have capitals,[1] and to her students became so familiar that it was designated merely by initials, M. A. M. When Mrs. Eddy arose in the morning she could ascertain, from the sort of depression that she experienced, or from the color of her mood and thoughts, just which kind of M. A. M. was being directed toward her, and which one of her enemies—Kennedy, Spofford, or Arens —was seeking to take control of her for the day. Sometimes all three set on her at once, and then the day was lost. The administrations of every student available would be required in these terrible emergencies.

During her Sunday talks in Boston Mrs. Eddy would usually wear a black silk gown with a bonnet in the fashion of the day; usually her gold-rimmed spectacles formed the most conspicuous part of her costume. She resented the spectacles, because she was often asked why she wore them, her teachings being what they were.

Her talks at these times, because they were partly addressed to newcomers and novices in her doctrine, dealt less with the horrors of M. A. M. and more with other points in Mrs. Eddy's theology; and in consequence the power that she had shown on previous occasions of moving an audience to a high degree of emotional exaltation—a mood which is associated with some manifestations of hysteria—was more effective than ever before.

Following her platform talk Mrs. Eddy would come down

[1]Mrs. Eddy eventually became most particular how capitals were used in connection with her dogmas. Vd. *Miscellany*, page 225: "A correct use of capital letters in composition caps the climax of the old 'new tongue.' Christian Science is not understood by the writer or the reader who does not comprehend where capital letters should be used in writing about Christian Science."

and shake hands with her audience personally. Asa meanwhile
would stand off to one side shaking hands again, and—whenever he found an interested newcomer—suggesting the wisdom of joining one of his wife's classes. If such a newcomer
showed anything more than passing interest, Mr. Eddy would
doggedly but politely get his address, and call later in person;
he had learned the value which every salesman sets upon per-
sistency.

Mr. Eddy always walked and talked softly, and glanced
around often to see if any mesmerists were on his trail. Every
now and then, it is told, he would duck into a doorway and
wait a few moments so that if any evil influence were following him it would pass on by.

As early as 1878 Mrs. Eddy had debated fleeing from
Lynn; and in this year she and Asa did depart temporarily,
leaving the house to the tenants, and living for a while in Boston boarding-houses. Even then it was her conviction that M.
A. M. was getting too close a hold on their Lynn quarters to
make living there comfortable. With one of her students,
Arthur T. Buswell, who at the moment was enjoying her
favor, Mrs. Eddy had got out a map of the United States
and examined it to find a more promising spot than Lynn for
carrying on her efforts. The map unfortunately did not indicate the areas where M. A. M. was distributed most sparsely,
but they finally decided that Cincinnati might be a likely place
to try out. The choice of Cincinnati was made because of
its central location and the number of railroads which ran
through that metropolis. Whether railroad facilities meant to
Mrs. Eddy a centre of wealth or a mere convenience for swift
exit if M. A. M. pursued her, is not recorded.

Following this decision Mr. Buswell was sent at his own
expense to Cincinnati to found a haven there, with the understanding that Mrs. Eddy and her household would follow in
some six weeks. She did not find it convenient to go, however,
for shortly thereafter she evidently found herself in a more
buoyant state of mind in which the perils of M. A. M. temporarily did not loom so large. Thus when Mr. Buswell wrote to
inquire about the delay and to say that he needed some money

if he were to continue eating, Mrs. Eddy was righteously annoyed. She replied that M. A. M. must be very terrible in Cincinnati and that Mr. Buswell must be very inefficient in defending himself against it, if he found himself in the condition he described. Mr. Buswell's correspondence with Mrs. Eddy was thereafter abruptly terminated.

She would occasionally revert, however, to the idea of making Cincinnati a refuge, whenever M. A. M. in Lynn seemed to renew its grip upon her; and on one of these occasions in 1878 she bethought herself of her son, George Glover, who all this time had been growing up and getting married and founding a family of his own in Minnesota.

So she sent him a telegram, asking him to come to Cincinnati at once and join her there. The telegram sounded almost as if she were dying, and George got on the train at once. But when he arrived in Cincinnati there was no mother. He waited for quite a while, growing more anxious every minute. Finally he wired the Chief of Police in Lynn. No answer came for days. Eventually, however, a telegram came from Mrs. Eddy herself, saying that she was in Boston and bidding him to hurry to her there. Once again a day or two of better health had made a flight to Cincinnati unnecessary, and she had abandoned the plan.

When George reached Boston after three days' travel he found the Eddys living there in a boarding house, taking a brief vacation from Lynn and its horrors. This was in 1878, a year, it will be remembered, when Mrs. Eddy was girded almost constantly in shield and buckler for her sorties in the law-courts. Her state of mind during this period is best described by her son himself.

Regardless of the fact that he had been farmed out to strangers all his life, he always spoke of his mother with an admirable gentleness and respect, and once severely rebuked a reporter who asked whether Mrs. Eddy spoke truly in referring to a "plot" that robbed her of her boy. "I do not agree with my mother in her version of the facts," he said with dignity. "But I shall never open my lips to contradict her. She is my mother, and my lips are sealed."

Mrs. Eddy had corresponded with her son during his life in the west at rather irregular intervals—more regularly at times when her own affairs were not going satisfactorily and she felt alone and deserted in the midst of ungrateful students. In 1865, when she heard that he was seriously ill, she temporarily became very alarmed. Quimby was not yet dead, and she immediately sat down to write the old doctor for help for George, saying that she was going to attempt a trip to see the lad.

She had corresponded with Quimby regularly ever since she met him, asking him constantly for treatment and mental help. She addressed him on July 29, 1865, to say that she had just received a letter which had "well-nigh separated soul and body," and that her first thought had been to seek Dr. Quimby, "like the Mother of old." George, it appeared, had "consumption of the bowels." He had travelled as far as Enterprise, Minnesota, on his way to reach his mother, and had there collapsed. Mrs. Patterson's letter continued:

> If I am with this body next Mond. I shall start for him with it although I am sick to-day and know nothing of the route to him. O Doctor, tis only in you I have any hope and can't you save him? . . .
> All I ask all I hope for is that he may be spared to me. Save him, save him if you can. . . .[1]

George was saved, and evidently without necessitating a trip west by his mother or his own journey to Lynn. At least, there is no record of any meeting between mother and son at this time. It was apparently not until 1878 that they finally came face to face in Boston, after his long wait in Cincinnati.

When George reached Boston, he found his mother and Mr. Eddy, now called "Doctor" Eddy, living in a large room in a boarding house, and wholly at the mercy of fears which the son did not at first understand. "Within a week of my arrival in Boston," the New York *World* later quoted Glover as saying, "I learned strange things. The strangest of these was that rebellious students were employing black arts to harass and destroy my mother.

[1] Vd. the first edition of *The Quimby Manuscripts*, edited by Horatio W. Dresser, for the complete letter.

"The longer I remained with mother, the clearer this became. Pursued by the evil influence of the students we moved from house to house, never at rest and always apprehensive. It was a maddening puzzle to me. We would move to a new house and fellow lodgers would be all smiles and friendliness. Then, in an hour, an inevitable change would come; the friendliness would vanish under the spell of black magic, and we would be ordered to go. But mother made it all very clear to me."[1]

Mrs. Eddy told her son just what she had told all her students—that Spofford, Kennedy and Arens were seeking her life with their mystic rites. Mrs. Eddy seemed exceedingly thankful to have her son close to her, grateful for a new and younger strength to lean on at a time when she was convinced that all the world was against her. She refused to think of George's returning to Minnesota, even though his wife was expecting the birth of a child. She talked almost continually of her enemies. If one is to credit the amazing interview with Glover recorded almost thirty years later by the New York *World*, her son finally became as convinced as she of the reality of this diabolic attack, and prepared to beard M. A. M. in its den. The following is a part of the lengthy statement attributed to him by *The World*:

It was Kennedy that mother talked of most. He was a master hand at the black arts, as mother pictured him daily to me, until at last I made up my mind to cut him short in his evil work. But I kept my plan to myself. One morning I slipped my revolver into my overcoat pocket and left our boarding house. . . .

I had never seen this man, but I knew where he had offices, and I walked straight there. He was doing business as a healer, and his name, lettered on a brass plate, was on the door of his office. Every detail of that visit is as clear in my mind today as if it took place only a week ago.

The girl who admitted me asked if I was a patient, and I answered "Yes." . . . The unsuspecting girl led me straight to Kennedy's office, on the second floor of the house, opened the door, bowed me into the room, and hurried away. Kennedy was before me, seated at his desk.

He looked up smilingly and asked, "Are you in need of treatment?"

Pulling out my revolver I walked to him, pressed the cold muzzle against his head, and said, "I have made up my mind that *you* are in need of treatment."

[1]Vd. New York *World*, March 3, 1907.

There, while he shook like a jellyfish in terror, I gave him his one chance to live. I told him that my mother knew of his black art tricks to ruin her and that I had made up my mind to stop him or kill him.

"You needn't tell me that you *aren't* working your game of hypnotism to rob her of friends and drive mother into madness," said I. "My one word to you is this: if we have to move from another boarding house I will search you out and shoot you like a mad dog."

I shall never forget how that man plead for his life at the end of my weapon and swore that the black art accusation was false and that my mother had deceived me.

But it did the business all right. We were not ordered out of another boarding house that winter.[1]

With the pitfalls of a newspaper interview in mind, one must, in fairness to Glover, discount this extraordinary bit of self-revelation, particularly since it came so many years after the event, but it remains an interesting illustration of the strange atmosphere in which his mother involved those who were around her at this time. Mrs. Eddy, according to her son, was not entirely pleased over what he had done, but she did not scold him. Whether she, too, attributed to his efforts the change of atmosphere which they struck in boarding houses, there is no way of knowing. Her son related, however, that her health immediately began to improve and he was shortly allowed to return to his wife and his new son.

It was early in 1882 that Mrs. Eddy decided to pack up and put Lynn forever behind her. She and her husband took a house in Boston at 569 Columbus Avenue, leased for $1,000 a year. Placed on the front door was a large silver plate bearing the words, "Massachusetts Metaphysical College."

Mrs. Eddy's college had been organized during the preceding year, and had originally been an experiment devised with the hope of rehabilitating her declining fortunes in Lynn. Mrs. Eddy rather liked the title of "College," and it seemed to her that it might lend some dignity to her teaching efforts. Actually, in organizing a college she indeed made a brilliant move. It was never a college that had any quarters but her own home,

[1] N. Y. *World*, March 3, 1907.

or any faculty except herself and immediate family; but the name had important publicity value in appealing to potential students in other parts of the country.

Mrs. Eddy obtained a charter for her college under a Massachusetts act of 1874, a measure so illy devised and so lenient in its requirements that it resulted in the founding of a number of institutions whose diplomas were so misleading that in 1883 medical institutions chartered under the act were forbidden to confer degrees.

The Massachusetts Metaphysical College received its charter January 31, 1881, with the purpose, as stated in the articles of agreement, of teaching "pathology, ontology, therapeutics, moral science, metaphysics, and their application to the treatment of diseases." Mary B. G. Eddy was listed as president. Between 1881, when the college was opened, and 1889, when it was closed, some four thousand students[1] were listed for the twelve-lesson courses, which later were reduced to seven lectures. The tuition price was $300 for the elementary course, and all students who could possibly pay for more than an elementary course were made to feel that any investment which would bring them nearer to divine understanding was well warranted. Allowing only for those who took the first course, however, such figures would indicate that the college earned at least $1,200,000. Occasionally a charity student would be taken for the elementary course, but never for the higher ones.

Not long after the Eddy effects were established in the Boston house, Mr. Eddy took to his bed after an extended period of weakened health. Mrs. Eddy from the start knew what was wrong with him. It was Mr. Arens, who was living in Boston, not far from the Eddy residence on Columbus Avenue. As has been noted, whenever Mrs. Eddy felt any symptoms of

[1]These were the figures claimed by Mrs. Eddy herself, and originally there seemed no reason for questioning them. Since accepting them, I have been informed by an ex-official of her church that the Board of Directors sought to make a check of all the names of the college students and to record them for the Mother Church records. According to this authority, less than seven hundred names were found.—E. F. D.

arsenical poison in herself she knew that she was suffering from M. A. M. being sent out by Arens. Now, when Mr. Eddy came down with sickness, he described feelings much like Mrs. Eddy herself endured when she was suffering from the Arens hostility. She was thus able to diagnose Mr. Eddy's illness with absolute certitude. He was ill with arsenical poison.

Being a passive soul and accustomed to believing exactly what he was told, Asa became worse and worse, Mrs. Eddy meanwhile treating both herself and her husband against a cruel arsenical death. Mr. Eddy lost his appetite; he could not sleep; he felt malicious animal magnetism closing in on him from every direction until he complained that he was being suffocated.

In this new terror Mrs. Eddy summoned Dr. Rufus K. Noyes to the bedside. He took a look or two and said "heart disease." Mrs. Eddy protested. She knew arsenical poison when she saw it. During Asa's final hours we are told that Mrs. Eddy sat by him constantly, with her face close to his and murmuring, "Gilbert, Gilbert, do not suffer so."[1] He died at daybreak on June 3, 1882, when his wife was in bed asleep. His body was taken back to Tilton, and buried in the cemetery on the banks of the Merrimac, a charming spot for a weary soul. Mrs. Eddy did not accompany the remains, leaving that task to the husband of Mrs. Choate. Mrs. Choate herself was delegated to the task of delivering a eulogy in Hawthorne Hall. Her subject was, "Blessed are they who die in the Lord."

Before the body was shipped Mrs. Eddy decided to show Dr. Noyes he was wrong. She called him up to make an autopsy, even though she had written, just the year before, a proscription of such proceedings: "A metaphysician never gives medicine, recommends or trusts in hygiene, or believes in the ocular or the post-mortem examination of patients."[2] And again, "Many a hopeless case of disease is induced by a single post-mortem examination."[3]

[1] Sibyl Wilbur, *Life of Mary Baker Eddy*, page 279.
[2] *Science and Health* (1881), vol. I, page 269.
[3] *Ibid.*, page 163.

Yet Mrs. Eddy was human enough to prefer self-justification to metaphysical theory, and she was confident that a post-mortem examination would show that her own diagnosis had been the correct one. So Dr. Noyes was sent for, and when he took out the gentle Asa's heart it revealed clearly the evidence of the defective tissues.

But Mrs. Eddy utterly refused to believe. She called in a "Doctor" Eastman, an accommodating gentleman who had no recognized medical degree but who was dean of the "Bellevue Medical College," an institution organized under the same act by which Mrs. Eddy's own college had been founded. The Bellevue institution was later closed as fraudulent. "Dr." Eastman's private practice had dealt largely in abortions; he had already been indicted at least once when Mrs. Eddy made him a director, and in 1893 he went to prison for five years.

These facts become of public interest for only one reason; Mrs. Eddy in a statement issued to the local press broadcast Dr. Eastman's corroborating opinion that it was metaphysical arsenic which had killed Asa. She sat down on the very day that she had viewed poor Mr. Eddy's heart and wrote a thousand-word letter to the Boston *Post*.[1] Among other things she said:

My husband's death was caused by malicious mesmerism. Dr. C. J. Eastman, who attended the case after it had taken an alarming turn, declares the symptoms to be the same as those of arsenical poisoning. On the other hand, Dr. Rufus K. Noyes, late of the City Hospital, who held an autopsy over the body today, affirms that the corpse is free from all material poison, although Dr. Eastman still holds to his original belief. I know it was poison that killed him, not material poison, but mesmeric poison. My husband was in uniform health, but seldom complained of any kind of ailment. During his brief illness, just preceding his death, his continual cry was, "Only relieve me of this continual suggestion, through the mind, of poison, and I will recover." . . .
There was such a case in New York. Every one at first declared poison to have been the cause of death, as the symptoms were all there; but an autopsy contradicted the belief, and it was shown that the victim had had no opportunity for procuring poison. I afterwards learned that she had been very active in advocating the merits of our college. Oh, isn't

[1] Published June 5, 1882.

it terrible, that this fiend of malpractice is in the land! . . . Circumstances barred me taking hold of my husband's case. He declared himself perfectly capable of carrying himself through, and I was so entirely absorbed in business that I permitted him to try, and when I awakened to the danger it was too late. . . . Today I sent for one of the students whom my husband had helped liberally, and given some money, not knowing how unworthy he was. I wished him to come, that I might prove to him how, by metaphysics, I could show the cause of my husband's death. He was as pale as a ghost when he came to the door, and refused to enter, or to believe that I knew what caused his death. Within half an hour after he left I felt the same attack that my husband felt— the same that caused his death. I instantly gave myself the same treatment that I would use in a case of arsenical poison, and so I recovered, just the same as I could have caused my husband to recover had I taken the case in time. After a certain amount of mesmeric poison has been administered it cannot be averted. No power of mind can resist it. . . . One of my students, a malpractitioner, has been heard to say that he would follow us to the grave. . . .

Once again, in that letter, Mrs. Eddy was struggling with reality. She wrote primarily not to convince a doubting public, who could not possibly have been interested in the cause of the unknown Asa's death, but rather in a desperate effort to justify her theories and abilities to herself. If she was unable to cope with the ailment that had attacked her husband, it was necessary to find a reason that would not destroy the validity of her own life philosophy. This is why, on the very day of the autopsy, Mrs. Eddy was moved in the pitiful fulness of her heart to sit down and write a thousand words which proved nothing except that no possible evidence would ever persuade her to admit a mistake.

A little while after Asa's death Mrs. Eddy produced the poem which may be as confidently looked for in her hours of grief as an egg from a bird in the nesting season. This effort, rather extensive and ambitious, was entitled, "Meeting of My Departed Mother and Husband," and described a dialogue held in Heaven. Asa said to his mother-in-law:

> Years had passed o'er thy broken household band,
> When angels beckoned me to this bright land,
>   With thee to meet.

She that has wept o'er me, kissed thy cold brow,
Rears the sad marble to our memory now,
    In lone retreat.[1]

A granite shaft was reared to mark the spot where Asa was laid.

[1] *Miscellaneous Writings*, page 385 ff. This bit of verse has a rather interesting history. Examination of copies of Mrs. Eddy's early manuscripts, some of which have been made available to the biographer, has shown that this poem was originally inspired by the death of her first husband. Upon Asa's death, she merely revised a few lines to make the verse fitting for a more recent occasion.

XIII

Even Mrs. Eddy's letter regarding her husband's death was effective publicity. Unnumbered thousands who had never heard of Mrs. Eddy or of malicious animal magnetism went to bed on the night of June 5, 1882, wondering what this dread force was against which Mrs. Eddy could offer protection if she "took hold in time."

For a while the death of Mr. Eddy was an inconvenience as well as a grief; and that it was a grief may not be doubted, for Mrs. Eddy always dramatized her direr moments. In these early and enthusiastic days of her movement's history, not a few students—and at times even Mrs. Eddy herself—thought that the doctrine might indeed abolish death. Certainly, since Mrs. Eddy had denied that a body had any organs, it was utterly impossible to admit that Mr. Eddy had died of a defective heart. Indeed, Asa's death in any event seemed rather to cast reflection on him personally, as if he had not grown sufficiently in Science. Thus there were a number of reasons why the arsenical poison theory was a convenient one for all concerned; and Mrs. Eddy's students accepted it wholeheartedly, and resolved to bestir themselves more ardently so that the fiend of M. A. M. might not gain a foothold in their midst again.

The position which was vacated in Mrs. Eddy's home by her husband—the position which involved waiting on her every want and whim, of acting as secretary, comforter, stabilizer, footman, butler, messenger, bookkeeper, and chief factotum—was shortly to be filled by one of the strangest characters in Mrs. Eddy's annals. His name was Calvin A. Frye.

In her unreasoning terror when her husband first died, Mrs. Eddy's first thought was to get some man into the house to lean on. Thus she immediately wired once more to her son in Minnesota, George Glover, with whom she had been carrying on a desultory correspondence ever since his previous visit.

George, however, felt under no obligation to his erratic and neglectful mother; he was without funds for railroad fare, and this time he did not make the trip. Mrs. Eddy also wired to Arthur Buswell, who was still in Cincinnati but no longer stranded.

Mr. Buswell, following his rebuff at Mrs. Eddy's hands after she sent him to Cincinnati, had allowed all correspondence to lapse until one day he received a message asking him to give Mr. Eddy absent treatments—Mrs. Eddy had marshalled all her resources against the Fiend. When he received a subsequent message to come to Boston, he resigned his position as Superintendent of Public Charities and went to her aid at once. He arrived to find Asa's body carefully laid out and Mrs. Eddy and her entire household frantic with fear and trembling. She told Mr. Buswell that she had resuscitated her husband twice, but when he sank for the third time all had been ended. Cruel critics later opined that to raise a third husband a third time would have been a feat to tax the resources even of Mrs. Eddy.

Mrs. Eddy herself rallied bravely for the purposes of writing press notices and putting out interviews, then went up to Mr. Buswell's home at Barton, Vermont, to spend the summer. She was in a nervous and exhausted condition, and there were many nights when Mr. Buswell was called to treat her for the same hysterical attacks with which all of her students who were near to her for any length of time had to deal.

Whatever the horrors of the frantic night, Mrs. Eddy usually managed to gather herself together during the day; and between attacks she was constantly planning and arranging for the winter's work in Boston. Her movement had become literally her life. She dreamed of nothing else, talked of nothing else. Her whole thought was taken up with only two things: planning for the extension of Christian Science, and devising recipes for escape from the constant emotional conflicts in which she found herself, with a physique that told her one thing and a philosophy that told her another. During her periods of good health Mrs. Eddy could forget awhile about M. A. M., the device which formed her avenue of escape from the conflict. But during periods of illness she was subject to double torture—not alone the physical pain, but the obsession of overpowering evil which gripped her in dread and fear.

It was while planning for the winter's lectures in Boston, the additions to the ranks of practitioners, and the enlarging of the church work, that Mrs. Eddy came also to the problem of her own household; she reached the conclusion that she needed a man who could take charge. In times of practical need she always turned to the male of the species.

Mrs. Eddy had passed the time when she would take any individual merely on faith, for she had found that as far as the practical world was concerned there was nothing which counted like evidence, in court or out. Even before Asa's death she had been looking around for a reliable student who could be useful in time of need, and she had sent her husband to Lawrence to investigate the record of Frye. The report had been favorable, and Mrs. Eddy now asked Buswell to telegraph Frye to meet her in Plymouth, New Hampshire, as she was returning to Boston.

The interview that resulted in putting Calvin Frye in charge of Mrs. Eddy's household thus occurred on the train. Terms were agreed on—$12 a week and board.

Frye had become interested in Christian Science through Mrs. Choate, who had treated his mother for an insanity from which she suffered for many years. Under Mrs. Choate's treatment Mrs. Frye apparently recovered to some extent; but at the end of four years the more violent insanity returned and she suddenly expired. This mental history is not without significance in the subsequent story of the anomalous position which Frye occupied in Mrs. Eddy's household.

He came of a good line, with a grandfather and great-grandfather who fought respectively during the wars of 1812 and the Revolution; Frye Village, Massachusetts, now absorbed in Andover, is said to have been named for the family. His grandfather had a milling business there, dealing in grist and lumber, and he had sent his son, Calvin's father, through Phillips Andover Academy and Harvard. Enoch Frye's Harvard Class of 1821 was the one made famous by

Emerson, Francis Cabot, and Edward Loring. With a lame leg and a softer character than his father, Enoch did not seem to prosper financially; and with four children and an insane wife—a fifth child having died in infancy—he was unable to do more for Calvin than send him to the small school in Frye Village.

At the age of twenty-eight Calvin married; his wife died within a year without issue. Having been early apprenticed as a machinist in the machine shops of Davis and Furber in North Andover, after his wife's death Calvin continued living at Lawrence with his father and insane mother, and worked in the Natick mill as an overseer.

This is the simple background of the man who was destined to become one of the powers behind the throne in Mrs. Eddy's empire. His arrival in her household coincides almost to a year with the time she first began to rise as a queenly figure in the fabulous world of her own creation.

After becoming interested in Christian Science through Mrs. Choate, Frye had taken a course of lessons under Mrs. Eddy, as had his sister Lydia. Calvin and Lydia both practised healing for a short time after finishing their course, and when Calvin joined Mrs. Eddy, Lydia shortly followed and did the housework.

When Lydia finally returned to Lawrence in ill-health, she underwent a surgical operation from which she never fully recovered, and she died still an enthusiastic Christian Scientist, proclaiming almost to her last breath that "there is no death."

Calvin soon became an established fixture in the Eddy household. Mrs. Eddy found him particularly malleable, peculiarly suggestible. He sensed her desires, her thoughts, her swift changes of whim and mood almost without the need of a word. Slow, taciturn, at first glance apparently even dull-witted, he was peculiarly shrewd, calculating, and even suave. There was no service in the Eddy ménage too small and mean for him to perform. He put the same energy into answering Mrs. Eddy's mail and shopping for the groceries. Mrs. Eddy soon became his entire existence. She was the centre of his world, the sun about which he revolved. In his devotion there was evident no sign of warm affection; it was a subtler relationship, such as is maintained between the hypnotist and his subject. There was almost a psychic quality in the bond between them. Mrs. Eddy, on her part, absorbed Frye, enveloped him completely, regarded him henceforth as part of herself. He was the one being in the world from whom she shortly had no secrets, and for whom she had no pose.

After entering her service he lived literally in obedience to her written reminder that Jesus was without family ties and would have us call no man father.

Georgine Milmine relates that when Enoch Frye died in 1886, Calvin went to the funeral, started for the cemetery, stopped the carriage en route, and dashed to the station to get the next train to Boston. When his sister died in 1890 he did not even acknowledge the message telling of her death, or a request for help in paying the funeral expenses. He had been completely absorbed by Mrs. Eddy, and he had inscribed on his soul the same command that for long was written above the door in Lynn which faithful Christian Scientists flocked by thousands to see—the door to the attic room where their text book had been born:

THOU SHALT HAVE NO OTHER GODS BEFORE ME.

After Mrs. Eddy's return to Boston with Frye and Buswell she moved her home and college to 571 Columbus Avenue, adjoining the building at 569 which she had previously leased. It was the typical stone dwelling that during the eighties lined Boston and New York streets in droves—a narrow façade, with a large bay, containing three windows abreast in each story, that rose from the ground to the mansard roof. There were three main floors, in addition to an attic floor under the mansard roof and the usual basement.

Mrs. Eddy had never acquired much furniture, and because her venture in Boston still was surrounded with uncertainties she furnished the Columbus Avenue house simply and even poorly. Mrs. Eddy was never a spendthrift with her money, and she now utilized every method to keep down expenses. The classroom on the second floor was laid with oil-cloth, and even the parlor of the house looked almost as bare as an office.

Mrs. Eddy was surrounded by some half dozen students who dwelt in the house, or, as they preferred to think of it, at the college. They all lived on a cooperative plan, paying expenses pro rata while Frye hired and fired servants, did the marketing, kept accounts, and supervised the ménage generally. On the first floor was an office where these resident students could see their patients; for from the first each student endeavored to make Mrs. Eddy's teaching pay its own way. The office was used in rotation, each budding "doctor" having office hours and seeing his patients at set times. Among these resident students in the early eighties were Hanover Smith, who later became insane; Arthur Buswell, E. H. Hammond, Julia Bartlett, and a Mrs. Whiting. Mrs. Emma Hopkins and Luther M. Marston joined the establishment a little later.

Mrs. Eddy comprised the institution's entire faculty. As from the beginning, twelve lessons completed the course. By this time, she knew her lectures almost by heart; for they were almost always the same with slight variation. Methods by which one could defend oneself against the wiles of malicious animal magnetism formed an important part of all her discourse. Actually, her talks were much more to the point than her writings, and dealt less with theology than with aspects of the use of mental suggestion. The actual practice of her theories was not nearly so involved, mysterious, nor profound as the reading of her voluminous textbook would imply. One simply concentrated his mind on the patient to be healed, visualized him as well and healthy, and verbally asserted that he was so. For obstinate cases "arguments" were provided, to the effect that the disease could not exist since God, Good, was all.

In treating the "Fiend," otherwise known as malicious animal magnetism, a variation of the same method was adopted. One merely concentrated his mind on the person suspected of sending baleful messages through space, and visualized him as powerless to harm, at the same time verbally asserting his impotence. If the case of "malpractice" were particularly aggravated, one could even assert that the human embodiment of the "Fiend" was himself suffering from the very ills he sought to induce. It was believed possible, in other words, to use mental power to create either good or evil. By proper concentration it was considered possible to inflict disease or death on the malpractitioner in the same way that he sought to inflict it on one of Mrs. Eddy's loyal students or on herself. All that was necessary was a sufficiently concentrated state of mind, so imbued with consciousness of infinite power, God, that it shared a divine omnipotence.

Such, in the language of the man in the street, seem to have been the essentials of Mrs. Eddy's teachings, when stripped of her theological lore and the various theses of her philosophy.

Her brief daily class periods left her abundant time to turn her attention to other things, from revising her book to checking up on the household expenditures. Mrs. Eddy continued to revise her book until her dying day; the method was always the same. She would cross out a word or sentence she wished to change with a lead pencil; and write in the new reading between the lines of the printed page.

Between times she attended to her correspondence, which now was growing apace. She was an inveterate letter writer, and there were few people who came in contact with her who did not eventually get a letter signed in her own hand. This, of course, was an excellent method of promoting herself, for it stimulated a personal interest which created dividends in the form of new pupils for her classes.

In addition, it was a dull week when she could not find some subject for a press notice, which Mr. Buswell was delegated to take around to the local papers in the hope that an editor would need an extra stick of type. Frequently one did, and when he used the material a constant reader would occasionally write in to take issue with it. Such disputes offered Mrs. Eddy one of her best opportunities for getting some real publicity, for she always wrote a reply that received much more space than her original notice. All editors find news in controversy, and like to keep an argument going.

On Sundays she frequently preached at Hawthorne Hall, and as her students built up their healing practice, attendance at Mrs. Eddy's Sunday meetings slowly increased. In addition, she occasionally made talks in the homes of patients whom various students had treated successfully and who had become interested in the strange old woman to whose doctrine was given the credit for the cure. Boston, particularly intellectual Boston, was fertile ground in those days for any new and mysterious cult, and this redounded markedly to Mrs. Eddy's advantage. Even though her talks left the intellect rather unsatisfied, the various works being accomplished by her healers seemed to warrant faith that there must be something in the doctrine, after all. Indeed, the mysteries of Mrs. Eddy's philosophy were in a way an advantage; for the curiosity of newcomers was stimulated by the very fact that they could not understand what they had heard.

Accordingly Mrs. Eddy, after students had established for her some personal contacts, was passed from hand to hand until she occasionally was invited to speak in a home of influence and wealth. Hostesses even in that day were not averse to being able to offer a strange "lion" to their friends at an afternoon reception, and Mrs. Eddy was strange enough to make a really curious attraction. In her black shawl and her curls she was rather unlike anything previously seen. In addition, her old ability to rise to the spirit of social gatherings and exude a rather supernormal energy stood her in good stead. When she made her little talk about the wonderful mysteries of the new God she had discovered, her eyes flashed, her head was dynamically atilt, her body erect, her fluttering hands eloquent in gesture. As always, she had that invaluable gift of imbuing an audience with a feeling if not with an idea.

Apparently Mrs. Eddy had finally learned to admit, in the privacy of her own conscience, certain of her limitations. Thus she began very soon even to drop some of her ungrammatical habits of speech, to discard the rustic graces which she had affected all these years, to study the demeanor of those around her and adapt it to her own needs. For a woman of her years this adaptation was in itself an admirable achievement. She seemed to acquire a wholly new appreciation of grammar, and even submitted her various writings, press letters and pam-

phlets to some of her students for editing. Her letters of
this period are better phrased, punctuated and penned than those
written twenty years previously. Most important, she adopted
the habit of seeing visitors and of showing herself publicly
only when she felt at her best. Even in her college she managed to build up a certain formal barrier between herself and
her students, seeing them only at certain hours and occasionally declining to receive them at all.

She dropped the habit of trying to preach at Hawthorne
Hall every Sunday, appearing only on those occasions when
she felt the sweep of that emotional exaltation which she desired to induce in her audience. Sometimes when she was
scheduled to speak she would delegate a student to talk for
her, making this decision at the last minute. Again, when some
student was named as substitute she would decide at the elev-
enth hour to give the lecture herself, and rush to the hall at
the last minute after all arrangements had been made to hold
the meeting without her.

It was at a meeting in a fashionable home on Monument Hill
in Charlestown that she first met Augusta Stetson, in 1884.
Mrs. Stetson was then a woman of about forty, medium in
height; well formed, with the large bust so esteemed in fashion
plates of the period; eyes widely set in a rather mobile face;
small nostrils above a generous, determined mouth. She was
destined to become a figure whose influence in Mrs. Eddy's
world was second only to that of Mrs. Eddy herself.

She had been born of old Puritan stock in Waldoboro,
Maine, about 1842. In after life she shrouded her past in mystery, refused to tell her age, and the town records were eventually burned. She grew up as one of five children in a house
which her father, Peabody Simmons, carpenter, built with his
own hands. When the family moved to another Maine town,
Damariscotta, Augusta was organist there in the Methodist
church and a singer in the choir. At twenty-four she married
a shipbuilder, Frederick Stetson, who was partially an invalid
as a result of imprisonment in Libby Prison during the Civil
War. As his wife she went to England where he secured employment with a British shipbuilding firm. Later he was sent
to Bombay, and here she had an opportunity to delve into

a subject in which she had an instinctive interest—the oriental philosophies. In these philosophies affirmation and denial play an important rôle, and a pantheistic God is postulated—a God who is the Universe, whose mind is All, and of whose mind matter, like force, is but one manifestation or expression in the midst of many.

Mrs. Stetson at the time she met Mrs. Eddy was studying to be an elocutionist under Professor Blish; elocution in the eighties was as popular an attraction indoors as bicycling was on open roads. Unlike the usual mystic immured in a shadowy life of negation, she was a dynamic individual, with the same rare gift of pouring a sort of liquid emotion out over those who listened to her talk which Mrs. Eddy in her better moments also shared. Mrs. Eddy, always with an eye out for new pupils, noted the attractive Mrs. Stetson seated in the fashionable audience, finished her lecture, went up stairs for her wraps. She saw Mrs. Stetson standing at the foot of the stairs when she came down to the door. Reaching into her bag, Mrs. Eddy drew out a card, and handed it to the stranger with her best smile. "Will you come to see me?" she asked.

Mrs. Stetson did not give an affirmative answer, but she did give her name and address at Mrs. Eddy's request. Mrs. Eddy duly noted it—she had learned the value of new addresses. Three or four months later Mrs. Stetson got the usual note from Mrs. Eddy, again inviting her to call. And Mrs. Stetson went.

During the visit the conversation was so steered that Mrs. Stetson invited Mrs. Eddy to talk at the home of her parents, with whom she resided. This was the beginning of an association of a unique kind. In late autumn Mrs. Stetson received another note from Mrs. Eddy, inviting her to join a class in the Massachusetts Metaphysical College. Mrs. Stetson demurred. She had recently spent a year and a half and a good deal of money in preparing herself to become a public reader and lecturer, and she felt that it would be much wiser to continue in a field in which she was greatly interested than pause for a course in a teaching that had not particularly impressed her.

It was then that Mrs. Eddy offered to give Mrs. Stetson the

$300 course as a compliment. Perhaps Mrs. Eddy had already sensed some of the possibilities in Augusta Stetson. As it happened, even Mrs. Stetson's lessons in elocution were to serve her admirably. She was destined to become the founder of the largest and wealthiest church in Mrs. Eddy's entire organization, and to put on the front pages of the metropolitan press one of the most amazing stories written in a modern age.

From the first Mrs. Stetson proved one of the most valuable additions to the Eddy entourage. At the close of her twelfth lesson she immediately started into healing work. Going back to Maine, her native state, she had several experiences which seem to have established her self-confidence, and soon she had a great number of patients seeking her out in the rural districts between Skowhegan and Portland. Mrs. Eddy's restrictions against lectures by her students had not yet been handed down, and Mrs. Stetson lectured on Christian Science whenever the opportunity offered. As published later in *The Christian Science Journal,*[1] some of these cures included:

Miss F . . . B . . . of Cambridgeport, cured in two treatments, of painful menstruation from which she had suffered intensely for four years. Mrs. W . . . D . . . of Portland, Me., cured of two cancers in one breast, and a tumor in the other; was treated one week. She rejoices from deliverance from the operation the specialists had advised. . . . Miss E . . . B . . . of Camden, Maine, had diphtheric throat, high fever, and pain in back and neck throat filled with white patches, badly swollen. One treatment was given at night. In the morning she was perfectly well. Miss H . . . E . . . L . . . of Skowhegan, Maine, was pronounced incurable, and had been unable to stand or walk for six months, from spinal trouble. After one treatment, she walked several times across the room, and after the third was perfectly well. . . .

The founding of *The Christian Science Journal* was nothing less than a stroke of genius. It was another approach to the publicity which was now serving Mrs. Eddy so well. *The Journal of Christian Science,* afterward called *The Christian Science Journal,* appeared first on April 14, 1883, an eight-page paper issued every other month. Small as it was, it was to prove one of the most effective allies Mrs. Eddy acquired in her

[1] Vol. III, page 79.

march to renown. It was small enough and cheap enough to enable her to send out a number of free copies of every issue; with an unerring business instinct she directed them out into far-away places and small towns where life was drab and a new emotional interest of any sort met an eager response. Mrs. Eddy's theology offered this emotional appeal, with the promise of release through its doctrines from all the ills flesh is heir to. In *The Journal* Mrs. Eddy regularly published, from the start, lists of cures that her Science had accomplished. Such lists read much like the testimonials in the old medical almanacs; there was absolutely no human ill which has a name that was not at some time or other listed in the cure column. Such publicity was irresistible. It struck sparks wherever it landed.

Arthur Buswell was the first associate editor of the paper. Mrs. Eddy herself retained the title of Editor, also writing extensively. Buswell did not last long. He had indeed been suspected of malicious animal magnetism for some time. On one occasion the Rev. Dr. Andrew P. Peabody of Cambridge had been engaged to preach before the Christian Science Congregation at Hawthorne Hall. Mrs. Eddy had assigned Calvin Frye to introduce the guest speaker to the audience. When the time came, however, the Reverend Doctor ascended the platform alone without an introduction. Several days passed thereafter, no comment being made. Then, late one night, Frye tiptoed up the stairs and knocked on Mr. Buswell's door, saying that he was wanted downstairs in the parlor. Mr. Buswell hastily got out of bed, dressed, and descended; Mrs. Eddy and a number of her students were sitting silently around the room. Mr. Buswell went in and joined the circle. All was silent. Then Frye arose.

"Mr. Buswell," he said very formally, "I charge you with having worked upon my mind last Sunday, so that I could not introduce the speaker."[1]

Mr. Buswell defended himself. Mrs. Eddy listened intently. Eventually everyone silently went off to bed.

But Mr. Buswell's place in the camp was shortly empty.

Mrs. Emma Hopkins became the associate editor of *The*

[1] Vd. Georgine Milmine, *Life of Mary Baker G. Eddy*, page 303.

Journal after he departed. This was the Mrs. Hopkins who later became widely known in Connecticut for her leadership in the New Thought movement. Her name first appeared in *The Journal* in February of 1884. She lasted just about a year. At the end of that time she and Mrs. Mary H. Plunkett entered into a practising partnership, deserted Mrs. Eddy, and put out a paper called *The International Magazine of Christian Science*. This publication, which escaped the infringement of copyright and consequently Mrs. Eddy's righteous wrath, caused Mrs. Eddy much annoyance for a number of years.

Thereafter a succession of associate editors came upon the scene, and one by one they became apostates to Mrs. Eddy's cause: Mrs. Sarah Crosse; the Rev. Frank Mason; William G. Nixon. The incidental defections among the converts to Mrs. Eddy's cause always maintained an extraordinarily high ratio. Now, however, for the first time in her career, Mrs. Eddy was establishing the machinery by which she could make converts faster than she was losing them. There are two ways to build up either a population or a congregation—increase the birth rate or lower the death rate. The recipe on which Mrs. Eddy finally stumbled achieved the former.

All in all, the years from 1882 to 1885 saw rapid advancement of her cause. Mrs. Eddy herself was almost constantly on the watch and in the saddle. Writing, editing, preaching, teaching, consumed practically all of her time. She had little recreation, and gave no time whatever to social intercourse; occasionally she indulged in a drive. She was never heard to discuss anything but her religion or her business with any one, either student or stranger. When the conversation veered to any other topic she was absent-minded. She read little beside the articles her own students wrote, the local newspapers, and the New York *Ledger,* which she had grown accustomed to when a young woman. In her more secular days she had rather liked such flowery novels as those of Mrs. E. D. E. N. Southworth, but recreational reading of this character was now banned from her life and she did not permit it for her students. Strangely enough, she took great and constant pleasure in reading from *Science and Health.* She never grew tired of picking up her own volume and industriously perusing its pages.

Her grip over her students constantly tightened. She ruled them with a power that was absolute. As early students left her and went back to their home towns, they took patients and created new prospects for Mrs. Eddy's classes. *The Journal* was also doing a most valuable missionary work. In addition, the very name of her college was an ever active benediction. Boston culture and learning carried a high rating in every town and hamlet west of the Adirondacks. A degree of "Doctor" from the Massachusetts Metaphysical College at Boston was something that had more than a religious sanctity to recommend it. It not only bestowed on its possessor a title of distinction; it could be gained in a comparatively short term of weeks; the remarkable healing powers that were supposed to go with the degree gave its owner a new asset with which to make a living; and to many the price did not seem prohibitive considering the advantages it secured.

In consequence students now began to arrive in greater numbers. Prosperity was in the ascendancy. Mrs. Eddy's house gained something besides oil-cloth on the floors and blank shades at the windows. An impressionable woman reporter for the *Ohio Leader*—the doctrine was rapidly stirring curiosity wherever copies of *The Journal* or wandering students wended their way—described the atmosphere there as follows, in an article dated July 2, 1885:

Accordingly at eight o'clock on that evening I rang the bell of the large and handsome residence on Columbus Avenue near West Chester Park, known as the Metaphysical College. A maid ushered me into a daintily furnished reception room where pictures and bric-a-brac indicated refinement of taste. Presently Mrs. Eddy came in and greeted me with a manner that, while cordial and graceful, was also something more, and had in it an indefinable element of harmony; and a peace that was not mere repose, but more like exaltation. It was subtle and indefinable, however, and I did not think of it especially at the time, although I felt it. The conversation touched lightly on current topics and finally recurred to the subject of metaphysics. . . .

Publicity of that nature was the sort that corporations to-day are willing to pay hundreds of thousands of dollars for every year. It went into homes in which the local newspapers possibly provided the only topic of conversation at the dinner table. The reporter went on to tell how she felt after the interview:

I remembered afterwards how extremely tired I was as I walked wearily and languidly up the steps to Mrs. Eddy's door. I came away, as a little child friend of mine says, "skipping". I was at least a mile from my hotel and I walked home feeling as though I were treading on air. My sleep that night was the rest of Elysium.

Very probably it all happened. And undoubtedly the writer found the very sort of good personal experience story that she was seeking for her news article.

Mrs. Eddy by this time had taken another important step. She was holding Thursday evening meetings in her house—meetings that had a slight social flair along with their religious atmosphere. Sliding doors connected all her first floor rooms; and she could throw these open to accommodate a fairly sizable gathering. It became rather the fashion in Boston to go down and take a look at her, and the question "Have you met Mrs. Eddy?" made further valuable advertising. Mrs. Frances Hodgson Burnett made a call. Bronson Alcott, always the dilettante, dropped in when he was in town; and his daughter Louisa followed him. Louisa as a literary light spread the news among her many acquaintances and others went. Bronson, who had been heard to say of *Science and Health* that "only a fool or a woman could have written it," wrote Mrs. Eddy a testimonial that was duly printed in *The Journal:*

The profound truths which you announce, sustained by facts of the immortal life, give to your work the seal of inspiration—reaffirm in modern phrase the Christian revelations. In times like these, so sunk in sensualism, I hail with joy your voice, speaking an assured word for God and immortality, and my joy is heightened that these words are of woman's divinings.

Mrs. Eddy, who had always possessed a penchant for a literary atmosphere, revelled in such visits, and, whenever she could, made them the occasion for further publicity. When Louisa Alcott wrote an article for *The Woman's Journal,* telling about Mrs. Eddy's doctrine in a manner that indicated no great kinship with the views of her transcendentalist father, Mrs. Eddy promptly replied in *The Christian Science Journal.* Other literary material failing, Mrs. Eddy could always take pen in hand and talk about literary figures; George Eliot and Rose Elizabeth Cleveland received praise in *The Journal's* columns impartially.

During all this steady upward rise in her fortunes, with new students coming in and new issues of *The Journal* always going out, Mrs. Eddy continued to have steady recurrences of her old attacks and to wage persistent war on malicious animal magnetism. The death of Mr. Eddy had made malicious animal magnetism a very real thing to every student in Mrs. Eddy's house, and whenever she had a nocturnal illness the whole household knew that the Fiend was again at hand.

It was one of the principal duties of the students residing in the house to surround Mrs. Eddy with mental defense against these attacks. All of her students, as has been said, were subject to whatever discipline she cared to impose upon them. It was, for instance, not uncommon for Mrs. Eddy to send telegrams to students who had departed from Boston instructing them to report to her at the college immediately. No explanations of the order would be given. When the students arrived, Mrs. Eddy would say that she had merely been testing their loyalty, and experimenting to see how readily they would come in the event of emergency. Such fire drills seemed to give her a tremendous amount of satisfaction and pleasure. She particularly demanded that on the Fourth of July no student should leave Boston, but should remain in readiness for her call. It was on the Fourth, she explained, that "mortal mind was in ebullition," meaning that animal magnetism was then roaming abroad more generally.

Mrs. Eddy's racking physical attacks, for which the heaviest defense against animal magnetism had to be reared, occurred usually around midnight, and sometimes later. At these times

Mr. Frye was invaluable. Mrs. Eddy would call him to do his duty; he would hastily arise, get into his clothes, and run down the halls knocking on the doors of the various resident students. They knew their cue, just as does the ambulance corps catching forty winks in time of war. Rolling out of bed, jumping into their waiting garments, they rushed to the post.

Meanwhile Mr. Frye would pull on his coat and go out to arouse the other students who were living in houses in the neighborhood. One by one they would straggle in, sleepily trying to hold their eyes open. Talking in low, mysterious tones, they would wait until called one by one into Mrs. Eddy's bedchamber.

Sometimes she would be sitting up in bed distraught, wringing her hands, her hair all tangled, her cheeks feverish, her lips muttering unintelligible phrases. Again she would be in a comatose condition, lying wholly senseless for several hours. Each student would go in alone, sit by the bed and treat her silently for some twenty minutes, then depart by another door than that by which he entered. Thereupon the redoubtable Frye would admit another warrior against M. A. M. to take the defense.

On at least one occasion in this period when Mrs. Eddy had a raging toothache, metaphysical treatment was abandoned and several of her students scoured Tremont Street in the middle of the night, trying to find an obliging dentist.[1]

Animal magnetism had by this time become with Mrs. Eddy an explanation for anything which went awry in the routine of her life. If the water pipes froze, or one of the best dinner plates dropped, or a letter went astray in the mails, or the wash boiler leaked, it was M. A. M. that was once again working its evil spell. Since none of her own students knew Mrs. Eddy's real case history, animal magnetism was readily accepted by most of them as being the explanation of her strange attacks, as well as any ailments of their own that got the better of them. When influenza spread through Boston and some of her students disturbed the peace of the classroom with their

[1]Related by Georgine Milmine, *Life of Mary Baker G. Eddy*, page 302.

sneezes, Mrs. Eddy announced that Spofford and Kennedy were up to their old tricks. These two students never completely left her consciousness.

Adverse treatment against M. A. M. had now become a system and was regularly a part of the college routine. In later years Mrs. Eddy vigorously denied, and at least once in her old age rather piteously denied, ever trying to work ill to any one. Testimony regarding what went on at these defense sessions rather conflicts. A regular society called the "Private meeting," and usually referred to as "P. M." was formed to gather in Mrs. Eddy's parlor and to "take up the enemy" in thought. The students sat with their eyes closed, and their thoughts concentrated on the personal enemy to be influenced.

Stories that gained general circulation about the weird goings-on at these sessions at last became fairly general, and caused much criticism. In 1888 Mrs. Eddy took occasion in *The Christian Science Journal* to deny some of the stories, admitting that she did organize "a secret society known as the P. M.," but insisting that its "workings" were not " 'terrible and too shocking to relate.' "[1]

It was at this time that Mrs. Stetson gained her training in Christian Science methods under Mrs. Eddy's direct tutelage. Mrs. Stetson in many ways was the emotional counterpart of Mary Baker Eddy, and lacking, similarly, in the well-balanced intellectual fly-wheel which makes for critical discernment. She was one of the few students close to Mrs. Eddy in those days who remained loyal after attaining leadership in wider circles than those bordering on Columbus Avenue.

As Mrs. Stetson went into new horizons she took the strange doctrines of malicious animal magnetism with her. Much of this teaching was carefully expurgated from Mrs. Eddy's published writings as time went on. As Mrs. Eddy abandoned personal teaching and slowly built up a barrier between herself and the outside world, she ceased to scatter her darker doctrines abroad with such a lavish hand—doctrines that were

---

[1] Vd. *Miscellaneous Writings*, page 350, where this statement, with revisions, still appears as a report from *The Journal* of September, 1888.

born in the depths of a hideous physical and mental suffering.

But Augusta Stetson believed and taught what Mrs. Eddy had personally taught her students at the house in Columbus Avenue. And thereby hangs the strange story of a cataclysm that in later years shook Mrs. Eddy's empire to its foundations, and made the ruler herself tremble in aged fear.

XIV

As Mrs. Eddy's publicity sense developed, she made a point of always insisting that as many ministers as possible be invited to attend any gathering which she addressed. Once in Boston, in the days when she was being taken up by hostesses who wished to present this new curiosity to their friends, she agreed to speak one afternoon at the home of Mrs. James Sanborn, whose husband was associated with the Boston firm of Chase & Sanborn. Mrs. Eddy had stipulated, as usual, that Mrs. Sanborn should have ministers present.

In this procedure Mrs. Eddy seems to have desired to accomplish two things. The presence of ministers to hear her lent an impress of authority and dignity to the occasion, an authentic flavor to the atmosphere, which she hardly could have created by her own presence no matter what her eloquence. Second, any possible disagreement of these ministers with her doctrine offered an excellent possibility for advertisement. Nothing is more effective for the arousing of public interest than controversy and disagreement. One of Mrs. Eddy's happiest days was the first Sunday that a Boston minister rose in his pulpit to denounce her.

When Mrs. Eddy arrived to lecture at the home of Mrs. Sanborn, she went upstairs as usual to remove her wraps, and then descended to the drawing rooms where a large crowd was gathered. She looked around her, scanning the men and women. She saw no ministers, and turned to Mrs. Sanborn. "Where are the clergy?" she asked.

Mrs. Sanborn explained that no ministers had been able to come.

Mrs. Eddy nodded her head. "Good afternoon," she said abruptly, went out in the hall, and climbed the stairs. When she came down she had her wraps on, and she left the house without another word.

There were even occasions when an audience had been assembled in which the ministers were sprinkled liberally, on which Mrs. Eddy again failed at the last moment to speak. She had now reached the point where she never hesitated, if she decided an hour or two before the scheduled lecture that she did not feel at her best, to refuse to appear. In such emergencies she would expect a student to conduct the proceedings. On one occasion she arranged with Augusta Stetson to procure a hall in Reading, Massachusetts, where Mrs. Stetson had been healing and teaching. The Congregational Church granted its auditorium for Mrs. Eddy's scheduled lecture, and when the evening came four ministers were sitting in special chairs at the foot of the platform. Mrs. Stetson was herself an able promotion expert, and she had drawn to the scene most of the representative citizens of the town.

The hour struck, and there was no Mrs. Eddy. Mrs. Stetson was frantic. She had already met three afternoon trains to no avail. Until the last minute she hoped for some miracle that would show Mrs. Eddy sitting serenely on the platform as the auditorium doors were closed. This did not happen, and Mrs. Stetson herself walked into the pulpit, apologized for Mrs. Eddy's absence, and talked for an hour and a half. It was her first effort to lecture without notes; but Augusta Stetson was a woman of great reserve force and infinite resources. She talked bravely and eloquently, and the next day returned to Boston to say she thought it most unkind that Mrs. Eddy should have put her in such a position.

Mrs. Eddy by this time had recovered from her bad half-hour of the day before, and was quite self-contained and smiling. Even when Mrs. Stetson asked her why she had not come to Reading she remained unruffled. "I was there," she insisted gravely. And then, as if to prove she had been spiritually present to lend Mrs. Stetson her moral support, she added, "You stood, Augusta. You stood, you did not run!"

And so there arose among some of Mrs. Eddy's students the tradition that she could be in many places at one time, and that in her omnipresence she could see all, understand all. Because she now allowed these students only to see her at her best, she appeared to them a wholly different woman than her neighbors had known in the old Lynn days. She was stern, but as God was stern; she was exacting, but so was Divine Justice. And when she arose to talk about this subject that had now become not merely an obsession but her entire existence, there were times indeed when she seemed transfixed—her voice throbbing with emotion, her eyes glistening, her muscles tense with the thrill that comes to every great actress when she knows instinctively that her audience has momentarily lost itself utterly in the eloquent words of her own soul.

For Mary Baker Eddy believed her doctrine with a belief that burned like fire. And there were times when her belief so consumed her that she was like a disembodied being. Under the adulation of her students she herself evinced a real change. Growing up around her was a tradition she desired to live up to. There was being established in her students' minds an ideal of her which she was not, but which she hungrily desired to be. And so, in her worse moments, she secluded herself in her room; and her students came to know that at this time she was communing with her God, and became even more hushed and worshipful. And when she again came down the stairs, to beam upon them radiance and a sense of well-being, none knew about those terrible moments she had spent in the fight against herself and her physical torture.

When, in the middle of the night, the alarm was called and the students gathered at her bedside to see a Mrs. Eddy who was utterly unknown, who writhed and twisted like a tortured victim of the Inquisition, it was not difficult for them to believe that in this state she was indeed possessed; that she was overcome with horrors that were not her own; that she was suffering under the lashes of others. She was taking on herself, as she said, the sins and illnesses of her students; she was fighting with the Fiend that Spofford and Kennedy and Arens were directing toward that peaceful household of God.

And so, like a mist slowly rising from the water, a tradition grew, expanded, gradually diffused itself until it completely enveloped all that it touched.

It was not difficult to believe that there was indeed something mysterious in this woman that set her apart, that rendered her unique. The name of Mrs. Eddy seemed commonplace for a woman who spoke so familiarly of God. The name of Mother seemed to have a little more of holiness. Sometimes they called her simply "Teacher"; Mrs. Eddy had a personal preference for the "Mother" title.

Under the influence of such suggestion around her—Mrs. Eddy was thoroughly susceptible—she was now certain of the divinity of her mission; and there were even times when she began to wonder about the divinity of herself. In the first issue of *The Journal* in 1883 the prospectus for the paper said:

While we entertain decided views as to the best method for elevating the race physically, morally, and spiritually, and shall express these views as duty demands, we shall claim no especial gifts from our divine origin. . . .

The use of the phrase, "our divine origin," leaves the reader wondering—as often, in her writings—what she really meant; but it indicates the presence of a thought in her mind even then. Two years later, in November, 1885, the idea had progressed so far that *The Journal* exuberantly exclaimed:

What a triumphant career is this for a woman! Can it be anything less than the "tabernacle of God with men"—the fulfillment of the vision of the lonely seer on the Isle of Patmos—the "wonder in heaven", delivering the child which shall rule all nations? How dare we say to the contrary, that she is God-sent to the world, as much as any character of Sacred Writ?

The "child" which is mentioned here came to be identified as *Science and Health*. Just as Jesus was the traditional offspring of Mary's communion with God, so did Mrs. Eddy's book come to be regarded in her circle of enthusiasts as a product of her own communings. This idea was elaborated in unmistakable terms in an article called "Immaculate Conception"[1] in *The Journal* of November, 1888:

[1] Incidentally, such a use of "immaculate" conception, to imply a virginal birth, is a theological *faux pas*. "Immaculate," as applied to a conception, is not properly a synonym for parthenogenesis, and in Christian theology does not relate to the Virgin's conception without intervention of a male. The term implies, instead, a birth free from the original sin of Adam—the Adam through whose fall men "sinnéd all," and so are tainted from the moment they issue from the womb until such sin is washed away in baptism. Christ's conception was immaculate because he was born free of original sin, and not necessarily because he was born of a Virgin.

Let us come in thought to another day, a day when woman shall commune with God, the eternal Principle and only Creator, and bring forth the spiritual idea. And what of *her* child? Man is spiritual, man is mental. Woman was the first in this day to recognize this and the other facts it includes. As a result of her communion we have Christian Science.

You may ask why this child did not come in human form, as did the child of old. Because that was not necessary. . . . As this age is more mental than former ages, so the appearance of the idea of Truth is more mental.

The idea of God as a feminine as well as masculine entity, combining the best features of both, had been familiar to Mrs. Eddy since her girlhood days, when Shaker teachings were the subject of wide neighborhood gossip. However much of these she consciously remembered, the historian can have no doubt but that they made a marked indent on her impressionable childish mind, and that as she heard some of Quimby's theories she indeed felt that many of them were a reiteration of ideas that had been slumbering in her mind from girlhood. Even Quimby's conviction that he took on himself the ailments of his patients, or that he could treat patients by mental processes from afar, was a concept familiar in connection with the Shakeress Ann Lee.[1]

And so Mrs. Eddy came to quote about herself the same Scriptural reference concerning the Woman of the Apocalypse that Ann Lee's followers had read as a prophecy of their own leader:

And there appeared a great wonder in heaven; a woman clothed with the sun, and the moon under her feet, and upon her head a crown of twelve stars. . . .

The child which this woman bore came to be regarded as Christian Science. The more she thought about this verse, the more did Mrs. Eddy come to regard it as a direct reference to her own teachings, and so she eventually included it in *Science and Health*. There is now a chapter there called The Apocalypse, in which the author quotes significantly from Revela-

---

[1]Mrs. Eddy eventually found Scriptural passages which she quoted to prove that Jesus, like herself, suffered because of the doings of others. Thus she says, on page 38 of *Science and Health*, that "his sufferings were the fruits of other people's sins, not of his own."

tion. Mrs. Eddy used guarded interpretations, preferring to let readers draw their own conclusions. But no discerning and loyal student could fail to sense the significance of the scriptural lines:

And she being with child cried, travailing in birth, and pained to be delivered.

What could be a more obvious reference to the days when she wandered from house to house, and was even set out in a night of rain?

. . . And the dragon stood before the woman which was ready to be delivered, for to devour her child as soon as it was born.

What more certain than that the dragon stood for malicious animal magnetism, which was always seeking to devour her work?

And the woman fled into the wilderness, where she hath a place prepared of God. . . .

It was not difficult for Mrs. Eddy, as she read that verse in Revelation, to remember her flight from Lynn.

And she brought forth a man child, who was to rule all nations with a rod of iron: and her child was caught up unto God, and to His throne. . . .

A little study of the Scriptures made it possible for Mrs. Eddy to find there an absolutely irrefutable prophecy of all the major events in the development of her life and her Science. Her more enthusiastic followers believed this without qualification. In a sermon which *The Journal* published after it had been delivered in Chicago by the Reverend George B. Day, "M. A., C. S. B.," it was claimed:

We are witnessing the transfer of the gospel from male to female trust. . . . Eighteen hundred years ago Paul declared that man was the head of the woman; but now, in "Science and Health," it is asserted that "woman is the highest form of man."

The Reverend Mr. Day was no more enthusiastic than

many of Mrs. Eddy's other students. Mrs. Eddy's book shared
in the same divine aura which was now surrounding herself.
Answering a query concerning the status of this book the editor of *The Journal* declared:

> Would it not be too material a view to speak of "Science and Health"
> being *based* upon any edition of the Bible? . . . The Chosen One, al-
> ways with God in the Mount, speaks face to face. In other words, "Sci-
> ence and Health" is a first hand revelation. . . .

Mrs. Eddy was never entirely sure of her own mind as to
her status. She often wavered. Under the rain of caustic criticism that eventually descended upon her from profane quarters she occasionally would qualify some of her previous
claims. But not to any great or permanent extent. She sensed
instinctively that to establish her Science as a divine revelation
would render it immune from really effective human attack,
and likewise make it irresistible to many followers. And so she
came to distinguish between her own Science and all other
modes of thought by the simple claim:

> "Human systems of philosophy and religion are departures from
> Christian Science."[1]

The obvious inference is of course that her Science was not
to be compared with any mere man-made doctrine. And occasionally she put it on a plane even above the Bible. Thus she
could write:

> Even the Scriptures gave no direct interpretation of the scientific
> basis for demonstrating the Spiritual Principle of healing, until our
> heavenly Father saw fit, through the Key to the Scriptures in Science and
> Health, to unlock this "mystery of godliness."[2]

As to her own rôle in the picture, even though her followers took their cue from this delusion of grandeur that was
sweeping over her, and themselves came to proclaim her as a
sort of female Christ, she was never wholly certain. She could
only say:

[1] *Retrospection and Introspection*, page 57.
[2] *Ibid.*, page 37.

No person can take the individual place of the Virgin Mary. No person can compass or fulfill the individual mission of Jesus of Nazareth. No person can take the place of the author of *Science and Health,* the Discoverer and Founder of Christian Science. Each individual must fill his own niche in time and eternity.[1]

At least in that statement Mrs. Eddy had the satisfaction of putting herself on a par with the Virgin Mary and Jesus in reserving for herself an individual niche beside them. Her *Journal,* as it wound its way through the mails every other month, was constantly developing the idea that there was in her a divine power above that of ordinary men. Thus, in an unsigned editorial:

To day truth has come through the person of a New England girl. . . . From the cradle she gave indications of a divine mission and power which caused *her* mother to "ponder them in her heart."

Under the force of such claims the circulation of *The Journal* increased constantly. There are always people who want to believe in miracles and wonder-workers. The thought of a mysterious Mrs. Eddy who could indulge in miraculous relations with God brought an unknown thrill of titillation into their care-worn lives.

In addition, much of the philosophy contained in *The Journal*—that much which its readers could understand—contained ideas of broad and substantial human appeal. To many readers in that day it came as a releasing revelation that God was not a long-bearded human with stern lips and a glassy stare, as portrayed in the local church windows, not a being thundering wrath and hell-fire and damnation and jealousy, but rather a principle, a force—a serene, tranquil entity which every man might discover for himself in his own heart. This idea was not new with Mrs. Eddy; nor was it new when Quimby found it. It goes back into human history to the forgotten beginnings of all idealistic philosophy. But to many people struggling with fear and poverty and disease in the joyless rounds of their drab lives, such a concept was a tremendous discovery. A concept of God as Power, as Love, as En-

[1] *Retrospection and Introspection,* page 70.

ergy, as Health, as Peace, a force utterly impersonal until it was expressed through the individual, when it became his own highly personalized expression of the God Mind—such a thought of God was a release into an entirely new realm of life.

Those reared in the orthodox theology of the nineteenth century had been brought up in fear and trembling before a God whose main duty and delight was the chastisement of a wicked mankind for its sins, and whose worship was properly carried on only by denying oneself every natural human joy and pleasure. A release from such a God was for many people a greater boon than release from disease. For not even a life of disease is as horrible as a life of fear. Mrs. Eddy, who lived a slave to fear until she died, was thus the strange instrument by which a new concept of God was spread abroad in which Fear was utterly abolished.

Strangely enough, Mrs. Eddy in her calmer moments was herself entirely aware of the deleterious effects of fear, and went so far as to assert without qualification that it lies at the foundation of all disease. Thus she wrote in *Science and Health:* "Fear is the fountain of sickness. . . . Fear, which is an element of all disease, must be cast out to readjust the balance for God."[1] And again: "Always begin your treatment by allaying the fear of patients. Silently reassure them as to their exemption from disease and danger."[2] Still again she said: "To succeed in healing, you must conquer your own fears as well as those of your patients, and rise into higher and holier consciousness."[3]

For this knowledge, wholly familiar to the modern psychologist, of the damage which fear may wreak in the human mind and body, Mrs. Eddy undoubtedly had Quimby again to thank.[4] Unfortunately for herself, however—regardless of her intellectual understanding of the unhappy effects which fear creates in humanity—Mrs. Eddy was unable to eliminate her own emotional maladjustments. It was from her own bot-

---

[1]Page 391.   [2]Page 411.   [3]Page 419.

[4]Vd. *The Quimby Manuscripts*, page 288: "*Where there is no fear there is no torment. Fear is error, Wisdom casts out fear, for it knows no fear.*" Italics are Quimby's.

tomless wells of fear that her whole horrible doctrine concerning M. A. M. emerged and expanded like the evil jinn of Aladdin's lamp. Her intellectual understanding of Quimby's God of Love never served thereafter to destroy the jinn; she could only bottle him up again for brief intervals. There came times, indeed, when she could write: "Never fear the mental practitioner, the mental assassin, who, in attempting to rule mankind, tramples upon the divine Principle of metaphysics, for God is the only power."[1] Such moments of intellectual logic, however, never served to deliver Mrs. Eddy from the terrors to which she became more and more enslaved.

Few people other than those who lived in personal reach of Mrs. Eddy's obsessions ever took her M. A. M. preachments seriously. Indeed, in a world where God was All and God was Love, the ascription of any reality to a devilish force such as M. A. M. was for most logical minds utterly impossible. Thus it was natural that Mrs. Eddy's textual references to such a factor in the world's work and in human lives did not make any great impression on the minds of her readers in the face of this other overwhelming idea that came to them like a refreshing wind in a desert.

To the extent that she was an agent in publicizing a greater and loftier conception of God it may be said that Mrs. Eddy rendered a magnificent human service; and this service is no less because of the fact that the idea of God as Principle was not new with Mrs. Eddy.

This concept of God is indeed pantheistic in its connotations; and despite the fact that Mrs. Eddy's denial of matter put her at permanent odds with pantheism, which she attacked at every possible opportunity, it was a concept of great beauty and power. It does not matter that Mrs. Eddy did not invent it, that she did not fully understand it, and that she lived out her own days with a God imaged through terror. Nor does it matter that Greek philosophers and Egyptian priests had

---

[1] *Science and Health*, page 419. Vd. also page 445: "The teacher must thoroughly fit his students . . . to guard against the attacks of the would-be *mental assassin*, who attempts to kill morally and physically. No hypothesis as to the existence of another power should interpose a doubt or fear to hinder the demonstration of Christian Science."

reached this concept long, long before her day, and that modern philosophers and scientists alike were glimpsing the same idea at the very time Mrs. Eddy was deriving it from Quimbyism. One may accord her honor in that she merely promoted and gained popular acceptance for a concept that previously had been apparently too erudite and scholastic for the mass mind. It was no mean achievement to make men behold a God of Love in a day when most churchmen were still slaves to a God made out of their fathers' subconscious horrors. It was surely no less an achievement for a woman who was constitutionally unable to grasp the full connotations of her preachments.

The idea that God dwells in all men, inspiring them alike with his Spirit, passed from Mrs. Eddy's philosophy into her theology in such a way that it soon became very natural for her to sense a special divinity of her own. The God that dwelt in Jesus, in the Eddy theology, was the Christ. Christ, that is, is God in man. In Jesus the Christ was manifest to a complete and perfect degree; in other men to a lesser degree.[1] So far as Mrs. Eddy felt herself to manifest more of the Christ than other men, she believed herself more divine than others. The extent of her conviction of her divinity depended merely on the extent to which she could believe that she manifested the Christ mind or consciousness.

It was natural that as her power expanded and the worship of her impressionable personal following grew, her suggestible mind was convinced that she manifested divinity in a unique degree.

The extraordinary results attending her visit to Chicago in 1888 did much to establish this conviction.

[1]This idea was derived straight from Quimby. The quotations that could be marshalled are almost innumerable, since the theme runs throughout his manuscripts. Vd.: *The Quimby Manuscripts*, page 201: "I will try to . . . show that [the name] 'Christ' never was intended to be applied to Jesus as a man, but to a Truth superior to the natural man." Again, page 244: "Jesus was the oracle and Christ the wisdom shown through this man." And finally, page 303: "*The Christ is the God in us all.* Do you deny that you have a particle of God in you?"
Italics are Quimby's.
For direct comparison of idea the casual reader may turn to page 333 of *Science and Health:* "Jesus was a human name. . . . Christ expresses God's spiritual, eternal nature." And on page 332: "Jesus demonstrated Christ."

She had been in Chicago previously, in 1884. Students who had gone there to practise healing, and copies of *The Journal* which reached the hands of local readers, had created a tremendous stir of curiosity about the mysterious Mrs. Eddy, and a demand arose that she come in person and establish a centre of teaching there.

Mrs. Eddy at the time felt that she had her hands full in Boston. Her correspondence was growing to enormous proportions; her classes were expanding constantly; she was preaching on Sundays and lecturing on Thursdays and meanwhile writing extensively on any and every subject that came into her mind. What she most enjoyed was the opportunity to write replies for newspaper publication to the attacks which the clergy were making on her with increasing frequency. Every bomb was an advertisement for her battle, and she flung these grenades back promptly and with enthusiasm. When the newspapers would not give her space, she could always use her *Journal*.

Such were her occupations when she tried to get Mrs. Choate to go to Chicago for her in 1884. Mrs. Choate declined. She had a large and lucrative practice of her own in Boston, had a home established for her family there, and saw no reason why she should pull up stakes to repair to Chicago, which at that time was regarded by well-bred Bostonians as an outpost in the wilderness.

Mrs. Eddy demanded from her students instant and unquestioning obedience regardless of their wishes or convenience, and from this day arose a coolness between her and Mrs. Choate which soon ended in a permanent rupture. Meanwhile Mrs. Eddy decided that she would make the trip herself. She took the invaluable Frye and Mrs. Sarah Crosse, went to Chicago for a month, and taught in the two front parlors of a house on the west side. The results of the trip were most successful. The classes were crowded to capacity for the entire period, and immediately the movement in the west gathered swift momentum. These new students went out all over the United States and extended Mrs. Eddy's teachings. Before many months had passed the California Metaphysical Institute had been founded at San José, California; the Illinois Christian Science Institute was incorporated at Chicago; and by 1888 thirty so-called "academies" were in existence.

Mrs. Eddy by this time had seen a vision of her movement entirely outgrowing the bounds of Boston. In 1882 she had been practically immersed at Lynn in a mire of failure. Within four years she had not only established herself financially on a firmer foundation than ever before in her life, but could actually establish a National Christian Scientist Association.

Delegates from the "Massachusetts Metaphysical College" and from organizations of students in other states met in New York on February 11, 1886, and the National Association was then agreed on. It was a small gathering, but the seeds of expansion were there. Before the year was out Mrs. Eddy sent Mrs. Stetson down to New York to establish a permanent New York centre.

She was canny enough to see that it was in the large cities that her Science could be most profitably promoted. Explaining the organization of her National Association, she wrote that "for many successive years I have endeavored to find new ways and means for the promotion and expansion of scientific Mind-healing."[1] Large as had been the impression which *The Journal* was making on the minds of small town populations, Mrs. Eddy knew that mass distribution would be accomplished only in cities. Four years' experience in Boston had been quite enough to convince her of metropolitan advantages. She said so frankly. About 1890 she wrote that "at this period my students should locate in large cities, in order to do the greatest good to the greatest number, and therein abide."[2]

On June 13, 1888, the National Christian Science Association held its second annual meeting in Chicago. By this time there were Christian Scientists carrying the new doctrine to all parts of the country, and *The Journal* was still rolling up new interest. Eight hundred delegates attended. The Chicago newspapers therefore chronicled the Association meeting as a matter of rather curious news, not failing to mention the fact

[1] *Retrospection and Introspection*, page 52.
[2] *Ibid.*, page 82.

that the "prophetess," as they called Mrs. Eddy, was attending the gathering in person. She was accompanied on her trip by the indispensable Frye and by one Ebenezer Foster, a young medical student who had recently entered her college and of whom she was growing very fond.

The first day's session was held without undue event in the First Methodist Church, at Washington and Clark Streets. On the second day the assembly was moved over to Central Music Hall for the delivery of addresses by practising students.

When the doors were opened not merely eight hundred delegates walked in—over three thousand others, curious citizens of Chicago attracted by the newspaper accounts, crowded into the seats and sat with craned necks trying to locate Mrs. Eddy.

She was behind the scenes, wholly unconscious of a very important fact—that she had been advertised as the speaker of the day. The advertisement explained the crowd. It had been inserted by George B. Day, pastor of the First Church of Christ, Scientist, in Chicago, who had probably gathered from previous experience that Mrs. Eddy's consent to speak meant nothing until she had actually been escorted to the platform.

Thus he gave her no chance to change her mind at the last minute and delegate a student to perform for her. He told Mrs. Eddy the news as he escorted her to a seat on the stage where a number of other students also sat. She protested—not very emphatically. As it happened, Mrs. Eddy was in a period of very good form on this particular day. As the pastor insisted, she felt surging over her that first wave of ecstasy which was always a signal of her inspiration. She walked to the front of the stage, stood there a moment, gazing out over the throng in front of her. Some mysterious vital force seemed to flow out of her into the vast audience.

Suddenly the whole assembly rose as if by one accord to greet her.

Slowly, serenely, as a hush fell upon them, she recited the first verse of the ninety-first psalm: "He that dwelleth in the secret place of the most High shall abide under the shadow of the Almighty."

It was a wonderful text, extraordinarily suited to the occasion, a superb choice for an audience that had come to hear a mystic priestess anointed of God.

It was an unprepared speech, delivered without notes, and poured out upon the audience like a stream of molten gold. She thrilled her hearers in words that have been described as "pentecostal." It was said later, in explanation of the inadequate newspaper résumés of the talk, that even the reporters were so spell-bound they forgot to take notes. The substance of the talk was later written for *The Journal* and republished in Mrs. Eddy's *Miscellaneous Writings,* but something, at least, was lost in the transcription, for it gives no clue to the reason for the extraordinary reaction of her audience.

When she came to an end the scenes enacted in that audience of four thousand were so amazing as to be utterly unprecedented. The whole throng arose as one man and started to sweep forward to the stage. Men surged up on the platform and pulled women and children after them. They fought to grasp her hand, to touch her dress. Women who could not bring their children near held the youngsters up calling for a blessing. Others shouted that they had been healed instantaneously. Feeble old women struggled to avoid being trampled by the swaying mass and to hold up palsied hands for her attention. Mrs. Eddy was herself almost crushed.

"Strong men turned aside to hide tears as the people thronged about Mrs. Eddy with blessings and thanks," said the Boston *Traveler.* "Meekly and almost silently she received their homage until she was led away from the place, the throng blocking her passage from the door to the carriage. What wonder if the thoughts of those present went back to eighteen hundred years ago, when the healing power was manifested through the personal Jesus? Can the cold critic, harsh opposer, or disbeliever in Christian Science call up any other like picture through all these centuries?"

That night similar hysterical scenes were repeated at the Palmer House, where she was staying. So effective had been the cumulative publicity that hundreds thronged to the hotel hoping to catch a glimpse of her. There were the curious and the credulous, the skeptic and the convert, the rich and the poor, the lame and the halt. So insistent were they in demands for a sight of the goddess, that Mrs. Eddy decided to come down into the parlors of the hotel to greet them. She herself was amazed. She had been learning a great deal in the last six years about the virtue of publicity, but she had never dreamed of the extent of the mad rhapsody which that publicity could create.

When news of her decision to see the crowd in the Palmer House parlors was made known through Frye, the hotel management hastily decorated the rooms with flowers; and the mobs that filled the streets pressed steadily into the building until all the public rooms and the corridors and stairs were thronged. Women lost clothes and flowers and jewels in the crush. They fought with each other to get near enough for Mary Baker Eddy's healing touch.

Mrs. Eddy, at the end of sixty-seven years, had at last been successful in publicizing a new God. And lo, men being what they are, the prophet of this God had herself become a deity!

XV

Mrs. Eddy returned from Chicago as an old woman with a magnificent future assured. Her enormous and wholly unexpected personal success at the Chicago convention had provided newspaper publicity national in scope. The humble name of Eddy had now been established in the minds of important editors everywhere. Hers was the sensational "human interest" story at which any canny editor would prick up his ears. A new religion, a miracle-working high priestess, thousands of followers with mysterious powers of the mind—it was stuff with which to conjure many columns of space, and news of the mysterious Mrs. Eddy would henceforth find eager reception.

And she was now enjoying much more than mere *réclame*. Material wealth was flowing into her exchequer in a steady river. She could form as many classes as she could find time to teach. There was no other member of her college faculty besides herself—she comprised the entire institution; but she managed to teach between thirty and fifty students in each three weeks' term. Each class, in other words, brought her between nine and fifteen thousand dollars.

In addition to the primary class, for which the standard tuition of $300 was charged, and which had previously been the only course taught at the college, there were now three other courses, each consisting of six advanced lessons. The tuition for the Normal Class was $200; for the class in Metaphysical Obstetrics $100; and for the class in Theology, $200. Any student taking the entire series of courses thus paid Mrs. Eddy a total of $800. A husband and wife taking a course together paid only a single fee, being considered as one; and there were also occasional charity students, Mrs. Eddy being particularly delighted to give free tuition to ministers of other creeds. On the whole, however, a million and a half dollars would be a very conservative estimate of Mrs. Eddy's income from her college alone in the nine years ending with 1889.

An advertisement describing her various courses, taken from *The Journal* of September, 1886, is as follows:

MASSACHUSETTS METAPHYSICAL COLLEGE

Rev. Mary Baker G. Eddy, President

571 COLUMBUS AVENUE, BOSTON

The collegiate course in Christian Science metaphysical healing includes twelve lessons. Tuition, three hundred dollars.

Course in metaphysical obstetrics includes six daily lectures, and is open only to students from this college. Tuition, one hundred dollars.

Normal class is open to those who have taken the first course at this college; six daily lessons complete the Normal course. Tuition, two hundred dollars.

No invalids, and only persons of good moral character, are accepted as students.

All students are subject to examination and rejection; and they are liable to leave the class if found unfit to remain in it.

A limited number of clergymen received free of charge.

Largest discount of indigent students, one hundred dollars on the first course.

No deduction on the others.

Husband and wife, entered together, three hundred dollars.

Tuition for all strictly in advance.[1]

Schooled in frugality and want all her life, she spent as little of her income as possible. When, in 1886, her students and members of her church in Boston decided that they should have a church building, it was the students themselves who endeavored to raise the necessary funds. They secured a piece of land on Falmouth Street, in a tenement district of the Back Bay neighborhood; and all through the latter years of the eighties they gave fairs, bazaars, picnics and concerts in order to reduce the mortgage. In addition, appeals were made to

---

[1]Mark Twain, who was aroused by Mrs. Eddy's financial demands to the statement that she never "allowed a dollar that had no friends to get by her alive," took equal delight in baiting her for those Eddyisms which he called her "literary trademarks." For an amusing discussion of her verbiage in this advertisement see his *Christian Science*, page 160 [Harper's *Authors National Edition*].

every member and to all students in Mrs. Eddy's college to set aside a weekly stipend for the mortgage payments.

Mrs. Eddy conserved her own money carefully, and seldom consulted any one except the stolid Frye as to its investment. All her life in the frugal New England atmosphere she had heard preached the value and desirability of bonds; and so it was bonds that she bought, usually government issues, which have always been as sacred to the New England farmer as to the peasant of France. She had a unique yet workable system of deciding on bond values. She would look up the population of a state, and its products; and if the people were numbered in large figures and seemed to be producing wealth at a satisfactory statistical rate, Mrs. Eddy decided that their securities were a worthy risk.

By no means was all of her time taken up with teaching. Her correspondence was tremendous. In New York, Chicago, Denver, and scores of smaller cities, young church congregations were being organized by her graduate students, and she kept in constant touch with such leaders by mail. In these years the leading spirit in a new church served the congregation as pastor, preaching sermons of his own devising with texts chosen from the Bible and *Science and Health*. Some of these pastors were brilliant entrepreneurs, attracting to their congregations some of the wealthiest and most influential citizens in the communities they served, and in at least one or two instances building up a personal revenue almost as large as that being enjoyed by Mrs. Eddy herself.

Unlike the original disciples of Christ, who had a philosophy that appealed only to the poor and downtrodden of the world, Mrs. Eddy's students carried with them a teaching that offered boon to rich and poor alike. To both it advertised relief from all human ills and from bondage both of flesh and mind. Most important, far from abjuring wealth, as did early Christianity, the God of Christian Science was not merely a loving Father-Mother but in addition was a Good Provider. A poor man was one deficient in the full knowledge of God as Good—the knowledge that God could manifest in his life as wealth. One of Mrs. Eddy's favorite quotations was that beautiful and serene text from the mystic words of Saint Paul to the Athenians, "For in Him we live, and move, and have our being."

With a psychology that healed the body, and a religion whose God promised to free the trammelled mind from care while not denying to the body its comforts and luxuries, the pastors of Christian Science offered in their preaching far more than competing ministers in any other creeds pretended to extend; and the marvellous strides achieved by Mrs. Eddy's teachings in those years were made all the easier by the rather pale and puerile comforts which were advertised in other pulpits. Darwin, Huxley, and their brother scientists had done much to weaken established orthodoxy; and, anomalous as it may seem, these great students of the material universe did much to shake communicants away from the old creeds into a new theology that denied the objective existence of all matter.

If it seems strange that Mrs. Eddy's illogical philosophy should have found adherents even among the wealthy, the cultured, and the influential, let it be remembered that no conversions to religion are ever made through the intellect; and if the established churches had not utterly lost most of their emotional appeal long before the eighties even Darwin and his *confrères* could never, through their mere factual evidence, have undermined faith and created occupants for Mrs. Eddy's pews.

The truth of it is that men are ultimately led by their emotions and not by their minds. It is further true that not even the unusually competent thinker is equipped to give intelligent examination to an abstract philosophy, unless he has received a type of education which is rare.

Thus it was that Mrs. Eddy's unique philosophy did not hinder the acquisition by her church of an ever-increasing membership of a calibre such as few other churches of the time could boast. The proselyting carried on by some of her abler pastors was amazingly efficient. The work of Mrs. Stetson, whom Mrs. Eddy had sent to New York in 1886, offers an excellent example. Mrs. Stetson, as she gathered converts one by one, did not seek to extend her teaching merely by the ordinary channels. She and her students went in search of "prospects" with all the astuteness of the super-salesman. If, for instance, Mrs. Stetson desired to gain the interest and support of a woman who was interested in music, she would have the prospect approached by a local church member who could talk music knowingly and with appreciation. Thus a common ground would be established. Eventually the prospect would be invited to hear some fine religious music, and would attend a musicale given in the parlors of one of the fashionable New York hotels by Mrs. Stetson and her followers. It should be said that these musical programmes were usually excellent and executed with faultless taste.

With the prospect introduced into local church circles on this social footing, Mrs. Stetson would lead her gradually into an active interest in the new church and its tenets. Every effort would eventually be made also to attract the interest of the husband. This system of proselyting worked with a marvellously small percentage of wasted effort. Its efficiency was determined largely by the personality of those in active charge of the campaign. With pastors as dynamic and able as Mrs. Stetson the personal appeal seldom failed.

Thus skilfully was the force of personal sales work added to the publicity which was now constantly extending Mrs. Eddy's influence as well as her wealth. Had she been able to continue the arrangement she sought to establish in the early days of her teaching, when she stipulated that students should pay her a ten per cent royalty on their practice, her wealth in a very few years would actually have become fabulous. Without any such percentage revenue, however, money was coming in at a rate that appears amazing even in later years when dollars are counted in millions more frequently than they were in the nineteenth century.

Mrs. Eddy took a small portion of her funds and in the fall of 1887 bought herself a new house. *The Journal* described this acquisition in glowing terms, in an article entitled "Material Change of Base":

At Xmastide Rev. Mary B. Glover Eddy began to occupy the new house which she purchased on Commonwealth Avenue, No. 385. The price is recorded in real estate transactions as $40,000. It is a large house in the middle of the block and contains twenty rooms. . . . The spot is very beautiful and the house has been finished and furnished under the advice of a professional decorator. The locality is excellent. For the information of friends not acquainted with Boston, it may be stated that Commonwealth Avenue is the most fashionable part of the city. . . . Within a few yards of Mrs. Eddy's mansion is the massive residence of His Excellency, Oliver Ames, the present Governor of Massachusetts. To name the dwellers on this Avenue would be to name scores of Boston's wealthy and influential men. On Marlboro Street, which is the next toward the river, are many more families of note; while everybody knows that Beacon Street, which is next in line, claims the blue blood of Boston for its inheritance, especially on the water side.

That notice bears the direct impress of Mrs. Eddy's own pen, and its description of the blue-blooded circles in which Mrs. Eddy had now come to dwell is a self-evident Eddyism. There was, however, a faction in Mrs. Eddy's church who followed her logic in a fashion differing from her own adaptation of it; who insisted that, since Christian Science denied the entire material world, one should try to dispense as far as possible with material conveniences. It was a small faction; and Mrs. Eddy never gave it any of her own sympathy, for she never followed her philosophy to such an inconvenient conclusion. But some unkind comment arose from these other logicians regarding Mrs. Eddy's new mansion, with references to Biblical texts concerning the "foxes which had holes" and "the birds of the air" with their nests; and eventually *The Journal* published a pseudo-apology for the hyperbolic announcement about Mrs. Eddy's new home.

To the end of her life she was destined henceforth to have trouble in reconciling her own delight in wealth with that escape philosophy which she had formulated in earlier days— days when she moved in drab poverty and sought deliverance by denying material realities.

Once, during her pastorate, when it was the custom to pass up questions in writing for her to answer, she found the query, "How can a Christian Scientist afford to wear diamonds and be clad in purple velvet?"

Mrs. Eddy did not attempt to refer to her philosophy, which

denied such esteemed realities. Instead, she denied that her adornment had cost her anything. She answered in a statement that was subsequently published in *The Journal:*

> This ring that I wear was given me several years ago as a thank-offering from one I had brought from death back to life; for a long time I could not wear it, but my husband induced me to accustom myself by putting it on in the night, and finally I came to see it only as a sign of recognition and gratitude of my master, and to love it as such; this purple velvet is "purple," but it is velveteen that I paid one dollar and fifty cents for, and I have worn it for several years, but it seems to be perpetually renewed, like the widow's cruse.

Thus did Mrs. Eddy squelch the critic, and turn the occasion into an opportunity to suggest again that she enjoyed the benefit of miracles. There is no doubt whatever that she did indeed spend comparatively little of her own money for the luxuries of the world; she was quite able to husband her own resources while her followers supplied her needs with gifts. Most of her clothes, for instance, were for years personal gifts from Mrs. Stetson in New York.

Mrs. Eddy had as carefully cultivated titles as she had husbanded prosperity. She was now president of the "Massachusetts Metaphysical College"; editor of *The Journal of Christian Science,* which had grown from an eight-page paper issued every other month to a voluminous monthly; president of the Christian Scientists' Association; and pastor of The First Church of Christ (Scientist).

She had been ordained to her pastorate by herself and her students, taking formal office in 1881, and thereafter she used the title of "Reverend" in almost all of her official and formal signatures.

As her wealth and power grew she developed astoundingly in her ability to direct and manage, to formulate plans and carry them to successful conclusion, to analyze a problem and put her finger on the underlying difficulty. The psychologist holds that there is no more able and efficient personality than the introvert who through some change of circumstances acquires or develops some extrovert tendencies. Such was the nature of the change which had temporarily come over Mrs.

Eddy. Suddenly released from the necessity of turning her gaze away from a bitter and ugly world into her own dream life, she grew overnight into an able and dominant personality.

It was a change, of course, that inflicted on her new problems of its own; for, unlike the ordinary individual who can change his philosophy of life as his experience grows, Mrs. Eddy had put her own early philosophy on record, included it in a regular system of thought, and marketed it at a price. She could never, for instance, retract her earlier denials of the reality of the material universe. She had made her syllogistic bed and must lie upon it.

This circumstance in itself created new conflicts which she never met quite successfully so far as her writings were concerned, though she added to them constantly in an effort to make them more harmonious with her changing concepts. That her logic never improved despite these efforts is not to be wondered at. Hers was the virginal mind which is never married to reality—a mind that, whatever its sorties into the world of experience, always returns to sleep only with its dreams.

Her seizures of paroxysm and hysteria never ceased. They came on her with particular frequency whenever she was faced with some problem in her material affairs which worried or perplexed her. As before, the attacks occurred usually in the middle of the night, and Calvin Frye had come to be her principal comfort on such occasions. Frye's impressionable mind had not only swallowed bodily her own explanation that these attacks were the result of the malicious magnetic messages sent out by her enemies; he even discovered a remedy that seemed to ease them. Gradually some of her students in the house learned of this, and it was a peculiarly disconcerting discovery for all concerned. The facts were not in sympathy with any of Mrs. Eddy's preachments; for her denial of the reality of matter had included a very rigorous denial of validity to drugs. As time went on she therefore made every effort to have in her household only students who were so closely bound to her that their loyal silence could be counted on, no matter what the emergency. Meanwhile she occasionally found it necessary to deny rumors that leaked out of the household

ing editorials with which she heads every issue she "commands and countermands" to her subscribers, "thunders to the sinner," pulls out all the organ stops and shakes the very basement; again her copy has tremolos of gladness, mounts to coy facetiousness. Her students construct an artificial pond for her on her lawn, and she asks them to "ponder."[1] Some Canadian followers give her a boat to float upon the pond's small bosom, and she considers thanking them in a "boat song."[2] With Mrs. Eddy the gift of a piano becomes a "memento." It is still the identical Mary Baker who in her girlhood correspondence could be studiously playful and indulge in the "mood lachrymal" by turns. In the same issue Mrs. Eddy would include a card of thanks for a twenty-pound turkey sent her for New Year's; a denunciation of the wiles of animal magnetism; and a list of Christmas gifts comprising everything from a "sweet, illustrated poem" to a photograph from Mrs. Mattie Williams—"a large fine photograph of her beautiful home in Columbus, Wisconsin."

In 1889 Mrs. Eddy published her account of her Christmas gifts under the suggestive head of "List of Individual Offerings." The "offerings" were extremely numerous. There were "hosts of bouquets and Christmas cards"; but many things more tangible. There were also a Sèvres china tea-set; two "fat Kentucky turkeys"; "a pansy bed, in watercolors,"—a picture with a bronze frame; a barometer; some "perfumery" —Mrs. Eddy's students did not generally know that she did not use it; a "plush portemonnaie"; a "stand for lemonade-set"; a "charm slumber robe"; a book called *Beautiful Story,* containing 576 pages; a silver "combination set"; and everything else that a lady of the eighties would probably find use for, from pin cushions to embroidered scarfs, "Bible Pearls of Promise," and a "Work of Art" entitled "White and Franconia Mountains."

Mrs. Eddy's publisher of the era, William G. Nixon, advised her in the following year that a detailed list of her "offerings" might with propriety be omitted from the paper.

[1] Vd. *Pond and Purpose,* now published in *Miscellaneous Writings,* page 203 ff.
[2] Vd. *Miscellaneous Writings,* page 142.

Mrs. Eddy thought otherwise. She wrote right back that she was constantly being told by students that they had felt the *"mental* impression" not to give her a present that year, and that they found that it strengthened and "blessed" them to overcome the temptation. And so, to quell "mental malpractice" and to hearten those who successfully opposed it, she wanted the notice published.[1]

Of all departments in *The Journal* the healing department and the testimonials were the most effective aid in Mrs. Eddy's promotion work. There were always being circulated, even in these days, stories that Mrs. Eddy never accomplished any healing of her own. In a department called "Questions and Answers," which she conducted and signed, she nipped all such rumors in the bud. Thus:

Question: Has Mrs. Eddy lost her power to heal?
Answer: Has the sun forgotten to shine and the planets to revolve around it? Who was it discovered, demonstrated, and teaches Christian Science?[2]

The list of cures which *The Journal* regularly and continuously publicized included every possible ailment that flesh can be heir to. There was the lady who after handling numerous victims of pregnancy, lung and brain fever, and nervous prostration, wrote *The Journal* that she had brought one patient "out of a Plaster cast into Truth," in addition to having had "some fine cases of spinal curvature." One healer had cured a case of spinal trouble in sixteen absent treatments, eliminated scrofula in thirteen, and remedied a lame back with a single application of her science. Another healer reported that she gave birth to a child without any pain whatever, and got up the next day and carried water from the well.

[1]Mr. Nixon eventually parted from Mrs. Eddy under rather painful circumstances, and it is for this reason that some of the confidential correspondence between Mrs. Eddy and her official family during this era has reached the public. Copies of a great deal more such correspondence are held in what are now alien hands, and some of this material will quite possibly see the light of day before much more time has elapsed. The letter referred to was furnished by Mr. Nixon to Miss Milmine, in whose work it appears on page 317.

[2]This still appears on page 54 of *Miscellaneous Writings*, which is a compilation of many of Mrs. Eddy's contributions to her *Journal* during these years.

Cancer, heart trouble, dropsy, lockjaw, Bright's disease, paralysis, insanity, kidney complaints, consumption, broken bones, scrofulous growths—there was no ailment which was not featured in the list of cures obtained by various healers out in the field. Such cures not only produced new converts for Mrs. Eddy immediately; testimony regarding them brought new hope into countless lives, and produced innumerable purchasers for the Eddy literature. Some of the testimony was so sincere that even the confirmed skeptic must pause and wonder; and there can be small doubt that the therapeutic psychology which formed a part of Mrs. Eddy's teaching in many instances accomplished healing results which would well justify the belief of the patient that it was a divine power. Only the untrained mind may find satisfaction in Mrs. Eddy's philosophic sophistries; but only the closed and dogmatic mind can doubt that the therapeutic psychology which formed a part of her system conferred an almost inestimable boon on many of those brought under its influence, no matter on what grounds these many described cures may be explained. It matters not to the victim whether the complaint from which he feels recovery be described in retrospect by skeptics as having been an imaginary ailment; he only knows that whatever it was, he suffered keenly, that his torment was real, and that he is rejoiced at release.

The cures claimed for Mrs. Eddy's Science did not end with humanity; customers wrote in testimonials for animals. Mrs. M. E. Darnell writes in *The Journal* of October, 1887, that she cured her dog after it had been bit on the tongue by a rattlesnake. Another woman told how she had treated a valued colt which had got into the oats bin overnight and had eaten until he had swollen up "tight as a drum." In a single morning, she wrote, she had made him "all right," and was delighted to have discovered that Mrs. Eddy's Science could be adapted to "the good of animals."

It was natural that in the practice of the Eddy philosophy and theology a great deal of obvious bunkum should creep into the system; for when all objective reality is denied, what then is truth? Puzzling over this very important philosophical problem, a correspondent asked some pertinent questions regarding some of its concrete aspects in a letter to *The Journal* of June, 1892:

All healers have some instantaneous cures, but if we mention only these does it not imply that we have no lingering cases? I call to mind a lady Scientist who wanted to make an impression in a new field where she hoped to get business. After talking of the many wonderful cures which she had effected, she added that she herself was cured in three treatments of a life-long malady. Now, while that was substantially correct, the shadows of her belief were not wholly effaced for over two years, and this was known to others in Science. Would it not have been better had the Scientist qualified her statement as to the time required?

Do not Scientists make a mistake in conveying the impression, or what is the same thing, letting an impression go uncorrected, that those in Science are never sick, that they never have any ailments or troubles to contend with? There is no Scientist who at all times is wholly exempt from aches and pains or from trials of some kind. . . .

This problem of the distinction between subjective and objective truth lived with Mrs. Eddy all her life and, far from ever solving it, she never even admitted that it had existence.

There was, however, one problem at this time which received her careful and continued consideration. This was the question of giving polish and literary distinction to the text of *Science and Health*. The editorial columns of *The Journal* were no more formal than her daily speech, and she did not care to have them so; but she was endeavoring to cultivate and establish for *Science and Health* the status of a sacred revelation not second in standing even to the Holy Scriptures. She now constantly referred to it as "God's Book."

Mrs. Eddy learned very quickly; she had by this time become well aware of the many lapses in diction, grammar, and reference from which her book suffered. This is to her credit rather than otherwise; and it was wholly unnecessary for her in later years to attempt to belittle the boon which was bestowed on her treatise by some adequate literary collaboration. Perhaps her dissimulation resulted from her natural vanity; perhaps it had occurred to her that a book dictated by God should need no editing. The biographer in a later age can only guess.

The collaborator who played the part which Mrs. Eddy subsequently sought to shield from public gaze was the Rev. James Henry Wiggin, a courtly, charming and philosophic soul whom she sought out late in 1885. He has been described as a man of enormous bulk and stature and immense geniality, with a near-sightedness and a consequent hesitation in his gait that put his friends in mind of Dr. Johnson. He might well have been the model for the often quoted *homo sum; humani nihil a me alienum puto,* for there was almost no human activity in which he did not find a sympathetic interest. A theologian, he was passionately fond of the theatre, and after the fall of the curtain would frequently go back-stage to felicitate his older friends among the actors and encourage the younger ones. With Edward Everett Hale and others he organized the Playgoers' Club of Boston; famous stage folk of the day such as William Warren, Mrs. John Drew, Adelaide Phillips, Horace Lewis and Sol Smith Russell were his personal friends and warm admirers; he knew his Shakespeare so well that he could find an illuminating quotation for almost any bit of conversation.

He was a versatile music critic, went to concerts with the same zest with which he sat down to table, was a raconteur to delight the hearts of friends, and a scholar of far more than local note. Few knew him who did not love him. Long after he gave up his active ministry he would return to his old parishes to preach the sermon for an old friend or fill the place of the newer minister who was on vacation. He was always eagerly welcomed at the Monday Ministers' meeting in Unitarian headquarters on Beacon Hill. He took as active a part in the recondite theological discussions which went on there as in the talk of those young artists, actors, and newspaper men whom he would gather around him after the theatre for a late supper.

He had retired from his ministry in 1875 to devote his time to leisurely writing and editing. His old friend John Wilson, of the University Press, found Mr. Wiggin's scholarly services invaluable in the preparation of theological and technical manuscripts for publication, and it was probably through this connection that Mrs. Eddy first learned of his talents for her task.

In later years, when the part that the Reverend Mr. Wiggin had played in Mrs. Eddy's authorship had come to public attention and interested persons had turned back to early editions of *Science and Health* to investigate reports of its textual eccentricities, Mrs. Eddy took up her pen to defend both her authorship and her grammar. She wrote:

It was a great mistake to say that I employed the Reverend James Henry Wiggin to correct my diction. It was for no such purpose. I engaged Mr. Wiggin so as to avail myself of his criticisms of my statement of Christian Science, which criticisms would enable me to explain more clearly the points that might seem ambiguous to the reader. . . .

In Christian Science my diction has been called original. The liberty that I have taken in order to express the "new tongue" has well nigh constituted a new style of language. In almost every case where Mr. Wiggin added words, I erased them in my revisions. . . .

I hold the late Mr. Wiggin in loving and grateful memory for his high-principled character and well-equipped scholarship.[1]

Mr. Wiggin was one of the few people who ever made a contribution to Mrs. Eddy's career for whom she announced a "grateful and loving memory." And considering his personal standing in the community, it would have been foolish for Mrs. Eddy to make an announcement of any other sort of regard.

It was in August, 1885, that Calvin Frye called on Mr. Wiggin in the old Boston Music Hall, and stated that he was the secretary of a lady who had written a book which needed revision and also an index. Calvin was exceedingly agreeable and suave in his manner, and Mr. Wiggin inferred from the tone of his talk that the manuscript in question was probably in a fair condition demanding only, as he afterward said, "such literary advice and help as might be needed by an author of average education and literary ability."

But Mr. Wiggin had a real experience awaiting him. A few days later Mrs. Eddy herself arrived. In a manuscript left at

---

[1]New York *American*, November 22, 1906. Vd. also the *Sentinel*, Dec. 1, 1906, and *Miscellany*, page 317, where the item was reprinted.

his death with his literary executor, Mr. Wiggin has himself described what followed:[1]

She was a person of great, stately mien, perfectly self-possessed and disposed to be somewhat overbearing and impressive in manner. She had a huge package of manuscript which I learned was designed to serve as the material for a forthcoming edition of *Science and Health,* with *Key to the Scriptures.*

We talked over the matter of recompense and those details and she seemed satisfied with my terms, was very direct and businesslike; and we entered into arrangements, whereby I was to undertake the revision of the manuscript, although she was careful to give me to understand that she regarded herself as having already gotten the manuscript in approximately the proper shape for the printer. But there were, she confessed, "doubtless a few things here and there, that would require the assistance of a fresh mind." I did not then give the package more than a mere passing glance.

I was intending to go up to the mountains with my wife, on a few days' vacation, and I put the package away in my satchel, thinking that when I got up in the hills, I would set about the revision, which I supposed could be completed in a reasonably short time. Some days later I opened the package and began a scrutiny of the manuscript. Well I was staggered!

Of all the dissertations a literary helper ever inspected, I do not believe one ever saw a treatise to surpass this. The misspelling, capitalization and punctuation were dreadful, but those were not things that feazed me. It was the thought and the general elemental arrangement of the work. There were passages that flatly and absolutely contradicted things that had preceded, and scattered all through were incorrect references to historical and philosophical matters.

The thing that troubled me was: How could I attempt to dress up the manuscript by dealing only with the spelling and punctuation? There would be left a mass of material that would reflect on me as a professional literary aid, were my name to be in any way associated with the enterprise. I was convinced that the only way in which I could undertake the requested revision would be to begin absolutely at the first page and re-write the whole thing!

I tossed the package back into the satchel and did nothing more until I returned to Boston. I then had an interview with Mrs. Eddy and explained as kindly and gently as I could the situation as I found it. I told her I would have to rewrite the manuscript. I had rather expected some-

[1]The following excerpts from this manuscript are taken from the N. Y. *World* of November 6, 1906, in which paper it was published entire. The manuscript was also incorporated in a critique written by Livingston Wright in 1901.

thing of a scene and was ready to tell her, as I had occasion to tell one or two others in times past, that if I undertook the revision, I must do so conscientiously, and that I could not be placed in a position where I might be censured for a showing that was not my own. But instead of any hesitation or hint of annoyance, Mrs. Eddy in a calm, easy, thoroughly stately manner agreed to my declaration about the matter of a re-write, acceded to my terms of recompense, and it began to slowly dawn upon me that perhaps this thing of a revision "from the ground up" as it were, was the very thing she had intended that I should do in the first place.

In the course of our conversation, I reiterated to her, that she must understand, of course, that I was not a Christian Scientist, did not hold views according to her own, and did not ever expect to become a Christian Scientist. I wished this point to be thoroughly understood at the beginning, as I meant that literary revision and my own religious and ethical connections should have no affiliation, one with the other.

However, to all this Mrs. Eddy would respond in the blandest of manner, "Oh, we know you are not a believer now, Mr. Wiggin, but we hope that you may come to unite with us." And this continued to be her stereotyped comment, whenever the question of my attitude toward Christian Science came up.

So Mr. Wiggin set to work, and for four years was employed at a good salary not merely in revising and rewriting *Science and Health,* but also in doing editorial work upon *The Journal.* From this task he derived an infinite amusement. He regarded Mrs. Eddy as an uneducated woman ludicrously unconscious of many of her worst mistakes; and he had at heart, as he later explained, a genuine concern "to keep Mrs. Eddy from making herself absolutely ridiculous and to keep her from flatly contradicting herself."

Mrs. Eddy wrote in her memoirs that "at ten years of age I was as familiar with Lindley Murray's Grammar as with the Westminster Catechism; and the latter I had to repeat every Sunday. My favorite studies were natural philosophy, logic and moral science. From my brother Albert I received lessons in the ancient tongues, Hebrew, Greek and Latin. My brother studied Hebrew during his college vacations."[1]

Mr. Wiggin failed to find any evidence of such classical learning. Indeed, he said:

[1]*Retrospection and Introspection*, page 10.

The evidence of lack of education and of ignorance concerning the writings and teachings of the famous philosophers was so overwhelming that I could not trust her references, but had to look up everything for myself, to be sure, and to feel that I was doing work that was commendable to my own standard and just to her while I remained her literary aid and counsel.

It has been many times claimed for Mrs. Eddy, and she has claimed it herself, that she knew something of the ancient languages and literature. I can positively assure you that Mrs. Eddy knew nothing whatever of the ancient languages. She could not translate a page of Latin, Greek, or Sanskrit or give a synopsis of the teaching of the great philosophers of the ancients, were it to have saved her life. . . .

Thus it was that I tried to examine every sentence and to cut out whenever she would permit; for understand, there were many occasions when she insisted on using her particular words or expressions even though I had positively assured her that they had best be changed or taken from the context. So, of course, in they went! I hunted up texts and mottoes with which to head the various chapters and adorn or illustrate the reading matter. All of this was a bagatelle, however, compared to the maddening task of straightening out her weird English and bolstering up her lack of learning, to use the mildest term.

Another thing that I shall never forget was a chapter in which Mrs. Eddy had proceeded to arraign a group of physicians because her husband while under their treatment had died. Mrs. Eddy accused these men of causing the death of Asa G. Eddy by—to use her exact phrase —"arsenical poison mentally administered."

She scored the doctors dreadfully in this essay of hers, and as there was nothing whatever—an autopsy having been performed upon the deceased—to show any unprofessional, much less criminal, conduct on the part of the attending physicians, who were of well known high-class reputations in their professions, I knew, of course, that the publication of any such charges as these would immediately bring her into serious trouble.

I remonstrated with Mrs. Eddy about this chapter, but she seemed determined, at first, to have one chapter go in. I urged her to think well before she made any such preposterous charges as those in print. "You'll be arrested and convicted for criminal libel as surely as you print that accusation against those doctors," I declared. Mrs. Eddy replied that she "would think it over." I came later to learn that that was her way of preparing for assent to a point that she felt could not be safely carried. A few days later she asked me if I felt the same way about that chapter. "I certainly do," I answered. "Very well," she responded. Several days passed when she once more asked me if I was still of the same opinion. I said, "Yes."

After the lapse of a few more days she said to me, "Mr. Wiggin, I have decided to leave out that chapter." I felt relieved, as may be imagined, but was surprised to hear her next statement, as she said most impressively and with peculiar suavity of mien:—"Mr. Wiggin, I often feel as if the Lord spoke to me through you!"

The place vacated by this chapter which Mr. Wiggin persuaded Mrs. Eddy to eliminate was filled in a rather amusing manner. Mrs. Eddy had asked him to draw up for her the outline of a sermon which she could use before her congregation. He did so, writing it around the "Sacred City" that is described in Revelation as the one that "lieth foursquare."

When Mrs. Eddy delivered this message to her congregation they were enraptured. Mr. Wiggin himself was present, and as the audience had pressed up to her to render the usual adulation and obtain a handshake, Mr. Wiggin hung on the outskirts of the crowd smiling with amusement to himself. Mrs. Eddy suddenly saw him there, nodded in high good humor, and put her hand to her mouth in a husky side whisper. "How did it go?" she asked.

Mr. Wiggin assured her that it had gone very well, and after the crowd had scattered told her that the sermon would make the very thing with which to fill up the gap in *Science and Health*.

Mrs. Eddy agreed, and the chapter on "Wayside Hints" ran through many editions. Mr. Wiggin always referred to it thereafter as "his chapter" in the book. Then one day Mrs. Eddy got to thinking. "Mr. Wiggin," she said, "whose chapter do you regard 'Wayside Hints'?"

"Why, Mrs. Eddy," he said, "it is unquestionably my chapter. It consists of my own words from start to finish. It is most assuredly my chapter."

Thereafter the chapter disappeared from the book.[1]

The most important thing that Mr. Wiggin accomplished for *Science and Health* was not the grammatical corrections he inserted so freely; not the antecedents he granted to pronouns, the subjects he assigned to participles, or new moods and tenses to which he introduced the verbs. His greatest ac-

[1]Some remnants of it, however, may be found in paragraphs beginning on page 575.

complishment was the restating of Mrs. Eddy's confused
ideas in language that was more or less intelligible on the first
or second reading. It is not necessary to do more than compare
a page or even a paragraph from the 1884 and the 1886 editions of the book to discover how much he really gave it.

Mr. Wiggin did not turn *Science and Health* into noble
English. He merely made it fairly intelligible English, inso-
far as that was possible for a treatise which—as far as its
philosophy and theology go—is not always logically intelligible. He never quite recovered from the amusement which his
task brought him. With tongue in cheek he wrote a number of
churchly articles for Mrs. Eddy's *Journal* which he signed
with the pseudonym Phare Pleigh. Under this name he also
turned out a rather amusing pamphlet which defended Mrs.
Eddy's cult on Biblical grounds, entitled *Christian Science and
the Bible.* He later said, "I found fair game in the assaults of
orthodoxy upon Mrs. Eddy, and support in the supernatural-
ism of the Bible; but I did not pretend to give an exposition
of Christian Science, and I did not know the old lady as well
as I do now."

Mrs. Eddy had never been in close contact for any length of
time with any one with a rich sense of humor. Those whom her
doctrine attracted were usually lacking in this boon which ordinarily is the fruit of an intellectual sense of proportion. Thus
Mr. Wiggin was a decided novelty, and for a while he and his
venerable patroness got along famously. Once she asked him
with a slight twinkle in her eye why he was so obdurate in re-
fusing to join her church. "Mr. Wiggin," she said with the
twinkle still showing, "Christian Science is a good thing. I
make ten thousand dollars a year at it."

Mr. Wiggin did not cease his efforts with *Science and
Health.* He tried to smooth down some of the rough spots in
Retrospection and Introspection, her "autobiography"; in *Miscellaneous Writings,* which included a number of Mrs. Eddy's
articles that had found previous publication in *The Journal;* in
the pamphlets called *Unity of Good* and *Yes and No.* In addition he did some doctoring on her poems, which he called "remarkable effusions."

"I know," he said, "that a deal of sport has been made over her poems, attention having been drawn with some interest and amusement to the prosody and rhyming. I planed off a good many of her poems and if they lack, after going through my hands, something in measure and comprehensibility, I surely don't know what the literary critics would have thought of the originals as they came to me."

One of Mr. Wiggin's duties was to answer criticisms regarding Mrs. Eddy's literary undertakings. He refused, however, to indite a refutation of the many charges that she had derived from Quimby much of the material which she had later published as her own. It was in 1882 that Julius Dresser returned to Boston from California, and to his amazement discovered that Quimby was playing Jonah to Mrs. Eddy's whale. In a letter published in the Boston *Post,* February 24, 1883, Mr. Dresser took up the cudgels for his old teacher and began publication of the facts as he knew them. To say that Mrs. Eddy was annoyed would express the situation mildly. For several years thereafter she was busy denying any debt to Quimby, whom she called "an ignorant mesmerist" whose manuscripts were "scribblings" and "ignorant pennings." She insisted that Mr. Wiggin should assist her in inditing these replies. He declined flatly, with the statement, "There is nothing to say."

Mrs. Eddy never yielded wholly to Mr. Wiggin's guidance, and there were many times when she insisted that she knew her own mind and that she was going to express it as she desired. "She would get in changes of her own in spite of me," he complained, "and thus mar or often turn my own sentence into an absurdity. This will explain why it is that even copies of the same edition do not read exactly alike. Part of the edition would be off the press when she would take a notion to have a change made here and there, and it had to be done."

Such hasty changes were made not only in her textbook, but also in *The Journal,* whose printers were often driven almost to distraction by Mrs. Eddy's last-minute demands that they halt the presses after the issue was actually running, in order to make a correction or insert new material. Sometimes these changes robbed even Mr. Wiggin of his sense of humorous forbearance. Turkeys were a very usual gift for Mrs. Eddy in holiday time, and Mr. Wiggin tells the history of one of them with a charming despair. It was during his period of editorship of *The Journal,* and he says:

> I had the copy all up one evening and had come home from the printers when they were about ready to start the presses. Imagine my surprise and annoyance to find that when I read my copy of the new issue, there was a notice that I knew nothing of, right on the editorial page, at the end of the left hand column, said notice being headed "Turkey!" There followed a card of thanks to some fellow living way down in Kentucky who had sent the Editor—as the card inferred—a 16 pound turkey. The card was signed "The Editor."
>
> Now fancy an editorial page which I had carefully arranged and sought to imbue with as much dignity as I could, consistent with the fact that this publication dealt with Christian Science, being splotched at the last moment and unknown to me by a "card of thanks" for a blooming old turkey. Think of it. Now it was just such things as those that would be foisted on my work at the last minute and in the most unexpected ways. But that wasn't all with regard to the turkey. While the card plainly inferred that the turkey had been sent to the Editor, I have to confess that I never saw the worthy bird! I did not get so much as a mouthful of him.

Mrs. Eddy even called Mr. Wiggin in on her perennial hunt for famous ancestors. She was resolved to have some worthy forebears with which to furbish up her coat of arms. She broached to Mr. Wiggin the subject of Hannah More. Mrs. Eddy had always admired Hannah More in her own authoress days, and the fact that Mrs. Eddy's great-grandmother was named Marion Moor suggested a possible tie-up.

Mr. Wiggin was not optimistic. "Why, Mrs. Eddy!" he exclaimed. "Hannah More was an old maid, lived an old maid, died an old maid. You certainly do not want to be claiming to have descended from Hannah More."

Mrs. Eddy decided not to use the word "descent," but she got in her reference. Her own memoirs state that her great-grandmother's family was "said to have been related to Hannah More."

Under Mr. Wiggin's constant "planing" Mrs. Eddy's text-

book began to gain greatly in its possible appeal to new readers, if only because it had gained so enormously in mere intel-
ligibility. Old readers and old students were not always pleased
at the changes; they liked the previous editions better. As Mr.
Wiggin said, these early editions "sounded more *like* Mrs.
Eddy." He once wrote to a friend:[1]

> The truth is, she does not care to have her paragraphs clear, and
> delights in so expressing herself that her words may have various read-
> ings and meanings. Really, that is one of the tricks of the trade. You
> know sibyls have always been thus oracular, to "keep the word of prom-
> ise to the ear, and break it to the hope." . . .

In general, Mr. Wiggin described Mrs. Eddy as "an awfully
smart woman; acute, shrewd, but not well read nor in any way
learned." The two got along rather amicably, for Mrs. Eddy
always had a respect for real scholarship, and she found his
genial and versatile talent exceedingly useful. Eventually,
however, his sense of humor rather palled on her. For one
thing, she did not like his notations on her proofs, accusing
him of "the most shocking flippancy." Mrs. Eddy's own sense
of humor was strictly limited. She wrote her publisher, Mr.
Nixon, that "when he returned his first proofs a *belief* (*but
don't mention this to any one*) prevented my examining them
as I should otherwise have done, and, to prevent delay, the
proof was sent to the printer. The second proofs have the most
shocking flippancy in notations. I have corrected them, also
made fewer of them, which will involve another delay caused
by Mr. Wiggin."[2]

Mrs. Eddy's "belief," which she mentioned in strict confidence, referred to one of her perennial illnesses. A few months
later she was again writing to Mr. Nixon to say that Mr. Wiggin's delays were due to his being affected by M. A. M. And
she added, "I will take the proof-reading out of Wiggin's
hands."

The association definitely came to an end in 1891. Mr. Wiggin died on November 4, 1900. His were not the last hands

[1] Letter quoted by Georgine Milmine.
[2] *Ibid.*

to contribute to the clarity of *Science and Health,* but his collaboration was perhaps more important than any other. The first four editions issued before he came on the scene not only showed no successive improvement, but rather had gone from bad to worse. Mr. Wiggin lifted the book out of its lingual deficiencies, and started it on the road to wide circulation, at a minimum profit per copy of two dollars and fifty-three cents. Mrs. Eddy got a royalty of a dollar a copy and her publisher received the rest. When the 1891 edition was exhausted, approximately 150,000 copies had been sold since the appearance of the first edition.

This did not mean that 150,000 people had read the book. As fast as a new edition appeared with its various changes Mrs. Eddy withdrew authorization from previous printings. Every healer, student and church member was required to obtain the latest edition as soon as it came out. In addition every loyal follower was required to purchase as much of Mrs. Eddy's other literature as he could afford.

Mrs. Eddy had developed into an excellent business woman. "You see," said Mr. Wiggin once, "Mrs. Eddy is nobody's fool."

XVII

When Mrs. Eddy returned from her Chicago triumph she walked into a certain amount of real tribulation which had been brewing for some time. Despite the years of prosperity, —the almost miraculous prosperity that had come upon both Mrs. Eddy and her movement,—the same old sort of trouble was astir. Many of her students were dissatisfied. Mrs. Eddy in some ways had changed for the better with advancing years; but less impressionable students who were with her long always ended up with the conclusion that something about Mrs. Eddy was radically wrong.

Mr. Wiggin was once told by one of Mrs. Eddy's feminine followers that if she saw Mrs. Eddy commit a crime with her own eyes, she would believe the fault lay in her sight and not in Mrs. Eddy's conduct.

Not all of Mrs. Eddy's followers, however, were born to play the rôle of ostriches forever; and gradually, as they came more closely to observe some of her growing claims to godlike glory, her delusions of grandeur, and her very human failings, a real dissatisfaction arose.

This was augmented by the fact that Julius Dresser was now carrying on an extensive campaign to publicize Quimby, denouncing Mrs. Eddy as a plagiarist, to use the mildest word. In 1883, at the time Mrs. Eddy was suing Arens for plagiarism, Mr. Dresser republished in the Boston *Post* the article on Quimby's healing which Mrs. Eddy had sent to the Portland *Courier* in a burst of enthusiasm twenty-five years previously. He also republished her poem, "Lines on the Death of Dr. P. P. Quimby, who Healed with the Truth that Christ Taught," as well as other material from her fluent pen. In 1887 he expanded this material into a pamphlet called *The True History of Mental Science,* and the pamphlet was later followed by essays in book form.

Mrs. Eddy by now had long been absolutely convinced that

what she taught was entirely her own, and faced with the ghost of a Quimby come to discredit her, she did not find it difficult to reach the conclusion that Quimby himself was a charlatan and quack of the first order. As for Mr. Dresser, she characterized him in her *Journal* as an errant fake who "has loosed from the leash his pet poodle to alternately whine and bark at my heels."

The forgotten articles in praise of Quimby, which Mr. Dresser now showed that Mrs. Eddy had indisputably written, were denounced without a blush. Mrs. Eddy wrote to the Boston *Post,* which she made her open forum, that the illiterate Quimby had given her nothing; that he had not even healed her. "In his day," she says, "Mind Science was utterly unknown to me; and my head was so turned with animal magnetism and will-power, under his treatment, that I might have written something as hopelessly incorrect as the articles now published in the Dresser pamphlet."[1]

Mrs. Eddy was becoming thoroughly alarmed. Her whole system was now built up around her claim that *Science and Health* had been her exclusive Divine Revelation. She searched her memory to recall who might have copies of the old Quimby manuscripts from which she had taught in her early days, and she sent messengers to try to get hold of them. In 1883, at the time she was suing Arens for plagiarism, she sent Mrs. Crosby a note that oozed sweet and loving regard for an old and intimate friend. "Now dear one," she wrote after a lengthy introduction, "I want you to tell this man, the bearer of this note, that you know that Dr. Quimby and I were friends and that I used to take his scribblings and fix them over for him and give him my thoughts and language which as I understood it, were far in advance of his."[2]

Mrs. Crosby flatly refused to give such an affidavit, and Mrs. Eddy's alarm was not decreased. The Dresser controversy was having an effect most unfortunate—for Mrs. Eddy —on the minds of her students; and meanwhile another im-

[1] Boston *Post*, March 7, 1883.

[2] Letter preserved in affidavit sworn to by Mrs. Crosby and published by Georgine Milmine in *The Life of Mary Baker G. Eddy*, page 101.

portant adversary was rising to confront her. This was the
Reverend Warren F. Evans, who had been a devout Swedenborgian until he had gone to Quimby for treatment a year
after Mrs. Eddy's first visit to Portland. He had become enthusiastic about the Quimby system, had at once begun to
practise it at his home in Claremont, New Hampshire, and
later conducted a kind of mind-cure sanitarium at Salisbury,
Massachusetts, which he called "Evans Home." In his latter
years he wrote voluminously concerning Quimby's and his
own theories, and published two volumes even before *Science
and Health* appeared—*The Mental Cure* in 1869, and *Mental
Medicine* in 1872. He followed these volumes with *Soul and
Body* in 1875, *The Divine Law of Cure* in 1881, *The Primitive Mind Cure* in 1885, and *Esoteric Christianity* in 1886.

Dr. Evans' writings had a sanity, clarity, and conservatism
which were wholly lacking in Mrs. Eddy's book, and they gave
a rather thoughtful and reasoned presentation of their subject which entitled them to critical consideration. Dr. Evans
and Mr. Dresser, with the students they gathered around
them, eventually established on the basis of the Quimby teachings the New Thought movement as it is known to-day.

Mrs. Eddy, as she saw some of her students buying the
Evans books and overheard them discussing the Dresser and
Evans contentions, sensed an imminent danger. Dr. Evans
was making no attempt to found a school of thought; he was
establishing no dogmas; he was merely setting forth his own
views for the consideration of others and for their testing in
their own experience. Since a philosophy or a psychology can
never compete with a religion in public drawing-power, there
was no real danger here for Mrs. Eddy's own establishment;
but the mere fact that some of her students had turned an ear
to a rival mode of thought inflamed Mrs. Eddy's imagination.
She had almost lost possession of her Science too many times
previously to view the present developments with any sort of
complacency.

In her alarm she immediately went to extreme lengths. She
issued instructions that Christian Science students should read
no works on mental healing other than those she herself had

written. In addition, she decided to prohibit even discussion of any sort of healing besides her own among her students; thus she introduced into the Christian Scientists' Association a radical by-law stipulating that two or more members should not meet for the discussion of Christian Science or mental healing unless all members of the Association were invited to be present.

She did not even stop there. It occurred to her that if schism was to be prevented it would be necessary to stifle not only free discussion but also an independent Science literature. In 1888 Mrs. Ursula Gestefeld of Chicago, who had been a member of Mrs. Eddy's class when she went to Chicago to teach in 1884, published a book of her own on Christian Science. It was called *A Statement of Christian Science,* with the subtitle of *An Explanation of Science and Health.* It was nothing more than a rather successful effort to clear up some of the mysterious logical depths which lurked in Mrs. Eddy's own opus; but Mrs. Eddy was furious.

Mrs. Gestefeld immediately joined the ranks of the mesmerists, as far as Mrs. Eddy was concerned, and was expelled from the Chicago church. *The Journal* declared that her metaphysics "crawled on its belly instead of soaring in the upper air."

Mrs. Gestefeld did not take her exile silently. She published a pamphlet called *Jesuitism in Christian Science,* which pointed out the very obvious truth that if *Science and Health* were a divine revelation, a discovery of universal principle and truth, then Mrs. Eddy could not possibly keep people from writing and thinking about it, any more than they could be restrained from writing about a principle of mathematics or a law of physics. Only if it were a figment of her own imagination could she enclose it in a fence.

Mrs. Eddy, however, had a strong possessive sense; and she would have preferred even to see *Science and Health* wholly unrecognized and locked in her own pasture than wandering abroad as a universal truth which was not branded as her own. Her claim of inspired authorship was never intended as a delegation of credit; by advertising God as a partner she had managed merely to magnify the significance of her own share in the proceedings.

It should be noted, in passing, that the by-laws which she eventually designed for her church are a most amazing monument to this strong instinct for ownership. By every device of which she could conceive, she made her Science exclusively her own. So fearful was she that it might come under the influence of some other mind that for years she would not permit *Science and Health* to be translated into a foreign tongue, although she could thus have established a wider circulation for it.[1] She knew nothing whatever about foreign languages, and would have been unable to ascertain whether or not the translator was making a faithful transcription of her text. Only her current periodicals were permitted to undergo translation.

Her high-handed methods, which sought to control not merely the personal activity of her students but even the content of their minds, undoubtedly caused a large part of the unrest in her Boston circle that eventually resulted in rebellion. But there were numerous other causes which affected various students differently. There was, for instance, her attempt to secure a larger revenue for herself at the expense of other teachers of her Science.

Her own students had gone out into other parts of the country and were making rapid progress and very handsome livings. By 1887 there were nineteen "academies" and "institutes" advertised in the pages of *The Journal*. A great many of her normal students had gone into teaching as well as healing. Mrs. Eddy felt, as she reflected on the situation, that these normal students were enjoying revenues from students who might otherwise have come to Boston and paid tuition into her own exchequer. Therefore she issued a new ruling that no primary students could henceforth enter her Normal classes unless they had taken their primary course in her own college. This meant that new students who took their primary course from Mrs. Eddy's graduate students would be forever barred from securing a higher degree in Christian Science. Obviously

[1] *Science and Health* now appears in French and German translations, with the English version presented on alternate pages. There is also an edition in Braille.

such a ruling would accomplish just what Mrs. Eddy intended —less competition for herself from other teachers, and a larger income.

So great a furore did this ruling raise, however, that she was shortly obliged to rescind it. But the bitterness which her attempt at monopoly aroused still remained. The situation finally came to a climax with the Corner case.

Mrs. Eddy, always in quest of revenues, now that prosperity was going to her head, had recently introduced into her college a course in metaphysical obstetrics. Mrs. Eddy obviously knew less about obstetrics than a good village midwife, and she was the only teacher her college possessed. But these handicaps did not bother her. She had taken students in large numbers for the course, which consisted of six lessons for a hundred dollars. The six lessons consisted almost entirely of discourses on malicious animal magnetism, and how to grapple with this scourge. Nothing about childbirth was taught except that the proper way to deliver a child was to make constant denials of everything, except the fact of the child itself. Spinsters and girls who hardly knew the difference between the two sexes went out to help women bring children into the world.

It was Mrs. Eddy's theory that the practitioner should sit by the bedside and make mental denials of the possibility of premature birth; this done he should proceed to deny the possibility of pain or suffering during the delivery. One student's notes for the entire course covered just about half a page of letter paper.

This course was obviously added to the college as a drawing-card and revenue producer, for Mrs. Eddy's students had for years been treating confinement cases without any special instructions other than those she had given them for the treatment of general human ills. Mrs. Eddy not only approved of their so practising, but had taken no little pride in the fact that some of her students had gained a reputation for handling confinements with real success.

Mrs. Abby H. Corner was an Eddy student who was not so successful. In the spring of 1888, shortly before Mrs. Eddy had left for the Chicago convention, Mrs. Corner attended her own daughter in childbirth. The daughter and infant both died. A public furore ensued, for the newspapers in many different cities were now coming to feature deaths which occurred to patients in the hands of Mrs. Eddy's practitioners. Mrs. Corner was prosecuted.

Mrs. Eddy was horrified. She was already becoming sensitive to the newspaper attacks that dealt with cases which in some instances were absolutely heartrending. To most of her students this seemed an occasion which demanded a united front toward a hostile world, and they began to raise a defense fund. Mrs. Eddy, however, decided otherwise. She was a woman peculiarly eager for laudation, peculiarly sensitive to attack. Thus she washed her hands of poor Mrs. Corner.

Mrs. Corner had handled her daughter's accouchement in the same fashion that other Eddy students had followed ever since Mrs. Eddy's first teaching efforts at Lynn. Mrs. Eddy, however, found an easy way out by declaring that since Mrs. Corner had not taken the recently installed course in obstetrics at the Metaphysical College, she was a quack. A statement to this effect was prepared for the Boston *Herald* of April 29, 1888.

The lamentable case reported from West Medford of the death of mother and her infant at childbirth should forever put a stop to quackery. There has been but one side of this case presented by the newspapers. We wait to hear from the other side, trusting that extenuating circumstances will be brought to light. Mrs. Abby H. Corner never entered the obstetrics class at the Massachusetts Metaphysical College. She was not fitted at this institute for an accoucheur, had attended but one term and four terms, including three years of successful practice by the student, are required to complete the college course.

The notice was signed "Committee on Publication, Christian Scientists' Association," but it sounds very much like Mrs. Eddy herself. At any rate, Mrs. Eddy utterly washed her hands of poor distracted Mrs. Corner, and tried to persuade as many of her students as she could to do likewise. Mrs. Corner's defense costs—amounting to $200—were nevertheless eventually paid out of the Association's funds. She was acquitted on somewhat technical grounds—that her daughter death occurred from a hemorrhage which might have caused death even though a registered physician had been in attendance.

From this time on Mrs. Eddy rather modified some of her teachings. She eventually even issued a ruling that no followers should use the titles either of "Doctor" or "Reverend" unless these had been legally conferred. She had been thoroughly frightened at the great surge of public indignation caused not only by this case but by other similar occurrences. She changed her obstetrical course by engaging a teacher who was a graduate M. D. and who had recently taken a course in her college—Dr. Ebenezer J. Foster. Mrs. Eddy announced in *The Journal* that "Dr. Foster will teach the anatomy and surgery of obstetrics, and I, its metaphysics. In twenty years' practice he has not had a single case of mortality at childbirth." She also issued instructions to her classes that a surgeon might be called in surgical cases. In the classroom she was once asked by a student who evidently had more experience in accouchements than most of the scholars, "What if I find a breech presentation in childbirth?"

"You will *not,* if you are in Christian Science," said Mrs. Eddy sharply.

"But if I *do?*"

"Then," said Mrs. Eddy sagely, "send for the nearest regular practitioner!"

A great many of her students were bitterly indignant over her desertion of Mrs. Corner. They could not help but observe that Mrs. Eddy herself not only failed to attempt any healing work, but actually refused either to accept patients for treatment or to give advice on treatment. She would not even accept in her classes a student who was ailing,—fearing, apparently, that she might be called on for a cure which she might not be able to produce. Mrs. Eddy already had discovered an important secret: that a reputation as a miracle worker could be established by the proper publicity without any undue effort of her own. To promote such a reputation only one thing was required—a passive inaction. To destroy it only one thing was necessary—a public failure.

Mrs. Eddy continued her policy of risking no failures.

It was therefore natural that her more observing students should reach the conclusion that Mrs. Eddy was allowing them to stand all the difficult burden of demonstrating Christian Science before the public, while she remained safely in the background. The Corner case cemented this conviction. Mrs. Eddy's previous attempts to get her fingers on the earnings of other teachers, her efforts to dictate to her students not only what they should do but even what they should think—all these things resulted in a general explosion.

The aggrieved faction in Mrs. Eddy's following desired only one thing—to withdraw from the Association without being branded as mesmerists. Mrs. Eddy's teachings to her inner circle on the subject of malicious animal magnetism were not yet modified, and many of her students had a sincere and honest fear of it. Most of them hoped, if they succeeded in getting safely away from Mrs. Eddy, to practise their healing work independently, and a public branding as mesmerists might be a serious hindrance to financially successful practice.

More than this, many of the students were seriously afraid of Mrs. Eddy herself. There were many rumors among them that Mrs. Eddy did not stop in her efforts to cope with malicious animal magnetism merely with seeking to turn such currents away from her own person; it was claimed that she sought actually to direct such evil forces against those who had aggrieved her. Mrs Eddy's actual power to hurl at her enemies disease, death or destruction was unknown; but for this very reason few cared to risk it. Mrs. Eddy herself had made a broad claim to such power. In the days before she found it convenient to deny that she had ever tried to bring harm to any one,[1] she had written in a moment when evidently overcome by a sense of persecution:

They should have fear for their lives in their attempts to kill us. God is supreme, and the penalties of their sins they cannot escape. Turning the attention of the sick to us for the benefit they may receive from

[1] Vd. *Science and Health*, page 457: "Since the divine light of Christian Science first dawned upon the author, she has never used this newly discovered power in any direction which she fears to have fairly understood. Her prime object, since entering this field of labor, has been to prevent suffering, not to produce it

s not safe, for if we feel their sufferings, not knowing the individual, we shall defend ourself, and the result is dangerous to the intruder.[1]

None of Mrs. Eddy's students wished to risk trying out her potentialities in black magic. All they wanted was to withdraw from her circle peacefully. But Mrs. Eddy had so designed the by-laws of her Association that this appeared impossible. In an effort to prevent any recurrence of the trouble which had overtaken her in Lynn, Mrs. Eddy had drawn up two of the by-laws as follows:

"*Resolved,* That every one who wishes to withdraw without reason shall be considered to have broken his oath.

"*Resolved,* That breaking the Christian Scientist's oath is immorality."

Mrs. Eddy's students felt that they faced a very difficult problem in getting away from her. They even discussed possible methods by which Mrs. Eddy might be expelled from her own Association and Church, leaving the students in control. But no practical plan appeared.

A way out came into view when Mrs. Eddy went to attend the Chicago convention. While a new and strange public was worshipping at Mrs. Eddy's feet, back in Boston some two score students took possession of the Association books. William B. Johnson, the Association secretary, was in Chicago with Mrs. Eddy. Some of the students called at his home and persuaded his wife to give them the Association records. They put these documents in the hands of an attorney, telling Mrs. Eddy on her return that she could have them only after she gave each student a letter of honorable dismissal from the Association.

Once again Mrs. Eddy was wholly amazed. When she heard that the students had actually considered expelling her from her own Association, she was frightened as well as angry.

[1] *Science and Health,* 1885 edition, vol. I, page 244. In her conviction that she was being robbed of health by the sick who turned their "attention" to her, Mrs. Eddy had in mind a parallel between herself and Jesus, whose ability to use a mental "touch" she describes in *Science and Health,* page 86: "Jesus once asked, 'Who touched me?' Supposing this inquiry to be occasioned by physical contact alone, his disciples answered, 'The multitude throng thee.' Jesus knew, as others did not, that it was not matter, but mortal mind, whose such called for aid."

Fresh from the adulation of that meeting of four thousand in Chicago, she had momentarily thought herself safe and established, and now she found herself facing the same possible calamity which had crashed down upon her only six years before.

She temporized. She had Mr. Johnson write an appeal asking the students to sit down and talk the whole thing over amicably. Quoting Mrs. Eddy herself, Mr. Johnson described Mrs. Eddy's conviction that "now is the only time for us to meet in Christian love and adjust this great wrong done to one who has given all the best of her years to heal and bless the whole human family."

The students, however, refused to yield, and remained as obdurate as those other students in Lynn. For a whole year the dispute wore on, the Association books remaining sequestered. In this year Mrs. Eddy did some stern thinking. Plans were again forming in her head. In her sixty-eighth year she reached a decision to tear down her entire organization and build it up anew in such a way that it would be absolutely impregnable to any assault.

Meanwhile she gave the students the thing they wanted— their letters of dismissal. Thirty-six withdrew at this one time, from a congregation that did not total more than two hundred. Many of those who departed were among the leaders in the organization, the most successful practitioners and teachers.

Mrs. Eddy, however, was prepared for the loss, had already made her plans far ahead. All her life she had learned through slow and painful lessons. She had now reached the time when she had first begun to realize the really immense possibilities in the idea on which she had her hands. She had made many fumbles in her efforts to develop it, and somehow she had always pulled through. It was now time to do things on a wholly grand scale, to tear everything down, to build all over again to rear a structure that would really be worthy of herself and her divine revelation.

At the age when most people have reached the grave, Mrs. Eddy was just beginning to create her empire.

XVIII

The years of 1888 and 1889 formed a period of flux and flow in which Mrs. Eddy's personal affairs seemed to get nowhere, but during which great schemes were completed in her mind. She had just begun to understand the real strength of her position as she pondered over the remarkable ovation which she had received in Chicago—an astonishing thing which she could not get off her mind. One fact, at least, was evident; far more honor was awaiting her outside of Boston than at home. And slowly she began to understand the reason: her writings and her *Journal* were doing for her a work which she could not do personally. They were going into far hidden homes which she herself could not enter, were achieving for her a fame and honor which she could not win in personal association with those around her. Most important, it must have occurred to her that such a group of scattered followers necessarily provided for her much stronger support than those around her who had opportunity constantly to put their heads together and plot sedition.

She determined to find a way in which she could utilize such a situation to her advantage. Meanwhile she made further attempts to prevent the circulation among her cohorts of any of the heretical literature which was being published on all sides by disaffected Eddy students as well as by followers of Quimby. She even ventured in *The Journal* of October, 1890, to instruct her students to lay aside the Bible itself in devoting their energies to a study of her own books. *The Journal* said:

A student—in the tongue of the world called a patient—who says to Scientist, "I take so much comfort in reading my Bible," if guided wisely, will be answered, "Let your Bible alone for three months or more. Don't open it even, nor think of it, but dig night and day at *Science and Health.*"

This seemed to be going rather far, and when the indignation it aroused became overwhelming, the Christian Science Publication Committee voted that it was "unauthorized, unwise, and not the thought of our committee." Mrs. Eddy nevertheless did not intend to retract too much. She was quite overwrought at the sight of former students doing a prosperous business in healing and teaching and even publishing their own literature under the Christian Science name. "Burn every scrap of 'Christian Science Literature,' so-called," cried Mrs. Eddy's *Journal,* "except *Science and Health,* and the publications bearing the imprint of the Christian Science Publishing Society of Boston."[1] To the end of her days she forbade her followers to read any book which might throw doubt on the validity of her own teachings.[2]

This period found Mrs. Eddy mentally in a state of turmoil. Her age was already telling on her, and in the face of important problems her nerves would become easily overwrought. To make matters worse, she was now beginning to suffer from a palsy which was destined to become more evident as time went on.

It was a time in which she wanted to be alone; and yet, because she was a creature of contradictory moods, she found herself lonely. George Glover, her son, had written her in the fall of 1887 that he wanted to come to see her and bring his wife and children. She had told him not to come. "I must have quiet in my house, and it will not be pleasant for you in Boston," she assured him forbiddingly in a letter of October 31, 1887. She continued:

The Choates are doing all they can by falsehood, and public shame such as advertising a college of her own within a few doors of mine when she is a disgraceful woman and known to be. I am going to give up my lease when this class is over, and cannot pay your board or single dollar now. I am alone, and you never would come to me when called for you, and now I cannot have you come.

I want quiet and Christian life alone with God, when I can find it

[1] *Journal,* October, 1890.
[2] Vd. *Retrospection and Introspection,* page 78: "I recommend students not read so-called scientific works, antagonistic to Christian Science, which advocate materialistic systems; because such works and words becloud the right sense of metaphysical Science."

ervals for a little rest. You are not what I had hoped to find you, and I
m changed. . . .

Promising to send for him when her public labor was over,
he continued:

. . . you will injure me by coming to Boston at this time more than I
.ave room to state in a letter. I asked you to come to me when my husband
ied and I so much needed someone to help me. You refused to come then
1 my great needs, and I then gave up ever thinking of you in that line.
Now I have a clerk who is a pure-minded Christian, and two girls to assist
1e in the college. These are all that I can have under this roof. . . .[1]

Mrs. Eddy even as early as October, 1887, was considering
he advisability of taking herself out of the public eye and
stablishing a kind of retired papal existence where she could
nove in stately grandeur. She had already progressed so far
1 her rise to wealth and established position in Boston that she
vidently wished to avert the disturbing possibility of a visit
rom her son and his entire family. The Glover family,
owever, arrived in 1888, regardless of her chill welcome.
Mrs. Eddy developed a dislike for Mrs. Glover at the first
neeting, and no subsequent meeting between the two women
eems to have occurred. George took a house in Chelsea for
.is wife and four children, and they dwelt there for the win-
er. The Glovers attended a few Christian Science social af-
airs, but made no extended impression, and shortly trailed
.ome again. About a year later, when Mrs. Glover was taken
eriously ill and her life was despaired of, George wired to a
Christian Science practitioner in Boston to give his wife treat-
nent, and Mrs. Glover recovered. Her husband regarded it as
 miraculous cure. He later explained that he did not call on
.is mother for such a service because of her dislike of his
vife.

[1]This is one of the group of letters to George which eventually Senator
handler sought to put on record as evidence in the Next Friends' suit. The
riginal of the letter was apparently returned to Mrs. Eddy's trustees when
.e suit was settled, according to the agreement then entered into. The letter
ppears entire in Georgine Milmine's *Life of Mary Baker G. Eddy*, page 454 ff.
 was first published in the New York *World* of March 10, 1907.

It was in this same year, when Mrs. Eddy failed to find any pleasure or delight in her rather rough and stalwart son, that she adopted another son more to her liking. The man she chose was the Dr. E. J. Foster whom she had previously made an instructor in obstetrics in her college.

Dr. Foster was then about 41 years old, a rather baldish man with small nostrils, large ears, dainty hands, and a certain sleekness about his well-rounded cheeks. Like almost all the men whom Mrs. Eddy had around her, he was rather negative in personality and without dynamic force of character.

Mrs. Eddy was taken with "Bennie," as she called him, from the start. He had been practising homœopathy for a number of years, ever since his graduation from the Hahnemann Medical College in Philadelphia. While in Boston on a visit to an aunt he paid a call on Mrs. Eddy, prompted primarily by curiosity. He had become interested in her through the experience of an old army comrade who had thought himself healed through reading Mrs. Eddy's book.[1]

Mrs. Eddy could always charm when she wanted to; and particularly at a time when she felt that people around her were not giving her adequate appreciation she would go to great lengths to be attractive to a newcomer. Mrs. Eddy revelled in her old art of making a good first impression. From a new friend she derived a thrill which she could never receive from an old one. It was at a time when she felt herself unappreciated and rather deserted that she told "Bennie" how much she wanted him to be her student.

Dr. Foster went away feeling extremely flattered and appreciative of the woman who combined faded gentleness with a gay vivacity in a way that reminded him of his mother. He entered her class the next day, and from the first was a favorite and preferred student. After he was graduated and had returned to Waterbury Center, Vermont, where he was practising, he shortly received an invitation to accompany Mrs. Edd

---

[1] Mrs. Eddy claimed many such healings. Vd. *Science and Health*, page 440. "A thorough perusal of the author's publications heals sickness. If patients sometimes feel worse while reading this book, the change may either arise from the alarm of the physician, or it may mark the crisis of the disease. Perseverance in the perusal of the book has generally completely healed such cases."

to Chicago on her convention trip. He accepted, and when Mrs.
Eddy was ready to return to Boston decided to stay west for
a while to visit a brother in Wisconsin. Mrs. Eddy meanwhile
arrived in Boston to find her followers in an open rebellion.
She immediately had one of her old attacks of feeling sorry
for herself. On such occasions she always liked to secure a
strong soul to lend support and give her sympathy. She
thought immediately of Bennie. She sent him a telegram asking him to come at once. Then she changed her mind and wired
him not to come. Then she veered once again, and before he
could unpack his valise sent another telegram reiterating the
request to join her.

On his arrival she not only installed him in her college as a
teacher of obstetrics, she gave him a room in her house and
said that she foresaw the relation between them was to be a
very close one. He was rather abashed; but she explained that
the relationship which she foresaw was that of a mother and
a son.

Many years later, after he had been subjected to numerous
indignities, Foster said, "I shall never forget the tenderness
of the greeting I received in Boston. Frankly she told me of
her love for me—mother love—and asked me to become her
son in the true legal sense. She was old and far from strong.
The men and women around her were strangers to her blood.
She clearly needed the loyal love and care of some one near to
her. I think that in that moment I really learned to love her
and I love her still."

On November 5, 1888, the Doctor became legally Ebenezer
J. Foster Eddy. Mrs. Eddy avowed in her petition to the Court
that "said Foster is now associated with your petitioner in
business, home life, and life work, and she needs such interested care and relationship."

Mrs. Eddy for some years derived a great deal of satisfaction from this bizarre relationship. As it had been a long time
since she had had a real man of her own about the house, she
felt a new sense of security. Even now, when she was 68 years
old, there were times when she was at heart the same clinging,
wistful and rather lonely girl that the bluff Doctor Patterson

had married. In moods like these it was very pleasant to hear
a man's tender voice call her "mother."

For Dr. Foster, however, life in the household was not en
tirely a bed of roses. For one thing, he had signed on for a per
manent engagement there without an inkling of the variou
ramifications of malicious animal magnetism. By this time ma
licious animal magnetism had managed to acquire a thor
oughly real and actual sort of individuality for every one per
sonally associated with Mrs. Eddy; it was just like anothe
boarder in the household. If the thing had been a sort of ma
niac imprisoned in the cellar and ready at any moment to breal
its chains and come crashing up through the floor, it could hav
been no more real and menacing. Denying such an evil was o
no avail. If Mrs. Eddy heard any denial, she immediatel
knew that such a person was himself in league with the mes
merists, and ejected him from the house promptly.

Accordingly Bennie himself shouldered the task of sitting
up with Mrs. Eddy during nocturnal paroxysms when sh
was being attacked by mesmerists. In the night-time he labore
with the subtleties of mesmerism; in the daytime with th
jealousies of other members of the household. Almost withou
exception each one there seemed to feel that he or she shoul
have been the one adopted if any adoption had been justl
scheduled.

The atmosphere of Mrs. Eddy's house was like a little self
contained and closed universe. Nothing was real or of signifi
cance except that which went on in Mrs. Eddy's mind. Ove
all hovered a subdued air of constant expectancy. Mrs. Edd
was surrounded by a little group or clique of students of whos
orbits she was the entire centre of gravity. What she did, sai
or thought was the only subject of any final importance. It wa
natural in such a chimerical world that the main occupation c
her satellites should consist of a constant manœuvring for pos
tion. As Mrs. Eddy retired more and more from the extern
world of affairs, the brooding life in her household became th
more fantastic.

By the early part of 1889, Mrs. Eddy was once more in a
overwrought and highly nervous condition, worrying over th

state of her affairs and wondering what should be her next step. She was distrustful of the loyalty of all her students, and on occasion said bitter things about some of them—acid which often filtered through to the student so characterized.

Mrs. Stetson, busy building an organization in New York, was occasionally the butt of such ill-tempered comments. She was being very successful in making converts, and Mrs. Eddy constantly wrote her long letters praising her efforts; but Mrs. Eddy did not always speak to her intimates as she wrote to her friends. Thus, when Mrs. Stetson followed Mrs. Eddy's example and took on an attractive young man to add atmosphere to her household, Mrs. Eddy was most indignant. "See!" she exclaimed, "How Stetson apes me!" Eventually she took a more public course of expressing displeasure by including in her church Manual a by-law forbidding "illegal adoption." Mrs. Stetson had not made her young man her legal heir. "Illegal adoption," according to the Eddy definition in the by-law, meant merely a relationship which was not made permanent by legal means. But it was a twist of words which formed a nice innuendo for Mrs. Stetson to worry over.

Mrs. Stetson heard about some of Mrs. Eddy's sharp remarks through the inevitable underground channels, and wrote to inquire about them. The reply intimated that Mrs. Stetson was being attacked by malicious animal magnetism, and reminded her that victims of M. A. M. always thought that Mrs. Eddy was herself the victim. By way of gentle rebuke, she added:

It is indeed true that malicious minds are trying to separate us by blinding you, that they know I have had such joy and I fear pride in. But they cannot blind me as to what they are trying to do, nor prevent my efforts to help you, if only you will name them.[1]

Mrs. Eddy on occasion, and in her worse moments, could say very sharp things. She once told Mrs. Hopkins, one of her earlier students, "you're so full of malicious animal magnetism your eyes stick out like a boiled codfish's." Later she usually

---

[1] Stetson, *Sermons and Other Writings*, page 26.

repented of such outbursts, and at times she was serene, lovable, and wholly electric with dynamic charm.

It was as if quite different souls would take possession of her slight body. No one ever knew when the sudden change would come—the transformation would occur as suddenly as a new light on a stage can immediately recolor and revalue an entire scene. This explains, perhaps, why none of those around her ever knew the real Mary Baker Eddy—and why posterity also may never really know her. Somewhere, behind the fleeting transitions of mood, was the reality which was the woman.

Between her moments of tension, ill-health, and suspicion Mrs. Eddy was working toward a new plan of church organization. Remembering the effort to expel her from her own Association, she informed a number of her students and leaders that she was considering abandoning organization altogether as an unspiritual excrescence. She again voiced this sentiment in later years—although at heart she was too much a born ruler really to mean it. But some of her students took the idea seriously. Mrs. Stetson wrote from New York to inquire if Mrs. Eddy wished her entirely to cease activities to get a church together. By this time Mrs. Eddy had reconsidered She replied: "Do not make a move until you understand just what God[1] means." She explained that her students were not to break up their organizations immediately, but that she wanted them to regard "spiritual unity" as their sole objective. Her concluding words are significant:

> Your devotion is beyond that of Ruth's, it is like the women at the cross. Oh child of my heart, God is ripening for you His hour.[2]

It will be seen from that letter how Mrs. Eddy was already confusing her own plans with those of the Deity, and in what theological terms she now was addressing her coterie. By 189 she was writing to Mrs. Stetson as follows—having just put on the market a new edition of the phœnix-like *Science and Health:*

[1] *i. e.* God speaking through Mrs. Eddy, who by this time handed out her pronouncements as if they were divine messages inspired in herself as an oracle.

[2] Stetson, *Sermons and Other Writings*, page 26.

My Beloved Disciple:

You ask to be this, or ask if you are? Yes, and the answer is, lovest thou me? Again, yes, for you are feeding my sheep . . .[1]

There followed a gentle reproof for Mrs. Stetson, who evidently had urged her to visit the New York congregation. It lay in the suggestion that the new edition of *Science and Health* was itself a visitor in which Mrs. Eddy was to be seen—an "angel visitant" which would "hold thee up in hands."

As Mrs. Eddy's delusions of deistic grandeur developed, she quoted the words of Christ with increasing frequency in the first person without ascribing previous authorship.

By this time, also, she could unblushingly sign a letter to Mrs. Stetson as "Ever thine own Israelitish Mother."[2]

Meanwhile, far from conquering her old fears of malicious animal magnetism, she felt herself becoming more and more enmeshed in their coils. The delusion of persecution developed apace with that of grandeur, and she was now convinced that she was being spied upon; that her friends, her clothes, her house, the chairs she sat in and the food she ate, even the most trivial inanimate objects with which she came in contact, were infected by the virus of this deadly mental poison which enemies were putting in her path. Often she would have a letter which she wished sent unscathed by mesmerism despatched for mailing to some near suburb to avoid the infection of the local mailboxes.

So great was her horror of this force in her life that her teaching and daily routine had become seriously interfered with. Most of her time was spent in talking about M. A. M., in discovering its imaginary plots against her and her work, in trying to thwart and protect herself against its advances. Many of her students bitterly resented lectures which dealt with nothing but malicious animal magnetism after they had paid their money to learn how to treat the sick; for Mrs. Eddy did not hesitate to pause in the discussion of any subject to announce that she felt herself being attacked, and to devote the rest of the period to an analysis of the symptoms.

[1]Stetson, *Sermons and Other Writings*, page 29.
[2]*Ibid.*, page 29.

Even her closest students, her most loyal friends, were not immune from the accusation of having turned against her. She could never be sure, for any length of time, of the probity or integrity of any one around her. Suspicion had come to dominate her life.

By the spring of 1889 she had become so obsessed with the conviction of persecution that she complained time and again to the son of her adoption, Foster Eddy, that she must flee from Boston immediately. She mentioned Cincinnati and Pittsburgh, but could come to no decision. Finally she burst out that it did not matter where she fled—that she must get away no matter where or how.

Foster Eddy took her up to Barre, Vermont, with Frye and a few women of the ménage, to a house that he knew to be available. The town band, however, had a custom of performing its concerts in the square in front of this house every night, and refused to yield to any bribing when Frye urged it to change locations. Mrs. Eddy therefore marched back with her troupe to Boston. The atmosphere of Boston, however, was as brimful of M. A. M. as before, so Mrs. Eddy left again, this time taking a furnished house at 62 State Street in Concord. Here again she felt the baneful influence of her enemy, and sent Dr. Foster Eddy out to reconnoitre for another location. She stipulated that to be safe it must be a certain distance from mailboxes, post-offices, telegraph and express offices, and stations; all such terminals she regarded as the favorite lurking spots for M. A. M. sent out by her enemies—just as dark doorways make good lairs for hold-up men.

A house and garden was finally found in Roslindale. Mrs. Eddy bought it, moved in, suddenly decided that the neighbors were tainted with M. A. M., and immediately moved out again and went back to Concord to the house she had previously deserted at 62 State Street. Here she stayed for about three years. It was, for her, a fortunate exile, which would be deepened as time went on. For she was already approaching a period of decline when for long intervals crowds of people definitely oppressed her and sometimes even terrorized her. This too, is the symptom of a definite mental state familiar to every psychologist.

In preparing her flight from Boston and her retirement from the public eye, Mrs. Eddy resigned from active editorship of *The Journal* in May of 1889. The resignation was made with a grand and sacrosanct flourish. Said *The Journal* of this event:

As our dear mother in God withdraws herself from our midst, and goes up into the Mount for higher communings, to show us and the generations to come the way to our true consciousness in God, let us honour Him and keep silence; let us keep from her and settle among ourselves or with God for ourselves, the small concerns for which we have looked to her.

Mrs. Eddy thereupon issued what she called "seven fixed rules," intended to protect her from all intrusion either by person or letter. They read as follows:

NOTICE

SEVEN FIXED RULES

1. I shall not be consulted verbally, or through letters, as to whose advertisement shall or shall not appear in the *Christian Science Journal*.

2. I shall not be consulted verbally or through letters, as to the matter that should be published in the *Journal* and *Christian Science Series*.

3. I shall not be consulted verbally, or through letters, on marriage, divorce, or family affairs of any kind.

4. I shall not be consulted verbally, or through letters, on the choice of pastors for churches.

5. I shall not be consulted verbally, or through letters, on disaffections, if there should be any between students of Christian Scientists.

6. I shall not be consulted verbally, or through letters, on who shall be admitted as members, or dropped from the membership of the *Christian Science Churches or Associations*.

7. I am not to be consulted verbally, or through letters, on disease and the treatment of the sick; but I shall love all mankind—and work for their welfare.

Next came Mrs. Eddy's withdrawal from her college. Since she was the entire teaching staff, except for the fact that her adopted son taught "the anatomy and surgery of obstetrics," her departure from Boston made it necessary to close the college doors.

This was unfortunate from the financial standpoint, for the college had been producing a magnificent revenue, and Mrs. Eddy was loath to sacrifice such a return. She tried for a short time to have Foster Eddy do the active teaching work while she remained president *in absentia;* but Foster Eddy completely lacked the dynamic personality which could make itself felt in a classroom. In consequence the student clientele immediately fell off. Mrs. Eddy announced that since it was her personal instruction that students seemed to want, the college must be closed altogether. She regretted this decision almost as soon as it was announced, and decided to call General Erastus N. Bates from Cleveland, where he was a very successful healer, to reopen the institution. General Bates had been conducting classes for less than a month, however, before Mrs. Eddy once again veered and sent him home over his protest. Thus ended her activities in the college.

Thereupon the Massachusetts Metaphysical College Association was also disorganized and its constitution and by-laws abrogated.[1] The National Association was similarly disorganized at its next meeting in New York.

Then Mrs. Eddy tore down the organization of her church In her *Journal* for February, 1890, it was declared:

> The dissolution of the visible organization of the church is the sequence and complement of that of the college corporation and association. The college disappeared that the spirit of Christ might have freer course among its students and all who come into the understanding of Divine Science. The bonds of the church were thrown away so that its members might assemble themselves together to "provoke one another to good works" in the bond only of love.

Mrs. Eddy, whenever she got discouraged, would criticise what she called "material organization." Thus she once wrote in a mood of weariness: "Despite the prosperity of my church

[1] Ten years later, in 1899, the college was again reopened with Mrs. Eddy as president, but its ownership was vested in her church, by which it was administered through a Board of Education; and Mrs. Eddy's association with its labors of preparing teachers for Christian Science was merely titular. The revenues went to the church.

it was learned that material organization has its value and peril, and that organization is requisite only in the earliest periods of Christian history."[1]

Be that as it may, Mrs. Eddy, far from ever loosening the reins of organization, spent most of her later days seeking means to draw them tighter.

Much of the disorganization of her church in 1890 existed only on paper. Members of the Association, for instance, continued to meet "as a voluntary association of Christians to promote growth in spirituality." Similarly, the church continued to hold its regular services just as before, and if an outsider had dropped in he would have noticed no difference. Actually, just one difference existed. No business was being transacted. Mrs. Eddy did not want any interference during a period when she was formulating the most ambitious plans she had yet conceived. She had no objection to churches whatever—she wanted them tremendously. At the very time that she had effectively put a stop to any business meetings in Boston she was urging workers in other cities to make haste to get their churches together. Mrs. Stetson already had a strong organization completed in New York. Mrs. Eddy now wanted something more—an imposing church building there. So she wrote to Mrs. Stetson in February, 1891:

I hope the cloud from Boston has not reached you. God reigns. He is showing me through it. His face is so sweet in the gloom, His love so true! . . .

Now, darling, I entrust you with another momentous move, namely, our memorial of Christian Science, that the ages will look upon it and be lifted up. . . .[2]

At this time Mrs. Eddy was taking no one into her confidence, was slowly and laboriously planning alone. As she wrote to Mrs. Stetson, "My household would send love but I and my folks here are *distinct*. I never take them into counsel and they seldom know when I write."[3]

[1] *Retrospection and Introspection*, page 45.
[2] Vd. Stetson, *Sermons and Other Writings*, page 29, for entire letter.
[3] *Ibid.*, page 29.

Mrs. Eddy wanted to have even her plans and designs recognized as solely and exclusively hers. There were now two dominant ideas in her mind—a monumental church in Boston, and another one in New York. She rightly considered that these two cities at that time formed the centre of the American intellectual universe. In sending Mrs. Stetson to New York Mrs. Eddy had given a tremendous opportunity into another's hands, and she knew it. In moments of doubt and suspicion there were already times when she wondered whether Augusta Stetson were wholly and sufficiently loyal to use this opportunity for Mrs. Eddy's advantage instead of personal glory. And yet—the only way to get a church into New York would be to trust Augusta Stetson, whose success in organization was already so great that Mrs. Eddy sometimes felt the twinges of jealousy.

There were times when Mrs. Eddy must have wished she were twins.

XIX

The thing that Mrs. Eddy now visualized, that was now almost in her grasp, was a group of churches so loosely organized that no successful amalgamation of any rebellious forces would ever be possible; and yet so cleverly organized that she would be in absolute, unshakable and final control. She spent months in trying to devise a system that would forever be immune from the dangers which had almost ruined her in Lynn, and had seriously frightened her in Boston.

The solution of her dilemma came with the idea of a central Mother Church, of which her perpetual control would be assured by giving this church a membership of followers from all parts of the United States. Scattered in village and town, in city and countryside, these members would be afforded no opportunity to assemble with sufficient frequency to confer over possible grievances or to plot insurrection.

It was a brilliant idea. Like all of Mrs. Eddy's other ideas, it had a growth rooted in her years of conflict. The selection of the name "Mother Church" for this central organization must have occurred to her as another happy thought. It not only signified the parent church from which branches would emanate, in the same sense in which the Shakers had used the term; to Mrs. Eddy it also meant a church peculiarly and uniquely the property of herself who was known as "Mother." All her followers were encouraged to use this title, and her new by-laws were to stipulate:

The Title of Mother. In the year 1895 loyal Scientists had given to the author of their textbook, the Founder of Christian Science, the individual, endearing term of Mother. Therefore, if a student of Christian Science shall apply this title, either to herself or to others except as the term for kinship according to the flesh, it shall be regarded by the church an indication of disrespect for their Pastor Emeritus, and unfitness to be a member of the Mother Church.[1]

[1] *Manual*, XXII, 1, in editions previous to 1903, when a new by-law was substituted.

Having devised a method for making the Mother Church safely and perpetually her own, Mrs. Eddy's next problem was that of the other churches and their control.

She reached a unique and again a brilliant solution. She decided not to try to control them. Instead, she emasculated them. She took away from them all prestige, influence and standing as individual organizations. No persons who merely held membership in a branch church were henceforth to have any recognition in Mrs. Eddy's system of government. Branch churches hereafter were to be only buildings where non-resident members of the Boston Church could meet, sing hymns, and hear Mrs. Eddy's book read. Membership in such a church was to mean little besides the right to contribute to the cost of the upkeep of this local meeting-place.

To have any real standing in Christian Science, a branch church member would necessarily have to become also a member of the Mother Church. Only members of the Mother Church could take the course of study ending in a degree of C. S. B. or C. S. D., becoming "Bachellor" or "Doctor"; only such members could teach; only such members could be Readers in branch churches.

If, under such regulations, Mrs. Eddy found a member of her Mother Church acting disloyally, she could expel him without any danger of his making undue trouble. For, with the membership of the Mother Church scattered all over the country, he could hardly organize a group of sympathizers and other troublemakers large enough to make effective protest and endanger Mrs. Eddy's own control of the Boston organization. And once expelled from this organization he would have no political standing as a mere member of his branch church—whether that branch church also disciplined him or not.

To make sure that branch church members would never unite to make effective rebellion, Mrs. Eddy stipulated that "no conference of churches shall be held." Even in laying a corner stone a branch church should not allow a "large gathering of people." Furthermore, "each branch church shall be distinctly democratic in its government, and no individual, and no other church, shall interfere with its affairs." The word "democratic" illustrates again how unique could be the effects which Mrs. Eddy obtained with language—her church was henceforth to be an absolute monarchy. Further to hold down the branch churches, she decreed that "the branch churches shall be individual, and not more than two small churches shall consolidate under one church government." Eventually, as will be seen, Mrs. Eddy even stipulated that a branch church should not hold an overflow meeting. In every way that she could conceive of she made certain that no branch church could ever acquire political power, or a membership large enough to attempt to wrest leadership from her.

She put all of her power into one bank, which was The Mother Church. Over this she gave herself absolute control. No branch church could hope in any way to gain dominance over this one. Thus she stipulated that "The Mother Church stands alone; it occupies a position that no other church can fill. Then for a branch church to assume such a position would be disastrous to Christian Science. Therefore no Church of Christ, Scientist, shall be considered loyal that has branch churches. . . ."

The article "The"[1] was reserved for use in position only before the name of The Mother Church, which "shall be officially controlled by no other church."

Having thus devised an organization that seemed rebellion-proof, Mrs. Eddy next devised a government for it that would respond to her will alone.

Because she realized the vital necessity of retiring from public gaze, Mrs. Eddy did not mean to resume the pastorate in her new church. She took for herself the title of Pastor Emeritus, which meant little, and did not at all indicate her actual status. Active pastors were shortly to be abolished.

[1]Characterized by Mark Twain as "that imperial word." . . . "For show, and style, and grandeur, and thunder and lightning and fireworks it outclasses all the previous inventions of man. . . . It lifts the Mother Church away up in the sky, and fellowships it with the rare and select and exclusive little company of the THE'S of deathless glory—persons and things whereof history and the ages could furnish only single examples, not two: *the* Saviour, *the* Virgin, *the* Milky Way, *the* Bible, *the* Earth, *the* Equator, *the* Devil, *the* Missing Link—and now *The* First Church, Scientist. . . ." Vd. *Christian Science*, page 238 (Harpers, Author's National Edition).

The Board of Directors was to elect the president—with her approval.

The treasurer and the clerk were to be appointed by the board, her creation.

Readers in the Church—after the abolishing of pastors—were to be elected by the Board of Directors, again subject to Mrs. Eddy's approval. And Mrs. Eddy reserved the right peremptorily to remove a Reader from office in any church.

She gave her church a sort of Elders' Council called the "First Members," and later "Executive Members,"—a group consisting of not more than 100 honored individuals. Such First Members had no political power, this being vested solely in the Board; they could not attend business meetings; their chief business was to fix the salary of Readers and to pass on the qualifications of new members for the church. All candidates for a place among the First Members had to receive Mrs. Eddy's approval.

Mrs. Eddy, in other words, was henceforth her whole church. The organization was so devised that it could function without her at any time when she was indisposed, or had no desire to interfere; but if occasion required she had absolute control of the entire church—its government, its finances, its membership.

This was the impregnable organization which she desired to create when she dissolved her former church and association. With these iron-clad provisions now outlined in her mind, although they were not to be issued as by-laws until a little later, Mrs. Eddy had set about the business of securing a building to house The Mother Church that she had planned.

It will be remembered that her old organization had paid down some money on a site in Falmouth Street. She now set her mind to work to find a way to get the land away from the individual members of that now dissolved organization She had no intention of letting them hold on to it.

The procedure she followed showed a clever if not wholly irreproachable business ability. The former church members had paid a total of $5,800 on their property, thus reducing the indebtedness to $4,963.50. Mrs. Eddy could have bought the property from them outright; such a transaction would have cost her at least $10,000, on the basis of the purchase price three years before, and the land had subsequently doubled in value.

But she discovered a cheaper method. With the old church organization dissolved, no regular business transactions were made, collections fell behind, and payments on the mortgage were neglected. Mrs. Eddy therefore stepped in and bought the mortgage, her lawyer acting for her. The mortgage was assigned to her by the former holder on December 6, 1888, and she paid for it exactly the amount which still was due. The next year, in August of 1889, she foreclosed on the mortgage; and at the ensuing foreclosure sale she allowed the land to go to the brother of her lawyer, George H. Perry, for exactly $5,000. She was keeping her own name entirely out of the transaction. Perry then deeded the land over to one of Mrs. Eddy's favorite students of the moment, Ira O. Knapp, for $5,100. Mr. Knapp then conveyed the land to Mrs. Eddy—the real owner all the time—for one dollar. Doubtless no real money changed hands except the extra $100, which presumably went to Perry as lawyer's fees. All the rest of the transaction evidently occurred only on paper, and took place for the one purpose of hiding the fact that Mrs. Eddy was the person behind it.

Thus at a total cost of about $5,000, plus lawyer's fees, Mrs. Eddy had secured a piece of land worth actually at least $20,000, taking it away from a group of owners she did not trust for delivery to a group of trustees of whose loyalty she could feel assured. These trustees, appointed by herself and subject entirely to her pleasure, were now held in the hollow of her hand. She could make them or break them at will. They were her creatures.[1]

She told no one else of her plans. She now converted her trustees into "The Christian Science Board of Directors." There were four of them; Ira O. Knapp, William B. Johnson, Joseph S. Eastaman, and Stephen A. Chase. To these Direc-

[1] For Mrs. Eddy's own account of this transaction see her *Message to the Mother Church for 1902*, page 13.

tors she conveyed the land which she had so cheaply acquired.
In return she pledged them to build upon this site, within a
period of five years, a church costing not less than $50,000.

This gift, which her *Journal* subsequently lauded as such
a generous one, was not made without strings attached. Said
The Journal:

Let us endeavor to lift up our hearts in thankfulness to . . . our
Mother in Israel for these evidences of generosity and self-sacrifice that
appeal to our deepest sense of gratitude, even while surpassing our comprehension.

However general were such sentiments, Mrs. Eddy's deed
of trust was perfectly comprehensible. Dated September 2
1892, and to this day published in the Church Manual as a
warning for all to read,[1] it required the Board members to use
Mrs. Eddy's real estate gift for nothing else than a church
building; required them to maintain such regular services here
as Mary Baker G. Eddy designed; and stipulated that if the
provisions of this trust deed were violated both the lot and the
church building must be reconveyed to Mary Baker G. Eddy
her heirs and assigns forever. There would henceforth never
be a question raised as to whose church this was.

After secretly organizing her Board, Mrs. Eddy showed her
hand sufficiently to make an announcement in *The Journal* that
she wanted contributions for a church building. Money imme
diately began to flow in. In the fall of 1892 the official organi
zation of church government was completed by the Board
But no public announcement of this important fact was made
For a whole year, until the first annual meeting of The Mother
Church was held on October 3, 1893, in Chickering Hall
Christian Scientists generally supposed that Mrs. Eddy had
meant what she said when she abolished all formal church
organization as an advance in spiritual grace.

They little knew Mrs. Eddy. By the time she was ready to
announce the formation of her new organization, she had been
collecting money for a church building for more than a year
By the fall of 1893 she had put all her plans in effect and had

[1] Page 128.

created what amounted to a closed corporation. When her followers at large finally learned what really had happened, they were face to face with an accomplishment against which they could not make a single effective protest. While they slept Mrs. Eddy had quietly moved them out of house and home, moved in herself, and locked the doors. And none of the old occupants would get back in without her special permission.

Besides her officers Mrs. Eddy had herself chosen twelve charter members for her church. She selected as these members only adherents of whose loyalty she was absolutely sure. All future applicants for admission to the church must be balloted on by these twelve. There was no other possible way to get in; even old church members who had trailed after Mrs. Eddy for years now had to pass the inspection. Needless to say, every person with the least taint of mesmerism, of disloyalty, of independence, or of heresy, was rigorously excluded. The new congregation was handpicked. Those left out in the cold were no longer Christian Scientists.

This done, Mrs. Eddy now issued through *The Journal* an invitation to all her loyal followers, everywhere, to line up, pass inspection, and get inside the door. The invitation amounted to a command. Reverend D. A. Easton, pastor of The Mother Church—pastors not being abolished until 1895—announced in 1893:

. . . Mrs. Eddy has invited Scientists everywhere to unite with The Mother Church. To obey cheerfully and loyally marks a growth in Science.

> Theirs not to reason why,
> Theirs but to do and die.

Dr. Foster Eddy wrote in *The Journal* that "the chaff has been separated from the wheat in a most marvelous manner." And indeed it had.

Under the watchword of obedience Mrs. Eddy's followers all over the country now began to apply for membership in her church. By October 2, 1894, a total of 2,978 such members was reported. "Experience, and above all, obedience, are the tests of growth and understanding in Science," wrote Mrs.

Eddy in her *Journal*. Every one took the cue, and contributed to the church building fund to his utmost ability. The corner stone was laid May 21, 1894. When the financial panic of 1894 slowed down contributions, Mrs. Eddy made a personal appeal to fifty of her wealthier followers to give $1,000 apiece. They did. For eighteen months the building went up stone by stone —the building which Mrs. Eddy described as a memorial "for her through whom was revealed to you God's all-power, all-presence, and all-science."

While the building went on, Mrs. Eddy completed her plans to keep her Science forever and ever her own. She had chained her new church to her with iron-clad provisions for its organization and government. She would not rest content until she had chained her theology in the same way, had rendered it impossible for any individual ever to make an infinitesimal change in her doctrines.

Thus was born a series of decrees as remarkable as any ever evolved for a church. All her provisions for church government, for enforcement of her decrees, and for discipline of members, were embodied in her Manual which she issued in the same year her congregation moved into the new Mother Church building.

It was in this year, 1895, that she decided to abolish pastors and have merely Readers. Mrs. Eddy had carefully watched some of her pastors in their pulpits every Sunday, inspiring large audiences with their eloquence, gaining new converts and many personal adherents by their elucidations of the Eddy doctrines. Mrs. Eddy knew that pastors were dangerous. Remembering her experience in Chicago, she knew how easy it was for an audience to arouse itself to a frenzy of adulation. Mrs. Eddy did not intend her pastors to receive any such personal acclaim. She herself was now out of the pulpit. She did not want any one else before the footlights, gaining homage that should be hers. Particularly she did not want pastors enjoying an opportunity to express free personal opinions that might slowly undermine her own teachings in *Science and Health*.

Thus she took pastors down out of their pulpits, and decreed that henceforth *Science and Health* should be the only pastor in her churches. This should be read aloud each Sunday, with additional readings from the Bible. She stipulated that her name should be announced as author whenever the Reader lifted up his voice to pour forth the contents of her book.

She ordained that the Reader must read from her own copyrighted book, and not from a manuscript or transcribed copy, and also that he was at no time to make remarks explanatory of what he read. As an additional and final safeguard Mrs. Eddy reserved the right to remove any Reader from office at her pleasure.

Even now she was not quite through. When Septimus J. Hanna, First Reader in The Mother Church, became remarkably influential even though he could speak no words of his own, Mrs. Eddy issued an additional by-law limiting Readers in The Mother Church to an office tenure of only three years.[1]

Having thus removed any danger of heresy developing in the pulpit, she sought other means for preventing any discussion of her philosophy or theology by assemblies of members.

She therefore ruled that before any meeting of church members could be called by the clerk she must be notified of the time and purpose of the gathering.

She prohibited any church member from engaging in public debate on Christian Science without previously notifying and gaining the consent of the Board of Directors.

She stipulated that after a lecture in her church there should be no general discussion; individuals should depart "in quiet thought."

She added to these rules as the years went by. When, for instance, her followers got into the habit of flocking into Boston from all parts of the United States for her church communion season, she abolished communion in her Mother Church. She meant to keep all opportunity for unduly large

[1]This by-law did not apply officially to the branch churches, for the simple reason that these churches technically had no political standing in Mrs. Eddy's organization, and hence technically were not subject to laws which she issued. Mrs. Eddy, however, expressed the "hope" that the branch churches would adopt a similar by-law restricting the tenure of office of their own Readers, and such measures were generally adopted. The time had now come when Mrs. Eddy's wish was law, as far as the branch churches were concerned. They had been rendered utterly dependent on her continued good will for any recognition Christian Science they hoped to enjoy.

gatherings and ensuing general discussion out of their reach

In order to carry on church propaganda work and yet avoid the evils attendant upon personal preaching, she organized a "Board of Lectureship." This Board was in reality a sort of promotion department, consisting of public speakers assigned to lecture upon Mrs. Eddy's Science. It was their business not only to promote the church but also to spread good news about Mrs. Eddy personally. She very much resented some of the stories that were leaking into circulation about the vagaries of her early life. Thus she wrote that "It is the duty of the Board of Lectureship . . . to bear testimony to the facts pertaining to the life of the Pastor Emeritus."[1] Probably never before in the history of a religion did the founder make such a decree.

She organized a system of perpetual censorship for these publicity lectures by decreeing, "Each member (of the Board) shall mail to the Clerk of this Church copies of his lectures before delivering them."

In all these measures Mrs. Eddy was endeavoring to prevent the sort of free religious discussion which has split the organized Christian Church into sects almost too numerous to count. But she was not yet through. She had not devised measures for preventing free writing on her Science.

She therefore sat down to design a series of provisions that would make her Science and her Church free in perpetuity from any literature whatever except that of her own creation

First, she decreed that her name should be announced as the author of any writing of hers which was quoted in any connection whatever. This provision henceforth would apply not only to quotations by Readers from *Science and Health* and to all hymns of her authorship sung in her church; it even applied to all excerpts from her writings quoted by individual church members. And members were further warned to instruct their students to obey the injunction.

Only her own writings and literature published by her publishing company could be sold in church reading rooms.

No book or writing of hers was to be published or republished without her consent.

[1] *Manual*, XXXI, 2.

No church member should publish an article deemed "false or unjust" either to Mrs. Eddy's Science or to Mrs. Eddy herself, under penalty of excommunication.

No church member should use "written formulas," or permit his patients or pupils to use them, in making healing statements for the sick, or in teaching. Mrs. Eddy stated that "whatever is requisite for either is contained in the books of the Discoverer and Founder of Christian Science." By this time Mrs. Eddy was using capital letters for words referring to herself.

No church member was permitted "to publish profuse quotations" from Mrs. Eddy's opus or to "plagiarize" her writings. This measure, she stated frankly, was intended to "prevent Christian Science from being *adulterated*."

She prohibited any church member from buying, selling, or circulating "literature which is not correct in its statement of the divine Principle and rules and the demonstration of Christian Science."

She forbade any of her members to patronize stores having for sale "obnoxious books."

All papers by students being instructed in Christian Science were to be destroyed after class room use.

Thus did she try to emasculate the mind and thought of any one who ever came into her church and subscribed to her doctrines. Individualism either in thought or in leadership was mercilessly abolished. And her followers calmly accepted the ultimatums. It should be said for them that for the most part they probably did not know what all these decrees were about. It is not in the nature of average men to study by-laws very carefully, or to ask their implications. They sign the agreement on the dotted line without bothering about details.

Applicants for admission to Mrs. Eddy's church would henceforth actually sign on such a dotted line. Not only would they have to present recommendations from persons already church members, but they would have to sign a statement agreeing to "subscribe to the Tenets and the By-Laws of the church."

Mrs. Eddy never intended to have another insurrection if

she could help it. She meant to have no more plagiarism. Indeed, she meant even to free herself from lawsuits. She eventually designed a most important by-law which read:

A member of this Church shall not employ an attorney, nor take legal action on a case not provided for in its By-Laws—if said case relates to the person or to the property of Mary Baker Eddy—without having personally conferred with her on said subject.[1]

When she wiped her pen after finishing her remarkable Manual she must have breathed a sigh of relief. At last, now, she thought herself safe. At last she could retire from the turmoil, and go up into what *The Journal* so unblushingly called her "Mount," and be able to go to sleep at night without constant fear that some one would steal her church or her book by morning. She announced that her by-laws "were impelled by a power not one's own."[2] Perhaps indeed she thought they had been.

No voice was raised in protest to Mrs. Eddy's all-embracing measures. Even her deposed pastors fell at her feet and made self-abnegating murmurings of Thy Will Be Done. L. P. Norcross, one of the pastors now demoted, wrote with humility in *The Journal* of August, 1895:

Did any one suspect such a revelation, such a new departure would be given? No, not in the way it came. . . . Such disclosures are too high for us to receive. To One alone did the message come.

Pronouns referring to Mrs. Eddy were now often being capitalized.

The Mother Church which she had reared with such scrupulous care saw its building finished on the night of December 30, 1894. The structure was in no sense an architectural triumph, and not many years passed before its members desired to enclose it completely in a more handsome and more luxurious creation. It may be stated in passing that Mrs. Eddy never permitted any such proceeding. Those gray granite blocks of its walls represented, each one of them, one more step up which

[1] *Manual*, XXII, 9.
[2] Vd. *Church Manual*, page 3; also *Miscellaneous Writings*, page 148.

she had laboriously climbed to a pinnacle almost unique in human history. Many men and women have come to seem godlike after their death. But Mary Baker Eddy, afflicted soul that she was, saw altars reared to herself even as she shuddered at night from ghostly terrors in her bed. And she did not intend to see a single altar razed.

While she was thundering down the law to her followers, and being unquestioningly obeyed, a chapel was being created for her in her church. It was called The Mother's Room. It was a chamber provided for the exclusive use of the prophetess when she should come into her temple. The shrine was fitted up by the children of Christian Scientists organized into a society known as the "Busy Bees." In this room was a picture before which a light perpetually burned. It represented the garret manger in Lynn.[1]

Mrs. Eddy herself used this strange chamber only once, on the night of April 1, 1895. She and the members of her Concord ménage came with her to see the newly completed church. That night Mrs. Eddy occupied the folding bed in the Mother's Room. Her household attendants slept all night in the pews.

To this chamber came her loyal followers in throngs each day, to pause a moment and meditate. Over the doorway was a sign stating that but four persons would be admitted at a time; these four would remain but five minutes, whereupon a bell would be sounded and would they please retire.

All day the crowds would wait to become one of a group of four. They would enter silently, with worshipful gaze. As they looked up at the illumined portrait set in a recess of the wall, the woman in attendance, Mrs. Sargent, would drone in monotonous voice the nature of the various appointments furnished by the Busy Bees. . . . "The mantelpiece is of pure onyx . . . and the beehive upon the window sill is made from one solid block of onyx . . . the rug is made of a hundred breasts of eider-down ducks . . . the toilet room you see in

[1] There is conflict in the testimony about the portrait in this room, which was long ago closed. Some reports relate that the original portrait hallowed by the perpetual light was a representation of Mrs. Eddy herself. If such was indeed the truth, the picture was eventually changed as a result of ribald comment then current.

the corner is of the latest design with gold-plated pipes . . . the painted windows were inspired by the Mother's poem, *Christ and Christmas* . . . that case contains complete copies of all the Mother's works. . . ."

The chairs which furnished the room were supposed to be those occupied by Mrs. Eddy while her opus was being revealed, and across their arms were stretched white ribbons as a bar to the materiality of all profane hips.

The reverent gazers would talk in low whispers; and then the bell would ring; and they would tiptoe softly out while four others were admitted, and the keeper of the shrine once more began her monotonous chant . . . "The mantelpiece is of pure onyx . . . and the beehive upon the window sill . . ."

Years before, in a burst of confidence to the boyish Richard Kennedy, Mrs. Eddy once had paused a moment and looked intently at him.

"Richard," she said suddenly, "you will live to hear the church bells ring out my birthday."

Before long that strange prophecy would now come true in her own church in Concord, where she dwelt.

The Mother Church was dedicated to her. Across the front of the temple, where the inscription to the Deity usually appears, were the words:

"A Testimonial to Our Beloved Teacher, the Rev. Mary Baker G. Eddy, Discoverer and Founder of Christian Science, Author of *Science and Health with Key to the Scriptures*, President of the Massachusetts Metaphysical College, and the First Pastor of This Denomination."

The faith of men is itself the greatest miracle of all the miracles which faith engenders.

XX

When Mrs. Eddy fled from Boston in 1889, and took refuge in Concord, she settled down into an unostentatious and even secret personal life of which her new neighbors knew next to nothing. Those who were aware of her at all regarded her as an old broken-down spiritualist come up from Boston to eke out her final days and die. Meanwhile her fame was being spread from coast to coast, and the name of Mrs. Eddy was becoming a household word in New York, Chicago and Denver.

Her real burst of local fame came with the dedication of The Mother Church and the newspaper publicity attendant upon this remarkable event. Only now did Concord come to take notice of a drama that had been unfolding under its very nose. Thereafter Mrs. Eddy became a subject of pronounced and increasing public interest, and her walks and drives always drew a crowd of gaping citizens anxious to behold this mysterious old lady, in her seventy-fourth year when her Boston altar was dedicated, as she rambled around her garden or went out for air in her carriage.

In 1892 she had bought herself a new dwelling-place in Concord, uniting two estates and remodelling the old rambling farmhouse on one of them into a structure that she called Pleasant View. This was henceforth to be her home for many years—as she grew older and older and older, and more mysterious and venerated with each passing birthday.

By 1892 she had thoroughly tested out all the local retreats of malicious animal magnetism, and Pleasant View struck her fancy as being quite untrammelled by this malevolent curse. Lying about three miles outside of the Concord limits, Pleasant View had a broad outlook, and from here Mrs. Eddy could gaze away to the east where her birthplace of Bow lay hidden in the foothills, and down to the southwest where Monadnock reared its peak into the low-hung mist.

She remodelled the frame house in rather a splendid fashion for that day. She gave it two towers in the latest post-Victorian style, hung a balcony from one side, and put on the front a lengthy porch with a lot of railing and columns. She finished her parlor in old-rose and gilt.

Mrs. Eddy took for herself some rooms attached to one of the towers, where she could look down the valley toward the old farm at Bow and occasionally remind herself how far she had come up the road of achievement. Externally her estate had every aspect of a jaunty and freshly painted home that was ideal for a grandmotherly and jolly old lady. There was nothing about it to suggest the mysteries that were immured within. The gardens were always kept in apple-pie order; no blade of grass ever peeped up its head in the wide, crushed-stone driveway; the hedges were sheared within an inch of their lives.

Every day Mrs. Eddy herself made a tour of inspection around the estate. She could spot the smallest detail that was out of order. If in the sweeping of a room a chair had been moved so much as an inch out of its former place, Mrs. Eddy could detect that inch and would call for some one of her household to come running. If the smallest gewgaw on the mantel or the what-not was not replaced to its exact mathematical place of former repose after being dusted, Mrs. Eddy' observing eye took note. Since her house was rapidly becoming a sort of museum, as a result of the offerings sent to Mother from all sorts of people living in all parts of the Union, the daily dusting in Mrs. Eddy's home soon became a rite in itself

She had now, however, solved her servant problem in unique fashion. In her church by-laws she stipulated that any church member, if called on to serve her in her home, must come without question, and on ten days' notice. The period of service required was at first a year; it was later raised to three years. The sonorous by-law which embodied this requirement added that, "a member who leaves her in less time without the directors' consent or who declines to obey this call to duty, upon Mrs. Eddy's complaint thereof, shall be excommunicated from The Mother Church."

As the years went by and it became desirable to withhol

from the world the facts concerning some of the eccentric rites that went on in Mrs. Eddy's home, the selection of the proper servants became an important problem. Meanwhile the Eddy publicity had made every one of her followers eager to get inside her sacred portals. Not every one can have an opportunity to wash floors or cook in the dwelling-place of a living deity, as Mrs. Eddy was now coming to be regarded by the more enthusiastic or impressionable of her flock. No one ever had to be asked twice to go. As the Reader in one of her churches who later became a Mother Church Director once said when he was asked to repair to Pleasant View, without any suggestion of the duties he would have to perform, "I'd shovel snow to be with Mrs. Eddy."

To those in far places who had used the therapeutic psychology embodied in Mrs. Eddy's teachings, and recovered health thereby, it was easy to believe that she and her theology were miraculously anointed by God. They immediately joined their voices of praise to the general melody, and could feelingly write her such lines as these:

DEAR MOTHER:—The most blessed of women! Oh, how I long to sit within range of your voice and hear the truth that comes to you from on high! for none could speak such wondrous thoughts as have come from your pen, except it be the Spirit that speaketh in you.[1]

The author of these lines was healed of "endometritis and prolapsis uteri of over twenty years standing." The further way from Boston such followers were located, the higher their reverence for the old lady who took her walks around the pond at Pleasant View would mount. And it was by no accident that eventually Mrs. Eddy's servants were almost invariably chosen from distant cities and farms.

When some of her students decided that they would make Mrs. Eddy the present of an artificial pond for her estate, and came up personally to superintend the installation, they made their contribution to her life almost as if performing a rite. Mrs. Eddy's letter of gratitude was later published in a pamphlet like a papal bull. This document was called *Pond and*

[1] *Miscellaneous Writings*, page 415.

Purpose, quoted Solomon's remark that "as in water face
answereth to face, so the heart of man to man," and was extremely theological. In Mrs. Eddy's eloquence the pond seemed
to grow into a whole river, and she wrote to those who had
arranged this large libation:

> Above the waves of Jordan, dashing against the receding shore, I
> heard the Father and Mother's welcome, saying forever to the bap
> tized of Spirit: "This is my beloved Son."[1]

Life at Pleasant View was maintained in a wholly unevent
ful manner. Mrs. Eddy rose early, and went to bed early, and
took a nap just before dinner, which she always had at noon
Members of her household lived in the same fashion, just a
if they had each been the old lady their mistress was. She stil
had with her Calvin Frye as secretary and general factotum
and when she went for her drive promptly at two o'clock it wa
Calvin who in livery mounted the footman's box before th
driver could say "get-up" to the horses. Mrs. Eddy was a littl
afraid of horses all her life. With Calvin along she felt quit
safe. For his part, like all other members of her household
there was no service too menial for him to perform, althoug
in the house he now occupied a position of respect and autho
ity.

It was the business of all in her household to assist her i
defending herself against the attacks of malicious animal mag
netism that visited her in Concord just as regularly as they ha
in Boston and Lynn. Knowledge of such attacks was general
withheld from the outside world, where profane believer
might have scoffed at Mrs. Eddy's explanation of these occu
rences.

Nor did she always rely merely on mental defense. Whe
the pain grew great she sought her old remedy. Foster Edd
who as a graduate M.D. had not wholly deserted his pharma
copœia even though he had taught in Mrs. Eddy's college, wa
quoted years later in an interview in the New York *World* a
saying that he kept a supply of the drug in his own room, an

[1] *Miscellaneous Writings,* page 206.

that this was drawn on for use whenever Mrs. Eddy's own supply ran out. *The World's* statement included a description of one such occasion. Once when Frye came to his room in the middle of the night to ask for a tablet he followed the secretary back to Mrs. Eddy's chamber. "Mrs. Eddy," *The World* quoted her adopted son as saying,[1] "was outstretched upon the bed in the agonies of one of the strange fits that frequently seized her. Her distorted face was turned toward me. With her thin hands she beat furiously at Frye as he bent over the bedside. An instant later she was shrieking. But Frye forced the morphine tablet into her mouth and held her firmly down among the pillows. That is what I saw with my own eyes. . . ."

Frye had already become utterly indispensable to Mrs. Eddy.

Between her physical attacks she could always rise up as a dominant, autocratic, energetic old woman, ruling her household and her church with a rod of iron, writing for long hours each day, issuing instructions in every direction, planning, designing, scheming.

Her sense of persecution extended even to her writings,[2] and she was often convinced that her enemies were seeking to hold up her publications by malicious animal magnetism. In the autumn of 1889, for instance, she had even ordered William G. Nixon, her publisher, to pick up *The Christian Science Journal* and flee with it from Boston to some other city where M. A. M. was not ensconced. Mr. Nixon had every reason for wanting to stay in Boston; he had brought his family from the far northwest and settled them there. And it was no simple matter to pick up a periodical from one city and take it to some other one—all between publication dates. But protests were quite useless. In any difference of opinion Mrs. Eddy always won. There was no possible reply that could be brought to bear when she advanced her foot, threw back her head, and said with very

[1] Quoted in N. Y. *World*, May 8, 1907.

[2] Evidences of this persecution complex still abound in *Science and Health*, despite its innumerable editings. In this connection Mrs. Eddy was particularly fond of recalling the persecutions of Jesus. Vd. pp. 316–317: "The spiritual idea of God, as presented by Jesus, was scourged in person, and its Principle was rejected. . . . Whosoever lives most the life of Jesus in this age and declares best the power of Christian Science, will drink of his Master's cup. Resistance to truth will haunt his steps, and he will incur the hatred of sinners. . . ."

low and ominous accents, "God has directed me in this matter
Have you anything further to say?"

Mr. Nixon hastily went to Philadephia, made a contrac
with a printer, and thereupon received a telegram ordering hin
to escort *The Journal* back to Boston at once.

When Mrs. Eddy was getting out her 1891 edition of *Sci
ence and Health* she was convinced that mesmerism was delay
ing the proceedings. In consequence she assigned members o
her household to "treat" the various persons and machine
that were engaged in the printing task. She assigned to he
adopted son, Foster Eddy, the most important rôle of treating
the printer himself, John Wilson of Cambridge, and of look
ing after the mental state of the man in charge of the bindery
Others of her confidants who were to assist in the task of rear
ing a mental bulwark about the production of the new editio
were Captain Eastaman, Miss Bartlett, Mrs. Munroe, M
Johnson, and Mr. and Mrs. Knapp.

Mrs. Eddy herself wrote out a formula for use in givin
mental treatment to the presses and the persons engaged i
operating them. "When the book goes to the bindery," sh
wrote, "then stop the press aid and turn all their force there.
Evidently she feared that such a concentration of treatmer
might possibly prove an overdose for the unaccustomed print
ing establishment, for she also instructed that "if I or M
Frye write or telegraph to you, then you must stop at once th
students' argument."[1]

Treatment did prove, as things happened, to be overdon
the press-room fell into real confusion, and Mrs. Eddy hastil
called off all treatment except that being administered by Fo
ter Eddy himself. "At once dismiss your help," she wrote, "an
confine your treatment to the Proprietor."

Mrs. Eddy was vastly pleased when the new edition can
out. As she wrote to Mrs. Stetson in 1891:

Oh, the marvel of my life! What would be thought of it, if it w
known in a millionth of its detail? But this cannot be now. It will tal
centuries for this.

[1]For the complete document, together with several of Mrs. Eddy's letters
her assistants embodying other similar instructions, see Milmine, *Life of Ma
Baker G. Eddy*, page 393 ff.

I have improved my version of the Lord's Prayer once more, and now pronounce it, *perfect*. Be sure and get the 3rd edition of the last Revised book. It will contain fifty improvements; sometimes one word, again a sentence, sometimes the meaning is flashed forth like lightning by these little touches. . . .[1]

It is plain that Mrs. Eddy herself could occasionally find time to wonder over the miraculous glory that had come to her. One cannot doubt that sometimes she herself was even convinced that a supernatural power had established itself in her career.

But always she took a very human pleasure in tinkering with her book. She enjoyed rearranging its paragraphs and lines until they were just so, in exactly the same fashion in which she adjusted the ornaments on her what-not until she achieved an approved effect.[2] It was a habit that gave the critics a merry opportunity. Of one of her Lord's Prayer revisions Mark Twain wrote:

It seems to me that this one is distinctly superior to the one that was inspired for last year's edition. It is strange, but to my mind plain, that inspiring is an art which does improve with practice.

As Mrs. Eddy improved her productions she took great care to sequester her earlier and less polished efforts and give authorization only to those which had received her mature consideration. In 1891 she wrote to Mrs. Stetson, who had now become her most prominent disciple, to instruct her to provide the important libraries in New York with copies of the latest revision of *Science and Health*. She herself, she said, was substituting this new version—"so much clearer, because I took time enough to make it so"—for the three hundred copies she had previously placed in libraries.[3]

[1] Stetson, *Sermons and Other Writings*, page 31.

[2] For Mrs. Eddy's own explanation of her revisions, vd. *Science and Health*, age 361: "I have revised SCIENCE AND HEALTH, only to give a clearer and fuller pression of its original meaning. Spiritual ideas unfold as we advance. . . . That hich when sown bears immortal fruit, enriches mankind only when it is understood,—hence the many readings given the Scriptures, and the requisite revisions of SCIENCE AND HEALTH WITH KEY TO THE SCRIPTURES."

[3] Stetson, *Sermons and Other Writings*, page 30.

As Mrs. Eddy's conviction of personal greatness increased, she became surer of her unique human standing; and there were times when she got to wondering quite seriously if she was not indeed a modern manifestation of Christ. She wrote Mrs. Stetson in 1900:

Jesus was the man that was a prophet and the best and greatest man that has ever appeared on earth, but Jesus was not Christ, for Christ is the spiritual individual that the eye cannot see. Jesus was called Christ only in the sense that you say, a Godlike man. I am only a Godlike woman, God-anointed, and I have done a work that none others could do.[1]

Mrs. Eddy's use of that little word "only" is interesting.

In darker moods, when she had to meet the attacks of critics and a rebellious following, her sense of persecution found an outlet in comparing herself to Christ on the Cross, and there were many times when she felt a deep sense of loneliness. "Everybody is fighting like fiends over every move that I make that God bids," she complained in 1893, "every one, I mean who hates Good; and my students leave me to meet it, as of old, alone in the sweat of agony."[2] Again, "As Paul was not understood and Jesus was not understood at the time they taught and demonstrated, so I am not."[3] Then, even more pointedly in a letter written during the Next Friends' Suit that came to overwhelm her late in life, "Do *not allow* the *evil one* in your midst to turn you away from me in this hour of crucifixion, or history will repeat itself, and Christian Science will once more be lost as aforetime. . . ."[4]

As early as 1895 Mrs. Eddy developed a habit of thinking of herself as Christ crucified whenever she felt something going wrong in her affairs. In this year that saw the dedication of her Mother Church she referred to herself as the modern embodiment of the "spiritual idea," threatened by such desert

[1] Stetson, *Sermons and Other Writings*, page 40.
[2] *Ibid.*, page 32.
[3] *Ibid.*, page 40.
[4] *Ibid.*, page 191. This refers to the idea that "Christian Science," as taught by Jesus Christ, was "lost" to the world after his crucifixion and was not again retrieved until Mrs. Eddy appeared on the scene.

ion as Jesus in turn had suffered about eighteen hundred and sixty-odd years previously. She wrote to Mrs. Stetson in 1895 on Thanksgiving day:

If all the students of C. S. should desert the spiritual idea and its embodiment at this period, as they did in the first century and suffer the consequence, our Cause would not be lost, but the thought of this is all that gives me the sharp sense of the time required to undo such error as this would again introduce, even the groans of Gethsemane and at times the sweat of agony. . . .[1]

Although in her later years Mrs. Eddy was forced by merciless wit and criticism to let go some of her claims to divinity, just as she was forced by numerous deaths to modify some of her proscriptions against consultations with doctors and to warn her followers not to treat contagious diseases, during all of the eighteen-nineties she thought of herself quite often as a complete religious institution.

When the meeting of the National Christian Science Association was held in New York in May of 1890, the secretary was instructed "to send to our Mother greetings and words of affection from her assembled children."

Mrs. Eddy was charmed. She wired right back:

ALL HAIL! HE HATH FILLED THE HUNGRY WITH GOOD THINGS AND THE SICK HE HATH NOT SENT EMPTY AWAY
                                        MOTHER MARY

Mary, of course, was a much happier and more fortunate name for theological uses than the rather commonplace Eddy. On the other hand, it was a name in fairly common circulation. So the President of the Association considerately sought to give Mrs. Eddy an established claim upon it. In his opening address he said:

There is but one Moses, one Jesus; and there is but one Mary.

Incidentally it is not amiss to note here that Mrs. Eddy's telegram is an excellent illustration of the manner in which

[1] Stetson, *Sermons and Other Writings*, page 36.

she adapted the Scriptures to her philosophy either by use of her *Key to the Scriptures* or by indirect rephrasing. The scriptural quotation on which her telegram was based was taken from St. Luke:

> "He hath filled the hungry with good things, and the rich he hath sent empty away."

When eventually Mrs. Eddy made a move to cement her ownership of the "Mother" title with a by-law, her followers for several years already had willingly accorded it. Few were those in her church who were loath to yield her exaltation. There is in almost every human breast some instinct which leads its owner to seek an object worthy of worship; and the higher men can raise their idols the greater is the reflected glory which they feel at their devotions. Mrs. Eddy's followers themselves, far from ever laughing at her, now took her even more seriously than she took herself. And it was not these worshipful satellites who eventually caused Mrs. Eddy to come down several steps from the peak of the Mount on which she had ensconced herself; it was only the ridicule of the general public who eventually became informed of some of her claims.

The greatest single assistance to establishing Mrs. Eddy's unique standing in the conceptions of her followers was not her publicity, but her retirement. Those who came in personal contact with her usually lost most of their awe before they had been with her long.

She first began to establish herself as an important figure when she sent out her publications to readers located far from her centre of activity. Her retirement in Concord now removed her from the sight even of the Boston disciples. It was therefore not difficult for legends to grow apace. As these myths developed and evolved, even some of those who had known Mrs. Eddy, had seen her in action, and had been utterly disillusioned, now began to hear of her wonderful and mysterious achievements to such an extent that they began to question their own previous judgment. Such is the power of effective and repetitious advertising on the human mind.

In Concord, Mrs. Eddy now showed herself but seldom. She

did not even go on foot around the town as when she first moved there, but took her airings only in a carriage. By the middle of 1895, after her Church had been dedicated, there were many of her followers all over the country eager to see her, so remarkable was the picture of her they had formulated in their minds. Mrs. Eddy had been to the new Mother Church only infrequently. On her visit when she spent the night in the Mother's Room, few others were present besides loyal disciples who could be trusted to give the properly rapt description of the manner in which Mrs. Eddy swept down the long aisle and knelt prayerfully before her own altar. On May 26 she had again appeared at the church to preach from its pulpit, to eagerly adoring crowds. These two appearances, however, did not satisfy the curiosity of the many out-of-town disciples who longed for a view of the Eddy countenance.

Thus when the Church held its first June Communion, in 1895, Mrs. Eddy decided to give church members another fleeting glimpse of herself, it being an occasion on which she felt in good health and capable of creating the impression she desired to disseminate. She telegraphed an invitation to the congregation to come up and be received at Pleasant View; a hundred and eighty of them boarded the train and journeyed up to Concord, and Mrs. Eddy proudly threw open her new house to them and did the honors of the occasion. She shook hands with each delegate, talked with many, and all went away happy at the thought of this brief contact with a Messiah.

Thereafter for a few years Mrs. Eddy made a point of allowing her worshipful following short views of her on special occasions, and for some time the pilgrimages to Concord took on the status of sacred journeys to a shrine. What an outlet for human yearning, rapture and religious exaltation these ceremonials provided is best described in the words of a follower whose account of her ecstasy on first seeing Mrs. Eddy was published in *The Journal* of June, 1899:

When I decided to attend I also hoped to see our Mother. . . . I saw that if I allowed the thought that I must see her personally to transcend the desire to obey and grow into the likeness of her teachings, the mistake would obscure my understanding of both the Revelator and the

Revelation. After the members of the Board had retired they reappeared upon the rostrum and my heart beat quickly with the thought, "perhaps *she* has come." But no, it was to read her message. . . .

The following day five of us made the journey to Concord, drove out to Pleasant View, and met her face to face on her daily drive. She seemed watching to greet us, for when she caught sight of our faces she instantly half rose with expectant face, bowing, smiling, and waving her hand to us. Then as she went out of our sight, kissed her hand to all.

I will not attempt to describe the Leader, nor can I say what this brief glimpse was and is to me. I can only say that I wept and the tears start every time I think of it. Why do I weep? I think it is because I want to be like her and they are tears of repentance. I realize better now what it was that made Mary Magdalen weep when she came into the presence of the Nazarene.

In 1896 Mrs. Eddy made only one appearance, preaching one Sunday in February in her church. In 1897 she made another lone public appearance, this time again inviting the communicants to come up to Pleasant View. Almost three thousand made the journey, so many that every available carriage in Concord was hired for the three-mile drive and hundreds had to cover the distance on foot. Wearing a purple silk dress adorned with black lace, with a bonnet on her head, Mrs. Eddy addressed them in a body. By this time she had established her membership in the Daughters of the American Revolution and she wore the D. A. R. insignia executed in diamonds and rubies. At her throat she flashed a diamond cross. On occasions like this Mrs. Eddy could be wholly delightful—a vivacious old lady ready to talk about anything from her family connections to her efforts to raise a fine garden. To an untutored observer listening-in on her informal conversation she would not have seemed greatly different from any affable grandmother who had taken a little too earnestly to religion in her declining years.

How she had engaged the imagination and awe of her followers, however, is illustrated by the vortex of wonder into which she threw them when she intimated that she did not desire to receive them at the communion in 1898. The real reason for her lack of hospitality at this time lay evidently in the fact that she was not feeling quite at her best, for 1898 marked the beginning of a more serious invalidism than she had known for many years. She had no desire, in this condition, to put herself on close display. But her disciples could not know this, and some of them were utterly at sea as to what they should do. As Mrs. Stetson has told the story:

I accepted this, of course, as her final word, and I never thought of going to Concord. The next morning Miss M. E. of Boston, who was visiting at Pleasant View, called me on the telephone at the Touraine, where I was staying, and asked if I were coming to Pleasant View with my students.

I said, "Of course not, after Mrs. Eddy requested us to discontinue our pilgrimage."

Miss E. urged me to reconsider it, and said she knew what she was talking about. I said, "I cannot do this unless I have it from higher authority than you."

She telephoned me again the next day and again requested that I consider going to Pleasant View with my students. I thought this was strange, and that I had better go at once myself that morning to Pleasant View. Upon my arrival I called for Mrs. Sargent and asked her what this request from Miss E. meant. I asked, "Does Mrs. Eddy want me to come?" She replied, "I do not know."

I asked again, "But who does want me to come?" and she replied, "I do not know."

I asked: "Is it right for me to come? What does this mean?" Again she replied, "Why, if you want to come, there is nothing to hinder you from doing so."

I said: "Well, what about this request of our Leader's not to come? I cannot disobey that. I am going to ask Mr. Frye." I called for Mr. Frye and he came to me. I put the question to him and he answered in the same evasive way. By this time I was aroused and I said: "What does all this mean? I do not wish to come unless I know that Mrs. Eddy desires me to do so. Did she tell you, Mr. Frye, that she wanted me to come?"

He said, "No." I asked, "But does she want me to come?" He replied, "I should do just as I wanted to do." I said a second time, "I cannot disobey that request of hers."

He said: "If a mother told her children she did not want to see them for a year or so and the children should all agree without a murmur to stay away, would you not think it looked as if those children felt glad they did not have to go?"

Then I suspected that this had been discussed and that Mrs. Eddy's knowledge of it was to be kept secret. I then asked, "Well, would you come?" He did not answer. I asked: "If I were to come to Concord where should I assemble with my students? Should I come to Pleasant View?"

He replied: "No. I should stand around the church. When you go
back, stop at the church and talk with Mr. Tomlinson about it."

I went and saw Mr. Tomlinson. He was very agreeable, and advised
me to stand near the church. He seemed to know something about it.
He said: "Mrs. Eddy drives by every day and you will have a chance
to see her. Be here at two o'clock." Then it dawned upon me that I had
better go back and collect my students who had not returned to New
York.

The next day we went to Concord and stationed ourselves in front of
the church. In a little while Mrs. Eddy drove past. It had been raining
slightly and we had put up our umbrellas. When she drove by, the rain
ceased, the umbrellas went down, and we saw our Leader. She recognized us by bowing, waving, and kissing her hand to us. She drove past
us three times. We took our blessing and went home.[1]

In 1899 Mrs. Eddy also failed to issue an invitation to
Pleasant View, but on June 5 she came to Boston, where the
church was holding its annual meeting the next day. She spent
the night at her old Commonwealth Avenue House, which she
had not sold, but had decided to keep, evidently for the sake of
its associations. By this time she had presumably forgotten
about the animal magnetism which had attacked her under its
roof. Even in keeping the house, however, she showed good
business management. She loaned it to The Mother Church to
be used as a residence for its First Reader, with the stipulation
in her by-laws that the church should pay the taxes and rent on
the property, "attend to the insurance before it expires," and
keep it in repair and suitably furnished. Mrs. Eddy, no matter
how long the church had carried her house in this fashion, reserved to herself the right to recover it at her request.

Here, then, she stayed for the night of June 5 as the guest
of the First Reader, Septimus J. Hanna, who had not yet become such an influence in the pulpit as to cause Mrs. Eddy to
remove him to another field. The next day she appeared before
the audience at the church meeting and was saluted with a wild
waving of handkerchiefs.

Thereupon she spoke briefly upon a favorite text, "Prove
me now herewith, saith the Lord of hosts, if I will not open
you the windows of heaven."

[1]Stetson, *Reminiscences, Sermons and Correspondence*, page 31 ff.

Mrs. Eddy did not again make a formal public appearance until 1901, when once more she invited her disciples to journey up from Boston after the Communion service. Three thousand again made the trip. They were not admitted to the house, and Mrs. Eddy appeared only briefly upon the balcony.

In 1902 no formal Communion pilgrimage occurred, although groups of communicants went up to Concord to seek a glimpse of the Leader on her daily drive. Her health had become too feeble for her to appear abroad; she took this occasion to announce a break of "any seeming connection between the sacrament in our church and a pilgrimage to Concord."[1]

By 1903 Mrs. Eddy was actually under the care of physicians. Despite a severe attack of *renal calculi* in May of this year,[2] she had rallied sufficiently by June to receive a large delegation of communicants. As she grew older there had developed in her face a frail, ethereal quality which could seem infinitely gentle and moving during those periods of calm that fell between her storms. Mrs. Eddy, as she smiled faintly upon these thronging worshippers at Pleasant View, may well have seemed to many of them a body attenuated almost to pure spirit.

Her last scheduled appearance before her church members was in 1904. It occurred not at Pleasant View, but in front of the recently completed Church at Concord. In this year when she was eighty-three years old, Mrs. Eddy drove in stately form up to the church while the throngs massed outside were hushed in reverence. The horses came to a halt, and Mrs. Eddy motioned to a high official of The Mother Church to come up and hear what she had to say. He thus received personally the greeting that she wished expressed to the whole church organization. By this time she had aged greatly, and her voice on this day did not have the sonorous carrying quality that in previous years had held whole audiences enraptured. But Mrs. Eddy had a lot of life left in her yet.

[1] *Message to the Mother Church for 1902*, page 20.   [2] Vd. p. 367.

PART IV

THE SECRET PLACE OF THE MOST HIGH

". . . Growing diffident of the protection and assistance of the gods, and suspicious of friends."

—PLUTARCH.

XXI

One thing that Mrs. Eddy's Concord retirement did for her was to provide a great deal more time for writing. Authorship was now her main source of revenue. She had invested almost a million dollars, for she was very sparing with her expenditures, and lived in such a manner that she had no great opportunity for ostentation. This capital, representing the profits from her college, was sufficient alone to supply her with a very handsome income in a generation when dollars were worth at least twice as much as they were a quarter of a century later.

But Mrs. Eddy saw no reason why she should live on past achievements, nor why she should not have constantly increasing revenues even though she had given up teaching. It never occurred to her to reduce the price of her book now that her own worldly comfort had been established. Instead, she spent a great deal of time planning ways by which her sales and revenues could be increased.

In some of her sales devices she was rather ingenious. Even the Busy Bees did not escape her attention. This association was made up of about 2,600 children who not only had furnished the Mother Room and provided its solid onyx beehive, but had engaged to keep it supplied with fresh flowers and to maintain a perpetual light burning in this holy of holies.

Mrs. Eddy was moved by this expression of childish fealty, and so she dedicated to the Busy Bees her next book, called *Pulpit and Press*. It was a thin and wholly uninspired volume consisting largely of reprints of newspaper articles on The Mother Church and Mrs. Eddy. It was priced at $1.00 a copy, postage 6 cents.

Mrs. Eddy immediately added 2,600 copies to its circulation by offering to sell each Busy Bee a volume at half price. Such an offer was a command, regardless of the fact that most of the Busy Bees as yet could hardly even read. Eventually, when some criticism arose concerning Mrs. Eddy's bland acceptance even of children's pennies as offerings at her shrine, she capitulated by dissolving the Busy Bees organization. At the same time she set aside $4,000 in bonds to be held in an interest-earning fund for distribution to the "dear children" when they came of age.

Her most effective method of promoting *Science and Health* was her constant issuance of new and revised editions. Following the edition of 1891, in which she had at last turned out a Lord's Prayer that was "perfect," she published still newer editions in 1894 and 1896. This policy caused criticism in Mrs. Eddy's own ranks, and Foster Eddy and Nixon had both argued against it, though to no avail. Mrs. Eddy knew her own mind. Every loyal church member was required to obtain a new edition as soon as it emerged from the press. It did not matter how many old editions he already possessed; these were utterly useless and passé when a new edition appeared, regardless of how minor were the changes effected. Sometimes, of course, these changes were important, such as Mrs. Eddy's permission to call a surgeon in cases needing surgical attention; or her permission to use morphia to quiet intense pain that mental treatment would not remove. Criticism of the many deaths in the hands of her healers caused the first change; her own experience doubtless led her into making the second. One of her several references to morphine, in present editions of *Science and Health,* is as follows:

If from an injury or from any cause, a Christian Scientist were seized with pain so violent that he could not treat himself mentally,—and the Scientists had failed to relieve him,—the sufferer could call a surgeon who would give him a hypodermic injection, then, when the belief of pain was lulled, he could handle his own case mentally.[1]

It was expected that every loyal follower would buy copies of every book that Mrs. Eddy produced. New books were not infrequent after she repaired to Pleasant View, for she had a great deal of time to devote to the task of getting together all her old notes and writings and pamphlets and speeches and newspaper letters and everything else that she had ever put on

[1] *Science and Health,* page 464.

paper, and paring the material down into shape suitable for inclusion in a bound volume.

Such was the sort of material that went into *Miscellaneous Writings,* a volume published in 1897. In order to promote the sale of this rather heterogenous work Mrs. Eddy issued a daring decree. It not only demanded of her followers that they should all buy the book: it stipulated that they cease teaching Christian Science entirely for a year and devote their efforts to promoting this new contribution to literature. About fifty academies were operating at this time, and untold hundreds of persons were making a living teaching Mrs. Eddy's precepts to those willing to pay for the instruction. The decree meant that all these academies must close on a week's notice; that all the teachers for a full year must find some other method of support; and that everybody within the church, without receiving a cent of commission, should endeavor to promote sales under penalty of excommunication. Mrs. Eddy's notice in *The Journal* of March, 1897, read as follows:

Christian Scientists in the United States and Canada are hereby enjoined not to teach a student of Christian Science for a year, commencing March 14, 1897. "Miscellaneous Writings" is calculated to prepare the minds of all true thinkers to understand the Christian Science text book more correctly than a student can. The Bible, *Science and Health with the Key to the Scriptures,* and my other published works are the only proper instructors for this hour. It shall be the duty of all Christian Scientists to circulate and to sell as many of these books as they can.

If a member of the First Church of Christ Scientist shall fail to obey this injunction it shall render him liable to lose his membership in this church.

It was in 1891 that Mrs. Eddy published her *Retrospection and Introspection,* informal memoirs written in her seventieth year. By this time she had come highly to idealize everything that had occurred in her childhood, and to the circle immediately around her in her home she did not hesitate to repeat tales even more remarkable than those she wrote in the pages of *Retrospection and Introspection*. It now developed that Mrs. Eddy's mother had lived in a state of divine exaltation for an entire eight or nine months before Mary was born.

Mrs. Eddy would repeat to her household with great solemnity what Mrs. Baker, heavy with child, told her neighbor, old Mrs. Gault. The expectant Mrs. Baker confided to Mrs. Gault that she could not keep her thoughts away from the strong conviction that she was going to have a child that would be holy, consecrated, and set apart for wonderful achievements.

As Mrs. Eddy retold these tales to her awe-inspired home audience, she undoubtedly felt that they were quite true, and from time to time could even produce in her reminiscences of childhood a recollection of an early miracle or two. In one of these confidential accounts to her ménage Mrs. Eddy would tell how her brother Sam cut his leg as he was chopping wood with an axe. He was put to bed in pain, and lay there suffering until Mary's father called her into the invalid's room. Old Mark Baker took Mary's hand, turned down the bedcovers, and touched her hand to the bandaged leg. Lo, the wound was instantly healed!

This was a great story for the entertainment of the household in the twilight, and Mrs. Eddy never got tired of repeating it. Her attendants lived just as she did, arising and retiring at the same hours, never dining out, never leaving the place except for some assigned mission, never receiving friends, never seeking entertainment. Mrs. Eddy was their all-in-all. Her naps, her dreams, her meals, her various employments during the day, formed the only punctuation marks in their existence. It was not strange that they hung raptly on her words.

Yet all was not calm in their midst. Despite the fact that an outside world supposed the Eddy home to be the very shrine of peace and love, the group around her had their own intense enmities and jealousies. Mrs. Eddy at all times had a favorite and at all times this favorite was the object of jealous regard from the other members of the circle.

No matter what her mood toward the others, Mrs. Eddy could always find a warm word for the one who held her tender regard at the moment; indeed, she could flatter and cajole in a manner that would have made vanity incarnate blush. In such remarks one could always trace the euphemisms of the small town poetess; and her references to "the touch of fairy fingers," or the "music of footfalls," or "the gracefulness of a nymph" would pour from her lips with daring aplomb. Georgine Milmine relates how she once told one young man that if she could paint a portrait of Jesus Christ, she would put on canvas a face that looked like his own.

Dr. Foster Eddy held on to his place in her regard for a surprisingly long period. Just as Mrs. Eddy had in turn breathed to Kennedy, Spofford, Arens and Buswell, one after the other, that each was to be the one chosen to sit at her right hand and carry on her career, so she had dazzled Foster Eddy with great visions and hopes. After his failure to carry on her college he still did not lose in favor with her, and she apparently derived a great deal of unalloyed satisfaction from the loyal affection which he gave her. He was at first horrified, then puzzled, by her strange night attacks, and often was called on to treat her at these times. Medical school graduates of that day knew little enough about abnormal psychology; his professional training therefore did not help him. And neither he nor any of the other students, nor indeed Mrs. Eddy herself, ever succeeded in curing her of her ailments by practising her own Science. Thus it was that for really effective treatment Mrs. Eddy finally fell back on Frye, who, canny, silent, resourceful, had found somehow the remedy. Frye now accompanied Mrs. Eddy everywhere. During her drives he got into a uniform and occupied the footman's box. At other times he had the general supervision of the house, opening all her mail, consulting her about its answering, transcribing her messages, keeping her accounts, occasionally even helping her to manage her investments.

Frye was not fond of Foster Eddy, and Foster Eddy early developed a strong aversion for the sleek and unctuous Frye. Each regarded the other as a possible adversary who required watching.

Bennie, as Mrs. Eddy always called Foster Eddy, had no formal work after the closing of the college. He ran around on errands to publishers; wrote some of her letters when Frye was engaged otherwise; occasionally addressed meetings at which Mrs. Eddy wanted representation; and on at least a few occasions helped in the kitchen, washing the dishes. When his mother was in pensive mood in the twilight after-supper hour he could play the piano and sing for her.

For a brief while Mrs. Eddy sent him to the Boston School of Oratory to develop his voice for speaking purposes. She took a certain pride in having her son appear in public with a style and elegance befitting her own present station in life; on these occasions he wore a long fur-lined coat, and affected a diamond ring which she had given him.

In the course of events William G. Nixon, Mrs. Eddy's publisher, resigned his post. Mrs. Eddy had made things rather uncomfortable for him for some time. Relations came to a climax during the period of making plans for the Mother Church building. Mr. Nixon insisted that the lot which Mrs. Eddy had shoved around in so many manœuvres should have a title-search. When the Massachusetts Title Insurance Company refused to insure the title Mrs. Eddy was most disturbed, asserting that "the title was from God, and no material title could affect God's temple." And she became actually angry when she discovered that Nixon, acting on the report of the Title Company, had returned to some donors the money they had contributed to a building fund.

Mr. Nixon resigned very shortly thereafter, toward the close of 1892. Mrs. Eddy thereupon decided to give the post to her adopted son. Bennie knew nothing whatever about publishing, but Mrs. Eddy hopefully thought he could learn. This was a very lucrative post, and Mrs. Eddy desired to have it in the family.

She had been trying to get a closer hold on her publishing affairs for some time. In 1889 she had given The Christian Science Journal to her old Christian Science Association. At that time The Journal was heavily in debt, and Mrs. Eddy was very glad to donate what Mark Twain characterized as "this sorrow to those lambs."

Mr. Nixon thereupon took The Journal and the other various projects of the Publishing Society and worked and prayed over them for some three years. When he started there was not a single dollar in the treasury and the Society owed bills for printing and paper to the amount of several hundred dollars; in addition, it had large contingent liabilities representing subscriptions paid in advance.

Mr. Nixon shouldered this collection of liabilities and in three years put *The Journal* on its feet. By 1892 he reported six thousand dollars in the bank and all bills paid. Mrs. Eddy thereupon looked over her records to see who really owned *The Journal*. As with all her gifts, she had presented *The Journal* to her old Association with conditions as well as liabilities attached; as Mark Twain phrased it, "she had tied a string to its hind leg, and kept one end of it hitched to her belt."

With the dissolution of the Association she believed that she could consider *The Journal* rightfully hers again. She wrote a letter to the old officers of the Association and so stated. She rather thought, she explained, that *The Journal* had "already fallen into her hands." At any rate, she asked for a formal vote to that effect. "I see the wisdom," she explained, "of again owning this Christian Science waif."

When she got *The Journal* safely back, Mrs. Eddy put it in the hands of The Mother Church, where she had concentrated all her other mundane affairs. She now put Bennie in charge of all her publishing. Not only did she want to provide a good job for Bennie—this being one of the most lucrative she could offer; she also desired to get a larger income for herself.

Previously, with *Science and Health* selling for three dollars a copy, plus postage, Mrs. Eddy had been getting only a dollar royalty. Since the book cost only about forty-seven cents to manufacture, this meant that the publisher made a very handsome profit—about a dollar and fifty-three cents a copy. There was virtually no sales or promotion cost, for every Church member and every copy of *The Journal* was a salesman; the publisher's net return—which in early days had been very narrow—was consequently rather large.

Mrs. Eddy decided that she would therefore raise her royalty to a dollar and a half, which under the circumstances was fair enough. Bennie himself made two-thirds as much; and with what he saved during his career in publishing he made himself very comfortable in his later years. His payments to

Mrs. Eddy indicate how her own income from her writings was mounting at this period; in 1893 he turned over to her royalties of $11,692; these rose to $14,834 the next year, and to $18,481 by 1895. Thereafter they mounted much more rapidly, so that by the early 1900's Mrs. Eddy's income from royalties alone must have amounted to between fifty and one hundred thousand dollars a year.

Bennie lasted in this job less than four years. If jealousy had existed in the Eddy household before, it was now enlarged into an envy that whispered on every hand. Nor was this feeling confined to Pleasant View; it was echoed in Boston. Not only was the head of the Publishing Society a very lucrative office; it was a most important and influential one. A man in this position was no mere editor; he was actually a director of publicity for a great and increasingly wealthy corporation. In some ways, in his influence over the Eddy destiny, he was even more powerful than Mrs. Eddy herself. For Mrs. Eddy in the last analysis was a creature of publicity.

Thus no one who had access to Mrs. Eddy's ear failed to carry to her the latest whispers that were going the rounds about Bennie. These varied from the story that Bennie was running around with women, to the tale that Bennie was seeking to usurp his Mother's place by killing her off with malicious animal magnetism.

Mrs. Eddy's horrible hallucinations about malicious animal magnetism grew with the years. Once Frye came in anguish to Bennie's door in the middle of the night to say that his mother was going absolutely insane. "Come quick," he said. "Your mother is mad! She thinks that a tumor is growing out on her breast, and she is calling for you."

Foster hurriedly slipped into a bathrobe and literally ran into Mrs. Eddy's bedroom. She lay there with the covers tossed off, her thin limbs half-showing through her gown, her wispy hair smeared back from her face, her mouth writhing with words that were not always intelligible. "It's growing," she shrieked with her eyes rolling wildly. She smoothed her hands over her breast as if she felt a bulbous protuberance. She grew hysterical with sobs.[1]

[1] Quoted from statement of Foster Eddy in N. Y. *World*, March 12, 1907.

Her adopted son sat with her until daybreak, talking to her soothingly, quietly.

The suggestion that even her own adopted son might be seeking to harm her needed only repetition to Mrs. Eddy to make it seem plausible. Indeed, this was probably the most powerful weapon against Bennie which jealous members of the household could use. But for once, at least, the old lady sought to ward off these suggestions. She had been genuinely fond of Bennie, and occasionally there were times of calm when she realized the treachery to old friends and counsellors of which in her more distraught moments she was capable.

Once, when she and Bennie were alone, she hungrily drew him down to the sofa with her and took his hand. "Bennie," she said despairingly, "Bennie—if I ever ask you to go away from me, do not leave me."

Frye had already discovered unconsciously a very simple and marvellous way to control Mrs. Eddy. It consisted merely of reiterated verbal suggestion, particularly when linked up with suggestions that she was being made the subject of malicious influence. From the accounts of every one who told of his experiences in Mrs. Eddy's home during the years of her retirement, this conclusion must be drawn. There were times when Mrs. Eddy feared the close-lipped Frye greatly, times when she abhorred him; she herself described him as utterly disagreeable. But in her periods of weakness she found herself more and more unable to resist the persistent attack of any mind, no matter how ignorant, that was more direct and less scattered than her own. Less and less could she fight off any suggestion that made appeal to her deep-rooted fears and errors. In the words of Foster Eddy: "Gradually her strength failed, and periods of frenzy seized her. I have seen her rush round her room, filling the house with her cries. In these paroxysms she was uncontrollable."[1]

The story was now brought to her that Bennie had been caught falsifying his books. Bennie heard the news at the same time that it reached his foster-mother. In the greatest haste and with extreme difficulty he got together vouchers to disprove the charges.

[1] N. Y. *World*, March 12, 1907.

Next came the story that Bennie was carrying on with a woman in his own office. He had given employment in his office to the widow of an old friend who was supporting her daughter. That he wooed her is improbable, for Bennie was now about fifty years old and had never displayed any characteristics that go with a roving eye. Be that as it may, Bennie got on a train for Concord within an hour after he himself had heard the story in Boston. He rushed out to Pleasant View, climbed the stairs to Mrs. Eddy's room, found her seated at her desk.

At sight of him she sprang to her feet, shrieked aloud, and rushed out into the hall. He followed, thinking that she had merely been seized by one of her attacks. Then she screamed "Murder!" Stumbling, falling, dragging herself through the house in terror, she kept up the cries of "Murder!" until she had thrown herself, sobbing, at Frye.[1]

Bennie turned away, left the house, and Mrs. Eddy soon notified him that he was removed from her publishing business. She placed the business in the hands of Joseph Armstrong, a devout Scientist who had formerly been a banker in Kansas City. This was in 1896.

Foster Eddy's mind worked slowly. After mulling over the situation for three weeks he decided that some one must have told Mrs. Eddy that he wished to kill her. So he went back to the house and besought an interview. Mrs. Eddy was in another mood, a soft, tearful, saddened mood rich with sentiment and loneliness.

She put her trembling, palsied hands into his and begged him never again to leave her. "You know how things are here," she moaned. "I want you to promise me that when you receive an order from me to go away, to do something in another city, do not obey it. Remember, my boy, I shall have been forced to make the order. . . . I shall not mean it. . . Promise me, my son. . . ."[2]

Foster Eddy promised. He left the house wondering. Not long afterward he received an order from Mrs. Eddy to go to Philadelphia and build up a new church there.

[1]Foster Eddy's statement in N. Y. *World*, March 12, 1907.   [2]*Ibid*.

The day he sailed Mrs. Eddy sent flowers to his ship, and a number of church members were at the wharf to see him off. It was Mrs. Eddy's method of farewell. Letters were sent ahead of him to Philadelphia advising church members there to have naught to do with him.[1] Rebuffed in Philadelphia and not knowing what to do, he went to Washington for a few days, then returned to Boston, dismayed. Mrs. Eddy at his beseeching granted him an interview in the home where not long previously he had sat at the head of the table. In the midst of their talk she turned her back on him and went upstairs.

She wrote him one letter after this dismissal. She accused him of the inevitable crime. "I am not or cannot be mistaken now in whose mind is on me," she wrote. . . . "You were governed by hypnotism to work against me and yourself. . . . You say those with whom you now are love you. I hope this will continue to be so."[2]

It was, in a way, a pitiful letter. From that time on Frye, who daily sat on the box of Mrs. Eddy's carriage, also presided at the head of her table.

He was not a genial master for Mrs. Eddy's home, but he could be a useful one. In a letter to her son George, she wrote of Frye—after expressing her disillusionment in Foster Eddy, whose books, she said, were so incorrect that they could not be audited—that he was, though the most disagreeable person to be found, at least an honest man, "if there is one on earth." Frye had learned, she said, to surmount the mesmerism that once had influenced him, and could be relied on not to "steal, commit adultery, or fornication, or break one of the Ten Commandments."[3]

She might have added another attribute: Frye could keep his counsel and be discreet.

[1] New York *World*, March 12, 1907.

[2] For entire letter vd. Milmine, *Life of Mary Baker G. Eddy*, page 422 ff.

[3] Miss Milmine's biography presents this letter in full on page 449. It first appeared in the N. Y. *World* of March 11, 1907.

XXII

With Foster Eddy out of the house Mrs. Eddy erased him
utterly from her consciousness. For her he no longer existed
He was still legally her adopted son; but she made no effort to
break the legal tie, and ignored him as utterly as if he had
never come into her consciousness. Christian Science circles in
which he had been received as the crown prince with almost
the same gusto as Mrs. Eddy herself—regardless of any jeal
ousies or personal animosities—now ignored him likewise. He
departed from Boston, travelled in the far west, and finally set
tled at Waterbury Center, Vermont. He did not even practis
medicine there, feeling that Mrs. Eddy and her coterie migh
not like such reversion to species. He indeed told friends in
later years that he was in fear for his life from various of the
Eddy followers. He, too, had perhaps become infected with the
persecution complex.

A greater semblance of temporary peace in her househol
meant that Mrs. Eddy could once more focus her attention o
her affairs in Boston. She seldom took her mind wholly off he
church, no matter what personal affairs were occupying he
attention; indeed, her church was so intimate a part of her lif
that during the late nineties she and her institution functione
as one. Hardly a day passed that she did not send for some ex
ecutive to come up and report to her on his handling of affair
No detail was too small to hold her interest, no project to
large for her now to entertain. Even after nights of absolu
agony, even in moments of the greatest emotional and hy
terical distress, she could somehow calm herself to hear ho
her congregations were getting along.

During her absence from Boston her affairs there prosper
amazingly. There were of course the same old stories th
Mrs. Eddy had lost her healing power, that she took drug
that she stole her religion from Quimby, that she had be
known to neighbors in Lynn as an absolute virago—such r

nors were forever cropping up. They in no way affected Mrs.
Eddy's loyal following, because that following was travelling
n a will to believe, and such rumors were put down to the mali-
ious jealousies against which all loyal followers were in-
tructed to defend themselves. Defense against malicious ani-
nal magnetism was—and still is—enjoined upon the church
nember in Mrs. Eddy's *Manual*.[1]

Meanwhile Mrs. Eddy's publicity department was function-
ng efficiently as usual; and as a counter to the less reputable
umors there circulated other and far more glamorous ones
bout the pure and self-abnegating life of the old high-priest-
ss immured in the chaste gray-green walls of Pleasant View.
ome of the more enthusiastic church members had reached
he conclusion that perhaps Mrs. Eddy already was preparing
erself for a final great miracle, that of conquering death and
iving herself life eternal. She had, indeed, denied the reality
f death along with the other materialistic things which she
:outed in her text-book.[2] Mrs. Stetson, at the head of the New
ork church, was openly preaching physical immortality, dearing not only that Mrs. Eddy was immortal but that she
erself was going to demonstrate immortality too. These
ings, when mentioned, were usually talked of in bated
reath, and Mrs. Eddy became more mysterious and revered
ith each passing year.

Mrs. Eddy herself rather prospered under the arrangement
y which she was relieved of all the petty detail of church man-
gement, and could devote her time to leisurely consideration
: the problems that weighed upon her. She was able to take a
nger time in making her decisions, was thus less prone to

XXVI, 3: "Teachers shall instruct their pupils how to defend themselves
ainst mental malpractice." VIII, 6: "It shall be the duty of every member of
s church to defend himself daily against aggressive mental suggestion. . . ."
Vd. *Christian Healing*, page 18: "You must admit that what is termed death
s been produced by a belief alone." Also *Science and Health*, page 42: "Death
l be found at length to be a mortal dream." *Ibid.*, page 164: "If you or I
uld appear to die, we should not be dead." *Ibid.*, page 428: "Life is real,
d death is the illusion. . . . Man's privilege at this supreme moment is to prove
e words of our Master: 'If a man keep my saying, he shall never see death.' . . .
e great spiritual fact must be brought out that man *is*, not *shall be*, perfect
d immortal. . . . The author has healed hopeless organic disease, and raised
e dying to life and health through the understanding of God as the only Life."

"command and countermand" and then countermand again
Thus her church and her publications themselves functioned
more smoothly. Meanwhile she had the benefit of the care of a
group of household attendants whose one worldly duty was to
wait upon her every wish and need, and soothe her constantly

One situation arose in Boston, however, which worried her
extremely. Once Mrs. Eddy had settled in Concord, those of
her followers who were able to exercise a strong personal in
fluence on their students now operated much more freely than
when Mrs. Eddy herself was preaching every Sunday. Mrs
Eddy's congregations, indeed, had always been built up by per
sonal influence. Even Mrs. Eddy herself, with all her limita
tions, had done more for actual church-building by her occa
sional public addresses than by all her writings. People can ge
inspired over a book, but they don't stay inspired over it.

What Mrs. Eddy never realized to her dying day was thi
important fact. She herself had never been a great person
leader. But this lack of hers was more than counterbalanced b
leadership supplied by ecstatic healers who went out and at
tracted students and made these students into church mem
bers. Readers of Mrs. Eddy's book sent in testimonials, bu
students of Mrs. Eddy's teachers joined the church and mad
donations to new building funds.

It was therefore not necessary for Mrs. Eddy to hold th
front trenches all the time. With personal leadership supplie
by her captains, she needed only to stand on the ramparts, tak
observations, hand down the orders, issue regular exhortation
of encouragement, and show herself occasionally. She made
vital historical mistake when she sought to tear out person
leadership in her church. She succeeded—almost succeeded-
in accomplishing this design before she died. As a result h
church slowed down in its rate of expansion within two de
ades after her death.

Mrs. Eddy wanted only one leader recognized—herself. U
fitted as she was for permanent appearance in such a rôle, s
had nevertheless clothed herself during her declining yea
with a glamorous mystery which concealed her defects a
magnified her strengths. Her followers took the Queen's ra

nent for the Queen, and were inspired to ardor accordingly. Thus, during her last few years, Mrs. Eddy's enterprise flourished temporarily without the personal leadership of those able captains who had done such valiant work in whipping it together, and whom Mrs. Eddy then demoted. But, with such leaders gone, the propelling force back of Mrs. Eddy's church lessened promptly with her demise. The most expertly drawn rules, regulations and by-laws could not hold a following together effectively without the driving force of personal inspiration. No army can win and hold recruits unless it is inspired by able commanders as well as by patriotism.

In her giant egotism, however, streaked as it was with vanity and jealousy, Mrs. Eddy never once realized what her healers and teachers had done for her, just as she never once realized what Kennedy and Spofford had done for her. In the declining years of her life she grew even more intolerant and more suspicious of any leadership beside her own.

This explains her final destruction of Mrs. Stetson. It also explains her assault on Mrs. Woodbury, whose career was far less gorgeous than that created by Augusta Stetson but provided far more comic relief.

Josephine Curtis Woodbury was the only Scientist in Boston who ever threatened seriously to rival there the influence of Mrs. Eddy herself. Mrs. Woodbury was an exceedingly dynamic, self-confident woman, quite untroubled by repression of complexes, and therefore as wholly unlike Mrs. Eddy as possible. She was clever, beautiful, and charming. She could write as fluently as Mrs. Eddy and talk much more engagingly. She was an expert at theatrical display, and could dramatize herself with consummate skill. Her personal influence over her students was amazing.

She had first studied with Mrs. Eddy in 1879, and had become one of the most influential healers and teachers in Mrs. Eddy's movement. Her contributions appeared regularly in *the Journal;* she had travelled as far as the Rocky Mountains preaching and lecture tours to spread the Eddy gospel; and through her efforts had made large contributions to the cause, both in converts and money.

Mrs. Woodbury exacted the same kind of personal adora
tion and attendance-dancing from her following that Mrs
Eddy herself required; but over Mrs. Woodbury's coterie wa:
a glamour of well-being which never descended on the harassec
souls who battled unceasingly with the baffling clouds of mali
cious animal magnetism hanging constantly over the Edd:
household. Mrs. Woodbury and her students had a royal good
time. She collected around herself young artists and actors an
musicians, handsome young men and charming young girls
and these pleasant creatures lived raptly in a play-world tha
was all their own. Mrs. Woodbury would take them to Europ
with her; and on their return they would point up their thec
logical conversations with little phrases in French.

Mrs. Woodbury, who herself could find a romantic adven
ture every time she walked down the street, taught them th
art of making drama from the most ordinary every-day event:
And so her young folk kept mental trysts and had revelation
and premonitions; saw miracles flowering under their eyes
could find a mystic portent or prophecy in the most casual oc
currence; and all in all lived a life of marvels.

All of this was wholly different from Mrs. Eddy's grim ex
perience of religion, for even in her most inspired moment
Mrs. Eddy's head never got very far into idealistic clouds, an
her feet were most heavily anchored in the earth. Her desir
were never expressed by idealization; she never sublimatec
Instead, her tempestuous emotions merely burst into occasion:
flame that consumed but could not illumine.

Mrs. Woodbury, living in a world of her own, had sorte
out from Mrs. Eddy's doctrines the less prosaic of the motif
and had woven from these an exceedingly romantic fabri
Mrs. Eddy, for instance, had dourly denied the virtues of ma
riage and the marriage-bed. She had a skepticism about tl
love relationship born of long experience. To the questio
"what do you think of marriage?" she replied with blasé su
cinctness:

That it is often convenient, sometimes pleasant, and occasionally a lo
affair. Marriage is susceptible of many definitions. It sometimes preser
the most wretched condition of human existence.[1]

[1] *Miscellaneous Writings*, page 52.

In her active teaching days Mrs. Eddy did not hesitate to speak much more frankly. She advised complete celibacy as the only real spiritual state.[1] Such advice would indeed be the only consistent conclusion warranted by her philosophy. Marital intercourse being based on physical sensation, and physical sensation being based on matter, which is Error, there could be no logical room for usual marital relations in a life which tried to adjust itself even partly to Mrs. Eddy's philosophy. Many of Mrs. Eddy's earlier students, teaching in the day when Mrs. Eddy was making unqualified statements, and had not yet learned to insert Ifs and Buts,[2] took these earlier injunctions of hers regarding marriage quite literally. Mrs. Stetson swallowed the doctrine whole, preached it far more openly than Mrs. Eddy ever had, and eventually made quite a stir about it in the metropolitan press. Mrs. Woodbury similarly had taken very seriously these dogmas handed down from the classroom platform. Mrs. Eddy had not hesitated to intimate that parthenogenetic conceptions could be arrived at when a person became sufficiently spiritual.[3] She stated in *Science and Health*:

The propagation of their species without the male element, by butterfly, bee and moth is a discovery corroborative of the Science of Mind, because it shows that the origin and continuance of these insects rest on

[1] Even to-day *Science and Health* expresses itself quite coolly, even if a little obtusely, on the subject of physical relationship between husband and wife. Id., page 61, in the chapter on *Marriage:* "The scientific *morale* of marriage is spiritual unity. If the propagation of a higher human species is requisite to reach his goal, then its material conditions can only be permitted for the purpose of generating. The fœtus must be kept mentally pure and the period of gestation have the sanctity of virginity."

[2] Mrs. Eddy inserted many as time went by. Vd. *Science and Health*, page 64: "Until it is learned that God is the Father of all, marriage will continue. . . . Spirit will ultimately claim its own,—all that really is,—and the voices of physical sense will be forever hushed."

[3] *Science and Health* still intimates this very thing in studied terms. Vd. page : "The time cometh of which Jesus spake, when he declared that in the resurrection there should be no more marrying or giving in marriage, but man would be as the angels. Then shall Soul rejoice in its own, in which passion has no part. *When white-robed purity will unite in one person masculine wisdom and feminine love, spiritual understanding and perpetual peace.*" The italics here are the biographer's.

Immediately following this bold prophecy Mrs. Eddy qualified herself thus: "Until it is learned that God is the Father of all, marriage will continue."

Principle, apart from material conditions. An egg was never the origi
of man, and no seed ever produced a plant.[1]

The fact that Mrs. Eddy was wholly wrong about the wa
that butterflies, bees and moths are propagated, could hardl
have occurred to students who subscribed so blandly to a num
ber of her other ultimatums. Fabre was still unknown and th
mystic Maeterlinck had not yet written his *Life of the Be*
Subsequently Mrs. Eddy read Agassiz, thereupon revisin
some of her own views regarding the propagation of the sp
cies, and incidentally obtaining numerous quotations whic
seemed to corroborate certain of her other ideas, and whic
she therefore salted liberally through her texts.[2] She eventu
ally removed from her treatise the statement regarding th
negligible part played by the "male element" among bee
moths and butterflies; but one still may find there the opinio
that "an egg is an impossible enclosure for Deity."[3]

In consequence, Mrs. Woodbury lined her room with pi
tures of Madonnas, and her students affected nun-like an
monkish cells for sleeping quarters. They all lived in the be
traditions of romantic chivalry, and with the hot idealism o
youth thought they meant what they said.

This was the state of affairs when Mrs. Woodbury a
nounced that she herself was going to have a virginal co
ception, or rather, that she already had it. It was a great da
in the Woodbury camp. Her students were utterly thrilled. Th
birth occurred in June of 1890, and Mrs. Woodbury name
her big bouncing boy "The Prince of Peace." Mrs. Woodbur
of course, had a husband. But this state of affairs was ce
tainly not wholly without precedent; thus the point was on
which only skeptics would care to discuss. Mrs. Woodbur
would not permit her son to address Mr. Woodbury
"father"; Mr. Woodbury was to be called Frank, and she he
self was to be known to the boy as "Birdie."

[1]*Science and Health* (1886), page 472.

[2]Another source for many of Mrs. Eddy's glib references to medical history a
scientific experiment lay in the *History of Four Thousand Years of Medici*
She also quotes from De Quincey, Jahr, and Darwin, and apparently read so
of the current medical magazines, as evidenced by brief quotations in *Science o
Health*, pages 162–164.

[3]*Science and Health*, page 550.

Prince was baptized in a pool at Ocean Point, Maine, which Mrs. Woodbury reminiscently called "Bethesda." She wrote about the event as follows:

There occurred the thought of baptizing little Prince in a singularly beautiful salt pool, whose rocky bottom was dry at low tide and overflowing at high tide, but especially attractive at mid-tide, with its two feet of crystal water. A crowd of people had assembled on the neighboring bluffs, when I brought him from our cottage not far away, and laid him three times prayerfully in the pool and when he was lifted therefrom, they joined in a spontaneously appropriate hymn.[1]

Mrs. Woodbury felt very proud over her advertised achievement, and even intimated that the august Mrs. Eddy herself had foretold the event. Six months previous to the lying-in Mrs. Woodbury paid a visit to Mrs. Eddy, and she quoted Mrs. Eddy as saying, "Go home and be happy. Commit thy ways unto the Lord. Trust him, and he will bring it to pass."

Mrs. Eddy was furious.

Obviously, if anybody was going to achieve a virginal conception in this modern day and age, such a distinction should not come to a mere follower instead of the founder of the system by which such miraculous results could be achieved. And Mrs. Eddy was not at the moment in a mood to believe in miracles concerning any one but herself. As a matter of fact, she never long entertained illusions about any one in the world except herself.

But it was hardly possible to discipline a lady who cared to make such a claim, particularly since her husband said nothing to the contrary; so Mrs. Eddy let the matter drift and bided her time. Since she had herself taught the doctrine, she certainly could not gainsay the possibility of Mrs. Woodbury's feat.

Thus matters stood for several years. When, in 1895, Mrs. Eddy reorganized her church, constructed a turnstile at the entrance, and carefully scrutinized every disciple who lined up to enter, she decided to keep Mrs. Woodbury out. Mrs. Woodbury was anguished. She wrote Mrs. Eddy asking her to use her influence with the First Members to rescind the decision—

[1] *War in Heaven*, page 51.

Mrs. Woodbury evidently sensing that it was Mrs. Eddy her-self who had barred the door.

Mrs. Eddy was adamant. She informed Mrs. Woodbury by letter she had made a rule that she herself should not be troubled with the question of membership applications, and she did not intend to interfere.

On reconsideration, however, Mrs. Eddy decided to admit the charming Mrs. Woodbury on a probation of two years. "I am not ignorant of your sins," she wrote, "and I am trying to have you in the church for protection from those temptations, and to effect your full reformation. Remember, the M. A. M. which you say in your letter causes you to sin is not idle, and will cause you to repeat them, and so turn you again from the church, unless you pray to God to keep you from falling into the foul snare."[1]

Mrs. Woodbury had not enjoyed her probationary member-ship a year before trouble broke. In 1896 suit was brought against her by Fred D. Chamberlain for the alienation of his wife's affections. Mrs. Chamberlain was a student of Mrs. Woodbury's. The Boston *Traveller* sensed a good story, and immediately started to scout for data. It soon discovered Mrs. Woodbury's previous claim concerning her "Prince," whom she had introduced to her friends as "little Immanuel," and even in a day before newspapers had learned the circulation possibilities of "sex appeal" it was obvious that here was a feature story.

The Traveller reported that Prince was now being sup-ported not by Frank Woodbury, but by Robert W. Rowe of Augusta, Maine, who was just then being sued by his wife Evelyn, for divorce on a charge of non-support. Mrs. Rowe claimed that her husband was contributing all his earnings to the education of the young Immanuel, who he devoutly be-lieved had been born as Mrs. Woodbury claimed.

In addition, *The Traveller* stated that attempts were being made by Mrs. Woodbury and her husband to finance the new Messiah by selling stock in an "air engine" to which Mrs. Woodbury held the rights. It was asserted that Mrs. Wood-

[1]For entire letter vd. Milmine, *Life of Mary Baker G. Eddy*, page 434.

bury was using her influence with her students to persuade them to buy stock, and interviews were published with several husbands whose wives, convinced of the miraculous conception, had sought to persuade their spouses to take some stock in the Woodbury enterprise.

All in all it was rather an unsavory mess, and Mrs. Eddy was thoroughly shocked at the resultant notoriety. Mrs. Woodbury, who had already been dropped and then again reinstated following her conditional admission the year before, was now excommunicated finally and forever. "How dare you—how dare you in the sight of God, and with your character behind the curtain, and your students ready to lift it on you, pursue the path perilous?" Mrs. Eddy wrote to her in stentorian accents.[1]

Mrs. Woodbury, however, was no longer in awe of Mrs. Eddy; and as if to emphasize her nonchalance walked regularly into The Mother Church to attend services even after her pew had been taken away by the Directors. She also sent Prince to the Sunday School. The surprised and innocent Prince was one day hoisted bodily by his little jacket and put out. Thereupon Mrs. Woodbury attempted what most others eventually did who separated from Mrs. Eddy—she went out to start a church of her own.

Such schisms had often occurred, and the resulting rival institutions were the bane of Mrs. Eddy's existence, as shown by her strenuous efforts to devise by-laws that would prevent the heresies resulting from these ruptures. Actually, however, rival churches started in this manner never seriously affected Mrs. Eddy's progress, for the simple reason that no one else ever dared, as she had, to claim exclusive and divine rights and privileges. Mrs. Eddy marketed her own teachings with the very modern advertising slogan, "this is the original—accept none other."[2] It is an effective slogan. No one wants something publicly labelled counterfeit.

[1] Milmine, *Life of Mary Baker G. Eddy*, page 435.
[2] Vd. *Message to the Mother Church for 1901*, page 18: "Those who laugh at . . . the Christian Scientist's religion or his medicine, should know the danger of questioning Christ Jesus' healing, who administered no remedy apart from Mind, and taught his disciples none other."

Thus it did not greatly matter, in so far as Mrs. Eddy's own income and prestige were concerned, that right in Boston Mrs. Crosse was operating a rival healing system; that Mrs. Gestefeld had broken away and started her own plant in Chicago; that Captain Sabin, who for a while had enjoyed Mrs. Eddy's warmest regard, had branched out for himself in Washington; and that in Brooklyn there was still another competing institution.

Mrs. Woodbury did what many others had attempted before her—she hired some rooms in the Legion of Honor hall and conducted services every Sunday morning. When she was unable to be present, her daughter Gwendolyn filled her place. No claims were ever made for Gwendolyn.

Mrs. Woodbury was now the latest mesmerist to be added to Mrs. Eddy's list of the proscribed; Mrs. Eddy had become convinced that Mrs. Woodbury was the worst mesmerist of all, beyond the competition even of Kennedy and Spofford. She lost no opportunity to denounce her. Mrs. Eddy feared Mrs. Woodbury far more because of her terror that Mrs. Woodbury would spout M. A. M., than because she dreaded the public attack attendant upon newspaper discussions of the Eddy doctrines. Mrs. Eddy always survived attack. But she could never surmount personal fear. It was at this time she wrote a pleading letter for mental help to Mrs. Stetson in New York. Under date of December 17, 1898, she said:

. . . I cannot remember anything but what serves to save our Cause from the jaws of the devourers. Another plot is, to organize churches within the vicinity of The Mother Church and no one in Boston lifts a finger against whatever is abusive to our Cause in such ways, but turns to me to meet it all. Will you not help put this down? . . .[1]

Mrs. Eddy doubtless suffered from the Woodbury incident far more than Mrs. Woodbury herself. For Mrs. Woodbury was a talented and resourceful woman. In 1897 she had opened her own attack by publishing a rather reserved account of the schism in a pamphlet entitled *War in Heaven.*[2] This account

---

[1] Stetson, *Sermons and Other Writings*, page 38.
[2] *War in Heaven—Sixteen Years' Experience in Christian Science Mind Healing.* Boston, Mass., Press of Samuel Usher, 1897.

however, was as nothing to the essay which she published in the magazine called *The Arena,* in May of 1899.[1]

In this article Mrs. Woodbury said that Mrs. Eddy had been a spiritualistic medium. She stated further that Mrs. Eddy was a subject of "demonophobia," or fear of demons. She entered into the Quimby controversy and announced that Mrs. Eddy had appropriated her thesis from the old Maine doctor. She criticised Mrs. Eddy's English. She accused her of an overweening greed of money and quoted Scriptural references about "trafficking in the temple."

Mrs. Woodbury also quoted some of Mrs. Eddy's statements which are of unusual interest because they show how Mrs. Eddy sought to establish herself as an efficient miracle worker with her own followers. Even though these quotations come from the lips of a disgruntled disciple, they are in harmony with other established records that they appear worthy of acceptance as approximately correct.

Mrs. Woodbury asserted that Mrs. Eddy claimed to have cured the Prince of Wales, later Edward VII, of his near-fatal illness in 1871, by the use of absent treatment. She quoted Mrs. Eddy as adding an even more fanciful detail—that it had been impossible to treat the Prince directly, because his "alleged immoral character" made it dangerous for her to approach him without an intermediary. Mrs. Eddy therefore treated the Prince indirectly through the Queen, his mother. Mrs. Eddy also claimed that she treated President Garfield after he was shot, and that she failed to save his life only because of malicious counter-currents set in force by Kennedy and Arens.

Mrs. Woodbury even dared to intimate in her *Arena* article that Mrs. Eddy had never healed any one at all:

Yet why should not the inspired teacher herself heal . . .? Example is stronger than precept. There are those living who affirm that the stupendous miracles she related to her first Lynn pupils, as having been wrought by herself—such as raising a dead child—were borrowed from Dr. Quimby's own cases. It is even said that Mrs. Eddy never herself

[1] *Quimbyism, or the Paternity of Christian Science,* reprinted in 1909 as a pamphlet, by the Garden City Press, Ltd., of Letchworth, England.

healed a single case; although her students may have healed many, and to them she has always referred applicants for help.

Mrs. Woodbury's assault was indeed more vicious than that of Mrs. Eddy's worst critics who had never been inside the fold. Scouting the claim that Mrs. Eddy had ever "discovered" anything, Mrs. Woodbury said:

> What she has really "discovered" are ways and means of perverting and prostituting the science of healing to her own ecclesiastical aggrandisement, and to the moral and physical depravity of her dupes. . . . What she has "founded" is a commercial system, monumental in its proportions, but already tottering to its fall.

It may safely be assumed from these sentences that Mrs. Woodbury was a very much disillusioned woman. Her keenest resentment rested on her feeling that she herself had been made one of the "dupes," and she blamed Mrs. Eddy entirely for the state of mind by which she herself had been led into proclaiming an "immaculate conception." What she told of Mrs. Eddy's class teachings on the subject of marital relationships was confirmed by other students of the period. Mrs. Woodbury said:

> One may well hesitate to touch this delicate topic in print, yet only thus can the immoral possibilities and the utter lack of Divine inspiration in Eddyism be shown.
>
> The substance of certain instructions given by Mrs. Eddy in private is as follows:
>
> If Jesus was divinely conceived by the Holy Ghost or Spirit, without a human father, Mary not having known her husband—then women may become mothers through a supreme effort of their own minds, or through the influence on them of an Unholy Ghost, a malign spirit.

In other words Mrs. Woodbury describes Mrs. Eddy's conviction that a supernatural conception might be obtained in one of two ways: through association with the Holy Ghost, as in Mary's experience; or through association with malicious animal magnetism—an "unholy ghost"—sent out by such a man as Spofford or Kennedy. This is a most interesting commentary on Mrs. Eddy's series of complexes. The psychiatrist is not unfamiliar with cases of sexual repression where women have hallucinations regarding their possible physical condition after being subject to delusions or obsessions in which a man plays a leading part.

For the psychiatrist it is a reasonable deduction that Mrs. Eddy suffered from a suppressed sexual urge toward most of the male students who had come in contact with her. That sex had played a large part in her neurosis even from her early girlhood is indicated in the testimony of old neighbors that her fainting spells came on most often in the presence of a group of young men, some of whom would usually have to carry her home. This is a phase of exhibitionism which again is representative and not unique. Sex neurosis played an important part in Mrs. Eddy's subsequent violent antagonisms. With a rigidly Puritanical training, promiscuous sex desire was abhorrent to her understanding. Her rational mind bade her suppress it,[1] but so strong was this urge toward such young men as Arens, Kennedy and Spofford that in suppressing and ignoring it she set up conflicts in her inner self of whose nature she was wholly unaware. As always in such circumstances, she began by abominating the instinct, and ended by transferring her hatred from this instinct itself to the person who had aroused it.

Such would be one psychological interpretation of the manner in which Mrs. Eddy's violent repulsions were formed. But this repulsion was not the sole result of the inner conflict from which she suffered. Basically the sexual attraction still persisted in her subconscious mind, since it had in no way been sublimated. In consequence there was born the subconscious desire to consummate this sexual urge. With this came an associated desire of the subconscious to bear a child to the man who was playing such a large part in her dream life. This desire she would also suppress in turn. She thus denounced the efforts of such a "mal-practitioner" as Kennedy to bring pregnancy upon an innocent woman. And she warned her girl students against a similar eventuality. There is little doubt that

[1] Vd. *Science and Health*, page 57: "Chastity is the cement of civilization and progress . . . without it one cannot attain the Science of Life."

Mrs. Eddy's subconscious mind would regard these girl students as rivals, in its dream life, for the attentions of the very man whom consciously Mrs. Eddy would denounce.

It is not uncommon for the psychiatrist to find conflicts of this nature in women who are well beyond the years of middle life. Physical impotency apparently does not affect the strength of the subconscious desire. It is well to remember, also, that Mrs. Eddy did not even begin to mature emotionally until far along in life. Had her first husband lived she might indeed have reached an emotional maturity—a state of emotional balance—which she never attained. She had loved Glover passionately; her letters to him[1] indicate a desire of extraordinary physical intensity. With Glover's premature death this passion never found physical expression, even in her subsequent marriage with Patterson, which, it may be deduced, brought her only an unsatisfied yearning. The resulting agony of unfulfilled desire undoubtedly must have played a part in the hysterical illness which fell upon her with renewed strength after the Patterson alliance. The same hysteria was renewed in exaggerated form at the time of her marriage to Eddy. Frustrated emotion had caused such hysteria with her since childhood.

There can be little doubt that it was Mrs. Eddy's frustrated emotional life which gave birth to much of her philosophy. Like all humanity, she sought to rationalize desires and fears. These attempts at rationalization again brought further conflicts, and so she swung around in a vicious circle, becoming further mired with every turn until the efforts at rationalization ended actually in delusion. In most such instances only the victim himself is affected. But Mrs. Eddy was a teacher of impressionable students to whom she passed on her obsession and her fears. Thus it was, for instance, that she impressed girl students with the necessity of guarding against the sexual

[1] Some of her letters to "Wash" Glover are now in the possession of John V. Dittemore, the last surviving member of the Board of Directors that served Mrs. Eddy's church during her lifetime. Shortly before Mrs. Eddy's death Mr. Dittemore purchased from the son of Samuel Baker, Mrs. Eddy's oldest brother, a mass of biographical material, including many letters which Mrs. Eddy wrote in her early years. Samuel, it will be remembered, was a close friend of "Wash" Glover, with whom he worked in the building business.

dvances of disembodied demon mentalities—"unholy ghosts."
Mrs. Woodbury said in her *Arena* essay:

Women of unquestioned integrity, who have been Mrs. Eddy's stu-
ents, testify that she has so taught, and that by this teaching families
ave been broken up; that thus maidens have been terrified out of their
its, and stimulated into a frenzy resembling that of deluded French
uns, who believed themselves brought into marital relations with the
orified Jesus, as veritably the bridegroom of his church. Whatever her
enials may be, such was Mrs. Eddy's teaching while in her college; to
hich she added the oracular declaration that it lay within her power to
ssolve such motherhood by a wave of her celestial rod.
The selfish celibacy of nuns and clergy, Christian or heathen, with
onsequent ecclesiastical interference in family life, have been, and are,
ischief-breeding blunders, fatal alike to morals and health. One result
f this interference on the part of Mrs. Eddy is that Christian Science
amilies are notably childless.

When Mrs. Woodbury put her opinions in print in this fash-
n Mrs. Eddy was extremely indignant. The *Arena* article
ppeared in May, only a month before Mrs. Eddy was sched-
led to write her yearly message to her church on the occasion
f its annual communion. In June, when Mrs. Eddy's disciples
ssembled in Boston, they were regaled with some Biblical quo-
tions which are seldom referred to in modern pulpits. This
ortion of Mrs. Eddy's message had all the austere and terrible
orce of a Papal Bull:

The doom of the Babylonish woman, referred to in Revelation, is being
lfilled. This woman, "drunken with the blood of the saints, and with
e blood of the martyrs of Jesus," "drunk with the wine of her fornica-
on," would enter even the church,—the body of Christ, Truth; and, re-
ining the heart of the harlot and the purpose of the destroying angel,
uld pour wormwood into the waters—the disturbed human mind—
drown the strong swimmer struggling for the shore,—aiming for
uth,—and if possible, to poison such as drink of the living water. . . .
d a voice was heard, saying, "Come out of her, my people" (hearken
t to her lies), "that ye receive not of her plagues. For her sins have
ached unto heaven, and God hath remembered her iniquities . . .
uble unto her double according to her works: in the cup which she
th filled fill to her double . . . for she saith in her heart, I am no
dow. . . . Therefore shall her plagues come in one day, death, and
urning, and famine; . . . for strong is the Lord God who judgeth

her." That which the Revelator saw in Spiritual vision will be accomplished. The Babylonish woman is fallen, and who should mourn over the widowhood of lust, of her that "is become the habitation of devils, and the hold of every foul spirit, and a cage of every unclean . . . bird"?[1]

It was the same old Mary Baker Eddy being consumed with an uncontrollable rage. The only difference was that she now expressed herself in a Biblical vocabulary and knew how to use a Concordance to find good quotations for what she wanted to say. Mrs. Woodbury burned with mortification. Although her name had not been mentioned in the pulpit, she apparently believed that many who heard that message would think she was the one referred to by Mrs. Eddy as the "harlot," "drunk with the wine of her fornication," sunk in "the widowhood of lust," and become "the cage of every unclean bird."

In consequence Mrs. Woodbury immediately sued for libel asking damages of $150,000. The case came to trial in the following June when Boston was again filled with Mrs. Eddy's disciples come once more to commune. Many of them were called as witnesses. All of them were horrified at the thought of Mrs. Eddy being subjected to a libel suit; one was heard to express the earnest opinion that to bring a suit against her was like seeking to fight against God. Mrs. Eddy herself did not appear, sickness being given as the reason. Only one witness, William G. Nixon, Mrs. Eddy's former publisher, admitted on the witness stand that he had understood Mrs. Eddy's message to apply to Mrs. Woodbury. All the others denied that they had ever even thought of Mrs. Woodbury when Mrs. Eddy referred to a Babylonish woman and harlot.

So Mrs. Woodbury lost her case. She believed that the trial had been affected by constant mental treatment which had been administered to the judge and jurors by followers of Mrs. Eddy who thronged the courtroom during the trial. So she would not even permit an appeal, but retired to private life.

How ardently Mrs. Eddy's church members did devote their mental attentions to the judge and jurors in the trial is ind-

[1] Mary Baker Eddy, Message, "Communion" June 4, 1899. Vd. *Miscellany* pages 125–126.

cated in a current letter written by Mrs. Stetson to one of her students. Mrs. Stetson, like so many of Mrs. Eddy's supporters, stayed in Boston and "worked" during the entire suit. And she wrote:

I have been so constantly occupied with the work on this trial, that I have felt it wise not to write or think outside of it if possible, and I knew that so far as I could, I must leave my students to do their own work. . . . The victory has come at last. We have demonstrated the *powerlessness* of hypnotism, witchcraft and mental diabolism to overthrow the Cause of Christian Science and the work of our beloved Leader, Mrs. Eddy. . . . The error was made so unreal that instead of three weeks, which the Judge gave for the trial, it was over in four days.[1]

Just before Mrs. Eddy's raging message was read in The Mother Church, Mrs. Woodbury's husband had died. Not a few of Mrs. Eddy's followers saw divine judgment in the event. When they reconsidered part of Mrs. Eddy's message, they were sure. For she had said: "Therefore shall her plagues come in one day, death, and mourning, and famine." It was whispered that perhaps Mrs. Eddy herself had co-operated with God and had shot this thunderbolt—she who dwelt in such mystery that there were only vague rumors about her powers.

No one could ever know or be sure; but many of her followers were thrilled by the thought that there ruled over them a sort of god, whose power was an illimitable and supernatural thing which as ordinary mortals they could not even comprehend, whose smile was beneficent, but whose just wrath was terrible to behold.

Who would dare, convinced of the supernatural nature of that power, to testify in open court against Mrs. Eddy?

Mrs. Eddy, after all this unfortunate publicity, did some more revising of *Science and Health*. By this time she had undoubtedly changed her mind regarding the matter of virgin conceptions; and so she wrote with a passing fling at Mrs. Woodbury's honesty:

I never knew more than one individual who believed in agamogenesis; she was unmarried, a lovely character, was suffering from in-

[1] Stetson, *Reminiscences, Sermons and Correspondence*, page 466.

cipient insanity, and a Christian Scientist cured her. I have named her case to individuals, when casting my bread upon the waters, and it may have caused the good to ponder and the evil to hatch their silly innuendoes and lies, since salutary causes sometimes incur these effects. The perpetuation of the floral species by bud or cell-division is evident, but I discredit the belief that agamogenesis applies to the human species.[1]

As usual, Mrs. Eddy had the last word. And—as usual—she picked the most imposing word which she could find in the dictionary, even if not the one quite applicable to the problem in hand.

[1] *Science and Health*, page 68.

XXIII

It was in 1898 that George Glover came again to see his mother. He had made a previous visit in 1892 that had been mutually very pleasant; for this time he had brought along his little son, George Junior, instead of his wife, and Mrs. Eddy seemed to enjoy the wholly novel rôle of being a grandmother. George Junior had sat on her lap; and once, when he inquired about a button on her desk, Mrs. Eddy told him he might push it if he wanted to.[1]

George Junior pushed, there was a wild clamor of bells all through the house, and Mrs. Eddy's whole staff came running into the room, led by the hurrying Frye. Mrs. Eddy leaned back in her chair and laughed and laughed and laughed, merely pointing to the youngster.

Mrs. Eddy's house had bells in every room. Every person in the house had a call, consisting of a certain number of rings. Mrs. Eddy was thus able to summon to her immediately any one of her ménage when the spirit moved her. When the bell rang clamorously and constantly, it was a signal that she wanted the entire staff to report. They would always come running in hot haste. Mrs. Eddy would not tolerate a moment's delay, and the last person inside the door always received a look of displeasure. Mrs. Eddy took promptitude as one of the proofs of loyalty.

In the six years between 1892 and 1898 Mrs. Eddy had climbed far up the ladder leading to her pinnacle. She had founded a Mother Church in Boston, and under the brilliant guidance of Mrs. Stetson the First Church in New York was making equally remarkable strides. George Glover therefore found a woman changed in many ways from the mother he

[1] Miss Wilbur, through some strange misunderstanding, relates this story as George Senior, instead of the grandson, had played with the bell. Compare her *Life of Mary Baker Eddy*, page 362, with Glover's own account in the New York *World* of March 3, 1907.

had seen six years before. There were now no heights that Mrs. Eddy did not dream of reaching. Obviously she thought of her religious following as if it were counted in millions instead of thousands.[1] She could refer nonchalantly to her correspondence with nobility as if she received letters with ducal crests and foreign stamps every day in the year. In 1897 she wrote the editor of the Concord *Monitor:*[2]

It would seem as if Christian Science were engirdling the earth. London lords and ladies throng to learn its teachings, it is in the White House of our national capital, in Windsor Castle, England, and the leading minds in almost every Christian land are adopting its essential theological points. . . .

As it is, if you were a candidate for the Presidency, mayhap I could give you one hundred thousand votes. . . .

The thronging lords and ladies strongly suggest the novels of Mrs. Eddy's old favorite, Mrs. E. D. E. N. Southworth, whose stories she had now abandoned; but her inveterate delight in advertising aristocratic connections persisted until she reached her grave. She had all of a parlor-maid's passion for the nobility, and by 1903 she had actually got herself a crest —the McNeil insignia—which first appeared on her personal stationery in this year.

While brushing up her ancestors, Mrs. Eddy also sought to provide herself with an imposing birthplace. She made a trip up to Bow where the old Baker homestead still stood, taking along with her an artist to create a picture. Old John Baker, a son of Mark Baker's brother, and Mrs. Eddy's cousin, told about this trip with some amusement. "She insisted that the old house as it now stands was reduced in size," he said, "and very different from what it was when she was born under it. roof. So she drew an imaginary sketch, continuing the roo and adding wings or extensions. Then she magnified the littl barn into a couple of vast granaries and did other things t

---

[1] Vd. *Message to the Mother Church for 1900*, page 1: "Judging from the number of the readers of my books and those interested in them, over a million of people are already interested in Christian Science." At this time the churc membership, by her own statement in the *Message*, was about 16,000.

[2] October 7, 1897.

make the picture look imposing. I told Cousin Mary that it wasn't as I remembered it, but she said I was getting old and didn't remember right. So I shut up and Cousin Mary got the man to draw a mighty fine house and surroundings."[1]

It is pleasant for the historian to be able to record that Mrs. Eddy's desire for aristocratic associations was not destined to go unrequited. In December, 1898, a real Lord and Lady actually did come over and call on her after having cabled back and forth for a year in making the necessary arrangements. Mrs. Eddy did not intend to receive a Lord and Lady except at a time when she felt at her best. They were the Earl of Dunmore, peer of the Scottish realm, and Lady Dunmore. The distinguished visitors were received at Pleasant View in a state that fulfilled Mrs. Eddy's ideas of noble splendor, and Lady Dunmore thereafter stayed in America until the annual communion of the following year. Her son, Lord Fincastle, left his regiment in India to come over and join her for the communion, and her daughter, Lady Mildred Murry, also arrived to swell the family group. It was a great day for Mrs. Eddy. She had a special pew reserved for them, *The Journal* explaining that this "was wholly a matter of international courtesy, and not in any sense a tribute to their rank."

Only three years later, in 1901, Mrs. Eddy took advantage of this fleeting contact with the British nobility to establish a closer understanding with the reigning family. On the death of Victoria she summoned her First Members and instructed them to send sympathetic regards to the British Government, and the bereaved King Edward. And when the lamented Lord Dunmore died in 1907, Mrs. Eddy addressed a forty-six word cable of condolence to "Countess of Dunmore and family, 55 Lancaster Gate, West, London, England."

She also condoled with Mrs. McKinley, wrote a tribute to the dead President, and published a lengthy essay on the reason why prayer had been unable to save him. She also wrote up her regrets on the death of Pope Leo XIII.

A letter which Mrs. Eddy sent to her son in April, 1898, gives such a remarkable illustration of how eagerly she sought

[1] Interview quoted in New York *World*, October 30, 1906.

personal distinction by exaggerating her associations with the
haut monde that it was later offered in court as evidence of her
delusions of grandeur. It read in part:

> I thank you for any interest you may feel in your mother. I am alone
> in the world, more alone than a solitary star. Although it is duly esti
> mated by business characters and learned scholars that I lead and am
> obeyed by 300,000 people at this date.[1] The most distinguished news
> papers ask me to write on the most important subjects. Lords and ladies
> earls, princes and marquises and marchionesses from abroad write to
> me in the most complimentary manner. Hoke Smith declares I am the
> most illustrious woman on the continent—those are his exact words
> Our senators and members of Congress call on me for counsel. But
> what of all this? I am not made the least proud by it or a particle hap
> pier for it. I am working for a higher purpose.[2]

The psychologist is not surprised to find side by side with
these pompous airs other paragraphs that indicate brooding
wells of self-pity—for the one forms compensation for the
other. By this time Mrs. Eddy was even pitying herself be
cause she herself had reached the heights of glory while her
neglected family could not speak correct English. George
Glover had never learned to read and write—his daughter
wrote his letters for him. And so Mrs. Eddy continued:

> Now what of my circumstances? I name first my home, which of al
> places on earth is the one in which to find peace and enjoyment. But m
> house is simply a house and a beautiful landscape. There is not one in
> it that I love only[3] as I love everybody. I have no congeniality with m
> help inside of my house; they are no companions and scarcely fit to be m
> help. . . .
> One thing is the severest wound of all, namely, the want of education
> among those nearest to me in kin. I would gladly give every dollar
> possess to have one or two or three that are nearest to me on earth pos
> sess a thorough education. If you had been educated as I intend[ed] to
> have you, today you could, would, be made President of the Unite
> States. Mary's letters to me are so misspelled that I blush to read them
> You pronounce your words so wrongly and then she spells them ac
> cordingly. I am even yet too proud to have you come among my societ

[1] Mrs. Eddy's church in 1898 had about 10,000 members.

[2] For the entire letter see Georgine Milmine's *Life of Mary Baker G. Eddy*
page 449, and the New York *World* of March 11, 1907.

[3] i. e., *otherwise than.*

and alas! mispronounce your words as you do; but for this thing I
should be honored by your good manners and I love you.[1]

Mrs. Eddy's correspondence with her son was exceedingly
irregular. Long periods would elapse and he would never enter
her mind. Then she would suddenly feel in an expansive mood
that called for writing, and she would send him a note. Thus,
while he wrote fairly regularly, he seldom received direct replies, for by the time Mrs. Eddy got around to writing she had
probably even forgotten what George's last letter said.

Finally Glover came to the conclusion that Frye was inter-
cepting his letters and keeping them from Mrs. Eddy. The
oftener he wrote and received no answer, the surer he became
that for some reason he was not reaching her.

When he went to Concord in 1898 he hung around Pleasant
View until he was sure Frye was out of the house, then went
up to the door. A girl he described as a maid servant answered
his ring. He asked to see Mrs. Eddy. The girl told him that no
one saw Mrs. Eddy except by appointment made through Mr.
Frye. Then she looked at him more closely. She remembered
him from his visit six years before. "Are you George Glover,
Mrs. Eddy's son?" she asked.

"Yes," said Glover, "I want to see my mother right now."

She let him in, and Glover, who knew the house, went
straight upstairs to his mother's study.

He told her immediately why he had come all the way from
the west. He needed money. His mining claims in the Black
Hills had been producing nothing. He was in debt. He asked
for $5,500, not as a gift, but as a loan, and offered his prop-
erties as security.

Surprised as she was to see him, she listened carefully, then
told him that she did not want security. She sat down at her
desk, wrote an order on her banker in Concord, and handed
him the slip of paper. It was for five hundred dollars less than
Glover had asked.

"This order covers my entire cash balance for to-day," she
told him. "But, my dear son, I will send you the rest right
away, by mail." She asked him about his mines, and he told

[1] New York *World*, March 11, 1907.

her about the quartz mill he hoped to erect. When she inquired what this would cost, he told her about $30,000.

"That can and shall be arranged at once," she told him.

At that moment Frye came into the room. He started at sight of the unexpected guest, put out a limp hand in greeting and told Mrs. Eddy to get ready for her drive.

"Under Frye's eye," said Glover in later years,[1] "mother was a different woman. The animation of a moment before had vanished. Her eyes fell and she moved away without a word.

"I lounged around the house and waited while mother took her drive. Frye accompanied her, dressed in his livery. I saw her only a moment after she returned from that ride. She was as white as a sheet and her hand trembled as it caught mine convulsively. 'Frye is angry, oh, so angry,' she whispered. 'He says that I shall not give you the money and we have quarrelled. You do not know the truth, George, but that man makes me account to him for every dollar—every penny.'"

She then told Glover to hurry away. He went in haste to the bank, got his money, and did not see his mother for another long interval. He carried with him the distinct impression that she stood in awe of her secretary-footman, and was even under Frye's control. One may well doubt, however, that her talk with Frye during her drive was entirely responsible for her change of heart by the time she reached the house again. Mrs. Eddy herself was quite capable of having changes of heart without consultation with any one—and she could veer like a weathervane in a minute. It is wholly probable that she regretted her unusual generosity to her son—for this was the first time she had ever given him money—before she stepped into her carriage. And she was undoubtedly anxious to get rid of him. His rustic manners and appearance in no way harmonized with the atmosphere with which she was seeking to surround herself.

She never sent him the five hundred dollars she promised, nor did he ever again hear anything about the $30,000 for the quartz mill. Eventually, however, she did decide to build him a house. He was living at this time in Lead, South Dakota,

[1] The substance of this interview, as well as the quoted conversation, is derived from George Glover's statement in the New York *World* of March 3, 1907.

where he owned a piece of property on the outskirts of the town. Frye sent up as superintendent of the building operations one Charles M. Howe, First Reader in a Christian Science Church at St. Joseph, Missouri. Why this strange choice of a building superintendent was made, history does not reveal.

The building venture fared badly. At the very time Mrs. Eddy's publicity department was making quite a news item of Mrs. Eddy's unparalleled generosity to her son, Glover was writing to his mother to ask for an extra $1,100 with which to repair building defects. The house had been so poorly constructed that large cracks immediately opened up in the plaster, the fireplace in the parlor caved in within a month, and windows began to sag. Glover sent his letter asking for an additional building allowance through the express office, this method being chosen because an express delivery would require her personal signature as a receipt. The report eventually came back that Mrs. Eddy refused to accept delivery personally; that she could not receive it except through her secretary, Calvin Frye.

In the end Glover authorized delivery to Frye, and in return received a letter signed by his mother dated August 21, 1900. Saying that she had already given him over $20,000, and that he had "resolved to throw away no more money" on him or his family, she declared:

My rule is that my secretary shall first read my letters. So, if you send another letter to me that breaks this rule and requires the expressman to deliver to me alone I shall return that letter to you unopened.[1]

By this time Mrs. Eddy was suffering periods of illness during which she had to depend almost entirely upon Frye to attend to her mail in such a manner that no one outside of her house would guess that she was indisposed. Frye answered personally what correspondence he could, and held the rest for Mrs. Eddy's attention when she could deal with it.

Mrs. Eddy had similarly become wholly dependent upon

[1] This excerpt is from another of the group of letters made public at the time the "Next Friends'" suit. Vd. New York *World*, November 2, 1907.

Frye for the keeping of her accounts. He received the moneys
that were paid into her hands, deposited them, made expenditures as purchases were necessary. Because Mrs. Eddy herself
demanded careful accounting and held Frye responsible for
keeping his books balanced, he in turn insisted that she list any
items of her own expenditure so that he could perform the
duties she assigned him. This is quite evidently the basis for
her statement that "Frye makes me account to him for every
penny." He did. If he had not insisted on such a course, Mrs.
Eddy's business affairs would very shortly have been in a woefully tangled state. For, as with everything else, Mrs. Eddy
could not keep her attention centred on her finances. She would
display a rapt and searching interest in them for a brief while,
catechize Frye thoroughly, rake him over the coals for some
minor error, announce that she was going to take all her business out of his hands; then she would abruptly forget the
whole matter until the next time.

Thus it was that Frye handled hundreds of thousands of
dollars a year, meanwhile drawing a salary that had risen by
stages to $1,000 per annum and then to $1,200. He was a
messy bookkeeper, but an entirely honest one. He had the passion for detail that is so often the mark of the small mind and
the cankered soul. He counted his dollars by pennies. Undoubtedly there were times when he got on Mrs. Eddy's nerves—
when he would have got on anybody's nerves. There were
undoubtedly times when she resented not only his disposition
but also his manner of supervision over her affairs. He was
petty even in his insistence that she should not spend a dollar
without his knowing it. In his small way he was a tyrant in the
Eddy household.

His delight in his tyranny was indeed his one compensation
in life. Frye was perhaps the only person in the world who was
never afraid of Mrs. Eddy. For the most part, he ruled her instead. And he was utterly indispensable to her. He shielded her
from the outside world. He made her appointments for her
when she could see people, made her excuses for her when she
could not. He not only attended to her finances and her mail; he
took on himself the burden of guarding her physical comfort.

He took her orders humbly one minute, and scolded her the next. He could even be dictatorial. Addressing her always as "Mother," he would seem by turns a deferential servant and an ill-mannered, truculent small boy. To Frye, Mrs. Eddy was hardly the anointed spiritual leader to whose image thousands in a great church bowed down; she was rather a flighty old lady who fumed and beamed by turns, and who needed not merely attentive service but also close and loyal supervision.

Eventually, despite Mrs. Eddy's rebuff to her son, Frye sent Glover the money he had requested to pay for alterations on his shaky new house, with instructions to have all expenditures covered by complete vouchers and to return any unexpended surplus. This Glover did. Three years later, in 1903, he went to Concord again, taking his daughter Mary with him. They registered at the Eagle Hotel, and sent a note asking if they might come up to Pleasant View for a call. But Glover was put off from day to day with various excuses. Mrs. Eddy was "too busy"—or could not be disturbed in her "great work"—or was "engaged for the day." She wrote Glover that he had done very wrong in coming to Concord at all, and that his best course would be to go away immediately.

He did not depart, and eventually Mrs. Eddy summoned him to Pleasant View. He was there just half an hour. Mrs. Eddy appeared agitated when he came into her room. One of the first things she asked was why Glover had returned some of the money she sent him. "Oh my son!" she said. "Why did you spurn your mother's proffered aid? Why did you throw my money back into my face?"

Glover was incredulous. He knew that she was referring to the money which he had returned from the extra expense allowance, along with the vouchers for paid bills, all in accord with her request. What he did not know was that Mrs. Eddy's memory at times was wholly unreliable, and that there were low periods in her life when she did not recall just what she had said in some mood that had gone before.

Glover had with him the letter from Frye instructing him to return any surplus with the vouchers. He drew it out, and Mrs. Eddy held it with palsied hands up close to her spectacled

eyes as she scanned the lines. "It *is* Frye's signature," she ex
claimed. "Would to God it had never been written!"

She grew more agitated. She took his hand and begged hin
to go at once. Suddenly she arose, told him good-by, ordere
him flatly to leave her immediately. "Start for home at once,
she told him harshly. "Don't delay."

George Glover left his mother after this fantastic interview
more sure than ever that things were occurring around her o
which she was ignorant and that she was merely an unwittin
dummy whose affairs were entirely in Frye's hands. Actuall
the truth lay in between. Mrs. Eddy's memory was never c
the best. It began fading even before she had produced all c
her writings. When she appeared so contradictory as in th
talk with her son, it was very easy to suppose that she was th
victim of another master mind that on occasion could eve
forge her signature. And this indeed was later asserted.

It is rather probable that on occasions such a "'forgery" c
Mrs. Eddy's signature happened—occasions when Mrs. Edd
was entirely too incapacitated even to put her name on a nece:
sary paper. On the whole, however, it would appear that as sl
advanced in years there were occasions when her memor
really did lapse; and there were other occasions when sl
found it convenient to give the impression that it had—just :
in this interview with her son, when she was obviously great
embarrassed by his presence in Concord, and undoubted
wished to get rid of him as swiftly and painlessly as possible.

How she could veer in feelings and change her mind wit
consummate ease is well illustrated by the offer she made in
letter to her son's family to pay for the education of the fo
children. She outlined very ambitious plans for the education
programme. Then she sent a remittance of three hundred dc
lars. It was the only money the family ever received for carr
ing the programme through. Eventually, however, Mr. Hov
was sent up from Missouri again, with instructions to take tl
children back to St. Joseph for schooling. When they arriv
there, they were all quartered for a while in a single hotel roor

---

[1]Described by George Glover in interview published in the New York *Wo*
of March 3, 1907.

hen farmed out by Howe among local church members. The
episode ended unfortunately not only because the schooling
plans were never carried through according to schedule, but
also because of personal complications.[1] The Glovers all
trooped back to Lead, and once again it was decided in the
family that something was certainly wrong with Grandmother
Eddy.

It is true that by 1900 Mrs. Eddy's health was obviously
precarious. She had done her last public teaching in the Christian Science Hall in Concord, on November 21 and 22, 1898.
Seventy persons were present in this class, one coming from
England, one from Scotland, and several from Canada. The
first lesson or lecture was about two hours long; the second ran
four hours. "Only two lessons," the faithful *Journal* sighed,
"but such lessons!" She taught the class gratuitously. Thereafter Mrs. Eddy's public appearances became much rarer. Her
appearance in Concord in 1904 was the last pilgrimage at
which she was seen, and those near enough her closed carriage
to obtain a real view of her remarked then on her enfeebled
state. It was in 1904 that Mrs. Eddy's church in Concord was
completed, and the pilgrimage there was in the nature of a
sacred jubilee for Mrs. Eddy's communion throngs. Here, for
the first time, chimes in her own church rang out her birthday,
just as she had once so boldly prophesied.

But perverse as she was, and ill and growing so very old,
Mrs. Eddy was not pleased. She wrote in due order to be published over her signature, "Why this meaningless commemora-
tion of birthdays, since there are none?[2] She did not like the
thought of advancing age. She had said in *Science and Health*,
'Never record ages.'"[3]

The church at Concord was raised as a special and personal
tribute to Mrs. Eddy, and although it was spoken of as her
gift to Concord, she in reality contributed only $100,000,
leaving the church to raise the rest as best it could. Thus appeals were broadcast to all loyal members of the Mother

[1] Vd. George Glover's statement in the New York *World*, March 3, 1907.
[2] *Miscellany*, page 235.
[3] Page 246.

Church to do their share, and Mrs. Stetson's church in New York contributed $10,000 for stained glass windows, while Mrs. Stetson donated an additional $1,000 personally.

In the early part of 1909 the startling fact developed that the church had hanging over it a mortgage that was coming due. Now Mrs. Eddy had made it an unwritten rule in her church that no church building was to be dedicated until it was wholly free from debt.[1] Debt in her philosophy had the same status as error; it did not, or at least should not, exist. An appeal was made to Mrs. Stetson, among others, to make an additional contribution that would free Mrs. Eddy's personal church from this extremely un-Scientific obligation. Mrs. Eddy's Board of Directors naturally were anxious to lift the obligation, if possible, without Mrs. Eddy's discovering the unfortunate truth. When they approached Mrs. Stetson, she flatly refused any assistance. Her letter of refusal had a logical ring to it which was unanswerable. But it made her no friends in Boston. She wrote Mr. Farlow of The Mother Church, in heavily underscored lines:

. . . Neither the *original* nor the *continued concealment* of this condition, from those entitled to know it, could have come from aught but error. Participation in the *concealment* of this fact is unwarranted in Christian Science. . . .

It is impossible, therefore, for me to contribute secretly to the cancellation of a debt upon the church, which existed when the edifice was dedicated. . . .

Upon careful reading of your letter, there seems to be another point. This call for aid is not for *support* from divine Love, in demonstration of Christian Science and its truth. The request is based upon the alleged inability of the church to demonstrate Christian Science. Fidelity to the teaching of our dear Leader, Mrs. Eddy, will enable any one, individual or church, to make a *complete* demonstration regarding *supply,* as well as that of overcoming sin, sickness and death. . . . Again, I must repeat, that it would be a pleasant and an easy thing to do to send the money to the church, but in this case, "I must be cruel, only to be kind."[2]

That letter was written less than a year before Mrs. Stetson

[1] In late years this unwritten law has not been taken so seriously, due perhaps to declining church revenues. See the U. S. Census of Religious Bodies for 1926, report for the Church of Christ, Scientist.

[2] Stetson, *Sermons and Other Writings,* page 267.

was cast out from Mrs. Eddy's church. Mrs. Stetson had now gravely offended the Boston Directors, and already she had frightened them. They had been fearing for some years that upon Mrs. Eddy's death Mrs. Stetson would attempt to seize the personal leadership of the church. And they had small desire to lose the temporal power which, with Mrs. Eddy's advancing years, was already falling more and more into their hands. Mrs. Eddy's Directors were rather ambitious and autocratic individuals who—however much they revered her or feared her—hardly believed that she was going to be immortal. They had no idea of her physical and mental ailments; with Frye's assistance she had concealed her private life even from the gaze of her church officials. On the other hand, these gentlemen knew very well that Mrs. Eddy was already a very old lady, and they did not wish to see Augusta Stetson benefit —at their own expense—by Mrs. Eddy's inevitable demise. For the most part they were men of no previous accomplishment who had gained their first taste of power and large income when Mrs. Eddy elevated them to the head of her organization. They had no intention of stepping down so that Mrs. Stetson could come up. Mrs. Eddy, for her part, had herself known long and haunting fears of Augusta Stetson. She had felt at various times, along with the Board, that Mrs. Stetson's dynamic ability was perhaps too dynamic.

But there was one great and overwhelming difficulty in dealing with Augusta Stetson. She loved and revered Mrs. Eddy.

XXIV

The relationship between Mary Baker Eddy and August
Stetson must baffle understanding unless it is remembered tha
Augusta Stetson sincerely regarded Mrs. Eddy as uniquel
divine.

This was not true during the early months of their associa
tion, as Mrs. Stetson sat in Mrs. Eddy's classroom and hear
the wiles of malicious animal magnetism denounced and tl
understanding love of God exalted. But Mrs. Stetson was
very imaginative woman. Unlike Mrs. Eddy, who reveale
but little of the temperament of the *religieuse,* Mrs. Stetso
was also a mystic. She could never find happiness unless at an
given moment she had a devout belief. For her peace of min
it did not so much matter in what this belief was centred, s
long as she was never without an idol on which she could poi
a constant libation of faith.

She was, in other words, a woman of great and burning e
thusiasms. She was not at first meeting particularly impresse
with Mrs. Eddy, but she had a highly suggestible mind. *A*
Mrs. Eddy's teachings worked more and more into her co
sciousness, Mrs. Stetson's native enthusiasm was awakene
and inflamed. She took Mrs. Eddy wholly seriously and lite
ally when that venerable lady wrote:

> It is authentically said that one expositor of Daniel's dates fixed t
> year 1866 or 1867 for the return of Christ. . . . It is a marked c
> incidence that those dates were the first two years of my discovery
> Christian Science.[1]

Mrs. Stetson never saw the very human Mrs. Eddy wl
was revealed to so many others who were associated with th

[1] *Miscellany*, page 181. Vd. also *Message to the Mother Church for 1900*, page
"Some modern exegesis on the prophetic Scriptures cites 1875 as the year
the second coming of Christ. In that year the Christian Science text-book, *Scie*
and Health with Key to the Scriptures, was first published."

mposite personality for any length of time. She herself wor-
ipped until the end. As she wrote of Mrs. Eddy in 1904:

What she says and does is *always right.* I am able to say that no mat-
what she may do—however human reason may try to argue against
r moves—I would regard these arguments as the "evil one" trying to
rken me as to her wisdom and leading, and would *instantly accept* and
low, without a question, wherever she leads.[1]

Even after she had suffered a humiliation greater than can
er come to many, in that it befell her in such high place, she
rote, "I would go to the scaffold or the stake to defend the
achings of Jesus the Christ, and of Mary Baker Eddy."[2]

Mrs. Stetson did not merely believe in Mrs. Eddy's divinity;
occasions she could even convince herself that Mrs. Eddy
as going to be immortal. Indubitably in Mrs. Eddy's varied
ritings are to be found claims that spiritual man is wholly
mortal and never dies. Like Lydia Frye, Mrs. Stetson pro-
imed to the end of her days that "there is no death," and
sisted that she would live forever.

Mrs. Eddy herself had at times made such claims. In *Sci-
ce and Health* she wrote that "Man *is,* not *shall be,* perfect
d immortal,"[3] and since she was regarded as the perfect
rthly expression of the man-idea, some of her followers as-
med that if anybody was going to be immortal Mrs. Eddy
ould certainly be that one. But so unstable were many of the
inds in Mrs. Eddy's movement that there were few who held
such a venturesome opinion consistently. Certainly Mrs.
ldy wavered in her own opinion on this question. She did not
glect, for instance, to make a will. On the other hand, when
lward A. Kimball died—a loyal student of whom Mrs. Eddy
as very fond—the old lady could write boldly that "there is in
ality no evil, no disease, no death. . . . My beloved Edward
Kimball . . . is here now as veritably as when he visited me
ars ago."[4] In a mood less hopeful, Mrs. Eddy could blandly
verse herself again and write: "To say that you and I, as

Stetson, *Reminiscences, Sermons and Correspondence,* page 733.
Ibid., page 691.   [3]Page 428.   [4]*Miscellany,* page 297.

mortals, will not enter this dark shadow of material sens
called *death,* is to assert what we have not proved."[1]

Mrs. Eddy believed on this question, as on so many other
just what she wanted to believe at the moment. Mrs. Stetso
was at one time apparently convinced that Mrs. Eddy wa
dead—and was mistaken in so thinking. As a rule, howeve
Mrs. Stetson usually proclaimed and taught that both she an
Mary Baker Eddy were immortal. Thus she wrote Mrs. Edd
the following letter, dated November 1, 1906:

> My students, assembled to-day at the annual meeting of their Ass
> ciation, unite with me in conveying to you our loyal love. We re-affir
> our instant, constant allegiance. We are individually watching and worl
> ing with you, realizing that we also rise with you in proportion to or
> understanding and demonstration of your teaching, by precept and exan
> ple, of the eternal law which governs and controls all created things. B
> cause, in this sacred hour, from your cloistered communion in the secr
> place of the Most High, *you* are demonstrating the immortality of Li
> manifest in individual man, *we* look for the appearing of the ideal ma
> made in God's image and likeness, never to disappear,—reflecting fo
> ever the presence, power, and peace of the eternal Mind.

This remarkable document, in which the italics are Mr
Stetson's, was published quite casually in *The Sentinel* of N
vember 10, 1906, indicating that its point of view was not cor
sidered in any way extraordinary at that moment.[2]

Mrs. Stetson to the end of her days insisted that Mrs. Edd
was Christ in modern embodiment. She wrote unhesitating
that "Mrs. Eddy occupies the position before the world to-da
which Jesus occupied two thousand years ago."[3] She asserte
further, "I believe that our revered Leader, Mary Baker Edd
was God-anointed and God-inspired to write *Science an
Health with Key to the Scriptures.*"[4]

Mrs. Eddy herself did not permanently retain the views cor

[1] *Unity of Good,* page 40.

[2] The version presented here is that of the corrected letter, as reprinted the f
lowing week in *The Sentinel* of November 17. The only changes were in capit
ization and punctuation.

[3] Stetson, *Sermons and Other Writings,* page 855. The letter was written
February, 1911, two months after Mrs. Eddy's death. It was in reply to cri
cism of an article Mrs. Stetson wrote called "The Demonstration of M
Eddy," and published in *The Independent* of January 26, 1911. In this remar
able article Mrs. Stetson had declared: "Mary Baker Eddy *lives.* . . ."

[4] *Ibid.,* page 832.

rning her own divine status that she promulgated in those
rlier years when she was overwhelmed and astonished at the
·lated success which met her proselyting. Similarly, she lost
l delusions about her personal immortality before she died.
ckness, discouragement and ridicule all played a part in
odifying some of these hyperbolic claims during her declin-
g years. She suffered particularly from the ridicule that blis-
red upon the pages of numerous erudite critics as soon as
·r claims began to be headlined. Mrs. Eddy was unusually
nsitive to ridicule that came from intellectual circles; her
'elong ambition was to be considered a ranking intellect
nong the great. She was accustomed to dealing with denun-
ition. But so limited was her sense of humor that against
licule she had no weapons. Mark Twain's comments thus
ing her far more deeply than the weightier blows of less
·ver antagonists. To a unique degree he had a faculty of say-
g true things in an extremely cutting fashion. Not even Mrs.
ldy could ignore his sardonic humor; and she made a perfect
rget for his pen.

Thus Mrs. Eddy in her soberer moments reconsidered some
her earlier ideas concerning herself and did some retracting.
iere was one retraction, it is true, that she never made. She
sisted to the end that *Science and Health* had been inspired.
f her book she said, "I should blush to write of *Science and
ealth with Key to the Scriptures* as I have, were it of human
igin, and were I, apart from God, its author."[1] Even when
ark Twain announced that such divine authorship was dis-
oved by the fact that no foreigner could acquire copyright
the United States, Mrs. Eddy refused to recede from a
.im which by this time she probably regarded as wholly true.
But she did make public withdrawal of her previous bland
ceptance of the status of a divinity. She entirely abandoned,
r instance, her title of Mother. She stated in a public letter
Mark Twain: "Without my consent, the use of the word
read like wild-fire. I still must think the name is not appli-
ble to me . . . I regard self-deification as blasphemous."[2]
rentually the Mother's Room was closed, by Mrs. Eddy's spe-

Miscellany, page 115.   ²Miscellany, page 302.

cial order. She said in explanation that "there is nothing in th
room now of any special interest. Let 'the dead bury the
dead,' and the spiritual have all place and power." And a ne
by-law was passed to replace the one which gave her sole rig
to the Virgin-like name. It said that "In the year nineteen hu
dred and three and after, owing to the public misunderstan
ing of this name, it is the duty of Christian Scientists to dr
the word *mother* and to substitute Leader, already used in o
periodicals."[1] This time the word "Mother" was not capita
ized. She established exclusive right to the new title of Lead
by forbidding any other church member to use it.

Mrs. Eddy explained her various changes of front—and
doctrine—by the following news item:

TAKE NOTICE

What I wrote on Christian Science some twenty-five years ago I
not consider a precedent for a present student of this Science. The b
mathematician has not attained his full understanding of the princi
thereof, in his earliest studies or discoveries. Hence, it were wise to
cept only my teachings that I know to be correct and adapted to
present demand.[2]

When it came to the previous claims of her *Journal* in u
mistakable language, and of herself in unmistakable hints, th
she was a modern Christ, she retracted completely. Two diff
ent by-laws were inserted in the *Manual* to cover the subje
Mrs. Eddy announced that "careless comparison or irrevere
reference to Christ Jesus is abnormal in a Christian Scie
tist, and is prohibited."[3] She added that "in accord with all
Mrs. Eddy's teachings, members of this Church shall neitl
entertain a belief nor signify a belief in more than one Chri
even that Christ whereof the Scripture beareth testimony
It was an extraordinary pair of by-laws, viewed from a
standpoint. Probably no such injunction was ever necessa
for any other Christian congregation in all the history of
past two thousand years. It was undoubtedly rather a diffic
provision to enforce. Having established an idea in the ima

[1] *Manual*, XXII, 1.   [2] *Miscellany*, page 237.
[3] *Manual*, VIII, 3.   [4] *Manual*, VIII, 7.

ation of her more enthusiastic and hysterical followers by
ow pounding over an extended period of time, she could
arcely hope to change it by a mere by-law. She could hardly
vitch convictions on and off in her congregations as the jani-
r switched the electric light.

And so it happened that Mrs. Stetson went on believing in
Irs. Eddy's divinity even after Mrs. Eddy herself had once
ore changed her mind. Mrs. Stetson continued to teach that
hristian Science would make its followers immortal. And she
so went on preaching the horrors of malicious animal mag-
etism, which she had learned at Mrs. Eddy's knee.

Mrs. Stetson, in other words, remained a fundamentalist
iring a period when Mrs. Eddy's doctrines were being planed
f—to use Wiggin's word—and smoothed down for wider
iblic consumption. This planing process began as soon as
Irs. Eddy had retired from active teaching while a business-
ke Board of Directors took charge of her mundane affairs,
• that she had time to ruminate and revise her texts. In conse-
ience Mrs. Stetson eventually came to be preaching a doc-
ine much bolder than that accepted by more recent converts
Mrs. Eddy's church. This explains why she could finally be
mvicted of heresy even though she taught nothing but Eddy
ogmas. The one trouble was that Mrs. Stetson taught doc-
ines that had become like former editions of *Science and
ealth*—wholly out of style.

It is probable that Mrs. Stetson would never have met her
agedy had she not developed a blind faith in Mary Baker
ddy. Like most of the other leaders in Mrs. Eddy's move-
ent, Mrs. Stetson presents an involved study for the psychia-
ist. She undoubtedly had many intellectual gifts—she was
dowed, indeed, with both intellect and personality of a cali-
r far superior to that of Mrs. Eddy. On the other hand she
as undoubtedly—like Mrs. Eddy—a slave to emotion. She
ver possessed a sense of balance. She was utterly lacking in
tellectual discrimination, in ability to appraise objective val-
s.

This explains why she trusted Mrs. Eddy as blindly as a
gh priestess would trust her god. And it offers at least a par-

tial clew to the reason for the remarkable love which August
Stetson bore for Mrs. Eddy—a love wholly unique and show
ing signs of being allied with a deep-lying complex.

Religious instinct is rooted in mysterious and often ur
plumbed emotional depths. A letter which Mrs. Stetson wrot
to Mrs. Eddy in 1896, telling how a dream gave her inspira
tion in a moment of great weariness, suggests much tha
would undoubtedly be of interest to a student of humanit
schooled in Freud. For she said:

I dreamed this: That you sent for me. I was shown into a larg
square room with one window, and one large door which opened on
lawn. In the room was a very large bed. You approached me, and smi
ing, whispered, "Rest, dear, rest." You then glided to the bed and la
down on the edge. I followed and laid myself on the other side. As
lay there I thought it was night and I said to myself, how quiet she i
Oh, how sweet and peaceful to be with her; I wonder what she wants n
to do! I must not sleep; when she awakes she will tell me. Then
seemed to be morning.

You quietly arose and went to a dressing table and began to arrang
your hair. I said, "Oh! Mother dear, may I dress it?" You immediate
sat down and whispered, "Yes, dear." I carefully arranged it, feeling
happy that I was permitted to do it. I exclaimed, "Oh, your hair is
lovely, dear Mother!" Then you arose and went to the door. Turnin
to me you again whispered, "Come."[1]

This letter obviously contains many sexual symbols. Mr
Eddy's early teachings recommending immaculate relation
ships between husbands and wives—the teachings which le
poor Mrs. Woodbury so far astray—found fertile soil in Mr
Stetson's mind, and she adopted them to the final letter. She i
sisted that her married students should live like "brother an
sister." Years later, having warmed to a young newspaper r
porter sent to interview her, Mrs. Stetson inquired if he wer
married. He said that he wasn't.

"Be thankful for that!" she exclaimed with fervor. "We a
know the dreadful thing that goes on in marriage. It belong
down there with Adam,"—and she pointed to the ground.

Mrs. Stetson never ceased to decry the marriage relation
ship. For her, a single love sufficed—her love for Mary Bak

[1]Stetson, *Reminiscences, Sermons and Correspondence*, page 163.

Eddy, whom she addressed as a Christ. She was one of the few students associated with Mrs. Eddy in her early Boston days who kept her first loyalty untarnished by disillusion. She bore for Mrs. Eddy an adoring respect never displayed by any other student.

It is probable that when Mrs. Eddy sent Mrs. Stetson into New York in 1886 the founder of Christian Science did not recognize the full scope of the opportunity for proselyting which lay in the city that was destined to be the cultural and financial capital of the United States. Mrs. Eddy, small-town New Englander that she was, regarded Boston as the hub of the universe. And Boston was indeed for Mrs. Eddy a mighty metropolis after the days of Stoughton and Amesbury and Lynn. What she then hardly realized was that the centre of culture was already shifting from Boston to New York; that New York with its rapidly growing wealth and population and its friendliness to new ideas promised greater power and wealth to the priestess of a new religion than Boston itself could ever hope to offer.

It is likewise probable that Mrs. Eddy in no way visualized the extraordinary heights to which Augusta Stetson would climb in the metropolis to the south. Mrs. Stetson herself did not want to go. She insisted to Mrs. Eddy that she did not know a soul in the city. "Is not God there?" inquired Mrs. Eddy optimistically. Mrs. Stetson could give only one answer to this leading question, and her answer carried her promptly to New York.

During her first years there she requested several times to be relieved of her post, so little did she relish the task of trying to make the still small voice of a new religion heard above the city's uproar. But Mrs. Eddy was obdurate. And Mrs. Stetson obeyed without further question. She lived in a furnished room in a cheap house on West 31st Street, did her own sweeping and cleaning, and depended quite literally on Providence for her food and clothes.

She brought to New York letters of introduction from Mrs. Eddy to two former students, Mrs. Leonard of Brooklyn, who was later to assume an important place in Mrs. Eddy's house-

hold, and Mrs. Laura Lathrop. Both of these women regarde(
Mrs. Stetson as an intruder into their reserve. They had com(
back to New York to make a good living out of their Science
as most of Mrs. Eddy's students intended to do. Mrs. Stetson
being sent down as an outsider to be a leader for that field, wa
eyed with distrust from the time of her arrival. This dislik
did not bear its full fruit until twenty years later, when Mrs
Leonard had direct and constant access to Mrs. Eddy's ear
But as early as 1888 Mrs. Eddy was hearing gossip abou
Mrs. Stetson.

Mrs. Stetson started healing and teaching at once, takin
patients and students wherever she could find them. Like Mr
Eddy, she realized the value of publicity. The first articl
which ever appeared on Christian Science in the New Yor
press was a letter she wrote to *The Sun,* published in th
paper on February 25, 1887. She wrote it so well that the ed
tor gave it an excellent advertising head, which proclaimed:

CHRISTIAN SCIENCE

It Is Proclaimed To Be The Healing
Taught By Jesus of Nazareth

In this same year Mrs. Stetson obtained a church charte
and preached the first Sunday sermon. When it came time
sing she stepped down from the rostrum and played tl
hymns. This first service was held in the old Columbia Ins-
tute. The next week the church moved to a meeting hall ov
a drugstore on Fifth Avenue at 47th Street where servic
were continued all winter. The congregation consisted prin(
pally of eight students who had studied with Mrs. Eddy
Boston, along with any new converts Mrs. Stetson was able
bring into the fold. Jealousies between Mrs. Stetson and M
Eddy's other students developed even during this first wint(
They felt that she was entirely too anxious to lead the wh(
show. Once in those early days when Mrs. Stetson wrote
Mrs. Eddy for advice on dealing with these very human syn
toms, and explaining how she was "treating" such unhap
manifestations of M. A. M., Mrs. Eddy feelingly replied:

Do just what you are doing with the ones you named, overcome any temptation to make it public. Vengeance is mine, saith the Lord. It is just what broke in on my church in Boston, what has broken up the church in Chicago and will yours if it can.[1]

But Mrs. Stetson prospered tremendously, despite minor backbiting. Her church moved from its drugstore location to Crescent Hall. It grew so fast that within four months' time it moved to Hardman Hall at Fifth Avenue and Nineteenth Street. In 1894 another move was made to Scottish Rite Hall, and the organization still expanded so rapidly that it was able in 1896 to buy and rebuild an old church building in West 48th Street at a round cost of $100,000. This was only two years after the $200,000 Mother Church was completed in Boston. But Mrs. Stetson did not stop even here. By 1899 continuing growth had made it necessary to expand again; a site was obtained on Central Park West, and architects engaged to design a church with a seating capacity of 2,200 people. Work was thereupon begun on a magnificent building that upon completion in 1903 had cost $1,250,000. It was entirely paid for when it was dedicated—a marvellous achievement for a woman who had come into New York almost poverty-stricken only a few years before. But Augusta Stetson could consistently inspire an audience to a degree such as Mrs. Eddy apparently achieved only once—in Chicago. She had the further advantage over Mrs. Eddy of being able to maintain the flow of dynamic power which she poured into her work. She had fewer conflicts to fight within herself.

Her secret of raising money was a mystery to the curious New York press until the day she died. She was at times even accused of using undue influence and—worse—hypnotic influence on the large numbers of wealthy converts she gathered around her. One observer once told amusingly how she looked a visitor in the eye, drew back her head, raised her hand in the air in the gesture of taking an oath, and said slowly, impressively, in a magnificent voice, "I—can—demonstrate—money."

She could and did. She raised millions even after she was

[1] February 10, 1890. Stetson, *Sermons and Other Writings*, page 27.

cast out of her church. She died leaving very little money
after spending with lavish magnificence until the end. She
always said that she never kept any accounts, that when she
needed money it was provided, that it was useful only when i
was used. Once when asked the source of her funds, she said
with a quizzical smile, and a Biblical reference, "Out of the
fish's mouth."

The imposing marble temple which she dedicated in 190?
completely outshone the unimpressive Mother Church struc
ture in Boston, magnificent as that $200,000 building had ap
peared to Mrs. Eddy only a few years before. Mrs. Stetson
was conscious of the disparity, and more than aware of the
glory of her own unequalled demonstration. Thus she wrot
to Mrs. Eddy in 1903:

> We shall dedicate without any debt. Our money is all in. The churc'
> is attracting a great deal of attention. . . . The edifice is only a type
> I know, but a better symbol than the old church, for the love that throug
> us has laid in the outstretched hands of God one million two hundre
> and fifty thousand dollars proves that much of self-love and trust i
> money has been destroyed. . . . The press has been clamoring for week
> to get matter for publication concerning us, but our doors have bee
> vigilantly guarded, and we shall give them only what is proper fo
> them to know. We shall not announce the date until next Saturda
> From now until the dedication is over, I pray for grace and strength t
> stand against the argument of the enemy of good in aggressive ment
> suggestion.[1] I know in whom I trust. This could not have been made pos
> sible but for your watchful, loving, protecting, and wise guidance.[2]

As Mrs. Eddy remembered her own modest church buildin
in Boston this letter could not have been wholly pleasing. Au
gusta Stetson was at least wise enough on a few occasions t
realize that even qualified praise of herself was not alway
music to Mrs. Eddy's ears. Several years later, for instanc
she wrote Mrs. Eddy in reference to an article in the *Broa*
way Magazine in 1907:

> We are not pleased with this story, because it says too much in prai
> of *our* church and of me, and for this reason we do not think it wise to ci
> culate it.[3]

[1] A synonym for M. A. M.
[2] Stetson, *Reminiscences, Sermons and Correspondence*, page 170.
[3] *Ibid.*, page 188.

When it came to dedicating her church Mrs. Stetson proceeded with consummate tact. Wm. H. Taylor, of the New York Board of Trustees, had suggested that the church should be dedicated "To the Glory of God." Mrs. Stetson demurred. "Let us," she said, "make two plans on tablets of cardboard,—inscribe one, 'To the Glory of God,' and the other, 'A Tribute of Love to our Leader and Teacher, Mary Baker Eddy.' Then we will send them to Mrs. Eddy and let her make her choice."

It developed during this conference that only a few weeks previously Mrs. Stetson had visited Mrs. Eddy in Boston and inquired whether she would object to having the New York Church dedicated to her.

"Why," Mrs. Eddy demanded, "should I object to an expression of love and gratitude from you and your students?"

The matter was consequently handled in accord with Mrs. Stetson's suggestion. The two sample inscriptions were prepared and sent to Boston. Mrs. Eddy considered them carefully. And then she wrote:

My Beloved Brethren: What if your church edifice in the far future be desecrated and used by others? Then your inscription "To the Glory of God" would be a stumbling block. I advise you not to engrave that assertion on stone, but write it on your hearts. . . .

As a result of this reasoned reply the church was dedicated to the glory not of God but of Mary Baker Eddy. Mrs. Eddy was profoundly pleased. The inscription was not confined to a corner-stone, but was carved on a stone panel as large as a bill-board. For burial in the corner-stone Mrs. Eddy sent Mrs. Stetson a special memorandum:

To Mrs. A. E. Stetson:

Beneath this corner-stone, in this silent, sacred sanctuary of earth's sweet songs, pæans of praise and records of Omnipotence, I leave my name with thine in unity and love.

The expressions of love which passed between Mrs. Eddy and Augusta Stetson were in those days legion. The two were on closest and most confidential terms. There were few persons whom Mrs. Eddy trusted, but in these early years she usually believed in the integrity of Augusta. She wrote, for instance, in 1898, at the time when the Woodbury matter was still scandalizing delighted readers, that she intended seeing no more reporters as soon as "all this" was over. Announcing that "God will guard, guide, protect us," she continued:

> We will trust Love. When you seal a letter with wax, use an impress that has a design. Wish I could run out and get one for you! I send the enclosed to show you how easily the letter could be opened. Use care send only by Express *unpaid*.[1]

Mrs. Eddy, who was practical enough not to trust wholly to God as long as sealing wax could be obtained, was simultaneously astute enough to appreciate to the full the invaluable and extraordinary work that Augusta Stetson was doing Thus any occasional twinges of jealousy she may have felt were not openly expressed. When Mrs. Eddy drew up her bylaws for the restraint of branch churches she had Mrs. Stetson's organization in the front of her mind as she wrote many of the provisions. But she did not admit this publicly. When on occasion she was inclined to feel that the New York church was already putting the Mother Church in the background she could quietly re-read those by-laws and feel safe.

Meanwhile she could always secure confidential information concerning events in New York from any one of half a dozen excellent sources. All of her own students had withdrawn from the Stetson circle with some display of temper. Mrs Laura Lathrop went first, and formed the Second Church. The Third, Fourth and Fifth Churches were formed in rapid succession, in each instance after the founders had felt heart burnings in their old pews.

Mrs. Stetson herself resented these schisms, which she regarded as unchristian, unnecessary, and unduly weakening the strength of her rapidly expanding organization. She told her own students that these other churches were not founded in Science, since Science taught love instead of jealousy and hate. She suggested to her other students, indeed, that they might well remain away from these schismatic organizations.

[1]Stetson, *Sermons and Other Writings*, page 37.

This news, also, was eventually carried back to Boston. It was told in such a way as to imply that Mrs. Stetson said hers was the only Christian Science Church in New York. Mrs. Eddy found it politic to ignore such reports—at the time.

In those days Augusta even provided most of the clothing that Mrs. Eddy wore. In November of 1900 Mrs. Eddy wrote: "Your wonderful gift of warmth and beauty, the ermine cape, is most acceptable, needful, and received with more gratitude than pen or lips can tell." In 1901: "I never wear my bonnets without *gratitude* to *you* for breaking the law that I shall have nothing fit to wear." Again, in December of the same year, "Your diamond crown is very beautiful. I thank you deeply. . . . Be strong in the right and never return evil for evil, but vice versa. . . ."

The diamond crown mentioned was a brooch that for years was one of Mrs. Eddy's favorite ornaments.

Mrs. Stetson continued to send clothes. In January of 1902, "a beautiful tea jacket." In 1904, a hood which "is very nice now, your love and faithfulness have again triumphed." In January of 1905 Mrs. Eddy actually grew eloquent on the subject of these regular gifts: "God *bless* my dear precious student who helps me to clothes while I am helping to clothe her with righteousness, the robes of heaven here and now."

Mrs. Eddy not only accepted graciously; she had no hesitancy about asking. Here, for instance, was a gentle hint: "I am in great need of summer suits of clothing, will you send me samples of these? Oh how good you are to me: What can I do to pay you, tell me, dearest one? You are all the student that I can depend upon to clothe me, and inasmuch as you have done it unto me, ye have done it unto the Father."

This letter was not signed "Mother," since that signature and form of address was being abandoned by general order.

Two weeks later Mrs. Stetson responded by sending "beautiful summer gowns," for which she was duly thanked in a letter signed with underscores, "Lovingly *ever* thine *own*."

Mrs. Eddy had cause to be doubly thankful. Mrs. Stetson's gifts multiplied, like the loaves and the fishes. For other students, to whom Mrs. Eddy mentioned Augusta as a shining

example, took the hint. So Mrs. Eddy wrote, "Your kindnes
to me has been an example for others and I shall not forget i
nor cease to speak of it as the great cause of your prosperity.'

The signatures on all of these letters from Mrs. Eddy wer
as warm as the endearments that a schoolgirl indites to he
favorite crush. "With thanks and love, always thine," "Eve
tenderly, lovingly thine," "As ever yours lovingly," "Eve
yours tenderly," "With love unbounded."

The prosperity which Mrs. Eddy mentioned had indeed ar
rived for her star student, and in an almost fabulous way.

Mrs. Stetson had laid down her pastorate uncomplainingly
when Mrs. Eddy abolished preaching in her churches, assume
the office of Reader, and later, when the terms of Readers wer
limited, relinquished even this office to become merely a mem
ber of the Board of Trustees of the New York First Church
But just as Mrs. Eddy's title of Pastor Emeritus gave no clev
to the real position that was hers, so did Mrs. Stetson's nom
inal office on the Board of Trustees give no hint of her power
ful leadership in her church's affairs.

Hers was a leadership based on two factors: not only he
almost unlimited dynamic energy, but also an apparently grea
gift for her work as a healer. Mrs. Eddy from her early day
of proselyting had shrewdly seen the importance of healing a
an aid to the rapid building up of her Christian Science or
ganization. Mrs. Eddy, however, had done most of her healing
in private, if at all; and the only available records of her suc
cesses were to be found in her own writings about herself.

This line of action—or inaction—hardly detracted, o
course, from Mrs. Eddy's final prestige; for her carefull
cloistered life rendered her a personage of such mystery tha
she perforce captured the public imagination. Under the cir
cumstances the publicity given to her claims of healing prow
ess made these claims just as effective as if she had actuall
gone down to the Common and in public view healed leper
every day.

On the other hand, this same retirement gave August
Stetson a unique and unplanned opportunity without curren
competition. For with Mrs. Stetson healing was literally a bi

business. It was the sort of business which brought her great fame, thousands of followers, and enormous power in church affairs.

When Mrs. Stetson and her architects planned the church building on 96th Street, some twenty-five rooms had been incorporated in the structure and furnished luxuriously for the exclusive use of healers and patients. Mrs. Stetson, in other words, had not tried to maintain an option on the healing art; she insisted that her students should also master it. In all, some forty healers were connected with Mrs. Stetson's church. Hither flocked the maimed and the halt and the blind of New York. And most of them, to the amazement of the incredulous, went away cured of their "errors." In 1908 three thousand and four different patients were received, four thousand seven hundred and four diseases were treated, three thousand three hundred and thirty-one diseases were reported as healed. Nothing quite like this Armageddon of inflictions had ever been seen before.

Mrs. Stetson was a proud woman, and she was proud of her extraordinary achievements in the church. And yet as every year she added hundreds more to the membership of her flock, healed the thousands, and garnered the millions, she never ceased to render constant and humble tribute to the woman she called her teacher, her Leader, and her Dearest One—Mrs. Eddy. Scarcely a week went by—and sometimes not a day—that she did not sit down to her desk and write some letter such as this:

MY PRECIOUS LEADER: . . . To-day at both services the auditorium and the overflow were filled to their utmost seating capacity, except a few seats out of sight behind the large columns. Never was there such appreciation of *you,* dearest; never such recognition of your wonderful message to the world, and never, oh, never, such love and loyalty as we felt for you, our beloved, our precious Guide to eternal Life, as to-day. I can do anything for you, dearest, will you let me know?

I am working and watching and praying, and demonstrating the healing power of Christian Science. Last Sunday a boy nine years of age was attended by a consulting physician, who declared that but one thing more could be done, and that was an operation which was most serious. I was called to calm the mother, who was nearly beside herself. I went

into the room in the absence of the nurse, and spoke audibly to the child.
Then I realized for myself just a few moments, that Love filled the
room, and I went out and to church. In an hour the surgeons came with
the doctors, when they were amazed to find the boy in a nearly normal
condition. This was the end of the disease. The boy quickly improved
and is the wonder of all interested.[1]

It is doubtful if letters like this made Mrs. Eddy wholly at
ease. All her life she had been subject to jealousy, suspicion
and fear. And she had never given her permanent trust and
faith to any one. Even though Augusta was doing miracles in
Mary Baker Eddy's name, Mrs. Eddy could occasionally find
room in her doubting heart to feel uneasy about Augusta. Nor
did such fears and jealousies lessen as Mrs. Stetson ascended
more and more into the spotlight, while Mrs. Eddy spent her
mysterious days within the walls of Pleasant View with age
and illness creeping upon her.

The years only added to Augusta Stetson's wondrous renown. Her healing department continued to be run wide open
to the public gaze for the marvel of all who would come and
see. She herself dominated it, ordered it, supervised it, inspired
it. She was here, there, everywhere constantly among the visiting throngs. She had said of her tasks in the days of her early
struggles that she worked twenty hours a day. Now, in the
years of her wealth and glory, she worked hardly less. Her
correspondence was enormous; she answered much of it in her
own hand. She wrote prolifically, most of this work being done
at night. During the day she directed the practice of the healers, consulted with them on the more difficult cases, taught
classes of students, held conferences on innumerable details of
church operation, found time to extend useful personal contacts with wealthy members. No phase of church operation
was too large or too small to engage her attention and energies. Because the Board of the church was composed entirely
of her students, she controlled the Board. Over both her students and healers she exercised a rigid personal jurisdiction
that extended to the most intimate details of their private lives.
Augusta Stetson was the motive force of her entire church.

[1] May 12, 1907, Stetson, *Reminiscences, Sermons and Correspondence*, page 19

Hers was wholly a personal leadership. She was in no way a mere creature of that printed publicity to which Mrs. Eddy owed so much of her own standing. Augusta Stetson was always in the midst of the crowd, exhorting, pleading, inspiring, directing. It was her business to enthuse the multitude—then direct that enthusiasm to her own ends.

Among her throngs she moved as imperious as a priestess of the royal blood. Long past were the days when she lived in a room that she swept with her own hands. She ruled in magnificence and dwelt in beauty. In 1905 her students had given her a great home adjoining the church on 96th Street. Even the linens of this home were a gift. When she stood poised at the top of the great Carrara marble stairway in her mansion, robed in sweeping lace and gorgeous in jewels, and started slowly to descend with her train floating behind her and a light hand on the rail, to the guest awaiting below she seemed nothing less than an empress, untouchable in her serene beauty.

Mrs. Eddy in Boston had a Mother Church whose members were scattered all over the United States, wholly removed from the personal influence of a dominant leader. It was a weak form of organization; Mrs. Eddy had intentionally made it so. Compared to the enraptured organization Mrs. Stetson had evolved, and then maintained in regularly renewed states of ecstasy, The Mother Church was characterless and impotent. Mrs. Eddy had inserted in her by-laws every possible provision she could devise to prevent just such a situation. But no by-law—even if it took away every title which Mrs. Stetson held—could emasculate her great personal influence over every one with whom she came in contact. Mrs. Stetson rivalled Mrs. Eddy even though she had no more official standing in the New York Church than membership on its Board of Trustees. Mrs. Eddy could fortify her own position by taking away all titles from her followers; but she could not hope so easily to take from them the abilities and capacities which she herself did not possess.

Mrs. Stetson's personal wealth grew with the extended range of her personal influence. It was said that the former mayor of a thriving city in New York State gave in association with his wife over $400,000 to Mrs. Stetson in a single year and that a certain rich woman donated her entire fortune during her lifetime. Others of lesser means gave large shares of whatever they possessed. Mrs. Stetson made generous giving a condition for the receiving of divine favor. It was suggested constantly in the experiences and testimonies given at the Wednesday night meetings, in teaching lectures, and in private talks with members, that one should trust entirely to Divine Supply, put all faith in Divine Principle, for any material support needed. The surest way to evidence such faith and to destroy personal fear of lack was to give generously of all present resources. Other important sources of revenue came through partnerships secured by Mrs. Stetson when business men in her congregation offered her shares of stock in return for giving their enterprises "mental treatments" for prosperity. It is related that she secured large returns in this way from numerous capitalists. All of her church leaders were wealthy.

Poverty and lack, or any confession of it, were regarded by Mrs. Stetson as shameful error. If poor communicants came into the church, they were taught the disgrace of staying poor, or at least of confessing poverty and impersonating it. In the secret rooms of the church, which few even of the members knew about, were maintained complete wardrobes of clothing which could be dispensed to those members who for some reason were slow in "demonstrating" new clothing of the properly prosperous fashion. The wealthy members of the congregation kept this wardrobe well supplied.

The church was designed almost as Mrs. Stetson's personal citadel. Back of the floor above the main auditorium were doors leading to rooms never seen by the general public and known only to a few members. Here were reception rooms, bedrooms, a dining-room and kitchen, and here lived members who were in the heart of Mrs. Stetson's inner mystical circle. The church building proper was connected with Mrs. Stetson's adjoining home by a covered passageway. In the church tower she had her own secret retiring rooms, to which she would mount alone when she sought absolute solitude.

It was indeed a singular creation, with a glamour such as nothing which Mrs. Eddy created had ever approached. In this atmosphere, extraordinary doctrines were taught—no less extraordinary than Mrs. Eddy's own. Mrs. Stetson did not permit couples in her church to marry without first seeking her approval, and marriages were abandoned on occasions when this approval was not forthcoming. Wives were taught that the highest spiritual existence was the sexless life of the nun. Those who had advanced to the more mystical inner circles of the church were instructed that sex life was utterly unspiritual; that husbands and wives who, desirous of children, used the usual means to produce them were "perpetuating the error of belief in physical birth."

Practitioners in the Stetson fold were not allowed to marry, and were reduced to the rank if they did. Such teachings were not given in open services; they were extended to those initiates sufficiently advanced in "spiritual understanding" to be ready for them. They in no way differed from the teachings that Mrs. Eddy herself had stressed in the days when she gave personal instruction in her Metaphysical College.

Naturally these highhanded methods brought a certain amount of revolt, even before the church had grown very far. In January of 1904 Mrs. Stetson wrote, "If there are, as has been reported, persons who are disturbed at my methods, they have never entered one complaint to me." That was perhaps true, but there were frequent complaints voiced abroad. When a prominent member resigned from the church after openly expressing his own hostility, his wife soon died. It was then whispered that Mrs. Stetson and her students had united to direct malicious animal magnetism against the unfortunate woman. Another woman in the church was firmly convinced, according to lurid accounts published in the New York press, that Mrs. Stetson had filled her husband with malicious mental currents, but she went on attending the church regularly because she felt in fear for her own life. One member whose misfortune it was to enter into a dispute with Mrs. Stetson left the church, opened up an independent practitioner's office, and immediately went insane. He was carried to the asylum loudly declaring that Mrs. Stetson's malicious animal magnetism had broken him in mind and body. And eventually there were several suicides which some critics attributed to a fear of Mrs. Stetson's mental wrath.

According to newspaper reports, these malicious mental treatments were carried on in much the same way that Mrs. Eddy had taught her students in the old College days. Mrs. Stetson would assemble her practitioners at noon of each day, except Sunday. The lesson would be read aloud, and then the leader would announce the name of the person who was believed to be attempting to harm Mrs. Stetson and her work.

"He does not want to harm the church," the leader would announce aloud.

Immediately all practitioners present would take up this thought and "make it real," picturing the subject as holding this state of mind.

After a few moments of meditation the leader would again say aloud, "He cannot hurt the church; he has no power."

All would hold this sacred thought, concentrating and visualizing.

The leader once more would continue, "He is confused—he is confused."

Then all would picture the man in a state of mental confusion.[1] If after such treatments, lasting sometimes half an hour a day for many months with the mental efforts of thirty people behind them, the victim did finally go insane, the outside world was allowed to understand that he was insane before he came into the church or he would never have defied Mrs. Stetson. Initiate members would be told that by the removal of the disobedient one God had protected his church.

Actually, direct suggestion played a real and a large part in these "treatments." If the practitioners were treating a person with the object of "confusing" him, giving him incapacitating disease, or rendering him unfit to conduct his business word was allowed to reach the intended victim of the proceedings being followed. Those who already believed in the potency of mental power easily were impressed with the horror which

[1]For this description of a "treatment" vd. New York *World*, October 31, 1909

was hanging over them. It would not be strange if, in numerous instances after receiving such news of the practitioners' activities, members actually began to be sick and ailing.

How the imagination of the more impressionable and hysterical members of the congregation was caught in a whirlpool of fear much like that in which Mrs. Eddy had engulfed herself may best be illustrated by the words of some of the sufferers.

"When I refused to yield my will to Mrs. Stetson," one church member related, "I aroused her enmity. One night as I lay in bed I felt that my hour had come, that mental forces which were almost irresistible were being directed against me. I called on God and for an hour I fought the fight. During that hour I developed such psychic faculties that I was able to make my body pass through the walls of my room. At last I conquered and have been safe since."

In cases where the practitioners thought themselves dealing with a particularly vicious enemy, the half-hour treatments were much extended; in the fashion Mrs. Eddy had established in years long past, a sort of guard mount was instituted, and the practitioners would take two-hour periods for the duty of holding it. One victim who had been told that he was being treated in this manner said that "the strain of the malpractice on me was so great that to get peace of mind I rode in the noisiest cars and went into the noisiest parts of the city. I could hug the noise for the relief it gave me."

Such were the works of the obsession which had first been born in the imagination of a sick woman, and had thence spread out its tentacles into lives utterly removed and remote from her own secret existence. And through all the tentacles, seen dimly but still seen, was Quimby's serene thought that God was All, and God was Love.

But fear can be a useful tool for an absolute ruler. And even though Mrs. Stetson lost numerous church members who could not bear with her, who broke away from teachings that seemed so foreign to a theology that sought to deny evil, such losses did not threaten her power. Disaffected students had not permanently damaged Mrs. Eddy—nor did they Mrs.

Stetson. Always there were new recruits eager to learn the mysterious secrets of gaining the health and wealth which seemed to be poured out upon loyal members of Mrs. Stetson's congregation in an endless supply.

But far in the background there was a woman watching, watching, with a tremulous fear which her letters carefully concealed. Mary Baker Eddy, as she peered out from the shadows of her throne-room like an old Queen who hears the crowds already cheering her successor, heard something besides the cheers. There were vague, low whispers.

Mrs. Eddy had long been aware of the scattered rumors that she was not really in voluntary retirement; that actually she was confined helplessly to her bed; that she was rapidly dying; that she was in fact dead and her death was being carefully concealed from the world. Those rumors had been current as early as 1900. They were particularly rife during the Woodbury trial, at which Mrs. Eddy did not put in a personal appearance.

As Mrs. Eddy now listened grimly, there came the sound of whispers fainter still. They said that Augusta Stetson was trying to make the rumors about Mrs. Eddy come true; that, seated in the marble whitenesses of her temple in New York, she was brewing for the Leader a storm of malicious animal magnetism so awful that even Mrs. Eddy with her divine power must succumb.

Mrs. Eddy heard, and shivered.

Mrs. Stetson, told about this mysterious rumor, was horrified. She wrote to Mrs. Eddy a long and ardent letter, eagerly denying, loyally protesting:

Oh, dearest, it is such a lie! No one who knows us can believe this. It is vicarious atonement. Has the enemy no more argument to use, that it has to go back to this? It is exhausting its resources and I hope the end is near. You know my love for you, beloved; and my students love you as their Leader and Teacher; they follow your teachings and lean on the "sustaining infinite." . . .

Your Father is *our* Father. He will protect *us* as He *has* and *ever will* protect *you*. We have much to do to stand in this hour, but we trust in God. . . .

This lie cannot disturb you nor me. I love you, my students love you, and we never send out such thoughts as are mentioned.[1]

"We never send out such thoughts." Doubtfully Mrs. Eddy must have rolled that sentence over and over in her mind, querying it, comparing it, always wondering. . . .

Kennedy . . . Spofford . . . Arens . . . Woodbury . . . Stetson. . . .

One can understand how she came to halt over that final name, Stetson. . . .

Mrs. Eddy, perhaps, wanted to believe in the love of Augusta Stetson. But when the long nights would come—those endless nights when she lay awake in her bed, time and again there would mount around her the cloud of vague, smothering fears—slowly, slowly choking her until she would scream for Calvin Frye. . . .

[1] For entire letter vd. Stetson, *Reminiscences, Sermons and Correspondence*, page 192.

PART V

THE TWILIGHT OF A GOD

"When Alexander had given way to fears of supernatural influence, his mind grew so disturbed and so easily alarmed that, if the least unusual or extraordinary thing happened, he thought it a prodigy or a presage, and his court was thronged with diviners and priests whose business it was to sacrifice and purify. . . .

"So miserable a thing is incredulity . . . and so miserable, also, superstition, which like water where the level has been lowered, flowing in and never stopping, fills the mind with slavish fears and follies. . . ."

—PLUTARCH.

PART I

THE TWILIGHT OF A GOD

XXV

At Pleasant View Mrs. Eddy maintained a veritable institution, surrounded by secretaries, servants, companions, and mental practitioners. For the first few years of her residence there her health remained as usual, with periods of violent attack and others when she seemed still at her radiant best. Gradually, however, there now came times when she took to her bed and remained there for rather extended periods. At these times she suffered terrible agonies.

It was after 1900 that her health began its definite decline. There were now long interims when she was an exceedingly difficult person for her household to endure, for her own agony was at times so great that it was then impossible to play the part of the gentle, gracious, serene old lady whom the world visualized as busily communing with her God behind the walls of Pleasant View.

Mrs. Eddy had thoughtfully established this picture of herself in the public mind by her own description. In *Science and Health* she wrote:

It has been said to the author, "The world is benefited by you, but feels your influence without seeing you. Why do you not make yourself more widely known?" Could her friends know how little time the author has had, in which to make herself outwardly known except through her laborious publications,—and how much time and toil are still required to establish the stately operations of Christian Science,—they would understand why she is so secluded. Others could not take her place, even if willing to do so. She therefore remains unseen at her post, seeking no self-aggrandizement but praying, watching, and working for the redemption of mankind.[1]

Servants in Mrs. Eddy's bizarre household came and went often. Mrs. Eddy's by-law demanding that any church member should on ten days' notice come to her home to render personal service gave her a wide range of choice in attendants.

Since at this time there were only three or four people in the whole world who knew the real situation in Mrs. Eddy's home —not even her church officials understood what really went on there—all loyal Scientists longed eagerly for an opportunity to come to serve at Concord and bask in the Divine Love which Mrs. Eddy was supposed to generate.

It was not easy to find persons suitable for Mrs. Eddy' purpose. For one thing, she took violent and sudden dislikes and if a new attendant came on a day when she had a mor strenuous attack of pain than usual, she concluded inevitabl that the new arrival had brought along a fresh supply o M. A. M. in his trunk, and would send him back to his hon town immediately.

Companions and servants for the household were importe from all over the world. A committee of three members wa maintained by the Board of Directors of Mrs. Eddy's churc with the specific duty of scouring the country to find th proper members for her household. One very amusing inc dent occurred in this connection when the committee brougl a cook from England. When she was examined at Ell Island the inspectors discovered that she had a wooden le and refused her admission on the ground that she migl become a public charge. The woman was most indignant. Sl insisted that she could cook for Mrs. Eddy just as well as she were a centipede.

As a matter of fact, Mrs. Eddy was herself even more pa ticular about the health and antecedents of those who cam into her house than any inspector at Ellis Island. She was eve particularly anxious to avoid having in her home any one wl might become sick or—horror of horrors—die. Such an o currence would unduly reflect on the traditions which no surrounded her. No one not thought wholly immune to tl baneful effects of M. A. M. was ever permitted inside tl Eddy threshold.

In addition to the usual servants attending to ordina household work, Mrs. Eddy had with her the ever prese Frye, who in turn had an assistant secretary, and eventual two assistants. Mrs. Laura Sargent and Mrs. Pamelia Leo

rd had by this time become fixtures in the family. Mrs. Sargent was utterly loyal; she had been a student in Mrs. Eddy's
irst class in Chicago and had later become custodian of the
Mother's Room in Boston. Mrs. Leonard, after experienc-
ng a number of inauspicious contacts with Mrs. Stetson, had
inally built up a flourishing healing practice of her own in
Brooklyn. Despite several notorious and unpleasant incidents
n which patients died and unfortunate newspaper publicity
esulted, Mrs. Leonard had become an important figure in
New York circles, and might perhaps have gone much fur-
her there had it not been for competition from Mrs. Stetson.
t was perhaps the reputation she developed in church circles
s a healer which accounted for her being called to reside at
Pleasant View. Another woman inmate of the house was
Miss Clara Shannon of Montreal.

In addition to these attendants several mental practitioners
were eventually added to the staff. These practitioners were
endowed with the specific duty of defending Mrs. Eddy and
er household from malicious animal magnetism.

So sheltered was this existence she led that rumors were
orever cropping up that she was dead. In consequence, the
figure of the old lady muffled in her closed carriage came to be
closely scanned by all church members who found their way
o Concord, and on many occasions groups of loyal followers
would gather around her house waiting for her exit in order
o glimpse the hallowed form. This custom soon came to
annoy Mrs. Eddy exceedingly. It was provocative of many in-
conveniences, not to mention dangers. As her health declined
and she was incapacitated for longer periods, it was not advisable that all the proceedings in her household should be
under close inspection. Eventually she issued a by-law prohib-
iting her followers from loitering near her residence.

Between the periods of Mrs. Eddy's illnesses there were
days and sometimes even weeks when the heavy clouds that
enveloped her seemed to her household to lift, and she became
gentle, lovable, and slightly vivacious old lady, who could
be as charming as a spoiled grandmother surrounded by an
adoring family. At times like this Mrs. Eddy forgot utterly

about the horrors of malicious animal magnetism, wandered
out to the barn and made pleasantries with the coachman,
complimented the servants, and told childhood reminiscences
to her companions. She had no sense of humor in any situation involving herself, but in her better moments she could
point up a story with apparent relish.

One of her favorite tales concerned a horse which her
father went to buy from an Irishman. When old Mr. Baker
looked the animal over, related Mrs. Eddy, he decided that
it was too skittish for his purposes. "Why," he remarked,
"that horse would jump if you said Boo to him." The owner
insisted that Mark Baker was wrong. So it was agreed that
a test should be made, Mark standing behind a tree and then
jumping out suddenly with a cry of "Boo!" as the owner
drove by.

The Irishman mounted the horse, Mr. Baker bided his
time, and then jumped out with a wild waving of the arms
and a "Boo" as loud as a shout. The horse shied across the
road, threw his rider, and galloped off into the distance. The
Irish owner got up ruefully and dusted himself off. "Well,
Mr. Baker," he said regretfully, "I think that was too big a
Boo for such a small horse."

A second story that Mrs. Eddy enjoyed telling when she
was in a pleasant mood concerned another Irishman whom
Mark had employed on his farm. The man, however, was exceedingly lazy, and Mr. Baker decided to fire him. But the
Irishman pleaded to be allowed to stay, even if he worked only
for room and board. Old Mark was obdurate. "Why," said
he, "you aren't even worth your week's room and board."

"Then," said the Irishman, "let me work two weeks for it."

In some of her confidences Mrs. Eddy would regale her
household with tales of the miracles which had surrounded
her from childhood. With bated breath she would repeat her
version of the radiant experiences of her mother before her
birth, would tell once again how her childish hand had healed
her brother's leg, would dwell on the manner in which she
heard a mysterious voice calling "Mary" in moments when
she was alone. By this time Mrs. Eddy had developed a sequ

to her "Mary" story as she had related it in her memoirs. In words breathing awe she would now tell an enraptured listener how she had lain awake in her little bed, and a voice came clearly, distinctly, calling her name. As her mother had instructed, she said, "Speak, Lord, for thy servant heareth." Here Mrs. Eddy would pause dramatically. "Then," she would announce, "my body was lifted entirely off the bed, to the height of at least a foot. This happened three times in succession." In such descriptions of a "levitation" Mrs. Eddy was undoubtedly drawing on her memories of early dabblings in Spiritualism.

When those in her household heard these tales, they reflected on the great privilege they enjoyed of living in the shadow of such miracles, and their hearts grew warm within them. As Mrs. Eddy sat in her chair in the twilight and droned on in her monotonous and aged treble, even her story of how as a child she went out to the pigsties on winter nights, and sang the little pigs to sleep, became in her hearers' minds a transcendent incident in the life of a child destined to become a Mother of Truth.

By the time she reached her eighties Mrs. Eddy had a great recollection for miracles of all sorts, in many places. Just as she had impressed her classes as far back as the days in Lynn with recitals of the manner in which she could reach out her hand and cure the ailing, so now she told how she had wrought miracles throughout the length and breadth of the New England states in all lives with which she had come in contact. She did not hesitate to incorporate such accounts in her writings. Again the biographer must not doubt her own belief in such occurrences. Her will to believe had grown rather than lessened with the years. She, who had always sought the centre of the stage, could not sit back inertly while her followers told glowing stories of their own success in using her Science to bring divine marvels into stricken lives. During all her life she had never been able to distinguish between her desires and external reality; and her consuming desire to remain always the Leader well explains how she would take pen in hand after reading in her *Journal* the mar-

vellous experiences of her healers, and write claims for her
self such as these:

After my discovery of Christian Science, I healed consumption in it
last stages, a case which the M.D.'s, by verdict of the stethoscope an
the schools, declared incurable because the lungs were mostly con
sumed. I healed malignant diphtheria and carious bones that could b
dented by the finger, saving the limbs when the surgeon's instrument
were lying on the table ready for their amputation. I have healed at on
visit a cancer that had eaten the flesh of the neck and exposed the jugu
lar vein so that it stood out like a cord. I have physically restored sigh
to the blind, hearing to the deaf, speech to the dumb, and have made th
lame walk.[1]

Nor did she fail to take credit even for such minor phe
nomena as second sight and third sets of teeth which croppe
out among any of her aged acquaintances. She could writ
with grave aplomb:

I have seen age regain two of the elements it had lost, sight and teet
A woman of eighty-five, whom I knew, had a return of sight. Anoth
woman at ninety had new teeth, incisors, cuspids, bicuspids, and on
molar.[2]

Mrs. Eddy's visions of herself as a harbinger of huma
welfare were in some instances extremely amusing, for ther
was no fact too irrelevant to be seized to serve her ends. Thu
a newspaper clipping describing Chicago's increase in popu
lation could lead her into the following panegyric, which sh
addressed to her new Chicago Church:

Thirty years ago (1866) Christian Science was discovered in Ame
ica. Within those years it is estimated that Chicago has gained from
population of 238,000 to the number of 1,650,000 inhabitants. Th
statistics of mortality show that thirty years ago the death rate was
its maximum. Since that time it has steadily decreased.[3]

In seeking in this manner to take credit for a reduced deat
rate—caused indubitably by the national discovery of laws
hygiene to which Mrs. Eddy had even denied existence—sh

[1]*Miscellany*, page 105.   [2]*Science and Health*, page 247.
[3]*Miscellany*, page 181.

was merely indulging in another skirmish in her perennial war with logic.

Despite the fact that there were still days when she appeared to be her old energetic self—days when she wrote industriously, planned assiduously, and was as active as formerly—by 1904 Mrs. Eddy had reached the point where she did not care to trust herself to a public appearance. Her last real sortie into the public gaze was in this year, when she appeared at her new Concord Church. Thereafter her health took a very marked turn for the worse, and by 1906 Mrs. Eddy was in a very serious condition. She was suffering from gallstones, in addition to the old hysterical ailments that had been with her since girlhood. In 1903 her pain had assumed such terrible proportions that doctors were called in.[1] By 1906 she was presumably resorting to morphine with some regularity to ease her agonies. In February of 1906, after one of the attendants in her household had received professional instruction on the administration of the drug, she asked her directors by letter to have three more students taught by a doctor the technique of giving morphine by hypodermic injections.[2] The board at the time generally did not know the reason for this strange request.

Doctors were no new experience to Mrs. Eddy. She had, for one thing, been utilizing the services of dentists over a long period, and finally entered into an agreement with one of them by which she paid $500 a year for the care of her teeth, which were rapidly decreasing in number. By 1903 all those in her

[1] Frye's diary of May 3, 1903, contains the following entry:
"Mrs. E. was suddenly attack (ed) with severe pain at 11.30 tonight and the 4 C.Ss in the house P.V. proved unable to relieve her She sent for Rev. I. Tomlinson neither did he help her. She then sent for Dr. E. Morrill & he is out of town: she then sent for Dr. S. Morrill. He was sick & could not come. She then sent for Dr. Conn and he remained with her from 2.15 until 4 Monday morning. But the pain was so intense & slow to respond that he called Dr. Billings for consultation who was here from 3 to 4." The entry for the following day continues: "After Conn left, Mrs. E. was a little relieved and at about 5 a. m. she slept for about one hour. But suffered every hour this forenoon from paroxysms of pain. . . . It was called renal calculi . . . then she called Dr. E. Morrill & he gave her a hypodermic." For a history of the Frye diaries and other excerpts see Appendix A.

[2] This fact is established through a copy of this letter which has been furnished the biographer with an affidavit affirming its authenticity. See Note, page 514.

upper jaw were missing, and she relied solely upon an uppe
plate for masticating purposes.

Mrs. Eddy had also condoned the use of physicians by oth
ers, despite the fierce assertions in her earlier writings tha
doctors could avail nothing. Not only did she order her grand
children to be vaccinated, giving George Glover the mone
for the bill, but in 1902, for instance, she paid a Boston sur
geon to operate upon her sister-in-law, Mary Ann Baker, fo
cancer of the breast. This was one of the few charities sh
ever extended to the Baker family. Mary Ann was the widow
of Mrs. Eddy's brother Samuel, of whom she had been ver
fond. When she first learned of Mary Ann's condition, sh
engaged a Christian Science practitioner, Mrs. Jeanette I
Weller, to give the anguished woman mental treatment. Whe
Mrs. Weller failed even to establish relief from pain, Mr
Eddy sent her sister to Dr. H. S. Dearing of Boston, afte
the woman had been in agony for seven years. Dr. Dearin
performed an operation and was paid by Mrs. Eddy's ow
check.

Her own extensive recourse to the services of the medic
profession was undoubtedly responsible for leading Mrs. Edc
to qualify her earlier denunciations of human weaknesses. Sh
never had sufficient courage to retract all of her unqualifie
pronouncements in *Science and Health*, but she did insert th
following paragraph, in addition to other addenda[1] permittir
the use of an anæsthetic:

> If Christian Scientists ever fail to receive aid from other Scientis
> —their brethren upon whom they may call,—God will still guide the
> into the right use of temporary and eternal means.[2]

In her *Manual* Mrs. Eddy went a step further, and som
what more boldly added a by-law which specifically count
nanced the use of physicians in certain emergencies. Thus, a
though she had written in *Science and Health* that "a patie
hears the doctor's verdict as a criminal hears his death se
tence,"[3] she inserted the following provision in her *Manua*

If a member of this Church has a patient whom he does not heal, and those case he cannot fully diagnose, he may consult with an M.D. on the anatomy involved. And it shall be the privilege of a Christian Scientist to confer with an M.D. on Ontology, or the Science of being.[1]

That carefully phrased provision may be interpreted in divers ways, inasmuch as conferences with a physician on the subject of Ontology might mean anything. In previous statements Mrs. Eddy had always belittled the "anatomy involved" in any illness, insisting even that testimonials of healing should not include a description of symptoms or suffering."

In her *Manual* Mrs. Eddy also made provision for an autopsy—which previously she had denounced utterly. She permitted vaccination, intimating that this measure was devised only to permit her followers to comply with the law of the land. And she put a stop to all further denunciations of the work of the medical profession by over-enthusiastic believers in her doctrine. Mrs. Eddy had largely recovered from her own excess enthusiasm over the possibilities of her Science. And so she wrote:

A member of this Church shall not publish, nor cause to be published, an article that is uncharitable or impertinent towards religion, medicine, the courts, or the laws of our land.[2]

In *Science and Health* Mrs. Eddy also finally inserted permission for her disciples to call on surgeons. This forms only another instance of the manner in which her early ecstasy succumbed to reality. Thus she said:

Until the advancing age admits the efficacy and supremacy of Mind, it is better for Christian Scientists to leave surgery and the adjustment of broken bones and dislocations to the fingers of a surgeon, while the mental healer confines himself chiefly to mental reconstruction and the prevention of inflammation.[3]

If Mrs. Eddy's own secretive resort to dentists and physicians appears strange to one familiar with her preachings, let

it be remembered that all her life she lived in two differe
worlds, between which there was a closed and locked doo
For the world of external reality she had only a repulsion ar
disdain. Again and again she would seem to throw this dee
rooted complex off; momentarily she would cease to be tl
introvert and would reach out to grapple with the realities
the universe around her in a fashion wholly brilliant, darin
and amazing. The by-laws which she designed for her churc
for example, reveal a mind become suddenly extrovert, dea
ing with a practical problem in a manner that can only asto
ish because of its handling of detail, its analytical tracing
cause and effect, its ability to classify, analyze, and resolve.

But such periods with Mrs. Eddy were of the briefest dur
tion—strange interludes from which she always returned
the hidden dream life within herself. Such journeys forth we
indeed often accompanied by actual physical symptoms n
greatly dissimilar to the rendings and retchings experienc
by some mediums in coming out of a trance. Even Mrs. Eddy
household, untutored as they were in psychological mysteri
and wholly without grasp of cause and effect, noticed th
previous to issuing a new by-law Mrs. Eddy always suffer
an attack of what they knew as malicious animal magnetisi
As a matter of fact, Mrs. Eddy all her life suffered a peri
of unusually severe illness before each and every accomplis
ment in her career. Her progress to power, fame, and weal
was made upward on steps formed by seizures of hysteria
pain. From one such extended attack she arose to develop e
thusiasm over Quimby; after a long period of hysterical wa
derings she went in partnership with Kennedy; hysteria c
stroyed this association and sent her into business, as it we
independently; from her hysterical experiences in Lynn s
fled to Boston; after further progress there, when she ev
organized a church, she once again was seized with a peri
of maladjustment which turned many students against l
and resulted in her tearing her church to pieces; from this e
perience she arose to found a new organization which was t
greatest achievement of her entire career.

Always, after each period of strain and conflict, she we

orth into the external world and made one more step upward
o her final goal. And yet, once this step had been taken, she
lways returned to her inner realm and closed the door on ob-
ective reality. In this inner world she lived the greater part
f her existence. While there she recognized no logic and no
onsistency. She did not even recognize objective truth—for
n the dream world there is no standard by which truth can be
neasured. Only one measure exists there—the measure of the
lesires. Thus it was that Mrs. Eddy could even lie to those
round her, and be unconscious that she lied. She asserted
hat which she wanted to believe; she desired so earnestly to
elieve it that for her the desire was a realized truth.

The student of abnormal psychology will observe here
ymptoms which are neither rare, unique, nor unclassified.
hey are indeed commonly found in varying degrees in con-
ection with persons esteemed as the soul of probity and
arnestness. It is wholly doubtful if Mrs. Eddy saw in
er secret use of medical services any reflection on her per-
onal character. It would scarcely have occurred to her that
uch a course need reflect on the sincerity of her preachments.
here can be no possible doubt that Mrs. Eddy believed in her
reachments utterly, completely, and with her whole soul. In
er dream life her philosophy was completely valid. Because
he kept this philosophy locked up in one room, and never took
out to be aired in the external universe, its validity remained
or her unquestionable. Her objective experience she at-
mpted to ignore as wholly unimportant and even as unreal.

If this psychological process seems obscure, as well it may
the normal mind, then let only the conclusion be empha-
zed: Mrs. Eddy repaired to doctors without any feeling of
le hypocrite, without any thought that she ought to be prac-
sing what she preached. She always preached what she be-
eved, that is, what she wanted to believe. She always did
hat the exigencies of the occasion required. After all, viewed
this aspect, she was not greatly different from the ordi-
ary run of men. Let those without sin cast a stone.

Strange as it may seem, none of Mrs. Eddy's church offi-
als, or her disciples, was in any way aware of her actual

physical condition, or had the slightest grasp of her psychology. Stranger still, no one in her household had any
real inkling of the psychological drama in which they were
playing dumb parts. As far as the ignorance of Mrs. Eddy's
household was concerned, the explanation lies in what she
told them regarding malicious animal magnetism. This
well-worn hobby had been such a useful device for release
during Mrs. Eddy's earlier life that it had become with her
an explanation for any situation which seemed difficult to supply with an answer. Beyond a doubt she blamed her declining physical condition on malicious animal magnetism
showered on her by hostile minds. Every attack in a periodical
or newspaper indicated one of the channels for this foul force
which so harassed her. It was animal magnetism that robbed
her of her teeth; it was animal magnetism which crystallized
in her as gallstones; it was animal magnetism which made her
unable to heal herself with her Science and hence forced her
to send for medical aid.

Thus did she rationalize the strange situation in which she
found herself. The members of her ménage accepted her explanations unquestioningly, and believed as sincerely as she
believed. When the time came that Mrs. Eddy was unable to
take her daily drive, she was horror-stricken to think that her
enemies might notice that their attacks were at last having
the desired effect. Thus, in order to foil the enemy, Mrs. Eddy
apparently instructed one of her white-haired companions to
substitute for her in the carriage at one o'clock, the usual driving hour, on afternoons when Mrs. Eddy was unwell.

Firm in the implicit belief that animal magnetism must be
foiled, this double, in Mrs. Eddy's own cloak, evidently journeyed forth as Mrs. Eddy ordered. The carriage had a closed
top, the windows were kept closed, and the curtains were always
partly drawn; but to make deception doubly sure, the occupant
carried a small black parasol with a heavy lace fringe, adjusting it always so that her face was shielded from any person
whom the carriage might pass.

Anomalous as an open parasol in a closed carriage might
seem, it attracted no more attention than would any of a

ld lady's eccentricities. Small though Concord was, and
amous as Mrs. Eddy was, this deception passed entirely with-
ut notice. Mrs. Eddy had become such a recluse by the end
f 1904 that even the small town where she resided knew of
er only as a myth, of which the only visible evidence was a
arge estate a few miles beyond the town, and an imposing
arriage in which a dimly seen old lady took a stately drive
with coachman and footman every day.

None of Mrs. Eddy's Board of Directors knew of the actual
tate of affairs, nor of her extended periods of illness, and
Mrs. Eddy considered it none of their business. Far from her
wing any duty to her Directors, she considered that they
were her creatures. The church they officered was her church.
he had organized it in such a fashion that she could rule it
when she willed, could let it take care of itself when she so
esired. There were times when she displayed vitally active in-
erest in it, so that Archibald McLellan was jumping on trains
o come up to see and consult with her almost daily. There
were other times when she seemed to ignore her officials com-
letely. It all depended on her state of mind and her state of
ealth. Those who eventually visualized Mrs. Eddy's church
s exercising complete control over Mrs. Eddy were looking
hrough the wrong end of the telescope. Mrs. Eddy was the
ueen who sometimes deigned to play with affairs of state,
nd at other times wholly ignored both her affairs and her
inisters. Such periods grew more extended toward the end
f 1905.

If, at such times, any of Mrs. Eddy's officials sought to see
er, a perfect answer was always ready. Mrs. Eddy was too
usy. She had weighty cares wholly beyond the comprehen-
ion of mortal mind. She was communing. She was guarding
er flock.

Far from giving any hint that Mrs. Eddy was physically
nable to grant an audience, such a response only increased the
ervor of the disciple to whom it was addressed. It served to
dvance the Eddy tradition, and on all minds a sacred picture
as impressed—Mrs. Eddy immersed in constant prayer and
ommunion on her Mount, seeking the answer to mysteries of

which no ordinary human mind could ever hope to conceive

Thus it was that Frye ceremoniously turned away visitor:
whenever it was not in order for visitors to be received. H
did not even hesitate to rebuff officials who believed that the
had urgent business to discuss. It was intimated that nothin;
could be so urgent for Mrs. Eddy as her own need to com
mune. Frye himself believed whole-heartedly in the maliciou
magnetism theory. And he was completely loyal to Mrs. Eddy
He understood what she herself emphasized: that at times whe
M. A. M. sought to attack her no one must know the succes
that had met the assault. When Mrs. Eddy's physician rec
ommended a galvanic battery to restore some of her failin,
strength, Frye assisted in procuring this as another mode o
defense against the established M. A. M. Mrs. Eddy's wome
companions gave her treatments with it just as they gave he
constant mental treatments—to keep the Fiend away.

It is probable that Mrs. Eddy might have passed her d
clining years in a mystery that would gradually have dee]
ened until her death. But publicity, which had served to exa
her so high, was now destined to drag her down again an
bring to her a humiliation no less great than her glory.

The world first began seriously to wonder about Mrs. Edc
and her retirement when she was unable to be present at tl
dedication of her new church building in Boston in 1906.

XXVI

The project of erecting a more magnificent church building in Boston had been begun in 1902. Mrs. Stetson's own
glorious temple, then well along toward completion, and her
well-advertised feat of raising $1,200,000 for its construc-
tion, rather put the humble Mother Church building to shame.
Overjoyed as were Mrs. Eddy and all her loyal followers to
see the glory of their Science being demonstrated as Mrs.
Stetson was then demonstrating, their satisfaction was di-
luted with some little envy. Mrs. Eddy, indeed, must secretly
have felt that the unpretentious building which housed the
Mother Church was rather a reflection on her own demonstrating abilities. She did not care to take a seat behind Mrs.
Stetson.

Thus it was that in June of 1902 the Directors of the Boston Church voted to raise two million dollars—or any necessary part thereof—for a church addition that would seat from
four to five thousand members. The total membership of the
church at this time was about twenty-four thousand.[1] Since all
loyal branch-church members always sought membership in
the Mother Church, this membership figure was not far from
the total of Mrs. Eddy's entire following, who then numbered
approximately thirty thousand. Due to Mrs. Eddy's addiction
to grandiose statements and her effective publicity methods,
the world at large already had an idea that the membership
figures for her organization were much larger than was actually the case. She had not hesitated, on more than one occasion, to mention the "millions" of her followers, and she could
speak of Christian Science being in the White House with an
air that almost gave her doctrines the sound of a politically
established religion.

When Mrs. Eddy learned in 1902 that she was going to be

[1] This is the figure quoted by the Christian Scientists themselves, at their
annual meeting of The Mother Church in 1902. Vd. *Miscellany*, page 8.

honored with a new and still grander memorial, she could
hardly contain herself. She wrote the following effusive letter to the members of her church:

I am bankrupt in thanks to you, my beloved brethren, who at our
last annual meeting pledged yourselves with startling grace to contribute
any part of two millions of dollars towards the purchase of more land for
its site, and to enlarge our church edifice in Boston. I never before felt
poor in thanks, but I do now, and will draw on God for the amount I
owe you, till I am satisfied with what my heart gives to balance accounts.[1]

A great deal of discussion now arose as to what disposal
should be made of the original Mother Church building.
Architecturally it had little to recommend it; and even though
it had a seating capacity for some nine hundred souls it
looked most humble in comparison with Mrs. Stetson's shining new temple in New York and the new plans under way
for a still more imposing shrine for the Mother. Many members were in favor of demolishing the structure entirely; others were for including and enclosing it in the immense structure that was now to take form on drafting-boards.

But Mrs. Eddy would have neither alternative. That old
church building might be utterly without any architectural
parentage, but it was still her child. It might have no claim
either to beauty, distinction, or grace; but it had a Mother's
love. She had dreamed over it, labored over it, gloried over it.
And so she passed another by-law:

The edifice erected in 1894 for The First Church of Christ, Scientist,
in Boston, Mass., shall neither be demolished, nor removed from the
site where it was built, without the written consent of the Pastor Emeritus, Mary Baker Eddy.[2]

The work of clearing the land for the new structure was
started on property adjoining the original Mother Church in
October of 1903. In 1904 the corner-stone was laid; and by
1906 the snow-white temple of Bedford stone and granite
raised its dome, in the words of Judge Hanna, "to a heigh

[1] *Miscellany*, page 9.   [2] *Manual*, XXXIV, 3.

of two hundred and twenty-four feet, one foot loftier than
he Bunker Hill monument." The original Mother Church
had been designed in the form of a cross; the addition with
its dome was meant to represent a crown. These symbols were
particularly dear to Mrs. Eddy; her diamond cross, and the
diamond crown given her by Mrs. Stetson, were her favorite
ornaments.

In the year which saw its completion The Mother Church
had 40,011 members,[1] of which 4,889 had been admitted at the
church meeting on June 5. The number of branch churches
now totalled 682; in addition there were 267 societies. And a
total of some 400,000 copies of *Science and Health* had been
sold since Mrs. Eddy's publication of the work, meaning
that she had derived about half a million dollars from her book
alone. This income now came to her automatically. She did
not have to worry about it. Under her agreements with her
Publishing Company her royalties were turned over with the
regularity of the incoming tides. From the Church itself Mrs.
Eddy did not derive an income. Technically she owned it all;
actually she let it run itself as a fundamentally independent
institution, merely handing down a new by-law when anything got out of gear.

The dedication of the new building was a cause of editorial
comment in every paper of any size in almost every city and
town in the United States. The church was paid for before
dedication, and a request was finally issued that no more donations be sent to the building fund. The imagination of newspaper editors was immediately gripped. Accustomed as they
were to the inevitable pleadings and moanings of their
local Methodists, Baptists, Presbyterians, Congregationalists,
Campbellites and other such sects who sought continually to
raise enough money to pay the janitor and the preacher;
inured as they were to constant fairs, bazaars, ladies'-aid
sociables, picnics, and any other entertainment that could be
invented to entice into church tills a few dollars to repair the

[1]For these and the following figures on membership vd. *Miscellany*, page 57,
where they are presented as a part of the "Report of the Clerk" to the annual
meeting.

parsonage roof or buy a new carpet for the Sunday school
resigned to perennial plaints of poverty from every church
with which they had ever been associated, most of the news
paper editors were simply overwhelmed by Mrs. Eddy's new
demonstration. They could not get over it. Some papers ran
articles every day for a week. Overnight Mrs. Eddy and
Christian Scientists generally gained a reputation for being
miracle workers of the first water. The general attitude to
ward the miracle was well expressed by the Boston *Journal*
which opined that "the money to provide it was pledged with
the readiness and despatch of an ordinary mortal passing out
a nickel for carfare."

The entire secret, of course, lay in Mrs. Eddy's emotional
hold on her membership. This hold, indeed, was the founda
tion of her whole belated success.

The emotional appeal is like fire; it has tremendous danger
as well as great uses; it almost destroyed Mrs. Eddy before
she learned to control it, before she lit upon the secret of
keeping personally far enough beyond its reach to use it safely
for her designs. But undoubtedly she had finally learned her
lesson. And her life was spared long enough for her to profit
by it. For when her new church was dedicated she was eighty
five years old.

The newspapers gasped over the achievement. The Boston
Globe spoke only representatively in declaring that "When
these people enter this new cathedral or temple . . . they
will find themselves in one of the most imposing church edi
fices in the country—yes, in the world." The descriptions of
filled columns for the delectation of readers in Europe, Can
ada, and Mexico as well as in towns and hamlets all over the
American continent. Reporters supplied almost endless de
scriptions of the marble for the Readers' platform; the twelve
exits; the seven marble and bronze staircases; the seventy
two bronze lamps each suspended by eight chains; the utter
lack of any pillar or post to support the roof and obscure the
view; the checking-room for three thousand wraps; the great
organ; the one mile and a half of pews.

For the dedication ceremonies all railroads ran special

rains to Boston, and estimates of the number of arrivals
aried from twenty to forty thousand. Most editors preferred
he larger and more sensational figure. Undoubtedly every
member of the church who could get to Boston went. Since
ew editors were in a position to know the actual membership
r organization of Mrs. Eddy's congregation, the fact that
0,000 Eddy followers were reported gathered in Boston sug-
ested other untold thousands hovering in the rear. Most edi-
ors were therefore inclined to estimate with the Topeka
Daily Capital, which declared:

. . . The great meeting of the church now being held in Boston will
ome as a revelation. In 1890 the faith had but an insignificant follow-
ng. Today its adherents number hundreds of thousands, and if the
rowth continues in like proportion through another decade every other
ect will be left behind in the race for numerical supremacy.

Some obscure editorial writer on *The Mexican Herald,* in
he City of Mexico, sat far removed from the scene as he de-
cribed the dome "which rivals that of the famous old Massa-
husetts State House," and wrote two paragraphs that were
orth many pages of the wondering exclamations that ap-
eared in the American press. He said in simple words:

The faith of these people is certainly great. They go about telling of
miracles performed in this twentieth century when "advanced" clergy-
en of other denominations are avowing their disbelief in the miracu-
us.
The higher critics and the men of science may think they can banish
aith in the supernatural, but no religion of growth or vitality exists
ithout faith in the things unseen.

This brief comment explains much regarding Mrs. Eddy's
emarkable achievement. The fact that she herself was one
f the "things unseen" played an important part in creating
he ecstatic faith which imbued her following. Mrs. Eddy as
mysteriously invisible high priestess had far greater power
ver the miracle-hungry imaginations of her disciples than
ould ever have been possible had they known or beheld the
Mrs. Eddy of reality—a pain-racked old woman almost ready
or her grave.

Of all the newspaper comment on the dedication it was per-

haps a paragraph in the Boston *Post* that most delighted Mrs
Eddy's eager eyes, for the clipping was among her paper;
when she died. This home-town journal was looking for a
fresh "news slant" after having exhausted almost every other
and so it said with complete and awesome gravity:

The gates of Boston are open wide in welcome to nobility. Never be
fore has the city been more frequented by members of the titled aris
tocracy of the old world than it is now. From all the centres of Europ
there are streaming into town lords and ladies who come to attend th
dedication of the new church for Christian Scientists.

That brief paragraph proves just one thing: that publicit
operates automatically, once the wheels start turning. Giv
enterprising newspapers one good suggestion, and they wil
do all the rest.

There can be no doubt that public opinion everywhere i
the United States was tremendously impressed, if not mysti
fied. "If," said the Boston *Globe,* "you ask a Christian Scien
tist how they do it, the reply will be in the form of a quotatio:
from *Science and Health.* 'Divine Love always has met an
always will meet our every need.'"

The dedication ceremonies were as impressive as the hug
temple itself. Six different times during the day some fiv
thousand people knelt in silent communion, six different time
recited in unison their Leader's version of the Lord's praye:
six times raised their voices to sing Mrs. Eddy's hymn, "She;
herd, Show Me How to Go."

This is a beautiful hymn, and one replete with the lovelines
of simplicity. Because it is unlike much of the doggerel whic
so liberally bestrews Mrs. Eddy's pages, it would be quit
possible to argue in the fashion of Mark Twain that it wa
not born of Mrs. Eddy's tortuous pen. And yet a student c
men must know that there comes to each one some momer
of inspiration, some day when the imagination is transfigure(
in which every man reaches heights which are strange eve
to his own soul. The *Sonnets from the Portuguese,* for e>
ample, are the perfect songs of a woman whose voice for on
brief spell was transformed by love into a lyric melody whic
never before nor after could it attain.

Unless one senses the extent to which gorgeous and enraptured exaltation may sweep in upon a life and momentarily illumine its every thought into a thing of limpid beauty, like a light flashed back of a painted screen, he will find it difficult to see in the lines to the Shepherd the Mrs. Eddy who would scream invectives concerning the Babylonian harlot. And yet, Mrs. Eddy is here, too:

> Shepherd, show me how to go
> O'er the hillside steep,
> How to gather, how to sow,—
> How to feed Thy sheep;
> I will listen for Thy voice,
> Lest my footsteps stray;
> I will follow and rejoice
> All the rugged way. . . .
>
> So, when day grows dark and cold,
> Tear or triumph harms,
> Lead Thy lambkins to the fold,
> Take them in Thine arms;
> Feed the hungry, heal the heart,
> Till the morning's beam;
> White as wool, ere they depart,
> Shepherd, wash them clean.[1]

Six times during the day were the thousands of voices raised in Mrs. Eddy's gleaming new temple to sing those words. The crowds for the first service had begun to gather as early as half-past-five in the morning. The doors were thrown open an hour later; within that hour the chimes began to play the hymns which they rang out all day, and at seven-thirty the first congregation saw the first of the six dedication ceremonies begin. Again and again the pews were filled by throngs led in by the two hundred ushers, as one congregation filed out so that another might come in. At noon a special service was held for the children. The last congregation before which the ceremonies were repeated did not gather until evening.

When, at the church meeting on the following Wednesday, it was announced that testimonies would be received from those whom Mrs. Eddy's Science had cured, voices rose from all

[1] Hymn 161, *Christian Science Hymnal*. One verse is omitted here.

over the building. Such public testimonials in church meet
ings had always played an important part in revivifying th
faith of old followers, in kindling hope in the breasts of new
comers. Now, as instructions were given for each person testi
fying to name as he arose the place where he lived, cities a
over Europe and America were called. "Chicago!" "London!
"Kalamazoo!" "Habana!" "San Francisco!" "Wichita!
"Dresden!" "Peoria!" "Indianapolis!" "Duluth!"

It was a marvellous gathering, a miraculous occasion. Neve
had staid Boston seen its equal.

And Mrs. Eddy was not present.

Seventy miles away, at Concord, Mrs. Eddy sat in her stud
hidden from the world while chimes pealed out her glory. Sh
was an old, old woman, ravaged by pain and weakened wit
age. On her better days she still took her drive. But the re
of her life she lived practically in three rooms. She could n
always think as clearly as a few years before; she would for
get easily. Her slight body—she now weighed less than
hundred pounds—had never been an adequate vehicle for th
tremendous dynamo which turned and churned inside. Fro
the beginning this wasted, suppressed power had sought
break through its restraining physical barriers. Time an
again it had shattered and destroyed bits of its own mech
anism in its paroxysms. Now in its old age the whole machi
was disintegrating.

As with so many who reach a ripe old age, the spirit whic
was Mary Baker Eddy seemed gradually, and at first almo
imperceptibly, to withdraw from the body which had nev
served it well.

Sometimes she would sit in the twilight for long, long mi
utes, her eyes wide open, her face serene and wholly cal
seeming to gaze out through the mists beyond the windov
that looked toward Bow into some world that no one else wa
conscious of. Often in these twilights Mrs. Sargent wou
read to her, almost always from the book that had for
many years been her life.

"Laura," she would sometimes interrupt and ask, "what
that you're reading?"

"Why, Mother, this is your own book. I am reading from 'cience and Health."

"Why, Laura, that is beautiful . . . perfectly beautiful. . . ."

And Mrs. Eddy would smile a gentle, sweet smile, and lean ack in her chair, and Mrs. Sargent would read on.

Sometimes for long periods Mrs. Eddy would show no interest in the affairs of the lusty and expanding organization to which she had breathed a virile life. It was as if she had now given it almost her last strength, so must lean back and usband what force she was not drained of. She had already ought to protect herself from the enthusiasms of her rapidly rowing following. All her life she had attempted to rule nose around her with a harsh sceptre. Suddenly even the ceptre had now grown too heavy for her palsied hands. She ought to withdraw as decisively as she had previously thrust erself forward. In an official notice to her followers she had lready said in previous years:

I hereby notify the public that no comers are received at Pleasant 'iew without previous appointment by letter. Also that I neither listen complaints, read letters, nor dictate replies to letters which pertain church difficulties outside of The Mother Church of Christ, Scienst, or to any class of individual discords. Letters from the sick are ot read by me or by my secretaries. They should be sent to the Christian cience practitioners whose cards are in the *Christian Science Journal*.[1]

There were two additional paragraphs in these "Rules of 'onduct," as they were called, designed to prevent all intruion upon her privacy. As time went on this proved a wise rovision. Despite the fact that until the end of her days Mrs. ddy enjoyed periods of comparatively good health and of iental fitness, she no longer could be sure of herself. There ere even periods when she was now definitely a subject to atatonia. This condition, familiar to physicians as associated ith hysteria and cataleptic symptoms, is characterized by oathy and indifference pertaining to events of everyday life, ie subject being susceptible to intense nervous excitement

[1] *Miscellany*, page 223.

when brought into contact with strangers or unaccustomed situations.

In consequence there were now times when Frye and his assistants necessarily handled a large part of Mrs. Eddy's mail without reference to her, answering all letters which did not absolutely demand her personal attention. All her life she had been a voluminous correspondent, writing in a sharply slanted and angular longhand familiar to almost every one of her personal students. By 1903 she resigned herself to dictating on many occasions. When she felt like adding a personal word she would often append a postscript in her own writing as when she said to Mrs. Stetson:

> I had to do as I do to others—have Mr. Frye typewrite this I am so oppressed with work for (others)[1] and the care for all

It seems highly probable that some of the letters which Frye wrote for Mrs. Eddy were signed in her name without ever having been referred to her. Calvin Frye could duplicate her signature so expertly that the untrained eye could not distinguish a difference. This was definitely proved in the trial of the Next Friends' suit, when a letter was put in evidence that had been written to W. G. Nixon, Mrs. Eddy's former publisher. It was signed "Mary B. G. Eddy per C. A. Frye," and the Eddy name was so written that it was apparently an exact duplicate of many signatures which were indubitably her own.

Because Frye died only seven years after Mrs. Eddy, probably no one will ever know the exact extent of Mrs. Eddy's authorship in some of her accredited correspondence during her final years. The historian must be the more puzzled because of the fact that Mrs. Eddy did not hesitate to deny authorship of some letter of hers which had been made public with disagreeable reverberations. Thus, when she desired to get the city of Concord to put some paving on Warren Street and North State Street, approaches to her house which found constant use during her drives, she was confronted with the

[1] This word "others" is written and then scratched out. Vd. Stetson, *Sermons and Other Writings*, page 147.

act that the local population had heard unfriendly tales con-
erning her recorded opinions of her neighbors. It looked very
much as if Mrs. Eddy might not get her paving done. Then
he wrote a letter to her townsmen called "Greetings," which
he concluded as follows:

> . . . Let brotherly love continue, I am sure that the counterfeit let-
> ers in circulation, purporting to have my signature, must fail to influ-
> nce the minds of this dear people to conclusions the very opposite of
> ly real sentiments.

After Mrs. Eddy's death, one of her former secretaries
vho had subsequently become a Director in her church, Adam
)ickey, was questioned regarding the handling of her mail
vhen he took the stand in the suit between the Christian Sci-
nce Board of Directors and the Trustees of the Publishing
ociety. Some of his testimony was as follows:

Q. What was your work?
A. That of secretary to Mrs. Eddy.
Q. In your work of secretary did you handle the incoming mail?
A. Yes, sir.
Q. Did you reply to some of the letters?
A. Many of them.
Q. And others were referred to her for her reply?
A. Yes.

There naturally came a time when it was convenient for
any of Mrs. Eddy's followers, some of them already in the
roes of internecine conflict even before her death, to cry
forgery" whenever confronted by one of Mrs. Eddy's writ-
n documents which made a point for the opposing side. Such
ccusations and counter accusations, combined with Mrs.
ddy's own occasional denials of her signature, present a
roblem which must be finally resolved, if at all, by some one
her than the biographer. Meanwhile the historian must be
ow to accept claims of counterfeit. Considering that Mrs.
ddy had a habit of changing her mind two or three times
vernight; that she could blow hot and cold almost in the
ame breath, and that her known signatures show at least **two**

or three radically different types of penmanship, with varying treatment of capitals and terminals,[1] it is obvious that mere variation either in thought or writing contains no adequate evidence that Mrs. Eddy's name was attached to important documents which she never saw. How far astray reliance on so-called internal evidence may lead even a clever critic is evinced in Mark Twain's analysis of *Science and Health*. On the whole, the biographer's one recourse is to judge documents attributed to Mrs. Eddy not according to how consistent they appear but rather how characteristic they are. Mrs. Eddy was a whole bundle of characteristics; she had utterly no consistencies. This fact kept those around her in a merry turmoil which did not lessen with the years.

As of old she could command and countermand and command again with a breath-taking speed that left her directors in a state of utter dismay. There was no telling, after a period of quiescence, when the old lady might come to life and change her mind with a thunderous pronouncement that would turn everything upside down. As in her youth, when she could rise from what seemed her deathbed with a vim that did not hint of the horror of a few hours before, so she could still astonish her companion-nurses by suddenly casting off her katatonic lethargy and undergoing complete metamorphosis. Once again she would be the dominant, eager, dynamic Mrs. Eddy, demanding her mail, demanding to see her directors, reprimanding, ordering, reproving, changing her mind. She had powers of recuperation which amazed every doctor who ever attended her.

To her household she was still the divinity who, when she was wrapped in apathy, was communing with God; who, when she was shrieking with pain, was fighting for life with the forces of malicious animal magnetism. When it was necessary to call physicians to her aid at these times, their presence was regarded as another indignity wreaked by M. A. M.—

[1] The reader interested in Mrs. Eddy's handwriting will find a large number of specimens, excerpts from over a quarter of a century's correspondence, readily available in facsimile form in Mrs. Stetson's *Sermons and Other Writings* as well as in her *Vital Issues in Christian Science, with Facsimile Letters of Mary Baker Eddy*.

ning to be hidden, prayed over, and denied. Since her household did not know that Mrs. Eddy had been subject to such seizures ever since her youth, it came to be a tradition that Mrs. Eddy at these times was wrestling to keep the forces of evil out of her organization. When it was further noticed that she often arose from such seizures in a serene state of mind, ready to dictate and promulgate a new by-law, there developed a notion that during these laborings she was giving birth to new ideas for her church. The neuropathologist would observe that on almost every occasion when she issued such a new by-law for her *Manual* she did it after suffering a paroxysm of fear. Her greatest fear was that some one would steal from her her power.

By 1906 Mrs. Eddy's condition had really become so serious she often could not leave the house. Not only was she more frequently subject to the katatonia which had already made its appearance; she was also greatly weakened physically. She had last been seen by a representative of the general public in May of 1905, when the Boston *Herald* was so insistent in demanding a personal interview that Mrs. Eddy talked with one of the paper's reporters for a few minutes in her home. It was rather a painful performance, even though the *Herald* representative was considerate, courteous, and quite willing not to press the questions that had been prepared for this occasion. These queries were left, instead, with Mrs. Eddy's secretaries for her to answer at leisure.

In this brief interview Mrs. Eddy said a little pathetically, "All that I ask of the world is time, time to assimilate myself to God. I would take all the world to my heart if that were possible; but I can only ask my friends to look away from my personality and fix their eyes on truth."

Even before this interview there had been reiterated reports that Mrs. Eddy was not secluded on her Mount for the mere purpose of communing with God. Even though she was surrounded with picked servants and companions who had been brought from far parts of the country and were thus widely separated from all friends, relatives and connections, it was inevitable that news regarding Mrs. Eddy's strange

situation should eventually leak through the barriers of se
crecy that had been reared around her.

Reports that she was a confirmed invalid, in circulation a
early as 1900, were so greatly resented by Mrs. Eddy tha
they often brought on a recurrence of the very physical con
dition against which she was struggling. Mark Twain's criti
cism of her, appearing first in the *Cosmopolitan Magazine* a
early as 1899, had made her actually and physically sick i
much the same way. Mark Twain did not question the realit
of the many cures which were coming to gleam upon the es
cutcheon of Christian Science; he indeed stated that he ha
personal knowledge of cures which were remarkable and com
plete. He instead attacked Mrs. Eddy at the point where sh
was most vulnerable—her claims to unique power and t
divine grandeur. And in the same breath he predicted tha
Christian Science was destined to have millions of follower
for the simple reason that it offered the stuff which ha
proved to have irresistible appeal to the imaginations of me
throughout all history.

Probably the most important result of the eminent Mar
Twain's sallies was the attention he centred on Mrs. Eddy
work and life. Few facts of her life, other than those whic
she herself had made public, were generally known. The ob
scurity of the background whence she had sprung was itsel
an incentive to curiosity.

Thus it was that in the end Mrs. Eddy's retirement actuall
defeated its purpose. Far from hiding her permanently fro
the critical gaze of an external world which she had alway
feared and had always sought to flee, her seclusion so stimt
lated curiosity that eventually she was almost undone.

The dedication of the great annex to her Mother Churc
in 1906, with a volume of publicity larger than Mrs. Edd
and her followers had ever expected, brought public curiosit
to a fever heat. The fact that Mrs. Eddy was utterly ina
cessible and hidden from all profane gaze was puzzling eve
to a large part of her own following. It must be remembere
in this connection, that her disciples, accepting literally h
published denials of the reality of all disease, sickness, drug

and death, were wholly ignorant of her actual physical condition. Many, indeed, had interpreted her conflicting statements regarding death to mean that she would never die but would go on and on forever. Many of them actually thought of her as immured at Pleasant View with only one purpose—the making of the final grand demonstration which would be eternal life. They were all wholly unprepared to visualize Mrs. Eddy as an old woman from whom the sands of life were slowly running out.

It was therefore natural that they should have expected to see her appear at the dedication of the great cathedral in Boston, even if she had had to interrupt her communings on the Mount for this purpose. Surely, it seemed, God would have been willing to excuse her for a few moments while she came down to show her radiant face to the spiritually-hungry thousands clustered at her new shrine.

As it happened, Mrs. Eddy was in a more helpless physical condition toward the end of 1906 than she had been in before her journey to Quimby. She had been disabled for the greater part of the year. She had gained her second sight, and was actually able for the first time in many years to read without recourse to the glasses which she had always resented. But otherwise she was extremely far from being the picture of serene health and enduring youthfulness which the highly retouched photographs distributed to her following indicated to the world.

For a moment, as she thought of the thousands who would flock into Boston for the church dedication, she must have had a touch of her old panic. For she herself well knew that they would irresistibly be drawn to Concord in the hope of seeing the blessed Mrs. Eddy on her well-known carriage drives. It was highly important that Mrs. Eddy's carriage should not be subjected to a too close scrutiny. And it was particularly desirable that none of her following should gather round her home to speculate about the entrance and egress of gentlemen of professional mien each carrying a little black case. This explains the following notice:

To the Beloved Members of my Church, The Mother Church, The

First Church of Christ, Scientist, in Boston:—Divine Love bids me say: Assemble not at the residence of your Pastor Emeritus at or about the time of our annual meeting and communion service, for the divine and not the human should engage our attention at this sacred season of prayer and praise.

In sending this notice to her Directors for publication, Mrs. Eddy explained that "now is the time to *throttle the lie* that students worship me or that I claim their homage." Poor, distraught Mrs. Eddy! Shortly after inserting this notice in her *Journal* she felt it necessary to make the prohibition permanent. So she created a new by-law for her *Manual,* which read under its caption of "The Golden Rule":

A member of The Mother Church shall not haunt Mrs. Eddy's drive when she goes out, continually stroll by her house, or make a summer resort near her for such a purpose.[1]

Mrs. Eddy's explanation to her congregation for not appearing at the dedication ceremonies was, like all her statements, given prominent position in her *Journal.* She wrote that "owing to the time consumed in travel, *et cetera,* I cannot be present *in propria persona* at our annual communion and the dedication in June next of The Mother Church of Christ, Scientist. But I shall be with my blessed church 'in spirit and in truth.' "

Mrs. Eddy's own following, long used to the injunction regarding "theirs not to reason why," did not seek to go back of the published pronouncements. But there were a few sharp observers, particularly among newspaper men, who were rather skeptical. They had heard rumors declaring not only that Mrs. Eddy was dying, but even that she was dead. When these rumors drifted into the editorial rooms of the New York *World,* it was determined to do some investigating. *The World* was an investigating sort of newspaper. Like old Mr. Wiggin, its interests were as unbounded as the infinitude of human experience.

The World was as much interested in literature as in trust-

[1] *Manual,* VIII, 27.

busting; thought that art could be made as exciting as scandal; knew that religion played as large a part in the lives of men as lust. And so it sent two men up to Concord to insist on an interview with Mrs. Eddy. They had instructions to let nothing stand in their way. This in itself seemed quite literally equivalent to bearding a lion in its den.

Mrs. Eddy's organization had its own method of dealing with newspapers.

XXVII

It was really Mrs. Eddy, and not the modern leaders of American "big business," who invented corporation publicity and devised the methods to make it work. The idea of assisting newspaper editors and readers to formulate their opinions through correctly prepared publicity material came to her as she pondered the attacks directed upon herself and her announced discovery.

When she reorganized her church she devised two important departments to deal with public opinion. One was the Board of Lectureship, whose members were "to include in each lecture a true and just reply to public topics condemning Christian Science, and to bear testimony to the facts pertaining to the life of the Pastor Emeritus."[1] Even more important than this Board was another department, called the "Committee on Publication." This committee consisted only of one man, technically responsible to the Board of Directors of The Mother Church, but, through the Board, to Mrs. Eddy personally. Indeed, Mrs. Eddy specifically reserved the right to appoint this "committee" if she so desired. In addition, she stipulated that a similar "committee" should be maintained by the branch churches in each state of the union and in each county of Great Britain and Ireland. The three largest branch churches in each such state or county should unite to select their "committee" and pay his salary. For some reason or other Mrs. Eddy allowed to California two "committees," one north and one south of "the 36th parallel of latitude." Probably she looked at her map and decided that California was a big territory.

Under this remarkable provision Mrs. Eddy had some fifty functioning publicity men scattered through the United States all employed for the sole purpose of disseminating good news

[1] *Manual*, XXXI, 2.

oncerning herself and her doctrine. No matter how small a news item in any newspaper in any city or town might be, it invariably came to the attention of the various Eddy "committees." If it met with their disapproval, a statement in correction of the offending item was immediately despatched to the editor. If he failed to publish such a correction, subsequent results were unpleasant. For Mrs. Eddy was entirely prepared against such a contingency. Under the duties of her Boston "committee" she had prescribed the following routine:

This Committee on Publication shall be responsible for correcting or having corrected a false newspaper article which has not been replied to by other Scientists, or which has been forwarded to this Committee for the purpose of having him reply to it. If the correction by the Committee on Publication is not promptly published by the periodical in which it is desirable that this correction shall appear, *this Committee shall immediately apply for aid to the Committee on Business.*[1]

The italics are the biographer's. Mrs. Eddy, through her own publishing experience, had happened on an important and useful fact. Newspapers are not published merely because their editors and owners like to see their views in print. They are published to earn revenue. Mrs. Eddy's own publications were earning approximately $400,000 a year, including advertising receipts, before she died. It thus became wholly obvious to her that a very short and quick route to an editor's heart would be through his pocketbook. And she was right.

If any city-editor ever dared ignore a communication sent out by the Committee on Publication, the managing editor would shortly receive a telephone call. He would not find the "committee" talking at the other end of the wire. Rather it would be one of his most valued advertisers. The advertiser would be extremely sorry to have learned that the Unionville *eagle* was so extremely prejudiced in its news columns. If the managing editor was incredulous, it would be explained that his paper seemed to have a desire to persecute and vilify the religious beliefs of the gentleman who now was speaking. If incredulity was still expressed, the managing editor would

[1] *Manual*, XXXIII, 2.

be told that he should look at the bottom of column six, on page seven, of his issue last Monday week; that he would find there a news item which was wholly erroneous, unjustified, and an insult to the advertiser who was now expressing complaint. The managing editor would look; would find a stick of type referring to Christian Science as a faith cure; would return to the wire; would try to learn what was the matter. Almost inevitably, before he had hung up, he had promised to print anything the gentleman at the other end wished to have published in correction.

The result was that the press was strewn with denials that Christian Science was in any way related to common faith cures; denials that Mrs. Eddy was aught but a luminous and vibrant and godly personality; assertions that her discovery was nothing else than a perfectly divine boon to man. So industrious were these various "publication committees" that editors very quickly came to avoid anything but the most reverent and studied approach to Christian Science, for they learned through bitter experience that the least slip would cause their telephones to begin a steady ringing that would not cease until they either had expressed public regret or had lost an advertiser.

The whole secret of this influence with the press lay not in numbers, but in organization. Mrs. Eddy's "committees" were picked for shrewdness and sagacity; in most instances they combined business acumen with religious zealotry; and they never rested until they cornered the offending editor with the most influential Eddy disciple in the community. They could pick with unerring accuracy exactly the right individual to assist the editor to revise his expressions of opinion.

It was natural that an editor, finding anything which he published on Christian Science subject to the most careful scrutiny, should reach the conclusion that the Scientists must be a remarkably numerous and influential sect; and Mrs. Eddy's "publication committee" encouraged this idea whenever possible. Mrs. Eddy's own hints concerning the million who responded to her will, combined with an editor's actual contacts with her disciples, left no doubt in thousands of editorial minds that the lady had untold legions of adherents. Probably few people would have believed, in 1906, that there were not many more than 60,000 Christian Scientists scattered all over the country.[1]

Mrs. Eddy herself lit upon a device to encourage this delusion. In her by-laws she inserted the following provision:

Christian Scientists shall not report for publication the number of members of The Mother Church, nor that of the branch churches. According to the Scripture they shall turn away from personality and numbering the people.[2]

It happened, when the New York *World* began really to get interested in the vague gossip regarding Mrs. Eddy in 1906, that its editors had only a glimmering of the real facts. But they sensed a tremendously vital human-interest story, and they were determined to get at the truth—regardless of the various wiles of the Eddy publication committees—if there were any possible way to arrive at it. *The World's* news and editorial columns had always maintained an attitude of complete *sang froid* toward the adjacent advertising columns; it was one of the few papers of the day which would have dared to send two reporters up to Concord to knock boldly and persistently at Mrs. Eddy's door. For undoubtedly malicious animal magnetism, by whatever name it is known, can be as big a bugaboo in a newspaper office as in a church.

The first act of the two reporters on arriving at Concord was to approach two men who were presumably close to Mrs. Eddy—J. Wesley Plummer, who was treasurer of Mrs. Eddy's church at Concord as well as the Deputy State Treasurer for New Hampshire, and Frederick N. Ladd, the Secretary of the Loan and Trust Savings Bank of Concord, who was Mrs. Eddy's second cousin. She did a great deal of her business with Ladd's bank.

The *World* reporters stated their mission to these men

[1] In June of 1906 the entire membership of The Mother Church totalled 0,000. The total number of Christian Scientists throughout the United States as 65,717, according to the U. S. Census of Religious Bodies of that year.
[2] *Manual*, VIII, 28.

quite frankly, explaining that they had heard apparently well
founded rumors that Mrs. Eddy was almost, if not quite, *hors
de combat,* and that she was wholly under the control of other
minds. Ladd and Plummer both laughed at such an idea.

"Isn't it enough that I tell you she is alive and well?" asked
Plummer with conviction. "I know it. But I fear it will be
impossible to see her. She is so overwhelmed with her great
work."

"How do you know she is well?" he was asked.

"Why, I see her every day in her carriage."

"But how do you know the woman you see in the carriage
is really Mrs. Eddy?"

"Why, I know it. I have been told so by Frye and others
whom I'd trust with my very life."

And then the fact was revealed that Plummer had never
once seen Mrs. Eddy face to face, despite the fact that he was
a leader in her Concord church and lived within half a mile
of her home. All he knew of Mrs. Eddy personally was what
he had heard. All he had seen of her was what he had glimpsed
as she drove abroad in her carriage. The carriage had a good
solid roof, the windows were almost never lowered, and the
old lady sitting in state within was always concealed almost
entirely by shadow.

Ladd was as certain as Plummer that Mrs. Eddy was on
deck quite as usual, in the state of good health which her re
ligion undertook to create and maintain for all its devotees
He laughed aloud at the suggestion that she was a pitiable in
valid. "Why," he said, "I have conferred with her personally
no longer than six months ago. She was a marvel of mental
alertness and physical vigor. Just look at her to-morrow in
her carriage, and you will see how ridiculous these stories
are."

The reporters however, refused to be convinced. They had
not yet played their trump card. They announced that they
had irrefutable proof that Mrs. Eddy had transferred a large
part of her property to Frye and to others. They had copies
of the documents of transfer.

There is every reason to believe that this was entirely new

Ladd and Plummer. They were horrified. They felt that this story must be scotched immediately. They said that they would get in touch with Frye at once and arrange to have the reporters see Mrs. Eddy personally.

Frye sent word that he would receive the men at noon. They drove up to the front door, which had hardly been opened since Lord Dunmore entered there, and rang the bell. The door swung open immediately, and a maid ushered them past a large steel engraving of Daniel in the Lions' Den and a reproduction of the McNeil coat of arms.

They were seated in the reception room on the right, and Frye shortly made his appearance—now a short, fat, sleek man, with an enormous nose, a receding chin, a little mustache trimmed and twirled at the ends into needle points, and white hair brushed close to his rounded skull. Frye, too, was getting along in years. He wore a black suit of rather ministerial cut, a white shirt with black tie, and kid slippers with soles as thin as dancing pumps.

He was businesslike and brusque. He inquired their purpose—although he had already been informed by Plummer and Ladd of the reason for their coming. The men said they wanted to arrange for an appointment with Mrs. Eddy. "Come back at three o'clock," said Frye pompously, "and I will give you ten minutes of my time."

At three o'clock the men were back again. This time they were received by Frye in company with his assistant, Lewis C. Strang, who had formerly been a dramatic critic. The World men once more repeated the reason for their arrival, and explained the rumors and the information which had brought them on their quest.

As Frye listened to their statement regarding rumors that Mrs. Eddy had been in his complete control for several years, and their evidence that he himself held title to all her property, he slowly dropped his composed address and became flushed and angry. "Well, what do you want me to do about it?" he at last demanded.

He was told that an interview was desired, and that The World would insist on having present at this interview Mrs.

Eddy's nearest neighbor, John F. Kent, in order to identify
her beyond a question.

Kent, who for some twenty years previously had been prin
cipal of the Concord High School until he had retired from
active work, had already been looked up by the reporters
they had discovered that he held Mrs. Eddy in very low es
teem. All courtesies between the two neighbors had been ende
in the course of a dispute over allocating the cost of paving
a nearby road. "Frye knows," Kent confided, "that I loo
upon Mrs. Eddy as a mountebank, that I have openly oppose
her, and that I regard Pleasant View as the home of frau
and trickery."

Kent therefore appeared an ideal man for the exposure o
fraud, if such existed. Frye and Strang both protested a
bringing such a man face to face with Mrs. Eddy. The re
porters insisted. Frye told them to go back to the hotel an
they would hear from him in twenty-four hours.

Frye always masked behind his rather negative exterior a
alert canniness. He was in no sense clever, but his profoun
loyalty to Mrs. Eddy made up for mental defects. He entere
in his diary every day verbatim accounts of her reprovals o
him and her angry outbursts just as faithfully as he tran
scribed her words of cheer or praise. "Mother was displease
with me to-day," he would write, "and called me an idiot.
must try to do better next time."

His very fealty to Mrs. Eddy, steady and unquestioning
like that of a rather stupid dog that has grown up in a family
made him peculiarly useful and quick to sense danger. Fry
immediately carried his report to Mrs. Eddy. Ill as she wa
she herself sensed the vital need of rising to the situation. Sh
had always at her command one important asset with whic
every actress is familiar, the inner glow of vitality whic
comes with a knowledge of a duty to one's public. The oft-re
peated reports that she was sick or dying were peculiarly hat
ful to her, and she resented them. They were, indeed, a publ
advertisement of her inability to cope with physical ill, an
thus a public challenge to her claims to priestly leadership :
her church. Accordingly she announced that she would a

:mpt to see not only the men from *The World*, but also her
eighbor next door.

True to his promise, Frye sent word to the reporters at the
otel that they might interview Mrs. Eddy the next day. The
World men themselves were fast developing a case of nerves;
ey had been in Concord but a few hours before they found
ome papers had disappeared from their rooms, and that night
hen they went for a walk, they were set upon by some
ugs.

The next afternoon Frye sent for them with Mrs. Eddy's
wn carriage. At Pleasant View they were met by Strang,
ad were seated in the parlor where they were shortly joined
y Kent. Strang buzzed in and out several times, then came
finally to say that Mrs. Eddy would receive them upstairs
her study. "Now follow me, if you please," said the urbane
trang, leading the way. In single file they started to climb
e stairs. Suddenly Strang paused, raising his hand to order
halt. A dead silence hung over them. Not a sound could be
ard in any part of the eerie house. Then, as Strang listened
ith uplifted head, they all heard a woman's voice come down
rough the shadowy stair well in a shrill whisper: "All right.
e quick!"

"Quick, now, please!" Strang repeated, and they all hurried
eir pace into a rush. Hastening through the hall into Mrs.
ddy's study, they lined up around the wall. They found them-
lves facing an aged woman who was standing in the centre
the room supporting her weight with her hands on a heavy
ble.

Subsequent events make it seem highly probable that they
ad arrived on one of Mrs. Eddy's worst days. And beyond
doubt 1906 was one of her worst years. She had amazing
cuperative faculties. Many times previously she had risen
om dire suffering to amazing displays of strength and en-
gy. And she would again. But to-day she needed to exert
ery effort merely to stand erect before these intruders.

She was woefully emaciated. Her hollow cheeks were
ight with rouge; her almost hairless brows were pencilled
jet black, and made a strange contrast with the whiteness of

the hair. At her lean throat sparkled the diamond crown tha
had been Augusta Stetson's gift. She reeled as she stood ther
a pitiful, appealing figure, trembling before the hunters wh
were upon her. Her eyes pleaded for mercy. Her lip
quivered.

And yet her indomitable, proud spirit refused to let he
yield. She raised her head, forced a sparkle into her eye
With an attempt at the surface vivacity with which Mar
Baker of old had once sought to win a hostile world she trie
to smile at the wondering Kent, whom she had not seen fo
seven years.

"My dear—dear—pro-professor!" she faltered. "H—H-
how glad I am to see you. Let me con-congratulate you o
getting back your position. I—I—I am so glad that you ar
at the head of our schools again." . . .

She was trying to force her poor, bewildered brain to re
member. She paused, gathered herself, tried to smile at Ke
once more.

"I—I—I ca-cannot understand your in-interest in poor m
Bu—but I ca-cannot be interviewed. . . ."

It was a torture no less for her listeners than for he
Newspaper reporters are men paid to do difficult jobs; b
it distresses them none the less, sometimes, to do the work. I
a corner of the room, as they stood before her, they all cou
clearly see the galvanic battery that had been hastily push
aside but not concealed, and a surgical basin half full of wat
with a sponge that was wet from use. The room itself reek
with the pungency of ammonia. The whole interview last
less than three minutes. As the men departed Mrs. Eddy sar
gaspingly into the chair behind her, her frail body shakir
with palsied spasm, and her face contorted in an agony
pain.

"Yes," said Kent as they went down the stairs, "she is Mr
Eddy beyond a doubt."

The World did not publish the account of this intervie
until two weeks later, on October 28, 1906. Meanwhile the r
porters remained in Concord, using their eyes and their ear
They very quickly discovered that Mrs. Eddy's carriage w

ierging regularly for afternoon drives, following always the
me route, and leaving and returning always at the same
ur. They were mystified. They were positive after their in-
rview that Mrs. Eddy was wholly unable to leave her rooms.
ie carriage was closed. Frye always rode in uniform in the
itman's box. Within sat a white-haired woman muffled to
e ears in fur, always holding a small sunshade before her
spite the fact that the carriage was entirely enclosed and
vered. Since the carriage moved at a rapid pace, and the
iman within always adjusted the angle of her parasol so
to shield her face from observers, it was difficult to iden-
y her. At that time newspapers did not have the advantage
long-range cameras with a fast lens, such as are in use to-day,
d the sorties of the carriage were puzzling.

The problem of identifying the occupant, however, was
ortly solved. The *World* reporters finally found a man, one
hn J. Hennesy, who had known Mrs. Leonard well in the
ys when he was employed in the Temple Bar Building in
ooklyn, and when she was taking patients for a dollar a
eatment. He named the carriage occupant as Mrs. Leonard.[1]
Less than a week after the *World* men had visited Con-
rd, Mrs. Eddy sent a public denial of any invalidism to a
iston newspaper. This item was in letter form, and read:

October 19, 1906

THE EDITOR OF THE BOSTON HERALD.

Dear Sir: Another report that I am dead is widely credited. I am in
ial good health, and go out in my carriage every day.

Truly yours, MARY BAKER G. EDDY.

On Sunday, October 28, *The World* broke forth with its
iry, describing not only Mrs. Eddy's wretched physical con-
tion but also the attempts to conceal it by such manœuvrings
these stage-set journeys of the Eddy carriage through the
incord streets. As a matter of fact, Mrs. Eddy's physical
bility was not nearly as extreme as the *World* men imag-
d, for the reason that their view of her in one of her less

That Mrs. Leonard ever substituted in this manner for Mrs. Eddy has been
ently denied by a member of the Eddy household of this period. Such con-
dictory evidence is the bane of the conscientious Eddy biographer.

buoyant moments left them without hint of the great re
cuperative powers that were hers. They had merely broke
in upon her at an unfortunate time. But they could not know
this, and so their paper openly charged that Mrs. Eddy ha
become merely the victim of a designing clique who ruled he
body and soul, and that she was no longer the master eithe
of her church or of her fortune. It was intimated that she wa
either mentally irresponsible or actually insane.

It was a sensational story, and within a few hours from
the time it appeared the Associated Press, the Publisher
Press, and various papers of prominence along the Atlant
seaboard had their own representatives in Concord. On
The World had picked up the scent the pack forgot all othe
considerations in eagerness to join in the chase.

Mrs. Eddy was frightened, and her church officers we
horrified. Alfred Farlow, Mrs. Eddy's "publication commi
tee" in Boston, hurried to her home and summoned there I
Cornell Wilson, who had been doing publicity work for Chri
tian Science in New York City. Wilson, like so many othe
holding prominent positions in Mrs. Eddy's church, had nev
met her until called in this emergency, and had seen her fro
a distance only once. Farlow himself had seen her only at ra
intervals and took most of his orders from her by letter. I
and Wilson both had reason to be surprised at the feeblene
of the Mrs. Eddy who now met their gaze.

As Farlow and Wilson hastily conferred with Frye a
Strang, every train coming into Concord was bringing mo
newspaper men to gather upon Mrs. Eddy's front lawn. T
whole situation was explained as tactfully as possible to M
Eddy. As usual in her periods of emergency, affidavits we
decided on. For a number of hours her "publication comm
tee" and his assistants worked at topmost speed. An impo
ing list of deponents was secured. The names of men atte
ing to Mrs. Eddy's mental and physical fitness included Ge
eral Frank S. Streeter, her attorney, who was later to defe
her sanity; J. E. Fernald, the president of the National Sta
Capital Bank; Frederick N. Ladd, her cousin, who was tre
surer of the Loan and Trust Savings Bank; Charles R. Cor

g, the mayor of Concord; and two New Hampshire editors, [. Meehan of the Concord *Patriot,* and George H. Moses of *he Monitor and Statesman,* subsequently of the United States enate.

These gentlemen were told that an emergency existed, and ere asked if they would do Mrs. Eddy the service of testiing that she was in good health and competent mind.

Their reassuring and entirely optimistic affidavits were imediately sent broadcast by telephone and telegraph over the untry; for by this time *The World's* preliminary story conrning Mrs. Eddy's enfeebled condition was being copied in pers from coast to coast. The officials of Mrs. Eddy's church ose manfully from their first horror to exert superhuman forts to protect their organization and its founder from these aledictions. All of the fifty-odd publicity men scattered over e country began immediately to earn their salaries. On the onday following the first Sunday story, two long distance lephones were in constant commission between Boston and ew York, Farlow sending the affidavits in this form to be ken down in New York via telephone and distributed there well as in Boston. Farlow by this time held not only the sition of chief "Publication Committee," but also the office President of the Mother Church. A statement two colnns long was given the telegraph companies with instrucns to send it free to any newspaper in the country desiring all tolls to be charged to the Christian Science officers. multaneously all local "publication committees" were wired put out a separate statement in their own localities.

The newspaper men gathered in Concord accepted the affivits politely when they were proffered, but insisted quite mly that affidavits were not what they came to Concord to cure. They wanted to see Mrs. Eddy. Consultations ensued. was finally decided that Mrs. Eddy would see the newsper representatives at one o'clock on Tuesday, October 30. Mrs. Eddy was quite certain that she could go through with ch an interview. Her marvellous will-power, her dynamic termination, were never more evident than at the time when se around her had despaired of her ability to recuperate.

There can be small doubt that her strange physical diffi
culties were unknown to those of her church officials t
whom the news was most important. It is also probable tha
none of them was in any way aware of the bottomless mer
tal complexes that lay concealed in her shadowy mind. M
Wilson, however, had a talk with her and decided on a pro
gramme. It was obvious that she could not possibly star
the strain of anything more than the briefest appearance. B
it seemed possible to attempt a showing of the venerab
woman under well guarded auspices. Mrs. Eddy insisted th
she was wholly able to go through with the ordeal. She wa
indeed confident that she could come downstairs and take
drive. This seemed a brilliant solution of the whole problem
if it could be arranged, in view of *The World's* assertio
concerning Mrs. Leonard. If all the assembled reporters cou
actually see Mrs. Eddy mount into her vehicle, the vicio
rumors ought permanently to be set at rest.

It is perhaps difficult for one not imbued with the atmo
phere that surrounded Mrs. Eddy and her church to sense t
sting of the *World* "exposure." It is particularly difficu
when it is realized that Mrs. Eddy was not the helpless du
of her household that *The World* had claimed. For even
her worst moments, Mrs. Eddy led every one who came
contact with her a merry chase. It was her will that rule
There was never a time, when she wished to gain an end, wh
she failed to bring not merely her household but also her Boa
of Directors cringing before her. Under such circumstanc
it appears at first glance remarkable that her following shot
have been concerned over a story that denied her mental r
sponsibility. It would seem that such a charge could ha
been easily disproved. But—it could not have been disprov
without showing Mrs. Eddy personally. And whatever h
mental condition, she was at the moment a very sick wom
physically, just as *The World* had said. *The World's* sta
ment that she was suffering from cancer was as near a dia
nosis of her ailment as its reporters had been able to come.

Now it happened that Mrs. Eddy was the one person in t
world who could never afford to make a public confessi

at she was sick. An admission of physical incapacity would
ave jeopardized her no less than proof that she was actually
sane. For she had built her whole life, her career, her fame,
er fortune, her church, upon claims that she had brought to
e world a means of remission from suffering. To her dis-
ples she was the great deliverer. She had sought to establish
e validity of her message on just one basis—its divine infalli-
ility. The whole fabric of her life and church was now
oven around that claim. And as always when claims to di-
ine infallibility are demonstrated to be fallacious, the valid-
y of the entire structure which she had built upon this
aim was now endangered.

The same thing has happened time and again in other
urches, to other religious leaders, who have erred in the
me way. When any message is preached to men that makes
s major claim to virtue the assertion that it is divine in
igin and hence infallible in operation, it bears the poison of
s own eventual destruction in its breath.

Thus in her old age the figments of human aspiration and
agination from which Mary Baker Eddy had built a lofty
eam castle to soar into the clouds began crashing down
ound her. She who had claimed infallibly to heal all who
ocked at her door must now humbly admit that she could
t heal herself. She who had taught men that she was
ointed of God to bring them the golden key that would
lock all Divine Good, must now bow her head to confess
at she herself could not use the key.

And yet—her pride burned within her. This should stand
her glory. Tortured as she was, she refused to recant. With
her pretensions now challenged, she raised her head, reared
rself to her feet. Even as the reporters hung in throngs
ound her doors, she steadied herself and looked Wilson in
e eye. "I will s-s-see them," she said.

And thus it was that she nerved herself for her ordeal,
d called for her women to bring her her finest clothes, and
s bathed, and rubbed and prepared.

Once again emergency gave her strength. All her life
reatened disaster had acted like a springboard for her ener-

gies. Once, when she was still Mrs. Patterson, sick in bed i
the shabby little house at North Groton, she heard cries
terror out in the side-lot. Dr. Patterson was there choppin
wood, when a neighboring farmer had come in with his so
and started an argument.

The argument developed into blows; the Doctor was felle
to the ground; and the enraged farmer motioned to his so
to take the axe and end the dispute with a murder.

At this juncture Mrs. Patterson rushed from the hous
With an unnatural strength in her arms, an unwonted ca
lousness to fear, she seized the farmer's son with his uplift
axe, overpowered him, held him until neighbors came ru
ning in answer to her shrieks.

Now in her old age it was the same Mary Baker who on
again saw disaster looming. This time it was not a husbar
who was endangered—it was herself and her child, the chur
to which she had given her very life's blood.

Wilson conferred with the newspaper men at their hot
"We have decided," he purred, "to let you see Mrs. Edd
Certain things must be arranged now and clearly understo
Of course it would be impossible to address a lot of questio
to Mrs. Eddy. It would not be proper, you know. Now it w
be best to select one of your number to ask certain questio
which should be prepared in advance. I suggest S. W. O'Brie
who represents *Ridgway's Weekly*. This lady interviewed M
Eddy several years ago, and will be the proper one to do t
questioning to-day."

The newspaper men did not at that time know that M
Sibyl Wilbur O'Brien was at that very moment engaged
writing some articles about Mrs. Eddy, with whom she h
recently held several interviews devoted to discussion
material.[1] Had they known, they might possibly have
jected, and Mrs. Eddy's ordeal would have been made s
more difficult. But it was agreed that Mrs. O'Brien shou
be the official spokesman, and she and Mr. Wilson prepar

[1] Mrs. O'Brien was eventually employed, at a salary of $200 a month an
contract giving her 20 per cent of future royalties, to write the present "auth
ized" biography of Mrs. Eddy.

ᴉree questions which were to be asked. The list of queries
ᴉey devised was as follows:

1. Are you in perfect health?
2. Have you any physician other than God?
3. Do you take a drive daily?

This list was read aloud to the assembled reporters.
"Is that all?" inquired H. A. Vivian of the New York *Times*.
"Why, yes," said Mr. Wilson amiably. "Those three ques-
ᴉons seem to cover every point."
"It does not strike me that way at all," said Vivian. "If
ᴐu have read the published statement in the New York
ᐟorld, you must know that the property interest of Mrs.
ddy forms a vitally important point. Who is handling her
ᴑoney?"
The other reporters chimed in their agreement with Vivian.
inally Wilson yielded to their insistence that a fourth ques-
ᴐn be added to the list. It was phrased to read:

4. Does any beside yourself administer your property or attend to
ᴑur business affairs?

When the questions were finally outlined, Wilson informed
ᴉe men that the reporter for the New York *World* would be
ᶍcluded. Wilson could not forgive either that newspaper or
ᵢ representatives.
Nine reporters, among whom Vivian of *The Times* was the
ᴉly New York representative, left the hotel at exactly twenty
inutes to one, riding in three carriages. They reached Pleas-
ᴉt View to be met at the door by Strang, who bowed them
ᴉo Mrs. Eddy's rose and gilt drawing-room, lifting heavy
ᴑrtieres to allow them to pass. As they passed, the portieres
ᵉre allowed to fall again, completely obscuring the view of
ᵉ hall and the stairway. Mrs. Leonard and Mrs. Sargent
ᴑrtly came into the room, richly and superbly gowned. They
ᵗroduced themselves, welcomed the guests with a show of
ᴀciousness, and went away.
Through the windows the men beheld the well-known Eddy

coach driven up to the door. Shortly the portieres were thrus
aside and a man in the dark green livery of a footman steppe
into the room, holding a top hat in his pudgy white hand. Som
one whispered "Frye" in an audible voice. Frye heard, hi
plump cheeks flushed, and he turned away and vanished agai
through the curtains. There was a long pause. The men set
tled into an uncomfortable silence.

And then, without a sound, without a warning step or
single preliminary indication, the great portieres were draw
to either side by hands that were not visible, and framed be
tween them the men saw Mrs. Eddy standing just beyond th
doorway.[1]

There she remained motionless for a moment, haggar
emaciated and palsied, her cheeks tinted brightly with roug
her gleaming, deepsunk eyes roaming around as if to seek
familiar object. She was dressed in brave extravagance,
finery reminiscent of nothing more than a marchioness in or
of her girlhood's favorite Southworth novels. Powdered, b
wigged, and bejewelled, fluttering with ribbons and plume
she would have attracted stares anywhere. She was at hea
still the Mary Baker Glover who all her life had sought
impress a difficult world with ill-chosen nuances of costun
that could make her nothing less than remarked and conspic
ous. But to-day she wore an ermine cloak instead of the b
ribboned wool dress of leaner years. It was the cloak given
her by Augusta Stetson. It parted at her shoulders to reve
a rose silk gown. At her throat were her diamonds. On h
head a hat nodded large, white ostrich plumes.

She took two steps forward to the portieres, and her glov
hands shook with palsy even as she reached them out to gra
the draperies and steady herself. Frye appeared at her rig
Strang at her left, moving out from the portieres which th
had previously drawn apart with concerted motion and whi

[1] In the description of this scene the author has compared the accounts w
ten by most of the reporters who were present. Evidences of personal bias
pear in some of the accounts, but the majority of the eye-witnesses agreed
to the essential details. In the main, the report of H. A. Vivian in the New Y
Times has been relied upon where there was variation in facts or any evide
of undue desire to prove a thesis.

ad until now concealed them. They stood there alertly, ready
ɔ support her if she should sway.

Once again Mrs. Eddy had been caught by intruders in an
ɪterim when the tide of her amazing vitality was at an ebb.
'o make matters worse, she was undoubtedly nervous, and
aint with the tremulousness of fear. But as the portieres parted
nd she stood revealed to the tense faces before her, she tried
ɔ smile. The smile died, and she hesitated like a very old lady
ʋho has been told to expect something, but has forgotten just
vhat and is trying to collect her mind. She mumbled a quite
ɪaudible sentence, and turned away as if to go to the front
ɔor. Edward M. Pearson, Secretary of State for New Hamp-
hire, was in the room with the newspaper men, with the an-
ɔunced purpose of identifying Mrs. Eddy for her interview-
rs. He had known the old lady for a number of years. As
ⅰrs. Eddy stood waveringly at the door he sought to catch
er eye. "How do you do, Mrs. Eddy?" he ventured politely.
ʋhe did not notice or hear him, gave no sign of recognition.
ⅼmong her other ailments Mrs. Eddy was contending with
ɪeafness. At this moment Mrs. O'Brien stepped forward, and
he men behind her closed in. She caught Mrs. Eddy's atten-
ɪon, but the old lady gazed at her without recognition.

"Are you in perfect bodily health, Mrs. Eddy?" asked Mrs.
ɔ'Brien deferentially.

There was a quick and very perceptible change in Mrs.
ɛddy's manner.

She caught herself, came back a step, and hesitantly leaned
hand against the doorway.

"Wha-at?" she inquired in her aged treble.

Mrs. O'Brien hastily repeated the question.

"Y-yes; y-yes, indeed I am," she murmured quite indis-
ⅰnctly.

"Have you any physician other than God?"

Again Mrs. Eddy's questioning gaze wandered pitifully
ver the faces of her audience. "W-what?" she reiterated.

Mrs. O'Brien repeated the second question, this time in a
ɔud voice.

Mrs. Eddy raised her head, as if taking a cue, then loosed

her hold on the portieres and flung out her arms. "No," sh
recited in a voice high-pitched and without accent. "No, Hi
everlasting arms are around me."

Here she half turned, swayed backward, and Frye hastil
steadied her with an extended arm. Mrs. O'Brien pressed for
ward. For Mrs. Eddy's own sake she had a duty to complete

"Do you take a drive daily, Mrs. Eddy?"

By this time Mrs. Eddy was staggering away from th
drawing-room door, half supported by Frye and Strang.

Advancing still further, Mrs. O'Brien repeated her ques
tion more loudly. "Do you take a drive daily, Mrs. Eddy?"

"Yes . . . yes . . ." answered Mrs. Eddy brokenly. Sh
was already turned away, her momentary strength gone, th
ninety-odd pounds of her slight body almost a dead weight o
the two men who were seeking to assist her in such a manne
that their support would not seem obvious. As Mrs. O'Brie
asked her last question, "Does any one beside yourself ad
minister your property?" Mrs. Eddy was already down th
hall. She did not hear. Half leading, half carrying, Frye an
Strang got her to the door. A reporter rushed forward to wal
beside her and gaze closely into her face. He was pulle
roughly back by one of the men in the household—Herman
S. Hering—the First Reader in the Concord Church.

For a moment, as the reporters watched, Mrs. Eddy sough
to shake off the hands that supported her. She tried bravel
under the skeptical stares to walk alone down the few step
that led to the carriage, waiting under the porte-cochère. Bu
her knees sank under her at the third step, and Frye put h
arm around her. He and Strang lifted her fragile frame al
most bodily into the coach. Strang wrapped rugs around he
placed a stool beneath her feet, tucked her carefully in. Sh
reached for one of the ribbons that hung from her throat; he
palsied hand could not grasp it; she let the hand fall and he
fingers began drumming ceaselessly on the rug tucked acros
her lap. Looking up again she motioned with shaking arm t
have the carriage door closed. She tucked her hands in he
muff; set herself primly in repose; gazed straight ahead
tried pathetically to compress her trembling lips into a straigl

ne. Frye mounted his box, and the coachman signalled the
at and sleepy horses to pick up their hoofs.

It was a remarkable and heroic piece of acting. As poor
Irs. Eddy leaned back wearily in her carriage, it would not
ave been strange if hot tears of relief had suddenly rolled
own her hollowed cheeks to make little furrows in the rouge.

The coachman clicked to the horses. Frye on his perch
azed vacantly at the sky, and the great carriage rolled pon-
erously through the Concord streets. Mary Baker Eddy
it huddled inside with the curtains half drawn, utterly alone.
he had been alone all her life. She had hungered alone, fought
one, suffered alone. There had never been any one near her
 help her. There were many to render her homage. There
ad never been one to give her understanding. And yet. . . .

After all, she was Mary Baker Eddy, anointed of God.
lone, yes. But to be unique is to be alone always. Only ordi-
ary men gain understanding. Only puerile souls find com-
deship. God is Himself alone for all eternity.

The white plumes nodded vigorously as she shook with con-
ant tremor. But she continued to gaze steadily, unseeingly,
raight ahead, as the carriage rolled ceaselessly on through
e quiet streets that the plump horses knew so well.

XXVIII

Among Mrs. Eddy's numerous fears, one that had plague
her ever since the beginning of her rise to financial prosperit
was a horror of losing her money. She managed eventually t
devise by-laws that would prevent her from losing her churcl
but she was not so sure about her fortune. Every time sh
reckoned up her accounts she had an attack of fright. He
fear was concerned not only with her ability to hold on t
her money during her lifetime; it extended to possibilities c
what might happen after her death. She was determined—
except on rare occasions when she had a momentary chang
of heart—that she did not want her son or his family to g
even a cent of her fortune upon her demise. She was particu
larly anxious that none of her valuable copyrights should fa
into his hands. She worried over this considerably, becau
she felt that in any suit to break her will Glover would prol
ably be a victor at law whether she sought to cut him off
not. Having pondered over such a possibility, she wrote
Nixon, her publisher of the period, on September 22, 189
declaring: "I see this morning the purpose of the enemy. It
to break my will at my decease if this can be accomplished
The "enemy" she mentioned was M. A. M., which she assert
would influence her son to make the contest. She continue

Now this I enjoin on you: Inquire of best copyright lawyers out
Boston, you can find, if I can assign my copyright of S. & H. and Uni
of Good in some one who would hold it if my will was broken and nev
name this party in my will or name it to whom it is assigned, whichev
would make it legal.

Kindly find this out at once and the way of conveyance of my cop
right so that if my will should be disputed or broken the publishing
S. & H. and Unity of Good could go on without hindrance.

There were some additional warnings, with instructions
"ask a lawyer or judge of the U. S. Circuit Court all about tl

question of legal conveyance . . ." The letter concluded with a postscript:

P. S. Be perfectly silent to all but the legal party about what I have written. The Boston lawyers whom I have employed are demoralized by M. A. M. *Note this.*[1]

Deep underscores marked the last two words.

Mrs. Eddy solved her problem momentarily by transferring her copyrights to E. J. Foster Eddy, this transaction taking place on October 8, 1890. There they stayed until 1896, the year when Mrs. Eddy finally changed her mind about Foster Eddy and took from him her publishing business. When she sent her adopted son packing and made Joseph Armstrong of Kansas City her publisher, Mrs. Eddy secured a reassignment of her copyrights, but she did not turn them over to Armstrong. By this time she had decided that Calvin Frye was probably her safest refuge. Thus on January 12, 1896, she transferred to Frye the copyrights to *Science and Health* and most of her other works; and on February 12 of this same year Mrs. Eddy also deeded to Frye all of her real estate holdings, including Pleasant View. Frye, of course, received no income from his holdings; he was acting merely as agent, and Mrs. Eddy secured her usual financial returns.

By the time three more years elapsed Mrs. Eddy had temporarily grown a little weary of Frye and had decided that it might be safer to take the copyrights away and assign them to some one else. This time she chose Edward A. Kimball, one of her most devout and loyal disciples, who for many years held a position on the Board of Lectureship. He was a dominating personality in her church, and was altogether far more level-headed and dynamic a personality than most of the men whom Mrs. Eddy's preachings attracted to her organization.

It must be evident to the observer that Mrs. Eddy and her doctrines held few men of outstanding qualities. All of the

[1] This letter, addressed to Mr. Nixon, came eventually into the hands of Senator Chandler, counsel for Glover in the Next Friends' suit, and was thereupon offered as evidence of the manner in which Mrs. Eddy's belief in M. A. M. affected "the contingent rights of relatives" in her estate. It was first published in the New York *World*, August 16, 1907.

personal leadership ever exercised in her church was exerte
by women.[1] Edward A. Kimball was rather an exception t
the general rule; he retained Mrs. Eddy's regard until the end
and when he died shortly before her own death she wrote
heartfelt notice of regret headed "There is no death," to de
clare that, "My beloved Edward A. Kimball is here now a
veritably as when he visited me a year ago." Incidentally, thi
pronouncement on Mr. Kimball's status was long used by Mrs
Stetson as an argument to show that Mrs. Eddy taught physi
cal immortality.

Mr. Kimball seems to have exercised a very sane and re
strained influence upon all of the rather excitable minds wit
which he came in contact. Once he was asked by a new arriva
in Mrs. Eddy's congregation regarding the real meaning c
malicious animal magnetism. "Well," drawled Mr. Kimba
"if I were really good at practising malicious animal mag
netism, and if there were somebody I wanted to try my pow
ers out on, I'd go out to the street where he lived and I'd rei
a house just across from his own. And then, whenever I
went out, and whenever he went in, I would let him see m
looking at him intently from out my window. And I shoul
make certain that he knew just what I was trying to do t
him. Then I would draw the blinds of my house, and slip ou
the back door, and go away on a nice long fishing trip. I real
think that this would work."

It was to Kimball that Mrs. Eddy assigned her copyrigh
on October 9, 1899, after she had had Frye deed them back t
her on October 6. Frye was allowed to retain his deed t
Pleasant View, however, until September 5, 1901. On May 2
1906, Kimball retransferred his copyright holdings to Mr
Eddy again, at her request. Thereupon Mrs. Eddy retran
ferred her holdings to Frye once more, including all her pe
sonal and real property.

---

[1] Mrs. Eddy herself realized this. Vd. *Miscellany*, page 355: "A letter from
student in the field says there is a grave need for more men in Christian Scien
practice.

"I have not infrequently hinted at this. However, if the occasion demands
I will repeat that men are very important factors in our field of labor for Chr
tian Science. . . ."

These were the transactions which the New York *World* had stumbled upon after long poring by its reporters over obscure legal documents registered with the county clerk, and it was these documents which were responsible for the conclusion that Mrs. Eddy was utterly irresponsible and merely the tool of dominating and grasping minds.

Nothing could have been farther from the truth. Mrs. Eddy was all her life the victim of no one but herself and her own dark and unreasoned fears. Neither Frye nor Kimball ever profited personally from their own parts in these obscure transactions; they were merely rendering friendly assistance to a tremulous old lady who grew less certain of providential protection and surer of the wiles of her enemies as the years went on. Frye, after all his years of service with Mrs. Eddy and his handling of an estate that eventually had a net value of three million dollars, ended his employment with about $11,000 of his own in the bank—the product of years of careful hoarding of his savings. When, in 1907, accountants went over his ink-splotched books, they found an error of only $677.41 for the eight years of Frye's stewardship between January 1, 1899, and March 6, 1907. And it was an error in Mrs. Eddy's favor, since this balance was money owing to Frye.

Unfortunately for Mrs. Eddy, however, only the most damaging conclusions could be drawn from the bare facts that such transfers and alienations of her property had taken place over a long period of years. Her interview with the assembled newspaper representatives at Pleasant View failed utterly in its purpose of dissipating the now growing conviction that she was utterly incompetent and perhaps a dotard at the mercy of the ambitions of others. Most reporters present at the interview agreed that she seemed a very weak and feeble old lady, approaching if not already immersed in her second childhood.

The ensuing incidents in the Eddy history prove what a great power a newspaper may exert not only in community affairs, but even in private destinies. The same publicity which in the past had done so much for Mrs. Eddy had now turned upon her with a pitiless and relentless glare. Publicity can break as well as make a tradition; and in a nation where newspaper readers thrive upon sensationalism there is always an eagerness to tear down an idol after it has once been exalted. From the dawn of human history it has been the tendency of an idolatrous populace to enjoy its sensations twice—once when it elevates its gods and heroes and again when it tears them down and tramples them underfoot. If anything, the second sensation is the more pleasurable one. This is as much a law of human nature in modern city streets as it was in the Roman forum. Nothing can build circulation for a newspaper so fast as front-page accounts regarding the very human weaknesses to which exalted specimens of humanity are subject.

This accounts for the fact that *The World* had no intention of letting Mrs. Eddy retire once more into her home and seal herself up again. It should be said for *The World* that its editors felt themselves to be performing an important public service. When told by the various officials of Mrs. Eddy's church that Mrs. Eddy's physical and mental condition was of no possible concern either to the public or the newspapers, *The World* registered emphatic disagreement. Its editors took the position that Mrs. Eddy had—or at least claimed to have—a million or more followers to whom her word was law and her wish command. She was in consequence a personage of great power over a great number of citizens, and should therefore be held wholly answerable to the bar of public opinion. By her own volition she had made her private affairs a matter of public importance. As a result neither she nor her associates had a right to expect or demand immunity from that inquiring public gaze which is the best guaranty enjoyed by a free nation that its established traditions and institutions can not be endangered.

The theory that a well informed public opinion is the best assurance of orderly progress in a nation under a republican form of government to-day amounts to a tradition in American journalism. It is a tradition that often appears to violate private rights and privileges; undoubtedly to Mrs. Eddy brought a great tragedy in her declining years. But here, as always, the interests of the individual are regarded as secondary to those of the group in which he moves.

As it was, Mrs. Eddy and the men around her were between Scylla and Charybdis. They could not possibly explain the unfortunate evidence that had now become public without producing other facts that might be construed as even more damaging. Undoubtedly, all of Mrs. Eddy's officials were themselves at a loss to explain some of the facts which the *World* investigation had produced. They themselves were not previously aware of her hazardous state of health; and Mrs. Eddy had taken good care to see that they had no previous knowledge whatever of her various transfers of property or the reasons therefor. When they questioned her tactfully regarding these unusual transactions, she refused to enter into any discussion or offer any reason. It thus appeared to her officials that the best and only procedure was to make no attempt at any explanation whatever. They sought only to use publicity in such a way as to perpetuate the tradition of Mrs. Eddy's usual good health. So, when Lord Dunmore made a trip to America in December of 1906, his arrival was seized on as a God-given opportunity to issue a bullish statement regarding the condition of Mrs. Eddy's health and mind. The interview was of the briefest duration, Mrs. Eddy saying only a few words after Lord Dunmore had been informed that she was quite too busy and involved in her great work to do more than welcome him briefly. Upon leaving he was asked to sign a prepared statement, which he did. This was the statement, which he afterward casually admitted to newspaper reporters did not represent his "individual effort":

I was immediately struck with Mrs. Eddy's personal appearance, and with the activity with which she got out of her carriage unaided and stepped into the hall. When I was ushered into her presence I could not help remarking to her that she was looking much better and younger than when I saw her last, and during the whole of our interview, which lasted upward of three-quarters of an hour, I was struck by the remarkable vigor of her mind and the extraordinary memory which she displayed for events that had taken place when I first had the privilege of seeing her, about seven years ago. She showed wonderful interest in everything that pertained to the Christian Science movement in Europe, and was most interested to hear how well the lectures were attended and received by the English people.

The efforts of Messrs. Farlow and Wilson to plant publicity of that nature were so obviously ill-advised as to defeat their own purpose. Utter frankness under the circumstances was admittedly almost impossible; but obvious dissimulation only added fuel to the fire of interest which was growing with every new fact about Mrs. Eddy now brought to light.

Until the close of 1906 the world at large had really known nothing whatever about her except that information which she herself had chosen to supply. Suddenly, however, the temple veils had been rent. Whole rivers of unexplained facts started to flow. Georgine Milmine, after months of personal investigation, inquiry and interviews in the New England communities where Mrs. Eddy had spent her life, was publishing in *McClure's Magazine* a biography so detailed and annotated that it was nothing short of a monumental piece of work.[1] Miss Milmine was not content to give mere facts; whenever she got hold of any particularly interesting or amazing facts, she presented them in the form of sworn affidavits from the persons who vouched for them.[2] Presented in this form, without sympathetic interpretation or explanation, much of the material seemed damning beyond description, and Mrs. Eddy chose to regard the resultant harshness of the *McClure's* articles as a wholly unjustified attack on her position and character.

Mrs. Eddy was not too ailing to write a long and indignant

[1] These chapters in *McClure's* were subsequently collected, edited, and revised to form *The Life of Mary Baker G. Eddy and the History of Christian Science.*

[2] A great many of these affidavits were collected by Frederick W. Peabody, Boston lawyer, who had prosecuted Mrs. Woodbury's libel suit, and who there after made it his life's work to "expose" Mrs. Eddy. Of Miss Milmine he said "She assured me she had searched the whole of Mrs. Eddy's life for a kindly a generous, an unselfish, a fine womanly deed, and would have been only to glad to have recorded it, but had not found one." (Vd. Peabody, *The Religion Medical Masquerade*, page 73.)

The *McClure's* biography was in many ways—although Miss Milmine did the greater part of the work—essentially the group effort of a staff of investigators and reporters who combed New England for facts for over two years.

eply to the first instalments of the Milmine biography; thereafter the evidence became so detailed and so unanswerable
hat even Mrs. Eddy gave up in despair and was thenceforth
silent. Meanwhile the facts that had now been revealed
brought forward people who had still more recollections at
heir disposal, and before the end of 1906 the public had heard
all about the collaboration of Mr. Wiggin in the revision of
Mrs. Eddy's text-book, and was being regaled with tales of
a woman so different from the generally accepted portrait
hat to enthusiastic disciples the stories were wholly un-
believable.

Meanwhile the New York *World* reached a determination
o stage an investigation of Mrs. Eddy's real status that would
be final and conclusive. It was decided to make the necessary
moves to bring Mrs. Eddy before the public in a court action
n which she could not be shielded behind the devotion of a
household.

This was the genesis of the famous "Next Friends" suit,
for which preparations were well under way in less than a
month after Mrs. Eddy's pitiful attempt to take a carriage
ride under the gaze of newspaper reporters. Such a suit could
egally have been brought by any representative citizen; but
n order to prosecute it most successfully it seemed best that
t should be brought not merely by "next friends" of Mrs.
Eddy but rather by her nearest relatives, who as heirs at law
would have a personal interest in maintaining her welfare and
guarding her estate. Mrs. Eddy's direct heirs at this time were
her son, George Glover, and his children. A nephew, George
W. Baker, also joined in the action.

George W. Baker was the only son of George Sullivan
Baker and of Mathy Rand, who had been Mrs. Eddy's dearest girlhood friend. It was not difficult to convince him that
his highly revered aunt was in such a questionable physical
and mental condition that some action should be taken to
guard the interests of her heirs. He was a printer by trade,
living in Bangor, Maine, and he had sought many times to get
n touch with Mrs. Eddy personally without ever receiving a
direct reply. He had appealed to his aunt in 1905 with par-

ticular anxiety, for at this time his wife was stricken with
epilepsy and he was financially unable to give her any medical
care. But he did not write asking Mrs. Eddy for charity.
Rather he inquired if she would buy from him a fine old watch
which had been the property of his uncle and Mrs. Eddy's
brother, Albert Baker.

Presumably this letter never was turned over to Mrs. Eddy
personally, for she had loved Albert dearly, and even though
her affections as well as her mind were extremely erratic it
seems probable that she would have been glad to own the
heirloom. Similarly, she had been extremely fond of George
Baker's father and mother. But she never made reply to
George's letter.

Eventually one of Frye's assistants, Gilbert C. Carpenter,
sent a rather curt answer. "The rules of the house prevent any
letters from being handed to Mrs. Eddy which do not pertain
to the great work she has in hand," wrote Carpenter with
enormous austerity. "I have not handed her your communication or told her of it. I know of some Scientists who desire to
make Mrs. Eddy a present, and if the watch could be bough
at a reasonable price I think they might like to purchase, with
the distinct understanding that Mrs. Eddy is to have it presented to her. What price will you dispose of it for?"

Carpenter finally bought the watch for twenty-five dollars,
after he had bargained and refused flatly to pay the fifty dollars which Baker said he needed. He sent with the money a
statement signed by Frye declaring that the watch had been
given to Mrs. Eddy in person.

In April of 1906 Baker wrote to Frye personally, making
a frank appeal for funds to assist his wife, who had just gone
to the hospital. This appeal went unanswered, and it was not
until a year later, when Mrs. Eddy's failure ever to contribute
to charity of any sort was being headlined in the metropolitan
press, that a check for one hundred dollars was sent to this
branch of the Baker family. It was addressed, however, not
to George, but to his mother, Mathy, as a gift to Mrs. Eddy's
"dear sister." Mathy Baker was then still living in Tilton.

Thus it was that George Baker was entirely willing to co-
operate in any way in a suit brought to determine whether

Mrs. Eddy or some one else was actually in control of her affairs. George Glover assented to play a part in the action with no less readiness when a representative of *The World* journeyed out to Lead.

Late in November of 1906 Senator William E. Chandler, United States Senator from New Hampshire and a rather eminent lawyer, had consented to take charge of the case for Mrs. Eddy's heirs, and the newspaper representative carried with him a statement from the Senator to that effect. Glover's was a suggestible nature, similar in many ways to that of his mother. He had no sooner seen Senator Chandler's letter, and heard of the suspicions entertained regarding Mrs. Eddy's helpless condition, than he was positive these were entirely true. Had he himself not been rebuffed by Frye when he sought to reach his mother? Had he not seen with his own eyes how his mother was a veritable slave to Frye's commands?

It was evident immediately that Glover would offer coöperation of a nature extremely satisfying to a newspaper editor's heart. It was arranged that he and his daughter Mary should at once take a train east. This they did, going first to Washington.

Before starting, Glover wrote his mother that he was coming east on a business trip and wanted to see her. This was obviously the first move to make in arranging any legal action. Mrs. Eddy and the officials who now buzzed protectingly round her had no inkling as yet that such a suit was being contemplated, and no idea whatever of the powers that would be behind it. But the arrival of Glover's letter nevertheless drew the Eddy household into consternation. Mrs. Eddy, beleaguered as she was by unfavorable publicity on every hand, felt that her son was the last person in the world she wanted in Concord with newspaper reporters thronging the street corners there. The officials of her church knew little enough of the events which had separated Mrs. Eddy and her son ever since his early boyhood, but they knew quite enough to agree with her that this was a disturbing incident best quelled promptly if possible.

Mrs. Eddy, weakened as she was, was exceedingly distraught. Her first thought—and that of her advisers—was that Glover should be summoned to Concord as promptly as possible and persuaded, bribed, or forced to go back to Lead. Accordingly a letter was despatched to him in Washington by personal messenger. Irving Tomlinson, a former First Reader in the Christian Science Church at Concord, called on the Glovers at their hotel at seven o'clock in the morning—just as soon as he got off his train. He presented a letter from Mrs. Eddy urging her son to come to Concord at once, adding that on arrival there he should shun all hotels and go with Mr. Tomlinson as a guest in the Tomlinson home. While George Glover talked to this unexpected caller he sent Mary across the street to fetch Senator Chandler. The Senator came running, and arrived just as another letter from Mrs. Eddy was delivered by post. This letter, handed to Mary, was written in Mrs. Eddy's familiar angular hand and said, " cannot see you for many months, terrible trouble is occupying all my time and the abuse of this N. Y. magazine will continue for months."

The two letters showed with what speed Mrs. Eddy could still change her mind. The letter advising Glover not to come to Boston was dated December 25; the letter borne by Tomlinson was dated the 26th. Both to Senator Chandler and Glover, rather unfamiliar with Mrs. Eddy's varying state of mind, it appeared that at least one of the letters was certainly a forgery—another evidence of the work of the clique which surrounded Mrs. Eddy.

Tomlinson spent most of the day with Glover and Senator Chandler in the hotel. One of the commissions which he bore was that of persuading Glover to return the eighty-odd letters which Mrs. Eddy had written her son over a period of years. Mrs. Eddy's church officials were just beginning to be aware of some of her eccentric habits of mind, and the manner in which she had incorporated herself in much of her informal correspondence. They were further aware for the first time of the possibilities of the sort of publicity to which Mrs. Eddy was now being subjected. They had instructed Tomlinson to get Glover's letters at all cost. At one stage of the talk

he excitable Tomlinson actually went down on his knees in
leading.

Glover, like his mother, had a native and rather backwoods
anniness. He did not once intimate that Senator Chandler
ad the letters at that very moment in a safe-deposit box in
Vashington, ready to offer them in court as evidence of Mrs.
:ddy's strange delusions. He played with Tomlinson like a
vhiskery tom-cat with a mouse. Tomlinson finally went back
vithout the letters. Glover stayed on in Washington. Shortly
hereafter Tomlinson went secretly to South Dakota to call on
ilover's wife, to persuade her to turn over to him the letters
vhich—as only Glover and Chandler knew—were actually in
Vashington. He naturally failed in his effort.

On January 2, 1907, Glover took his daughter Mary—
nder Senator Chandler's instructions—and went up to Con-
ord unannounced.[1] He arrived around noon, sent a message
o Pleasant View that he would like to call on his mother at
wo o'clock, and then had lunch. At two o'clock he and his
aughter presented themselves promptly, after walking up the
ong drive because their driver told them that all hackmen in
:oncord had been forbidden to enter the Pleasant View
rounds. Mrs. Sargent opened the door immediately upon
heir ring; she said no word, but merely inclined her head
vhen they asked to see Mrs. Eddy, and motioned them
hrough the hall toward the library. She departed, and father
nd daughter sat there in a silence which weighted the atmos-
here of the house like a heavy fog. Suddenly the stillness
vas broken by a vibrant, burring sound that penetrated the
vhole mansion. Glover looked questioningly at his daughter.
t was the sound of the galvanic battery, coming from Mrs.
:ddy's room on the second floor at the front of the house.

It went on for some ten minutes. Silence again fell, and
vithin a little while Mrs. Sargent returned. "Mrs. Eddy," she
aid, "awaits you in her study."

They climbed the heavily padded stairs. Mrs. Eddy was in
er small study adjoining her bedroom, seated in an arm-

[1] For Glover's account of the interview which follows, vd. the New York *World*
March 2, 1907, together with a brief resumé in the issue of March 3, page 2.

chair with a window at her right and a table at her left hand
It was the same setting in which she had received her son on
his last visit; but on that occasion the table, the floor, the en
tire room was strewn with papers. To-day it was orderly, se
rene. Mrs. Eddy held two sheets of writing paper up close to
her eyes as her son and granddaughter came into the room
Her hands trembled and the papers quivered as she scanned
them. She did not notice the arrivals. Mrs. Sargent stepped
forward quickly.

"Mother!" she said sharply.

Mrs. Eddy paid not the slightest attention.

"*Mother!*" Mrs. Sargent repeated.

Mrs. Eddy suddenly laid the papers on the table, looked up
pushed herself up from her chair with her hands on the arms
George stepped forward. "I am so glad to see you, my son,
she said with a slight break in her voice. She kissed him, an
he kissed her through his flowing whiskers and beard. George
Glover at this period in his life had a shock of unkempt hair
and a beard that was reminiscent of nothing less than Mose
in the wilderness. Mary then pressed up and her grandmothe
embraced her. Mary had been told to watch for "stimulants
on the old lady's breath. Mrs. Eddy kissed her on the cheel
and Mary lost all opportunity for detective work. Probabl
her quest would have been vain even in more favoring circum
stances. Over four months had elapsed since the unfortunat
interviews with the reporters, and Mrs. Eddy's ability to re
cover her energies swiftly even when she seemed almost a
death's door had once again stood her in good stead. To-day sh
appeared no more feeble than might any old lady of eighty-si
years.

"I am so glad to see you both!" said Mrs. Eddy fondl
"Are you both well?" She looked searchingly at George. "
know you are well, but you look thinner than when I saw yo
before."

Mrs. Eddy let herself down in her chair, leaned back, trie
to smile at them. She was wearing the black silk which she s
often affected, with white ruching at the neck and cuffs. A
her throat was Mrs. Stetson's brooch. On her left hand sh
wore a marquise ring. Her face was pale, with the fine sk

tretched like parchment. Her thin white hair, instead of be-
ng parted as in former years, was now curled in little indi-
idual strands that stood out all over her head, so as partly to
bscure the pink flesh of the scalp that shone through beneath
hem.

"I'm very busy writing for the press," said Mrs. Eddy, as
f to make conversation. "The papers have abused your father
utrageously, George."

The papers had all been stating that Mrs. Eddy's first hus-
and was buried in the Potter's Field.

"George," said Mrs. Eddy, "if there was ever a tender, lov-
ng husband, your father was one!" Then she mentioned the
eparted Doctor Patterson. She said the papers were also
busing her about Patterson, although it was all his fault.
People say I am dead, and all such things, and that it is only
n impostor in my place. You know me. I am your mother,
;eorge, am I not?" Her voice broke slightly again, trailed off.
Ier mind reverted to Patterson. "I have an affidavit," she
aid irrelevantly. "It is from the White Mountain Hotel
eeper."

Mrs. Eddy did indeed have an affidavit, which she had se-
ured in 1902, when talk about her adventures as the wife of
)r. Patterson was first beginning to be rumored in Boston.
.. D. Rounsevel had at that time taken oath that in 1874,
·hen Patterson was boarding with him at Littleton, New
Iampshire, the doctor declared that his wife had been "a pure
nd Christian woman . . . that if he had done as he ought,
e might have had as pleasant and happy a home as one could
·ish for."

Mrs. Eddy's mind came back to her son and granddaughter.
he asked Mary how she was getting along in Christian Sci-
nce. Mary replied that she did not know anything about
hristian Science.

"Why!" exclaimed the old lady, "didn't Mrs. McMann
·ach you?"

"No."

"Why, Mary Glover, some one is lying. Didn't Mrs. Mc-
Iann of—of—your city teach you, Mary, and your family?"

"Mother," said George, "who told you that?"

"No one told me. I read it."

"You read it, mother? Why, no such lady lives in Lead."

"I will get the letter," said Mrs. Eddy, firmly. She pressed her bell that hung from the end of a cord. Strang came into the room. "Have you got that letter of Mrs. McMann's?" Mrs. Eddy asked,—"the letter in which she said she taught my son and his family?"

"Yes, I think I have it," Strang answered. "But it doesn't read that way."

"It does read that way."

"No, I don't think so."

"I know I have that letter. Bring it to me at once!"

Strang went out with a tolerant smile on his face. Mrs. Eddy leaned laboriously forward, opened a drawer in the desk, took out a bottle, extracted from the bottle a key, and then opened another drawer. It was full to the brim of unassorted papers, and she fished around in them looking for her letter. George Glover, seeing how her fingers fumbled and trembled with nervousness, took the drawer clear out of its tray and placed it on his knees, hoping to make her task the easier.

"I would not look for it now, mother," he said kindly. "You will find it some other time."

"Yes," said Mrs. Eddy, "I will. Things are always disappearing. My will disappeared."

Glover was incredulous.

"Yes," she said. "One day a warning from God told me I had better look for it. I went to get it and it was not there. I could have sworn that it was there. I asked Mr. Frye where it was, and he said, 'I know where it is,' and went to get it, and it was gone. . . . Before the night of the day that will was taken, I made another will. I have got it in a good strong place, in a what do you call it—in a good, strong place. General Streeter has got it in his—his safe."

Glover, remembering his old suspicions of Frye, made a remark about Calvin's possible connivance.

"Mr. Frye is as honest as I am honest," said Mrs. Eddy, with assurance, "and you know I am an honest woman. If Mr. Frye is not an honest man I am not worth a penny in the world. I know he is honest, for he has been tested by the bank."

It was like Mrs. Eddy to have Frye tested without his knowledge, just as she originally had him investigated before employing him.

Mrs. Eddy ruminated a moment upon some of the other attempts that had been made to wrong her. "Two men came to my house," she said, "and told me you wanted me to come out where you live at—at——"

"At Lead?"

"Yes. I told them that I couldn't. I wanted to very much. But you know I could not stand the journey."

"Mother, how do you think the will was stolen?"

"Why, by those men who wanted me to go out to your place! They wanted to get me away and murder me for the will!"

"Why, mother, they couldn't get into the house, could they?"

"Oh, yes. Some one has been in and robbed the house, stole some of the furniture. But I have it all back now. They came in through the window. But now I have the windows fixed so that no one can get in when the doors are fastened."

Mrs. Eddy, once her mind had turned to the dangers which beleaguered her, could hardly stop. She mentioned a large team of horses, valued at six thousand dollars, which a Southerner had sent her as a gift. But she would never drive behind them. The horses would have run away," she said, "and broken the carriage, and thrown me out."

"Then you think the horses were sent for the purpose of killing you?"

She laughed a cackling laugh, and winked at him knowingly. "You have it."

She asked Glover about the reason for his trip east. He said that he had come on business. She inquired if he and Mary had seen the church, then explained how she had given the ground for the erection of the first building. When it came time to build a larger structure, she said, she told her people they could not tear down the original church. They replied they would build an annex. "I told them very well," related

Mrs. Eddy. "They say the new church is beautiful, and th
dome is some feet higher than the Bunker Hill monument.
She herself had not seen it.

The new church building made her think of Lord Dun
more, whom she regarded as one of its most distinguishe
communicants. Lord Dunmore had made his last visit to he
on December 17, only about a fortnight before.

"Lord Dunmore called on me and we had a talk," said Mrs
Eddy proudly.

"When was he here?" queried Glover.

Mrs. Eddy considered a bit and was uncertain. "It wa
within a year," she said. "It was since your last visit to me.

Glover saw that she was wearied. He said that he and Mar
must go.

"Mr. Tomlinson and his sister will make it pleasant fc
you if you wish to stay there overnight," said Mrs. Edd
hopefully. "His sister is a beautiful child. I have not a loung
or a bed, not even a bed to make with a blanket on the floo:
All of our sleeping apartments are occupied. I would keep yo
if I could."

Glover tried to make it easy for her. "Mother, I have a
appointment with a man on business," he said. "Thank M
Tomlinson for me, and tell him I appreciate his kindness ver
much."

She urged him to come again. "Oh!" she exclaimed, "yo
don't know how I love you, and I love all your family." He
quick change of mood softened her infinitely. "You are m
son and only child!"

Glover looked at her searchingly.

"You don't do any writing?" he inquired. "You have othe
do it for you?"

"I am very busy," she said.

Son and granddaughter arose to go. She kissed them affe
tionately without getting up from the chair. She watched the
wistfully, even a little hungrily, as they left the room. As the
passed through the door she dropped her head wearily in
her hands.

Downstairs Mrs. Sargent met them. Glover asked her abo
the robber. Mrs. Sargent said that some silver spoons and t

eather rug had been taken—evidently the rug of eider-down
reasts that had once adorned the Mother's Room before that
hrine was closed.

"Nothing else?" inquired Glover. "No papers were taken?"

"Oh, no," said Mrs. Sargent, "no papers. They did not get
pstairs."

Glover and Mary returned promptly to Washington. Their
ontinued presence there, and their association with Senator
Chandler, which was now known to the Boston officials as a
esult of discreet supervision, at first puzzled and then thor-
ughly frightened Mrs. Eddy's Board of Directors. By this
ime these officials realized that Mrs. Eddy, if not wholly ir-
esponsible as *The World* and other papers had claimed, was
t least in a position where unfavorable publicity—indeed,
ny publicity—was to be avoided at all costs. Every effort was
1ade to persuade George Glover, through his mother, to re-
1rn west. Even a mild form of bribery at last was tried.
Ioney was telegraphed to the National Bank at Lead, where
1lover had his home, and a wire was sent to Glover person-
1ly over Mrs. Eddy's name:

DONT LOSE ANY TIME HURRY HOME AND GET THE
MONEY THAT I HAVE SENT TO LEAD CITY ENJOY IT

Unfortunately for the peace of mind both of Mrs. Eddy
nd her church officials, the whole matter was too far ad-
anced to have its course changed by any such tactics. Glover
imself, after his interview in which Mrs. Eddy had re-
ealed obvious lapses of memory, was quite honestly con-
inced that she was in a helpless mental condition. Like his
1other, he had the gift of believing anything which he wished
) believe at the moment. The man who once thought that
ennedy was tormenting her could now quite as easily feel
1at Frye was abusing her. By this time it was even ru-
ored that Frye had become an addition to Mrs. Eddy's list
f husbands—the sole foundation for this newspaper gossip
ing the revelations concerning the transfers of Mrs. Eddy's
roperties. George Glover was even willing to believe that he
1ust take up the cudgels for his mother against a new step-
ather. Thus it was that on March 1, 1907, in Mrs. Eddy's

eighty-sixth year, suit was brought in the Superior Cour
at Concord, to ask the appointment of a receiver for Mrs
Eddy's temporal affairs. It was entitled a "petition of Mar
Baker Glover Eddy, who sues by her next friends, Georg
W. Glover, Mary Baker Glover and George W. Baker." The
defendants included not only Calvin Frye and Lewis C
Strang, but most of the influential figures at the head of Mrs
Eddy's church. In this group were Alfred Farlow, Presider
and Chairman of the Christian Science Publication Commit
tee; Joseph Armstrong, Mrs. Eddy's Publisher; Irving C
Tomlinson, Chairman of the Board of Trustees of the Con
cord Church; Ira C. Knapp, Director of the Mother Church
William B. Johnson, Secretary of the Mother Church; Ste
phen A. Chase, Treasurer of the Mother Church; Edwar
A. Kimball, teacher and lecturer; and Hermann S. Hering
First Reader of the Concord Church.

The plaintiffs declared that Mary Baker G. Eddy was men
tally incapable of managing her business affairs and fortune
that they had abundant reason for belief that she was help
less in the hands of designing persons; and that the defend
ants named were believed to be the individuals seeking to take
advantage of her decrepitude.

The suit came as a thunderbolt to every one in Mrs. Eddy
world. No one had ever thought it likely that George Glove
could find ways, means, or even desire to bring a legal actio
against his mother. When the suit first was filed Mrs. Edd
was not informed of it, most probably because no one coul
think of anything adequate to say. It was not merely Mr
Eddy who was affected; her entire church was involved.
was emphasized that the suit was in no sense an attac
upon Christian Science, but was directed only at safeguard
ing Mrs. Eddy's personal welfare. But Christian Science wa
bound so intimately to Mrs. Eddy that she and her discover
were almost one; and anything that would discredit Mr
Eddy must almost inevitably discredit her well advertised rel
gion.

Although the suit was entirely unexpected, publicity a
tendant upon any sudden and sensational move by Glover ha

een feared ever since his long stay in Washington had be-
ome a matter for speculation among Mrs. Eddy's church
fficials. In consequence it was decided to forestall any pos-
ible move Glover might make by creating for him a trust
und large enough to assure his active co-operation in avoid-
nce of any undesirable publicity. Only a day before the
apers were served upon Frye and the other defendants, Mrs.
ddy offered by messenger to create a trust for $125,000 in
avor of her son and his children.

When informed of this offer Glover refused to consider it,
vith the assertion that he was more interested in rescuing his
"feeble-minded" mother from her captors than in his own
nancial advantage. The following day the suit was filed, and
ie offer was withdrawn. Thereupon General Streeter, Mrs.
ddy's legal counsel, determined on an even more decisive
iove. He advised Mrs. Eddy to create a trusteeship for her
ffairs, and to turn over to her chosen trustees all her assets
nd the management of them.

This was thereupon done, and on March 6, 1907, Mrs.
ddy signed the necessary deed of trust which gave owner-
iip of her property in trust to three individuals: Archibald
IcLellan, editor-in-chief of her publications and periodicals;
)siah E. Fernald, president of one of the local banks; and
Ienry M. Baker, a cousin and a lawyer, whom Mrs. Eddy
ice described as "a very good man and as honest as any law-
r can be." These gentlemen took over a total of $871,861.46[1]
i bonds, cash, and cash assets, in addition to Mrs. Eddy's
al estate holdings, her personal property, and her exten-
ve and valuable copyrights.

If General Streeter thought by this action to discourage
eorge Glover, his associate plaintiffs, his backers, and his
)unsel from proceeding with their action, the General seri-
isly miscalculated. The issue was now merely changed to
ie question of whether, on March 6, 1907, Mrs. Eddy was
f sound mind and competent to put her signature to a docu-

[1]There appears to have been an additional amount of cash, not provided for
the trust agreement, which was previously taken over by the trustees and
iich brought Mrs. Eddy's total holdings up to slightly over $900,000. Just
iy this other sum was handled in this way seems not to have been explained.

ment creating a trusteeship for her property. In this form
the case marched into the courts, with a new plaintiff added
to the list of relatives. E. J. Foster Eddy had by now come
forward to add his complaints to the voluminous documents
already entered.

Mrs. Eddy herself, presumably under her counsel's direction, wrote a letter in her own hand to Judge Robert N. Cham-
berlin of the Superior Court under date of May 18, protesting her complete competence and sanity. She said:

RESPECTED SIR:—It is over forty years that I have attended personally to my secular affairs, to my income, investments, deposits, expenditures, and to my employees. I have personally selected all my investments, except in one or two instances, and have paid for the same.

The increasing demands upon my time, labors, and thought, and
yearning for more peace and to have my property and affairs carefully
taken care of for the persons and purposes I have designated by my last
will, influenced me to select a Board of Trustees to take charge of my
property. . . .

I selected said Trustees because I had implicit confidence in each one
of them as to honesty and business capacity. No person influenced me
to make this decision. . . .

This suit was brought without my knowledge and is being carried on
contrary to my wishes. I feel that it is not for my benefit in any way
but for my injury, and I know that it was not needed to protect my
person or property. The present proceedings test my trust in divine
Love. My personal reputation is assailed and some of my students and
trusted personal friends are cruelly, unjustly, and wrongfully accused. . . .

The whole affair dragged along in the courts until August,
due largely to the illness of the Judge, and not to the desire of
Mrs. Eddy's counsel to play for time. The long-drawn-out
publicity was driving poor Mrs. Eddy, as well as her officials,
almost frantic. Even in such eminent columns as those of the
New York *Times* the Eddy logic and doctrines were receiving thorough dissection, in the search for any evidence that
might bolster up the charge of an incompetent brain. Thus
The Times could say with unusual wittiness for its sober
pages:

Mrs. Eddy writes, "There is no pain in Truth and no Truth in pain;
thus we prove the same by the rule of inversion." And this notwith-

anding the fact that the "rule of inversion" is anything but infallible,
or while all elephants are quadrupeds, all quadrupeds are not elephants.[1]

The suit to test Mrs. Eddy's sanity, as it now was known,
ad come to be front-page news for papers all over the United
tates, despite the frantic efforts of Mrs. Eddy's publicity
epartment to encourage editors to speak softly. With the
ew York *World* bravely breaking out every day with some
resh angle of the case, the rest of the press could hardly ig-
ore it. None of them, it is true, could compete with *The
World,* for only *The World* had any of that golden material
alled "inside information." And even *The World* was often
eeling in the dark for guidelines as it sought to put together
ome of its astonishing facts.

So it happened that Mrs. Eddy, after creating for herself a
areer that had been crowned with honor, fame, and wealth
uch as few women have ever achieved, was brought to the
ar of justice to demonstrate that she was not a mental incom-
etent.

For a moment fear and horror almost submerged her. She
rote to Augusta Stetson only a day after she signed the trust
greement, evidently replying to a query from Augusta about
e truth of gossip which reported Mrs. Eddy's sharp remarks
ncerning her star student:

The leading students must not allow this attempt of the enemy to
ercome them, and *you* yield to it! The lies that are told about me, or
at I say of you, are not worth your notice or mine.[2]

Momentarily, in this hour of darkness, Mrs. Eddy must
ave regretted many things, even the harsh and biting things
e had said about Augusta Stetson. She needed unfaltering
yalty among her followers more than she had ever needed it
her life.

The correct quotation is as follows: "The divine metaphysics of Christian
ence, like the method in mathematics, proves the rule by inversion. For ex-
ple: There is no pain in Truth, and no truth in pain; no nerve in Mind,
d no mind in nerve; no matter in Mind, and no mind in matter; no matter
Life, and no life in matter; no matter in good, and no good in matter." The
rying capitalization is Mrs. Eddy's. Vd. *Science and Health,* page 113.
Letter dated March 7, 1907. Vd. Stetson, *Sermons and other Writings,* page 191.

XXIX

Senator Chandler's opening argument before the augus
court that was to decide Mrs. Eddy's competency was bui
around a detailed analysis of the phases of paranoia wit
which she was held to be afflicted. He announced his intentio
of presenting two forms of evidence: first, that she pa
pably suffered from delusions; second, that this mental stat
rendered her incompetent to manage her business affairs.

The Senator was in consequence dealing with one of th
finest distinctions in law—the hair-line distinction betwee
medical and legal insanity. It is a question by which lawyei
and courts both are often perplexed—the problem of how fa
a citizen's legal responsibility is affected by an observed path
logical condition.

Senator Chandler found his first evidence in the state of
mind that was revealed in the pages of *Science and Healt.*

"Mrs. Eddy's book," said he, "alone is proof that she
suffering from the following systematized delusions and d
mentia:

"The first one is the delusion—fundamental, widesprea
and deep-rooted—of the non-existence and non-reality of th
physical universe, organic and inorganic. All her delusions a
built upon this fundamental delusion, and they are system
tized so that they are a part of her whole being. They a
built upon and about a single insane delusion as to the no
existence of the reality of the physical universe."

This is a most important commentary on Mrs. Eddy's ph
losophy. But the problem involved here is not the sort whi
lends itself easily to the incisive analysis of the purely leg
mind. It is much too large for any court room. In the end,
can be resolved only in the human laboratory.

The philosopher, even the amateur philosopher, must o
serve that the whole structure of Mrs. Eddy's philosoph
theories was originally based upon a logically false premis

434

he pathologist and psychiatrist would in turn be inclined to
eny her sanity just to the extent that this original false
remise had become an accepted guide to all action in her life.
ll men make errors in logic; but no sane men make such
rrors consistently and without discovering them. In other
ords, just to the extent to which Mrs. Eddy had allowed
ne delusion to color all other motivation in her mental proc-
sses without becoming aware of her false start, to that de-
ree the pathologist would judge her insane according to the
sual human norms.

The most potent argument for her relative sanity is the fact
1at her subsequent actions were so often inconsistent with
1e premises she took for her philosophic dissertations. The
0mpletely insane mind—the mind so wrapped in delusion
1at it is unaware of any external reality whatever—is usu-
1ly utterly consistent within itself. Once having accepted one
1lse premise, it thereafter follows that premise out to a com-
etely logical conclusion. The man who becomes convinced,
0r instance, that he is Napoleon, will act out the entire part
f Napoleon with complete logic and consummate perfection.
1is mind differs from the normal mind only in its inability
1 judge the validity of the first premise which motivates his
1bsequent conduct. The normal and responsible mind is con-
antly engaged in rechecking, comparing, and revising its
remises during all of its active existence. This is the func-
0n of the intellect, which is rational, as opposed to the sub-
1nscious, which is emotional.

The fact that Mrs. Eddy acted so frequently without ref-
rence to the philosophic theories in which she found emo-
0nal consolation may be regarded as reliable evidence that
r rational processes were not wholly divorced from the nor-
al human standard. Whatever the periods of delusion to
hich she was a prey, periods in which she fled abjectly
om the world of reality which she so abhorred, there were
1merous connective periods in which she proceeded without
1y reference whatever to the philosophic tenets which she
lieved and sought to promulgate.

Had she actually endeavored in all her conduct to follow

to a logical conclusion some of the irrational tenets in whic
she took emotional refuge, her story would indeed have con
to a swift and early end. Unwashed, unfed, unhoused, ur
clothed, she would so utterly have spurned all material ac
juncts to living that her mundane existence would have bee
brought promptly and decisively to a very natural close.

This, of course, did not happen. Mrs. Eddy seldom allowe
her abstract theories to conflict with her concrete necessitie
Her emotions undoubtedly and very naturally colored her ir
tellect; they did not usually rule it so completely as to inval
date all of its normal processes.

Pathologically there could have been no question regar
ing her pitiable emotional condition, which was all predicate
upon fear. And yet, even in their severest symptoms, Mr
Eddy's delusions were typical rather than otherwise. Psychi
trists find these symptoms duplicated time and again in ir
numerable cases that come under their observation. There a
indeed few individuals, however near they seem to approac
that vague standard known as normal, who do not show son
evidence of maladjustment to their environment. Such sym
toms do not necessarily or usually render the individual su
ficiently irrational to be incompetent; oftentimes the ma
adjustment acts rather as a tremendous stimulus to admirat
achievement. Paranoia, which is delusion born of maladjus
ment, is never a matter of mere symptoms; it is inevitably
question of degree.

Abstruse considerations of this character, however gre
their importance in reaching a balanced estimate of Mrs. Edc
as an actor on the human stage, had only one application
judging her competency as the executor of a trust deed. Th
one matter which the Superior Court of New Hampshire w
called upon to decide was this: had Mrs. Eddy's belie
affected her rational processes in any such manner as to e
danger the contingent rights of relatives in her estate?

It was the contention of Senator Chandler that Mrs. Eddy
theories regarding the material world and her relation to
were delusions so monstrous as to render questionable ev
her competency to sign a deed of trust.

"The world," said Mr. Chandler in presenting his analysis, s known to astronomers, to geologists, to physicians, chem- ....s, naturalists, and to the lawmakers of the country. Mrs. ...dy, controlled by her delusion, believes that the world is ...ither real nor existent. . . .

"From this one fundamental delusion of Mrs. Eddy's, I ...ve built up six or seven other delusions which I am about ... state.

"The second delusion is that of the supernatural character ...the Science she calls her own and of the supernatural man- ...r in which it was discovered by her. She believes as an in- ...ne delusion that she was miraculously and supernaturally ...ected by Almighty God to receive divine revelations di- ...tly from God, to herself alone, of the greatest gift ever ...en to the world—a new and supernatural mode of curing ...ease.

"Third, she has been possessed all these years of a delusion ...to the cause of all the diseases of mankind; a delusion as to ... cure of disease; a delusion as to the prevention of disease. ...d this insane systematized delusion of Mrs. Eddy comprises ...d includes a complete system as to the mode by which alone ...ease is cured and as to the only way by which disease can ...cured or prevented. . . .

"Fourth—the delusion of the relation of the Science she ...ls her own to philosophy and Christianity. Mrs. Eddy has ...ieved all these years that her revelations as to the cause of ... physical universe, including man, have also the important ...ysical mission of supplanting all present systems of phi- ...ophy and religion and that henceforth and hereafter the ...ught and progress of the universe is to be developed only ...ough the Science that she calls hers.

"Fifth—the delusion as to the existence of animal magnet- ... or malicious animal magnetism. This insane systematized ...usion possessed by her is one that involves the idea of per- ...ution and diabolism. These are the names which she gives ...it: 'Electricity of Mortal Mind,'—'The Red Dragon,'— ...e Trail of the Fiend,'—'The Sting of the Serpent.' And ... delusion envelops and embraces a large portion of her

mental life. It is intimately related to her personal comfo
and business ability.

"Red dragon, fear, inflammation, sensuality, horror,—a
animal magnetism. Why, she says the mild forms of anim
magnetism are disappearing and its aggressive features a
coming to the front. 'The looms of crime hidden in the dar
recesses of mortal thought are every hour weaving webs mo
complicated and subtle.'[1] . . .

"Sixth—the delusion as to the operation of alleged m
licious animal magnetism in the causing and curing of di
ease. It will appear that she believes malicious animal ma
netism is capable of producing all manner of evil; of poisonir
mankind; of producing death itself. . . .

"The evidence is going to be overwhelming from her pu
lished works; letters signed by her, and from all testimor
that these are the delusions in which this woman has lived
these years past and beyond all question they have reach
the stage of senile dementia.

"These delusions of hers include two well-known systen
tized delusions—the delusion of grandeur and the delusion
persecution. In a study I am now making with the aid of
scientific friend, I find these are the most common delusio
namely, the delusions of grandeur and greatness, and the c
lusion that the person who is being investigated is being p
secuted.

"This dementia of Mrs. Eddy's is continued and progr
sive. Take the delusion of grandeur. In 1890 she said, 'I a
heard and obeyed by 300,000 people at this stage, and m
of the distinguished newspapers ask me to write on the m
important subjects. Lords and ladies, earls, princes, marqui
and marchionesses from abroad, write me in the most fam
iar manner. Hoke Smith declares that I am the most illustric
woman on the continent. These are his exact words. C
Senators and Members of Congress call on me for counsel

"This she said to one of her students: 'Obey. When I

---

[1] Quoted from *Science and Health*, page 102. Mrs. Eddy frequently repea
herself—thus part of the same quotation appears in her *Message to the M*
Church for 1901, pages 20-21.

ise, obey strictly. Never question it, because I am God's
mouthpiece, and God demands that you obey his commands
without understanding why.'

"This case, very briefly stated, is the unfortunate case of
Mrs. Eddy which we shall be obliged to submit to you during the proof. These proofs will show amazing things of malicious animal magnetism. All writings of Mrs. Eddy are full
of it. Her life has been surrounded by it. She lives in an atmosphere of it, going back many years and coming down to
April 27 of the present year.

"Now that belief of malicious animal magnetism, as Your
Honors will see, is a horrible doctrine, if it is a doctrine. It
is a horrible belief, if it is a belief—that one person, or half
a dozen persons, mal-practitioners, sons of the devil, if they
are fit to do so, can by fixing their minds on people they hate
produce any disease to the objects of their hatred, which they
desire. They can produce poison in the veins. They can stop
a man's being, and all done without the possibility of detec-
tion because it is silent, mental influence exerted by these
workers.

"On the other hand, this system of Mrs. Eddy's which has
formed so vast a part of her life undertakes to guard against
this, the evil effects of malicious animal magnetism.

"When it is believed by Mrs. Eddy that enemies, her enemies, enemies of Christian Science, are working this malicious
influence, her friends, the Scientists, get a counter-influence
going to counteract and destroy the influence of the mal-prac-
tioners." . . .

Much of the substance of Senator Chandler's speech, however interesting as analysis, was of no avail as argument, so
far as the legal proceedings were concerned. For the court
ruled that proof of Mrs. Eddy's alleged delusions should not
be presented from years back of 1890. In this, Mrs. Eddy's
counsel won an important point, in line with their contention
that only one question was before the court—Mrs. Eddy's
state of mind on March 6, 1907, when the deed of trust was
signed. For this important ruling of the court meant that
Christian Science itself, and all its literature, would not have

to stand trial in a sanity test. The literature practically a
antedated 1890 in origin. The defense problem was therefor
greatly simplified. For undoubtedly it would have been diffi
cult and unpleasant to attempt public justification of some o
Mrs. Eddy's strange dissertations to critical and unemotiona
intellects. No one in the employ of Mrs. Eddy's prosperou
church was willing to see the sensational aspects of her be
liefs headlined constantly by the clever reporters of the me
ropolitan journals. Christian Science, among other things, ha
become a big business institution, and public attacks on th
character of its merchandise were doing a great deal of harn

It was therefore far preferable—if a choice of evils ha
to be made—to defend Mrs. Eddy singly than to defend he
in connection with her religious and philosophical literatur
Fortunately for the peace of mind of Mrs. Eddy's counse
she was in much better health than during the preceding yea
when interviewed by newspaper reporters; she had recupe
ated some of her strength, and though partly paralyzed, w
well able to conduct a coherent and sustained conversatio
It therefore seemed that the easiest and most obvious way o
would be to produce the old lady for a personal examinatio
This was exactly what Senator Chandler and his clients d
sired, was what the New York *World* had wished to brin
about all along.

Mrs. Eddy's counsel, however, were not sure that she cou
withstand the cold scrutiny of alienists; for they themselv
recognized only too well the narrow demarcation betwee
medical and legal insanity, and they were not at all sure wh
the critical judgment of alienists might conclude. Thus, wh
Judge Robert N. Chamberlain of the Superior Court a
nounced that he would appoint three Masters to determi
the mooted question of Mrs. Eddy's competency, her couns
argued hotly against the inclusion of alienists in the grou
They lost their point, however, and when the three Maste
were named, one of the most noted alienists in Boston, I
George E. Jelly, was appointed as one of the three, togeth
with Judge Edgar Aldrich of the U. S. District Court a
Hosea W. Parker of Claremont. The sole business of th

ommission was to decide whether or not Mrs. Eddy was
gally competent during the month of March, 1907, when
ɪe signed the trust agreement alienating her property from
er control.

It was made plain that Mrs. Eddy's religion would be in-
ɔlved in the inquiry only as it affected one single point. Judge
ldrich said:

Now if Mrs. Eddy is in a condition of health and strength to submit
an examination upon these questions, it [the Commission] would be
ɪmpetent to go into that [her religion] not because it is a delusion in
spect to religion, not because a large number of people think it is not
delusion, not because others think it is, not because it relates to Chris-
ɪn Science—but because it shows a frame of mind which might make
possible that the delusion would operate unfavorably and prejudi-
ɪlly to the contingent rights of relatives.

Thus it was that the three Masters journeyed to Pleasant
iew, accompanied by Senator Chandler, senior counsel for
ɪe "Next Friends"; Frank S. Streeter, counsel for Mrs.
ddy; and the court stenographer. George Glover had wished
• be present, but was not permitted to accompany the in-
ɪisitors. The examination at her home was arranged for by
ɪe Court in deference to Mrs. Eddy's advanced age and in-
ɪlidism.

Mrs. Eddy had been prepared to receive them in the library,
here the heavy curtains were half-drawn so that the room
as almost in twilight. Even in the shadows, however, her
ɪce was emaciated, her eyes hollow, her hands thin and
ɪavily veined. Feeble, but nerved for the ordeal with every
ɪuscle in her body tense, she stood to receive her visitors,
ɪen lowered herself haltingly into her armchair. She seemed
ɪmost to be acting a well-learned part—a voice high-pitched
ɪd unmodulated, her answers given for long minutes without
falter, only the nervous flutter of her eyes and fingers occa-
ɔnally betraying her anxiety.

It was almost an unprecedented situation in the annals of
ɪe great. It was even a situation which might well have jus-
ied in this strange old woman burning indignation and dis-
ɪin. She, who had built for herself a kingdom in which her

rule was absolute, had now in her declining years actually t
submit to the indignity of demonstrating that she was able t
rule.

All her life she had lived in humiliation—as a girl when sh
was a weakling in her family; in her middle years as she wan
dered from house to house with only Quimby's idea to pa
her way; in her later success as she fought off accusation tha
she had stolen from Quimby instead of creating that whic
was her own. And she had battled against each humiliatic
successfully, somehow always finding from it an escape. An
now she sat trembling in the shadows of her library, trappe
by humiliation in her old age.

It was a tragic scene—no tragedy that ever had come
Mary Baker Eddy compared to this. Around her, defendin
her, were only paid hirelings. Somewhere—it did not matte
—was the son who had never seemed a son. It was he, the
told her, who was bringing this final and climactic mortific
tion into her long career. . . .

She was an old woman now, almost ready to die. And sh
did not have a single friend in the world. "I am as alone as
solitary star." . . .

As she now peered uncertainly around the room that w
filled with men whose names she did not remember, her ey
became a little frightened. Her gaze roved questioningly ov
the grave faces that confronted her. Her eyes lost their focu
She moistened her lips. . . .

A voice broke in upon her consciousness.

"Well," said Judge Aldrich pleasantly, "the gentlem
present want to ask you some questions."

Mrs. Eddy craned forward slightly, clutching her la
shawl with palsied hands. "And I beg pardon? My only dif
culty is a slight deafness. I can see to read common pica, b
I can't hear distinctly without some difficulty."

"If you feel fatigued," said the Judge, raising his kind, lo
pitched voice, "we want to have you speak of it and let
know."

"Thank you," replied Mrs. Eddy eagerly, in her sing-so
soprano—her voice had lost the sonority of its earlier yea

I can work hours at my work, day and night, without fatigue,
hen it is in this line of thought; but when I go to worldliness
am sometimes fatigued by it—and yet these things are indis-
nsable and I regard them as sacred."

Judge Aldrich paused a moment, collecting his train of
ought. "Did you acquire all this property here, at the out-
t, or did you acquire it gradually?"

"I purchased it at the outset," said Mrs. Eddy. "And I sug-
sted every construction and arrangement of my grounds
roughout and I still attend to it," she added with quick and
vious pride.

"How many acres have you?"

Mrs. Eddy thought a moment. "I don' know the number
acres."

"Well," said the Judge, "that is something women don't
ways carry in their minds."

The old lady, ruminating, had suddenly thought of one of
r favorite topics. She pointed out the window. "This little
nd was made for me by my friends. It is an artificial pond.
have a boat down there in the boat house."

"Do you raise fruit here on the place?" queried Mr. Par-
r. "I can see fruit trees."

"Yes, sir," she replied deferentially.

"Oh, you do?"

"—And there were no trees except Normandie pines when
came here. The rest of the trees I planted and when I sug-
sted a large tree be planted they laughed at me and I said,
ry it and see if it will succeed.' Every one of these trees
ound here was planted by myself—that is, not by myself,
t by my direction."

"Did you come directly from Boston here?" continued Mr.
arker.

"I did,"—briefly.

"To this very place here?"

"Yes, sir. They laughed at me for taking this place, and I
id, 'You will see it will be pretty, pretty soon.' The old lady
uckled slightly over her recollection.

"Some one was telling me," said Judge Aldrich, "that you

had given to the public streets—the improvements of stree
in Concord. Is that so?"

"I have,"—proudly—"$10,000 at one time."

"Where was that expended?"

"It has been expended on this street and other streets-
Main Street and other streets," she repeated, with slight u
certainty.

"Was that done at the suggestion of any one, or was
your own idea?"

She ruminated, her veined hands quivering in her lap. "
can't decide strictly where it was expended," she said, loo
ing up. "I know it was on the streets."

"The original idea, the idea of giving money to Conco
for the streets, was it your idea or suggested by some one?'

"It was mine. They consulted me with regard to it. My st
dents contributed toward it also and left the decision to me
There was a self-satisfied note in Mrs. Eddy's voice.

"Now about your investments," said the Judge with a ge
tle deliberation. "We will touch on these just a little to-da
Not much. About your investments—you have some incon
I suppose, now?"

The old lady smiled archly. When she spoke there was
hint of caution in her voice. "Some income? Yes, my life i
surance is coming due pretty soon, and I want to make a go
use of it."

"What do you consider good use of it? What do you co
sider good investments?"

"I don't put it into life insurance," she replied with sere
and contradictory satisfaction. "Never. God insures my life

"How would you invest money?" . . .

She carefully smoothed out her dress, her eyes downc
for a moment as she considered her words. She recognized
crucial question. When she looked up there was a watch
gleam in her eyes.

"Well, I should invest it in the hands, at my age, of Tr
tees, that I could vouch for from my own knowledge. A
why? Because, when I found my church was gaining ov
40,000 members and the field demanding me all over t

world, I could not carry on the letters, make answers to the inquiries that were made of me, then I said, 'Which shall I do? Carry on the business that belongs to property, or shall I serve God?' And I said—and it came to me from the Bible—'Choose ye this day whom ye will serve. Ye cannot serve God and Mammon.' Then I chose and said, 'So help me God,' and I launched out, and I gave my property—I gave nine hundred thirteen thousand dollars to the trusteeship for the benefit of my son, but . . . no, nine hundred and thirteen thousand dollars to the trusteeship for myself." She caught her words and glanced warily up at the men facing her. "For my son I gave one hundred and twenty-five thousand dollars into trusteeship for himself and family."

Judge Aldrich turned to her gravely. "Where did that idea of putting your property into the hands of trustees originate—with yourself, or somebody else?"

Mrs. Eddy's fluttering hands came to repose with a slight air of satisfaction. "Utterly with myself. It came to me in an hour, in this room, and I think the first one that I named it to was Laura Sargent, and I said to her: 'Don't speak of it; but I feel impressed that it is my duty.'" Her voice quoted herself with a sibillant impressiveness.

"When was that?"

"That was in February, 1907." She paused, ruminated. "I think it was May . . . February . . . I don't mean May. I mean February, 1907." She nodded her head positively.

"You mean last winter?"

She craned her neck. "How?"

Judge Aldrich reconsidered his approach. "Now this is all interesting and useful, but I still have not quite made myself understood. For instance, without regard to your Trusteeship, now if you had $100,000 to invest to-day—and we will lay aside for the purposes of this question the matter of Trusteeship—what kind of investments would you consider sound? Municipal bonds, or government bonds, or bank stocks, or what?"

"I prefer government bonds," she said with the conviction of a connoisseur. "I have invested largely in government bonds,—and I prefer bonds to stocks. I haven't entered into stocks."

"Why?"

"Because I didn't think it was safe for me. I didn't want the trouble of it, that was all. I always selected my own investments."

"How do you select them now?"

Archly:—"I leave them to my trustees."

"Before that?"

"I will tell you." She adjusted herself in her chair as in settling down for a real confidence. "I had books that gave definitely the population of the states and their money values and I consult these, and when I see they are large enough in population and valuation to warrant an investment, I make it.

The Judge was intrigued. "Well, now, upon what philosophy do you base your calculation upon population?"

"Upon population?" The phrasing of this question puzzled her.

"Upon population—that is, why do you take population as the standard?"

She was a little impatient with his ignorance. "Because think they can sustain their debts, of course, and pay them—can't they?"

Dr. Jelly, who had sat silent during the entire talk, now turned to her with a question along a different line.

"Mrs. Eddy, are you willing to tell us something about the development of your special religion? Are you willing to tell us about that? How the matter came about and how it has existed and developed? It would be interesting to us to know you are willing to tell us about your so-called Christian Science." Dr. Jelly was too much the scientist to resist the use of that *so-called*. "Tell us something about the development of that. Are you willing to do that?"

The old lady brightened up immediately, a new eagerness in her shadowy eyes. "If you will sit nearer, I can tell you more distinctly."

They all shoved their chairs forward a little, and Mrs. Eddy surveyed them with a pleased interest. Dr. Jelly repeated his query.

"What I ask, Mrs. Eddy, is if you are willing to tell us something of the development of your so-called Christian Science."

"I would *love* to do it."

"Tell us as fully as you please. I think we would all like to hear it. . . ."

She started at once, her soprano voice pitched without inflection, as if reciting an oft-conned piece. "I was an invalid born in belief. I was always having doctors——"

"When you say 'born in belief,' " interposed the doctor, "I perhaps do not understand what you mean."

The old lady looked at him severely and with reproof. "I mean born according to human nature—born not of God, but of the flesh. That is what I mean. I was an invalid from my birth."

"Can you tell us something about the way in which you were an invalid, if you can recollect it?"

"No . . ."—uncertainly—"I cannot recollect it. I was weak and a dyspeptic."

"I asked you to tell me something about the development of Christian Science. Will you go on, if you please?"

She was a little impatient with him. "I would gladly do it, as I said."

"Go on, if you will," he urged.

"My father employed doctors of the highest character. And they were estimable men. Dr. Renton was one, and he said, and the others said: 'Don't doctor your child: she has not too much brain for her body. Keep her out of doors, keep her in exercise and keep her away from school all you can, and don't give her much medicine' . . ." She paused to explain to a younger and ignorant generation: "—Then it was all allopathy, you know."

"Can you tell about how long ago that was, please?"

"No . . . I should say I was eighteen years old—along here—about there—and it came to me . . . no, I wasn't so old as that, I think . . . and it came to me through Dr. Merrill that he was a homœopath, and I had never heard of that before. It was a new subject in New Hampshire, and Father says, 'Well, I thought he was a fine fellow, but he must have

gone mad to have taken up homœopathy.' . . . Well, tha
was the general idea of things, and when he came to Concor
people thought that of him generally, I think, but he healed th
cases that the other M.D.'s did not and my father employec
him, and I got well under his treatment. . . . But—yot
asked me to tell my footsteps?"

"I did."

"I studied homœopathy." Her voice trailed off, and she
moistened her lips, and looked at the inquisitors before her a
little piteously. "May I lean back in my chair?"

"Yes—and if you get tired, say so."

She settled herself more easefully and resumed the rôle tha
was so difficult before these grave, solemn men. "Then I said
'I will study homœopthy.' I did. I was delighted with it.
took a case that doctors up there considered hopeless and
cured the case and she was like a barrel in the bed, full o
water and I cured her right up——"

Now that the flood-tide of her recollections was unloosec
she went on garrulously, endlessly—a grandmotherly and pa
thetic old lady who had at last found an appreciative audienc
for the sort of things she liked to talk about. Stocks, bonds
investments, unimportant details about making roads an
trusts, held no interest for her. It was much more fascinatin
to dwell on the long and romantic past, the years of struggle
the climb from obscurity, the rebuffs by cruel enemies . .
and now look at her, Mary Baker Eddy, enthroned in her ol
age so that even her smallest recollection was of great impor
tance to these eminent Masters appointed by the Suprem
Court. . . .

She never took her eyes off her inquisitors, those shinin
eyes in her withered face. Back and forth her hands flutterec
now touching the diamond ornament at her throat, now pull
ing at her black shawl, now smoothing at her dress or twinin
in her lap. Her droning voice never wavered. It was wit
difficulty that the Masters brought her to an end; thanked he
formally for receiving them; paused to hear her play th
graphophone which she displayed with childish delight as he
"artificial voice"; ushered themselves out of the penumbrou
room.

Hardly were they in the hall when they heard the sharp langor of a bell echo through the house. In an instant Frye came hurrying after them, to say that Mrs. Eddy had not nished her statement, and wished to complete it. Back to the ibrary the eminent visitors hurried. Mrs. Eddy sat in the rmchair where they had left her, upright and rigid, excitenent in her pale face. "I felt I did not answer you fully," she old them with a new forcefulness in her voice. "I dropped ay subject before I concluded it with regard to the footsteps ɔ Christian Science."

Judge Aldrich told her that he had not really wished to ush this line of inquiry further, that he not only desired not ɔ weary her but, most important, did not desire to have his uestions appear to be an attack on her doctrines.

Mrs. Eddy insisted that she would deem it a favor to be llowed to explain these mysteries.

"When I came to the point that it was mind that did the ealing," she said, "I wanted to know what mind that was. Vas it the mind that was in Christ Jesus? Or was it the human mind and human will? Then I went to an investigation f spiritualism, mesmerism, and hypnotism, to see if I could nd out and I didn't find good there; therefore I turned to ɔd in prayer and said: 'Just guide me, guide me to that mind hich is in Christ,' and I took the Bible and opened it at the ords: 'Now go write it in a book.' I can show you where it is ı the Bible."

She spoke almost without pause, just as if she were repeatng one of the well-learned talks that she had used for so any years in her classroom.

"I then commenced writing my consciousness of what I had ⅰen and I found that human will was the cause of disease inⅰead of its cure; that hypnotism and mesmerism as human ɔnceits did not heal; they were the origin of disease instead f its cure; and that the Divine Mind was the healer. And ıen I found it through the Scripture, 'He healed all our disⅰses.'—'Go into the field, preach the Gospel, heal the sick,' nd I felt there was my line of labor and that God did the ealing and that I could no more heal a person through morıl mind or will-power than I could heal them by cutting off their hands, and I could not hurt them by it, for I don't know how to use will power to hurt the sick;—I don't know how to do it. . . ."

Her voice broke for a moment, memories crowding in on the old accusations that she had sought with incantations to kill Spofford and Kennedy and Arens. . . .

"When they began to talk mesmerism first I began to doubt it, and I said to a facetious student, 'Hanover Smith, you go into the other room and see if I can sit down and tell lies enough to make you suffer.' He went into the other room and I commenced what they said they said to make folks sick, and I did my best talking it and he came in and I said, 'Hanover do you feel *mean?*' And he said, 'I never felt better in my life than I do now. I feel better than when I went in. I feel rested.' "

"A Christian Scientist," she went on in her thin treble "can no more make a person sick than they can be a sinner and be a Christian Scientist. They can no more make them suffer or injure them in any way; they have not the power to do it. All the power that they have comes from on High. We have no other power and no faith in any other power. Now I have finished. I thank you for your kindness and attention very much."

The old lady made a motion of dismissal with her hand graciously, imperiously, and leaned back in her chair with contentment on her face, utterly weary with excitement, but satisfied. She had made her defense, had been given an opportunity wholly to confound those old accusations of enemies who had tried to paint her a sorceress of evil.

She rested wanly against her cushions, a lonely old woman eager for understanding. And the Masters went back to ponder the evidence, and consider what their decision would be.

XXX

The question of Mrs. Eddy's legal competency was never allowed to reach adjudication. Before the end of August, Senator Chandler withdrew his suit, and the whole matter was eventually compromised.

But no one who heard Mrs. Eddy talk to the distinguished Masters could have believed her any less competent to manage her business affairs than any other old lady of her years, or that, in the words of Judge Aldrich, any of her possible delusions "would operate unfavorably and prejudicially to the contingent rights of relatives." There can be small doubt that to the end of her days Mrs. Eddy was well able not merely to garner money, but also to keep it after she got it. Dr. Allen McLane Hamilton, an alienist employed by her own counsel, said in a formal statement, "I am firmly of the opinion that she is competent to take care of herself and that she is not coerced in any way. In fact it would appear as if she takes the initiative upon all occasions."

On the other hand, posterity is not greatly concerned with the small issue of how competently Mrs. Eddy directed her business affairs during her declining years. Rather must its interest be centred on a question of much broader implication: the manner in which her complex mind was related to the ordinary human norms.

In the last analysis, posterity can be the only final judge regarding the degree of Mrs. Eddy's sanity. And in its deliberations many considerations must be involved. It is easy to conclude that a man is sane as long as he accepts the common standards of the community in which he moves; and just as easy to pronounce him insane as soon as he varies widely either from the motivations or conclusions which impel his neighbors. Yet the outstanding difference between the genius and the madman is often only the fact that the genius eventually makes his own unique logic accepted by his fellow men,

while the madman never convinces his neighbors of the real
ity of the world as he himself views it.

Thus many a genius has been regarded as a lunatic unti
men came gradually to share in some of his convictions. And
conversely, history presents the record of many lunatics who
temporarily achieved the status of a genius, merely becaus
they were able for a brief time to cast the spell of their delu
sion over some of their fellows.

It must be obvious, at least, that sanity is merely a rela
tive state. A man in the midst of society might be adjudge
hopelessly insane; yet, if he is placed alone on a desert island
and is able there to fend for himself and carve out of his nat
ural environment the needs of his human existence, he ha
every right to regard himself as completely rational. He i
setting his own norms in a world of his own creation. Th
only standard by which he may be judged is his ability t
continue animal existence in his environment, either by ad
justing his needs to the limitations of the environment or els
by adjusting the environment to his needs.

This is to an extraordinary degree a parallel of the re
markable career of Mrs. Eddy. She created for herself
unique universe, in which she herself established all standard
She created it after finding herself in complete conflict wit
the world in which her fellows moved by norms that wer
utterly at variance with her own nature. In the new worl
which she moulded, after having battled unsuccessfully wit
the old one for more than half her life, she did not succeed i
eliminating conflict. But she at least designed and built a li
tle enclosure of her own, in which she satisfied a fair po
tion of her desires, in which she alone made the measures, i
which she alone was arbiter. And she lived and moved in th
environment of her own design with perhaps as much succe
as other beings generally demonstrate in adjusting themselv
to the other world which the majority of mankind accepts
its natural habitat.

Had Mrs. Eddy taken ship from her own isolated islar
and returned to the world known to the majority of men, sl
might possibly have been classed as a paranoiac. But Mr

Eddy never returned. She lived and moved and reigned in isolated state, building herself an empire and eventually attracting, from among passers-by, visitors who stopped off and remained to be ruled. Thus it was that she not only created her universe but populated it. She herself chose the inhabitants. None of those who passed her port was allowed to stop off unless he, too, had a cast of mind that could subscribe to the norms Mrs. Eddy herself accepted. If occasionally there landed some one whose mental processes differed from those of Mrs. Eddy and were more like those in the old world which she had left behind, then he was cast out immediately. For judged by the standards of Mrs. Eddy's world it was he who was insane. If he could not accept and subscribe to the conceptions which she had established in her island universe, if he found himself at variance with the majority there, it was he who was irrational, and not the rest.

Had Mrs. Eddy failed in her task of creating a separate universe for herself, had she been unable to maintain herself in this new enclosure, then the world she left behind would have nodded sagely and its every man might have tapped his finger to his head. Since she not only tamed her wilderness, but attracted to her novel empire many others willing to give her fealty, the world can well recognize her unique achievement. She achieved, indeed, what not many men or women in history have ever attained. For few individuals who have found themselves utterly at variance with all other men have ever succeeded in going forth and establishing, apart from the rest of humanity, a world of their own design.

It is a mark of genius in man when he is not content to adjust himself to his environment, but attempts instead to remould his circumstances more in accord with his desire. It is this gift of re-creation which above all distinguishes a man from lower beasts, to the degree to which he may possess it. It can not be denied that Mrs. Eddy demonstrated the possession of such a gift in an extraordinary way. She started by seeking flight and escape; she ended by tearing down every obstacle in the world around her, and then rebuilding her realm to suit her desires and needs. She flung bridges where

she found chasms; levelled mountains with magnificent dar
ing where she desired plains; distorted the course of whol
rivers when she thought them inconvenient; reared entire citie
when she wanted a bit of shelter, raised innumerable temple
when she wished to worship, built vast gaols when she had .
subject she wished to condemn. The prodigality of her energy
her ambition, and desire, the lavish scale on which she oper
ated, can only amaze and confound.

Had Mrs. Eddy's own hopes and dreams been fulfilled, sh
would eventually have had the majority with her. She neve
ceased to dream that all mankind would some day desert th
old world which she herself had found unbearable, and ente
into her own universe to enjoy the lofty fantasies which sh
had erected there. She was a sick woman, and thought that a
the world was ill. She desired escape, and thought that all hu
manity must need release. So it was that she beckoned to th
multitudes.

And she indeed lured many to share her refuge.

But the millions to whom she gestured never came. It no
seems probable that her hope of building for the majority c
men, and of drawing all humanity within the boundaries c
her mysterious country, will never be fulfilled.

Probably the majority will always be on the outside. Bu
posterity should be exceedingly slow to pronounce on Mr
Eddy the usual verdict of the majority when it judges the b
ing who has refused to accept the validity of the realit
known to the mass mind. It can well afford to temper i
judgment with admiration and acclaim for a unique achieve
ment. It can wisely give careful consideration to Mrs. Eddy
empire to see if men may not discover there some laws c
building which can be more widely applied in the wor
which the majority calls real. If a single principle can l
found there which is useful to the world in general, then h
manity need not quarrel with her memory. It will not matt
even that she may not have been the first to employ this pri
ciple; her contribution will be no less if she merely demo
strated it, helped to test it, managed to bring it to the attentic
of others who might never otherwise have known that it e

sted. Her empire may even fall into rack and ruin; yet if from its towers one contribution to human knowledge can be salvaged, then Mrs. Eddy's strange universe was an advance in the evolution of worlds.[1]

As so often happens with those who have achieved momentously, Mrs. Eddy lived too long. Had she died even ten years before the expiration of her allotted span, she would have blazed out in consummate human glory. The illness of old age, the weakness to which all flesh is heir despite the ever-renewed eagerness of its denials, was her undoing. Her pride was tarnished by her own misery. Vandals broke into her isolated universe from the other world she had thought to be escaped from forever, and before they had been repelled she had been struck to the heart as she sat gasping on her throne.

The case which sought to demonstrate her mental incompetence was withdrawn for probably just one reason: Senator Chandler must have feared that the decision might go against him, due to the court rulings which restricted the evidence that he might offer. The action had gained one end, so far as the interests of Mrs. Eddy's possible heirs were concerned, in that she had appointed trustees who would conserve the resources of the estate. Meanwhile it seemed wiser for Senator Chandler to avoid any decision adverse to his clients, withdraw his case while he could, and prepare to attack from a new angle. It seemed to him probable that he could have better hope of success by starting an entirely new action to test not merely Mrs. Eddy's competence to make a deed of trust but rather her entire mental status over a long period of years.

The menace of a suit of this nature was regarded by the officials of Mrs. Eddy's church with extravagant horror. Whether Mrs. Eddy were eventually adjudged to be legally sane or insane, a normal person or a paranoiac, the whole action might be dragged through the courts for endless

[1] A suggestive and rather impartial little treatise on the subject of Mrs. Eddy's contribution may be found in the final chapters of the last work of Sir William Fletcher Barrett, F. R. S., entitled Christian Science: An Examination of the Religion of Health (Henry Holt & Company, New York, 1926). The work was completed and published by his sister, Rosa M. Barrett.

months, and the resultant publicity would have possibilities o
damaging her church to an irremediable degree. Accordingl
General Streeter, attorney for Mrs. Eddy, opened negotia
tions for a compromise. Offers to create generous trust fund
out of Mrs. Eddy's estate for all the plaintiffs were extended
In view of his duty to his clients, it seemed wise to Senato
Chandler to accept such an offer.

Mrs. Eddy, as she thought over the whole situation, wa
by moods indignant, tearful, and horror-stricken. She blame
the whole situation on malicious animal magnetism. He
physical health, instead of declining after 1906, had for
while showed encouraging improvement. But mentally sh
was extremely distraught. While the Next Friends' case wa
still hanging in the courts, it was arranged that Arthur Bris
bane, who had some close Christian Science friends, shoul
interview her and write a friendly article that might be use
ful for general publicity purposes. He asked her the reason fo
the suit.

"Greed of gold, young man," exclaimed Mrs. Eddy. "The
are not interested in me, I am sorry to say, but in my money
and in the desire to control that. They never tried to help m
when I was working years ago and when help would hav
been so welcome."

Mrs. Eddy never ceased to speak of her son as if it were h
who had deserted her in time of need; just as in stressing hi
illiterate uncouthness and the manner in which it reflected o
her own standing she never once seemed to realize that sh
herself might be responsible for George's lacks.

But she seemed genuinely affected when young Brisban
then at the beginning of his fame as a newspaper man, aske
her why George had joined in the action. Tears filled her eye
her voice broke, and she could not go on. Finally she turne
to General Streeter, who was present at the interview t
make sure his client had wise guidance in what she said. Sh
blinked her eyes a little rapidly, and tried to smile. "You kno
what they say, General," she said brokenly, "—'A mother i
a mother all her life; a father is a father till he gets a ne
wife.'"

Before Brisbane left, Mrs. Eddy had recovered her poise, and also some of her feeling of indignation. "Young man," he remarked with a sonorous gruffness that recalled her compelling voice of earlier years, "I made my money with my pen, just as you do. And I have a right to it."

Immediately after Mrs. Eddy was told that Senator Chanler was willing to withdraw his suit, and would accept an offer from Mrs. Eddy's attorneys for a compromise that would protect the financial interests of his clients, she had a great overflowing of the heart. She suddenly felt that God was in his heaven after all, and that it was a time for general rejoicing. She decided to have a great jubilee. She instructed General Streeter to have all the papers ready to be signed a week before Christmas day. Then on Christmas she would stage a general homecoming, and invite all her exiled family to gather around her—the Glovers, the hitherto ignored Bakers, and even Foster Eddy. Foster Eddy indeed received a letter from her that completely overwhelmed him with its warm friendliness. He had dropped a line to Mrs. Sargent, expressing concern for Mrs. Eddy's health; the reply was written in Mrs. Eddy's own hand. It said, under the date of August 30, 1907, that she had seen his kind letter to Mrs. Sargent, and continued:

If you would like to call upon me now, I have a little leisure and would be pleased to see your dear face once more for a chat with you after the old way.

She would, she added, make an appointment to see him if he would drop her a line.[1]

Apparently no appointment was ever made for Bennie to call again upon his adopted mother, but meanwhile all preparations went forward for creating the trust funds and signing the papers in time for the Christmas homecoming, which Mrs. Eddy had invited even her attorneys to attend.

On Monday, a week before Christmas, all the attorneys were assembled in Boston, with their clients sitting within brief call. Glover, who had returned west, was at home packed

[1] For entire letter, see New York *World*, January 5, 1908.

and waiting for the telegram saying that his inheritance wa
ready for collection. Foster Eddy had already arrived in Bos
ton in time to select a new motor car which he meant to pui
chase in celebration of getting his share of the Eddy million

As the attorneys and their assistants all sat talking ger
ially around a table waiting for the arrival of Henry M
Baker, who was to bring the signed papers from Pleasai
View, Mr. Baker burst in almost breathless.

"Gentlemen," he said dramatically, as he stood in the centi
of the floor without removing his coat, "I have just come fror
Pleasant View. It is my duty to inform you that Mrs. Edc
refuses to go on with the reconciliation. She says that she wi
not sign; that she will never admit Glover and Dr. Eddy 1
Pleasant View; that she never wants to see either of thei
again."

The meeting broke up in general dismay and consternatio:
No one present doubted that the sudden change of mind ha
come from Mrs. Eddy herself, and that her attorneys were :
no way responsible. What had actually happened to Mrs. Edc
was merely a sudden burst of fear that her advisers were su'
ject to malicious animal magnetism. Once again she ha
characteristically reversed herself.

Chandler announced immediately that he would enter a ne
suit and bring the whole matter into the federal courts. Mi
Eddy told her horrified church officials that Chandler cou
do what he pleased. She had thought of a more pleasant u
for her money than turning it over to mere relatives by na
ural selection and adoption.

The nature of this more pleasant use was revealed in a le
ter she wrote to Archibald McLellan, her editor, on D
cember 14, and which was first revealed to the world when
was published in *The Sentinel* on December 21. *The Sentin*
was a weekly publication which had been organized to suppl
ment the monthly efforts of *The Journal*. Mrs. Eddy's lett
here said:

MR. ARCHIBALD MCLELLAN:
  My dear Trustee: I desire to commence immediately to found
Christian Science institution for the special benefit of the poor and t

neral good of all mankind. The founding and endowment of this in-
itution will cost at least one million dollars. Please come to me at your
rliest opportunity and I will give you further details.

Most truly yours,
MARY BAKER EDDY.

Probably this bright idea had been born in Mrs. Eddy's
ind as a result of the searching investigation of numberless
porters to discover traces of those extensive charities which
rs. Eddy hinted, ever and anon, that she had extended to a
edy universe. The reporters were forced to announce to
at reading public that no traces of such charitable appro-
iations from Mrs. Eddy's coffers were ever found.[1] Her
ajor donation was a matter of some $10,000 to the city of
ncord, to be devoted to building and improving some nearby
ads that she used constantly in her drives. Even this fund
nsisted partly of contributions from the faithful, and it
rdly recompensed Concord for a very human conservativism
own by Mrs. Eddy in her tax payments. It was revealed
ring the Next Friends' suit that Mrs. Eddy—although she
ust have had over half a million dollars worth of taxable
operty at the time—signed in 1901 a statement to the local
x assessors that she was worth only about $19,000 for tax
rposes. The same amount was sworn to by Calvin Frye, in
ccessive years, time after time, until it was eventually raised
$55,000, where the valuation stood at the time of the suit.
Mrs. Eddy's idea for a million-dollar Foundation was there-
re an answer to the innuendoes she resented so warmly.
million dollars comprised approximately the total of her
rsonal cash assets at this period, as opposed to those of her
urch, which had cash resources of some twelve million.
t Mrs. Eddy's project for a great foundation was never
alized, for eventually her advisers prevailed upon her to
mpromise the Next Friends' suit. By the end of 1908 Mrs.
ldy was again involved in turmoil. She was busily engaged
finding ways and means to excommunicate Mrs. Stetson.

The Christian Science view-point regarding charity, as commonly expressed,
hat needy humanity would not need charity if it subscribed to Christian
ence, and thereby used Mrs. Eddy's system of attaining well-being.

The resulting sensational publicity made it necessary for the Christian Science Church to take in every sail that could possibly be reefed on a sea that had suddenly become so stormy that catastrophe was threatening on every hand.

In consequence Senator Chandler was asked once more to sit at a round-table, and eventually, on November 10, 1909 an agreement was signed by which George W. Glover received a total of $250,000, and E. J. Foster Eddy acquired title to $50,000. Glover's patrimony was inclusive of the original trust fund of $125,000 which had been previously set aside for him and which at that time he had refused. This trust was now increased to $150,000, and he received in addition $100,000 in cash. The agreement with Glover stipulated that he should return all letters which Mrs. Eddy had ever written him.

Undoubtedly it was the scandalous attitude of the newspapers toward Mrs. Eddy and her church during the litigation and the other untoward events of 1906 and 1907 that brought to her the idea of publishing a newspaper of her own —a paper that would carry to her disciples news of the day without thrusting under their eyes in banner headlines the story of Mrs. Eddy's sensational struggles with generally recognized realities. Thus in one of her reflective moods she decided on the following letter, which on August 8, 1908, she addressed to the Christian Science Board of Trustees:

BELOVED STUDENTS:—It is my request that you start a daily newspaper at once, and call it the *Christian Science Monitor*. Let there be no delay. The Cause demands that it be issued now.

You may consult with the Board of Directors, I have notified them of my intention.

                              Lovingly yours,
                                MARY B. G. EDDY.[1]

When on September 19, appeals went out for funds to enlarge the Christian Science Publishing House, no reason was given for this need, but money started pouring in immediately. As usual, Mrs. Eddy meant to let her disciples do the contributing and Mrs. Eddy's church would do the owning.

[1] Vd. Sibyl Wilbur, *The Life of Mary Baker Eddy*, page 372.

t was not her idea, for instance, to sell stock for her new
nterprise and thus raise the necessary capital for its flota-
ion. Such a procedure would have made the stockholders part
wners. Until she breathed her last breath Mrs. Eddy was a
ood business woman.

When a notice was published in *The Sentinel* asking
cientists who were journalists to volunteer their services for
he newspaper, so many responses were received that only a
raction could be accepted. The first issue of the paper ap-
eared the day before Thanksgiving, November 25, 1908.
rom the beginning *The Monitor* was successful, its an-
ounced policy being the publication of news devoid either of
ensationalism or descriptions of human weaknesses. In ex-
laining the founding of *The Monitor, The Sentinel* quoted
previous statement from Mrs. Eddy printed in her *Miscel-
neous Writings* under the heading of "A Timely Issue."

Having suffered all her life from a fear so insensate that
was pathological, Mrs. Eddy had blandly written:

Looking over the newspapers of the day, one naturally reflects that
is dangerous to live, so loaded with disease seems the very air. These
escriptions carry fear to many minds, to be depicted in some future
me upon the body. A periodical of our own will counteract to some
xtent this public nuisance; for through our paper, at the price at which
e shall issue it, we shall be able to reach many homes with healing,
urifying thought.

With *The Monitor,* Mrs. Eddy's church became possessed
f five periodicals carrying her ideas to the ends of the earth.
irst came the famous old *Journal,* a monthly. There followed
he *Christian Science Quarterly,* first published in 1890. *The
hristian Science Weekly,* founded in 1898, had later become
he *Sentinel. The Christian Science Herald,* first copyrighted
1903, was in 1905 dropped in its English form and given
German setting under the name of *Der Herold der Chris-
an Science.* This circulated widely abroad. None of these
ublications, however, could occupy the field *The Monitor*
as destined to fill. With the appearance of this daily it be-
me thenceforth unnecessary for any one of Mrs. Eddy's
llowers ever to obtain news regarding the world's activi-

ties and ideas from any other source than Mrs. Eddy's ow
organization.

In the same year that *The Monitor* was founded Mrs. Edd
startled the world by moving herself and her household ou
of Pleasant View. Mrs. Leonard, one of Mrs. Eddy's atter
dants, her close confidante in her declining years—the wo
man who had taken her place on the carriage drives whil
Mrs. Eddy was ravaged by illness—died on January ;
1908. She was nearly sixty-nine years old. Her death wa
caused by diabetes, according to a doctor who was called in a
the end. During the previous summer Mary Tomlinson, th
sister of the former First Reader of the Concord Church, an
another attendant in the Eddy household, had committed su
cide by hurling herself out of a window of the Parker Hous
Hotel in Boston.

Mrs. Leonard's death, on top of the suicide, convinced Mr
Eddy that malicious animal magnetism was becoming so fata
and so horrible at Pleasant View that she must flee immed
ately. She felt that M. A. M. was entirely responsible no
merely for her own ill health, but also for the cruel even
attending the *World* exposé in 1906 and the subsequent san
ity trial in 1907. The fact that even the people around he
were succumbing to the poisonous darts of the Fiend mac
her fear actually for her own life, and time and again she to
her companions around her that she feared, unless they gav
her adequate mental protection, that she might be killed a
night when she slept and was unaware.

Finally she reached the state of mind from which she ha
suffered in Boston. She felt that she must get away fro
Pleasant View anywhere, anyhow. During the last twen
years of her life she had come to love the rambling old hou
at Pleasant View so dearly that in her will she had even stip
lated that she wanted to be buried there. But overnight th
feeling was changed. Pleasant View had become a house o
horrors where slimy and ghostly fears sought to choke h
almost hourly. She said that it did not so much matter whe
she went, but she must go immediately. On second though
she decided that it did matter a great deal where she wer

he must get out of New Hampshire. If the laws of New Hampshire had been different, it might not have been possible or her to have been publicly maltreated in such an outrageous manner. She told her Trustees that she must leave New Hampshire at once. If she stayed there she might lose every ent she had to her name.

In this emergency her Trustees found a magnificent house a Chestnut Hill, Massachusetts, surrounded by twelve acres f woodland. They purchased it for her at a cost of $100,000, nd had it altered, furnished, and decorated without Mrs. ddy's ever seeing it. The most extraordinary haste was made ith the alterations. A force of several hundred laborers was nployed, the men working in shifts that ran through the full venty-four hours. Huge arc-lights were employed to turn e night into day. Despite such an unusual proceeding amid e quiet retreats of Chestnut Hill, news of Mrs. Eddy's ans to flee Concord did not leak out until the flight was actu- ly made. Mrs. Eddy indeed had every step of this new under- king guarded with jealous secrecy. As always in the past, e feared that some of the mesmerists might discover her ans, and seek to betray the enterprise with their wiles.

The house at Chestnut Hill, which is a suburb of Bos- n, had been owned by Robert P. Walker, a Chicago real tate dealer and a leading Christian Scientist in his own city. was a great stone mansion with some thirty-four rooms de- gned in the best of modern architectural traditions and sug- stive of nothing less than a baronial château. Extensive terations were made for Mrs. Eddy's residence. Her own ite of rooms was laid out in the southeast corner of the sec- d floor. She insisted when the house was bought that her rsonal chambers should exactly match in design and plan e three rooms in which she had spent her life for the last ten ars at Pleasant View. This injunction was scrupulously eyed. Directly in front of her boudoir was installed an elec- ic elevator to carry her to and from the lower floors.

The whole mansion was magnificently furnished and deco- ted. On the upper floors suites of bedrooms were laid out such a manner that each had a bath. These were designed

for the use of mental practitioners, whom Mrs. Eddy now
maintained around herself in an ever increasing throng.

The hallways of the mansion were provided with stately
staircases of steel. On each landing at the second and third
floors an enormous steel safe was built into the walls for the
guarding of Mrs. Eddy's documents. These were increasing
rapidly in number. They included not only the original manuscripts and the proofs for Mrs. Eddy's voluminous writings, but also documents far more obscure. Beginning about
1890, Mrs. Eddy had loyal agents engaged in a task of literally scouring New England to gain possession of all biographical material which might throw on her career a light
different from that in which she herself envisioned it. The
material she then secreted but, strangely enough, never destroyed. She had managed to secure a number of the manuscripts from which she had originally taught; she obtained
possession of letters which she had later regretted; she sought
affidavits from every soul willing to subscribe to a statement
which seemed favorable to her conception of herself, or unfavorable to those whom she regarded as her enemies. No
quest was too laborious to be performed in this task of vindicating Mary Baker Glover Eddy. When, for instance, it
was rumored that Glover had been buried in the Potter's
Field, one of Mrs. Eddy's officials went south and searched
for days for data which would counteract this gossip. The
Lodge to which Glover had belonged had long been dissolved.
Many of its papers had been burned. It was finally discovered
that some of its records had been transferred to another lodge
and then stored in an old barn. These were ransacked and
pored over until an account of the Masonic funeral provided
for the "Major" had been discovered.[1]

The removal of Mrs. Eddy's possessions into the new mansion, henceforth to become famous as "Chestnut Hill," was
effected entirely at night. No one outside of her Trustees, not
all even in her household, and only two or three high officials

[1] Much of this material was subsequently published in *Miscellany*, where
lengthy accounts of Major Glover's standing in life and resting in death still appear in rebuttal of the gossip which pained Mrs. Eddy so greatly. Vd. pages
329–336.

f her church, knew that the move was to be made until it was
ctually consummated. The last baggage was transferred
n Saturday night. The next day, Sunday, January 26, 1908,
Irs. Eddy and her ménage were transferred in a state as
nagnificent as if she had been an empress or a queen. One
comotive went before her train to make sure the tracks were
ear; another followed in the rear to prevent any collision
rom behind. Thus were precautions taken to prevent mali-
ous animal magnetism from appearing even in the form of
n unruly switch or an unexpected impediment on the track.

Mrs. Eddy was gowned for this brief journey through the
orders of the outside world in soft gray velvet, a gray velvet
at, and gray furs. Heavily veiled, she stepped into her train
ith elaborate assistance from the men in her household. Dr.
lpheus B. Morrill, Concord physician and one of Mrs. Ed-
y's many second cousins—the Bakers had relatives all over
ew England—accompanied the party. After she entered
e great house at Chestnut Hill the doors were closed and
arred from within, and six armed men went on watch that
ght outside the house. Mrs. Eddy had always been a victim
f fear. Now, in her very old age, the things she feared had
ome upon her.

XXXI

Even in her last days Mrs. Eddy retained her gift of rally
ing immediately in times of stress. *The World's* enterprisin
reporters had arrived to knock at her door at perhaps the lea
auspicious moment of her uneasy life; and yet even from th
tremendous shock Mrs. Eddy arose promptly, bravely, an
with magnificent gusto, ready to lay around her on all side
with her broadsword and stoutly defend her fortificatio
from the worst attack she had ever had to face.

Her pen could still be as biting as ever, and there we
times when she yet could rise to use it with her old jab an
twist. She could still find energy, for instance, to write a thre
thousand word reply to *McClure's Magazine,* and demand wi
vim:

Who or what is the *McClure* "history," so called, presenting? Is
myself, the veritable Mrs. Eddy, whom the New York *World* declar
dying of cancer or is it her alleged double or dummy heretofore
scribed?

If indeed it be I, allow me to thank the enterprising historians f
the testimony they have thereby given of the divine power of Christi
Science, which they admit has snatched me from the *cradle* and t
grave, and made me the Leader of the good men and women in o
own and in other countries. . . .

Mary Baker Eddy was a warrior until the end. And s
still needed every resource. For she had yet to deal with A
gusta Stetson.

For days, for months, for years, Mrs. Eddy had be
craftily, fearfully biding her time. She knew now that th
time had come. Perhaps, indeed, she had delayed too lor
There were times when she must have regretted that she h
not acted years before. For she now was certain that in A
gusta she had been deceived. Augusta's honeyed words we
only the words of the Fiend.

Mrs. Eddy had a great deal of outside assistance in reach-
g this conclusion. Almost from the beginning of the sensa-
onal newspaper publicity that broke upon Mrs. Eddy in late
)06, the metropolitan press intimated that Augusta Stetson
as Mrs. Eddy's logical successor. Enterprising newspaper
porters did not find it difficult to locate Christian Scientists
New York who were convinced that Mrs. Stetson was di-
cting streams of malicious animal magnetism against the
fortunate old woman at Pleasant View in order to hasten
e dawn of a new regime when she herself could inherit the
ingdom. It was at this time that "M. A. M." first was seen
the headlines of the metropolitan press, and so mysterious
as the strange symbol that no fancy seemed too improbable
r the imaginations of excited newspaper reporters. It was
inted in all seriousness that Mrs. Stetson and Frye were in
ental league to influence Mrs. Eddy's weakened mind to
ake Augusta Stetson the Eddy heir.

Such wild rumors gained currency so rapidly that few of
e faithful could resist believing them; thus it was that the
irst Reader of the Concord Church could write gravely to
ornell Wilson, publicity man in Mrs. Eddy's household:

Would it not be well to protect Mrs. Eddy from the Stetson argument
ecifically, or are the workers doing so? It has troubled me but "helped"
e[1] to hear that Frye was a channel for that diabolism. We are all
rking to know that stuff has no power over the suit.[2]

Enterprising newspaper editors know that conflict is the
sence of good drama, and good drama on the front page is
hat helps to build circulation. They consequently traced
wn with all eagerness every rumor that Mrs. Stetson was
eking to oust old Mrs. Eddy from her Boston throne.

Mrs. Stetson, being a woman of vast emotions and enthusi-
ms, was like Mrs. Eddy in that she had tempestuous moods,

A typical example of the Eddy influence. The writer means that he is not
ually troubled—for a confession of being in trouble would be a confession of
ng in "error." Thus: "I am sick—but am well"; "I am poor, but am rich,"
.

This letter was found on the street, according to the New York *World*, in
ich paper it was published in full in the issue of May 6, 1907.

when words rushed to her tongue that gave later cause fo
regret. And like Mrs. Eddy, she alienated followers who wer
only too glad in later years to describe some of her worse mo
ments.

Then it was that the New York press learned how Mr
Stetson had once referred to Mrs. Eddy as "that woman,
declaring that "she never healed anybody." One of Mrs. Ste
son's old friends was glad to relate how, during the time whe
Mrs. Stetson was studying at Mrs. Eddy's college and wa
living in Mrs. Eddy's house, she exploded in resentment ove
Mrs. Eddy's adoption of Foster Eddy. "That little pupp
dog!" exclaimed Mrs. Stetson. "I'll get him out of here. Sh
should have adopted me, not him!" Another old friend re
called hearing Mrs. Eddy say, as far back as 1896, that "Mr
Stetson has admirable qualities; but I do not admire her.
Others asserted that Mrs. Stetson had always discourage
students from going to Boston to study in Mrs. Eddy's co
lege, offering them cheaper tuition if they would take her ow
course.[1] Still another remembered hearing Mrs. Stetson re
mark that she was going to "put the screws on" all Eddy fo
lowers who stood in the way of her own ambitions.

Probably the majority of these things were actually sai
under some guise or other, for Mrs. Stetson had a temper, a
well as an ambition, and few who were associated with he
for any length of time failed to notice it. And there can b
small doubt that Mrs. Stetson expected to succeed Mrs. Edd
to the leadership of the Christian Science Church. Mrs. Ste
son in later years always denied this, by inference, assertin
time and again that neither she nor any one else could eve
take Mrs. Eddy's place. The truth was, of course, that Mr
Stetson did not expect to take Mrs. Eddy's place as the "di
coverer and founder" of Christian Science, but she un
doubtedly had expected to inherit the mantle of directorshi
over the church organization, and so informed some of he

[1]This was real treason in the inner circles. Vd. Mrs. Woodbury's *War
Heaven*, page 46: "It was generally understood among Mrs. Eddy's Norm
students that they should not themselves teach affluent or prominent app
cants, however worthy, but send them to her college to quench their thir
and this we gladly did."

ssociates. As she pondered over this probability, she decided
1at after Mrs. Eddy's death she would move the headquar-
:rs of the church from Boston to New York; she intimated
s much to several of her confidants of the moment. Revela-
ons of this nature were also published in the New York
apers in 1907. The New York editors even discovered that
-hen collections were being taken up to furnish Mrs. Stet-
on's new home, one devotee begged for donations with the
lea, "We all want to be in on this—it's going to house the
'hrist."

Mrs. Eddy was well aware of all this talk of *lèse-majesté*,
: only because Mrs. Stetson sat down and wrote a letter pro-
:sting absolute loyalty every time some eager city-editor gave
:ace to a new story describing her ambitions.

By this time, however, Mrs. Eddy was in a mood beyond
onvincing. Her whole universe was crashing and thundering
own around her, her carefully devised retreat had been
tterly violated, and she was being dragged before the public
or a sanity test. Mrs. Eddy knew what she knew. As she
ad written an infinite number of times, she could always tell
-hose mind was upon her.

It is possible that had she dared she would have put Au-
usta out of her church during the storm of 1907. She had
a her by-laws one provision which made such an excommu-
ication possible, and without the possibility of any appeal:

Members of this Church shall not learn hypnotism on penalty of be-
g excommunicated from this Church. . . . If the author of Science
ad Health shall bear witness to the offense of mental malpractice, it
all be considered a sufficient evidence thereof.[1]

But Mrs. Eddy did not dare to put this by-law into effect.
irst, one of the indications of her insanity as alleged by
handler was her very belief in the power of the malpracti-
oner. To excommunicate Mrs. Stetson under such a by-law
ould thus play straight into the hands of her legal per-
:cutors. Second, Mrs. Eddy was becoming by this time so
:arful of the mysterious powers of Mrs. Stetson that she

[1] *Manual*, XI, 9.

herself did not want to make a move that might excite Au
gusta's wrath against her. Fear of Augusta now amounte
practically to an obsession with Mrs. Eddy. Third, it was
serious question whether Augusta could be put out of th
church without losing from the Christian Science fold th
entire First Church congregation in New York. If August
were excommunicated, she had so much personal influenc
that she might easily take most of her congregation out wit
her, if she so desired; and it was the largest and wealthie
congregation among the branch churches, in many ways mo
powerful than The Mother Church itself.

This was the difficult problem which Mrs. Eddy faced i
her old age, as she dwelt in the shadowy chambers at Ches
nut Hill and faithful practitioners watched the night throug
seated outside her door.

Already Mrs. Eddy had passed one by-law intended to cu
Augusta by halting her rapidly expanding church. She ha
forbidden overflow meetings. Until this measure was pr
mulgated Mrs. Stetson was holding a regular Sunday ove
flow meeting in her Reading Rooms, and even from this se
ond meeting she was turning hundreds away.

Mrs. Eddy waited a little while, and then devised a secor
by-law aimed at Augusta's overweening power. She ha
watched with amazement and even jealousy the thousan
who went annually to Augusta's shrine to be healed. She no
passed a by-law forbidding healers to have offices in ai
church building. Mrs. Stetson and her students had to mo
out of their practitioners' offices on less than twenty-fo
hours' notice. Mrs. Stetson said no single word of protest.

Mrs. Eddy herself had always stressed the need for ef
cient healers in her church. She repeated time and again th
it was healing, not mere teaching, that made converts f
Christian Science. She had cut down the charges allow
teachers time and again in order to force them out into hea
ing work. She herself had written Mrs. Stetson in 1902:

> I want you to give most of your time to healing. This department
> Christian Science is the one in which no student has equalled me. It
> the one to which every student should aspire more than to any other.
> is the one most vacant at present. . . .

It was in healing rather than in teaching or church-making that she wanted the members of her church to lead, wrote Mrs. Eddy, adding in conclusion: "Healing is the foundation of Christian Science."[1] And she was right.

The healing department in Mrs. Stetson's church was perhaps the greatest single factor in its marvellous expansion, the most important pillar and support ever designed for the Eddy hierarchy. But in one moment of jealousy and fear, with one sweep of the pen, Mrs. Eddy cast it out. A single sentence from a letter which she wrote to Augusta far back in 1894 explained this characteristic ruthlessness perfectly.

"You see," Mrs. Eddy had said, "Mother cuts off right hands if they are made offensive."

Between January and November of 1908 Mrs. Eddy so immured herself at Chestnut Hill that once again the old rumors were revived that she was dead. In May of 1908 Mrs. Eddy had found it once again necessary to issue a general denial of disability, and she phrased it with an acerbity that revealed a growing resentment. She wrote to the New York Herald on May 15:

Permit me to say, the report that I am sick (and I trust the desire thereof) is dead, and should be buried. Whereas the fact that I am well and keenly alive to the truth of being—the Love that is Life—is sure and steadfast. I go out in my carriage daily, and have omitted my drive but twice since I came to Massachusetts. Either my work, the demands upon my time at home, or the weather, is all that prevents my daily drive. . . .

On the next day Mrs. Eddy wrote another notice which was eventually published in her *Sentinel*. Having thought about the matter overnight, she had grown extremely indignant over the continuing public interest in her state of health, following her experiences with newspapers in 1906 and 1907. She said with all of the old Eddy fire and spirit:

TO WHOM IT MAY CONCERN

Since Mrs. Eddy is watched, as one watches a criminal or sick person, she begs to say, in her own behalf, that she is neither; therefore to be criticized or judged by either a daily drive or a stay at home, is super-

Stetson, *Sermons and Other Writings*, page 42.

fluous. When accumulating work requires it, or because of a preferen
to remain within doors she omits her drive, do not strain at gnats
swallow camels over it, but try to be composed and resigned to tl
shocking fact that she is minding her own business, and recommen
this surprising privilege to all her dear friends and enemies.

Her drives were no longer a recreation for Mrs. Eddy
any sense of the word. She went forth on them with an ir
determination to show the world that the stories whisper
about Mary Baker Eddy were only lies. Once she said to
new secretary who found her painfully trying to draw h
gloves on her shaking hands, "Mr. Dickey, I want you
know it does me good to go on this drive. I do not mean th
the physical going for a drive does me good. But the enen
have made a law that it hurts me to go on this drive, and th
are trying to enforce it."

Despite her heroic and magnificent efforts to overcome t
M. A. M. of the enemy, to conquer the body that had alwa
served her so poorly, and to combat the constant renewal of t
rumors about her earthly presence, these whispers were i
peated in ever increasing volume, and credence grew with t
repetition. By 1908 numerous loyal Christian Scientists the
selves had become convinced that Mary Baker Eddy w
actually no more, and that only a designing Board of Dir
tors was endeavoring to maintain the fiction of her existen
There is abundant evidence to indicate that Mrs. Stetson h
self came to credit these rumors, so often were they reite
ated. She presumably had had no direct word from Mrs. Ed
since April.[1] And she now realized what the Board of Dir
tors in Boston themselves believed: that there must shor
be a struggle for power between the Board and herself. S
had no way of knowing positively whether Mrs. Eddy w
in mental stupor, or dying by degrees, or perhaps dead a
buried. But she had no intention of allowing church leadersl
to pass into any hands but her own.

Accordingly, in November of 1908, news leaked out
the press that Mrs. Stetson was planning to build on Riv
side Drive, in New York, a branch church of the First Chu

[1] Vd. Stetson, *Reminiscences*, for Eddy letter dated April, 1908.

f Christ, Scientist, that would exceed in magnificence any-
ning which Christian Science had yet demonstrated. It would
e even larger and more costly than the Mother Church an-
ex in Boston. It was apparently her first open move to make
erself and her New York church supreme in the Christian
cience world.[1]

Neither Mrs. Eddy nor her Board could read this announce-
nent with any feeling but horror. Only the Mother Church
as permitted to have branches. Augusta's announcement
hat she was going to organize a branch for her own temple
ould only mean that war was now declared and that the re-
ellion was on.

Mrs. Eddy was in a strange quandary. Obviously the situa-
on called for prompt action. But undoubtedly she was dis-
raught with fear—not merely fear that she was at last to be
usted in her old age from the position of leadership in which
he had fought for a lifetime to establish herself, but an even
ore personal fear for her physical safety.

Meanwhile, as she nervously pondered, Archibald McLel-
n, Editor-in-Chief, inserted the following editorial in *The
entinel* of December 5:

A newspaper of Nov. 30 announces, on information said to have been
ceived from the First Church of Christ, Scientist, of New York City,
aat: "It is proposed to have a church edifice, rivalling in beauty of
chitecture any other religious structure in America. . . . Mrs. Eddy
known to be profoundly pleased at this new evidence of growth and
osperity in the church of which she is Founder. . . . It was learned
st night that Christian Scientists here have aspired to build another
d more splendid edifice, ever since the Boston Christian Scientists
ected the $2,000,000 Mother Church."

Concerning these news items, it is to be said that Mrs. Eddy was not
known to be profoundly pleased" with what purports to be plans of
irst Church of Christ, Scientist, of New York City, for she learned of

[1]There can be no doubt that Mrs. Stetson had previously become aware of
rs. Eddy's feeble condition through first-hand knowledge. In August, 1906,
st before Mrs. Eddy's privacy was violated by reporters and at a time when
e was in almost constant physical pain, Mrs. Stetson came to Pleasant View
her summons to give her treatments. Apparently Mrs. Stetson gave her tem-
rary benefit (vd. *Reminiscences*, p. 746); but Mrs. Eddy was quite capable of
aching the conclusion, in retrospect, that Augusta had actually harmed her
nile pretending temporarily to help.

this proposed rival to The Mother Church, for the first time, from tl
daily press.

Three leading facts remain immortal in the history of Christian Sc
ence, namely:

1. This Science is already established, and it has the support of ¿
true Christian Scientists throughout the world.

2. Any competition or rivalry in Christian Science is abnormal, ar
will expose and explode itself.

3. Any attempt at rivalry or superiority in Christian Science is u¡
christian; therefore it is unscientific. . . .

In many of our large cities when a congregation has outgrown i
church building, then other branch churches are organized and ne
edifices erected to accommodate the increasing members; but ea
branch at once becomes an individual church, and has immediate co¡
nection with The Mother Church, so that the later organizations are ¿
directly attached to the parent Vine as are any of the earlier branche
The members of each new organization are in no wise connected ¿
affiliated with their former church. . . .

Were one branch church to depend upon a neighboring branch f¡
training and support, this action would tend to sever its connection wi
The Mother Church. The essential condition for fruit-bearing is und
vided attachment to the parent Vine. On the other hand, no bran¡
church, however large, is privileged to oversee or supervise anoth
branch.

Side by side with this editorial was another one, also signe
by the Editor-in-Chief. It said, among other things:

Are you striving, in Christian Science, to be the best Christian ¡
earth, or are you striving to have the most costly edifice on earth? . .

The more modest and less imposing material superstructures indica
a spiritual state of thought; and vice-versa.

At that moment the writer appears to have remembere
some of the things that were being said about Mrs. Eddy
luxurious new abode, with particular reference to its ve¡
material elegance, for he immediately swept into the follov
ing paragraph:

The house which Mrs. Eddy now occupies is larger than she nee
because she could not find exactly what she wanted; but it is a pla
house, and its furnishings are not extravagant. Mrs. Eddy has declar
against the display of material things, and has said that the less we ha
of them the better. Since God has taught her that matter is unreal a¡
Spirit is the only reality, any other position would be unscientific.

It is obvious that Mr. McLellan was undertaking a burden which Mrs. Eddy never assumed—that of striving for consistency. Mrs. Eddy herself thought about the astonishing church situation for quite a while, and then leisurely wrote the comment which appeared six weeks later[1] in *The Sentinel:*

I have crowned The Mother Church building with the spiritual modesty of Christian Science, which is its jewel. When my dear brethren in New York desire to build higher,—to enlarge their phylacteries and demonstrate Christian Science to a higher extent,—they must begin on wholly spiritual foundation, than which there is no other, and proportionately estimate their success and glory of achievement only as they build upon the rock of Christ, the spiritual foundation.

Mrs. Eddy obviously hesitated to make her words too harsh. The thought must have occurred to her that it would be wise generalship to play for time, and meanwhile sound out the depths of various possibilities. As always in the face of calamity, she nerved herself to energetic action. Thus she sent letter to Mrs. Stetson on December 7, exactly a week after the first newspaper announcement, and two days after Mr. McLellan's denunciations of the New York Church had appeared in *The Sentinel:*

My Beloved Student: I have tried and hoped all through the past season to have you come to me and take a drive with me around the Chestnut Hill Reservoir but have failed hitherto.[2]

If the season was not too far advanced for Mrs. Stetson to enjoy such a drive, Mrs. Eddy asked that she designate a day and hour, adding that she usually took her drive between one and two o'clock of an afternoon. She signed the letter "Lovingly yours." Never was there a more disarming document.

No one will ever know the mixed emotions which Mrs. Stetson felt when this letter came to her by post. It was typewritten, but it was concluded with a signature that appeared veritably Mrs. Eddy's own. It was like a voice from the grave. Mrs. Stetson immediately got on a night train, went to Boston, and let Frye know she was there as soon as she got off

[1]January 16, 1909.
[2]Stetson, *Sermons and Other Writings*, page 180.

the Pullman in the morning. Mrs. Eddy sent back a note to
the Touraine, which Mrs. Stetson always made her Boston
headquarters. It was very brief; it simply asked Mrs. Stetson
to come to Chestnut Hill at one o'clock that afternoon for a
short drive. This time, however, the note was in Mrs. Eddy'
own hand. It was unmistakably authentic.

Augusta arrived at the exact hour. She remembered only
too well Mrs. Eddy's love for absolute promptness; Mrs
Stetson in turn had exacted this same tribute from her own
students. She was informed when she rang the bell that Mrs
Eddy was already in her carriage at the porte-cochère. Mrs
Eddy by this time had had installed another elevator which
took her down from her second-floor apartment direct to the
carriage entrance.

The day was cold, and her attendants had wrapped around
her a white lamb's wool blanket, putting over this soft cover
ing a heavier and darker rug.

It would not have been strange, as Mrs. Stetson stood there
if she had been at a momentary loss for words. But August
Stetson, like Mrs. Eddy, was a woman of many resources
She stepped into the carriage, and Mrs. Eddy took both her
hands, kissed her, and said how glad she was to see her dear
student. When Mrs. Stetson was seated Frye made a move to
cover her with the dark rug that Mrs. Eddy shared. "Remove
that," instructed Mrs. Eddy, "and put Augusta under the
white robe with me." Mrs. Stetson protested that the carriage
rug was quite sufficient. "No," Mrs. Eddy answered, "I want
you to share this with me."

Thus was re-established the old atmosphere of intimacy
that Mrs. Eddy at the moment so greatly desired. They drove
for three-quarters of an hour. No record of the actual con
versation during the drive exists.[1] But there can be small
doubt, from Mrs. Stetson's subsequent accounts of the in
cident, that Mrs. Eddy in every sentence carefully probed
What she wanted was information—to know whether Au
gusta was also playing a part, or was sincere in maintaining

[1] After the above was written there was found, among Mrs. Stetson's paper
a group of her notes concerning this drive. These have now been deposited i
the Union Theological Seminary, New York. They seem to confirm the biog
rapher's thesis.

hat old deferential manner of loyal student to cherished
eacher.

As for Augusta, she perhaps remembered a time when she
old a member of her Board of Trustees, "You will never see
Mrs. Eddy again." Perhaps she remembered how she had pre-
iously proclaimed that Mrs. Eddy would be immortal. And
ow, like Peter, she had then lost faith.

As she sat there beside Mrs. Eddy on that chill December
fternoon, Augusta Stetson's soul must have burned within
er. At any rate, she never ceased after that day to proclaim
hat Mary Baker Eddy was immortal; and for her, indeed,
Mrs. Eddy had actually come back from the grave.

Mrs. Stetson made compensations, too.

For Mrs. Eddy this drive was undoubtedly a calculated
nove to learn first-hand just how far Mrs. Stetson had carried
er plans in conspiring to bring rebellion and secession into
he church that she herself had sought so hard and long to
nake inviolable. One may imagine her with trembling fingers,
nd a voice that faltered with eager nervousness despite her
very effort to control it, endeavoring to learn the worst—
teering the talk casually from topic to topic, chatting inti-
nately, discussing her household, asking finally about Au-
usta's own affairs, striving with every word to peer beneath
ie mask of affectionate humility which Augusta wore with
uch aplomb.

And she could discover nothing. With protestations of
ve and reverence Mrs. Stetson denied that she ever meant
) do what the newspaper had reported. She was planning only
) create a new branch—not for her own church—but for
Mrs. Eddy's own Mother Church. It was to have been an-
ther monument to Mary Baker Eddy—the most glorious
nonument in marble that had yet been erected. But the news-
apers had discovered these plans while the whole thing was
nly under consideration. They had written ignorant stories
ull of lies. The newspapers always lied. Mrs. Eddy herself
new why they lied. They were always motivated only by
I. A. M. "Oh, dearest, this is *such* a lie! No one who knows
s can believe this! . . ."

Thus might Augusta have protested, full of horror **with**

every thought of how greatly she had erred, how tremendously
she had sinned in her momentary weakness when she doubted
the existence of her immortal leader. No one will ever know
whether she confessed this error to Mrs. Eddy as they drove
that afternoon for three-quarters of an hour. But she did
make a promise. The project for a new church in New York
would be dropped immediately. Since the newspapers had so
terribly misinterpreted it, Augusta would abandon the idea
completely.

On hearing this, Mrs. Eddy's heart must have trembled
with joy. She could not possibly desire anything more. For
the moment, at least, her leadership and her organization were
safe. Whatever Augusta's real intentions and ambitions might
be, an open break could for a while be averted. No matter what
the future might hold, catastrophe was temporarily post-
poned.

There was still time for Mrs. Eddy to save her church.

The drive ended and the two returned to the house. Mrs.
Eddy was helped directly into the elevator from her carriage
and was taken upstairs. Mrs. Stetson meanwhile entered the
house and went into the drawing room. Mrs. Eddy removed
her wraps, took a chair, and sent for Mrs. Stetson to come up.
Despite her feeling of assurance that all was still well, she
wanted to make doubly sure. Augusta came into the room
radiant now and poised. Mrs. Eddy looked at her searchingly
and once more felt safe.

"How healthy and strong you are," Mrs. Eddy exclaimed
enviously.

They said good-by, and Augusta went downstairs again
to be met by Mr. Dickey, the secretary, who offered to show
her Mrs. Eddy's private reception room, where a number of
the more lavish presents sent to Mother had been arranged.
Mrs. Eddy by 1905 had collected so many presents that in a
mood of sudden decision she issued a notice forbidding her
followers to send her any more Christmas gifts. This was a
great relief to the servants in the Eddy household, but the
order puzzled the Church congregations, many of whom interpreted it as a ban on Christmas giving in general. Had the

een able to see Mrs. Eddy's museum, they would have un-
erstood.

Into Mrs. Eddy's feeling of gratification as she sat in
er study, there must have crept a flicker of doubt, for she
ing for Mr. Dickey, asked if Mrs. Stetson had left, and said
ie wished to see Augusta again. Mrs. Stetson entered the
oom, approached her Leader, dropped suddenly to her knees
efore the low chair in which Mrs. Eddy was sitting. Involun-
arily, almost, Augusta bowed her head. Mrs. Eddy took both
f Augusta's hands in hers, and for a few moments was silent.
ow she knew. Now she had no remaining doubt that her
Mother Church, her hierarchy, was safe.

"This is the happiest day of my life on earth," she said,
id paused. And then, slowly, with ecstasy in every word,
God bless you, forever—and forever—and forever."

Mrs. Eddy waved her hand. It was a signal for Augusta
go. As she approached the door of the room in which she
lought she had been alone with her Leader, she saw Mr.
ickey and Mrs. Sargent standing together beside the door,
ce sentinels. Only at that moment did a little wonder stir
ithin her. Never before had she had a personal interview
ith Mrs. Eddy except when they had been alone.

The two sentinels swung the door open silently. Mrs. Eddy
ould never see Augusta Stetson again.[1]

Mrs. Stetson went back to New York. She told her Board
Trustees merely that the general sensation which resulted
om their announcement of new building plans made it wise
abandon the entire project. The Board agreed with her; the
oard always agreed with Mrs. Stetson. Public announce-
ent of the change in plan did not refer to Mrs. Stetson's
lk with Mrs. Eddy. Indeed, Mrs. Stetson addressed her an-
ouncement to Mrs. Eddy personally, just as if the old lady
d never even heard the news. It was a letter meant pri-
arily for public consumption, with an introduction so
arased that an ordinary reader would be led to assume that

The quoted conversation in this final interview between Mrs. Eddy and Mrs.
tson is taken directly from Mrs. Stetson's own accounts. The indirect con-
sation is inferred from her many references to the incident, which are scat-
ed throughout her writings.

the whole news had just broken in the papers. Mrs. Stetso
was writing on December 14, 1908, two weeks after *Th
World* published its sensational story, nine days after M
McLellan's denunciation in *The Sentinel*, and five days afte
she had had her personal interview with Mrs. Eddy. And sh
said:

MY PRECIOUS LEADER:

Lest you may have seen the reports of the New York press in regar
to the contemplated new branch of your Church—The First Church
Christ, Scientist, Boston, Massachusetts—which was to have bee
formed from an overflow of First Church of Christ, Scientist, Ne
York City, I am writing you a true statement of facts as they o
curred. . . .[1]

There were almost a thousand words more, and a poem. Th
poem began "Build thee more stately mansions, O my soul."

But the announcement that Mrs. Stetson and her Board c
Trustees would abandon their building project came entire
too late to save Augusta Stetson. Mrs. Eddy had alreac
made up her mind. Augusta was not to be trusted for at
other moment. There was only one problem to be solved: ho
to get rid of her safely.

The Board of Directors of The Mother Church agree
with Mrs. Eddy fully. They felt that their position, the
power as the natural heirs to the control of a great churc
were in serious jeopardy. With the suit to determine Mr
Eddy's sanity still unsettled, and Mrs. Eddy's death a po
sibility at any moment, the Directors realized that they fac
a hazardous future. They knew that Augusta Stetson wou
try to seize control of the church the instant Mrs. Eddy di
appeared from the scene.

If they hoped to avert this grim eventuality, they must g
rid of Augusta Stetson before anything happened to Mr
Eddy. They had indeed seen this necessity approaching ov
a period of several years. But there was no longer time to d
lay. With their church already under fire from every side, th
indeed felt that they would have a tremendous task, followir
Mrs. Eddy's demise, to pull the organization together, witho

[1]Stetson, *Reminiscences, Sermons and Correspondence*, page 203.

lso having to face a civil war with Mrs. Stetson and her nu-
nerous loyal supporters.

In consequence rumors began to reach Mrs. Stetson that
he Board of Directors meant to take from her the church she
ad spent her life in building; that they were seeking a way
o destroy her influence and to cast her out from the church
ntirely. Mrs. Stetson was inclined to be incredulous. She
ooked back upon the long years of devoted association with
Mrs. Eddy, recalled the innumerable expressions of love and
onfidence which Mrs. Eddy had directed to her, and remem-
ered that Mrs. Eddy was still alive. She could not see how
he Boston Board could succeed in its design. She was well
ware that she had no friends among the church officials in
Boston. But she needed no friends there if Mrs. Eddy was
n her side. She counted on her Leader with a whole heart. If
ver a doubt came to her, she had only to remember Mrs.
Eddy's parting words in that last talk: "God bless you—for-
ver—and forever—and forever. . . ."

Serene in her renewed faith in her Leader, Mrs. Stetson
elt secure. And then suddenly, unwittingly, she gave Mrs.
Eddy and the Boston Board the very opportunity they were
o eagerly seeking—an opportunity to slide her smoothly out
f the Church on doctrinal grounds.

In February of 1909, Mrs. Stetson had written to one of
er students, "The day is nearly over—the time for the Sun-
ay evening service is at hand. . . . Everything is so quiet.
. . There seems to be something strange impending. . . ."

There was. It hung on until July. Late in the afternoon of
riday, July 9, a group of Mrs. Stetson's practitioners had an
dea. They would make her a present of gold. Needless to say,
he earnings of the practitioners of the First Church were
arge; they thus had every reason to feel indebted to Mrs.
tetson because of very tangible blessings. When all had con-
ributed to the monetary collection, it occurred to them that
heir gratitude could not be fully expressed unless they also
ent a personal note. They wrote a composite letter, which
Mrs. Stetson received the next morning with a box contain-
ng the money.

Probably malicious animal magnetism was working over
time against Mrs. Stetson at that moment. For a reading of
the fond expressions of gratitude in the composite letter
brought to her the idea that she ought to send both the letter
and the money to Mrs. Eddy. It was Mrs. Eddy, after all,
who had made it possible for Augusta Stetson to become
teacher and preacher to men. It was Mrs. Eddy who should
really receive this gift and this praise.

The fact that Mrs. Stetson sent this gift to Mrs. Eddy,
seen in retrospect, seems so foolhardy as to appear utterly
unreasoned. What Mrs. Stetson did not know was that her
arch antagonist was not the Board of Directors of The First
Church of Christ, Scientist; it was a silent, watchful, fearful
old woman whose opportunity had now come.

In forwarding the money and the tributes from the twenty-
five practitioners Mrs. Stetson wrote her Leader:

> They were sent to me as expressions of loving gratitude the day be-
> fore our Communion service. I feel they belong to you, dearest, and are
> your fruit; for without your divine instruction and Christly guidance
> I should not have had them, so I send this copy of the dear letters to
> you, with the type of the gold of human character which is fast melting
> into spiritual understanding in each of these students.
> You asked me years ago this question, "Augusta, lovest thou me?"
> I answered, "Yes, beloved Leader, I love you." Again you repeated the
> query, "Lovest thou me?" and again I replied, "Yes, I love you, my
> Leader, Teacher and Guide to eternal Life." Then you said, "Feed my
> sheep." I have earnestly and prayerfully endeavored to do this. These are
> thine, Holy One; I trust they are all strong in Christ. . . . May none
> fall away! They desire to honor you, our great forever Leader; they
> have come up out of great tribulation, and have washed their robes
> . . . Precious Leader, my love for you is inexpressible. God grant my
> constant prayer that I may be worthy to be called Your faithful, obedi-
> ent, loving child."[1]

As these excerpts show, it was obviously a letter written in
a state of exalted religious ecstasy. Harried by ridicule, Mary
Baker Eddy had withdrawn all possible claims to divinity. But
there was at least one who now came to her and said, "Holy
One . . . my love for you is inexpressible."

[1] Stetson, *Reminiscences, Sermons and Correspondence*, page 215.

There was no humility in Mary Baker Eddy's eyes as she gazed. She turned from this tribute to her and scanned the enclosure, the tribute from the practitioners to Augusta Stetson. The practitioners had evidently written with the thought uppermost in mind that communion service was only two days away. Somehow they had taken the transubstantiation theory and had got it mixed up with Mrs. Stetson. One practitioner, for instance, had said: "Your unselfish life, fast approaching the perfect idea of Love, is to my hungry sense for Truth, 'the bread of heaven and the water of Life.' Eating this bread and drinking this water is to me eating the body of Christ, and drinking his blood."

As Mrs. Eddy held the paper in her shaking hand, and read these words which deified Augusta as a Christus, she felt that her long awaited opportunity had come. Here was evidence that provided doctrinal grounds to assure for Mrs. Stetson a perfect exit. So Stetson thought she was Jesus Christ, did she?

The Directors displayed firm orders received from Mrs. Eddy: "Act, and act quickly. Handle these letters according to *Science and Health,* and *The Mother Church Manual.*"[1]

To Mrs. Stetson, Mrs. Eddy dictated a letter which was a masterpiece of self-restraint. She said:

I have just finished reading your interesting letter. I thank you for acknowledging me as your Leader, and I know that every true follower of Christian Science abides by the definite rules which demonstrate the true following of their Leader; therefore, if you are sincere in your protestations and are doing as you say you are, you will be blessed in your obedience.[2]

The words almost froze upon the paper as they were dictated from Mary Baker Eddy's lips—the firm, thin lips that once had asked, "Lovest thou me?"

But there was more:

The Scriptures say, "Watch and pray, that ye enter not into temptation." You are aware that animal magnetism is the opposite of divine

[1] Stetson, *Reminiscences, Sermons and Correspondence,* page 217.
[2] Stetson, *Vital Issues in Christian Science,* page 155.

Science, and that this opponent is the means whereby the conflict agains
Truth is engendered and developed. Beloved! you need to watch and
pray that the enemy of good cannot separate you from your Leader and
best earthly friend.

Mrs. Eddy did not think it necessary to state just wha
steps she herself had already taken to bring about a separa
tion, with speed and permanence. Instead, she hastened on
her Motherly duty of issuing due warning fulfilled:

You have been duly informed by me that, however much I desire t
read all that you send to me, I have not the time to do so. . . .

It is here that Mrs. Eddy established her subsequent alib
for the whole delicate operation. Whatever her Board did
with the letters, Augusta could understand that Mrs. Eddy
personally was not concerned in the unfortunate business
Pilate had washed his hands. But even yet Mrs. Eddy was no
quite finished:

The Christian Science Publishing Society will settle the questio
whether or not they shall publish your poems. It is part of their duties t
relieve me of so much labor.

I thank you for the money which you send me which was given yo
by your students. I shall devote it to a worthy and charitable purpose.

Mr. Adam Dickey is my secretary,[1] through whom all my business i
transacted.[2]

It was a unique document, one of the most interesting in
the whole range of Eddy literature. The wheels of Mrs
Eddy's legal procedure thereafter began immediately to grind
The letters, after going to the Board of Directors, were pub
lished in *The Sentinel* with a denunciatory editorial. Th
Board made its plans.

And yet, one must conclude that as Mrs. Eddy lay awake in

[1]This does not mean that Frye had been demoted. His duties had become s
manifold that he really played the part of a general secretary. Dickey assumed th
more specialized rôle of corresponding secretary. Since Mrs. Stetson knew Fry
very well, from their old association in the Eddy camp, and since she did not know
Dickey at all, it seems quite possible that Mrs. Eddy's statement here wa
meant to raise a barrier to all friendly approach.

[2]Mrs. Eddy published this letter in the *Christian Science Sentinel* of July 1
1909.

er bed at night her courage momentarily failed her. She
eared Augusta more than any one else in the world. She
eared the malicious animal magnetism that might emanate
rom an enraged Augusta more than anything else in her uni-
erse. Perhaps, after all, it might be better to temporize.

So she wrote another letter, eleven days after the first one:

ly DEAR STUDENT:—Awake and arise from this temptation pro-
uced by animal magnetism upon yourself, allowing your students to
eify you and me. Treat yourself for it and get your students to help
ou rise out of it. It will be your destruction if you do not do this.
answer this letter immediately.[1]

Mrs. Stetson, in reply, wrote a long puzzled letter that
roped blindly for the reason behind these shattering thun-
erbolts. As a matter of fact, Mrs. Eddy never once resented
eification of herself; she only deprecated it. The by-laws for-
idding it were inserted at a late date merely in answer to
eneral public ridicule. The real trouble now was that Au-
usta's students were deifying not Mrs. Eddy, but "you and
1e." Mrs. Stetson now wrote with rather pitiful dismay:

I have always delighted to revere, follow and obey you. . . . I am
biding by the divine rules laid down in your writings. . . . Precious
eader, I am watching and praying that "the enemy of good" cannot
separate" me from you, my Leader and Teacher. . . . Beloved Leader,
ou are ever speaking to my heart. . . .

Your loving child, AUGUSTA[2]

Despite its reassuring tone, this letter seems not to have
rompted Mrs. Eddy to any immediate action, for she appar-
1tly did not write again to her Board until about a week later.[3]

[1] Stetson, *Vital Issues in Christian Science*, page 159. Mrs. Eddy published the
tter in the *Christian Science Sentinel* of October 16, 1909.

[2] Stetson, *Vital Issues in Christian Science*, page 161 ff.

[3] Mrs. Eddy's Directors evidently heard from her frequently in this crisis.
1 1926 John V. Dittemore, now the sole surviving member of her Board, re-
rred to seven letters on the subject of Mrs. Stetson and her activities written
Mrs. Eddy to her Board of Directors in this period. He cited the dates of
ly 20, 21, 24, August 2, 3, September 9 and October 12, and referred also to
tters on the subject written by Mrs. Eddy to Mrs. Lathrop and others of her
llowers. Vd. his paid advertisement in the New York *World* of April 1, 1926.

Meanwhile wheels had begun to turn. The Board of Direc
tors—highest tribunal of Christian Science—called Mrs. Ste
son to Boston before the end of July to catechize her concern
ing her doctrinal heresies and dismiss her from the church. But
while Mrs. Stetson was in Boston, Mrs. Eddy must have ha
another change of heart. She evidently decided that it would b
safer not to try to proceed with the business after all, for th
Board dismissed all the charges after hearing only one witnes
Mrs. Stetson was allowed to return to New York. The Direc
tors wrote the Trustees of Mrs. Stetson's Church that it ha
been decided to allow them to apply their own discipline to the
erring member.

One may fairly conjecture Mrs. Eddy's condition in thi
crisis—a body racked by the hysterical pain which the tortur
of uncertainty had always induced, a mind distraught by th
indecision of fear. She had no doubt of the consequences c
allowing Augusta Stetson to remain in the church. If, on th
other hand, she excommunicated Augusta, she would have t
face the terrors of M. A. M., so potent when it was directed b
an adept manipulator.

But Mrs. Eddy's Board was not as fearful of M. A. M. a
she was, and by this time they were thoroughly arouse
They had to take their orders from Mrs. Eddy, but they ha
no intention whatever of allowing Mrs. Stetson to stay in th
church. Furthermore, they had small hope that Mrs. Ste
son's own Board of Trustees would take any disciplinary ac
tion. Her Trustees were all her own students; they were a
much Mrs. Stetson's creatures as Mrs. Eddy's Board was th
echo of Mrs. Eddy.

Thus Mrs. Eddy's Board called all of Mrs. Stetson's pract
tioners to come up to Boston and be catechized. The Bosto
officials discovered many heresies in the testimony taken dur
ing a period of sessions that lasted over two weeks. The
learned that Mrs. Stetson was openly teaching that Mar
Baker Eddy was divine. Worse still, she had taught that sh
Augusta Stetson, was second in divinity only to Mrs. Eddy
She had said openly that only she could lead her students t
Mrs. Eddy and to God.

Yet even this did not shock the Board so much as further revelations that they themselves, Mrs. Eddy's chosen Directors, were being "treated" by Mrs. Stetson and her practitioners. Their names were being "taken up" at the noon meetings with the suggestion that they had lost all power. On one occasion Mrs. Stetson had gone so far as to tell them—in this absent treatment—to "go six feet underground." This could mean only one thing: she was seeking to bring upon them death. She was actually daring to attempt destruction of the chief officials of the Christian Science Church. Mrs. Stetson later explained that she meant only to tell the "Adam" in the Directors—that is, their evil and mortal nature—to retire to the nether world.

This was quite enough for the Board of Directors. They brought the hearings to a close, and then called to Boston the Trustees of Mrs. Stetson's church. In a conference in the Board Room of The Mother Church, held September 24, the Boston Board told the New York Board that action against Mrs. Stetson must be taken immediately.

Mrs. Stetson's loyal Board was quite incredulous. Mrs. Eddy's Directors therefore decided that it was time to crack the whip, and Mrs. Eddy, in a moment of daring to brave all the forces of malicious animal magnetism, consented. Thereupon her Board sent to Mrs. Stetson a letter admonishing her for her errors, finding that she was not "fit for the work of a teacher," and revoking her right both to teach and practise as a church healer. Her "card" was withdrawn from *The Christian Science Journal*, automatically revoking all recognition of her as a practitioner.

Thus, without excommunicating her, a way had been found to humble her. She could still go to her church and sit in the front pew in that magnificent temple where she had ruled so long. But no longer would she have any official standing whatever as a teacher and exponent of the faith.

When news of this action was brought to Augusta Stetson, signed with all the dignity and authority of the Board of Directors of The Mother Church, she gave no sign of the tragedy which was welling in her heart. She paused, waited

for a voice—the voice of the woman Augusta had loved and
served as "precious teacher." One single word from her would
turn this blow.

No word came. There was no sound from the woman clois
tered at Chestnut Hill. Dry-eyed, serene, Mrs. Stetson calml
called her Trustees together. She laid the charges against her
self before the members. She then retired from their delib
erations.

She was still waiting for a sign. Her life's work and lov
were suddenly crumbling around her. The sign came. It wa
Mrs. Eddy's voice speaking through *The Sentinel* of Octc
ber 16:

TAKE NOTICE

I approve the by-laws of The Mother Church, and require the Chri
tian Science Board of Directors to maintain them and sustain ther
These Directors do not act contrary to the rules of the Church Manua
neither do they trouble me with their difficulties with individuals
their own church or with the members of branch churches.

My province as a Leader—as the Discoverer and Founder of Chri
tian Science—is not to interfere in cases of discipline, and I hereby pu
licly declare that I am not personally involved in the affairs of tl
church in any other way than through my written and published rule
all of which can be read by the individual who desires to inform ther
selves of the facts.   MARY BAKER EDDY.

October 12, 1909.

Again and for all time, Mrs. Eddy was disclaiming respo
sibility for whatever fate befell Augusta Stetson. She ha
dissociated herself from the whole nasty business.

As for Augusta Stetson, it was her faith that finally ruin
her. Her belief in Mary Baker Eddy was her ultimate u
doing. Without making a move in her own defense she a
lowed her honors to be plucked from her, her robes of t
high-priestess to be torn away, her life's work to be shattere
And she only bowed her head.

At almost any moment before the end she could have gat
ered around her the remnants of her stately robes, tak
sword in hand, and vanquished every enemy. She could ha
appeared before her altar in the midst of her ecstatic wc
shippers, and with one hour of exhortation, and a final wo

f command, torn the Christian Science Church in half. Most
f her followers would undoubtedly have deserted all other
tandards to follow hers. They would have seceded eagerly
ad she made one single move to persuade them to journey
ut with her to new and more delightful promised lands.
'here were few indeed in her church who could resist her
ynamic power and eloquence when she chose to exert it.
Irs. Eddy, now only a myth to almost every one in her or-
anization, could not have availed against the extraordinary
ersonal appeal of Mrs. Stetson, had Mrs. Stetson sought to
aise her voice.

But she made no move. Even more than she loved power
nd wealth and influence, she worshipped her conception of
ie woman she knew as Mrs. Eddy—Mary Baker Eddy,
vhom she had thought dead, and now knew lived. Mrs. Eddy,
ad she only known it, had nothing to fear from Augusta
tetson. For Mrs. Stetson her slightest wish was a command.

Thus does faith work its miracles—and thus did it render
ervice to Mrs. Eddy even in her old age. Augusta Stetson
vent to her grave proclaiming that Mrs. Eddy was divine
nd could not err. She maintained that Mrs. Eddy stood by
vhile she was crucified by the Board of Directors for just
ne reason: Mrs. Eddy, in the rôle of Christ, was showing
Augusta Stetson how to rise to an even higher state of con-
ciousness, where one could build "on a wholly spiritual foun-
ation," and live entirely apart from the lower levels of either
material organization or a material world.

Humbly, worshipfully, Mrs. Stetson wrote to Mrs. Eddy
vhen she received news that she could no longer teach or
eal in the Christian Science Church:

Iy Precious Leader, Teacher and Guide:—I have heard your
ear voice in your letter which appeared in *The Sentinel* of October
5th. . . . I am today sending in my resignation as a member of the
oard of Trustees of First Church of Christ, Scientist, New York City.
am also notifying the Secretary of my Students' Association that I
iall not attend the approaching Annual Meeting. . . . I shall strictly
ot oppose the orders of the Board of Directors of The First Church of
hrist, Scientist, in Boston, Mass. . . . I am apprehending more and

more the meaning of "wholly spiritual" building, which you enjoine(
upon me and my church in your letter in the *Sentinel* of Jan. 16th
. . . My gratitude and love for my precious Leader are beyond all tha
human language can express. Your faithful child,   AUGUSTA.[1]

And so Mrs. Stetson lifted from Mrs. Eddy and her Boar(
the shadow of every fear which had plagued them. Mrs. Edd
breathed easily for the first time in months. Her Board pro
ceeded to finish trampling Augusta Stetson into the dust.

On the very day that Mrs. Eddy had written her Pilat
script, "Take Notice," she had written to Archibald McLellar
Chairman of the Board of Directors:

October 12, 1909

BELOVED STUDENT: Learn at once if The Mother Church can be prose
cuted for suspending a student or even expelling them, who is giving u
so much trouble as Mrs. Stetson does, and if it can be done safely dro
Mrs. Stetson's connection with The Mother Church.

Let no one know that I have written you on this subject. Lovingl
yours,   MARY BAKER EDDY.[2]

Mrs. Eddy always had trouble with relative pronouns i
times of excitement.

The Board immediately proceeded to its welcome assign
ment. Mrs. Stetson's own Trustees had presented a repor
entirely vindicating her. The congregation of Mrs. Stetson'
church had then voted to accept this whitewashing repor
after a sensational all-day meeting in which riots occurre
and policemen had to be posted at the church. For Mrs. Stet
son had enough enemies in her own congregation to make th
discussion of her status exciting. Virgil Strickler, the Firs
Reader of the Church, had finally taken sides against her; h
was the one who had supplied the Boston Board with much o
its evidence of the manner in which Mrs. Stetson had given it
members "death treatments," and he was the dominatin
leader of the minority opposition in the church.

[1] For entire letter, vd. Stetson, *Vital Issues in Christian Science*, page 96.

[2] John V. Dittemore, former Director of The Mother Church, made this le
ter public in a paid advertisement published April 1, 1926, in the New Yo
World, which also printed the document in its news columns of that date. Th
purpose of his advertisement was to refute assertions by Mrs. Stetson—the
still alive—that her excommunication had been caused by the Board of Direc
ors, and not by Mrs. Eddy.

Strickler's diary concerning the conversations at some of
the noon-day practitioners' meetings provides an extraordi-
ary commentary on the manner in which some of Mrs.
Eddy's habits of thought affected her impressionable follow-
rs. For Mrs. Eddy there were two different minds—the Di-
ine Mind, which could not err; and the mortal mind, which
was entirely error. How far astray this bit of dogma could
ead impressionable souls—including Mrs. Eddy herself—is
well illustrated in the following excerpt from Strickler's rec-
rd of a meeting Mrs. Stetson held with the practitioners
pon her return from her first hearing in Boston—the hear-
ng that was dismissed. The date was July 31, 1909.

I said: "Mrs. Stetson, if we tell this, they will expel you instantly
rom The Mother Church." She said: "I know it; what shall we do?"
fter awhile she said: "We must deny that I ever said any of those
ings. I deny that I ever said them." I said: "But Mrs. Stetson, you
d say them, and you have habitually taken up people by name and
eated them."[1] She replied that it was not her that took them up; that
was the human that said those things, and that the human was not her
al self, and that she could say that she never said them, and do it with
mental reservation that her real self had never said them. . . .
Miss ——, one of the practitioners, then broke in to say that she had
nied in this way in a certain lawsuit, and that it was perfectly proper
 deny something you had said if you only did it with the mental res-
vation that while the human self may have done the thing, it was the
al self that was denying having done it. . . .
Pretty soon Miss ——, another practitioner, said that she had been
 the witness stand for two days in the lawsuit mentioned, and had
tified throughout from the "absolute," and the opposing lawyer had
ver caught her once.
Not to be outdone, Mrs. ——, another practitioner, spoke up and
d that she too had been on the witness stand for a day and a half in
 same lawsuit and had done the same thing. . . .[2]

This explanation of the way in which some of Mrs. Eddy's
ctrine's may be utilized to heal a suffering conscience offers

According to Mrs. Eddy's writings, to "take up" people by name and with-
. their consent give them "absent treatment," was a mesmeristic practice
orgivable in a Christian Scientist. This prohibition reflected her own fears
being unwittingly "treated."

From excerpts from the diary supplied to the New York *World* and published
ts issue of November 7, 1909.

a perfect demonstration of the morass into which any ph
losophy must fall when it provides no standards for distin
guishing between subjective and objective truth. Once Mrs
Eddy had denied the reality of an objective material world
she stripped away all standards by which any truth could b
ascertained. No human idea can ever have its truth demon
strated until it is tested and compared with the objective rea
ity whose existence Mrs. Eddy utterly denied.

Thus does Mrs. Eddy's philosophy lead inevitably into th
traditional night where all cows are black. And that is wher
it led Mrs. Stetson. After she had been vindicated by her ow
church, the Boston Board summoned her for trial before i
own members. Neither Mrs. Eddy nor her Directors intende
to leave Augusta Stetson a leg to stand on. Even though he
recognition as a teacher and healer had been taken away, sh
might somehow manage to cause trouble if she were allowe
to remain in The Mother Church. So a new trial was calle
in Boston. Mrs. Stetson was charged with sins as various a
undue control of her students, malpractice against othe
Mother Church members, and self-deification. At the end o
the trial she was excommunicated from The Mother Churc
forever.

Mrs. Stetson to the end made no move of resistance of an
sort. Excommunication from The Mother Church did not en
her membership in the New York Church which she ha
founded. But as a mere member of a branch church she ha
no standing in Christian Science. She immediately handed
her resignation to her own congregation, and never aga
crossed the threshold of the temple which she had raised.

She never ceased to affirm that Mrs. Eddy was a moder
Christ, and that her own excommunication was only on
more step in her climb to Mrs. Eddy's Christ-like level—
level where one had shaken off all material bonds, and becom
pure spirit.

"Die?" she exclaimed once to a question. "Why, of cour
I shan't die. I haven't an organ in my body, not a one. I a
already on a plane that would mean instantaneous death
any one of you."

Never once did she admit a belief that Mrs. Eddy had turned
gainst her. Years later, when Mrs. Eddy's letter ordering her
xcommunication—"if it can be done safely"—was made pub-
c, Mrs. Stetson flatly denied the authenticity of the document.
he was quoted as saying, in an interview published in the New
ork *World*:[1]

Mrs. Eddy took no part in the unwarranted and arbitrary action of the
ard of Directors in dropping my name from the roll of the material or-
nization of the Christian Science Church in 1909. . . . I invite Mr.
ttemore and the Board of Directors to produce any such letter, or
ters, claimed to be from Mrs. Eddy, which they will submit to a hand-
riting expert for the examination of the signature. . . .
Mrs. Eddy never wrote such a letter. Can any one imagine her doing
ything in an underhand way?

Augusta Stetson lived to a ripe old age. In 1928, when she
ed of heart disease after a physician had been called to relieve
r intense suffering, she was still proclaiming that she would
immortal—"here and now."
To the very end she maintained that Mary Baker Eddy
me to her constantly, and that they communed together
ery night on planes too high for human ken.
April 1, 1926.

XXXII

Mrs. Stetson was formally excommunicated from T[
Mother Church on November 18, 1909; she resigned fro[
the New York branch church that she herself had created (
November 22, and within the next few months—the dang[
of her own presence removed—the Boston Board had excor
municated all of the Stetson trustees and practitioners. Eve[
official and leader in her church who had raised a voice in h
defense was thrust into outer darkness. Her memory w
torn out root and branch from the church that she had builde
and the fields in which it had flourished were sown with sa[

The eager interest with which Mrs. Eddy watched t[
course of these proceedings is attested by the words ascrib[
by one of Mrs. Stetson's students, Miss Mary R. Pinney, to t
First Reader of The Mother Church. When, after Mrs. St[
son's excommunication, the First Reader came to "admonis[
Miss Pinney in accordance with a by-law of the *Manual,* s[
disputed the right of the Board of Directors to impose on h
their own interpretation of Mrs. Eddy's teachings. Then,
quote Miss Pinney,

"Judge Smith made a statement to the effect that Mrs. Eddy had ne[
expressed so much active interest in any issue since the Woodbury tri[
I quoted the *Manual,* Article XXII, Section 7, that Mrs. Eddy is not[
be consulted in cases of discipline. Judge Smith replied, 'Mrs. Eddy [
made an exception in this case.' "[1]

To the end, however, Mrs. Eddy maintained her fiction
being entirely disinterested in and aloof from the confli[
Her last letter to Mrs. Stetson, the finale to their years [
warm and devoted correspondence, had been written on A[
gust 30, 1909. With cool unction Mrs. Eddy repeated the a[
surance of her love, and voiced her trust that God would (
rect Augusta's footsteps into the path of His flock. She urg[

[1] Stetson, *Vital Issues in Christian Science,* page 223.

494

er to follow the guidance of The Holy Bible, *Science and
ealth,* and The Mother Church *Manual,* and concluded:

I have not the time to think of the Students in all their varied duties
. life, but I have the faith to leave them in the hands of God, who
veth to all men liberally and upbraideth none.

As ever yours in Christ,

MARY BAKER EDDY.[1]

What Mrs. Eddy really meant was that she was leaving
ugusta in the hands of the Board of Directors. Mrs. Stet-
n never heard from Mrs. Eddy again. Mrs. Eddy did, how-
-er, address a few words to the New York congregation in
ovember after Mrs. Stetson had been forever exiled. She
id in a letter later published in *The Sentinel:*

ELOVED BRETHREN:—In consideration of the present momentous
estion at issue in First Church of Christ, Scientist, New York City,
am constrained to say, if I can settle this church difficulty amicably
 a few words, as many students think I can, I herewith cheerfully
bscribe these words of love:—
My beloved brethren in First Church of Christ, Scientist, New York
ty, I advise you with all my soul to support the Directors of The
other Church, and unite with those in your church who are support-
g The Mother Church Directors. . . .

It was not this appeal, however, which saved to Mrs. Eddy
e largest branch church in her organization. Only the fact
at Mrs. Stetson bowed her head for the executioner's blow
ithout a protest allowed Mrs. Eddy to die with her church
tact instead of sundered by revolution.

In her last years Mrs. Eddy's physical condition was pecu-
rly distressing to her Board, which had only now come to
low that she was a prey to very human ills which in no way
came a priestess whose powers of healing had been her-
led to the ends of the winds. During the days when with al-
rnate courage and vacillation she was directing the destruc-
n of Augusta, she was still subject to those same ill-
sses of hysterical nature which had been with her all her
e, and there was never assurance that one day which found
r active and able to direct her affairs with dynamic energy

For entire letter, vd. Stetson, *Vital Issues in Christian Scceince,* page 164.

would not be followed by another in which she might be er
tirely helpless.

She never left her house or indeed the three rooms in whic
she dwelt on the second floor except for her drives, and eve
with her iron determination and an elevator which carried h
direct to her carriage, she could not always find the strengt
for this habitual appearance. These periods of confinemer
accounted for the renewal of the rumors concerning her dea
and the fraud being practised on the public by her Directo
—the rumors which found such credence that even Augus
Stetson herself had been deceived.

Many others of less eminent position were also misled; ar
the Directors were constantly faced with the necessity of cor
bating the most unfortunate reports which refused to
downed despite the warmest denials. One particularly emba
rassing incident was involved.

In Brooklyn, on Dyker Heights, was a flourishing Chri
tian Science Church which had been built and fostered by
Mrs. Della Gilbert. Mrs. Gilbert was a tall, blue-eyed wom:
of highly emotional temperament who had never know
Mrs. Eddy personally, but had established quite a followir
in the Brooklyn residential districts.

In May of 1909, shortly before Mrs. Stetson sent to Mr
Eddy the fatal composite letter, Mrs. Gilbert decided—as h;
so many others—that Mrs. Eddy was either dead or "min
less," and that she was surviving only as a corporation. Ha
ing reached this conclusion, Mrs. Gilbert bought a ticket f
Boston with the determination to verify her opinion.

She went out to the great house at Chestnut Hill qui
unannounced, rang the bell, and was received by Mr. Dick
She was informed that she could not see Mrs. Eddy. She s
for some minutes with Mr. Dickey in the great silent rece
tion room, heard not even a sound in all the vast mansion, a
decided that she now knew all: Mrs. Eddy was no more. Wh
she left Mr. Dickey she went back to the Parker House, whe
she was staying, and wrote an ultimatum. Under the date
May 21, 1909, she said, in a letter subsequently published
the New York *World:*

Y DEAR MR. DICKEY:

I came to Boston to see the "Leader" and go into the home of Mrs. ddy. I did both. You, of course, working metaphysically, well know hat it means to enter a house and get the mental atmosphere that fills I accomplished all I wanted in that visit. I saw the only Leader when saw you—the only Leader that you or any one else in that house can oduce in the flesh.

For a long while I have been maturing my plans. I have back of me, oney, power and influence from a worldly standpoint and God from a iritual. It is not my purpose to attempt to overthrow the Christian cience organization, as I believe it was originally started right by Mrs. ddy, the author of the inspired text book *Science and Health*. The ok will stand. What I purpose to do with God back of me is to down is personally conducted tour of religion—this fetishism. The idol ist go. . . . God is our leader, is my leader, and with him to guide d govern me I shall commence my work—to tear down this idol. I all organize a church, a Christian Science Church in New York ty. . . .

There was much more. Mrs. Gilbert gave the Church au- orities three days to make a reply, before she put her plans to effect.

On the final day of grace she was visited by two high offi- als of the church organization. There was a long and an- iished meeting. The spokesman talked to her with tears in s eyes. He and his fellow officials were indeed in a most un- ortunate situation. They could not publicly produce Mrs. ddy, because of her physical condition; on the other hand, ey could not proceed as if she were really dead, for the sim- e reason that she was liable to rise up any day very much ive and with completely renewed energy, to overturn all that r officials had tried to accomplish during her indisposition. s Mrs. Gilbert later wrote in a published statement: "To e and talk with the hidden leader was all I asked. It was then at he wept. I had asked the one impossible thing."

The two officials pled long and ardently with Mrs. Gilbert see the error of her ways. They showed her recent letters ritten and signed by Mary Baker Eddy in Mrs. Eddy's own igular hand. They contended that Mrs. Eddy was still alive, d communing regularly.

Mrs. Gilbert finally capitulated. She agreed not to seek to

found a rival church. She later stated that one of her visitor
urged on her the possibility of bringing about "the purificatic
of the Church by other means than exposure." She furth
quoted him as saying:

"If you have made any financial sacrifice in this work, Divine Lo
will make up all your losses. Only abandon your plan. . . ."[1]

Mrs. Gilbert agreed graciously after hands had been shak
all around. The visitors departed, and she sat down ar
penned another letter. She stated that her expense in her u
dertaking had amounted to some five thousand dollars. "
Divine Love will send, give, or loan to me the sum of $5,000
she wrote, ". . . the money would tide me over the next fe
months . . . and enable me to start my church work in t
Fall in New York if at that time you think it advisable."

This finished Mrs. Gilbert. The Board of Directors sent h
letter to the newspapers, and immediately dropped the Gilbe
name from the roll of The Mother Church.

But the conditions in the Eddy household which made
possible for situations such as the Gilbert incident to ari
undoubtedly plagued Mrs. Eddy's harassed Directors to
extreme degree. After they consummated what they call
their "housecleaning" in Mrs. Stetson's church, and got t
Next Friends' suit settled so that all danger of a contest
relatives over Mrs. Eddy's will was eliminated, their life w
hardly easier. For Mrs. Eddy refused to die. She lived on a
on and on, querulous, commanding, ailing, suspicious. Even
the smallest matters she could keep her Directors in hot wa
constantly. A statue, for instance, had been ordered for pla
ing in the new addition to The Mother Church. The comm
sion was given to the sculptor after Mrs. Eddy had been cc
sulted regarding the design—the figure of a kneeling woma
When the work was completed, the Directors asked M
Eddy's permission to place the sculpture above the great c
gan. Mrs. Eddy refused flatly, then announced that she c
not want the thing in her church at all. When the Directc
pointed out that the commission for carving it had been plac

[1] New York *World*, June 7, 1909.

ith her express permission and that they were under obliga-
ons to receive it, she was no less adamant. She announced
at she had changed her mind.

She changed her mind constantly with no reference what-
er to anything that had gone before. When this habitude
ove her directors almost frantic, she would lean back with
benevolent smile to declare that God was speaking through
r, and nothing more was to be said. "Is a leader any less a
ider because she changes her mind?" she would inquire with
iality. "I do change my mind frequently. But when I do it is
id that changes me—He has given me additional light."

Thereupon Mrs. Eddy would say impressively that in over
rty years of Leadership she had never made a mistake.

She kept her secretaries in a constant dance by the same
rt of tactics. She would dictate a letter, have it all typed
t, and then revise it time and again until it had gone
rough so many drafts that the original version was unrec-
nizable. Sometimes she would ponder over a letter for
urs, seeking for what she said was the right word. In the
ne way she still toyed with *Science and Health* even in
ese final days, spending long hours, when she felt in the
od, in re-reading her work and revising it with notes be-
een the lines as had been her custom for years.

Some of these changes were made at the suggestion of cor-
pondents. One worshiper wrote in to point out that "cica-
zed joints" should correctly be made to read "ankylosed
nts." Mrs. Eddy consulted her three dictionaries, which she
t always beside her, and agreed. But she would not always
ld so graciously. When one correspondent wrote that "hec-
mbs of gushing theories" was a phrase that did not mean
ything, since a hecatomb was a sacrifice of one hundred
ls, Mrs. Eddy refused to amend this line in *Science and
alth*. The phrase sounded well, and she was satisfied. She
l her secretary that since the statement was used in a sense
ridicule, it quite fully expressed what she wanted to say.
eople do not always understand my sense of humor," she
plained.

Occasionally some of Mrs. Eddy's correspondents were not

wholly deferential in their suggestions for revising her use o
the English tongue. One woman, having read in *Miscellaneou*
Writings Mrs. Eddy's denunciations of a critic as a "bee
bulged, surly censor," wrote from England to suggest th
Christian Scientists should not use epithets. Had the lady on
known Mrs. Eddy's resources in epithets, she would have r
alized that the critic was getting off lightly. But this letter di
pleased Mrs. Eddy extremely.

Between her periods of literary activity the old lady cou
always find time to rearrange the furnishings of the thr
rooms in which she spent practically all of her waking a
sleeping hours. When she moved into the great house
Chestnut Hill, she decided that she did not like the rooms th
had been prepared for her. They were too large. Her stu
was twenty feet long, her desk being placed at the far end
the bay window. When she sat at her desk it took all of sever
seconds for a secretary to reach her side after he had open
the door. She declared that something must be done to sa
her time. Her bedroom was likewise so graciously commoc
ous that she felt as if she were voyaging across seas of carp
She announced that the entire scale of her living quarters mi
be cut down. Long consultations ensued. Finally an archite
was called from the West—no local residents were ever giv
a chance to see the Eddy establishment at close range.

As a result of the architect's deliberations, it was decid
that the entire scale of Mrs. Eddy's living quarters should
telescoped, and Mrs. Eddy retired to the third floor of t
mansion for three weeks while the necessary alterations we
being accomplished. Part of the extra space obtained in t
manner was utilized for the new elevator to carry Mrs. Ed
direct to her porte-cochère.

When Mrs. Eddy came back to her revised quarters s
spent long hours in rearranging their furnishings. She wo
take infinite time to decide about the positions to be accorc
the furniture, the ornaments, the *bibelots*, and all the otl
accoutrements with which she was surrounded. Mr. Dick
her secretary, won her heart immediately by an invention 1
trying out pictures in different positions before they we

ing. The invention consisted merely of a stick with a hook
the end; with the aid of this device a picture would be held
in a countless number of positions while Mrs. Eddy sat
ck and looked with appraising eye, trying every possible lo-
tion until she had hit on the right one.

Mr. Dickey was also a great convenience in assisting her to
just her extensive collection of souvenirs, samples from the
tensive accumulation of offerings at her shrine over a long
riod of years. A simple and enraptured soul if there ever was
e, he took an exquisite delight in co-operation with the old
dy to satisfy her whims. "She herself," wrote Mr. Dickey
ecstatic phrases, "named the spot on the mantel where each
nament should rest; while I, overjoyed at this rare privilege,
oved things back and forth at her command until everything
as placed as she desired it."[1]

Once Mrs. Eddy had decided on a location, she never forgot
Her rooms were dusted and swept whenever she went on
r drive; and if anything was half an inch out of position
hen she returned, woe to the housemaids. If they insisted
at everything had been returned exactly to its former posi-
on, an argument ensued which was very painful for all con-
rned. One gathers from Mr. Dickey's account that Mrs.
ddy was still a masterhand in using the epithets by which the
nglish lady had been pained.

Mr. Dickey solved this serious problem very simply—just
all great inventions are simple. He suggested the use of
cks to mark the exact location of everything in the room.
hen, when things were moved, they were put back exactly
the tacks. There could be no possible mistake.

This happy result of ingenuity so pleased Mrs. Eddy that
e was in a good humor for days. Mr. Dickey assumed the
atus of a genius. Almost her last official act before she died
as to appoint him to her Board of Directors.

Between her periods of energetic puttering Mrs. Eddy
ould time and again succumb to the physical suffering that

Adam H. Dickey, *Memoirs of Mary Baker Eddy*, page 61. The Dickey ac-
unt of proceedings in Mrs. Eddy's home is peculiarly valuable, inasmuch as
is the recital of a loyal disciple who was the senior member of the Christian
ience Board of Directors when he penned his revelations.

the household always knew as M. A. M. At such times eve
one in the ménage was on emergency duty just as happens
an army camp when the planes of the enemy are sighted. Mr
Eddy's household consisted of from twelve to eighteen pe
sons beside herself, the variation in number being account
for by the number of mental healers who were in servi
around her. Her personal servants consisted of a housekeepe
a houseman, a coachman, a night watchman, and two maic
one of whom prepared her meals while the other cared for h
rooms, her wardrobe, and her person.

Mrs. Eddy had grown exceedingly scrupulous and dain
regarding her person with the passing years; every day s
wore a fresh silk gown, with newly laundered lace or ruchi
at the throat and wrists; her nails were carefully manicure
her skin thoroughly bathed, her hair painstakingly arrange
Her maids were busily occupied almost from dawn, for Mr
Eddy regularly rang her electric bell for service every mor
ing at six o'clock. Punctuality had become so much of a feti
that clocks adorned every possible niche in her rooms, and s
even had an alarm clock hung at the foot of her bed.

The mental healers were never supposed to leave the
rooms unless they were specifically summoned. They we
spoken of as being "at post," and their instructions for ea
day would be sent up by the hand of Frye, Mrs. Sarger
or Mrs. Eddy's maid. Such instructions, contained in t
"watch," listed the specific evils or "errors" which the heale
were supposed to attack and combat. Evils which receiv
their special attention were unpropitious conditions in M
Eddy's church, the effects of malicious animal magnetism
Mrs. Eddy's personal health, and the vagaries of the weathe
Mrs. Eddy was never satisfied with their work on the weathe
In January of 1910 she instructed them in a general order
"make a law that there shall be no more snow this seasor
Every one in the household redoubled his efforts. Snowstorr
were a difficult manifestation to deal with, particularly
Massachusetts, where these phases of error had gained
unusually strong foothold—much stronger, for instance, th
in Florida, which was almost immune. Mrs. Eddy, howev

horted her people not to be discouraged. They also continued
work valiantly against thunderstorms, and here—at least
r that winter—they seem to have had more success. Mr.
ickey wrote in his *Memoirs* that during his sojourn with
rs. Eddy "there were fewer and fewer thunderstorms until
ey almost ceased to be." At times when Mrs. Eddy felt it
cessary to rebuke her household for failure in their mental
forts to control the elements, she often told how she had dis-
ated many a storm-cloud merely by looking at it.

Besides the work on the weather which was done in her own
usehold, Mrs. Eddy also appointed a committee of three in
ston to lend co-operation in this task. Whether this church
mmittee took its duties seriously cannot now be known.[1]

The watchers in Mrs. Eddy's household stayed on duty all
ght. Mrs. Eddy, as always, went to bed at nine o'clock. From
ne o'clock onward her healers had two-hour "watches" in
nich they were supposed to sit up and concentrate mentally
order to guard her from the evil mental currents being sent
t by her enemies.

Mrs. Eddy had no doubt whatever that her enemies were
eking to kill her. Under her own repeated assertions regard-
g this fear her household came to share her belief. When
new coachman died less than a week after he had been en-
ged, Mrs. Eddy and those around her knew that he had not
en strong enough to withstand the attacks of malicious ani-
al magnetism which were concentrated against Chestnut
ill more powerfully than any other spot on earth. Eventu-
y Frye himself gave the appearance of succumbing to this
ful influence. One night after Mrs. Eddy had gone to bed,
rs. Sargent came hastily to her door to say that Frye was
mpletely unconscious and could not be aroused.

Frye had had another one of his cataleptic seizures, which
his old age had become rather rare. None of those in Mrs.
dy's establishment at Chestnut Hill had ever seen him
icken in this manner. Mrs. Sargent and every one else

For details regarding Mrs. Eddy's efforts to eliminate snow from the New
gland climate vd. Dickey's *Memoirs of Mary Baker Eddy*, pages 20 ff., 49
53.

thought that he was dead. Mrs. Eddy rang immediately fo
her maid, tried to get out of bed, then dropped back to sa
that she would not wait to dress. She clutched a shawl aroun
her thin shoulders. "Bring him to me," she said hoarsel
"Bring him to me at once."

Calvin was hoisted to a large rockingchair and carried, st
slumping over in the chair, around through the hall, to be d
posited at Mrs. Eddy's bedside. Mrs. Eddy reached out
trembling hand and rested it on his shoulder.

"Calvin!" she exclaimed. "Calvin! Wake up! Disappoi
your enemies! You shall not go. I need you here. Calvi
Awake!"

The senseless Calvin eventually groaned, his eyes can
slightly open, his breathing assumed some regularity.

"I don't want to stay. . . . I want to go . . ." he mu
mured.

"The idea!" exclaimed Mrs. Eddy. "Just listen to that!"

Calvin was very shortly thereafter put to bed, and he wa
up and around the house at his usual tasks the next mornin
with his accustomed regularity. But the eyes of every one
the household were luminous. They had seen a miracle pe
formed. A man had been raised from the dead under the
very gaze! All spoke in hushed voices, and once again the
faith was warmed. All of them had heard echoes of the ide
—rumored in the outside world for years—that Mrs. Edd
had lost her healing power. Now, this lack of faith r
proached, they reconsecrated themselves to their tasks of mi
istering at the shrine.

Mrs. Eddy herself, as she remembered the deaths of P
melia Leonard, of Mary Tomlinson, of the new coachman; a
she recalled the times when even Calvin Frye had succumbe
founded though he was in the faith,—Mrs. Eddy would ofte
become panic-stricken.

"Mr. Dickey," she said once, "if I should ever leave he
—do you know what I mean by that? . . ."

"Yes, Mother."

"If I should ever leave here, will you promise me that yo
will say that I was mentally murdered?"[1]

[1]Related by Mr. Dickey in his Preface to his *Memoirs of Mary Baker Edd*

"Yes, Mother."

Mrs. Eddy had Mr. Dickey swear an oath to God that he ould not fail to keep this promise.

Mrs. Eddy was constantly exhorting her healers as a gen- al would his soldiers. Time and again—usually when she ffered one of her attacks despite the dutiful "watches" of er mental practitioners—she would accuse them of sleeping . their posts. "You don't any of you realize what is going 1," she would cry. "This is a dark hour for the cause and ou do not seem to be awake to it."

Her household to the day of her death attributed much of er physical suffering to the birth throes of new ideas for her urch. As Mr. Dickey phrased it, "she actually felt the needs the Movement in her body just as the mother of a young fant would feel the needs of the infant and supply them."[1] ntil she died Mrs. Eddy was passing new by-laws, and her nesses during these periods became a cause for holy wonder. Calvin Frye told me," said Mr. Dickey, "that these experi- nces always came to Mrs. Eddy in this way and that when- er any great revelation came to her, concerning that which emed necessary for the welfare of the cause, these struggles opeared in her body. This corroborates what she told me oout feeling the needs of the Movement in her body."[2]

It was in 1908 that Mrs. Eddy passed a most important y-law abolishing communion to The Mother Church. The ason she gave was that the number of communicants had rown so great that the church would not seat them. Actually is obvious difficulty could easily have been overcome by hav- ig more than one service, as on the day when the church was edicated. The real motivation back of the decree was un- oubtedly the fact that Mrs. Eddy's entire congregation was gog with the sensational events of the previous year—the ewspaper investigations, the Next Friends' Suit, which was ill unsettled, and the Stetson situation, which was just be- nning to be rumored. Mrs. Eddy did not want these matters scussed at any general meeting of her followers. She wor- ed until once more she became desperately ill. Then she

[1] Adam H. Dickey, *Memoirs of Mary Baker Eddy*, page 117.
[2] *Ibid.*, page 47.

passed her by-law forbidding all future communion gathe[r]
ings. With this practical solution arrived at she felt bett[er]
immediately, and once more her household marvelled at t[he]
process by which she gave birth to the ideas for the guidan[ce]
of her children.

It was for similar reasons that she issued a ruling disban[d]
ing all gatherings of Executive Members; once again sh[e]
afterward had an unwonted period of calm.

When Mrs. Eddy's illnesses were not caused by her ment[al]
confinement, so to speak, they were caused by her enemie[s].
Mrs. Eddy never got far away from her enemies until t[he]
end of her days. If she felt any attacks coming on her eith[er]
during the day or the night, she immediately looked at h[er]
clock, by which she had a light, and then consulted her cha[rt]
to see what healer was supposed to be holding watch at th[at]
hour. If the attack grew more severe instead of passing, s[he]
would issue the next day a sharp reprimand to the healer f[or]
not keeping his watch properly. Mr. Dickey has recorded th[at]
the watches "were far more frequently not kept than kept[."]
Undoubtedly, poor Mrs. Eddy had a hard time of it.

"If error can do this to me, what is it going to do to you[?"]
she would sometimes moan to her healers in agony. "If y[ou]
will keep the watch, I shall be a well woman. Where all t[he]
students have failed is in not knowing how to handle anim[al]
magnetism. The workers in the field are not healing becau[se]
they cannot meet the animal magnetism which says they ca[n]
not heal. It tried to overcome me for forty years and I wit[h]
stood it all. I am working on a plane that would mean insta[n]
taneous death to any of you. I am out in the front rank mee[t]
ing the attacks of the enemy alone. . . ."

In almost the last year of her life she dictated a new e[x]
hortation to be inserted in the pages of *Science and Healt[h]*
It read:

Christian Scientists, be a law to yourselves that mental malpract[ice]
cannot harm you either when asleep or when awake.[1]

Her greatest fear was that she might eventually be a[t]

[1] *Science and Health*, page 442.

cked by her enemies when she lay asleep and the watch was
rowsing at his post.

She had grown used to pain. All her life she had struggled
ith pain, had been stricken and conquered time and again, al-
ays rising once more to start the battle anew. It was now
eath that she feared. She could not think of herself as dead.
he could not imagine herself apart from the world that she
ad created.

And now she could feel this world of hers slipping from
er grasp—the protective organism which she had built up
round her to shield herself from the cold universe beyond.
eath would mean—what? She did not know. There was
ttle in her religion about death. She had always fled from
e very thought. She had not even provided her church with
funeral service.

Never had her philosophy made a place for the great prob-
ms which men have faced since the dawn of consciousness.
he had merely denied the existence of all problems. And yet
e now had come to days when she could not deny death.
agerly, hungrily, desperately as she had held to life, the
ought of death remained. The shadow drew nearer. . . .

For all men religion means a quest for a reality greater and
ore inclusive than the paltry data which the mere senses can
veal. From the beginning of time men have believed that be-
nd the materiality which they can touch and see lies a deeper
alm the senses do not apprehend. It is not another realm—it
the same world interpreted through another—perhaps a
reater—understanding.

The world of sensory experience has been infinitely enriched
r men who did not deny this visible realm—but rather en-
rged it by adding some inner glimpse of the further reality
hich eyes can never behold.

But this was not the experience of Mary Baker Eddy. In
eking the inner meaning of things, she lost the sensory uni-
rse she had sought to enrich and explain. Instead of gaining
greater Life, she merely sacrificed one partial beauty to seek
other meaning, no less incomplete.

Never once had the great universe around her ever seemed

to her a comrade. In her philosophy she could never gaze u
at the heavens and know that she and they were kindred. Sh
could not feel that because she was of the earth earthy, sh
was also of the stars. She could never experience the peac
that comes with lying on a hillside in a warm spring twiligh
and knowing that man and twilight and the trees and gras
are one, inseparable, for all eternity. Never could she sense th
serene fellowship that comes with gazing into a sunset, c
standing in the cathedral mystery of a forest, and remembe
ing that man and the world which surrounds him are friend
and lovers.

For Mary Baker Eddy there was only loneliness. All he
life she had stood alone, battled alone, against a Univers
which she had never understood. This one great Reality, whic
asks only understanding from men in order to give the
everything, had for Mary Baker Eddy been only a hosti
enemy from which to flee.

The time was now come when she could flee no longer. R
ality had outstripped her, and at last would not be denied.

And she had no philosophy to lend her strength, and n
understanding to give her peace. Death to her was merely—
death. Deny it as she would, it was now the end. Never befo
had she considered death seriously. Never had she thougl
about transition. In her philosophy there had been no place fc
transition, no room for experience.

Now the Universe was slowly closing in around her. R
ality drew near.

XXXIII

The Directors of Mrs. Eddy's church were greatly perturbed as they saw her end approaching. For never had she made permanent provision for their own status and that of her church. Her by-laws still required the formal consent of herself, as Pastor Emeritus, before they could be effective.

Mrs. Eddy had made her will, disposing of her own property. Outside of a few small personal bequests, practically all of her estate was to go to her church, which in effect she owned personally. The provisions of the will were therefore equivalent to a transfer of money from one hand to another. What would happen to the church when she died?

Mrs. Eddy herself wondered.

For years she had worried over this question, and for years she had tried to avoid the thought. Once, as far back as 1901 —soon after rumors that she was dead first gained credence —she was asked by a reporter from the New York *Herald* about the future of her hierarchy.

At that time she said, "No further change is contemplated in the rulership. You would ask, perhaps, whether my successor will be a woman or a man. I can answer that. It will be a man."

"Can you name the man?" she was asked.

"I cannot answer that now," she declared.

This statement, issued nonchalantly and for probably no more reason than that Mrs. Eddy was rather tired of women —considering what she had just endured from Mrs. Woodbury—had immediate repercussions. There were no men of importance in her church, but several women who felt that they had a right to be considered proper heirs to the Eddy power and leadership. Mrs. Eddy's pronouncement caused murmurings among all of them. Mrs. Eddy realized her tactical blunder, and immediately issued another statement:

I did say that a man would be my future successor. By this I did not mean any man today on earth.

Science and Health makes it plain to all Christian Scientists that t
manhood and womanhood of God have already been revealed to a d
gree through Christ Jesus and Christian Science, His two witnesse
What remains to lead on the centuries and reveal my successor, is m
in the image and likeness of the Father-Mother God, man the gener
term for all mankind.

This second statement was all very involved and tho
oughly qualified, but it at least may be taken as evidence tha
Mrs. Eddy had changed her mind. As a matter of fact, sl
seems never really to have made up her mind. There was on
one reality she faced in connection with her church: the ma
ter of her own leadership. She worked for years to desig
by-laws so impelling that this leadership could never be take
from her. Having gone thus far, her imagination could reac
no farther.

To the end she feared the men and women around her on
a little less than she feared death itself. Thus she had d
stroyed mercilessly every one in her church who ever gaine
any access of power that might endanger her own unique co
trol of her creation. This fear of others was so strong that sl
could not overcome it even when she knew that her span of da
was closing.

And yet, on evenings when she sat in the twilight after tl
supper hour, she wondered. She once told Mr. Dickey, p
thetically and with earnestness, that if she could only fir
someone with adequate spiritual gifts of leadership she wou
immediately put him at her church's head. But she died wit
out ever finding an heir. There was no human being in who
she had faith—no person whom she dared trust.

Her Directors in the last months came to her time ar
again. They were becoming panic-stricken. They knew that sl
was done. Over and over they had read their by-laws. Th
could find no provision for carrying on the church after sl
was dead. There was no single word or phrase to admit the po
sibility of her death. To the end of the world—according
those by-laws—Mary Baker Eddy was to go on decreein
supervising her officials, reserving the right to make all ne
laws, forbidding any single change in church governme

ithout consultation with her, stipulating implicit obedience
her every spoken or written command. The officials of the
urch were all her creatures; it was her church alone. No mat-
r how much her congregation ever contributed to it, they
d no voice in its government. They owned nothing in it. They
d no privilege except the right to come and sit in the pews
hile services were performed according to a ritual which
ary Baker Eddy had prescribed.

But what would happen to the powers which she had re-
rved to herself? Who would rule the church in her stead?

Her Directors came to her—often on days when she was
o weak to do more than sit idly in her chair, listening. They
eaded with her. They exhorted. Sometimes their words grew
impassioned as to seem more like threats than pleading.
hey begged that she write one new by-law—one single pro-
sion which would give them power to act in her stead when
e was gone.

And always she merely listened, silently, unmoved. Finally
e would raise her head in her old signal of dismissal. She
ould hear no more.

And then she would turn in her chair and again gaze out
the window—far away into horizons that seemed endless.
e would remain in the same position for minutes that passed
to hours—wordless, almost motionless, except for the trem-
ing that shook her withered limbs.

So the Directors would go away, perplexed and wondering,
d sometimes angered. Actually, had they but known, they
d little to fear. On Mrs. Eddy's death they merely took to
emselves the powers that formerly had been retained by her;
d they obtained voluminous legal opinions which apparently
mented them in this right. But before she died they could
t be sure that such an easy way out would be possible, had
certainty that they would not again have another formida-
e lawsuit to face in the courts.

For her own part, Mary Baker Eddy was not concerned
out her Directors. She had only one concern—herself. Her
urch apart from herself was not her church. If she was
t the Leader it did not matter. Her church was all she had

—it was all she was. She could not imagine herself apar
from it. She could not conceive of bequeathing it to any on
else in the world. No less difficult would it have been for he
to consider willing away some part of the body in which sh
had lived all her life.

And so she never once put her pen to a measure whicl
would admit the reality of her passing away from the churcl
she had created. She merely made the will which gave he
personal holdings to her church, which was herself. In addi
tion she left small bequests to Frye, Mrs. Sargent, and other
of her personnel, with a provision that Frye should have liv
ing quarters in the old Commonwealth Avenue house until hi
death. She left ten thousand dollars to each of her grandchil
dren; she set aside $100,000 as a trust fund to educate Chris
tian Science practitioners—this provision evidently being
reflection of her former desire to endow a million-dollar foun
dation; she provided for the lifting of the debt on the Secon
Church in New York. No Christian Science churches wer
supposed to have debts. This one had been founded by Mrs
Lathrop in opposition to Mrs. Stetson. Mrs. Eddy perhap
felt a personal interest in seeing its prosperity assured. T
Mrs. Stetson, Mrs. Eddy returned in her will the diamon
crown which Augusta had given her so many years befor
To Mrs. Lathrop she left her diamond cross. Nothing wa
left to charity. The entire personal estate represented in th
will was valued at approximately $3,000,000.

As she approached the end she would sit for long, lon
hours without a word, her eyes open but apparently quite un
seeing. It was as if she had finally reached a state of utte
unawareness of the entire external world—that unawarenes
of materiality which in her philosophy she had held up as a
ideal.

She who had sought to deny the existence of all extern;
reality was now come to a time when in truth all her exper
ence with an objective world was ended. She remained m
tionless in her chair, her hands clasped in her lap. Perhaps sh
was wrapped in contemplation; perhaps only in torpor. Son
men have said that she was in a stupor induced by drugs. Pe

aps we shall never know, and, after all, it does not greatly matter. She was an old, old woman, and—whatever their philosophies may be—old people should not be allowed to suffer without such comfort as medical science can afford.[1]

As she would sit thus endlessly, men in the world beyond were making glamorous explorations into the realities from which she had always fled. While twilight fell in her room, and her unseeing eyes wandered out of the great window to the dim lights of Beacon Street that stretched beyond, astronomers were somewhere gazing up to capture in their telescopes the light that had left stars millions of years ago. In far-off laboratories other men were peering through microscopes to discover infinitesimal but populous worlds of which the race had never even dreamed. They were analyzing matter to count its atoms; were exploring atoms to count the ions; were learning that matter and energy and light are only varying aspects of the same underlying reality; were discovering that the same laws of cause and effect apply equally to the life of the single ion and to the greatest galaxy of stars.

These others were seeking to master the universe not by denial but by understanding. They had thrown off the fears

---

[1] The present officials of Mrs. Eddy's church have disparaged all evidence that she ever resorted to drugs after her "discovery" of Christian Science. They characterize references to her use of morphine as "aggressive propaganda, apparently circulated to discredit Mrs. Eddy and to induce belief that she abandoned her own teaching."

They phrased a general denial in the following words, which appeared in the *Christian Science Sentinel* of January 26, 1929. The italics in the following paragraph are the biographer's:

"*As we are informed*, Mrs. Eddy did not, at any time after 1866, believe in the use of any drug as a *curative agent* in connection with the practice of Christian Science. Nor did she, at any time after she became a Christian Scientist, either use a drug or allow one to be used for her, except as *she employed, in a few instances, an anæsthetic for the purpose of temporary relief from extreme pain.*

"That she acted consistently with her teachings is shown by her statement about dentistry and surgery in the *Christian Science Sentinel* for December 6, 1900, and in *The Christian Science Journal* for January, 1901, and the paragraph in our text-book on the use of an anæsthetic (*Science and Health*, p. 464). As in a degree pertinent, it is to be remembered that the Master himself momentarily felt a sense of separation from his divine source, for he cried out, 'My God, my God, why hast thou forsaken me?' but he never abandoned his fidelity to divine Principle. Neither did Mrs. Eddy."

This carefully phrased denial, particularly interesting because of the parallel it seeks to draw between Mrs. Eddy and Jesus, appears to take refuge in the phrase, "As we are informed." For the rest, it seems to admit exactly what close

of their forefathers, had cast away the superstitions that ha
trammelled the race from its youth. Like Solomon, who whe
he gained understanding had all other things added unto hir
these earnest explorers who faced the universe with hone
eyes were being rewarded with a bounty inconceivable. H
manity was securing a power that previously had been thoug]
impossible except for a God.

personal associates of Mrs. Eddy have declared to be the facts: not that s
ever took morphine as a "curative agent"—no one ever took morphine as
"cure" for anything—but that she did find in its "relief from extreme pain"
temporary refuge. In this connection it should be observed that the Directc
do not define what they mean by "an anæsthetic" and "a few instances."

Numerous statements of Mrs. Eddy's old associates describing scenes in whi
morphine played an important part are given added meaning in the light
data which have more recently been revealed. The records in the Frye diari
excerpts from which the biographer is enabled to present in this edition
Appendix A, are not the only evidence that she found comfort in this "ana
thetic."

There has been made available to the biographer a copy of a letter alleged
have been signed by Mrs. Eddy and addressed by her to her Board of Directo
together with a sworn affidavit declaring upon oath that the letter was so sign
and addressed and that the affiant has personal knowledge that it is genui
and authentic. In this letter, dated February 4, 1906—a year in which l
physical condition seems to have been particularly precarious—Mrs. Eddy sa

"Three more Students who are *unmarried* and free from family obligatic
should be selected and instructed by Dr. —— (who taught Mr. —— how
inject morphine. He is an M.D. and qualified therefor—as I am told." M
Eddy stipulated that the instruction should be such that the students co
make the injections "*safely* as to puncturing a vein or injecting too large a d
of morphine." The italics indicate words underscored in the letter.

The names of the doctor and of Mrs. Eddy's attendant who had alrea
been instructed are omitted from the above excerpt, although they are set fo
in the letter. A copy of this letter with the accompanying affidavit, sworn to
a former official of the Christian Science Church and a person believed to
thoroughly responsible, has been deposited by the biographer in the Scrib
files.

This official states that it later was common knowledge among the Boa
members that the instructions contained in the letter had been complied wi
although the members did not at that time have any idea that the persons
tutored were being trained to administer morphine to Mrs. Eddy personal
With the possible exception of one official who, as the liaison officer between t
Board and Mrs. Eddy, made frequent trips to her home, the Board memb
believed at the time only what they had been accustomed to believe concerni
Mrs. Eddy's orders: that these embodied purposes so transcendental in natu
that they should only obey, and not necessarily seek to understand.

In an important entry in the Frye documents, Dickey is quoted as referri
to Mrs. Eddy's "morphine habit." (See Appendix A.) Unless further evider
becomes available, however, it seems fairer to assume that Mrs. Eddy ne
became a drug "addict" in the usual sense of that word, although there is ov
whelming evidence that the drug was for her, particularly in her latter days
useful and at times even necessary sedative.

In the world from which Mary Baker Eddy had fled men were learning to soar through the air with the birds; to travel with the speed of the wind; to harness the power of the lightning; to make their voices omnipresent at their will. By discovering the effects of each cause they were learning to foretell the future; to create any good for which they felt a need; to destroy age-old evils they had so long battled to no avail. Armed with knowledge learned in their new comradeship with an all-wise nature they were refashioning the face of the earth howsoever they desired; were turning deserts into gardens; were making rivers into light.

Such were some of the bounties of the universe which Mary Baker Eddy, never understanding, had denied and deserted in order to create another world of her own.

In this phantasmagoric creation of hers she had found honor and glory. Adulation and wealth had been showered upon her with fantastic prodigality. Willing subjects had come in throngs to share her kingdom with her. Her every material ambition had been satisfied. The realm which she created revolved around her alone. She, the creator, was at once the centre and boundary of her creation. In her own microcosm she was God, and there was nothing more.

And yet, even as she looked at her handiwork and pronounced it good, even as she thrilled at her power, she must have sensed that there was one thing which she had never found in the world of outer reality, nor created in the world she had spun from her own dreams. It was the thing she most hungered for, and as a woman had sought from the beginning. This was comradeship.

She was as alone among the populace who crowded in to dwell in her island universe as in the days when she wandered from house to house with only her book under her shabby arm. In no single heart did she find comprehension. There was always adulation, but never human love. In her prayer which was repeated every Sunday in her church was a line of pleading: "Feed the famished affections." This was her interpretation of the Lord's supplication, "Give us this day our daily bread." She hungered until the end.

So it was that as she now paused in the twilight that was looming up from her valley of the shadows, she groped for a bit of friendliness. From time to time she would rise from her chair to wander around her rooms and touch with trembling fingers the multitude of ornaments that cluttered up the furniture.

"Mr. Dickey, I have been thinking of this whatnot. It seems so childish. I believe I had better part with it. What do you think?"

"Mother, everything on that whatnot represents some one's love and appreciation for you, and there is no reason why you should not have it."

"Mr. Dickey, you always say the right thing. I'll keep it." So her days would pass.

As 1910 drew to a close, there seemed less and less reason for her continued existence. Weeks would go by when she was too distrait, and oftentimes too ill, even to make an inquiry about the progress of the great organization to which she had given life. Often she would arouse herself to take a drive. She insisted with almost childish petulance that these drives were necessary, and ordered her carriage even on days when she seemed hardly equal to the task of dressing. Her drives were her last grand and gallant gesture to a hostile and unbelieving world.

Mrs. Sargent usually drove with her during these last weeks of her life. With impersonal and churlish silence Frye would tuck the two old ladies into their robes, close the door, mount his box, and the coachman would drive off while Mrs. Eddy lay back with closed eyes.

Occasionally there were times when she could sit at her desk with her old energy, and write with trembling pen words that were still obeyed without question by every official to whom they might be addressed. Less than two weeks before her death she instructed her Board of Directors to make Adam Dickey a member of their counsels.

In the bay window in which her desk was set she could gaze over the lavish estates of her neighbors to the Blue Hills; but

[1] Related by Adam H. Dickey in *Memoirs of Mary Baker Eddy*, page 71.

lightly turning her chair she could look down her own drive where it was lost in the trees of Beacon Street that stretched beyond. It was here that she dreamed for hours through the late afternoons and early twilight, watching without a flicker in her gaze. The electric globes on either post of the iron gates would finally be lighted; the lights of Beacon Street would follow; far beyond, the stars would begin to appear as the glow in the west died; darkness would settle and enshroud the room, creeping out from the far corners until it enveloped the immobile, tenuous figure in the window.

Sometimes she would press a button that lighted a tiny globe on the desk, where a copy of *Science and Health* lay at her hand. Little more than the book itself was illumined by the small circle of light. She would open the volume at random, and with trembling finger running down the page read a few lines until she wearied. She would close the book, and put out the light, then once more lean back into her chair and gaze out into the night.

Mrs. Sargent would come into the room.

"Mother!"

No answer. Only silence, and the ticking of the many clocks.

"Mother!"

Still no movement in the darkness. Mrs. Sargent would reach for the light, then put her hand on Mrs. Eddy's thin little arm to which the silk of her sleeve clung closely.

"Mother!"

Mrs. Eddy would look up hastily, part her lips with a flicker of a smile.

"Yes, Laura!"

"It's nine o'clock, Mother."

"Yes, Laura."

Another day had run out.

Mrs. Eddy contracted a very bad cold before November closed, but she insisted on the first day of December that she would take her drive as usual. She came home with a cough that racked her frame. She was very weak and exhausted; she sank in the chair at her desk, and asked Mrs. Sargent to put a pencil and paper in reach of her hand. Mrs. Eddy fumbled for the pencil, righted it between thumb and forefinger, slowly wrote with painful trembling:

"God is my Life."

She leaned back in her chair, breathing with difficulty. Mrs. Sargent put her to bed, and brought her a little food as evening came. The next day, Friday, Mrs. Eddy managed to rise and imperiously insisted that she should be dressed. All day she sat in her chair, saying almost no word. In their own rooms the mental healers kept their watch, combating the magnetic approaches of the relentless evil. Word had come that Mrs. Eddy was again being attacked. Night came, and Mrs. Sargent helped her to disrobe. She was palpably weaker. There were times when she could hardly get her breath. A healer came to sit outside her door. The night watch was established.

On Saturday she was not able to rise. She merely lay with wide open eyes, saying no word, the thin hands clenching and unclenching on the coverlet. At a quarter to eleven on Saturday night Mrs. Sargent, sitting by her, noticed that she had ceased to breathe. The end had come quite easily and naturally, with none of the tense struggle that marked her life. She was open-eyed and conscious until the last. And not once did she admit, by word or gesture, that she knew her death was near.

None of Mrs. Eddy's church officials was aware that the end was so imminent. She had never taken them into her private confidence; nor were the members of her household accustomed to communicating with the officials except by her orders. No one from her great church was present as she passed quietly away, a very, very old woman in a flannel nightgown.

For an hour or so Mrs. Eddy's attendants were utterly lost. They experienced no great grief or shock; they merely were helpless, like an army that had lost its commander. They knew what had killed her, and were a little terrified. Malicious animal magnetism had finally overcome her in her bed, as she had foreseen.

Finally it was decided to send word to Archibald McLellan and Alfred Farlow, of The Mother Church. The two officials reached the great house about three o'clock in the morning. Mrs. Eddy was still lying in her walnut bed, her old-fashioned nightgown with its high neck covering her slight frame with decent circumspection. Mrs. Sargent had crossed the now motionless hands on her breast, and had closed her eyes.

Mrs. Sargent stood quite tearless at the foot of the bed. Frye was fumbling aimlessly around the room. Dickey paused expectantly inside the door. McLellan and Farlow took a close look to make sure that this important news was true, then spoke brusquely with business-like accents. They decided with Dickey, now a Director and hence their new associate in power, that a medical examiner had better be called to certify the death. It was most necessary that everything should be done with due attention to all orderly regulations. Great responsibilities were now coming into their hands. . . .

The medical examiner did not come until the middle of the next morning. He questioned Mrs. Sargent and Frye closely. They were vague in their knowledge of what had happened. Dickey said he thought pneumonia was the worldly cause of death; Mrs. Eddy seemed just to "fill up" before she died.

The doctor looked at the calm face on the pillow. It was not greatly furrowed; in death it had few lines, and the skin was fair and smooth. The cheeks and eyes were deeply hollowed. The mouth was firm—Mrs. Sargent had had enough presence of mind to slip in Mrs. Eddy's plates. Mrs. Eddy had lost every tooth in her head before she died.

The physician made out his death-certificate briefly: "Natural causes—probably pneumonia." He signed his name and the date.

The death was announced to the Boston Church at the close of the Sunday morning services. The congregation filed out, hushed and wordless. The Directors were busily talking to newspaper reporters.

"She just got sick and died," Farlow told them brusquely. "But I rather think she did it in a nice sort of way, and up to the very last—one might say—she was up and standing around."

A twist crept around the corners of his mustached mouth, and grew into a faint smile as he spoke the words.

Mrs. Eddy's officials laid her away quietly and with a complete absence of ostentation. There was no formal funeral, for the ritual of Mrs. Eddy's church made no provision for death. Two hundred persons, including reporters, the members of the household, the church officials, and others, assembled in the richly furnished drawing-rooms at Chestnut Hill where what was left of Mrs. Eddy lay in a bronze casket. She was garbed in a white silk gown. Over her shoulders had been gathered a shawl of filmy white lace, which flowed from throat to feet in an embracing tenderness such as in life she had never found.

As the clock struck the hour of eleven in the morning Judge Smith, First Reader of The Mother Church, read some psalms, the Second Reader declaimed Mrs. Eddy's poem, "Mother's Evening Prayer," and then Mrs. Eddy's last version of the Lord's Prayer was recited by all. They formed a procession to pass around the coffin and look upon the features of this strange old woman whom none of them had really ever known. The bronze container was then sealed and taken to Mt. Auburn cemetery, near Boston. It was placed in a tomb of cement and steel, and guarded night and day until sufficient time had elapsed for complete decomposition.

There were some hundred thousand souls who spoke reverently of her as "Leader" when she died on that December night in 1910. Some of them looked hopefully for her resurrection. Ecstatically they expected another miracle.

Mrs. Eddy's business-like successors to power and wealth discouraged this idea. They had seen enough of Mrs. Eddy in the four years before she died to be justified in a secret doubt concerning the possibility of a miracle.

They said as little as possible, however, and the ecstatic faith of many others was undisturbed. They wished to have it so.

This was the end of Mrs. Eddy's own story. Her church would indeed live on after her. But she had left it without a

eader; without a head to guide it, or a dynamic heart to in-
pire it to new conquests. As Alfred Farlow told reporters:

There will be no "Leader" named to take the place of Mrs. Eddy.
There is no need of any leader. In fact, the aim of Christian Science
doctrine is to do away with leadership. The whole teaching of the church
discourages independent leadership.

And so it was that within only a few weeks after Mrs.
Eddy's death her church had a renewal of its bickerings; and
the Board of Directors, instead of meeting once a week, were
gathering in all-day sessions to devise means for holding together the hierarchy they had inherited. Despite their best
efforts, despite the great wealth Mrs. Eddy had left them
for the financing of new conquests, their church, viewed to-
day from a perspective of two decades later, was destined to
become merely another minor sect among the many.[1] Her
dream of bringing all the world to worship in her temples remained merely a shadow of desire.

[1] The United States Census of Religious Bodies, 1926, showed a total of only
202,098 Christian Science church members in the United States, about two-
tenths of one per cent of the total population. Although this figure represents a
total increase of 207.5 per cent over the total shown by the preceding census
(1906) it is evident that in these twenty years the church's growth had slowed
down to a fraction of its previous rate. In the sixteen years between the census
of 1890 and that of 1906, the membership had increased 653.3 per cent, at the
amazing average yearly rate of 40.8 per cent of the 1896 total. In the twenty
years following the census of 1906, this rate diminished to a yearly average of
10.4 per cent of the 1906 total. Without discounting the large aggregate increase
of the church since 1906, the slackening of the rate of expansion must be regarded as significant.
    The debts of churches reporting have shown a large average increase. In 1906
the average debt on the 88 churches reporting debt was $4,447. By 1926 this
figure had risen to $23,451, the average for each of the 411 churches reporting
debt. This is perhaps another indication of decreasing vitality.
    These are statistics for territorial United States only, but from the 1926
census figures for the Mother Church, deductions as to the international figures
may be drawn. It is worth noting that on November 30, 1926, the Mother
Church had a total of 166,320 members, of whom 149,957 were in the United
States. This leaves a membership of 16,363 residing in extra-territorial United
States and in foreign countries.
    Of the Mother Church membership resident in the United States, 87,940 per-
sons were also members of branch churches. In addition, branch churches in the
United States had 52,141 members who did not belong to the Mother Church.
If this same proportion were preserved for foreign countries it would indicate—
on the basis of 16,363 foreign members of the Mother Church—a total of only
about 25,000 professed Christian Scientists outside the United States.
    Allowing for the probability that a smaller relative proportion of foreign

And yet, if some of her dreams were futile—if, measured
by the standard of what she desired to achieve, she must to-day
be regarded as having failed—hers was the defeat that is often
more gallant and magnificent than victory.

Such a will to achieve, in the face of every barrier which
reality and imagination could present, is the mark of a spirit
which after all does not need marble monuments. Nor need
she be ashamed in death to have her fellows know what were
the difficulties above which she fought to rise. For there are
few indeed who may not see their paltry weaknesses magnified many times in her own frail self, and, so seeing, understand how admirable was the will with which she coun-
tered them.

And indeed it was through her limitations, and not such
paltry virtues as some men have wished to shroud her with,
that she came finally to comradeship among the great. For
few have been the leaders of men who have not suffered from
some great handicap to which they owed their leadership; the
world's history has been written by souls who, striving to overcome some barrier, have gathered a momentum that finally
carried them far beyond mere compensation to heights of
fame.

If, when she reached her pinnacle, she failed to find there
the release from the disabilities against which she struggled
so long, this need not shadow the meaning of a woman who
shared a finite human destiny.

Christian Scientists are members also of the Mother Church, it seems likely
that there are not more than 250,000 professed Christian Scientists in th
entire world.

The statement of history, doctrine, and organization supplied by the Christian Science Board of Directors points out that the Sunday-schools of the de
nomination in 1926 enrolled 140,566 pupils not more than twenty years of age
of whom comparatively few were members of the church. It declares also tha
"in a sense, the Christian Science church can be said to include a large numbe
of persons who believe in Christian Science and attend its services, or study th
Bible with Mrs. Eddy's writings, but are not yet admitted to membership; an
the number of adherents who are not members is estimated as exceeding th
number who are."

For the United States Census figures vd. "Census of Religious Bodies, 1926–
Church of Christ, Scientist"—a sixteen-page report obtainable through th
Superintendent of Documents, U. S. Government Printing Office, Washington
D. C.

That indomitable will which keeps men always marching to goals they ever approach but never quite attain, that thing which Dostoievsky has called "man's quenchless yearning after Universality," is the force in man that relates him to eternity. Such a will, working through human finitude, is the soul of a Life greater than any individual.

So it was in her gallant struggle to achieve despite every human limitation that Mary Baker Eddy revealed whatever divinity may glow in man.

THE END

That inconsolable will which keeps men always miserable so goals they over-approach but never quite attain, that thing which Dostoievsky has called "man's quenchless yearning after... the unreal"; is the force in him that refers him to deity, and will, working through humanity, deify the real and so create, it may be, a God.

So it was in her call for worship to achieve, create a demand in man, Mrs. Mary Baker Eddy repeated whatever divinity may flow in her...

APPENDIX A

THE FRYE DIARIES

Since first publication of this work, opportunity has presented itself to include some additional and previously unpublished source material which strongly fortifies the biographer's interpretation, and which is intrinsically important because of its nature.

Agents of the Christian Science Church have particularly sought in their official publicity to impugn the author's sources. The Frye Diaries, from which excerpts can now be given in sufficient number to validate data from many other directions, present the evidence of an eye witness to the most intimate events in Mrs. Eddy's career, set down from day to day. This record, kept by an attendant who devoted almost his whole life to Mrs. Eddy's service, and whose attitude cannot possibly be accused of unfavorable bias, shows us a woman utterly different in almost every aspect from the conception of Mrs. Eddy which has been publicized by "authorized" agents.

The nature of this material was generally familiar to the biographer when he was still engaged in his work. Only sufficient excerpts are included now to show that certain sensational conclusions in the text, such as those touching Mrs. Eddy's illnesses, her mental condition, her use of morphine, and the attitude of her attendants, have ample foundation.

Calvin Frye died in 1917, living out his days in uneventful peace and enjoying, under Mrs. Eddy's will, the right to occupy his rooms in her old Commonwealth Avenue home until the end. His diary-records extend over the greater number of years he was in Mrs. Eddy's employ. All of the entries quoted here are taken from photostatic copies of the originals, of which duplicates have been deposited by the author in the files of his publishers. That portions of this material can now be included in this volume due entirely to the kindness of John V. Dittemore, who occupies what is to-day almost a unique position in Christian Science history.

Because Mr. Dittemore's relation to these documents is important in establishing their authenticity, some brief facts concerning his own career must be mentioned. Mr. Dittemore is the last surviving member of that group of men who were Directors of Mrs. Eddy's Church during her lifetime. He was made a member of the Board in 1909, eighteen months before her death, and resigned in 1924 from the Church. Before his resignation he had taken exception to a number of policies, pursued by his associates, which he considered high-handed, ill-advised, and calculated to bring the organization into eventual difficulty, and indeed resorted to legal measures in an attempt to force certain changes in some of these policies.

Having come into the Church with a high enthusiasm, born of the fact
that he had been suddenly relieved of a very serious chronic illness after
treatments on the Eddy-Quimby principle, he eventually came to realize
that certain convictions regarding Mrs. Eddy and her work were not justified. He was possessed of an inquiring mind and a great interest in establishing facts. As a result, he early became an indefatigable research worker,
desiring at the time to locate data which would refute Mrs. Eddy's critics
and establish her own claims. Many doors were opened to him because of
his position. As time went on, however, it became increasingly evident that
his growing mass of data would not serve his original purpose. To the contrary, it threw a wholly unexpected light on Mrs. Eddy's career.

Meanwhile, before his resignation, Mr. Dittemore assembled what is
probably the most important collection of original documents concerning
Mrs. Eddy's life extant. The material in the official files of the Mother
Church will perhaps never be released in entirety by the Church officials,
consisting as it does of many documents which these officials have certainly
shown no desire to make public in the past, and which were, in at least some
instances, presumably acquired to prevent publication. Mr. Dittemore, however, realizing at the time the historic importance of this material, and feeling that the public interest was involved, had photostatic copies made of
many of the more vital documents. In addition, he purchased from time to
time, for his own library, any additional original manuscript material which
came to light. The eventual publication of Mr. Dittemore's documents must
be eagerly awaited, providing as it will the final and conclusive evidence
concerning the many disputed points in Mrs. Eddy's career.

Concerning the manner in which the Frye documents came into his possession, Mr. Dittemore has made the following statement:

Just before the death of Mr. Frye, Mr. Charles H. Welch, a close friend and
the one whom Mr. Frye had named executor under his will, gave to me certain
portions of diary records of a personal nature which Mr. Frye had kept for many
years. These portions had been removed from the diaries at Mr. Frye's request
in order that upon his death, which he felt was imminent, they might not fall
into alien hands and be misused or perhaps destroyed. Mr. Welch immediately
gave these documents to me, as one of Mr. Frye's closest friends and adviser
during his latter days.

Other books and documents, relating to Christian Science and Mrs. Eddy,
which were in Frye's hands were given at this time to the Church. The portion
of the diaries given to me were never owned by the Mother Church, and indeed
I have always regarded my possession of them in the nature of a public trust.

Knowing the great dangers to which the existence of valuable historical material was likely to be subjected, I had the documents photostated as a precau-
tionary measure. This precaution was well taken, evidenced by the fact that
the originals were eventually burned.

That such evidence of supreme importance regarding essential facts in Mrs.
Eddy's life has nevertheless survived in photographic form must be extremely
gratifying to every historian who appreciates the value of the first-hand record.

While I have been reserving this material, in connection with a great many
other important and previously unpublished documents, for use in a history

which I have long been compiling to record for the first time the inside story of the Christian Science movement, I am now glad to make certain portions public. I do this from an impersonal sense of duty, feeling that the anti-social activities of Mrs. Eddy's Church have now become so pronounced that data of this nature is of great importance to the public interest.

Much of Frye's diary-record was written day by day on a desk calendar, similar to that which most business men keep in front of them for memorandums. Sometimes Frye would use the same pad for two years in succession, never tearing off a page and going back to January 1 to insert new entries on top of those for the previous year. His account is extremely matter of fact. Often statements obviously by Mrs. Eddy are inserted without ascription to her and without quotation marks. Part is in long hand and part in stenographic shorthand. Names will often be in shorthand—particularly Mrs. Eddy's own name—and the rest will be in script. All of the entries are written in the spirit of a faithful servant who believes exactly what he is told. Frye's lack of intelligence becomes a real advantage, his lack of discrimination between cause and effect an actual historical asset. Every event is described as it might have been seen through Mrs. Eddy's own eyes.

This following entry is important as indicating decisively the effect on Mrs. Eddy of her association with young Kennedy and Arens, as related in the biographer's early pages. It should be noted that Frye, like Mrs. Eddy, has no doubt that M. A. M. is the cause of her ills.

November 15, 1883

Mrs. Eddy has had a belief of difficulty of breathing for the last two days and got only temporary relief from it, this morning at about 4 o'clock she called me to help her. I attempted (to) do so for about ten minutes when she told me I made her worse afterwards told me she could not rise from the bed to speak to me because of the suffocating sense it produced; worked for (her) faithfully last evening with little result. When we were together this morning at about :30 she discovered that the mesmerists were arguing to her inflamation and paralysis of spinal nerve to produce paralysis of muscles of lungs and heart so as to prevent breathing & heart disease with soreness (?) between the shoulder-blades

She experienced the greatest relief when she and I took up Kennedy & Arens to break their attempt to make her suffer from aforementioned beliefs, and she said "I have not breathed so easy for two days"

                                                                CALVIN.

Frye's humility and self-abnegation persisted even in Mrs. Eddy's tantrums. As indicated in the text, he never questioned her pronouncements even when they reflected most personally on himself:

March 25, 1895

Mrs. E. was disturbed with my driving yesterday called me an idiot insane &c Last eve she asked me if I knew I was insane. She says WATCH, Do everything promptly dont put off.

Statements that Mrs. Eddy's seizures came on her usually at night and accounts of her fears of "mental poison"—the sort of M. A. M. tha she said killed Mr. Eddy—are confirmed in this entry:

August 26, 1899

Mrs. Eddy a terrible night last night fear & fever and poisoned to death ii belief. After I had attempted to mentally & audibly help & comfort her withou success she said Now stop entirely and go to sleep turn y(ou)r mind entirel away from me. If I dont speak to you again on earth, Goodbye darling.

That Mrs. Eddy could occasionally be tremendously upset by very smal matters that went awry in her routine, and that Pleasant View was no always the ante-room to Heaven which her devotees pictured, is atteste here:

April 7, 1900

Mrs. Eddy had a severe experience all day yesterday being tormented wit a sense of evil all day long. She found Clara told dressmakers wrong and there by had her dress skirt made 1½ in. too short in back & spoiled. Laura & I bot caused her trouble thro stupidity & sin so that she declared I was the cause c influencing others to abuse her. While driving she was confronted by questio of membership from Mother Church to — Church & jealousy. An atmospher & hate & revenge from testimony being taken in Montreal on W suit &c & Stewart case

The following evidently refers to one of Mrs. Eddy's early manuscript containing her copyings from Quimby, which had somehow come into Mr Stetson's hands and which Mrs. Stetson presumably mailed to Pleasar View with a request for information. It is of importance here as indicatin Mrs. Eddy's mental attitude in her latter days toward Quimby, in conne tion with her unacknowledged borrowings. It appears that the reawakene thought of Quimby, whose memory by this time she had doubtless almos suppressed, could make her physically ill:

February 14, 1902

Yesterday I showed to Mrs. Eddy what claimed to be an old manuscrij written by her in 1867 & I asked he(r) if it was in her handwriting & of her con position She replied no! & I intended to send such a reply to Mrs. Stetso After seeing it & all night long she was under great fear & old beliefs asserte themselves. She got but 2 hours sleep.

By 1903 Mrs. Eddy's physical condition had declined to the point wher regardless of her philosophy, she found it necessary to seek the services c doctors, as shown by these excerpts, also included in the text:

May 3, 1903

Mrs. E. was suddenly attack(ed) with severe pain at 11:30 tonight and th 4 C. Ss in the house P. V. proved unable to relieve her. She sent for Rev. I. (Tomlinson neither did he help her. She then sent for Dr. E. Morrill & he wa out of town: she then sent for Dr. S. Morrill he was sick and could not com

he then sent for Dr. Conn and he remained with her from 2:15 until 4 Monday
morning. But the pain was so intense & slow to respond that he called in Dr.
Billings for consultation who was here from 3 to 4.

May 4, 1903

After Dr. Conn left, Mrs. E. was a little relieved and at about 5 a. m. she
slept for about one hour. But suffered every hour this forenoon from paroxysms
of pain. . . . It was called renal calculi . . . then she called in Dr. E. Morrill
and he gave her a hypodermic.

Any disagreement between Mrs. Eddy and her associates, not uncommon in her irascible moods, was stated by Mrs. Eddy to be the result of
M. A. M. That such an explanation seemed entirely logical to the more
devoted of her followers is indicated by Frye's own attitude. He wrote of
one such occurrence:

October 20, 1907

Last evening, under the influence of M. A. M. Mr. Tomlinson told Mrs. Eddy
he was ungrateful and a tyrant.

As set forth in the body of this biography, M. A. M. from an outside
source was believed by Mrs. Eddy and her close associates to be the cause
of most of her suffering. Exposure and recognition of such malign currents
was regarded as alone often sufficient to counteract their effect. This entry
is of particular interest because it reveals at first hand the effect on Mrs.
Eddy of the many public rumors regarding her unfortunate physical condition:

Tuesday, July 28, 1908

At about 12 o'clock last night an editor of Boston *Herald* called Mr. Dickey
by telephone and asked at what hour Mrs. Eddy died! He said the rumor on
the street is that she is dead. She had been having a series of attacks for over
a week which kept her in bed and on the lounge almost the entire time and last
night she despaired of living until morning: but when this telephone was rec'd
it revealed cause of attacks & (she) gained much relief.

In repeated entries the Frye Diaries confirm the biographer's statements
that Mrs. Eddy in her latter years varied between resort to doctors and reliance on the "treatments" of associates in her household:

August 3, 1909

Intense pain last night—she requested an M.D. to administer an hyperdermic;
called W. H. B.

Frye's records show beyond any possible doubt what a difficult problem
the household had to contend with:

August 11, 1909

Monday night at about 10 oclk Mrs. Eddy awoke in a severe belief and called
for help but all seemed so dazed they were unsuccessful. She was surprised &
declared we wanted her to die & did not love. When I told her I love her more
than any other person on earth she said *"You lie!"* This morning I received a
bitter letter from Geo. W. Baker which he wrote Aug. 9th.

The Next Friends' suit was undoubtedly a terrible and tragic interlude for Mrs. Eddy; Frye's unadorned description of her agitation is most moving:

September 25, 1909

W. E. Chandler published in newspapers today that the "Next Friends" suit is to be revived again &c &c By Mrs. Sargent's advice, Mr. Dickey told Mrs. Eddy about it and it has nearly upset her. This evening I heard her pray Mr. Dickey to prevent it; He replied there will be no suit all the next friend want is money—to compromise Mrs. Eddy told him to get a settlement with them.

Mrs. Eddy called to her room L. E. Sargent, Mrs. Rathvon, Mr. Rathvon, I. C. Tomlinson, A. H. Dickey & myself and requested each to hold up his right hand and promise that we would not leave her but stand by her till this "next friend" threat was met—the threat to revive the next friend suit.

In these last days of her life Frye mentions Mrs. Eddy's resort to morphine for release from her sufferings as a "habit." The following entry alone would justify all the author's necessary references to this unfortunate matter:

Monday, May 9, 1910

Mr. Adam H. Dickey last night told Mrs. Eddy, that she shall not have any more morphine! She had for several days been suffering from renal calculi and had voided stones in the urine but yesterday the water seemed normal and so having had hyperdermic injections twice within a few days he believed she did not need it but that it was the old morphine habit reasserting itself and would not allow her to have it.

Frye's account of Mrs. Eddy's struggles in the last few months before her death, his description of her pathetic prayers to her "healers" for relief from her sufferings, and his simple statement that he felt "quite confused and discouraged," surpass in the drama of his unaffected narrative any possible comment which an author could make.

Monday, September 26, 1910

Mrs. Eddy called I. C. T., A. H. D., W. R. R., E. S. Rathvon, L. E. Sargent & C. A. F. and demanded of us to heal her, for she was tired of going on in this way confined to her bunk &c &c; she added that she would give any one of us $1000. to heal her.

A. H. D. said he would give $1,000. to be able to heal her &c. so said the others in substance. I did not reply for some time for I felt quite confused & discouraged, but finally said "Well all we can do is to keep up our courage and work on up to our highest understanding. She replied "Has it come to this! She afterward said If you all feel like that turn your (mi)nds away from me & know that I am well.

APPENDIX B

MRS. EDDY'S USE OF SOURCES

In biography one often approaches the greater problem by studying the lesser. In the instance of Mrs. Eddy's writings such a method can be fruitful.

Because many Christian Scientists, grateful for the healing and inspiration they have gained from Mrs. Eddy's psychology, have therefore subscribed to all of her other teachings whole, they have bitterly resented the biographical statement that her doctrines were not inspired direct from Heaven but came largely through the channel of an obscure and repudiated country practitioner.

Certain partisans have even sought to deny the authenticity of the Quimby Manuscripts *in toto;* they have even insinuated that the book which Horatio Dresser has edited under this name is itself a gigantic forgery. Before long the original manuscripts—at this writing still in Quimby's family—will doubtless be deposited in some public institution where they will be available at first hand for the study of scholars, thus putting an end to unfounded insinuations which impugn at once the honesty of Quimby, of the Dressers, and of this writer. Meanwhile it is quite possible to show from an entirely different angle that Mrs. Eddy, in her penchant for philosophical and theological musings, relied consistently on sources exceedingly mundane.

Quimby, though the most important, was by no means her sole source and inspiration. She secured from him her great idea and a certain amount of phraseology for it, but in the course of time she needed for her pages much more material than Quimby furnished. Thus she turned to other writers. When, for instance, Carlyle referred in *Heroes and Hero-Worship* to

the unseen and spiritual in them that determined the outward and actual

he could find undoubted inspiration for a text of *Science and Health*, where she instructed her readers to

work out the spiritual which determines the outward and actual. (Page 254.)

Thorough analysis of *Science and Health* from the standpoint of comparative literature has never yet been attempted. Because it has been through innumerable revisions and re-writings, has had the benefit of extensive editing at hands other than Mrs. Eddy's, has a bulk so large and a literary significance comparatively small,—for all these reasons no scholar has as yet had patience or incentive to give the book the critical analysis required to lay bare all its indebtedness.

Not many thrusts, however, are required to puncture the balloon of the claim that Mrs. Eddy's own statements as to her divine inspiration should be taken literally. A study of her lesser writings will show that she went boldly to several philosophers besides Quimby to seek not only inspiration but also the verbiage to express it. Nor did she give credit to those who met her need.

For an adequate understanding of Mrs. Eddy it must be realized, as have insisted elsewhere, that most of her career was born not of a desire t express to the world a vital message that defied repression. It arose not from a passion to save suffering humanity. It resulted not from a prophet's urg to preach to the world regardless of all cost to self.

Mrs. Eddy was not this fairly usual type of evangelist. Her literary effort sprang primarily from an urge for self-justification—a desire to attain im portance in a world which had previously ignored and spurned her. He church organization grew up out of these literary efforts—was her mean indeed, of marketing them. It was for her another device by which she coul impress herself on her environment. The measures she devised for its go ernment and operation stand as evidence of this.

To speak in homely language, Mrs. Eddy from the days of her girlhoo wanted fiercely "to be somebody." Literary distinction was the specific go she early set for herself. After all, the opportunities in the America of th 1800's for any woman, no matter what her endowment, to achieve se expression outside the family circle were limited largely to literary wor Mrs. Eddy, to the end of her life, took pleasure in the thought of being successful author. Even when she became a great power in her church, s seems to have prized her concept of herself as an important authoress r less than her position as a theological czarina. As she told Arthur Brisban "I make my money with my pen, just as you do."

New light can be thrown on this thesis through a little known intervie which appeared in the Boston *Globe* of June 16, 1907, at a time when Mr Eddy was being subjected to publicity owing to the Next Friends' sui That the interview was never repudiated is shown by the fact that it was r printed in a semi-official account of the trial sponsored by Christian Scien interests.[1] In contradiction in many respects of her previous versions of h relations with her son, she was quoted as saying:

When my son was eight years old I determined to leave my father's hou to pursue my literary work, and I selected as the woman best calculated to ca for the child, the wife of Simeon Cheney. . . . I was then able to earn $50 week by my writings, and I had been offered $3,000 a year to write for *The O Fellow's Covenant.* . . . I was very busily engaged in my writings, but I nev forgot my boy. He was a very smart boy, and the Cheneys grew very fond him, and they wanted to keep him for their own. I sent them money for education and support. . . .

That the untutored Mrs. Glover ever had such sums offered to her, in day when $3,000 was equivalent to $12,000 now, and, as such, a magni cent editorial salary, is strongly to be doubted. But her delight in posing a highly successful and widely read writer from her earliest days is evide

Now the great trouble with many who are ambitious for self-expressi in the field of literature, the reason why so many would-be authors fail make a lasting mark on their time, is that they never discover anythi

[1] *Mrs. Eddy and the Late Suit in Equity*, by Michael Meehan, published by the auth Concord, N. H., 1908.

impressive to say. Mrs. Eddy's success dates from the time when, largely by accident, she discovered something extremely important—a message which, so far as the public of her time was concerned, seemed new.

That it was eventually through a theological organization as much as through a book that Mrs. Eddy secured recognition for her idea and hence for herself, that the idea was not originally her own, that she never even learned to think or write about it adequately,—these things constitute one of those human anomalies which constantly arise to confound and amaze the student of the Eddy career.

All of this must be understood, however, for a fruitful study of Mrs. Eddy's sources of inspiration. In *Science and Health* she practically exhausted the thesis she had derived from Quimby. She had indeed exhausted almost all the variations which her imagination could weave around the central core of Quimby's thought. That she believed whole-heartedly in the Quimby doctrines—at least during most of her errant moods—cannot be doubted. Her passionate belief indeed came to be almost an obsession, so divorced was it from the usual reasoning processes. Her burning faith in her philosophy, however, seems primarily to have inspired in her a desire to obtain thereby her own salvation. When she sat down to write about her doctrines, her motivating impulse was less an eagerness to share salvation with the world than to win from this world mere acclaim for personal achievement. This conclusion is forced upon us for the simple reason that no other hypothesis will fit all the enormous contradictions in her career. This one explains the whole tragic history.

After completing her major opus, Mrs. Eddy eventually found herself in the unenviable position of a literary Trilby whose Svengali has expired. Her inspiration was no more. Meanwhile, *en route* to becoming a successful author, she had made herself into a high priestess. Her book sold only because the priestess publicized and pushed it. Acclaim arose, and with it a demand for further revelations. Thus do we behold Mrs. Eddy in the position of the temple oracle who—as in olden days when votaries gathered around the sacred shrine to hear prophecies—was forced to become occasionally vocal to maintain the enthusiasms of the worshippers.

Mrs. Eddy had very little left to say. And there was no high priest to hide behind the sacred image and to speak words of wisdom to the multitude through the mouth of the divine figure.

It was a difficult position. Mrs. Eddy was no more willing to confess her lack of inspiration than she was to acknowledge her lack of ability to practise her Science on herself. It was no mere matter of honesty or dishonesty. All her pride was at stake. And that vast inner egoism of hers, which had carried her so far after triumphing over seemingly impossible obstacles, refused to confess impotency.

So it was that she sought inspiration like any other mortal. But she could not bring herself to acknowledge this. Just as she secretly repaired to doctors, she secretly repaired to books.

She had never read widely, and was in many ways incapable of digesting

thoroughly what material she did peruse. What help she obtained seems t
have been largely from a few documents available in her personal librar

For a knowledge of what some of this help was, posterity is largely ir
debted to the curiosity of a Mr. A. A. Beauchamp, antiquarian and deale
in rare books, who was engaged by the Christian Science Board of Directo
to compile some memorabilia of Mrs. Eddy after her death. Working amon
her documents, he noticed that some of her books had pages heavily under
scored.

One volume which, at the time, hardly attracted his attention was a
old book entitled *The English Reader, or, Pieces in Prose and Verse from th
Best Writers; designed to assist Young Persons to Read With Propriety an
Effect; Improve Their Language and Sentiments, and To Inculcate The Mo
Important Principles of Piety and Virtue.*

It was compiled by Lindley Murray, and bore the imprint of Horati
Hill & Co., Concord, N. H. It was a reader with which many school childre
in the early 1800s must have been familiar.

Another book underscored and annotated in Mrs. Eddy's own hand wa
a small volume, quite modern, that would have slipped easily into a pocke
Entitled *Philosophic Nuggets*, it contained wise reflections from Carlyl
Amiel, Ruskin and Kingsley, which were compiled and copyrighted in th
form by Jeanne G. Pennington in 1899.

Eventually, moved largely by curiosity, Mr. Beauchamp obtained dupl
cates of these works. The discovery that their pages had been of materi
aid to Mrs. Eddy in her literary career thereupon resulted.

Only brief comparisons were required to make it evident that Mrs. Edd
had relied on the transcendentalists for inspiration to an unexpected degre
Their thoughts and phrases had both proved useful to her as an adjunct
her Quimbyisms. Once or twice, indeed, she borrowed whole passages—lor
enough to necessitate the conclusion that this indebtedness, at least, coul
not have been unconscious. A third source of her literary inspiration obv
ously lay in her scrapbook, a volume of newspaper clippings which Mr
Eddy had evidently kept for more than half her lifetime, and in whic
numerous items have been found that appear in somewhat altered form
her formal writings. Old newspaper columns headed "Dewdrops of Wisdom
and containing pithy exhortations to virtue, had evidently appealed to Mr
Eddy strongly. She had preserved these columns in large number; bri
comparison showed that parts of their contents had been further preserve
without quotation marks, in Mrs. Eddy's own writings.[1]

There is a quality infinitely pathetic in the picture we have of Mrs. Edd
an old woman now famous and renowned, burdened with the necessity
keeping her renown nourished. She has already passed the span of thre
score and ten, unhappy, pain-racked and lonely. Her one satisfacti

[1] Upon Mrs. Eddy's demise photostatic copies of this scrap-book were made, and o
such copy was retained as a souvenir of Mrs. Eddy by each director in her Church. It
one of these copies which was made available for study by the biographer; it is to be hop
that it will eventually be presented to some important library for permanent preservati
as source material relating to Mrs. Eddy's life.

in life is the knowledge that she has outwitted ignominy and achieved eminence. And yet this very achievement taxes her resources constantly, and will tax them the more as years go by. The time has come—it is 1895—when she must write an Annual Message to her church, the newly reorganized church which she has sought so hard to make her own, so that it will be her monument in perpetuity. Feebly she wracks her brains. Inspiration from heaven fails to come. And so she turns to the old Murray's Reader. There, on page 89, she finds a brief sermon by a now-forgotten Scottish Divine named Hugh Blair. It seems to fit her need.

Mrs. Eddy writes a brief introduction of her own, and then copies painfully from the Reader's yellowed pages:

MURRAY'S READER, p. 89

It will not take much time to delineate the character of the man of integrity, as by its nature it is a plain one, and easily understood. He is one who makes it his constant rule to follow the road of duty, according as the word of God, and the voice of his conscience, point it out to him. He is not guided merely by affections, which may sometimes give the colour of virtue to a loose and unstable character.

2 The upright man is guided by a fixed principle of mind, which determines him to esteem nothing but what is honourable; and to abhor whatever is base or unworthy, in moral conduct. Hence we find him ever the same; at all times, the trusty friend, the affectionate relation, the conscientious man of business, the pious worshipper, the public spirited citizen.

3 He assumes no borrowed appearance. He seeks no mask to cover him: for he acts no studied part; but he is indeed what he appears to be, full of truth, candour, and humanity. In all his pursuits, he knows no path but the fair and direct one; and would much rather fail of success, than attain it by reproachful means.

4 He never shows us a smiling countenance, while he meditates evil against us in his heart. He never praises us amongst our friends; and then joins in traducing us among our enemies. We shall never find one part of his character at variance with another. In his manners he is simple and unaffected; in all his proceedings, open and consistent.—BLAIR.

MISCELLANEOUS WRITINGS, p. 147

My Beloved Students:—Another year has rolled on, another annual meeting has convened, another space of time has been given us, and has another duty been done and another victory won for time and eternity? Do you meet in unity, preferring one another, and demonstrating the divine Principle of Christian Science? Have you improved past hours, and ladened them with records worthy to be borne homeward? Have you learned that sin is inadmissible, and indicates a small mind? Do you manifest love for those that hate you and despisefully use you?

The man of integrity is one who makes it his constant rule to follow the road of duty, according as Truth and the voice of his conscience point it out to him. He is not guided merely by affections which may some time give the color of virtue to a loose and unstable character.

The upright man is guided by a fixed Principle, which destines him to do nothing but what is honorable, and to abhor whatever is base or unworthy; hence we find him ever the same—at all times the trusty friend, the affectionate relative, the conscientious man of business, the pious worker, the public-spirited citizen.

He assumes no borrowed appearance. He seeks no mask to cover him, for he acts no studied part; but he is indeed what he appears to be,—full of truth, candor and humanity. In all his pursuits, he knows no path but the fair, open, and direct one, and would much rather fail of success than attain it by reproachable means. He never shows us a smiling countenance while he meditates evil against us in his heart. We shall never find one part of his character at variance with another.   Lovingly yours,
Sept. 30, 1895.   MARY BAKER EDDY.

For years Mrs. Eddy had raged against the thing she called plagiarism.

Any one who took, or merely adapted, a thought from *Science and Health* without due credit, was pilloried as a thief and robber. Her hatred of unacknowledged borrowings from her own writings was in direct proportion to her fierce desire to have her hard-won fame persist throughout the ages. Perhaps, with this in mind, she debated with herself about using Blair's forgotten words. Was acknowledgment necessary?

Having set those sentiments down, and reread them; having modernized the spelling, and sanctified the thought by capitalizing Truth and Principle, synonyms in Mrs. Eddy's Science for God, Mrs. Eddy evidently decided that no acknowledgment would be required. This message stands to-day as utterly her own, among the pages of her copyrighted *Miscellaneous Writings*.

As time went on, and further literary expression became necessary, she absorbed *Philosophic Nuggets*, always revising and rephrasing any inspiration she gained therefrom so that it would conform to Christian Science terminology. Sometimes, of course, such digestion was unnecessary. Carlyle's "time-world," which "only flutters as an unreal shadow," could serve as perfect inspiration without a change. "This time-world flutters in my thought as an unreal shadow," wrote Mrs. Eddy.[1] When Carlyle declared that the centre of things was "not a madness and nothing, but a sanity and something," Mrs. Eddy could refer with ease to her new church (this was in 1903) as being "not a madness and nothing, but a sanity and something from the individual, stupendous Godlike agency of man."[2] Often only a bit of editorial rephrasing was necessary to make the borrowed observation express her meaning. Ruskin's statement that "a little group of wise hearts is better than a wilderness full of fools," embodied Mrs. Eddy's own idea completely. She herself said: "A small group of wise thinkers is better than a wilderness of dullards."[3] This sentiment was expressed in her message on the dedication of her Concord church, which was hailed at the time as Mrs. Eddy's own gift to her congregations, its large mortgage not being generally known. Her health in that year was definitely on the decline; at such an advanced age as hers almost anyone might find it difficult to produce original thoughts suitable for a church dedication. Ruskin helped her again. Said he:

> We are all of us willing enough to accept dead truths, or blunt ones; which can be . . . shrouded and coffined at once out of the way . . . but a sapling truth, with earth at its root and blossom on its branches; or a trenchant truth that can cut its way through bars and sods; most men dislike the sight or entertainment of, if . . . such . . . may be avoided.

Without noting her source, Mrs. Eddy rewrote this as follows, losing in her paraphrase much of the rich metaphor:

> Most of us willingly accept dead truisms which can be buried at will; but a live truth, even though it be a sapling within rich soil and with blossoms on it,

[1] *Miscellany*, p. 268. [2] *Miscellany*, p. 14. [3] *Miscellany*, p. 162.

branches, frightens people. The trenchant truth that cuts its way through iron and sod, most men avoid until compelled to glance at it.[1]

It should be noted here that all of the quotations from Carlyle, Ruskin, and Amiel which are mentioned here—indeed, all that have ever been found in Mrs. Eddy's writings—are contained in *Philosophic Nuggets*. Apparently her familiarity with these authors depended on this one small book.

Sometimes, indeed, Mrs. Eddy's meaning would be rather obscure were it not for the fact that we can look at the original source of her passage and thence follow her train of thought. When, for instance, it was necessary in 1905 to become vocal, in answer to a request from the Boston *Herald* for an expression of opinion on divorce, Mrs. Eddy gravely set down, "I am as silent as the dumb centuries without a Divina."[2]

Is Mrs. Eddy here indulging in a Latinism? If so, why should centuries bereft of a seeress seem dumb? Could the authoress be purposely obscure? Or could she, rather, have failed to grasp Carlyle's own reference when he wrote, "The ten dumb centuries continued voiceless . . . had no Divina Commedia to hear"?

It was in the next line of this essay of hers that Mrs. Eddy found an opportunity to join with Carlyle in mentioning the flutters of her "time-world."

Usually Mrs. Eddy preferred to do some editing of her own on those *Philosophic Nuggets* which appealed to her. Sometimes she would change the mood of a verb. Amiel, announcing that "the redeemed are happier than the elect," inspired Mrs. Eddy to feel that, at least, "the redeemed should be happier than the elect."[3] Ruskin, observing that "as the thing is good or bad, so is the maker of it," led her to believe that "as the thing made is good or bad, so is its maker."[4] Carlyle, praising "him who is seen toiling for the spiritually indispensible," reminded her of David—"he that toiled for the spiritually indispensible."[5] Carlyle evidently stood at her shoulder throughout this message to her votaries. His mention of "the deadliest sin . . . that same supercilious consciousness of no sin," could lead her to exclaim about "a supercilious consciousness that saith there is no sin";[6] and when he inquired, "Of all acts is not for a man, repentance the most divine?" Mrs. Eddy had no doubt whatever. For her, the Passover, if "spiritually disconcerned," would be a passage over a "sea of repentance—which of all human experience is the most divine."[7]

Often a philosopher would make learned observations that fitted in with Mrs. Eddy's pet theories with a remarkable ease. During all of her latter years, for example, she heartily disliked what she called "quacks," meaning all practitioners of faith-healing by a system which was not her own. Mr. Dresser, for instance, was a "quack." So was Mrs. Woodbury after her dismissal. So was any other Christian Scientist who fell by the wayside.

[1]*Miscellany*, p. 160.   [2]*Miscellany*, p. 268.
[3]*Miscellany*, p. 229.   [4]*Miscellany*, p. 205.
[5]*Message for 1900*, p. 14.   [6]*Ibid.*, p. 15.   [7]*Ibid.*, p. 15.

Thus, when Carlyle declared that "quackery gives birth to nothing; give death to all things," Mrs. Eddy agreed heartily, and found therein a rea threat to any one of her flock who dared patronize an unauthorized healer With evident meaning she mentioned the "quacks, giving birth to nothing and death to all."[1]

In the end, perhaps, Mrs. Eddy did not render her votaries a disservice if she taught them to give a personal meaning to fine philosophic observa tions of which otherwise they might never have heard. Few in her church perhaps, would ever know that Amiel had advised one "to live, so as to keep this consciousness of ours in perpetual relation with the eternal." Mrs. Eddy, in counselling her flock "to live so as to keep human conscious ness in constant relation with the divine,"[2] perhaps gave to them an idea which they themselves would not have acquired more directly from the philosopher.

Many more instances could be presented to show by what various thought of her fellow men Mrs. Eddy was influenced, at the same time never daring to admit her indebtedness. To maintain her fame as the bearer of a mes sage, she rewrote and adopted to her own special needs any observation which promised to be useful, just as to win this fame she had started by re writing and revising Quimby. To her it did not greatly matter whether her mentor were Quimby, Ruskin, Carlyle, Blair. All her long, tragic life she had known only one urge—the necessity of Self. This persisted until the end

For the discerning mind no infinite number of quotations from her source is needed to prove the essentially human nature of this Self which drove her so mercilessly all her years. Endless comparisons could hardly show us a soul more finite and heavy with pathos than the woman we already know —Mrs. Eddy, pursued by uneasy fame into her painful old age, searching for new inspiration frantically, scouring the columns of writers she deemed obscure, to find bright thoughts that would save her from being revealed in barren, speechless ignominy before the world.

[1] *Message for 1901*, p. 30.
[2] *Miscellany*, p. 160.

BIBLIOGRAPHY

WRITINGS BY MRS. EDDY

While the following is not a complete list of Mrs. Eddy's publications, owing to the fact that she combined and recombined her many writings into various forms at different times, it includes all of her formally published works which are vital to a study of her career.

Since this listing was first compiled for publication, the Union Theological Seminary, New York, has received by gift from a student of Mrs. Stetson one of the most valuable collections of early editions of Mrs. Eddy's writings extant. Other rare works on Christian Science are included. The collection must be of great importance to all research workers.

Science and Health. Copies of the rare First Edition of 1875, now almost priceless, are available in four public libraries. These institutions are the Library of Congress, the New York Public Library, the Boston Public Library, and Harvard College Library.

Of the even rarer Second Edition of 1878, copies are preserved in the Library of Congress and the New York Public Library.

The Third Edition of 1881 may be found in the Library of Congress, the New York Public Library, the Boston Public Library, the Peabody Institute in Baltimore, the Harvard College Library, and the British Museum.

The present authorized edition, formerly published by the Christian Science Publishing Society and now by the Trustees, is available in almost all public libraries and in all Christian Science Reading Rooms.

The Science of Man, by Which the Sick Are Healed. Embracing Questions and Answers in Moral Science Arranged for the Learner. By Mrs. Mary Baker Glover (Lynn, T. P. Nichols, printer, 1876). Of this exceedingly rare and important first edition at least one copy is available for reference. This is in the New York Public Library.

Unity of Good (1887); *Christian Healing* (1886); *The People's Idea of God; Its Effect on Health and Christianity* (1886). Now published in one brochure.

Historical Sketch of Christian Science Mind Healing (1888). A copy of the Third Edition of this pamphlet (1890) is in the New York Public Library. The 1888 edition is presumably a revision of the pamphlet "Historical Sketch of Metaphysical Healing," published in 1885, from which numerous quotations exist but of which no copies now seem available.

Christian Science Series (Vol. I, 1889; Vol. II, 1890; Christian Science Publishing Society). This includes a series of brief treatises, partly by Mrs. Eddy, partly by her students. Now rare but unimportant.

Retrospection and Introspection (1891). This brochure of 95 pages is Mrs. Eddy's own account of her early life and the steps leading to the "discovery" of Christian Science.

No and Yes (1891).

Rudimental Divine Science (1891).

Christ and Christmas, a Poem (1893). This poem caused a great deal of amazement when it was first issued, since accompanying illustrations showed Mrs. Eddy in the company of Christ. The edition was eventually withdrawn. It has value primarily as a curiosity.

Poems. This volume of 73 pages contains verse published at odd times by Mrs. Eddy from her girlhood on.

Manual of The Mother Church, The First Church of Christ, Scientist, in Boston, Massachusetts (1895).

Pulpit and Press (1895).

Miscellaneous Writings (1896). This volume includes a large number of Mrs. Eddy's contributions to her *Journal* during the days when the paper was largely her personal house organ.

Christian Science versus Pantheism (1898); *Messages to The Mother Church for 1900; 1901; 1902.* Now published in one brochure.

Personal Contagion; What Our Leader Says. Pamphlet containing 5 pages of 12 pt., totalling approximately 120 words, which was copyrighted in 1909 as a reprint of two articles attributed to Mrs. Eddy and published in *The Sentinel.*

The First Church of Christ, Scientist, and Miscellany (1913). This book was published posthumously, by the Christian Science Trustees, to include various informal writings left behind by Mrs. Eddy, together with numerous newspaper clippings.

The Christian Science Hymnal, with five hymns written by Reverend Mary Baker Eddy.

MRS. EDDY'S PERIODICALS

The Christian Science Journal. Volume 1 begins with 1883. The Wisconsin State Historical Society is uniquely fortunate in having a complete file, beginning with Volume 1, of this remarkable record of Mrs. Eddy's climb to her pinnacle. The Boston Congregational Library has parts of Volumes 1, 3, 10, 15, 17, 22, 23, 25 and 28-32. The files in the Congressional Library and the Boston Public Library alike begin with Volume 3. The New York Public Library has a partial file of Volume 4 and a complete file of subsequent volumes. The Detroit Public Library's file starts at Volume 6, the Philadelphia Free Library with Volume 9, Harvard College with Volume 11, the University of Illinois with Volume 20.

The Christian Science Sentinel. This paper, founded in 1898, was issued as the *Christian Science Weekly* in the Volumes 1-21. The Congressional Library and the New York Public Library each has a complete file, beginning with Volume 1. Other libraries which have at least certain issues in Volume 1, with more or less complete files thereafter, are as follows: The Wisconsin State Historical Society, Madison; the Connecticut State Library at Hartford; Oberlin College; the Grosvenor Library, Buffalo; the Boston Medical Library. Files of the Public Library at Houston, Texas, start with issues in Volume 2, and the Boston Public Library has a complete file beginning with this volume. Harvard College has a complete file starting with Volume 3, and the University of Pennsylvania's file starts with issues in Volume 4, as does the file of the University of Illinois. The California State Library has a complete file beginning with Volume 12.

Note: The other periodicals of Mrs. Eddy's church belong less in a bibliography of Mrs. Eddy's personal career than in one pertaining to the history of the Christian Science organization. No quotations from them have been made in this biography. The interested reader will find them listed on Page 461.

BOOKS AND PAMPHLETS

Effort has been made briefly to sketch the history of the more important books listed here, and also to indicate the libraries in which rare publications vital to the student may be found. Where libraries are not mentioned, it may be assumed either that the book is generally available or that it is not important enough to warrant a general search. Almost all of the works included here are available in the New York Public Library.

Memoirs of Mary Baker Eddy (Adam Dickey, C.S.D.). Published in 1927—three years after the author's death—by his widow, Mrs. Lillian S. Dickey. The imprint was that of the Merrymount Press, Boston, Mass. An English Edition appeared under the imprint of Robert G. Carter, 29 Hogarth Road, Earl's Court, London. Mrs. Dickey, a member of The Mother Church in good standing, was promptly persuaded to withdraw the publication. All copies were recalled. The Dickey account of the atmosphere in Mrs. Eddy's home and the occurrences there forms one of the most extraordinary documents in her history, for it is the work of a loyal disciple who served in Mrs. Eddy's household for several years and died as one of the ruling officials of the church.

Only two copies are now available in the United States—those deposited under the United States copyright laws in the Library of Congress. The New York Public Library possesses a photostat print of the English edition, obtained from another photostat copy in the possession of John V. Dittemore, which copy in turn was secured from the original in the British Museum.

The Life of Mary Baker G. Eddy and the History of Christian Science, by Georgine Milmine (Doubleday Page and Co., 1909. Published in England under the imprint of Hodder & Stoughton, 1909). This book is composed of the articles published originally by Miss Milmine in *McClure's Magazine*, with revisions and additions necessitated by the large amount of additional information concerning Mrs. Eddy and her career which came into public possession after the magazine articles were published. The copyright was eventually purchased by a friend of Christian Science, and the plates from which the book was printed were destroyed, according to information which appears to be authentic and accurate. The author has been informed that the original manuscript was also acquired.

As a result, this most valuable source-book has become exceedingly rare. Copies are available in the Library of Congress, the New York Public Library, and the Boston Public Library.

The Life of Mary Baker Eddy, by Sibyl Wilbur (The Christian Science Publishing Society). This book, which is now "authorized literature," was first issued by the Human Life Publishing Company in 1907 as a reprint, with revisions, of the articles by Miss Wilbur in the *Human Life* Magazine. A former member of the Christian Science Board of Directors financed Miss Wilbur during the period when she wrote her chapters, according to his statement to the author.

The Quimby Manuscripts, Edited by Horatio W. Dresser (Thomas Y. Crowell Company, 1921). The first edition of this very valuable work, which contained the letters which the then Mrs. Patterson addressed to Dr. Quimby, is already exceedingly rare. Copies are available in the Library of Congress, the New York Public Library, and the Boston Public Library. The second edition, with the letters missing, is readily available in most public libraries and from the publishers.

The True History of Mental Science, by Julius A. Dresser (A. Mudge & Son, Boston, 1887). Revised by his son, Horatio W. Dresser, and reissued by The Alliance Publishing Co. (New York) and G. H. Ellis (Boston) in 1898.

This was the first of the Dresser salvos, fired on Mrs. Eddy when Julius Dresser found her teaching Quimby's doctrine as her own "revelation." The contents of the pamphlet were first delivered in lecture form by Mr. Dresser in the Church of the Divine Unity, Boston, February 6, 1887.

Julius A. Dresser was the most active of Quimby's followers in the period when Mrs. Eddy was under treatment. He was founder of the New Thought movement, which has had little formal organization, but which has built up a remarkably large following throughout the world.

The Philosophy of P. P. Quimby, by (Mrs.) Annetta G. Dresser (Boston, Geo. H. Ellis, printer, 1895). Mrs. Dresser was Dr. Quimby's patient in 1862. Her pamphlet contained numerous newspaper excerpts concerning his work, with brief quotations from his manuscripts.

A History of The New Thought Movement, by Horatio W. Dresser (T. Y. Crowell Co., 1919).

The Mental Cure, Illustrating the Influence of the Mind on the Body, Both in Health and Disease, and The Psychological Method of Treatment, by Rev. W. F Evans. (Colby & Rich, Boston. "Entered according to Act of Congress, in the year 1869, in the Clerk's Office of the District Court of the District of New Hampshire.") This highly important volume, published three years after Quimby's death and six years before the appearance of *Science and Health* should be available in some of its later editions in the larger metropolitan libraries. The New York Public Library has the eighth edition of 1886.

The Rev. W. F. Evans was one of Quimby's most intelligent enthusiasts Following *The Mental Cure* he published many other books; but this first volume is the most important in any consideration of Mrs. Eddy's career, for it shows indubitably the wealth of inspiration which Quimby generated.

The Philosophy of Electrical Psychology, by John Bovee Dods (Fowler & Wells New York, 1854). This is perhaps the first important treatise on suggestion and its effects published in this country. It is available in the New York Public Library.

Reminiscences, Sermons and Correspondence, by Augusta E. Stetson, C.S.D (G. P. Putnam's Sons, 1914).

Vital Issues in Christian Science, with Facsimile Letters of Mary Baker Eddy, by Augusta E. Stetson, C.S.D. (G. P. Putnam's Sons, 1914).

Sermons and Other Writings, by Augusta E. Stetson, C.S.D. (G. P. Putnam's Sons, 1924). This volume of 1277 pages contains all the facsimile letters published in connection with *Vital Issues in Christian Science*, with various other not included in the earlier book. Like all of Mrs. Stetson's other writings, thi book is on the "index expurgatorius," unofficial but efficacious, of Mrs Eddy's Church. On Page 406 Mrs. Stetson says: "My books . . . which contain all that I have taught and demonstrated for years, have been boycotted and the members of the organization forbidden to read them. I have even been told . . . that my books have been burned."

The Religio-Medical Masquerade, by Frederick W. Peabody, LL.B. (The Hancock Press, Boston, 1910). Available in the New York Public Library. Issued in 1915 in a new edition by Fleming H. Revell & Co., New York-Chicago.

A Complete Exposure of Eddyism or Christian Science, by Frederick W. Peabody (Boston, 1904). This is the substance of a lecture delivered at Tremont Temple, in Boston, August 1, 1901. Available in the New York Public Library

Copies of this and the previously listed treatise by Mr. Peabody are of primary interest because of his close association with contemporary Christian Scientists, and not because of any discrimination in his handling of his material. When Mrs. Woodbury's article on Mrs. Eddy's beliefs regarding sex matters was published in *The Arena*, the magazine was sued for a violation of copyright, in connection with an illustration it had reproduced. There was no suit for libel. Mr. Peabody was engaged to defend the magazine's interests, and he subsequently became Mrs. Woodbury's counsel in the prosecution of her unsuccessful libel suit. Later he assisted Senator Chandler in the prosecution of the Next Friends' Suit. Copies of his pamphlets are now exceedingly rare.

Quimbyism, or the Paternity of Christian Science, by Josephine Curtis Woodbury (Garden City Press, Letchworth, 1909). This is a reprint of Mrs. Woodbury's article in *The Arena* of May, 1899. It is available in the New York Public Library.

War in Heaven, by Josephine Curtis Woodbury (S. Usher, printer, Boston, 1897). A copy of this pamphlet is available in the New York Public Library.

Popular Bibles: Science and Health, by Woodbridge Riley, in the *Cambridge History of American Literature,* Vol. 4, first edition (G. P. Putnam's Sons, 1921). This chapter, which traced the origins of Mrs. Eddy's work without much reverence, met such a hostile reception in certain quarters that the publishers withdrew the entire volume. A new edition of the volume was issued containing an entirely new chapter under the same title, written by Lyman P. Powell. The first edition cannot now be purchased, but should be available in those larger libraries which acquire books promptly on publication.

Christian Science, by Mark Twain (Harper & Brothers, 1907). This often hilarious and always caustic attack on Mrs. Eddy and her organization is now generally available in libraries, though for years it was rather rare. It includes a number of magazine articles previously published in the *North American Review*.

Mary Baker G. Eddy, by Arthur Brisbane (The Ball Publishing Co., Boston, 1908).

Christian Science: Historical Facts, by Alfred Farlow (Puritan Press, Boston, 1902).

Mrs. Eddy and the Late Suit in Equity, by M. Meekan (Concord, 1908).

Little Journeys to the Homes of Great Teachers, by Elbert Hubbard (Vol. 23, East Aurora, 1908).

Mary Baker Eddy and her Book, Science and Health with Key to the Scriptures, by W. D. McCrackan (M. E. Starr, Tamworth, N. H., 1925).

The Passing of Mary Baker Eddy and Other Essays, by E. C. Farnsworth (Smith & Sale, Portland, 1911).

Christian Science: A Biographical Sketch of the Discoverer and Founder, by Septimus James Hanna (Gay Bros. & Co., New York, 1896).

The History of a House (Built by Squire Bagley, in Amesbury, Mass.), by Mary Beecher Longyear (The Zion Research Foundation, Brookline, Mass., 1925).

Christian Science and its Discoverer, by E. M. Ramsay (W. Heffer & Sons, Ltd., Cambridge, Eng., 1923).

Side Lights on Mary Baker Eddy-Glover—Science Church Trustees Controversy in the "Next Friends' Suit," by R. D. Kathrens (Kansas City, Mo., 1907). Pamphlet available in New York Public Library.

Sixty Years of Christian Science (A. W. Martin). Society of Ethical Culture.

Christian Science and Legislation (A pamphlet which includes three articles: *The Endeavor to Handicap Truth*, by Edward A. Kimball; *Christian Science and Legislation*, by Judge Clifford P. Smith; and *Christian Science: A Practical Religion*, by Judge Septimus J. Hanna (The C. S. Publishing Society, 1905).

Christian Science, the Faith and its Founder, by Lyman P. Powell (G. P. Putnam's Sons, 1907).

The Truth About Christian Science, by James H. Snowden (The Westminster Press, Philadelphia, 1920).

Christian Science as a Religious Belief and a Therapeutic Agent, by B. O. Flower (Twentieth Century Co., Boston, 1909).

Christian Science History: A Statement of facts relating to the authorship of the Christian Science Text-book "Science and Health with Key to the Scriptures," by S. J. Hanna (C. S. Publishing Society, Boston, 1899).

The Religion of Health: An examination of Christian Science, by Sir William Barrett; completed by Rosa M. Barrett (J. M. Dent & Sons, Ltd., London 1925).

Christian Science: Pure Metaphysics, by Francis J. Fluno (The Christian Science Publishing Society, 1917).

A Biographical Sketch of Reverend Mary Baker G. Eddy, by Hon. Henry Robinson (People and Patriot Co., publishers, Concord, New Hampshire).

The Good Side of Christian Science, by C. D. Larson (E. J. Clode, New York 1916).

Sophistries of Christian Science, by E. C. Farnsworth (Smith & Sale, Portland Maine, 1909).

Christian Science: Its Discovery and Development. Pamphlet by W. D. McCrackan, reprinted from "The Great Events by Famous Historians," a set of 20 books marketed *circa* 1911 by the "National Alumni Association," New York.

Three Thousand Years of Mental Healing, by George B. Cutten (Charles Scribner's Sons, 1911).

Miracles of Healing, by Charles W. Waddle. Thesis for Ph.D., Clark University 1909. Reprinted from *American Journal of Psychology* (April, 1909).

Mind and Health, with an Examination of Some Systems of Divine Healing, by Edward E. Weaver (The Macmillan Co., 1913).

Mesmerism and Christian Science—a short History of Mental Healing, by Frank Podmore (Methuen, London, 1909).

Our Hidden Forces (*La Psychologie Inconnue*), by Émile Boirac. Translated by W. de Kerlor (Frederick A. Stokes Company).

The Major Symptoms of Hysteria, by Pierre M. F. Janet (Macmillan, 1907).

GENERAL MAGAZINES AND PERIODICALS

Although the author has sought to avoid use of data which belong primarily to the history of Christian Science, and not to Mrs. Eddy's personal experience it has nevertheless been necessary to weigh and appraise a large amount of material on Christian Science which is certainly of indirect importance. It has been deemed wise to indicate to the reader the sources for some of this collateral reading, in addition to assembling sources to which direct reference has been made.

It has not seemed practicable to list current newspapers in this summary, since this would be largely a repetition of previous footnotes, where the important dates are all given in connection with the events to which they belong. The research worker should note, however, that the files of the New York *World* from 1900 onward contain in almost every year source material which is invaluable, even though due allowance must be made for its sensationalizing by enthusiastic reporters. *The World* has always displayed greater interest in the drama attending Mrs. Eddy's career than any other important daily in the United States. Frequent reference to the *World* columns has been made in the footnotes, with a statement of the date. The student who desires even more material will find that while *The World* has no index, it is possible to make good use of the New York *Times* index in this connection. *The Times* usually published brief résumés of current Christian Science news—which it seldom considered of enough general interest to feature—on either the same or the following day the *World* accounts appeared.

Because it is almost impossible, in dealing with the following material, to make any listing in order of importance, an alphabetical listing of the magazines, with dates in chronological order, is used. Reference is made here to all available non-Christian Science periodicals containing essays, studies, or data which the author considers germane to a study of Mrs. Eddy's career; but no effort has been made to present a complete roster of articles dealing primarily with Christian Science. Only an incidental number of articles in this latter class has been included, usually because of some apparent significance.

It is perhaps unnecessary to warn the student of bias which lurks in a great number of the articles referred to here. Little has been written regarding Mrs. Eddy that does not suffer from the writer's desire to prove a pre-formulated thesis, and this is even more true of magazines than of books, for in this instance an editorial bias was added more often than not to the writer's point of view.

The Prognosis in Eddyism (Henry Reed Hopkins). *American Medical Quarterly*, January, 1900. Reprinted as 12-page pamphlet in 1900.

Christian Science and Its Prophetess: Part I, *The Facts in the Case*, by H. W. Dresser. Part II, *The Book and the Woman*, by Josephine Curtis Woodbury. *Arena*, May, 1899. The second half of this article was subsequently reprinted in a pamphlet called: *A Complete Exposure of Eddyism or Christian Science* (The Garden City Press, Letchworth, 1909).

Christian Science and the Healing Art (W. G. Ewing, C. B. Patterson, J. B. Leavitt, J. W. Winkley). *Arena* (January, 1901).

Christian Science (J. B. Willis and Alfred Farlow), *Arena* (June, 1901).

The Recent Reckless and Irresponsible Attacks on Christian Science and Its Founder (B. O. Flower), *Arena*, January, 1907.

A Further Word on Christian Science, *Arena* (May, 1907).

The Meaning of Christian Science (William D. McCrackan), *Arena* (May, 1907).

Truths of Christian Science (J. B. Willis), *Arena* (July, 1907).

Fallacies of Christian Science (E. C. Farnsworth), *Arena* (July, 1907).

Seven Alleged Delusions of Christian Science (B. O. Flower), *Arena* (October, 1907).

Mark Twain's Attack on Christian Science (B. O. Flower), *Arena* (November, 1907).

God as Conceived by Christian Science (G. T. Moore), *Arena* (March, 1908).

Christian Science and Organic Disease (B. O. Flower), *Arena* (November, 1908).

Christian Science (J. D. Works), *Arena* (January, 1909).

Mark Twain on Christian Science, Athenaeum (London) (April 20, 1907).

What the Public Wants to Read (E. Wood), *Atlantic Monthly* (October, 1901).

Christian Science (J. W. Churchman), *Atlantic Monthly* (April, 1904).

Christian Science—Why Not? (C. Caverno), *Bibliotheca Sacra* (Oberlin, O.) (October, 1902).

The Source of "Science and Health" (Hermann S. Ficke, Ph.D.), *Bibliotheca Sacra,* (St. Louis) (October, 1928).

Christian Science in New York City (W. A. Johnston), *Broadway Magazine* (New York) (May, 1907).

What has Christian Science Really Accomplished? (W. A. Johnston), *Broadway Magazine* (November, 1907).

Mary Baker G. Eddy (A. P. Fitch), *Canadian Magazine* (Toronto) (January, 1907).

Cures of Christian Science (Francis D. McGarry), *Catholic World* (June, 1909).

Mrs. Eddy, a Creative Intellect (J. Martin), *Catholic World* (November, 1922).

The Mystery of a Personality (W. Irwin), *Collier's* (December 24, 1910).

Psychological Reasons for Pronouncing Mrs. Eddy a Paranoiac, Current Literature (November, 1910).

Mary Baker Eddy's Immense Achievement, Current Literature (January, 1911).

Mrs. Stetson on the Immortality of Mrs. Eddy, Current Literature (January, 1912).

Was Mrs. Eddy A Plagiarist? Current Opinion (May, 1922).

Christian Science—an Impartial Estimate (C. Klein), *Cosmopolitan Magazine* (February, 1907).

The Truth About Christian Science (C. A. Murray, Earl of Dunmore), *Cosmopolitan Magazine* (March, 1907).

Mark Twain, Mrs. Eddy, and Christian Science (E. A. Kimball), *Cosmopolitan Magazine* (May, 1907).

Christian Science Idealism (J. R. Mozley), *Cosmopolitan Magazine* (July, 1907).

An Interview with Mary Baker Eddy (Arthur Brisbane), *Cosmopolitan Magazine* (August, 1907).

Beecher and Christian Science (Margaret B. White), *Cosmopolitan Magazine* (August, 1908).

Mrs. Eddy—Her Purpose and Accomplishment (F. Dixon), *Cosmopolitan* (February, 1911).

Christian Science (E. W. Cook), *Contemporary Review* (London) (November, 1902).

The Truth About Christian Science (E. W. Cook), *Contemporary Review* (London) (October, 1903).

The Pedigree of Christian Science (Frank Podmore), *Contemporary Review* (London), Vol. 37 (January, 1909).

Mesmerism and Christian Science (F. Podmore), *Contemporary Review* (November, 1910).

The Christian Scientist (F. Richardson), *Cornhill Magazine* (London).

A Physician's Impeachment of Christian Science Cures, Current Opinion (March, 1920).

Christian Science from a Psychologist's Point of View (James R. Angell), *World Today* (April, 1905).

Christian Science (R. H. Benson), *Dublin Review* (London) (July, 1908).

The Magic of Nothing (F. V. Branford), *English Review* (London) (July, 1924).

Christian Science and Mortal Mind (M. A. Stobart), *Fortnightly Review* (December, 1902).

Christian Science and Government (A. Farlow), *Government* (Boston) (May, 1907).

A Defense of Christian Science (S. J. Hanna), *Government* (Boston) (February, 1908).

Malicious Animal Magnetism (J. Jastrow), *Hamton Magazine* (October, 1910).

My Meeting with Mrs. Mary B. G. Eddy (W. F. Smith), *Human Life* (June, 1907).

A Glance at the Personnel of the Christian Science Movement (Alfred Farlow), *Human Life* (January, 1907).

Glimpses of a Great Personality (Sibyl Wilbur), *Human Life* (Boston), 1907, January, February, March, April, May, August, September, October, November, December. The articles in this publication, which was so obscure that it was not even listed for the "Annual Library Index," were later reprinted in book form by the Human Life Publishing Company, after they had been subjected to extended editing and rewriting. The book was finally taken over by the Christian Science Publishing Society and became the "authorized" biography. (Listed on a preceding page.) Files of *Human Life* are available in the larger public libraries.

Truths and Untruths of Christian Science (W. Gladden), *Independent* (April 2, 1903).

Mrs. Eddy's Career, Independent (December 8, 1910).

Mrs. Eddy's Resurrection, Independent (January 12, 1911).

The Demonstration of Mary Baker Eddy (A. E. Stetson), *Independent* (January 26, 1911).

Mrs. Eddy and Mrs. Stetson (A. E. Stetson), *Independent* (October, 1913).

Mrs. Eddy (J. Arthur Hill), *Journal of the Society for Psychical Research*, Vol. 13, Pages 169 f., 199 f. (London, 1908).

Mrs. Eddy's Unpublished Poems, Ladies Home Journal (June, 1911).

Mary Baker G. Eddy (Georgine Milmine), *McClure's Magazine*, Vol. 28–29 (1907), January, February, March, April, May, July, August, September, October. Vol. 30 (1908), February, March, April, May, June. A file of these volumes is available on the shelves of libraries throughout the United States. These articles later formed the basis for the Milmine biography.

Christian Science Since Mrs. Eddy (B. J. Hendrick), *McClure's Magazine* (September, 1912).

Christian Science—What It Claims (I. C. Tomlinson), *Metropolitan Magazine* (June, 1908).

Some Intellectual Weeds of American Growth (George Milbry Gould), *Montreal Medical Journal* (August, 1904). Reprinted in 1904 as a 16-page pamphlet, now available in New York Public Library.

The Girlhood of Mary Baker Eddy, as revealed in letters written by Mrs. Eddy and now published for the first time (Isaac F. Marcosson). *Munsey's Magazine* (April, 1911).

Malicious Animal Magnetism in Christian Science, The Nation (May 19, 1910).

Christian Science and the Emmanuel Movement, The Nation (June 25, 1908).

Origins of Christian Science, The Nation (February 10, 1910).

Christian Science (C. S. Mack), *The New Church Review* (April, 1901).

Phineas Parkhurst Quimby (George A. Quimby), *New England Magazine* (March, 1888).

The Founder of Christian Science (H. H. Williams), *New England Magazine* (November, 1899).

The Growth of Christian Science (W. D. Quint), *New England Magazine* (July, 1909).

Mary Baker Eddy and Her Work (Alfred Farlow), *New England Magazine* (December, 1909).

Christian Science Faith Regarding Death (A. Farlow), *New England Magazine* (January, 1911).

Recent Growth of Christian Science in New England (C. A. Woodard), *New England Magazine* (April, 1914).

Christian Science and Its Legal Aspects (W. A. Purrington), *North American Review* (March, 1899).

The Absurd Paradox of Christian Science (J. M. Buckley), *North American Review* (July, 1901).

The Simple Logic of Christian Science (W. D. McCrackan), *North American Review* (August, 1901).

The Phantom Fortress of Christian Science (J. M. Buckley), *North American Review* (September, 1901).

The Strength of Christian Science: A Final Word (W. D. McCrackan), *North American Review* (October, 1901).

Christian Science (Mark Twain), *North American Review* (December, 1902; January, 1903; February, 1903).

Mrs. Eddy's Relation to Christian Science (W. D. McCrackan), *North American Review* (March, 1903).

Mrs. Eddy in Error (Mark Twain), *North American Review* (April, 1903).

The World Mission of Christian Science (F. Dixon), *North American Review* (November, 1922).

The Christian Science View of Sin (Alfred Farlow), *Outlook* (July 27, 1901).

Truth and Error in Christian Science, Outlook (June 23, 1906).

A Christian Science Case Explained (E. R. Cox), *Outlook* (December 11, 1909).

An Extraordinary Career, The Outlook (December 17, 1910).

Christian Science and the Sex Question, Outlook (September 13, 1913).

Christian Science (M. G. Kidder), *Overland Monthly* (September, 1908).

Christian Science—A Reply to M. G. Kidder (F. W. Gale), *Overland Monthly* (San Francisco) (October, 1908).

The How and Why of Christian Science (G. A. Miller), *Overland Monthly* (January, 1909).

Spiritual Healing Divested of Mystery (P. V. Ross), *Overland Monthly* (May, 1917).

Mary Baker Eddy (Morris Fishbein), *Plain Talk* (November, 1927).

Science and "Christian Science" (F. A. Fernald), *Popular Science Monthly* (April, 1889).

The Grain of Truth in the Bushel of Christian Science (C. C. Batchelder), *Popular Science Monthly* (March, 1908).

The Personal Sources of Christian Science (I. W. Reilly), *Psychological Review* (Lancaster, Penn., 1903).

The Menace of Eddyism (F. Ballard), *Quarterly Review* (London) (July, 1921).

The Founder of Christian Science, Review of Reviews (January, 1911).

Inverted Witchcraft, The Spectator (London) (May 25, 1901).

Christian Science Quackery, Saturday Review (London) (July 7, 1906).

The Essential Falsehood of Christian Science (F. W. Mueller), *Westminster Review* (London).

Christian Science (J. Knott), *Westminster Review* (London) (February, 1907).

Christian Science (W. N. Miller), *Westminster Review* (London) (May, 1907).

Mary Baker Eddy from the Christian Science Point of View (Clara L. Burnham), *World Today* (February, 1907).

Christian Science in England (F. Dixon), *World Today* (February, 1908).

Christian Science Without Mystery (R. L. Hartt), *World's Work* (December, 1907).

Trading in The Holy Spirit (C. Howard), *World's Work* (April, 1910).

TEXTUAL CHANGES IN THIS EDITION

(Other than typographical)

Page 165—Lines cut to permit insertion of footnote.

Page 167—"Doctor" Eastman was not the individual with a similar name who was a Director in the College; this confusion has been corrected.

Page 169—New material added in footnote.

Page 260—Membership in the Mother Church was not necessary to become a healer, the author is advised.

Page 287—Mrs. Eddy received a delegation of communicants at Pleasant View in 1903, a fact noted in this edition.

Page 331—Seventy persons attended Mrs. Eddy's last class; sixty-one was the number given in earlier editions.

Page 367—Cuts made to permit the insertion of documentary data concerning Mrs. Eddy's employment of morphine.

Page 372—Naming of Mrs. Leonard deferred until page 401.

Page 373—Only Archibald McLellan, and not the Directors, made regular official visits to Mrs. Eddy's home. The others seldom saw her.

Page 381—The testimonial meeting was held not Sunday but on Wednesday.

Page 401—Lines cut to permit insertion of footnote.

Page 406—Footnote inserted, correcting previous reference to Sibyl Wilbur, who was not employed to write the "authorized" biography until later.

Page 461—The Quarterly was correctly described in earlier editions as first copyrighted in 1901. But it was first published in 1890. It was not copyrighted earlier owing to its inclusion of the International Sunday School lessons.

Page 472—Exact date of Mrs. Stetson's most recent word from Mrs. Eddy established. Line changed to meet contention that Mrs. Stetson did not announce building plans personally.

Page 473—Lines cut to permit insertion of footnote.

Page 476—Lines cut to permit insertion of footnote.

Page 514—Footnote rewritten to include evidence from Mrs. Eddy's own correspondence with her Directors regarding the administration of morphine.

Page 520—Two hundred persons, according to one present, made up the approximate total at Mrs. Eddy's funeral—not fifty, as stated in earlier editions. In addition to this correction in fact, the author has gladly modified his earlier statement that "Mrs. Eddy's officials got her out of the way as quickly and as inconspicuously as possible." The actual facts—apart from all interpretation—are that Mrs. Eddy died late Saturday evening; the church officials learned of her passing early Sunday morning; the medical examiner arrived late in the morning; the funeral took place Thursday.

INDEX